# THE WODROW–KENRICK CORRESPONDENCE

## VOLUME 2

# The Wodrow–Kenrick Correspondence

1750–1810

Volume 2: 1784–1790

Edited by
MARTIN FITZPATRICK,
EMMA MACLEOD, AND
ANTHONY PAGE

Great Clarendon Street, Oxford, OX2 6DP,
United Kingdom

Oxford University Press is a department of the University of Oxford.
It furthers the University's objective of excellence in research, scholarship,
and education by publishing worldwide. Oxford is a registered trade mark of
Oxford University Press in the UK and in certain other countries

© Martin Fitzpatrick, Emma Macleod, and Anthony Page 2024

The moral rights of the authors have been asserted

First Edition published in 2020

All rights reserved. No part of this publication may be reproduced, stored in
a retrieval system, or transmitted, in any form or by any means, without the
prior permission in writing of Oxford University Press, or as expressly permitted
by law, by licence or under terms agreed with the appropriate reprographics
rights organization. Enquiries concerning reproduction outside the scope of the
above should be sent to the Rights Department, Oxford University Press, at the
address above

You must not circulate this work in any other form
and you must impose this same condition on any acquirer

Published in the United States of America by Oxford University Press
198 Madison Avenue, New York, NY 10016, United States of America

British Library Cataloguing in Publication Data

Data available

Library of Congress Control Number: 2020930747

ISBN 978–0–19–880902–9

Printed and bound by
CPI Group (UK) Ltd, Croydon, CR0 4YY

Links to third party websites are provided by Oxford in good faith and
for information only. Oxford disclaims any responsibility for the materials
contained in any third party website referenced in this work.

*In memoriam*
*Professor H. T. Dickinson*

# CONTENTS

| | |
|---|---|
| *List of abbreviated citations* | ix |
| *List of illustrations* | xi |
| *Acknowledgements* | xiii |
| *Editorial conventions* | xv |
| *Persons mentioned in Volume 2* | xix |
| *List of letters in Volume 2* | xxxv |
| Introduction to Volume 2 | 1 |
| Letters 79–155 (1784–90) | 69 |
| *Appendices* | 465 |
| *Primary sources cited in Volume 2* | 469 |
| *Secondary sources cited in Volume 2* | 485 |
| *Index* | 503 |

# LIST OF ABBREVIATED CITATIONS

The correspondents are often abbreviated thus: JW (James Wodrow), SK (Samuel Kenrick)

| | |
|---|---|
| Addison, Graduates of Glasgow | *A Roll of the Graduates of the University of Glasgow from 31st December, 1727 to 31st December, 1897*, compiled by W. Innes Addison (Glasgow, 1898). |
| Addison, Matriculation Albums | *The Matriculation Albums of the University of Glasgow from 1728 to 1858*, compiled by W. Innes Addison (Glasgow, 1913). |
| Alumni Cantabrigienses | John and John Archibald Venn, *Alumni Cantabrigienses: A Biographical List of All Known Students, Graduates and Holders of Office at the University of Cambridge, from the Earliest Times to 1900*, 10 vols (1922–53). |
| Alumni Oxonienses | Joseph Foster, *Alumni Oxonienses: The Members of the University of Oxford, 1715–1886*, 4 vols (Oxford, 1888–91). |
| Ancestry | *Ancestry Library*, www.ancestrylibrary.com. |
| Burns Encyclopedia | Maurice Lindsay, *The Burns Encyclopedia*, 3rd edn (1995). |
| Catholic Encyclopedia | *The Catholic Encyclopedia*, www.newadvent.org/cathen. |
| Clergy of the C of E | *Clergy of the Church of England Database*, https://theclergydatabase.org.uk/jsp/search/index.jsp. |
| CNF | Norah Kenrick, *Chronicles of a Nonconformist Family: The Kenricks of Wynne Hall, Exeter and Birmingham.* Edited by Mrs. W. Byng Kenrick (Birmingham, 1932). |
| DAO | *Dissenting Academies Online*, www.qmulreligionandliterature.co.uk/research/the-dissenting-academies-project/dissenting-academies-online. |
| Diaries of Mary Ann Wodrow Archbald | Diaries, 8 vols (1785–1806, 1839–40), Mary Ann Wodrow Archbald Papers, Sophia Smith Collection of Women's History, Smith College, Northampton, Massachusetts. |

# LIST OF ABBREVIATED CITATIONS

| | |
|---|---|
| Ditchfield, *Letters of Lindsey* | G. M. Ditchfield, ed., *The Letters of Theophilus Lindsey (1723–1808)*, Volume 1, *1747–1788* (Woodbridge, 2007); Volume 2, *1789–1808* (Woodbridge, 2012). |
| *DSCHT* | *Dictionary of Scottish Church History and Theology*, ed. Nigel M. de S. Cameron (Edinburgh, 1993). |
| *DSL* | *Dictionaries of the Scots Language/Dictionars o the Scots Leid*, https://dsl.ac.uk. |
| *FES* | *Fasti Ecclesiae Scoticanae: The Succession of Ministers in the Church of Scotland from the Reformation*, by Hew Scott, 10 vols, 2nd edn (Edinburgh, 1920). |
| *HPO* | *History of Parliament Online*, www.historyofparliamentonline.org. |
| Johnson's *Dictionary* | Samuel Johnson, *A Dictionary of the English Language*, 7th edn, 2 vols (1783). |
| *LBS* | *Legacies of British Slave-Ownership Database*, www.ucl.ac.uk/lbs/project/details. |
| Loeb Classical Library | Loeb Classical Library, www.loebclassics.com/page/aboutloeb. |
| *NRS* | National Records of Scotland, Edinburgh. |
| *NSA* | *The New Statistical Account of Scotland*, 15 vols (Edinburgh, 1845). |
| *ODNB* | *Oxford Dictionary of National Biography*, eds. Colin Matthew, Brian Harrison, Lawrence Goldman. and Sir David Cannadine (2004–), www.oxforddnb.com. |
| *OED* | *Oxford English Dictionary*, www.oed.com. |
| *OSA* | *The [Old] Statistical Account of Scotland*, ed. Sir John Sinclair, 21 vols (Edinburgh, 1791–99). |
| Surman Index | The Surman Index Online, https://surman.english.qmul.ac.uk. |
| W-K, I | Martin Fitzpatrick, Emma Macleod, and Anthony Page, eds, *The Wodrow–Kenrick Correspondence*, Volume 1: *1750–1783* (Oxford, 2020). |
| Wilson, *Dissenting Churches* | Walter Wilson, *The History and Antiquities of Dissenting Churches and Meeting Houses in London, Westminster and Southwark*, 4 vols (1808). |
| *Works of Joseph Priestley* | *The Theological and Miscellaneous Works of Joseph Priestley*, ed. J. T. Rutt, 25 vols in 26 (1817–32). |

# LIST OF ILLUSTRATIONS

1. Towns and cities of significance in the Wodrow–Kenrick correspondence. — xxxix
2. Parish map of Ayrshire. *Ecclesiastical Map of Scotland* by Aaron Arrowsmith (1825). — xl
3. 'Bewdley', from Thomas Sanders, *Perspective Views of Market Towns in the County of Worcester* (1770). — xli
4. Address panel. Letter 39: Samuel Kenrick to James Wodrow, 5 December 1759. — 4
5. Address panel. Letter 103: Samuel Kenrick to James Wodrow, 5 October 1785. — 5
6. Seal on Letter 103. — 211
7. Archibald Arthur's obituary for William Leechman, Glasgow, 8 December 1785, published in the *Caledonian Mercury*, 12 December 1785 (printed enclosure, Letter 108). — 230
8. Margaret 'Peggy' Wodrow, watercolour by Mary Ann Wodrow, n.d., Mary Ann Wodrow Archbald Papers, Sophia Smith Collection, SSC-MS-00006, Smith College Special Collections, Northampton, Massachusetts. — 423
9. Mary Ann Wodrow, watercolour self-portrait, n.d., Mary Ann Wodrow Archbald Papers, Sophia Smith Collection, SSC-MS-00006, Smith College Special Collections, Northampton, Massachusetts. — 424
10. Professor William Leechman, by William Millar, oil painting, 1774/1775, © The Hunterian, University of Glasgow. — 425
11. Worcester Dissenters' Resolutions, 27 January 1790, printed enclosure, Letter 153. — 449
12. Worcester Dissenters' Resolutions, 24 August 1790, printed enclosure, Letter 155. — 463

# ACKNOWLEDGEMENTS

We have continued to incur many debts in the course of editing the correspondence of James Wodrow and Samuel Kenrick. We are grateful to Hugh McGuire, Director of Dr Williams's Trust, and to the trustees again, for permission to publish the letters, and we thank him and the library staff, especially Lisa Cheetham, for enabling us to check our transcriptions. Lisa Cheetham pointed out the beautiful seal used by Samuel Kenrick for a letter sent while Helen Wodrow was staying with his family in Bewdley, reproduced in Plate 6.

For assisting in the transcription of the letters we thank Diana Barnes, Julia Bohlmann, and Maryanne Page. We thank Graeme Miles for help with translation from Greek, and Tony Rail for his translations from Samuel Kenrick's shorthand system. We are grateful to the Ayrshire Archaeological and Natural History Society for directing us to the journal of Mary Ann Wodrow, and to Smith College, Massachusetts, for making it available to us on microfilm. We would like to thank Grayson Ditchfield for his invaluable support for the project. Richard B. Sher provided substantial and essential assistance in checking the first draft of this volume, and we are very grateful to him, while recognizing that all remaining errors are of course our own. Warm thanks are also due to Cathryn Steele and Imogene Haslam at Oxford University Press for their support of this project and for their guidance and advice as it has progressed towards publication. Colleagues at the Universities of Tasmania and Stirling have offered enthusiasm and encouragement—we especially thank Gavin Daly in Tasmania, and David Bebbington, Ali Cathcart, Katie Halsey, Colin Nicolson, Angus Vine, Kelsey Jackson Williams, and the members of Eighteenth-Century Studies at Stirling. Finally, we thank our families for their constant support.

This volume is dedicated to the memory of Professor Harry Dickinson (1939–2024), who supervised Emma's PhD thesis, examined Anthony's, and was Martin's friend over many years, in celebration of his intellectual stature as a leading historian of eighteenth-century British politics, and with gratitude for his kindness and humanity.

# EDITORIAL CONVENTIONS

The Wodrow–Kenrick correspondence manuscripts have been carefully preserved, first in the Kenrick family and since by Dr Williams's Library: very little of the ink is too faded to read; the handwriting of both men is clear and regular; and the fact that the collection was produced by only two hands makes it easier to develop a working familiarity with them. Nevertheless, many of the letters contain blots, tears, creases, writing that is not easy to decipher, and similar challenges to transcription. There are also some passages of shorthand that have been helpfully translated by Tony Rail. In developing our editorial conventions we found it very helpful to consult the examples set in *The Letters of William Godwin, Volume I: 1778–1797*, ed. Pamela Clemit (Oxford, 2011) and *The Letters of Theophilus Lindsey*, ed. G. M. Ditchfield, 2 vols (Woodbridge, 2007 and 2012).

Each volume has a list of the letters it contains. We have also provided a list of people who appear in the correspondence, along with the number of the first letter in which they are mentioned and their birth and death dates (if known). We also identify family or close friend relationships to Wodrow and/or Kenrick.

Explanatory notes aim to help the reader understand and interpret the letters. Unless otherwise stated, biographical information is sourced from the *Oxford Dictionary of National Biography*. If a source is not in our List of Abbreviated Citations, full details are provided when first cited and a short title used for subsequent citations. Unless specified, the place of publication is London. Cross-references to other letters in the correspondence usually provide only the letter number, and some of the letters cited in this volume are forthcoming in Volumes 3 and 4.

Each letter begins with a heading that indicates its number in the chronological list of letters, the author, and the date. This is followed by information, if available, indicating the place where the letter was written, the address to which it was posted, and any postmarks, stamps, franks, and additional notes added—for example, Kenrick often noted when he had received and answered a letter. It is noticeable that there were commonly more postmarks on the letters in this volume than there were on the letters in Volume 1. We use a forward slash / to indicate line breaks in the address. If we have been able to determine additional information, this is included within square brackets.

In some cases the Wodrow–Kenrick correspondence includes partial drafts of letters, including some drafts in shorthand. Minor variations from the posted letter are included in the explanatory notes. This volume contains some passages written in shorthand by Samuel Kenrick (see Letters 116, 117, 143, and 148). Tony Rail kindly undertook the difficult task of translating these, and makes the following points: Samuel Kenrick's shorthand is based on the system taught by Jeremiah Rich, *Semographie; or, Short and Swift Writing…Invented by William Cartwright…Published by his Nephew Jeremiah Rich* (1644). This was promulgated at Philip Doddridge's Academy in Northampton and its successors. Kenrick displays some inconsistencies in the way phonic elements are joined, and he neglects many of Rich's arbitrary characters.

We have aimed to reproduce the text of the letters as they appear in the original manuscript. Every letter, transcribed from the microfilm copy, has been carefully checked by the editors against the microfilm copy in Dr Williams's Library. The following provides a guide to how we have addressed particular issues in transcription in the letters:

**Abbreviations.** When used by an author, abbreviations have been retained.

- Common abbreviations include: Birm$^m$., Birmingham; Ed$^r$., Edinburgh; Gen$^l$. Asly, General Assembly of the Church of Scotland.
- Wodrow and Kenrick frequently abbreviate Christianity as X$^{ty}$., Christian as Xian, Christ as X, and other slight variations.
- A List of Abbreviated Citations has been provided for some sources frequently cited in the explanatory notes.
- The correspondents are often abbreviated in explanatory notes as JW (James Wodrow) and SK (Samuel Kenrick).

**Brackets.** Both square and round brackets by Wodrow or Kenrick are rendered as round brackets (). Square brackets are used for editorial insertions: [London].

| | |
|---|---|
| [ ] | blank space in the text |
| < > | unreadable text |
| <—> | unreadable text also scored out by the author |
| <s> | uncertain text owing to poor legibility |

| | |
|---|---|
| [s] | Editors either adding a letter/word, or guessing a letter/word where the page is torn |
| [page torn] | page torn, and we cannot confidently guess the missing text |
| [blotted] | page blotted |
| [Am]erica | where we can confidently guess part of a word removed by a torn page, we supply the missing letters in square brackets |

**Contractions.** In cases where an author (usually Kenrick) indicates a contraction by leaving out a letter and placing a mark above the word, we have given the full word—for example, 'coment' becomes 'comment'.

**Dashes.** These are very common in Kenrick letters. Our standard formatting is to start the dash at the end of a word, but leave a space before the next word, thus: "'London– then go home'". Where a word is split between lines (often with a dash), we ignore the line break and the dash.

**Deletions.**

| | |
|---|---|
| ~~Glasgow~~ | deletion (mark-through) readable |
| <~~Glasgow~~> | deletion (mark-through) readable but unsure |
| <—> | deletion (mark-through) unreadable |
| <— —> | deletion (mark-through) unreadable more than one word |
| <-> | one letter deletion (mark-through) unreadable |

**Emphasis.** Underlining has been reproduced. Text is italicized in cases where the angle of writing has been changed and/or pen strokes made heavy for emphasis.

**Letters or words inserted by the correspondent above the line of text.** These are rendered thus: ^possibly^.

**Omitted words.** In cases where it is obvious that Wodrow or Kenrick inadvertently omitted a word, that word is supplied by the editors in square brackets.

**Punctuation.** Punctuation is reproduced as it appears in the original letters. However, if a stop is clearly visible (or a heavy pen flourish) but there is no capital for the following word, we supply the capital; or conversely, if a capital is visible but no stop, we supply the stop.

**Quotation marks.** When quoting someone, Wodrow and Kenrick often place "quotation marks at the start of every line. We ignore these and simply place quotation marks at the start and end of the quotation, and at the start of each paragraph in multiple paragraph quotations.

**Repeated words.** The last word on a page is often repeated at the start of the next page, and Wodrow and Kenrick sometimes mistakenly repeat a word. In such cases we only transcribe one word.

**Salutations and signatures.** The placement of these varies in the manuscript letters, but has been standardized in our transcriptions. Salutations start flush with the left margin of the page, while closing compliments and signatures are indented from the right margin.

**Spelling.** In all cases this is reproduced in the often inconsistent original form. For correct spelling of names, see the relevant entry in the Index.

**Superscript letters.** These are reproduced as they appear on the page. When superscript and a period are used for a contracted word, it is usually clear that the period comes after the superscript letter: M$^r$., L$^d$., w$^{ch}$., rec$^d$. We have standardized this practice.

**Translations.** English translations are provided in the footnotes. The translator is named in brackets at the end of the passage.

- Shorthand has been translated by Tony Rail.
- Where noted, classical Greek and Latin translations and explanatory notes have been provided by Graeme Miles, University of Tasmania.

# PERSONS MENTIONED IN VOLUME 2

Biographical details for an individual appear in a footnote at their first mention in the letters. Subsequent footnotes may add details relevant to the particular text, and sometimes refer back to the first footnote for the individual. The following list notes the first letter in which the individual is mentioned.

## Family mentioned in Volume 2

### Kenrick
Samuel Kenrick (1728–1811)
Elisabeth Kenrick, *née* Smith (*c.* 1726–1815), SK's wife (Letter 80)
Mary Kenrick (1754–1812), SK's daughter (Letter 80)
James Kenrick (1757–1804), SK's nephew, son of John Kenrick (Letter 142)
Timothy Kenrick (1759–1804), SK's nephew (Letter 112)
William Kenrick (1729–93), SK's brother (Letter 133)
Ralph Eddowes (1751–1833), husband of Sarah (Letter 142)
Sarah Eddowes, *née* Kenrick (m. 1777, d. 1815), SK's niece (Letter 142)

### Wodrow
James Wodrow (1730–1810)
Louisa Wodrow, *née* Hamilton (1733–93), JW's wife (Letter 84)
Gavin Wodrow, JW's son (*c.* 1761–81), JW's elder son (Letter 84)
Helen ('Nell') Wodrow (*c.* 1763–95), JW's daughter (Letter 82)
Margaret ('Peggy') Wodrow (1767–1845), JW's daughter (Letter 84)
Andrew Wodrow (b. 1752), son of JW's brother Robert (1711–84)
Elizabeth Wodrow, *née* Balfour (d. 1812), wife of JW's brother Patrick (Letter 120)
Margaret Biggar, *née* Wodrow (b. 1717, d. after 1786), JW's sister (Letter 84)
Marion ('Mainy') Wodrow, JW's sister (Letter 86)
Patrick Wodrow (1713–93), minister of Tarbolton, Ayrshire, JW's brother (Letter 106)
John Warner (1713–86), minister of Kilbarchan, cousin of JW (Letter 84)
Mrs Warner, wife of Patrick (Letter 114)
Patrick Warner (1710–93), brother of John Warner and cousin of JW (Letter 88)
Mary Ann Wodrow (1762–1841), later Archbald, JW's niece (Letter 114)
James Archbald, Mary Ann Wodrow's husband (m. 1789) (Letter 149)

**Others named in the correspondence, Volume 2**

Adam, John (1719–92), minister in Greenock (Letter 118)

Addison, Joseph (1672–1719), essayist and politician (Letter 85)

Adrian (76–138 AD), emperor of Rome (117–38) (Letter 118)

Ainsworth, Robert (1660–1743), lexicographer (Letter 105)

Allan, John (1737–1812), minister of Row, Dunbartonshire (Letter 125)

Alva, see Maxwell

Anacreon (b. c. 570 BC), Greek lyric poet (Letter 119)

Anderson, John (1726–96), professor of natural philosophy at Glasgow (Letter 91)

Andrews, Robert (1723–66), presbyterian minister at Bridgenorth (Letter 81)

Ankerville, see Ross

Anne, Queen (1665–1714, r. 1702–14) (Letter 96)

Annesley, Arthur (1744–1816), eighth viscount Valentia (Letter 133)

Apollonius of Tyana (c. 3 BC–c. 97 AD), Greek philosopher (Letter 117)

Arbuckle, Mr, previous pupil of JW (Letter 137)

Argyll, see Campbell

Aristotle (384–322 BC), Greek philosopher (Letter 131)

Arnot, Hugo (1749–1806), Edinburgh historian (Letter 87)

Arthur, Archibald (1744–97), professor of moral philosophy at Glasgow (Letter 108)

Ashworth, Caleb (1722–75), Dissenting minister and tutor at Daventry academy (Letter 112)

Athanasius of Alexandria (c. 298–373), Christian theologian (Letter 79)

Auld, William (1709–91), minister of Mauchline, Ayrshire (Letter 149)

Badcock, Samuel (1747–88), theologian and literary critic (Letter 79)

Bagot, Lewis (1740–1802), bishop of Norwich (Letter 88)

Bailey, Nathan (c. 1691–1742), lexicographer and schoolmaster (Letter 97)

Bailey, William (fl. 1783), directory editor (Letter 97)

Baillie, Lesley (1768–1843) of Mayville House, Stevenston, Robert Burns's 'Bonney Lesley' (Letter 132)

Baines, James (1710–90), minister of the Relief Church in Edinburgh (Letter 118)

Balfour, James (1741–1806), writer to the Signet in Edinburgh, Louisa Wodrow's cousin (Letter 129)

Balfour, John (1715–95), bookseller and printer in Edinburgh, Louisa Wodrow's uncle (Letter 84)

Balfour, Major and Mrs, relatives of Louisa Wodrow (Letter 108)

Barnes, Thomas (1747–1810), Presbyterian minister in Manchester and reformer (Letter 155)

Baron, Richard (d. 1786), Dissenting writer and editor (Letter 80)

Baxter, Andrew (1686/7–1750), natural philosopher and metaphysician (Letter 86)

Bayle, Pierre (1647–1706), Huguenot philosopher, theologian, and historian (Letter 119)

Beattie, James (1735–1803), poet and professor of moral philosophy at Marischal College, Aberdeen (Letter 83)

Bellamy, George Anne (c. 1731–88), actress (Letter 97)

Belsham, Thomas (1750–1829), Independent minister and tutor at Daventry academy, then at Hackney from 1786 (Letter 112)
Bertram (Ratramnus) (d. c. 868), monk in northern France who argued against transubstantiation (Letter 81)
Biggar, Matthew (d. 1806), minister of Kirkoswald, brother-in-law of JW (Letter 86)
Blair, Hugh (1718–1800), minister at St Giles's, Edinburgh, and professor of rhetoric and belles lettres at Edinburgh (Letter 85)
Blair, James Hunter, see Hunter Blair
Blair, Mrs, 'a Dorsetshire lady' (Letter 150)
Blair, Robert (1741–1811), of Avontoun, solicitor general for Scotland (Letter 154)
Bogue, see Boog
Boog, Robert (1746–1823), minister of the second charge in Paisley (Letter 151)
Boswell, James (1740–95), lawyer, diarist, and friend of Samuel Johnson (Letter 79)
Bourn, Samuel (1689–1754), English Presbyterian Dissenter and Arian (Letter 79)
Bowman, John (1701–97) of Ashkirk, banker and tobacco merchant in Glasgow (Letter 98)
Boyd, William (1748–1828), minister of Fenwick, Ayrshire (Letter 88)
Boyle, Elizabeth, née Ross (d. 1791), Lady Glasgow (Letter 84)
Boyle, Patrick (1717–98), Lord Shewalton, army chaplain and landowner (Letter 98)
Boyle, Mr, of Irvine (Letter 88)
Bradfute, John (1725–93), minister of Dunsyre, south Lanarkshire (Letter 120)

Brisbane, Mary (d. before 1807), sister of Robert Brisbane (d. 1807) (Letter 84)
Brisbane, Robert (d. 1807), kinsman of SK (Letter 81)
Brown, Malcolm (1694/5–1794), minister of Kilbirnie, Ayrshire (Letter 86)
Brydone, Patrick (1736–1818), son-in-law to William Robertson (Letter 99)
Buchan, Elspath or Elspeth, née Simpson (c. 1738–91) (Letter 84)
Bull, George (1634–1710), bishop of St David's (Letter 80)
Burke, Edmund (1730–97), Whig politician and political philosopher (Letter 80)
Burnett, James (1714–99), Lord Monboddo, Scottish judge and philosopher (Letter 124)
Burney, Charles (1757–1817), schoolmaster and book collector (Letter 121)
Burns, Robert (1759–96), Ayrshire poet (Letter 134)
Butt, George (1741–95), Anglican clergyman in Kidderminster and poet (Letter 155)

Cadell, Thomas (1742–1806), the elder, bookseller (Letter 138)
Caldwell, Andrew (1733–1808), barrister and architectural expert, MP in the Irish Parliament (Letter 133)
Calvin, Jean (1509–64), Protestant Reformer (Letter 115)
Campbell, Archibald (1682–1761), third duke of Argyll (Letter 98)
Campbell, George (1719–96), principal of Marischal College, Aberdeen, and minister of Greyfriars' Chapel, Aberdeen (Letter 87)

Campbell, Ilay (1734–1823), judge and politician (Letter 79)

Campbell, John (1708–75), writer and historian (Letter 122)

Campbell, William (1727–1805), Arian presbyterian minister in Armagh (Letter 146)

Campbell, Willielma (1741–86), Viscountess Glenorchy (Letter 88)

Cappe, Newcome (1733–1800), Dissenting minister and unitarian theologian (Letter 79)

Carlyle, Alexander (1722–1805), minister of Inveresk and leading Moderate (Letter 149)

Cassillis, see Kennedy

Cathcart, Archibald Hamilton (1764–1841), divinity student at Oxford, son of Lord Cathcart (Letter 106)

Cathcart, Charles Schaw (1721–76), ninth Lord Cathcart, army officer and diplomat (Letter 106)

Cato, Marcus Porcius the elder (234–149 BC), Roman soldier, senator, and historian (Letter 107)

Chambers, Ephraim (c. 1680–1740), lexicographer (Letter 105)

Charlotte, Queen (1744–1818) (Letter 80)

Charters, Samuel (1742–1825), minister of Wilton, in the Scottish Borders (Letter 96)

Chaucer, Geoffrey (c. 1345–1400), poet and author of *The Canterbury Tales* (Letter 131)

Chidlow, Mr, clergyman at Chester (Letter 142)

Chifflet, Pierre-François (1592–1682), editor of Vigilius (Letter 100)

Christie, Thomas (1761–96), political writer (Letter 130)

Cicero, Marcus Tullius (c. 106–43 BC), Roman orator and statesman (Letter 107)

Clarke, Samuel (1675–1729), Anglican clergyman, theologian, and Newtonian philosopher (Letter 86)

Clarke, Samuel (1684–1750), Dissenting minister at St Albans (Letter 119)

Clarke, Samuel (1728–69), Dissenting schoolmaster at Chiswick and minister at Birmingham (Letter 119)

Clarke, Sarah, wife of Samuel Clarke (1728–69) (Letter 119)

Clarkson, Thomas (1760–1846), abolitionist (Letter 135)

Clerk, John (1757–1832), advocate and Foxite Whig politician in Edinburgh (Letter 154)

Clow, James (d. 1787), professor of logic at Glasgow (Letter 98)

Collins, Anthony (1676–1729), philosopher and freethinker (Letter 80)

Colquhoun, Patrick (1745–1820), statistician, merchant, lord provost of Glasgow, and founder of the Glasgow Chamber of Commerce and the Thames police in London (Letter 121)

Copland, Patrick (1748–1822), professor of mathematics and teacher of natural philosophy at Marischal College, Aberdeen (Letter 99)

Cornwallis, Charles (1738–1805), first marquess (Letter 86)

Cowper, William (1731–1800), poet (Letter 134)

Coxe, William (1748–1828), historian and Anglican clergyman (Letter 93)

Craig, William (1709–84), minister of St Andrew's church, Glasgow (Letter 108)

Crauford, John (?1742–1814), politician (Letter 79)

Crawford, Mrs Barbara, sister of Quintin, student friend of JW, nabob (Letter 140)

Crawford, Jean, of Dalry (Letter 131)

## PERSONS MENTIONED IN VOLUME 2

Crellius, Johannes (1590–1633), a Polish-German Socinian writer (Letter 96)
Cullen, William (1710–90), chemist and physician (Letter 115)
Cunningham, Alexander (1756–90), eleventh laird of Craigends (Letter 114)
Cunningham, Ann, see Monteath
Cunningham, William, thirteenth earl of Glencairn (d. 1775) (Letter 146)
Cunninghame, Robert Reid (1744–1814) of Seabank House, Stevenston, coal company manager (Letter 84)

Dale, David (1739–1806), textile merchant in Glasgow and cotton manufacturer at New Lanark (Letter 86)
Dalrymple, Sir David (1726–92), third baronet, Lord Hailes (Letter 84)
Dalrymple, William (1723–1814), minister of the first charge of Ayr (Letter 125)
Dalzel, Andrew (1742–1806), professor of Greek at Edinburgh (Letter 149)
Davidson, Archibald (c. 1732–1803), minister of Inchinnan, Renfrewshire, then principal of Glasgow University (1786–1803) (Letter 108)
Dawson, Benjamin (1729–1814), Anglican clergyman (Letter 150)
Demosthenes (384–322 BC), Athenian statesman and orator (Letter 118)
Dempster, George of Dunnichen (1732–1818), politician (Letter 79)
Dilly, Charles (1739–1807), bookseller in London (Letter 139)
Dinwiddie, Mr and Mrs, of Redvale, near Manchester (Letters 98, 101)
Doddridge, Philip, Independent minister, writer, and founder of Northampton Academy (Letter 112)
Dolben, Sir William (1727–1814), MP for Oxford University (Letter 135)
Douglas, Dunbar Hamilton, fourth earl of Selkirk (1722–90) (Letter 80)

Douglas, Gavin (1476–1522), bishop of Dunkeld, poet, and translator of Virgil's *Aeneid* (Letter 131)
Douglas-Hamilton, Archibald (1740–1819), ninth duke of Hamilton (Letter 79)
Dow, Robert (1707–87), minister of Ardrossan, north Ayrshire (Letter 125)
Drysdale, John (1718–88), minister of the Tron Church, Edinburgh (Letter 149)
Dun, Alexander (1718–90), minister of Cadder, near Glasgow (Letter 154)
Dundas, Henry (1742–1811), lawyer and politician (Letter 98)
Dundas, Robert (1758–1819), solicitor general, then lord advocate for Scotland (Letter 154)
Dunlop, Alexander (1684–1747), professor of Greek at Glasgow (Letter 104)
Dunlop, Sarah, daughter of Alexander Dunlop (Letter 104)
Dunlop-Wallace, Thomas (1750–1835), of Dunlop and Craigie (Letter 84)
Dunmore, see Murray

Eddowes, Joshua (1724–1811), Dissenter and bookseller in Shrewsbury (Letter 153)
Edgar Ætheling (c. 1052–c. 1125), brother of Queen Margaret of Scotland, elected but not crowned king of England (Letter 148)
Edward VI, King (1537–53) (Letter 115)
Eglinton, see Montgomerie
Emlyn, Thomas (1663–1741), Dissenting minister and Unitarian pioneer (Letter 91)
Epicurus (341–270 BC), Greek philosopher (Letter 84)
Epiphanius (c. 315–403), early church father, bishop of Constantia (Letter 118)
Erskine, Henry (1746–1817), lawyer and politician (Letter 79)

Erskine, John (1721–1803), minister of the second charge of Old Greyfriars in Edinburgh and leader of the Popular party in the Church of Scotland (Letter 96)

Erskine, Thomas (1750–1823), renowned barrister and MP, brother of Henry Erskine (Letter 154)

Est, Willem Hessels van (1542–1613), Dutch Roman Catholic biblical commentator (Letter 87)

Euler, Leonard (1707–83), Swiss mathematician and physicist (Letter 112)

Eunapius (b. 346), Greek sophist, rhetorician, and historian (Letter 117)

Eusebius of Caesarea (d. 339), Greek bishop and historian of Christianity (Letter 123)

Evanson, Edward (1731–1805), unitarian schoolmaster at Mitcham (Letter 79)

Fagaras, Josephus Pap de (fl. 1780), minister and mathematician in Transylvania (Letter 84)

Farmer, Hugh (1714/15–87), Dissenting minister in Walthamstow, Essex, preacher at Salter's Hall in London, and theological writer (Letter 87)

Farnaby, Thomas (1574/5–1647), schoolmaster and grammarian (Letter 147)

Ferguson, Adam (1723–1816), professor of moral philosophy at Edinburgh (Letter 107)

Fergusson, Sir Adam of Kilkerran (1733–1813), politician (Letter 79)

Fergusson, Alexander (1689–1770), minister of the Abbey Church, Kilwinning, 'the Abbot' (Letter 99)

Festus, Porcius (fl. 60–62 AD), Roman procurator of Judea (Letter 129)

Fielding, Henry (1707–54), author and magistrate (Letter 144)

Finlay, James and Robert (fl. 1783–85), merchants in Glasgow (Letter 90)

Findlay, Robert (1721–1814), dean of the faculty of divinity at Glasgow and minister of St David's parish, Glasgow (Letter 106)

Fitzherbert, Maria, née Smythe, (1756–1837), unlawful wife of the Prince of Wales (Letter 113)

Fitzherbert, Thomas (1746–81), second husband of Maria Fitzherbert, née Smythe (Letter 113)

Fleming, John (1711–87), minister of Kilmacolm, near Paisley, Renfrewshire (Letter 79)

Fordyce, David (bap. 1711, d. 1751), professor of moral philosophy in Aberdeen (Letter 105)

Fordyce, James (1720–96), Scottish presbyterian minister and moralist in London (Letter 105)

Foulis, Andrew (d. 1775), printer to the University of Glasgow (Letter 110)

Foulis, Robert (1707–76), brother of Andrew, printer to the University of Glasgow (Letter 110)

Fownes, Joseph (1715–89), minister at High Street, Shrewsbury (Letter 150)

Fox, Charles James (1749–1806), politician (Letter 79)

Francis, St (d. 1226), Italian poet and founder of the Franciscan order (Letter 112)

Fullarton, William (1754–1808) of Fullarton, near Irvine (Letter 132)

Fullerton, Alexander (1737–87), minister of St Clement's and Futtie and master of Aberdeen Grammar School (Letter 84)

Fulton, William, distant relative of SK (Letter 84)

Geddes, Alexander (1737–1802), Roman Catholic priest and biblical scholar (Letter 138)

Geddes, James (1710–45), lawyer and writer in Edinburgh (Letter 110)

Gentleman, Robert (1743–95), Arian minister in Kidderminster (Letter 155)

George III, King (1738–1820) (Letter 80)

George, Prince of Wales, 80

Gerard, Alexander (1728–95), professor of divinity at King's College, Aberdeen (Letter 99)

Gibbon, Edward (1737–94), historian of ancient Rome (Letter 85)

Gibson, Peter?, merchant (Letter 106)

Gibson, Mrs, wife of Peter Gibson and cousin of Louisa Wodrow (Letter 94)

Glencairn, see Cunningham

Glenorchy, see Campbell

Gordon, Jane, duchess of, née Maxwell (1748/9–1812), political hostess and agricultural reformer (Letter 99)

Gordon, Lord George (1751–93), third son of the duke of Gordon (Letter 151)

Graham, James (1755–1836), marquess of Graham, third duke of Montrose (1790–1836), politician, and chancellor of Glasgow University (1780–1836) (Letter 79)

Grant, David (1750–91), minister of Ochiltree, Ayrshire (Letter 151)

Gregory (538–94), bishop of Tours (Letter 100)

Griffith [Gruffydd] ap Llewellyn, king of Wales (r. 1055–63) (Letter 148)

Griffiths, Elizabeth, née Clark (d. 1812), second wife of Ralph Griffiths, editor of the *Monthly Review* (Letter 119)

Griffiths, Isabella (d. 1764), first wife of Ralph Griffiths, editor of the *Monthly Review* (Letter 119)

Griffiths, Ralph (c. 1720–1803), bookseller, publisher, and editor of the *Monthly Review* (Letter 119)

Haddow (d. 1784) of Irvine (Letter 82)

Hailes, see Dalrymple

Hakewill, George (1578–1649), clergyman and author (Letter 112)

Hamilton, see Douglas-Hamilton

Hamilton, see McCormick

Hamilton, Anne (d. 1789), sister of Louisa Wodrow (Letter 146)

Hamilton, Lord Archibald (1673–1754), naval officer, governor of Jamaica, and MP (Letter 97)

Hamilton, Archibald (1740–1819), ninth duke of Hamilton and sixth duke of Brandon (Letter 97)

Hamilton, Elizabeth, née Millar (d. 1798) (Letter 84)

Hamilton, Frederick (1728–1811), son of Lord Archibald Hamilton (1673–1754) (Letter 97)

Hamilton, Helen (d. 1793), mother of Louisa Wodrow (Letter 146)

Hamilton, James (1721–82), minister of the Abbey Church, Paisley (Letter 82)

Hamilton, John (1740–92), Louisa Wodrow's brother in London (Letter 84)

Hamilton, Mrs, John Hamilton's wife (Letter 149)

Hamilton, Robert (1743–1829), professor of natural philosophy at Aberdeen, Louisa Wodrow's brother (Letter 87)

Hamilton, Robert, weaver in Stevenston (Letter 131)

Hamilton, Thomas (fl. 1757–81), professor of anatomy at Glasgow (Letter 98)

Hancox, Joseph, chair of the Worcester district of Protestant Dissenters (Letter 155)

Harris, James (1709–80), philosopher (Letter 131)

Hartley, David (bap. 1705, d. 1757), philosopher and physician (Letter 110)

Hastings, Selina, *née* Shirley (1707–91), Countess of Huntingdon, supporter of the Calvinistic Methodists (Letter 118)

Hatchet, Buckley, of Lee, Shropshire (Letter 142)

Hawkes, William (1732–96), Joseph Priestley's predecessor at the New Meeting, Birmingham (Letter 123)

Hawkes, William (1759–1820), Dissenting minister (Letter 123)

Hayley, William (1745–1820), poet and biographer (Letter 79)

Herschel, William (1738–1822), astronomer royal (Letter 120)

Hervey, James (1714–58), Evangelical clergyman and writer (Letter 110)

Hill, George (1750–1819), minister of St Andrews and principal of St Andrews University (Letter 154)

Hoadly, Benjamin (1767–61), bishop of Winchester (Letter 151)

Hollis, Thomas (1720–74), political propagandist (Letter 80)

Home, Henry (1696–1782), Lord Kames, judge and philosopher (Letter 98)

Hope, Lord Charles (1740–66) (Letter 93)

Horace, or Quintus Horatius Flaccus (65–8 BC), Roman lyric poet (Letter 123)

Horne, George (1730–92), dean of Canterbury (Letter 129)

Horne Tooke, John (1736–1812), radical reformer and philologist (Letter 131)

Horsley, Samuel (1733–1806), archdeacon of St Albans, then bishop of St Davids (Letter 80)

Howard, Charles (1746–1815), earl of Surrey, MP for Carlisle (1780–86), eleventh duke of Norfolk (1786–1815) (Letter 80)

Howard, John (1726–90), philanthropist and penal reformer (Letter 113)

Howard, Thomas (1747–91), third earl of Effingham (Letter 152)

Howes, Thomas (1724–1814), rector of Thorndon (Letter 118)

Huet or Huetius, Pierre-Daniel (1630–1721), French scholar and churchman (Letter 80)

Hume, David (1711–76), philosopher and historian (Letter 109)

Humphreys, Alexander (fl. 1777–85), student at Glasgow (Letter 98)

Hunter, Peter, writer in Irvine (Letter 84)

Hunter, William (fl. 1759–84) of Mainholm and Brownhill, Ayrshire (Letter 86)

Hunter Blair, James (1741–87), first baronet, banker in Edinburgh (Letter 86)

Huntingdon, see Hastings

Hurd, Richard (1720–1808), bishop of Worcester (Letter 79)

Hutcheson, Francis (1694–1746), professor of moral philosophy at Glasgow (Letter 80)

Ingram, John, student friend of JW (Letter 140)

Irvine, William (1743–87), lecturer in materia medica and chemistry at Glasgow (Letter 106)

Isocrates (d. 338 BC), Athenian orator (Letter 123)

Jackson, Cyril (1746–1819), dean of Christ Church, Oxford (Letter 135)

Jamieson, John (1759–1838), antiquary, philologist, and minister at Forfar (Letter 130)

Jardine, George (1742–1827), minister and professor of logic at Glasgow (Letter 96)
Jenyns, Soame (1704–87), author and politician (Letter 119)
Jerome (c. 342–420), Bible translator (Letter 118)
Jesse, William (c. 1739–1815), Rector of Dowles near Bewdley (Letter 100)
Jesus Christ (Letter 79)
Job, Old Testament saint (Letter 147)
John, writer of John's Gospel and the book of Revelation (Letter 79)
John the Baptist, Jewish preacher heralding the ministry of Jesus (Letter 124)
Johnson, Joseph (1738–1808), publisher (Letter 138)
Johnson, Samuel (1709–84), author and lexicographer (Letter 117)
Johnston, David (1734–1824), minister of North Leith (Letter 154)
Johnstone, Edward (1757–1851), physician in and near Birmingham (Letter 83)
Johnstone, James (1730–1802), physician in Kidderminster (Letter 144)
Jortin, John (1698–1770), Anglican clergyman, ecclesiastical historian and literary critic (Letter 122)
Joseph II (1741–90), Holy Roman emperor (r. 1765–90) (Letter 113)
Judas Iscariot, disciple of Jesus who betrayed him (Letter 154)
Julianus, Flavius Claudius (r. 332–63), emperor of Rome (Letter 109)
Justin Martyr (100–165), apologist and martyr for the Christian faith (Letter 79)
Justinian (r. 527–65), Roman emperor, author of the Institutes (Letter 119)
Juvenal, or Decimus Junius Juvenalis (fl. c. 100 AD), Roman satirical poet (Letter 131)

Kames, see Home
Kaye, Sir Richard (1736–1809), dean of Lincoln Cathedral (Letter 113)
Kästner, Abraham Gotthelf (1719–1800), German mathematician (Letter 143)
Kennedy, David (1727–92), tenth earl of Cassillis (Letter 82)
Kennedy, Thomas (1726–75), ninth earl of Cassillis (Letter 120)
Kennedy, Thomas (d. 1819), of Dunure and Dalquharran, Ayrshire (Letter 84)
Kippis, Andrew (1725–95), Presbyterian minister in Westminster and biographer (Letter 118)
Knox, John (c. 1513–72), Protestant Reformer (Letter 115)
Knox, Vicesimus (1752–1821), priest, headmaster, and writer (Letter 110)

Lang, Gilbert (1725–91), minister of Largs, Ayrshire (Letter 79)
Lang, James, deacon of the hammermen in Glasgow, 1787 (Letter 98)
Lapsley, James (1754–1824), minister of Campsie and Antermony (Letter 154)
Lardner, Nathaniel (1684–1768), Presbyterian minister in London and patristic scholar (Letter 122)
Latimer, Hugh (c. 1485–1555), Protestant Reformer (Letter 115)
Lauchlan(e), Mr (Letter 88)
Lauderdale, see Maitland
Laurie or Lawrie, George (d. 1799), minister of Loudoun, Ayrshire (Letter 96)
Lavater, Johann Caspar (1741–1801), Swiss theologian and physiognomist, philosopher, and poet (Letter 99)
Leechman, Bridget, née Balfour (d. 1792), wife of William Leechman and aunt of Louisa Wodrow (Letter 84)

Leechman, William (1706–85), professor of divinity and principal of Glasgow University (Letter 79)
Leland, Thomas (1722–85), historian and Church of Ireland clergyman (Letter 150)
Leslie, David (1722–1802), sixth earl of Leven (Letter 154)
Levi, David (1742–1801), writer on Judaism (Letter 131)
Lindsey, Theophilus (1723–1808), unitarian minister in London (Letter 79)
Locke, John (1632–1704), philosopher (Letter 131)
Loudon, John (1699–1727), professor of logic and rhetoric at Glasgow (Letter 122)
Lowth, Robert (1710–87), biblical critic and bishop of London (Letter 84)
Lunardi, Vincenzo (1754–1806), Italian hot-air balloonist (Letter 106)
Luther, Martin (1483–1546), Protestant Reformer (Letter 115)
Lyttelton, George Fulke (1763–1828) of Hagley (Letter 155)
Lyttelton, William Henry (1724–1808), baron Lyttelton and baron Westcote (Letter 80)

Macintosh/Mackintosh, James (1727–99), minister of Moy and Dalarossie, Inverness-shire (Letter 130)
Mackenzie, John (1743–1836), minister of Portpatrick, Wigtonshire (Letter 84)
MacKinlay, James (1756–1841), minister of the Laigh Kirk, Kilmarnock (Letter 126)
Macknight, Elizabeth (d. 1813), wife of James Macknight and sister of Edward McCormick (Letter 114)
Macknight, James (1721–1800), biblical scholar and minister of the Old Church, Edinburgh (1778–1800) (Letter 83)
Maclaine, Archibald (1722–1804), minister at the English church at the Hague (Letter 84)
Macleod, Hugh (d. 1809), professor of ecclesiastical history at Glasgow (Letter 96)
Macreddie, Mrs (Letter 84)
Madan, Martin (1725–90), Anglican clergyman associated with the Calvinist Methodists (Letter 144)
Madan, Spencer (1758–1836), rector of St Philip's, Birmingham (Letter 131)
Maitland, James (1759–1839), eighth earl of Lauderdale (Letter 154)
Mansfield, see Murray
Margaret, Queen of Scots [St Margaret] (d. 1093) (Letter 148)
Martin, Samuel (1740–1829), minister of Monimail, Fife (Letter 154)
Mason, William (1725–97), poet (Letter 79)
Maty, Paul Henry (1744–87), writer, editor, and teacher (Letter 122)
Maxwell, Elizabeth Hairstanes (b. 1717), Lady Alva (Letter 88)
Maxwell, Patrick (1747–1806), minister of Kilbarchan, Ayrshire (1787–1806) (Letter 130)
McCormick, Edward (1745–1814), advocate and sheriff of Ayr (Letter 114)
McCormick, John ('Jack'), wife of Edward McCormick (Letter 114)
M'Gill, Elizabeth (1765–91), daughter of William M'Gill (Letter 149)
M'Gill, William (1732–1807), minister of the Old Kirk, Ayr and heterodox theologian (Letter 79)
M'Indoe, David (d. 1826), student at Glasgow University and later minister at Newcastle (Letter 96)
McIntosh/Macintosh, Robert (Letter 154)

Melanchthon, Philip (1497–1560), Protestant Reformer (Letter 115)

Melmoth, William, the younger (c. 1710–99), translator of Cicero (Letter 107)

Millar, Andrew (1705–68), bookseller in London, relative of SK (Letter 134)

Millar, Henry (d. 1771), minister at Neilston, relative of SK (Letter 82)

Millar, John (1735–1801), professor of civil law at Glasgow (Letter 79)

Miller, Thomas (1740–1819), minister of Old Cumnock (Letter 84)

Milliken, Alexander (1743–65) (Letter 96)

Milliken, James (1741–63) (Letter 96)

Milliken, Jean, née Macdowall (d. 1791) (Letter 84)

Milton, John (1608–74), Puritan poet and polemicist (Letter 131)

Mitford, William (1744–1827), historian of ancient Greece (Letter 95)

Monboddo, see Burnett

Moncrieff Wellwood, Sir Henry (1750–1827), eighth baronet of Tullibole, minister of St Cuthbert's, Edinburgh (Letter 154)

Monteath, Ann (c. 1762–1848), née Cunningham (Letter 128)

Monteath, James Stewart (fl. 1784), previously rector of Barrowby, Lincs (Letter 88)

Montesquieu, Charles de Secondat (1689–1755), Baron de la Brède, Enlightenment philosopher (Letter 112)

Montgomerie, Archibald (1726–96), eleventh earl of Eglinton (Letter 86)

Montgomerie, Frances, née Twysden (b. 1762), married Archibald Montgomerie, eleventh earl of Eglinton (1783), divorced (1788) (Letter 125)

Montgomerie, Hugh (1739–1819), politician and army officer, twelfth earl of Eglinton (Letter 79)

Moodie, Alexander (1728–99), minister of Riccarton, Ayrshire (Letter 151)

Moor, James (c. 1712–79), professor of Greek at Glasgow (Letter 122)

Morgan, Miss, niece of Richard Price (Letter 140)

Morgan, Sarah (1726–1803), sister of Richard Price (Letter 140)

Morgan, William (1750–1833) or George Cadogan Morgan (1754–98), nephews of Richard Price (Letter 140)

Morthland, Matthew (fl. 1752–85), Glasgow University factor (manager) (Letter 98)

Moulson, Mr (d. before 1796), business partner of Ralph Eddowes (SK's nephew by marriage) (Letter 142)

Muir, George (1723–71), minister of the High Kirk, Paisley (1766–71) (Letter 114)

Muir, John (d. c. 1769), rector of Perth Academy (Letter 99)

Mure, Elizabeth (c. 1714–95), of Caldwell, sister of William Mure of Caldwell (1718–76) (Letter 120)

Mure, William, of Caldwell (d. 1831), army officer (Letter 79)

Murray, John (1732–1809), fourth earl of Dunmore, colonial governor and Scottish representative peer (Letter 119)

Murray, William (1705–93), first earl of Mansfield, judge (Letter 131)

Newton, Sir Isaac (1642–1727), natural philosopher and mathematician (Letter 110)

Nicoll, Mr, writer in Aberdeen (Letter 95)

North, Frederick (1732–92), second earl of Guilford (Letter 80)

Origen (c. 185–254), early church father in Alexandria (Letter 118)

Orton, Job (1717–83), Dissenting minister in Salisbury (Letter 119)
Oswald, George (1735–1819), of Scotstoun, Balshagray, and Auchencruive (Letter 86)
Oswald, Richard (1705–84), merchant, contractor, speculator, and British negotiator at the Peace of Paris in 1782–83 (Letter 86)

Pairman, William (1735–98), minister of Elie, Fife and nephew of William Leechman (Letter 84)
Paley, William (1743–1805), theologian and moralist (Letter 143)
Palmer, John (1742–1818), theatre proprietor and postal reformer (Letter 115)
Palmer, Samuel (1741–1813), Dissenting minister in Hackney (Letter 119)
Parr, Samuel (1747–1825), schoolmaster, Anglican clergyman, and writer (Letter 150)
Paterson, John (fl. 1789) of Craigton (Letter 97)
Paul (c. 5–64/65 AD), apostle and author of New Testament epistles (Letter 87)
Peebles, William (1753–1826), minister of Newton-on-Ayr (Letter 146)
Pennant, Thomas (1726–98), naturalist, traveller, and writer (Letter 93)
Pétau, Denis (1583–1652), also known as Dionysius Petavius, French Jesuit philosopher and theologian (Letter 80)
Peter, apostle, author of two New Testament epistles (Letter 92)
Phillips, John George (c. 1761–1816), MP for Carmarthen (Letter 152)
Phocas (547–610), Byzantine emperor (r. 602–10) (Letter 111)
Pindar, Peter, see Walcot

Piozzi, Hester Lynch (1741–1821), previously Thrale, writer and friend of Samuel Johnson (Letter 117)
Pitt, William the Younger (1759–1806), prime minister (1783–1801, 1804–06) (Letter 79)
Plato (c. 428–348 BC), Athenian philosopher (Letter 123)
Playfair, John (1748–1819), professor of mathematics at Edinburgh (Letter 99)
Plutarch (c. 46–c. 120 AD), Greek historian, biographer, and philosopher (Letter 117)
Polycarp (70–155 AD), bishop of Smyrna, martyr (Letter 124)
Pouilly, Louis-Jean Lévesque de (1691–1751), French philosopher (Letter 143)
Preston, William (1740–1808), foreman in Andrew Strahan's printing business (Letter 140)
Price, Richard (1723–91), philosopher, political reformer, and Presbyterian minister in London (Letter 117)
Priestley, Joseph (1733–1804), unitarian theologian and natural philosopher (Letter 79)
Priestley, Mary, wife of Joseph Priestley (1743–96) (Letter 85)
Prior, Matthew (1664–1721), poet (Letter 84)

Raikes, Robert (1736–1811), editor of the *Gloucester Journal* and philanthropist (Letter 113)
Rayner, Elizabeth (1714–1800), patron of Joseph Priestley and Theophilus Lindsey (Letter 118)
Rees, Abraham (1743–1825), Presbyterian minister at the Old Jewry congregation in the City of London, and tutor in Hackney (Letter 140)

Reid, Thomas (1710–96), philosopher and mathematician, professor of moral philosophy at Glasgow (Letter 83)

Richard III (1452–85), king of England (r. 1483–85) (Letter 94)

Richardson, Prof. William (1743–1814), professor of humanity at Glasgow (Letter 80)

Ridley, Nicholas (c. 1500–55), Protestant Reformer (Letter 115)

Roberts, Betty Carolina (1745–1817), wife of SK's banking partner Wilson Aylesbury Roberts (Letter 102)

Roberts, Wilson Aylesbury (1736–1819), banking partner and friend to SK (Letter 135)

Roberts, Wilson Aylesbury (1770–1853), son of Wilson Aylesbury Roberts (1736–1819) (Letter 135)

Roberts, Caroline Aylesbury, daughter of Wilson and Betty Roberts (Letter 143)

Robertson, John (1733–99), minister at Kilmarnock, Ayrshire (Letter 146)

Robertson, Mary, née Nisbet (1723–1802), wife of William Robertson (Letter 99)

Robertson, William (1721–93), historian, principal of Edinburgh University, minister of Old Greyfriars in Edinburgh, and leader of the Moderate party in the Church of Scotland (Letter 96)

Robertson, William (1753–1835), lawyer, son of William Robertson (Letter 99)

Rogers, Thomas (d. 1793), banker and leading Dissenter in London (Letter 118)

Rose, Samuel (1767–1804), student at Glasgow University then lawyer (Letter 108)

Rose, William (1719–86), schoolmaster and co-founder of the *Monthly Review* (Letter 116)

Ross, Andrew (1726–87), minister of Insh, Stranraer (Letter 150)

Ross, David (1727–1850), Lord Ankerville of Tarlogie, judge (Letter 117)

Rouet/Ruat/Ruet, William (1714–85), professor of ecclesiastical history at Glasgow (Letter 93)

Rouet/Ruat, Mrs, wife of William Rouet/Ruat/Ruet (Letter 96)

Rowan, Mr, Bewdley resident (Letter 143)

Rufinus, Tyrannius (c. 345–411), Roman theologian (Letter 100)

Russel, John (1740–1817), minister of the chapel of ease at Kilmarnock (Letter 151)

Seddon, John (1724–69), Dissenting minister and tutor (Letter 118)

Selkirk, see Douglas

Shaw, Duncan (1727–94), minister in Aberdeen (Letter 130)

Siddons, Sarah (1755–1831), actress (Letter 97)

Smith, Adam (c. 1723–1790), moral philosopher and political economist (Letter 83)

Socinus, Faustus (1539–1604), Italian theologian exiled in Poland (Letter 79)

Socrates, Greek philosopher (Letter 80)

Somerville, Thomas (1741–1830), minister of Jedburgh and memoirist (Letter 154)

Speirs, Alexander (1714–82) of Elderslie, banker and tobacco merchant in Glasgow (Letter 97)

Spens, Graham (c. 1771–85), son of Nathaniel Spens (Letter 96)

Spens, Nathaniel (1728–1815), Edinburgh physician (Letter 96)

Stanhope, Charles (1753–1816), third earl Stanhope (Letter 152)

Sterne, Laurence (1713–68), writer and Anglican clergyman (Letter 95)

Stevenson, Alexander (c. 1725–91), professor of the practice of medicine at Glasgow (Letter 106)

Stewart, Keith (1739–95), cousin of Archibald Montgomerie, earl of Eglinton (Letter 125)

Stillingfleet, Edward (d. 1795) or James (fl. 1772–1817), clergyman (Letter 117)

Stirling, James (1740–1805), banker and lord provost of Edinburgh (Letter 154)

Stirling, John (1654–1727), principal of Glasgow University (Letter 98)

Stirling, John (fl. 1779), translator of Virgil (Letter 147)

Stirling, Miss (Letter 139)

Strahan, Andrew (1750–1831), printer and publisher (Letter 140)

Stuart, Andrew (1725–1801), lawyer and politician (Letter 79)

Succoth, see Campbell

Sulzer, Johann Georg (1720–79), Swiss mathematician (Letter 143)

Surrey, see Howard

Sutherland, Elizabeth (1765–1839), countess of Sutherland (Letter 84)

Sydney, see Townshend

Sykes, Arthur Ashley (c. 1684–1756), latitudinarian clergyman (Letter 80)

Symington, William (1764–1831), engineer and steam-power pioneer (Letter 120)

Tait, Peter (fl. 1768–95), merchant, bookseller, and printer of the *Glasgow Journal* (Letter 84)

Tayler, Thomas (1735–1831), Dissenting minister at Carter Lane, London (Letter 138)

Tayleur, William (1712–96), Shropshire correspondent of Theophilus Lindsey (Letter 150)

Taylor, John (1694–1761), presbyterian theologian in Norwich (Letter 87)

Taylor, William (1744–1823), minister of the North or High Church, Glasgow (Letter 98)

Theocritus (b. c. 300 BC, d. after 260 BC), Greek pastoral poet (Letter 131)

Thompson, Seth (c. 1731–1805), schoolmaster in Kensington and clergyman (Letter 139)

Thomson, Thomas (1730–99), minister of Dailly, Ayrshire (Letter 149)

Thrale, Henry (1728–81), brewer and politician, first husband of Hester Piozzi (Letter 119)

Thucydides (c. 460–c. 400 BC), Greek historian (Letter 147)

Thurlow, Edward (1731–1806), first baron Thurlow, lord chancellor (Letter 131)

Toland, John (1670–1722), Irish philosopher and freethinker (Letter 80)

Toulmin, Joshua (1740–1815), unitarian minister and historian (Letter 79)

Townshend, Thomas (1733–1800), first viscount Sydney (Letter 96)

Trail, Robert (1720–75), professor of ecclesiastical history at Glasgow (Letter 109)

Trail, William (1746–1831), professor of mathematics at Marischal College, Aberdeen (Letter 99)

Tullideph, Thomas (1700–77), professor of biblical criticism and principal, University of St Andrews (Letter 87)

Urwick, Thomas (1727–1807), Independent minister at Grafton Square, Clapham (Letter 139)

Valentia, see Annesley

Vigilius Tapsensis, fifth-century bishop of Thapsus (Letter 100)

Viret, Pierre (1511–71), Protestant Reformer (Letter 115)
Virgil, or Publius Vergilius Maro (70–19 BC), Roman poet (Letter 123)
Voltaire, François-Marie Arouet (1694–1778), French Enlightenment philosopher and satirist (Letter 130)

Walcot, John (1738–1819), satirist whose pseudonym was Peter Pindar (Letter 119)
Walker, John (1731–1803), minister of Colinton and professor of natural history at Edinburgh (Letter 154)
Walker, Robert (1755–1808), minister of the Canongate, Edinburgh (Letter 154)
Warburton, William (1698–1779), bishop of Gloucester (Letter 109)
Warton, Thomas (1728–90), poet and historian (Letter 131)
Watson, Richard (1737–1816), bishop of Llandaff (Letter 135)
Wat(t), Hugh, brewer in Saltcoats, Ayrshire (Letter 104)
Watts, Isaac (1674–1748), English hymnologist (Letter 118)
Welsh, William (d. 1806), minister of Drumelzier, Tweed Valley (Letter 154)
Wesley, John (1703–91), evangelist and founder of Arminian Methodism (Letter 113)
Westcote, see Lyttelton
Whitbread, Samuel (1764–1815), brewer and politician (Letter 93)
White, Hugh (fl. 1782–83), minister of the Relief Church in Irvine (Letter 84)
White, Joseph (fl. 1784–85), Fellow of Wadham College, Oxford (Letter 112)
Whitefield, George (1714–70), leading Calvinist Methodist and evangelist (Letter 100)

Wigan, Thomas (c. 1744–1819), rector of Oldswinford near Stourbridge (Letter 88)
William III and II, King (1650–1702, r. 1689–1702)
Williams, Daniel (c. 1643–1716), presbyterian minister and benefactor (Letter 118)
Willis, Francis (1718–1807), clergyman and physician (Letter 147)
Wilson (fl. 1785), clerk to the faculty, Glasgow University (Letter 98)
Witherspoon, John (1723–94), leading Popular party minister, then principal of the College of New Jersey (1768–94) (Letter 83)
Wright, James (d. 1812), minister of Maybole (Letter 120)
Wyatt, Mr, colleague of Thomas Christie (Letter 143)

Xenophon (c. 435–354 BC), Greek historian, essayist, and military commander (Letter 124)

Yate, Benjamin, of Whitchurch, Shropshire, matriculated at Glasgow in 1746 (Letter 115)
Yorke, Sir Joseph (1724–92), baron Dover, soldier and diplomat (Letter 93)
Young, Edward (c. 1683–1765), poet, playwright, and satirist (Letter 80)
Young, James (1711–95), minister of New Cumnock, Ayrshire (Letter 151)
Young, John (1747–1820), professor of Greek at Glasgow (Letter 98)
Young, Mrs John (Letter 108)
Young, Stephen (1744–1818), minister of Barr, Ayrshire (Letter 151)

Zwicker, Daniel (1612–78), Socinian theologian and utopian (Letter 80)

# LIST OF LETTERS IN VOLUME 2

Extant and identified missing letters by James Wodrow (JW) and Samuel Kenrick (SK)

| No. | Author, place | | Recipient, place | Date |
|---|---|---|---|---|
| 79 | JW, Stevenston | to | SK, [Bewdley] | 1784, April 15 |
| 80 | SK, Bewdley | to | JW, Stevenston | 1784, June 2 |
| 81 | SK, Bewdley | to | JW, Stevenston | 1784, Aug. 13 |
| 82 | SK, Bewdley | to | Mary Kenrick, Glasgow | [Enclosed with Letter 81] |
| Missing | JW | | SK | 1784, Sept. 17 |
| 83 | SK, Bewdley | to | JW, Stevenston | 1784, Sept. 28 |
| 84 | JW, Stevenston | to | SK, Bewdley | 1784, Oct. 22 |
| 85 | SK, Bewdley | to | JW, Stevenston | 1784, Dec. 2–3 |
| 86 | JW, Stevenston | to | SK, Bewdley | 1784, Dec. 7 |
| 87 | JW, Stevenston | to | SK, Bewdley | 1785, Jan. 3 |
| 88 | JW, Stevenston | to | SK, Bewdley | 1785, Jan. 7 |
| 89 | SK, Bewdley | to | JW | 1785, Jan. 14 |
| Missing | SK | | JW | 1785, Jan. 28 |
| 90 | JW, Stevenston | to | SK, Bewdley | 1785, Jan. 19 |
| 91 | JW, Stevenston | to | SK | 1785, Feb. 6 |
| 92 | SK, Bewdley | to | JW | 1785, Feb. 22 |
| 93 | SK, Bewdley | to | JW | 1785, March 21 |
| 94 | JW, Stevenston | to | SK, Bewdley | 1785, March 25 |
| 95 | SK, Bewdley | to | JW | 1785, April 27 |
| Missing | JW | | SK | 1785, May 12 |
| 96 | JW, Edinburgh | to | SK | 1785, June 16 |

| No. | Author, place | | Recipient, place | Date |
|---|---|---|---|---|
| 97 | SK, Bewdley | to | JW, Stevenston | 1785, June 29 |
| 98 | JW, Stevenston | to | SK, Bewdley | 1785, July 21 |
| 99 | JW, Stevenston | to | SK, Bewdley | 1785, Aug. 5 |
| Missing | SK | | JW | 1785, Aug. 22 |
| 100 | SK, Bewdley | to | JW, Stevenston | 1785, Sept. 19 |
| 101 | SK, Bewdley | to | JW | 1785, Sept. 23 |
| 102 | JW, Stevenston | to | SK, Bewdley | 1785, Sept. 27 |
| 103 | SK | to | JW, Stevenston | 1785, Oct. 5 |
| Missing | SK | | JW | 1785, Oct. 22 |
| 104 | JW, Stevenston | to | SK, Bewdley | 1785, Oct. 31 |
| 105 | SK, Bewdley | to | JW, Stevenston | 1785, Nov. 11 |
| 106 | JW, Stevenston | to | SK, Bewdley | 1785, Dec. 1 |
| 107 | SK, Bewdley | to | JW, Stevenston | 1785, Dec. 1 |
| 108 | JW, Stevenston | to | SK, Bewdley | 1785, Dec. 27 |
| 109 | JW, Stevenston | to | SK, Bewdley | 1786, Jan. 9 |
| 110 | SK, Bewdley | to | JW, Stevenston | 1786, Jan. 21 |
| 111 | JW, Stevenston | to | SK | 1786, Jan. 23 |
| 112 | SK, Bewdley | to | JW | 1786, Feb. 11 |
| 113 | SK, Bewdley | to | JW, Stevenston | 1786, March 20 |
| 114 | JW, Stevenston | to | SK, Bewdley | 1786, April 11 |
| 115 | SK, Bewdley | to | JW, Stevenston | 1786, April 25 |
| 116 | JW, Stevenston | to | SK, Bewdley | 1786, May 2 |
| 117 | JW, Glasgow | to | SK, Bewdley | 1786, May 17 |
| Missing | SK | | JW | 1786, June 30 |
| 118 | SK, Bewdley | to | JW | 1786, July 3 |
| 119 | SK, Bewdley | to | JW | 1786, July 20 |
| 120 | JW, Stevenston; Tarbolton; Kirkoswald | to | SK, Bewdley | 1786, Aug. c. 9–15 |
| 121 | JW, Stevenston | to | SK, Bewdley | 1786, Aug. 28 |
| 122 | SK, Bewdley | to | JW | 1786, Sept. 28 |
| 123 | SK, Bewdley | to | JW | 1786, Oct. 7 |

## LIST OF LETTERS IN VOLUME 2

| No. | Author, place | | Recipient, place | Date |
|---|---|---|---|---|
| 124 | SK, Bewdley | to | JW | 1786, Oct. 16 |
| 125 | JW, Stevenston | to | SK, Bewdley | 1786, Nov. 23 |
| 126 | JW, Stevenston | to | SK, Bewdley | 1787, Jan. 9 |
| 127 | SK, Bewdley | to | JW, Stevenston | 1787, Jan. 19 |
| Missing | SK | | JW | 1787, c. early April |
| 128 | JW, Stevenston | to | SK, Bewdley | 1787, April 26 |
| 129 | SK, Bewdley | to | JW, Edinburgh | 1787, May 11 |
| 130 | JW, Stevenston | to | SK, Bewdley | 1787, June 15 |
| 131 | SK, Bewdley | to | JW, Stevenston | 1787, Aug. 23 |
| 132 | JW | to | SK, [Bewdley] | 1787, Sept. 2 |
| 133 | SK, Bewdley | to | JW, Stevenston | 1787, Sept. 28 |
| 134 | JW, Stevenston | to | SK, Bewdley | 1787, Dec. 13 |
| 135 | SK, Bewdley | to | JW, Stevenston | 1788, Feb. 13 |
| 136 | JW, Stevenston | to | SK, Bewdley | 1788, May 28 |
| Missing | SK | | JW | 1788, June 9 |
| 137 | JW | to | SK | 1788, July 3 |
| Missing | JW, Woodstock | to | SK | 1788, early Sept. |
| 138 | JW, London | to | SK, Bewdley | 1788, Sept. 16 |
| Missing | SK | | JW | 1788, Sept. 18 |
| 139 | JW, London | to | SK, Bewdley | 1788, Sept. 27 |
| Missing | SK | | JW | 1788, Sept. 29 |
| 140 | JW, London | to | SK, Bewdley | 1788, Oct. 15 |
| 141 | JW, London | to | SK, Bewdley | 1788, Oct. 25 |
| 142 | JW, Kendal | to | SK, Bewdley | 1788, Nov. 11 |
| Missing | SK | | JW | 1788, Nov. 28 |
| 143 | JW, Stevenston | to | SK, Bewdley | 1788, Dec. 25 |
| 144 | SK, Bewdley | to | JW, Stevenston | 1789, Jan. 16 and 20 |
| 145 | JW, Stevenston | to | SK, Bewdley | 1789, Feb. 5 |
| 146 | JW, Stevenston | to | SK, Bewdley | 1789, March 8 |
| 147 | SK, Bewdley | to | JW, Stevenston | 1789, March 20 |
| 148 | JW, Stevenston | to | SK, Bewdley | 1789, May 20 and 23 |
| 149 | JW, Stevenston | to | SK, Bewdley | 1789, Aug. 5 |

| No. | Author, place | | Recipient, place | Date |
|---|---|---|---|---|
| 150 | SK, Bewdley | to | JW | 1789, Aug. 10 |
| 151 | JW, Stevenston | to | SK, Bewdley | 1789, Nov. 9 |
| 152 | SK, Bewdley | to | JW, Stevenston | 1789, Dec. 16 |
| Missing | JW | | SK | 1790, Jan. 5 |
| 153 | SK, Bewdley | to | JW, Stevenston | 1790, Feb. 24 |
| Missing | SK | | JW | 1790, May 11 |
| 154 | JW, Edinburgh | to | SK, Bewdley | 1790, June 2 |
| Missing | SK | | JW | 1790, July 14 |
| Missing | JW | | SK | 1790, July 23 |
| 155 | SK, Bewdley | to | JW, Stevenston | 1790, Sept. 25 |

1. Towns and cities of significance in the Wodrow–Kenrick correspondence.

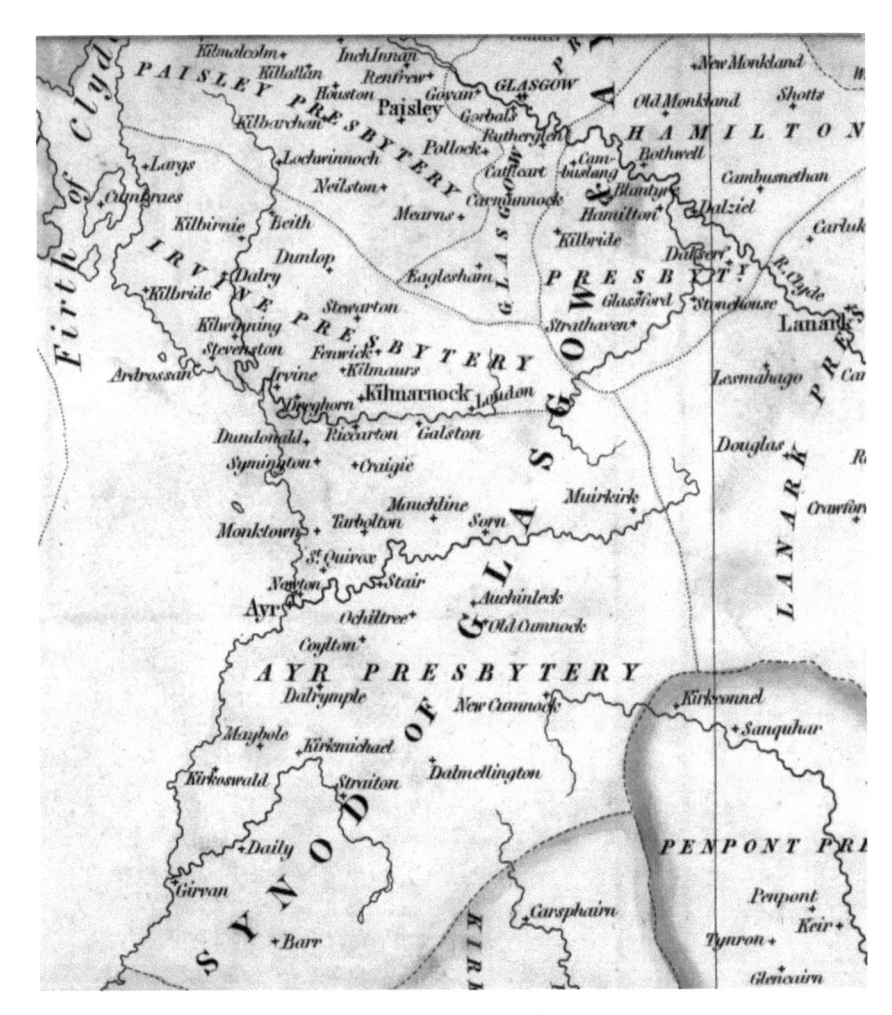

2. Parish map of Ayrshire. *Ecclesiastical Map of Scotland* by Aaron Arrowsmith (1825).

3. 'Bewdley', from Thomas Sanders, *Perspective Views of Market Towns in the County of Worcester* (1770).

# INTRODUCTION TO VOLUME 2

> Your Modesty tends you to consider them as interruptions or intrusions on my more serious or useful Occupations but in truth during the bussiest moment I ever had a Packet from Bewdley gives new fillip to my spirits & makes me go on with more alacrity.[1]

The second volume of letters between James Wodrow (1730–1810) and Samuel Kenrick (1727–1811) covers a much shorter period of time than the first (1750–83): only seven years, from 1784 to 1790, which contained neither the revolution in America nor that in France, other than its first eruptions. Nor was Britain at war during these years. Although the major political events that provoked such long, interesting letters from them in earlier and later periods are missing from the letters contained in Volume 2—and the letters written about the rights and wrongs of British government policy with regard to America in the 1770s are the best known of the whole correspondence—Wodrow and Kenrick had so much to write to each other about in this short span of years that Volume 2 nevertheless contains a very rich seam of material for historians of the late eighteenth century.

During the years 1784–90, Wodrow had reached his mid- to late fifties, and Kenrick entered his sixties, both now long established in successful careers. The University of Glasgow conferred on Wodrow the degree of Doctor of Divinity in 1786, and the heritors of Stevenston parish built him a new manse in 1788. Their daughters were adults, and a major segment of Volume 2 is taken up with Mary Kenrick's visit to Scotland to stay with the Wodrow family from June till October 1784, and Helen ('Nell') Wodrow's return with her to Bewdley, to become part of the Kenrick household until September 1785. Wodrow himself visited Bewdley, on the only occasions he ever did this, in early September and late October 1788, on his way to and from London to arrange for the publication of William Leechman's sermons. The reader's sense of missing what was said and experienced in these only meetings of such good friends since 1765 until the end of

---

[1] Letter 120, James Wodrow (JW) to Samuel Kenrick (SK), c. 9–15 Aug. 1786.

Wodrow's life in 1810 reinforces how fortunate it is that such a high proportion of their letters have survived to record their friendship, which was otherwise carried out on paper. Wodrow wrote to Kenrick from London, anticipating his second visit to Bewdley, on the road north:

I must leave many things in your last & former agreable Letters to be answered viva voce for I have met with so many persons & things in this new world if I may call it so as perfectly confuse my poor head when I sit down to give any account of them.[2]

There are a number of missing letters from this period (sixteen of which we are aware, besides the seventy-seven extant and published here in full). Of those which survive, there are eight letters written in 1784, a spike of twenty-three surviving letters in 1785 when Nell Wodrow visited Bewdley, sixteen in 1786, nine in each of 1787, 1788, and 1789, and three in 1790. Thus the correspondence in this period, while incomplete, is nonetheless remarkably full and fluent.

The General Introduction to Volumes 1–4, contained in Volume 1, should be consulted for introductions to James Wodrow, Samuel Kenrick, and the correspondence as a whole; for a general discussion of their principal contexts (the Enlightenment, religion, their regional locations, and the course of British politics in 1750–1810); and for an examination of the correspondence as a case study of friendship in the eighteenth century. This Introduction to Volume 2 provides an exposition and evaluation of the evidence contained in the letters of this volume, dealing with:

  i. Friends and family, 1784–90
 ii. Living the Enlightenment, 1784–90
iii. Theology and religion, 1784–90
 iv. Political concerns, 1784–90

# I. Friends and Family, 1784–90

'I cannot too often express to you, how happy your letters make me by their length & the variety of the matter they contain, which is entirely suited to my wish & taste', Kenrick replied in June 1784 to Wodrow's substantial missive of 15 April.[3] Wodrow's letter had indeed covered a wide range of content, from the Scottish system of poor relief and the growing denominational diversity in

---
[2] Letter 140, JW to SK, 15 Oct. 1788.
[3] Letter 80, SK to JW, 2 June 1784; Letter 79, JW to SK, 15 April 1784.

Scotland; to the doctrine of Christ and the published disputations of Joseph Priestley; to political events at Westminster in the wake of the fall of the Fox–North administration, and Scottish reactions to these; to a discussion of his and Kenrick's current reading matter; to a brief report on the health of the ageing Professor William Leechman (1706–85), principal of the University of Glasgow, Wodrow's mentor and an important influence also on Kenrick. It is a fine example of the breadth, depth, and candour of discussion that both men enjoyed so much in their letters, and clearly they took as much pleasure in their continuing friendship and its substance on paper as they ever had as young men, testified to by the steady flow of letters in each direction during this seven-year period. Kenrick was as ever affectionately impatient with Wodrow's characteristic insistence on obtaining franks for his letters to save his friend from paying postage when he received them: 'Adieu my dear friend. Never mind franks. I do not know where to buy real pleasure cheaper than at the post office.'[4]

Much of each letter was very often taken up by responding to the content of the previous letter, so that several threads of discussion were frequently simultaneously maintained—reports on friends and family, discussions of theology and current affairs, evaluations of books and journalism, and mutual advice on matters of concern. Their accustomed candour in correspondence meant that, while signalling the delicacy of what they sometimes felt necessary to convey—such as the prickled pride of Wodrow's friend William M'Gill when Kenrick had shown some of the manuscript of his *Practical Essay on the Death of Christ* to Joseph Priestley without prior permission—they nevertheless communicated fully.[5] As ever, sometimes the press of business and the length and number of unanswered letters building up caused them to delay replying: 'like other poor debtors I am beginning almost to grow averse to undertake the discharge of them', confessed Kenrick. 'And yet how pleasing is the task when I once sit down to it!—could I but secure undisturbed one hour or two to myself!'[6] His delight in writing to Wodrow was clearly reciprocated. Wodrow wrote in January 1786: 'Having a frank by me I write a short Epistle', a letter which, unusually, has not survived complete, but which even in its abbreviated state contains a part-transcribed, part-summarized sermon by William Leechman, and was clearly never 'a short Epistle'.[7]

---

[4] Contained in Letter 82, SK to Mary Kenrick, n.d. but enclosed with Letter 81, SK to JW, 13 Aug. 1784. See W-K, I, p. 36, for the pre-payment system of franking mail.
[5] For example, in Letter 87, JW to SK, 3 Jan. 1785.
[6] Letter 110, SK to JW, 1 Jan. 1786.
[7] Letter 111, JW to SK, 23 Jan. 1786.

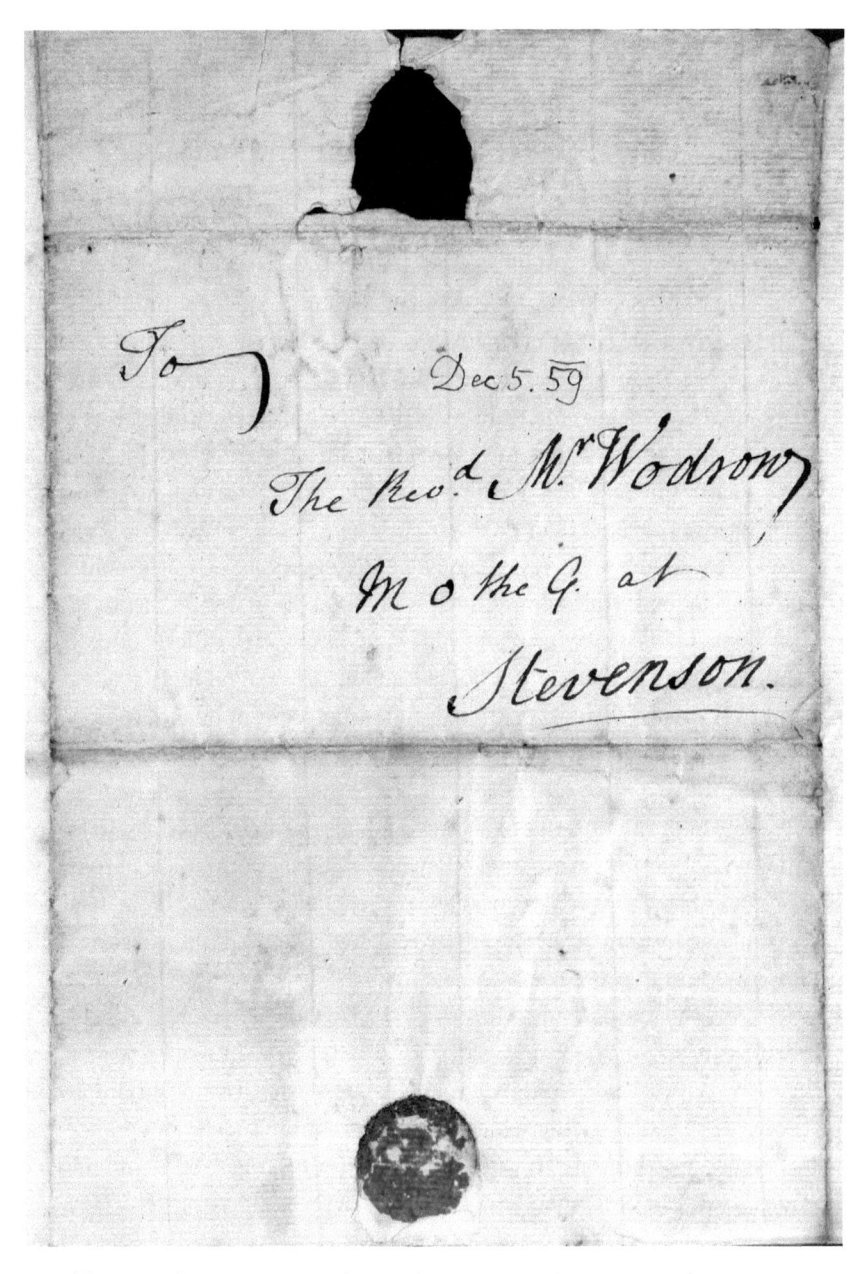

4. Address panel. Letter 39: Samuel Kenrick to James Wodrow, 5 December 1759.

5. Address panel. Letter 103: Samuel Kenrick to James Wodrow, 5 October 1785.

The development of the postal service in Britain by the 1780s can be seen in the increasing content of the address panels on letters (see Plates 4 and 5) which, by the mid-1780s, included not only the name and town of the recipient but also the name of the MP who provided the frank, and often rubber-stamped dates of posting ('JA/10' signifying 10 January, for instance) and postal towns through which the letter passed—Irvine and Carlisle are common stamps on Wodrow's and Kenrick's letters. Already by 1783 the one stagecoach journey run from Edinburgh to London per month in 1763 had become sixty, taking four days each instead of twelve to sixteen days.[8] Between 1784 and 1790, John Palmer of Bath reformed the British postal service with the support of the prime minister William Pitt, so that all the main post routes had a daily delivery by fast mail coach.[9] This also carried six passengers, and Wodrow travelled in one from Penrith to Carlisle during his journey home from Bewdley in 1788.[10] The regular allegations made by Wodrow and Kenrick in the early decades of their correspondence, of postal officials interfering to explain delays or mishaps in the mail, continued into the 1780s, but they also recognized the benefits of the new service, even if it cost more to use after the Act of August 1784.[11] Wodrow's anxiety in early 1785 for letters from Bewdley after Nell had arrived there in November is understandable, so that by 19 January, his only explanation for the lack of letters since early December was that 'some of the Harpies as you once called them, of Postmasters or Mistresses had laid their accursed paws on some Packet which we have been expecting every day for a fortnight past from you'. In fact, this letter crossed with a letter from Kenrick, and Wodrow acknowledged that, 'We must now drop all future censures on the Postmasters & Mrs's. for they have behaved most handsomely in the conveyance of the last mentioned packet'—furthermore,

I must intreat my friend to get tougher & more durable paper at least for the cover of his Letters. The frank without seeming to have suffered anything from the Weather or any other accident came to my hand quite open all round, & the direction worn off & separated from the rest. But some good friendly Postmaster or mistress had neatly tied it up with a piece of twist & sealed it a second time at the knott & thus preserved the contents quite safe till they reached their owner. Was not this a very kind Office to an unknown person?[12]

Nevertheless, their concerns about letters being carelessly or criminally handled by 'those sad fiends the postmasters & mistresses' continued,[13] and when possible

---

[8] Richard B. Sher, 'Scotland Transformed: The Eighteenth Century', in Jenny Wormald, ed., *Scotland: A History* (Oxford, 2005), p. 201.
[9] Susan E. Whyman, *The Pen and the People: English Letter Writers 1660–1800* (Oxford, 2009), p. 59; Letter 115, SK to JW, 25 April 1786.
[10] Letter 143, JW to SK, 25 Dec. 1786.
[11] National Debt Act, 24 Geo. III s.2 c.37; SK to JW, Letter 83, 28 Sept. 1784.
[12] Letter 91, JW to SK, 6 Feb. 1785; cf. Letter 92, SK to JW, 22 Feb. 1785.
[13] Letter 112, SK to JW, 11 Feb. 1785; cf. also Letter 103, SK to JW, 5 Oct. 1785; and Letter 111, JW to SK, 23 Jan. 1786: 'You know what happened not long ago, & our good Scots Proverb says "burn't bairns dread the fire".'

they sent letters also by relatives,[14] by acquaintances, and by commercial traffic between Birmingham and Glasgow, sometimes via London.

From the perspective of their personal lives, the major events contained during these years and treated at length in their letters were the visits of Mary Kenrick (1754–1812), Nell Wodrow (c. 1763–95), and Wodrow himself; and the deaths of William Leechman and John Warner. Mary's visit to Scotland, soon after Volume 2 opens, was the catalyst for an increasing closeness between the two families. Kenrick had often previously signed his letters 'S. E. & M. K.', but letters between the daughters became frequent after her stay had resulted in a still longer sojourn by Nell in Bewdley. We may guess that Wodrow would in any case have suggested breaking his own journeys to and from London in 1788 at Bewdley, but surely that became even more natural after Nell's extended stay there three years earlier. Each father was evidently close to his daughter, and swiftly developed great affection also for the daughter of his friend. Wodrow was delighted by Kenrick's 'amiable & accomplished Daughter' and wrote movingly of 'the parting we had with her at Glasgow which the joy of embracing her English friends will not yet have effaced the impression of'.[15] The Kenricks, meanwhile, persuaded Wodrow to allow his daughter to stay with them for months longer than he had intended, and were clearly bereft when she left: 'She has left a great blank at our fire side, by breaking our partie quarree wch. was so comfortable last winter.'[16]

It is not surprising that Mary Kenrick was the first to travel, 'this strolling daughter of ours', as Kenrick described her.[17] She was a regular traveller already on behalf of the family business, fitting the pattern of Leonore Davidoff's and Catherine Hall's Birmingham middling-order women, or Deborah Simonton's urban Scottish equivalents, much more closely than that of Amanda Vickery's or Katherine Glover's elite women who contributed to the family economy most substantially by managing complex households.[18] Nearly ten years older than

---

[14] Letter 84, JW to SK, 22 Oct. 1784, is annotated on the address panel, 'by Mary & Nell', who carried it with them from Stevenston to Bewdley.

[15] Letter 84, JW to SK, 22 Oct. 1784; Letter 86, JW to SK, 7 Dec. 1784.

[16] Letter 105, SK to JW, 11 Nov. 1785.

[17] Letter 82, SK to JW, enclosed with Letter 81, SK to JW, 13 Aug. 1784.

[18] For example, Letter 104, JW to SK, 31 Oct. 1785. Leonore Davidoff and Catherine Hall, *Family Fortunes: Men and Women of the English Middle Class, 1780–1850*, 2nd edn (2002), especially pp. 279–80, 285–86, 289; Deborah Simonton, 'Negotiating the Economy of the Eighteenth-Century Scottish Town: Female Entrepreneurs Claim Their Place', in Katie Barclay and Deborah Simonton, eds, *Women in Eighteenth-Century Scotland: Intimate, Intellectual and Public Lives* (Farnham, 2013), pp. 211–32; Amanda Vickery, *The Gentleman's Daughter: Women's Lives in Georgian England*

Nell, she travelled alone to Stevenston. She had been born in Ayrshire and was twelve before the family moved to Worcestershire. Her mother was also born in Maybole and, according to Mary, she was 'as much or more a Scotchwoman than ever that is enthusiasticaly fond of Scotland & it's honour'.[19] Mary enjoyed visiting family friends and relatives in Ayrshire and Glasgow, as well as sea-bathing and taking in the Scottish landscapes.[20] Nell Wodrow, just twenty-one when she left home, was escorted to Bewdley by Mary in autumn 1784 and accompanied home nearly a year later by her mother's brother, John Hamilton, a London merchant. Despite her father's anxieties about her possible awkwardness in new company, Nell clearly delighted in the Kenricks' social circle and made good friendships. Wodrow began to argue that it was 'high time she were thinking of her return to the bleak barren Mountains of the north' in March 1785,[21] which Kenrick brushed off for some time, telling Wodrow that it would 'be like tearing off a limb to part with her', despite agreeing that her parents must want to see her again.[22] That reunion did not happen until November, following a journey which took Nell from Bewdley to Birmingham, and on to Manchester, before returning to Stevenston.

There is no substantial evidence in the correspondence between Wodrow and Kenrick of their families being dramatically affected by progressive, Enlightenment feminist developments (though their daughters were clearly carefully educated in subjects beyond the domestic and 'accomplishments'), nor, on the other hand, of their wives and daughters being intentionally repressed by domineering patriarchy.[23] While Louisa Wodrow and Elisabeth Kenrick do not have the substantial roles in the Volume 2 letters that Mary and Nell have, they are a constant presence in them, and the overwhelming sense of the correspondence is of contented, companionate family lives. If they did not have the opportunities that Wodrow and Kenrick had to pursue fulfilling careers, or that the Wodrows' sons would have expected to have, had they lived, there is every indication that

---

(1998), pp. 127–60; Katharine Glover, *Elite Women and Polite Society in Eighteenth-Century Scotland* (Woodbridge, 2011).

[19] Letter 84, JW to SK, 22 Oct. 1784.
[20] Letter 82, SK to JW, enclosed with Letter 81, SK to JW, 13 Aug. 1784.
[21] Letter 94, JW to SK, 25 March 1785.
[22] Letter 97, SK to JW, 29 June 1785.
[23] See the thirty-six essays in Sarah Knott and Barbara Taylor, eds, *Women, Gender and Enlightenment* (Basingstoke, 2005) for a substantial, multifaceted, and transnational discussion of the impact of the Enlightenment on women and feminism; and Arianne Chernock, *Men and the Making of Modern British Feminism* (Stanford, CA, 2010), for an illuminating study of the roles of British men in the 1790s in supporting women's opportunities and rights, from the modest to the radical.

mutual respect, trust, and affection were the hallmarks of both families. In Mary Kenrick's case, she played an active part in the family business. There is little direct evidence to suggest the kinds of intellectual family life examined by Jane Rendall in Professor John Millar's family of six daughters, Professor William Cullen's four daughters and seven sons, and their friends, nor is there clear evidence otherwise either. It seems likely that Nell was challenged by dyslexia, yet also that both men regarded the three daughters as intelligent conversationalists.[24] And there is plenty of evidence to suggest the model of family life Rendall portrays, characterized by considerable companionship, and the education of daughters to be able to participate in 'an enlightened form of sociability, with a full awareness of the social and political issues of the period'.[25] When Wodrow sent Kenrick copies of two of Robert Burns's poems circulating in manuscript in Ayrshire—a landscape pastoral and a severe, current ecclesiastical satire—the verses had been copied out by Nell and Peggy for the whole Kenrick family to read and enjoy.[26] Kenrick's rare stray 'This is my wife's remark', after a telling point in the middle of a discussion of William M'Gill's ecclesiastical travails in Letter 150, indicates that full discussion of letters between the men by their families took place at least sometimes, and perhaps often. Jennie Batchelor's and Manushag Powell's work has established that periodicals apparently directed at either men or women were regularly consumed by all the members of a family who took them.[27]

As Wodrow saw Mary and Nell set out together from Glasgow for Bewdley in October 1784, he wrote, 'Very happy shoud I be did time & money & other... circumstances put it in my power to accompany them the whole way to Bewdley: but that is impossible at present.'[28] He never persuaded Kenrick to visit Ayrshire again, although to the end of their lives they each fantasized about the other coming to stay. 'Distance is now nothing', Kenrick wheedled. 'It is as easy to come to Bewdley, as to go to Glasgow or Edr. when you once set out. This gives

---

[24] On Nell, see *W-K*, I, pp. 138–39, 461–62.
[25] Jane Rendall, '"Women That Would Plague Me with Rational Conversation": Aspiring Women and Scottish Whigs, c. 1790–1830', in Knott and Taylor, eds, *Women, Gender and Enlightenment*, pp. 326–47, quoted at p. 331.
[26] Letters 134, 135, 151, and 152.
[27] Jennie Batchelor, *The Lady's Magazine (1770–1832) and the Making of Literary History* (Edinburgh, 2022); Jennie Batchelor and Manushag N. Powell, *Women's Periodicals and Print Culture in Britain, 1690–1820s: The Long Eighteenth Century* (Edinburgh, 2018).
[28] Letter 84, JW to SK, 22 Oct. 1784.

me a ray of hope that sometime I may see here my worthy friend.'[29] It is difficult not to conclude that the difficulties of leaving their professional obligations for the length of time so long a journey would entail appeared insuperable to each, until they were old enough that the physical demands now seemed too great. Wodrow's decision that Leechman's sermons should be published posthumously not in Edinburgh but in London, for the sake of reaching a greater readership, was therefore essential to the friends meeting in person once more.

Wodrow, whose father had died when he himself was only four years old, had been sent to Glasgow University at the age of eleven, where he came under the influence of Principal William Leechman (1706–85), attending his divinity lectures from the age of fourteen. He remained close to Leechman in later life, doubtless helped by the fact that the principal's wife, Bridget, was the aunt of his own wife, Louisa; and the Wodrows' sons, Gavin and Patrick, had lodged with the Leechmans as students.[30] Thus, when twelve years of 'asthmatic and gravellish complaints'[31] led to Leechman entering his short final illness in winter 1785, Wodrow was one of a small circle of close friends who often attended his bedside and kept company with him and his wife. He sent long, touching reports to Kenrick of the 'good death' of this prominent clergyman, blessing his household and the university professoriate, and looking forward to the joy of heaven. After Leechman's death on 3 December, Wodrow was named as one of five executors of his estate. He had no personal financial concern in it, but Bridget Leechman gave Wodrow a large, disorganized collection of sermon manuscripts and asked him to prepare them for publication, with any profits from the edition to belong to him. While Wodrow was not insensible to the financial element of this gift, it is clear that his primary desire was to publish a suitable memorial to his mentor.[32] Mrs Leechman also arranged that William Richardson, professor of humanities (Latin) at the University of Glasgow, the mutual friend of her husband, Wodrow and Kenrick, should offer to accompany

---

[29] Letter 100, SK to JW, 19 Sept. 1785.

[30] JW had copied out part of Leechman's letter to him on the death of Gavin, for SK to read, at the time of Gavin's death. When Mary and Nell left Glasgow for Bewdley in Oct. 1784, having just visited the Leechmans, he insisted on Mary taking the original letter with her for her father to see. W-K, I, pp. 451–52; Letter 84, JW to SK, 22 Oct. 1784.

[31] James Wodrow, 'The Life of Dr. Leechman, with some Account of his Lectures', in Wodrow, ed., *Sermons, by William Leechman, D.D., Late Principal of the College of Glasgow, to which is prefixed Some Account of the Author's Life, and of his Lectures, by James Wodrow, D.D., Minister at Stevenston*, 2 vols (1789), I, 1–102, at p. 83.

[32] Letter 136, JW to SK, 28 May 1788.

Wodrow to London to arrange the publication of the sermons, and hence the opportunity to visit Kenrick.

Not surprisingly, the letters convey little of Wodrow's days as a guest of the Kenrick family, other than his enjoyment of them. 'I now think with and speak with pleasure of my English Excursion especialy of the fortnight I spent at Bewdley by much the happiest part of part of it', he wrote on Christmas Day 1788, safely returned home.[33] Meanwhile, letters from Kenrick to Wodrow during Wodrow's travels are missing. There is much to glean, however, from Wodrow's long letters in autumn 1788, reporting his travels much as Kenrick had written about the early days of his first Grand Tour, with James Milliken in 1760.[34] Wodrow described himself as 'a young traveller though an old man'.[35] It is impossible, reading Wodrow's impressions of London as a first-time visitor, not to have in mind the visit to the British capital of John Galt's Rev. Dr Zachariah Pringle and his family in *The Ayrshire Legatees* (1821), Wodrow and the Pringles simultaneously fascinated and exhausted by the experience. Not to mention Wodrow's arrival back in Stevenston, where, if he was characteristically briefer in reporting it, his experience seems to have been similar to Pringle's: 'a wellcome reception from my family & Parish. The last seemed to think that they had lost me entirely, being little accustomed to such long seperations'.[36]

The other significant death during these years was John Warner's (1713–86), Wodrow's cousin and Kenrick's friend, beloved by both men. Warner had suffered a permanently debilitating stroke in 1775 and, by the time of Mary Kenrick's Scottish trip in autumn 1784, he was much reduced.

She saw Mr. Warner in one of his best situations, tho' looking miserably ill, yet was sensibly hurt & shocked once or twice & You woud have been infinitely more, from the recolection of his happier days.[37]

A few months later, Wodrow reported that Warner's condition had improved significantly since Mary had seen him. However, he reported a 'Catastrophe':

almost all his valuable Papers are lost—dissipated by the cursed infidelity of a female Servt. (who is yet greatly attached to him & her care & attention to his person & health

---

[33] Letter 143, JW to SK, 25 Dec. 1788.
[34] W-K, I, pp. 272–79.
[35] Letter 136, JW to SK, 28 May 1788.
[36] Letter 143, JW to SK, 25 Dec. 1788.
[37] Letter 84, JW to SK, 22 Oct. 1784.

absolutely necessary) among some of her own relations who can read them, but cannot relish them[38]

—including several sets of sermons Warner had been preparing for the press. When he heard that Warner had died in March 1786, Kenrick wrote, 'I do join you in declaring that he was the greatest & best of men I ever was acquainted with. Blest wth. the first rate talents to command admiration, he had every thing amiable & endearing to attract love & esteem.'[39]

One further illness was noted briefly at the same time as Warner's death:

A neice of mine here a Sister of the Capt$^n$. has had a tedious fever for six weeks past but is now on the recovery. I was obliged to leave her when at the worst & spend a week at Kilbarchan hapily our young folks have escaped it they left the house for some time.[40]

This was Mary Ann Wodrow (1762–1841), daughter of Wodrow's eldest brother Robert (1711–84), who had succeeded their father to the parish of Eastwood, Renfrewshire (1734–57) and was now living on the island of Little Cumbrae, off the north Ayrshire coast.[41] Her journal records her close friendship with Wodrow's daughter Margaret or 'Peggy' (1767–1845), and her gratitude to her uncle James for his care for her while she was seriously unwell while staying at Stevenston in early 1786: 'I shall never forget the Paternal tenderness with which my unkle traited me sitting whole hours by my bedside with the solicitude of a Parent who watched an only child.'[42]

'I believe few souls are more intimately united than your's and mine', Kenrick wrote in April 1786, in response to Wodrow's hope that their long friendship would continue uninterrupted 'till we meet in the regions of eternal friendship & join many of our worthy friends there whom we have now lost for a time'.[43] Continuing, Kenrick echoed him, both of them conscious of their loss of John Warner on 8 March: 'Yes, my dearest friend, I trust too that our correspondence

---

[38] Letter 88, JW to SK, 7 Jan. 1785.
[39] Letter 115, SK to JW, 25 April 1786.
[40] Letter 114, JW to SK, 11 April 1786.
[41] Robert's first wife Mary Craig had died in 1754, with whom he had two daughters and two sons. He married Anne Ruthven in 1755 and had a further son and four daughters, including Mary Ann.
[42] Sophia Smith Collection of Women's History, Smith College, Northampton, Massachusetts, Journal of Mary Ann Wodrow, volume 1, March 1786, f. 116. We are grateful to members of the Ayrshire Archaeological & Natural History Society who made us aware of this important journal. See also David A. Gerber, 'Mary Ann Wodrow Archbald: Longing for Her "Little Isle" from a Farm in Central New York', in *Authors of Their Own Lives: Personal Correspondence in the Lives of Nineteenth Century British Immigrants to the United States* (New York, 2006), pp. 281–308.
[43] Letter 114, JW to SK, 11 April 1786; Letter 115, SK to JW, 25 April 1786.

here will hold out 'till we meet in the regions of eternal friendship & join many of our worthy friends there whom we have lost for a time.' As the following pages proceed to discuss, the letters in Volume 2 are an invaluable source for understanding the rich literary, religious, and political culture of Britain in the 1780s; but if they only communicated the depth of the friendship between Wodrow, Kenrick, their families, and their friends, they would still be a wonderfully abundant historical resource.[44]

## II. Living the Enlightenment, 1784–90

By the mid-1780s the period of the 'high Enlightenment', dominated by some of the most famous names in philosophy, was waning—David Hume died in 1776, Jean-Jacques Rousseau in 1778, Lord Kames in 1782, and Adam Smith in 1790— but its impact in the intellectual and social strata just beyond them was substantial for decades to come.[45] The concerns they had generated regarding rational enquiry, freethinking, the value of the individual, political liberty, and scientific achievement—if they had ever been neatly capable of formulation as a discrete package—now continued to be diffused, worked out, and fought over in the writings of a vast number of less well-known figures across a spectrum of different scholarly and practical fields.[46] Romantic ideas would in due course soften, challenge, and replace the hard edges of radical, rationalist, Enlightenment views at the cutting edge of modern thought, but they never superseded them altogether in terms of their influence on wider society. In the 1780s, radical Enlightenment rationalism and liberalism continued to challenge the British establishment and

---

[44] See also below, p. 41 on the meaningful friendships that both men maintained, not only with clergymen of sympathetic theological views with their own, such as Thomas Wigan of Bewdley and their beloved John Warner of Kilbarchan, but also with ministers of 'high orthodoxy', such as William Jesse of Dowles and Robert Dow of Ardrossan. See also W-K, I, pp. 81–101 for an extended discussion of friendship in correspondence and the historiography of friendship.

[45] Aileen Fyfe and Colin C. Kidd, eds, *Beyond the Enlightenment: Scottish Intellectual Life, 1790–1914* (Edinburgh, 2023); Richard Whatmore, *The End of Enlightenment: Empire, Commerce, Crisis* (2023).

[46] Martin Fitzpatrick, Peter Jones, Christa Knellwolf, and Ian McCalman, eds, *The Enlightenment World* (2004); Jonathan Israel, *Radical Enlightenment: Philosophy and the Making of Modernity, 1660–1750* (Oxford, 2002); Israel, *Enlightenment Contested: Philosophy, Modernity, and the Emancipation of Man, 1670–1752* (Oxford, 2008); idem, *Democratic Enlightenment: Philosophy, Revolution, and Human Rights, 1750–1790* (Oxford, 2011); idem, *The Enlightenment that Failed: Ideas, Revolution, and Democratic Defeat, 1748–1830* (Oxford, 2019); J. G. A. Pocock, *Barbarism and Religion*, 6 vols (Cambridge, 1999–2010); Thomas Munck, *Conflict and Enlightenment: Print and Political Culture in Europe, 1635–1795* (Cambridge, 2019).

the status quo in politics and religion, as the next two sections will discuss. They were spreading increasingly widely and deeply in British society, as were ideas which opposed them, such as the 'conservative Enlightenment' advanced by John Pocock.[47]

Jon Mee has proposed a 'Transpennine Enlightenment' to describe the knowledge networks of the north of England and the south of Scotland in the period 1781–1830,[48] while Mark Towsey has pointed to the record of reading preserved in Rev. George Ridpath's diary as evidence of 'the extent to which the Enlightenment produced by such luminaries [as Hume and Smith] percolated through to readers in provincial Scotland'.[49] Similarly, as highly cultured, professional men, well educated at Glasgow University, acquainted with a wide range of thinkers famous both in their own day and in the twenty-first century, Wodrow and Kenrick were representatives of a less well-known circle of British society around the central core of Scottish and English Enlightenment literati. Forming a single but strong connection between the south-west of Scotland and the West Midlands, they discussed many of the latest ideas, they looked for their practical implications, they were aware of living in a changing world, and they did not always agree, either with each other or with what they read, despite Kenrick's cheerfully optimistic assertion: 'for candid & enlightened minds, cannot long or far disagree'.[50] Reading, writing, and publishing are three of the major preoccupations of the letters in Volume 2.

Both men took pleasure in good conversation, though it was not always readily available. Kenrick thought that, if Wodrow and Joseph Priestley could only meet in person and converse 'with calmness ease & freedom', his friends would be surprised 'to find how near [their] sentiments coincided'. Meanwhile, Wodrow complained about the 'unceasing Lig Lag about the families & trifling incidents in the neighbourhood' that dominated the table when his visit with his MP,

---

[47] J. G. A. Pocock, 'Conservative Enlightenment and Democratic Revolutions: The American and French Cases in British Perspective', *Government and Opposition*, 24 (1989), pp. 81–105. Central to this was a 'clerical Enlightenment' delineated in B. W. Young, *Religion and Enlightenment in Eighteenth-Century England: Theological Debate from Locke to Burke* (Oxford, 1998).

[48] Jon Mee, 'Transpennine Enlightenment: The Literary and Philosophical Societies and Knowledge Networks of the North, 1781–1830', *Journal for Eighteenth-Century Studies*, 38 (2015), pp. 599–612; Jon Mee, *Networks of Improvement: Literature, Bodies and Machines in the Industrial Revolution* (Chicago, IL, 2023).

[49] Mark Towsey, *Reading the Scottish Enlightenment: Books and Their Readers in Provincial Scotland, 1750–1820* (Leiden, 2010), p. 1.

[50] Letter 89, SK to JW, 14 Jan. 1785; Towsey, *Reading the Scottish Enlightenment*, especially pp. 233–305.

Sir Adam Fergusson, was joined by Col. William Hunter of Brownhill, 'a clattering eating & drinking man', instead of the discussion of 'any interesting subject of politicks Learning &c' that Wodrow had anticipated.[51] Their correspondence operated as a reliable form of good literary and philosophical conversation, as demonstrated by the writers' regular habit of responding methodically and often substantially to each topic covered by the letter to which they were replying. Thus, the many-twined thread of conversation was maintained, even when letters were written months apart.

In particular, Wodrow's and Kenrick's correspondence operated as a tiny, virtual, literary salon: a two-man book club. As David Allan has put it, 'Reading may safely be described as one of the great collective obsessions of eighteenth- and early nineteenth-century England.'[52] Moreover, reading, using libraries, and patronizing bookshops were not only solitary occupations but also an important aspect of Georgian sociability.[53] By the late eighteenth century, subscription libraries, circulation libraries, and book societies were common in small as well as large towns throughout the British Isles, while access to bookshops was also increasingly easy for professionals and members of the middling orders such as Wodrow and Kenrick.[54] Allan notes a range of contemporary estimates such that there may have been between 600 and 2,000 book clubs in England by 1820. There was no public library in Bewdley until 1819, when a bequest provided more than 3,000 books for its establishment.[55] Keith Manley identifies around a hundred subscription libraries in Scotland by 1800, 'of which at least half could be described as working-class', as well as many circulating libraries. The Ayr Library Society was founded in 1762, though the Saltcoats subscription library in Wodrow's parish did not emerge until 1825.[56]

---

[51] Letter 89, SK to JW, 14 Jan. 1785; Letter 86, JW to SK, 7 Dec. 1784.

[52] David Allan, *A Nation of Readers: The Lending Library in Georgian England* (2008), pp. 26, 172; Towsey, *Reading the Scottish Enlightenment*, p. 1. See also William St Clair, *The Reading Nation in the Romantic Period* (Cambridge, 2004).

[53] Peter Clark, *British Clubs and Societies, 1580–1800: The Origins of an Associational World* (Oxford, 2000), pp. 109–10; Mark Towsey and Kyle B. Roberts, eds, *Before the Public Library: Reading, Community, and Identity in the Atlantic World, 1650–1850* (Leiden, 2018); James Raven, 'Libraries for Sociability: The Advance of the Subscription Library', in Giles Mandelbrote and Keith A. Manley, eds, *The Cambridge History of Libraries in Britain and Ireland, Volume II 1640–1850* (Cambridge, 2006), pp. 241–63.

[54] Towsey and Roberts, eds, *Before the Public Library*.

[55] Allan, *A Nation of Readers*, pp. 60–61, 63, 65.

[56] There were also circulating libraries in Kilmarnock (1760), Ayr (1766), Irvine (1780), and Beith (1780). Keith Manley, *Books, Borrowers, and Shareholders: Scottish Circulating and Subscription Libraries before 1825: A Survey and Listing* (Edinburgh, 2012), pp. 73, 56, 145, 151, and *passim*. See also

Wodrow and Kenrick were both voracious readers and consumers of review periodicals. In good Dissenting tradition, Kenrick was a founder and very active member of the first book society in Bewdley (established in 1767).[57] In 1785 he reported to Wodrow the start of a second such club in the town, and explained how his own society operated:

not to rival ours which has now flourished 18 years, but because we had not room for them. Ours consists of 20 Members– & 14 have already subscribed to the new one. In ours we have high Church & low-church & no church, catholics & presbyterians– Drs. of divinity & Doctors of physic, gentlemen & tradesmen Foxites & Pittites.– Yet in all this medley, we have not the least dissension or animosity: & for the moderate expense of 7/6 annually, have 4 comfortable convivial meetings, & as many & whatever books we please.[58]

Wodrow admired this arrangement, and he was envious, 'not so much for the opportunity of reading many books but the time you can spare for doing it'.[59] While, as a young clergyman, sermon-writing had dominated much of his time, now it was consumed by parish business, attending to company, and 'an extensive correspondence by Letters from doing my own & cheifly other people's bussiness which everyone will have too much of who has any ability integrity & disposition to oblige', so that 'I have not the time to read the sixth part of the books I have it in my power & woud wish to read'. 'I often cannot spend above five or six hours in a week in reading', he concluded. Visits to Edinburgh, which he anticipated might have allowed him to catch up on the latest publications, tended to be overtaken by social obligations with friends and family.[60] Kenrick, while similarly wishing that 'Bank & business were far enough' that he might spend more time reading, envied his friend Joseph Priestley for his capacity to read swiftly. 'It is incredible the quantity he reads', he wrote.

---

Clark, *British Clubs and Societies, 1580–1800*, p. 110; St Clair, *The Reading Nation in the Romantic Period*, p. 246; D. D. McElroy, 'Literary Clubs and Societies of Eighteenth-Century Scotland, and Their Influence on the Literary Productions of the Period from 1700 to 1800' (PhD thesis, University of Edinburgh, 1951). For an overview of the different types of libraries active in this period, and the different terms associated with them, see Katie Halsey, 'Types of Libraries, Books and Borrowing 1750–1830: An Analysis of Scottish Borrowers' Registers', 9 Nov. 2020, https://borrowing.stir.ac.uk/types-of-libraries. Thanks to Katie Halsey and Josh Smith for advice on reading and libraries in this period.

[57] St Clair, *The Reading Nation in the Romantic Period*, p. 246.
[58] Letter 92, SK to JW, 22 Feb. 1785. See Allan, *A Nation of Readers*, p. 32: a membership of between six and thirty seems to have been optimal in book clubs and societies.
[59] Letter 94, JW to SK, 25 March 1785.
[60] Letter 94, JW to SK, 25 March 1785; Letter 96, JW to SK, 16 June 1785.

He does it in reality by rapid glances. He reads every book litterally thro' in the original. As he goes along he marks every passage on the margin to his purpose wth. a particular mark for the head or topic it belongs to. And when he has thus perused the Volume he gives it to his ammanuensis to transcribe. These transcriptions are then arranged for their different purposes– & he proceeds to the next book.[61]

Nonetheless, the evidence of the vast majority of their letters shows that both men consumed an impressive number of books and reviews, ranging from recent fiction to sixteenth-century and contemporary theology to ancient literature. In one twelve-month period between April 1784 and April 1785, the publications they mentioned or discussed included the poetry and drama of William Mason and William Hayley,[62] the theology and philosophy of Joseph Priestley,[63] Hugh Blair's *Lectures on Rhetoric and Belles Lettres* (1783),[64] the Scottish history of Hugo Arnot and Lord Hailes, William Mitford's Greek history,[65] and the travel writing of William Coxe and Thomas Pennant,[66] as well as some unspecified novels.[67]

Nor did Wodrow and Kenrick read simply to while away time, or to keep up with fashion. These were intellectually curious readers who loved learning. Kenrick delighted in reading Homer and Edward Gibbon for their own sakes, but he particularly enjoyed digesting footnotes and 'their collateral instruction', which turned reading into a conference:

---

[61] Letter 123, SK to JW, 7 Oct. 1786.

[62] William Mason, *The English Garden: A Poem in Four Books* (1772–81); William Hayley, *Plays of Three Acts; Written for a Private Theatre* (1784). Letter 79, JW to SK, 15 April 1784; Letter 80, SK to JW, 2 June 1784; Letter 84, JW to SK, 22 Oct. 1784; Letter 85, SK to JW, 2–3 Dec. 1784.

[63] Joseph Priestley, *An History of the Corruptions of Christianity* (Birmingham, 1782); Joseph Priestley, *Letters to Dr Horsley, in Answer to His Animadversions on the History of the Corruptions of Christianity* (Birmingham, 1783); Joseph Priestley, *Letters to Dr. Horsley, Part II: Containing Farther Evidence that the Primitive Christian Church was Unitarian* (Birmingham, 1784); Joseph Priestley, *An Appeal to the Serious and Candid Professors of Christianity* (1771); Joseph Priestley, *A Familiar Illustration of Certain Passages of Scripture Relating to the Power of Man to do the Will of God, Original Sin, Election and Reprobation, the Divinity of Christ and Atonement for Sin by the Death of Christ* (1772); Joseph Priestley, *The Triumph of Truth; Being an Account of the Trial of Mr E. Elwall, for Heresy and Blasphemy, at Stafford Assizes, before Judge Denton. To Which are Added, Extracts from Some Other Pieces of Mr Elwall's, Concerning the Unity of God* (Leeds, 1771). Letter 80, SK to JW, 2 June 1784; Letter 84, JW to SK, 22 Oct. 1784; Letter 87, JW to SK, 3 Jan. 1785.

[64] Hugh Blair, *Lectures on Rhetoric and Belles Lettres* (1783; 2nd edn, 1785). Letter 85, SK to JW, 2–3 Dec. 1784.

[65] Hugo Arnot, *The History of Edinburgh* (Edinburgh, 1779); David Dalrymple, Lord Hailes, *Annals of Scotland: From the Accession of Malcolm III, surnamed Canmore, to the Accession of Robert I* (Edinburgh, 1776); William Mitford, *History of Greece*, vol. 1 (1784). Letter 87, JW to SK, 3 Jan. 1785; Letter 95, SK to JW, 27 April 1785.

[66] William Coxe, *Travels into Poland, Russia, Sweden and Denmark*, 3 vols (1784); Thomas Pennant, *A Tour of Wales*, 2 vols (1784). Letter 93, SK to JW, 21 March 1785.

[67] Letter 87, JW to SK, 3 Jan. 1785.

These are like a constant comentary on the text as well as upon the authorities, where the author descends from his dictatorial chair & freely converses with his hearers upon what he has been saying. This is what I call learning– or it is the sort that pleases me best.[68]

This experience was replicated by their regular consumption of the *Monthly Review*, the pioneer of eighteenth-century review periodicals since its establishment by Ralph Griffiths in 1749. It had set a pattern for moving beyond abstracting new academic publications to poetry, novels, drama, and other more popular literary works, and also for providing critical evaluations. By the 1780s it had been joined by the *Critical Review* (established in 1756), the *English Review* (1783), and the *Analytical Review* (1788). All of them leaned towards liberal political and religious views, and the *English Review*, founded by John Murray and edited by Gilbert Stuart, and the *Analytical*, founded by Thomas Christie, whom Wodrow met in London in 1788, were heavily influenced by London Scots.[69] During the 1780s, the *Monthly Review* was still the periodical of choice for both Wodrow and Kenrick, and the one they discussed together, though they were both becoming somewhat disillusioned by it in this decade. Kenrick had known some of the writers of Ralph Griffiths's *Monthly* in the past; Dr William Rose (1719–86), a Dissenting schoolmaster, a Scot who taught in Chiswick and whose son Samuel Wodrow knew and admired, had been a frequent contributor. By 1786, however, Wodrow was suggesting that the liberal theological flavour of the *Monthly* was turning and possibly also their politics: 'They are surely a different set of men than when Mr Rose was among them.'[70] Kenrick agreed that 'that corps of critics are greatly degenerating from their predecessors in most of the walks of litterature', but he was in truth more surprised that they had held a consistent liberal line for as long as they had.[71] This precipitated a discussion of which periodical they might switch to. Wodrow asked his friend's opinion of the *Critical Review* and the *English Review*, but Kenrick replied that there was no other review he particularly recommended, though he had heard the *English Review* recommended for its material on foreign publications, and had good things to say about the *New Annual Register*.[72]

During their discussions in 1787–89 of two poems by 'our Airshire poet', Robert Burns, circulated locally in manuscript and copied and sent by the Wodrows to the Kenrick family, Wodrow and Kenrick extended an ongoing

---

[68] Letter 95, SK to JW, 27 April 1785.
[69] Derek Roper, *Reviewing before the Edinburgh, 1788–1802* (1978), pp. 20–22.
[70] Letter 116, JW to SK, 2 May 1786.
[71] Letter 119, SK to JW, 20 July 1786.
[72] Letter 121, JW to SK, 28 Aug. 1786; Letter 122, SK to JW, 28 Sept. 1786.

consideration of the transferability and comprehension of Scots language and local knowledge beyond the border with England. Wodrow had already been concerned about 'Scottisisms perhaps Vulgarisms' that he had slipped into while attempting 'an easy simple familiar stile' for his biographical essay on William Leechman, and about similar Scots expressions used by his friend William M'Gill in his *Practical Essay on the Death of Jesus Christ* (1786).[73] He was also apprehensive that Nell would be awkward at first in company in Bewdley because of her spoken Scots dialect.[74] This was a common concern among educated Scots, but Kenrick's view of all three instances, and also of Burns's poetry, was that language was not a barrier.[75] He himself was familiar with Scots language, having lived so long in south-west Scotland; but in any case, he pointed out, there were many dialects and accents also within England, which marked everyone below the upper classes.[76] M'Gill's book was, simply, 'a good book. For it cannot be read, without our being made better thereby. We forget the author & style & think of nothing but the subject & our own feelings'.[77] As for Burns's poetry in Scots, 'Every reader must understand something of him. What they do understand they admire, and *ex pede Herculem*, conclude from thence that what they do not understand must be equally excellent.'[78]

Behind the rich eighteenth-century culture of reading lay the great expansion of the trade in printing, publishing, and selling books.[79] Much of Volume 2 is taken up with discussions of two publications with which Wodrow had a great deal to do: Rev. Dr William M'Gill's *Practical Essay on the Death of Jesus Christ* (1786) and Wodrow's own two-volume edition of the sermons of Principal William Leechman (1789). Richard B. Sher's magisterial *The Enlightenment and the Book* (2006) has explored the scope, significance, and process of the publication of

---

[73] Letter 130, JW to SK, 15 June 1787; Letter 84, JW to SK, 22 Oct. 1784.
[74] Letter 84, JW to SK, 22 Oct. 1784.
[75] Towsey, *Reading the Scottish Enlightenment*, pp. 238–41.
[76] Letter 85, SK to JW, 2–3 Dec. 1784.
[77] Letter 133, SK to JW, 28 Sept. 1787.
[78] Letter 135, SK to JW, 13 Feb. 1788. See also 130–31, 133–34, 151–52; Emma Macleod, 'Burns and the Borders of Poetry in the Letters of James Wodrow and Samuel Kenrick', *Burns Chronicle*, 133 (Autumn 2024). For wider contemporary discussions of the merits or limits of Burns's Scots poetry by comparison with his English verse, see the collections in Donald A. Low, *Robert Burns: The Critical Heritage* (1974) and Corey E. Andrews, *Inventing Scotland's Bard: The British Reception of Robert Burns, 1786–1836* (Columbia, SC, 2022).
[79] See, for example, Thomas Munck, *The Enlightenment: A Comparative Social History, 1721–1794* (2000); Munck, *Conflict and Enlightenment*, especially pp. 25–70; Carla Hesse, 'Print Culture in the Enlightenment', in Fitzpatrick, Jones, Knellwolf, and McCalman, eds, *The Enlightenment World*, pp. 366–81.

books written by Scottish authors in Britain, Ireland, and America in the later eighteenth century, demonstrating 'that the move from author / text to book was a complicated, creative, and contingent process in which the book trade, and above all publishers, had a large role to play'.[80] Wodrow found that, after the time-consuming and difficult tasks of writing and editing texts were completed, the negotiations with publishers and further work on the text to comply with the size and scope of the books agreed on were more arduous and complex than he had anticipated. One decision that a new author or editor had to take was whether to risk adequate sales figures being reached to ensure that their book would not make a loss (in which case they might sell the copyright to the publisher), or to rally sufficient support before publication via a subscription list of guaranteed buyers.[81]

Wodrow's role with M'Gill's book was to try to ensure that it sold as widely and as well as possible, since M'Gill required to raise money by means of the tract to support his family, having lost a very substantial sum of money in the crash of the Ayr Bank in 1772.[82] An Edinburgh bookseller who had initially shown interest had taken cold feet because of its allegedly Socinian theology, so Wodrow was keen to make use of his Bewdley friend's understanding of English Rational Dissenting tastes in theological writings and of the English publishing market to help M'Gill. He sent Kenrick a copy of the table of contents in late 1784, carried by Nell in her luggage, along with some previous publications of M'Gill's that would give Kenrick some idea of his abilities.[83] Wodrow himself thought M'Gill ought to publish the book openly rather than anonymously, not only because that seemed

---

[80] Richard B. Sher, *The Enlightenment and the Book: Scottish Authors and Their Publishers in Britain, Ireland, and America* (Chicago, IL, 2006), quotation at p. xv. See also a recent intervention in this field, supporting Sher's contention quoted here, and broadening its scope by means of quantitative and social network analysis methodologies: Yann Ciarán Ryan and Mikko Tolonen, 'The Evolution of Scottish Enlightenment Publishing', *Historical Journal*, published online 2024, pp. 1–33, doi: 10.1017/S0018246X23000614.

[81] Sher, *Enlightenment and the Book*, pp. 228–35. See also Richard B. Sher, 'The Book in the Scottish Enlightenment', in *The Culture of the Book in the Scottish Enlightenment: An Exhibition, with Essays by Roger Emerson, Richard Sher, Stephen Brown, and Paul Wood*, Thomas Fisher Rare Book Library (Toronto, 2000), pp. 40–60, on the variety of forms and processes of book publication. For the widespread use of subscription publishing by Scots of the lower and middling orders in the eighteenth century in order to obtain reprints of older books, see Valerie Honeyman, '"That Ye May Judge for Yourselves": The Contribution of Scottish Presbyterianism towards the Emergence of Political Awareness amongst Ordinary People in Scotland between 1746 and 1792' (PhD thesis, University of Stirling, 2012), pp. 145–225.

[82] Letter 84, JW to SK, 22 Oct. 1784; Richard Saville, *Bank of Scotland: A History, 1695–1995* (Edinburgh, 1996), pp. 156–66.

[83] Letter 84, JW to SK, 22 Oct. 1784.

more honourable to him but also because he thought the sales would be better in Scotland, where M'Gill's name was known, despite the disapproval of 'the Orthodox at Edr.'.

Kenrick secured the opinions of his friends Thomas Wigan and Joseph Priestley on M'Gill's manuscript. While Wigan was 'quite in raptures' with the book,[84] Priestley was less optimistic; he thought it should be published locally in Scotland, and by subscription.[85] Nevertheless, Kenrick, chagrined that M'Gill had not approved of his showing his manuscript to Priestley, undertook to secure as many subscriptions to it in England as he could, should M'Gill choose to publish it that way rather than sell the copyright. M'Gill consulted the advice of London booksellers through the offices of Wodrow's brother-in-law John Hamilton, a London merchant, but in the event he published the book by subscription in Edinburgh, as Priestley had advised.[86]

Kenrick had anticipated as early as summer 1784 that Wodrow would be given William Leechman's papers to publish after the principal's death.[87] In fact, Leechman left them to his wife, who immediately gave them to Wodrow. He told Kenrick that

> this treasure...consists of five or six bundles put up by himself & marked in the outside with his own hand, they are cheifly Sermons, such as a bundle of those preached in the Colledge Chapel. Another entitled Sacramental Sermons. Another Sermons that may be used with a small change. A small bundle of Discourses delivered to the Literary Society.[88]

As Thomas D. Kennedy points out, it is not as easy as we might hope to recover the full extent of William Leechman's significance and stature during his lifetime because of the decision not to publish his secular writings after his death.[89] He was Francis Hutcheson's preferred candidate for the chair of divinity at the University of Glasgow in 1743 in order to establish the teaching of candidates for church ministry in Moderate rather than Evangelical theology.[90] On Leechman's successful appointment to the post, after a hard-fought battle in the Glasgow

---

[84] Letter 85, SK to JW, 2–3 Dec. 1784.
[85] Letter 89, SK to JW, 14 Jan. 1785.
[86] Letter 94, JW to SK, 25 March 1785; Letter 108, JW to SK, 27 Dec. 1785; William M'Gill, *A Practical Essay on the Death of Jesus Christ* (Edinburgh, 1786).
[87] Letter 80, SK to JW, 2 June 1784.
[88] Letter 108, JW to SK, 27 Dec. 1785.
[89] Thomas D. Kennedy, 'William Leechman, Pulpit Eloquence and the Glasgow Enlightenment', in Andrew Hook and Richard B. Sher, eds, *The Glasgow Enlightenment* (East Linton, 1995), p. 58.
[90] See Section IV.

Presbytery and the Synod of Glasgow and Ayr, Hutcheson's verdict was that 'we have at last got a Right Professor of Theology, the only right one in Scotland'[91]—although, in fact, Leechman had been greatly influenced by Professor William Hamilton at Edinburgh, Louisa Wodrow's grandfather and five times Moderator of the Church of Scotland, a man who similarly steered away from 'enthusiasm' in religion.[92] As Moderator of the General Assembly himself in 1757, and principal of Glasgow University from 1761 to 1785, Leechman was an influential figure during the period of the high Enlightenment. He published several individual sermons during his lifetime, as well as a Life of Francis Hutcheson which was prefixed to Hutcheson's posthumously published *System of Moral Philosophy* (1755) and 'remains the standard biography' of Hutcheson.[93]

Wodrow discussed the possibility of publishing some of Leechman's secular essays (a substantial number of which he excerpted and summarized for Kenrick)[94] with Leechman's professorial colleagues in the Glasgow Literary Society, since they had originally been read in that forum. They, however,

seemed to think that nothing coud appear with dignity under his Name but Sermons indeed I believe they are right in their judgment. There is a solemnity and strength in his manner that just suits the Pulpit & does not so well suit any other thing.[95]

This suggests a desire to present Leechman only in his role as a churchman and professor of theology, occupied wholly with sacred concerns; and, though Wodrow made clear that he was acting under the direction of the professoriate rather than taking the decision himself, this choice may have suited his

---

[91] Kennedy, 'William Leechman, Pulpit Eloquence and the Glasgow Enlightenment', p. 58, citing William Robert Scott, *Francis Hutcheson: His Life, Teaching and Position in the History of Philosophy* (Cambridge, 1900), p. 93.

[92] Kennedy, 'William Leechman, Pulpit Eloquence and the Glasgow Enlightenment', pp. 60–61; Thomas Ahnert, *The Moral Culture of the Scottish Enlightenment, 1690–1805* (New Haven, CT, 2014), p. 36.

[93] Thomas D. Kennedy, 'Leechman, William (1706–85)', *ODNB*.

[94] Letter 109, JW to SK, 9 Jan. 1786; Letter 110, JW to SK, 21 Jan. 1786. These were: a vindication of the national character of the Jews; a discussion of 'the Grandeur of the Hebrew Nation in its most flourishing times compared with other Nations of the World in the same Age'; 'An Enquiry into the Origin of the Heathen Mysteries'; 'The Importance of Moral Philosophy among the Sciences & in the After Life'; an essay warning against 'Metaphysical Disquisitions & their tendency to lead to Scepticism', especially in young minds; one on the life and character of the Emperor Julian; several disputing arguments in David Hume's *History of England*; 'On the spirit of Popery and Protestantism and its Effects on Literature Liberty and other great interests of human Society'; on religious intolerance in ancient Greece and Rome; and on an inherent tendency towards progress in human society.

[95] Letter 121, JW to SK, 28 Aug. 1786.

admiration for Leechman's ability in extempore prayer and knowledge of scripture. Material on devotion was what he hoped to find when he first took Leechman's papers home.[96]

On the other hand, he also suggested to Kenrick: 'Besides there is scarce any of these things fit for the public eye except the essay on Education & even that unfinished.'[97] Given the labour that transcribing, checking, and printing the sermons cost him, it would not be surprising if he was not anxious to extend the task to the essays.

[T]hey want the last polish of his hand. None of them are wrote a 2d. time but several of them improved by additions on seperate scraps of Paper by Interlineations such as render them in some places almost illegible. These passages must be wrote over on a seperate Paper & the whole put into the hands of somebody to make out a fair Copy for the Printer for none of them can be printed from his own Copy intended only for himself.[98]

'It is lucky he was a stranger to every kind of shorthand', he concluded, ruefully.

Moreover, Wodrow admired secular scholarship greatly, as the many discussions he had with Kenrick demonstrate—he was proud of his own father's secular scholarly achievements even while in ministry, so it is not clear that he would have been averse to publishing Leechman's secular as well as his sacred writings.[99] Kenrick, too, hoped that Wodrow would find a second, more complete, copy of Leechman's essay on Hume's *History* which could be published. Yet it was also Kenrick who proposed that a biography prefixed to the sermons ought to concentrate on Leechman's career as a churchman and professor of theology.[100] A year before he died, Leechman himself had expressed the desire to publish a volume of his sermons, which surely influenced his friends and colleagues.[101]

---

[96] Letter 108, JW to SK, 27 Dec. 1785.
[97] Ibid.
[98] Letter 128, JW to SK, 26 April 1787.
[99] W-K, I, pp. 5, 428–29; Letter 263, JW to SK, 5 July 1808.
[100] Letter 112, SK to JW, 11 Feb. 1786; Letter 118, SK to JW, 3 July 1786; Letter 120, JW to SK, c. 9–15 Aug. 1786. Cf. Letter 122, SK to JW, 28 Sept. 1786, on the decision only to publish Leechman's sermons: 'Mr. Wigan & I have nothing to say against the members of the College club– they are certainly much more competent to judge of the propriety of what of this great man's ought to be published than we can be– not to mention the weight of your own judgment. All we want is to see them [i.e. the published works].'
[101] Letter 84, JW to SK, 22 Oct. 1784. Indeed, JW implied as much in 'The Life of Leechman', p. 100–01: having noted that Leechman's papers contained the substance of his university lectures, of sermons, and of essays for the Literary Society, he continued: 'With respect to the two last articles, it is much to be regretted that this worthy man never found leisure or inclination to prepare any thing for the press... Yet, as he had consented, not long before his death, to revise as many of his sermons as, with those published by himself, would make up a single volume;

The choice of what to publish may well then have been influenced by the desire to promote a particular view of Leechman, the size of the task, and, perhaps, Leechman's own stated wish. Meanwhile, the decision which seems to have been taken at some later date to destroy the secular essays that Wodrow had been given, however regrettable for historians, may not have been motivated by an over-zealous desire to shape Leechman's reputation, but perhaps it was simply taken by Wodrow's family after the end of his own life.[102] Wodrow did publish a summary of Leechman's university lectures on the evidence of Christianity,[103] but even those were 'in such a confused state that [Leechman had] attempted himself to burn them but was prevented by Mrs Leechman'.[104]

Kenrick and others persuaded Wodrow to write a short biography of Leechman to be prefixed to what became the first of two volumes of sermons, a Life which eventually ran to around a hundred pages and was accompanied by an engraving of William Millar's portrait of Leechman, painted in 1774/75 (see Plate 10).[105] Although Kenrick encouraged him frequently, Wodrow felt diffident about his capacity to do justice to his subject, and he undertook substantial research by correspondence with Leechman's family and friends for this purpose.[106] Alongside writing the Life, reading the sermons preoccupied Wodrow for much

and many of his friends have expressed their earnest wishes to see more of his sermons in print; I have attempted to revise a few for that purpose.'

[102] A certain volume of Leechman's papers had been destroyed during the months before his death by his wife and his nephew, Rev. William Pairman of Elie, Fife. Letter 117, JW to SK, 17 May 1786. But JW took various letters to Leechman, lectures, and sermons home with him after the principal's death for his own pleasure in them. The Glasgow Literary Society, established in 1752, met weekly on Friday evenings from November to May for discussion of academic papers dealing with a wide range of scientific, philosophical, theological, and literary subjects. It was one of the most important literary societies of the Scottish Enlightenment. A typed transcript made in 1892 of the minutes of the Literary Society, 1764–79 is held in Glasgow University Archives and Special Collections, at GB 247 MS Murray 505, as is the original manuscript of the minutes 1790–1800, at GB 247 MS Gen 4/1. They show that Leechman delivered a discourse annually in mid-November, as the second most senior member after Robert Foulis, between 1764 and 1771. Four of his papers concerned education, two discussed aspects of David Hume's *History of England*, and one explored the life and character of Emperor Julian 'the apostate'. He also posed questions for discussion on eight occasions in this period: three on education, two on social improvement, one on civil liberty, and one on ancient Greek and Roman religion. There are no minutes extant for the years 1772, 1774, or 1775; Leechman was absent from the one meeting recorded in 1773, and he no longer seems to have been a member of the Society from 1776. We are grateful to Zubin Meer for sharing his expertise in relation to these minutes.

[103] Wodrow, 'The Life of Dr. Leechman', pp. 35–49.
[104] Letter 114, JW to SK, 11 April 1786.
[105] Letter 110, SK to JW, 21 Jan. 1786; Wodrow, 'The Life of Leechman', in *Sermons*, I, pp. 1–102.
[106] Letter 120, JW to SK, c. 9–15 Aug. 1786; Letter 121, JW to SK, 28 Aug. 1786.

of 1786 and 1787, most of them undated and incomplete, especially in their conclusions,

> where only perhaps two or three hints are given on the ground of what was delivered viva voce and the Principal's stile was so nervuous & so much his own that is will be difficult & dangerous for any other person to attempt to imitate it.[107]

Nevertheless, he admitted that 'The Labour has been pleasant as a grateful tribute of respect to the Memory of a man whom I loved & revered above all others.'[108] Eventually the tasks of writing and transcribing were complete, and Wodrow travelled to London in autumn 1788 for the purpose of seeking a publisher with a wider reach than Edinburgh publishers might have had, to negotiate terms, though on his return he continued to transcribe, having agreed with Andrew Strahan, the publisher, a larger size of volumes than had originally been envisaged.[109] The book was published in two volumes in 1789.

Together with this substantial labour of love, Wodrow acquired the papers of his cousin, Rev. John Warner of Kilbarchan, who died in 1786. Kenrick was astonished to hear that, while these documents, like Leechman's, had been found 'in the greatest confusion', many of them were 'much fitter for Publication than the Principals'.[110] Wodrow had also found some Italian books with Kenrick's name on them, and a clean copy of a translation made by Warner and transcribed by Kenrick in the 1750s of Louis-Jean Lévesque de Pouilly's *Theorie des Sentimens Agréables* (Geneva, 1747).[111] Pouilly's book was published in English in 1749 as *The Theory of Agreeable Sensations: In which the Laws Observed by Nature in the Distribution of Pleasure are Investigated; and the Principles of Natural Theology and Moral Philosophy are Established*. Warner's manuscript seems to have been a new translation with notes and commentary, which Kenrick had transcribed in the hope of having it published. While he was in London negotiating the publication of Leechman's sermons, Wodrow also investigated whether he could have this translation published, but Thomas Christie advised him that, while valuable, it was now probably out of date and was unlikely to sell.[112] In fact, in his first flush of enthusiasm in May 1786,

---

[107] Letter 120, JW to SK, c. 9–15 Aug. 1786.
[108] Letter 128, JW to SK, 26 April 1786.
[109] See Letters 136–43. For a discussion of Wodrow's negotiations in London and their outcome, see Sher, *Enlightenment and the Book*, pp. 247–49.
[110] Letter 114, JW to SK, 11 April 1786; Letter 115, SK to JW, 25 April 1786.
[111] See W-K, I, pp. 226–29, 232; Letter 114, JW to SK, 11 April 1786; Letter 121, JW to SK, 28 Aug. 1786; Letter 122, SK to JW, 28 Sept. 1786.
[112] See Letters 136–43.

he had thought to publish some of Warner's sermons and a Life,[113] but this possibility seems to have run into the sand, perhaps in recognition of the volume of work Leechman's sermons had cost him alongside his parish business. It occurred to him that Kenrick might have written a short biography of Warner, but, despite his repeated attempts to encourage his friend to put pen to paper in this cause, nothing came of this.[114]

As Wodrow sorted through the disorganized mass of Professor Leechman's papers after his death, he was particularly taken with an essay on education, which he quoted and summarized at length for Kenrick and his Bewdley friend, Thomas Wigan.[115] This led the correspondents into a discussion of the conceptions of and optimism in human progress held by Enlightenment writers. 'It has always been my opinion as well as wish', Kenrick wrote, candidly, 'that mankind are daily improving in wisdom and virtue.' The writings of the philosopher David Hartley (1705–57), as well as those of his hero, Joseph Priestley (1733–1804), and the seventeenth-century theologian George Hakewill (1578–1649), confirmed him in this view.[116] His ideas were akin to those of John Locke, Thomas Paine, and Mary Wollstonecraft, who held that human nature was fundamentally benign and that rational education would gradually lead to political and then social improvement, rather than like the millenarianism of other contemporary writers.[117] He was not sure if his views would conform to those of Scottish Enlightenment writers such as Adam Smith (1723–90), Lord Kames (1696–1782), and John Millar (1735–1801). These philosophers had discussed a theory of four stages of civilization, in which human societies developed from hunter-gathering to urbanization, via pastoral and agricultural phases, while Adam Ferguson had proposed a three-stage theory of moral progress; and, like the English radical reformers, they were optimistic that such progress was to be expected.[118] Wodrow summarized the Scottish stadial theory for Kenrick but suggested that he probably held a view

---

[113] Letter 116, JW to SK, 2 May 1786; Letter 117, JW to SK, 17 May 1786; Letter 127, SK to JW, 19 Jan. 1787.

[114] See Letters 144–47 in Jan.–March 1789.

[115] Letter 109, JW to SK, 9 Jan. 1786.

[116] Letter 112, SK to JW, 11 Feb. 1786.

[117] Clare Jackson, 'Progress and Optimism', in Fitzpatrick, Jones, Knellwolf, and McCalman, eds, *The Enlightenment World*, pp. 177–93; Gregory Claeys, *Thomas Paine: Social and Political Thought* (1989); Barbara Taylor, 'Mary Wollstonecraft and the Wild Wish of Early Feminism', *History Workshop Journal*, 33 (1992), pp. 197–219; Gregory Claeys, ed., *Utopias of the British Enlightenment* (Cambridge, 1994); J. F. C. Harrison, *The Second Coming: Popular Millenarianism 1780–1850* (1979).

[118] Emma Macleod, 'Revolution', in Aaron Garrett and James Harris, eds, *Scottish Philosophy in the Eighteenth Century. Volume I: Morals, Politics, Art, Religion* (Oxford, 2015), pp. 363–69.

more like Leechman's providentialism. The principal had not been convinced by the stadialist theory that progress was 'natural, gradual & uniform', but rather had believed in a version of the 'Great Man' theory of history—that 'great & unforseen causes under the direction of Providence' drove progress, particularly through individuals of vision and 'almost divine Genius' who precipitate progress in any one part of the world, which then gradually spread elsewhere by similar means—a view Kenrick agreed that he held.[119]

Education, the subject of Leechman's essay, was itself a regular theme in the correspondence, as it was for Enlightenment writers from John Locke, whose *Essay Concerning Human Understanding* (1690) and *Some Thoughts on Education* (1693) underlay much of the eighteenth-century discussion on education, to Jean-Jacques Rousseau, Joseph Priestley, and Mary Wollstonecraft, as well as conservative writers such as Sarah Trimmer and Hannah More. Wodrow and Kenrick themselves had less to say on the education of children in the 1780s than they had previously done, now that their own children had grown up, but the Scottish universities were powerhouses of the Scottish Enlightenment, and they continued to take a keen interest in Glasgow University, their *alma mater*. Elsewhere, as Margaret C. Jacob points out, universities were 'hardly in the vanguard of the Enlightenment', and Kenrick still enjoyed pointing out the progressiveness of the Scottish universities in relation to Oxford University, which he had been barred from attending as a Dissenter, resulting in his matriculation at Glasgow instead in 1745.[120] Now, when his Bewdley friend Wilson Roberts took his son to enrol at Christ Church College, Oxford, Kenrick contrasted the continuing concern with religious ritual at Oxford with its removal in Scotland and its replacement with the pursuit of modern knowledge.

is it not strange that at this time of day [Science] should still continue to be so [neglected], & these old forms so strictly adhered to: while wth. you, who pass for a religious people, the form should be dropped & the improvement of the human mind in every branch of Science should come in its room—[121]

He thought that Wodrow, in his 'Life of Leechman', ought to set out the advances made at Glasgow University under Leechman's principalship, which 'wd. be highly acceptable at this time & of advantage to the university when contrasted

---

[119] Letter 116, JW to SK, 2 May 1786; Letter 119, SK to JW, 20 July 1786.
[120] Margaret C. Jacob, 'Polite Worlds of Enlightenment', in Fitzpatrick, Jones, Knellwolf, and McCalman, eds, *The Enlightenment World*, p. 275.
[121] Letter 135, SK to JW, 13 Feb. 1788.

with the indolence & slovenly negligence wch. prevail at the two English universities– as published by Mr. Knox, & never contradicted'.[122] Kenrick was also concerned for the maintenance of Dissenting academies for the training of Dissenting ministers, and he was dismayed that those liberal-tending academies which had formerly existed at London, Exeter, Taunton, Derby, Warrington, and Kendal had all closed by 1786. He was pleased, however, by the establishment of New College, Hackney (or Hackney Academy), and also by the foundation of the New College at Manchester. He made a donation to the support of Hackney Academy in gratitude for the scholarship to Glasgow he had been awarded by the Dr Williams's Library.[123]

One of the longest and largest running concerns in their correspondence, respecting the University of Glasgow, was less a high-minded discussion of letters and learning in the age of Enlightenment and more a gossipy saga following the vendetta of their erstwhile friend, John Anderson (1726–96), the professor of natural philosophy, against William Leechman and an increasing majority of the Glasgow professoriate who sided with Leechman: 'a most terrible stramash', as Wodrow called it.[124] According to Lord Buchan, Anderson was 'by far the ablest Man in his profession of teaching Physics by experimentation in Britain', and indeed Wodrow's son Gavin had greatly enjoyed auditing his classes in 1775–76.[125] He had toured England with Kenrick and the young James Milliken (1741–63) in 1759.[126] He was a contentious figure at the university, however. Having voted for himself in the election to the chair of natural philosophy in 1757,[127] he proceeded

---

[122] Letter 118, SK to JW, 3 July 1786; Vicesimus Knox, 'LXXVII: On Some Parts of Discipline in our English Universities', in *Essays, Moral and Literary by Vicesimus Knox, M.A. a New Edition in Two Volumes* (1782), II, pp. 331–37. See also Roy Porter, *Enlightenment: Britain and the Creation of the Modern World* (2000), pp. 59, 347; Graham Midgley, *University Life in Eighteenth-Century Oxford* (New York, 1996).

[123] Letter 112, SK to JW, 11 Feb. 1786; Letter 118, SK to JW, 3 July 1786.

[124] Letter 91, JW to SK, 6 Feb. 1785. Copies of correspondence relating to Anderson's years of strife with Leechman and others at the University are held at the University of Glasgow Archives and are listed in Julie Gardham and Lesley Richmond, 'Research Resources in the University of Glasgow for Adam Smith and the Scottish Enlightenment' (University of Glasgow, 2009, rev. 2013, available at www.gla.ac.uk/media/Media_138989_smxx.pdf, pp. 8–13.

[125] Paul Wood, '"Jolly Jack Phosphorous" in the Venice of the North; or, Who Was John Anderson?', in Hook and Sher, eds, *The Glasgow Enlightenment*, p. 111, citing Glasgow University Library, MS Murray, 502, 201/76, f. 1; *W-K*, I, pp. 363–64.

[126] *W-K*, I, pp. 235–65, *passim*.

[127] Anderson was already the professor of oriental languages at Glasgow University, a position often used as a temporary post until a more suitable chair became available, and which he had held since 1754. Paul Wood, 'Anderson, John (1726–1796)', *ODNB*.

to bring a series of lawsuits against Leechman and his allies through the 1760s and 1770s.

By 1785 Anderson was so incensed by his failure to have Leechman's reputation destroyed because of the college bursar's financial mismanagement that he campaigned (unsuccessfully) for a royal visitation to the university in order to expose the principal and his supporters. He became obsessed with the issue far beyond the point of sense, rallying students to his cause and sending them into the town to gather signatures for his petition. Kenrick remembered his and Wodrow's student days, when Anderson had often come 'near to blows' with Adam Smith, then a young professor and 'as fiery & choleric as Anderson himself'—'when we poor souls tho$^t$. that all their attention was taken up in promoting the cause of litterature'.[128] Wodrow received a regular stream of news of events by the channel of his wife's aunt, Mrs Leechman, and he vented his own feelings, in turn, to Kenrick. 'Mr L. has got the lye in the rudest manner....I am much more hurt with these things than he is', he told Kenrick. 'He rests in the Integrity of his heart without being disconcerted with all they can say.'[129] Events escalated for more than a year until spring 1786 when Rev. Dr William Taylor successfully sued Anderson at law for libel, while Anderson himself lost all the several cases he had taken to the Court of Session against the University.[130] Wodrow had been anxious enough at one point that he asked Kenrick to do what he could to check any effects of Anderson's slander of the quality of teaching and student experience at Glasgow: 'I beg you will contradict these groundless calumnies.'[131] In fact, Adam Smith had written to William Cullen on 20 September 1774:

In the present state of the Scotch Universities, I do most sincerely look upon them as, in spite of their faults, without exception the best seminaries of learning that are to be found any where in Europe. They are perhaps, upon the whole, as unexceptionable as any public institutions of that kind, which all contain in their very nature the seeds and causes of negligency and corruption, have ever been, or are likely to be.

Nevertheless, he continued, 'That, however, they are still capable of amendment, I know very well, and a Visitation is, I believe, the only proper means of procuring

---

[128] Letter 92, SK to JW, 22 Feb. 1785. Indeed, Smith himself clashed with Leechman on a number of occasions: Ian Simpson Ross, 'Adam Smith's "Happiest" Years as a Glasgow Professor', in Hook and Sher, *Glasgow Enlightenment*, p. 90; Nicholas Phillipson, *Adam Smith: An Enlightened Life* (2010), p. 121.

[129] Letter 94, JW to SK, 25 March 1785.

[130] Letter 117, JW to SK, 17 May 1786; Letter 134, JW to SK, 13 Dec. 1787; Letter 136, JW to SK, 28 May 1787.

[131] Letter 108, JW to SK, 27 Dec. 1785.

them this amendment'—if the visitors likely to be appointed, and the reforms they might propose, were known and acceptable.[132]

Finally, the Scottish Enlightenment was characterized by a quest for 'useful knowledge' alongside the literary, historical, and philosophical achievements of its luminaries, and Kenrick's local context of Worcestershire and Birmingham also favoured interest in economic and technological improvement. Wodrow and Kenrick were both interested in advances in industry and especially infrastructure. 'This is an Age of Discovery beyond any other particularly in Mechanical invention.'[133] The navigable waterways of Britain had been under development since the 1720s, but the age of canal-building began in 1761 with the Duke of Bridgewater's coal canal from Worsley to Manchester. Thirty-three Acts of Parliament were passed by 1774 for inland waterway improvement in the Midlands and the north of England, and five in Scotland; most were relatively short but designed to link natural and manmade stretches of water strategically, as in Worcestershire.[134] In 1786 Wodrow was keen to 'hear more of your public Spirited scheme of the Water carriage', or canals, that Kenrick had earlier mentioned as being proposed to extend the River Severn for the benefit of the iron trade, though neither canal scheme was supported in Parliament that year, to Kenrick's disgust.[135] Wodrow sympathized and replied that the Forth and Clyde canal in Scotland was badly delayed because of local corruption.[136]

He did, however, enjoy telling Kenrick about a report of the demonstration of a steam engine driving a model carriage at Leadhills, a lead miners' community in south Lanarkshire—which, in an exemplary fusion of Scottish Enlightenment literary and industrial culture, was also the location of the first subscription library in Scotland, established in 1741.[137] Kenrick was sceptical of Wodrow's account of the capacities of the steam engine:

---

[132] Adam Smith to William Cullen, 20 Sept. 1774, *The Correspondence of Adam Smith*, eds Ernest Campbell Mossner and Ian Simpson Ross, in *The Glasgow Edition of the Works and Correspondence of Adam Smith*, vol. 6 (Indianapolis, IN, 1987), pp. 173–74. See also Ronald Lyndsay Crawford, *Scotland and America in the Age of Paine: Ideas of Liberty and the Making of Four Americans* (Aberdeen, 2022), p. 193.

[133] Letter 120, JW to SK, *c.* 9–15 Aug. 1786.

[134] John Rule, *The Vital Century: England's Developing Economy, 1714–1815* (1992), pp. 231–40.

[135] Letter 116, JW to SK, 2 May 1786; Letter 119, SK to JW, 20 July 1786.

[136] Letter 121, JW to SK, 28 Aug. 1786.

[137] For a career demonstrating a similar fusion, see Julian Glover, *Man of Iron: Thomas Telford and the Building of Britain* (2017).

Your Leadhills philosophic family exceeds every improvement yet made in this improving age. Like Miss Wodrow's story of the infant Doctor– it only wants one trifling circumstance– its being really a fact.–[138]

Although Wodrow's fancy had taken flight to suggest that this engine would in the course of time render canals

utterly useless & with them all the Carriage & draught horses in the Kingdom Ploughs Balloons &c, &c, for surely such a self moving Machine may easily [be] applied to the purposes of tillage of mounting in the air as it goes in every direction sailing on the sea & what not

—he was correct, though Kenrick's scepticism is understandable.[139] He was accurate, too, in the details with which he had supplied Kenrick of the as yet modest engine driving a model carriage, which could carry 1600lb at 10 miles per hour up or downhill. Its inventor, the engineer William Symington (1764–1831), was still a student at Edinburgh University, but he went on to design the first effective steam boat, the paddle steamer *Charlotte Dundas*, in 1803, and so he was 'the first [person] to demonstrate working examples of steam powered transport on both land and water'.[140] Automatons and hot-air balloons intrigued both men.[141]

Wodrow was interested that his MP, Sir Adam Fergusson, was touring the west Highland coast with his fellow MP, George Dempster, to reconnoitre good locations for establishing planned fishing villages.[142] He was impressed by Kenrick's report of the pledges totalling nearly £200,000 for the two Severn canals combined; as he was, also, by the £10,000 subscribed by Dissenters in London for the establishment of New College, Hackney. Whether for civic architecture or industrial support, he regretted, the Scots did not donate so abundantly.

You have a spirit in your part of the Island I mean a generosity of Spirit which animates such undertaking which we are strangers to in this part of the Island for I reckon nothing

---

[138] Letter 120, JW to SK, *c.* 9–15 Aug. 1786; Letter 122, SK to JW, 28 Sept. 1786.
[139] Letter 120, JW to SK, *c.* 9–15 Aug. 1786.
[140] Graeme Symington, 'William Symington 1764–1831: Engineer, Inventor and Steamboat Pioneer', revised 3 Nov. 2022, https://sites.google.com/view/williamsymington/introduction-and-contents; cf. I. G. C. Hutchison, *Industry, Reform and Empire: Scotland, 1790–1880* (Edinburgh, 2020), p. 49.
[141] Letters 105, 106, 108, and 110.
[142] Letter 121, JW to SK, 28 Aug. 1786; T. C. Smout, 'The Landowner and the Planned Village in Scotland, 1730–1830', in N. T. Phillipson and Rosalind Mitchison, eds, *Scotland in the Age of Improvement* (Edinburgh, 1996), pp. 73–106.

either in the Edr. schemes or that of our Fisheries compared with the Subscription of £10,000 in a single day.[143]

It was not easy to raise money for new capital investment, as Wodrow knew from his own corner of north Ayrshire, where schemes to deepen the harbour at Saltcoats required his representation to the local MP.[144] The harbour had been built in around 1700, and later extended, and a small canal to the local coalfields opened in 1772.[145] Shipbuilding and rope works were added in 1775; all of these explain the growth in the population of Wodrow's parish from fewer than 400 people in around 1700 to 1,412 in 1755 to 2,425 in 1791.[146] It was a thriving small community based on a very mixed economy; but the largest local landowners were more interested in investing in their parks and estates than in local industrial capital.[147]

Wodrow enjoyed visiting Edinburgh when he was a delegate from the Synod of Glasgow and Ayr to the General Assembly of the Church of Scotland, as he was in 1785. He reported then on the ongoing urban improvements in the Scottish capital, confident that Kenrick would be astonished by its size by this time, the New Town development only having begun in 1768, three years after the Kenricks had left Scotland for Worcestershire. By 1785, although much of what is now considered to be the classic core of the New Town was yet to be built—Charlotte Square, the George Street Assembly Rooms, and most of the residential buildings—St Andrew's Square was complete, and Wodrow reported that the foundations for many of the 200 houses contracted had been laid. Far from thinking this slow progress in eighteen years, he was amazed at the speed of events. Moreover,

The buildings are grand beautiful & have every convenience. The streets and squares so perfectly regular that a stranger after looking for five minutes at the plan of it or walking two or three times thro' it may find any street square or house in it without any embarrassment.[148]

---

[143] Letter 120, JW to SK, c. 9–15 Aug. 1786; Letter 118, SK to JW, 3 July 1786. SK did not suggest that the £10,000 had been pledged on a single day, however.

[144] Letter 88, JW to SK, 7 Jan. 1785.

[145] John Strawhorn, ed., *Ayrshire at the Time of Burns* (Kilmarnock, 1959), p. 267.

[146] James Wodrow, 'The Parish of Stevenston', in Sir John Sinclair, ed., *The Statistical Account of Scotland, Drawn Up from the Communications of the Ministers of the Different Parishes*, 13 vols (Edinburgh, 1791–99) (hereafter *OSA*), vol. 7 (1793), pp. 26–27.

[147] For example, see Strawhorn, *Ayrshire at the Time of Burns*, pp. 246, 291, 300.

[148] Letter 96, JW to SK, 16 June 1785. The 1768 plan of James Craig, the architect who won the competition to design the New Town, can be seen at Wikimedia Commons, File: 1768 James Craig Map of New Town, Edinburgh, Scotland, accessed 8 March 2023, https://commons.wikimedia.org/wiki/File:1768_James_Craig_Map_of_New_Town,_Edinburgh,_Scotland_(First_Plan_of_New_Town)_-_Geographicus_-_Edinburgh-craig-1768.jpg.

Meanwhile, the North Bridge was almost finished; and The Mound, now the site of New College, University of Edinburgh, and the Assembly Hall of the Church of Scotland, had appeared out of the rubble of the building works.

We learn less from the letters about the development of English towns such as Manchester, Liverpool, and even Birmingham, near Bewdley. Wodrow was looking forward to seeing those as he anticipated his journey south to London in 1788;[149] and Kenrick expected Nell Wodrow to have a fine time seeing the sights of Manchester on her return to Scotland in 1785, even in lieu of her long-expected trip to London. 'This goes wth. our dear Nell to Manchester', he wrote on the eve of her departure.

where I hope she will meet wth. much amusement & information. It is certainly one of the most enlightened spots in this Kingdom and she will be there at the celebrated Music Meeting wch. it is thought will not be in[fer]iour to the 2 exhibitions at Westminster Abbey. It has been advertised in the London papers for 2 months past.[150]

Manchester was, as Mee shows, a foundational 'node' in the transpennine Enlightenment. It grew from a population of fewer than 20,000 in the mid-eighteenth century to 70,000 by 1800, largely owing to the booming Lancashire textile industries and its cotton exchange. Its Literary and Philosophical Society was founded in 1781, however, a body 'concerned not just with the science and technology interface, but also with polite letters and general "improvement"'.[151] Wodrow and Kenrick, though curious about anything new and useful, were themselves primarily readers and thinkers, and their participation in the Enlightenment was principally located in pen and print.

## III. Religion, 1784–90

Religion is a key theme in this second volume, which illuminates the similarities and differences between radical English Rational Dissent and prudent Scottish Moderate Presbyterianism.[152] As outlined in the General Introduction to Volume 1, Wodrow and Kenrick were Presbyterians of the 'rational Christian' disposition who shared a common education at Glasgow but came to live in different religious contexts.

---

[149] Letter 136, JW to SK, 28 May 1788.
[150] Letter 100, SK to JW, 19 Sept. 1785.
[151] Mee, 'Transpennine Enlightenment', p. 599.
[152] Martin Fitzpatrick, 'The Enlightenment, Politics and Providence: Some Scottish and English Comparisons', in Knud Haakonssen, ed., *Enlightenment and Religion: Rational Dissent in Eighteenth-Century Britain* (Cambridge, 1996), pp. 64–98.

As a Presbyterian in England, Kenrick was a nonconformist, and became what was called a Rational Dissenter. There was a diversity of denominations and views among Dissenters, but a broad divide developed in the late eighteenth century between those Dissenters who remained orthodox and increasingly embraced Evangelicalism and Rational Dissenters who championed the right of private judgement, rejected doctrinal tests, and tended to develop heterodox theological views.[153] Dissenters from the Church of England were allowed to have their own chapels and academies under the Toleration Act of 1689, but they remained excluded from public offices and from matriculating at the University of Oxford and graduating from Cambridge by the requirement to subscribe to the Thirty-Nine Articles. This unequal legal status made Dissenters 'vulnerable to acts of petty victimisation by local figures of authority', and they lived with a 'sense of insecurity and injustice'.[154] While Rational Dissenting congregations tended to be composed of wealthy merchants and manufacturers, by rejecting orthodox doctrines they were technically outside the Toleration Act, and could be prosecuted under the Blasphemy Act (1698), as judge Blackstone pointedly reminded Joseph Priestley.[155] Becoming a prosperous banker in Bewdley, religion was largely a personal matter for Kenrick, and he maintained good relations with his Anglican neighbours, with whom he enjoyed discussing theology and publications. From this relatively safe and comfortable position, Kenrick became a keen advocate of religious liberty and Unitarianism.

In contrast, as a clergyman in Ayrshire, Wodrow was responsible for delivering sermons and other parish duties for the established Church of Scotland, had subscribed to its Westminster Confession of Faith, and owed his position to the patronage of the Earl of Eglinton. In the mid-eighteenth century the Scottish church became divided between Evangelical and Moderate clergy.[156] Wodrow was in the latter camp, and they generally tried to avoid theological dispute and focussed on preaching morality and writing on secular subjects such as history, philosophy, and languages. The Moderates became ascendant among the clergy, as they were increasingly appointed to parishes under the Patronage Act of

[153] Valerie Smith, *Rational Dissenters in Late Eighteenth-Century England: 'An Ardent Desire of Truth'* (Woodbridge, 2021), p. 5; see also W-K, I, pp. 61–63.

[154] John Seed, '"A Set of Men Powerful Enough in Many Things": Rational Dissent and Political Opposition in England 1770–1790', in Haakonssen, *Enlightenment and Religion*, pp. 157–58.

[155] Anthony Page, 'Rational Dissent and Blackstone's Commentaries', in Anthony Page and Wilfrid R. Prest, eds, *Blackstone and His Critics* (Oxford, 2018), pp. 78–81.

[156] On the Scottish religious context, see W-K, I, pp. 45–51.

1712.[157] This was attacked by the Evangelical 'Popular Party', who argued that parish elders and heritors should elect their ministers.[158] On either side, there was a diversity of views and dispositions. Among the Moderate clergy, for example, those around Edinburgh tended to focus on literary pursuits, with their leading figure being the historian William Robertson.[159] This focus on history, philosophy, and polite letters, particularly by leaders in the east of Scotland, traditionally led historians to characterize Moderate clergy as pragmatic and disengaged from theological controversy. As Colin Kidd has demonstrated, however, the situation was different in south-west Scotland, where Wodrow was a minister.[160] There a number of Glasgow-trained Moderate clergy explored heterodox theology, opposed enforced subscription to the Westminster Confession of Faith, and fought off charges of heresy against two of Wodrow's friends, Alexander Fergusson and William M'Gill.[161] In Kidd's words, 'the battles between Enlightenment and counter-Enlightenment were sharper and fiercer in Ayrshire and Renfrewshire, it seems, than elsewhere in Scotland'.[162]

Wodrow and Kenrick shared an Enlightenment commitment to the candid discussion of ideas, and to civil and religious liberty. In contrast to Kenrick's optimistic radicalism, however, Wodrow's experience as a Moderate minister in a Calvinist land fostered scepticism in him towards popular politics.[163] Rational religion might prevail among a majority of the clergy, but the Calvinist Reformation had sunk deep roots in Scotland, and Moderate sermons were being judged by

---

[157] Richard B. Sher, *Church and University in the Scottish Enlightenment: The Moderate Literati of Edinburgh* (Edinburgh, 2015), pp. 93–150; Ian D. L. Clark, 'From Protest to Reaction: The Moderate Regime in the Church of Scotland, 1752–1805', in N. T. Phillipson and R. Mitchison, eds, *Scotland in the Age of Improvement: Essays in Scottish History in the Eighteenth Century* (Edinburgh, 1970), pp. 200–24.

[158] Richard Sher and Alexander Murdoch, 'Patronage and Party in the Church of Scotland, 1750–1800', in Norman Macdougall, ed., *Church, Politics and Society: Scotland, 1408–1929* (Edinburgh, 1983), pp. 197–220.

[159] Colin Kidd, 'Subscription, the Scottish Enlightenment and the Moderate Interpretation of History', *Journal of Ecclesiastical History*, 55 (2004), pp. 502–19.

[160] Colin Kidd, 'Enlightenment and Anti-Enlightenment in Eighteenth-Century Scotland: An Ayrshire-Renfrewshire Microclimate', in Jean-François Dunyach and Ann Thomson, eds, *The Enlightenment in Scotland: National and International Perspectives* (Oxford, 2015), pp. 59–84.

[161] Colin Kidd, 'The Fergusson Affair: Calvinism and Dissimulation in the Scottish Enlightenment', *Intellectual History Review*, 26 (2016), pp. 339–54. On M'Gill, see below, near the end of this section.

[162] Colin Kidd, 'Satire, Hypocrisy and the Ayrshire-Renfrewshire Enlightenment', in Gerard Carruthers and Colin Kidd, eds, *International Companion to John Galt* (Glasgow, 2017), p. 18.

[163] On the link between Unitarianism and radicalism in England, see Stuart Andrews, *Unitarian Radicalism: Political Rhetoric, 1770–1814* (Basingstoke, 2003).

'village Calvinists'.[164] 'The Clergy of Scotland are not so much respected...by their own people as when you were in the Country', Wodrow told Kenrick. 'I believe the cheif cause is a difference in their Theological sentiments'. In some places, congregations seceded and appointed ministers who would preach 'more calvinistisck' sermons that were 'suited to the books they are accustomed to read'.[165] A combination of personal temperament and context made Wodrow a cautious Moderate, who was happy to discuss theology in private but tried to encourage his friends to be prudent in their publications. He disliked theological dispute and thought it undermined the promotion of the essence of Christianity.

An insight into Wodrow's religious context is provided by the journal of his niece, Mary Ann Wodrow (1762–1841). The daughter of his eldest brother, Mary Ann lived on the Isle of Little Cumbrae and became a very close friend of James's daughter, Margaret ('Peggy') Wodrow (1767–1845). Intelligent young women, there was a 'great similarity in our Sentiments & Feelings' and their minds could have been 'cast in the same Mould'. They enjoyed 'wildly pleasing scenes & romantic Walks' on the isle, and Mary Ann described Peggy as having 'a ready turn of envention and her ideas were striking (to me at least) & uncommon' and she 'afforded much amusement'. Yet they differed on religion. As an orthodox Calvinist, Mary Ann

regretted the difference in our education about Religious matters she [Peggy] being led to expect happyness hereafter from our own Merit & taught to think we were only frail, not corrupted creatures alas how little hope might we have if there was no better Righteousness than our own to trust to– fain would I have brought on this subject but was not qualified for it & Perhaps would have enjured the cause I wished to support.[166]

James had raised Peggy with the Arminian theology he had learned from William Leechman, which rejected Calvinist predestination and claimed that faith and good works could lead to salvation.[167] The relationship between these two young women illustrates the intensely religious context in which James Wodrow ministered during the 'Age of Reason'.

---

[164] Luke Brekke, 'Heretics in the Pulpit, Inquisitors in the Pews: The Long Reformation and the Scottish Enlightenment', *Eighteenth-Century Studies*, 44 (2010), pp. 79–98; Valerie Honeyman, '"That Ye May Judge for Yourselves": The Contribution of Scottish Presbyterianism towards the Emergence of Political Awareness amongst Ordinary People in Scotland between 1746 and 1792' (PhD thesis, University of Stirling, 2012).

[165] Letter 79, JW to SK, 15 April 1784.

[166] Diaries of Mary Ann Wodrow Archbald, I, ff. 55–56.

[167] Martin Fitzpatrick, 'Varieties of Candour: English and Scottish Style', *Enlightenment and Dissent*, 7 (1988), p. 38.

The eighteenth-century Enlightenment faith in the power of reason saw varying responses by Protestants in Britain. All believed that God was revealed in his two books, Nature and the Bible, and attacked the common enemy of deism in the early eighteenth century.[168] Protestants were divided, however, on how much faith could be placed in reason as a tool for interpreting God's revelation. Conservatives emphasized the limits of reason in religious matters and defended the necessity of subscribing belief in established creeds, with some doctrinal points being inherently mysterious and incomprehensible. As Bishop Samuel Horsely put it: 'it is not expected that we comprehend, but that we believe; where we cannot unriddle we are to learn to trust; where our faculties are too weak to penetrate, we are to check our curiosity and adore'.[169] Liberal-minded theologians, on the other hand, argued that critical study of scripture and history could identify the essential core truths of Christianity, and encouraged toleration of a variety of opinion on disputed non-essential doctrines. In the late eighteenth century, Rational Dissenters in England led the way in arguing that deism was best countered by cleansing Christianity of the orthodox theological 'corruptions' that had developed in its early centuries and restoring what they argued was the pure, primitive, practical religion that Jesus had taught, and which could be embraced by any rational individual. In this view, the Enlightenment could be seen as a 'second Reformation'.[170]

Rational Dissenters, along with some Anglican Latitudinarians, tended to develop heterodox theological views, rejecting the core orthodox doctrine of the Trinity as three 'persons' in one God: the Father, Son, and Holy Spirit.[171] They

---

[168] John Redwood, *Reason, Ridicule and Religion: The Age of Enlightenment in England 1660–1750* (1996).

[169] Samuel Horsley, *An Apology for the Liturgy and Clergy of the Church of England* (1790), p. 67; F. C. Mather, *High Church Prophet: Bishop Samuel Horsley (1733–1806) and the Caroline Tradition in the Later Georgian Church* (Oxford, 1992), pp. 205–08; Peter B. Nockles, *The Oxford Movement in Context: Anglican High Churchmanship, 1760–1857* (Cambridge, 1994), pp. 203–04; see also Young, *Religion and Enlightenment in Eighteenth-Century England*, ch. 4, 'The Way to Divine Knowledge: The Mystical Critique of Rational Religion'. Horsley was a first cousin of Louisa Wodrow and is discussed several times in the Wodrow–Kenrick correspondence. JW reported that William Leechman was 'amazed at a man of Horsley's abilities appearing at this day as a defender of the Athanasian doctrines'. Letter 84, JW to SK, 22 Oct. 1784.

[170] John Walsh, Colin Haydon, and Stephen Taylor, eds, *The Church of England, c. 1689–c. 1833: From Toleration to Tractarianism* (Cambridge, 1993), pp. 37–38; Anthony Page, 'The Enlightenment and a "Second Reformation": The Religion and Philosophy of John Jebb (1736–86)', *Enlightenment and Dissent*, 17 (1998), pp. 48–82.

[171] For a perceptive discussion of differing views on Christology among Dissenters, see Alan P. F. Sell, *Christ and Controversy: The Person of Christ in Nonconformist Thought and Ecclesial*

argued that this mystery was a theological invention of the early years of the Church, and lacked sufficient evidence in scripture. Arguing for the unity and supremacy of God the Father, anti-trinitarians were divided on the question of Christ's nature. Arians argued that Jesus Christ was divine and had pre-existed his life on earth, but was a subordinate being to God—in essence, a super-angelic being.[172] Socinians, on the other hand, argued that Jesus was a human, given a special commission by God, and then resurrected and exalted following his crucifixion. Arianism and Socinianism were attacked by orthodox theologians because they both depicted Christ as a 'creature' who was subordinate to God rather than part of the incomprehensible Holy Trinity. Anti-trinitarians tended to also reject other doctrines such as original sin, atonement, and eternal punishment.

Rational Dissent, with its theological diversity but broadly anti-trinitarian position, gave way in the last years of the century to a narrowly defined Socinian Unitarianism. In 1774 the renegade Anglican, Theophilus Lindsey, established a Unitarian chapel at Essex Street in London that was patronized by some of Britain's elite, such as the Duke of Grafton.[173] Yet the spread of Unitarianism owed most to the prolific and combative Yorkshire polymath Joseph Priestley— whose works are frequently discussed in this volume of the Wodrow–Kenrick correspondence.[174] Raised a Calvinist, he became an Arian in the 1750s and then a Socinian in 1768. In the words of Bob Webb:

In the heat of that new conviction, Priestley published a series of brilliant polemics, intended to convert not only Arians, but Calvinists, Methodists, Anglicans, and sceptics to his newly won theological position, and to persuade them as well to the philosophical necessarianism he had drawn from David Hartley.[175]

Samuel Taylor Coleridge called him 'the author of modern Unitarianism'.[176] Kenrick appears to have been one of the early converts to Priestley's Unitarianism, and was eager to meet 'this wonderful man' when he moved to nearby

---

*Experience, 1600–2000* (Eugene, OR, 2011), ch. 3; more broadly, see Jonathan C. P. Birch, *Jesus in an Age of Enlightenment* (New York, 2019), especially ch. 7.

[172] Maurice Wiles, *Archetypal Heresy: Arianism through the Centuries* (Oxford, 2004), p. 146.

[173] Theophilus Lindsey, *The Letters of Theophilus Lindsey (1723–1808)*, ed. G. M. Ditchfield, 2 vols (Woodbridge, 2007–12).

[174] For a detailed two-volume biography, see Robert E. Schofield, *The Enlightenment of Joseph Priestley: A Study of His Life and Work from 1733 to 1773* (University Park, PA, 1997); idem, *The Enlightened Joseph Priestley: A Study of His Life and Work from 1773 to 1804* (University Park, PA, 2004).

[175] R. K. Webb, 'The Emergence of Rational Dissent', in Haakonssen, *Enlightenment and Religion*, p. 36.

[176] Cited in H. N. Coleridge, *Specimens of the Table Talk of the Late Samuel Taylor Coleridge*, 2 vols (1835), I, p. 166.

Birmingham.[177] Priestley sought to monopolize and promote the term 'Unitarian'. 'In my opinion', he wrote in 1786, 'those who are usually called Socinians (who consider Christ as being a mere man) are the only body of Christians who are properly entitled to the appellation of Unitarians.'[178] And his Unitarianism was an extreme version of Socinian theology—for example, unlike the early Socinians, he rejected the immaculate conception and did not allow prayers to Christ. Priestley's success is revealed by Google Books Ngram, which shows that use of the word 'unitarian' rose sharply in the late 1770s and reached an all-time peak in the mid-1780s.[179] Priestley's intellectual sparring partner, Richard Price, a leading Arian, joined the Unitarian Society when it was established in early 1791 but died a few months later. Had he lived, he would no doubt have been as disappointed as Wodrow was that they adopted a divisive platform that unambiguously defined Jesus as human and excluded the Arian doctrine of his pre-existence.[180]

The spread of anti-trinitarianism led to dissatisfaction with enforced subscription to the orthodox doctrine of the established churches. Following the publication of Francis Blackburne's *The Confessional* (1766), in the early 1770s around 200 Anglican clergy petitioned Parliament to remove the requirement that they subscribe to the Thirty-Nine Articles of the Church of England. This was rejected on two occasions, and several resigned, with Theophilus Lindsey establishing the Essex Street Unitarian Chapel in 1774. Under the Toleration Act, Dissenters also had to subscribe belief in the orthodox doctrine contained in the Articles, and they also unsuccessfully petitioned for relief from this obligation in 1772 and 1773. They were successful in 1779, however, when the Nonconformist Relief Act substituted a simple declaration of belief in the Bible.[181] By the mid-1780s, however,

---

[177] Letter 72, SK to JW, 15 Aug. 1781, in W-K, I, p. 455.

[178] Joseph Priestley, *An History of Early Opinions Concerning Jesus Christ* (Birmingham, 1786), pp. 80–81. Priestley acknowledged that his 'Arian friends' would be 'particularly offended at my not allowing them the title of *unitarians*' (p. xvi).

[179] Based on a Google Ngram Viewer search showing how frequently the word 'unitarian' appears in Google Books that were published in Britain in the period 1650–2019. https://books.google.com/ngrams/graph?content=Unitarian&year_start=1650&year_end=2019&corpus=en-GB-2019&smoothing=3, accessed 6 April 2024.

[180] Robert K. Webb, 'Price among the Unitarians', *Enlightenment and Dissent*, 19 (2000), p. 162; G. M. Ditchfield, 'Anti-Trinitarianism and Toleration in Late Eighteenth Century British Politics: The Unitarian Petition of 1792', *Journal of Ecclesiastical History*, 42 (1991), pp. 39–67, at 46–48. JW was 'grieved' to see 'that such a liberal minded society shoud start upon any narrow or party principles, which will exclude nine tenths of the rational Xians in Britain'. Letter 164, JW to SK, 16 June 1791, W-K, III.

[181] G. M. Ditchfield, 'The Subscription Issue in British Parliamentary Politics, 1772–79', *Parliamentary History*, 7 (1988), pp. 35–80.

leading Rational Dissenters had become dissatisfied with toleration and were demanding religious liberty. They began a campaign for repeal of the Test and Corporation Acts that was successively moved and defeated in Parliament between 1787 and 1790, during which Kenrick became the secretary of the Worcester Protestant Dissenters.[182] No equivalent petitioning campaign against subscription arose in north Britain, though Wodrow had helped a young friend, John Mackenzie, to publish a Scottish equivalent of Blackburne's *Confessional* in 1771.[183] Only after the failure of repeal in 1790 did the Scottish clergy ask Parliament to exempt members of their church from the *English* Test Act when being appointed to *British* public offices. The application failed, and Wodrow was particularly disappointed that a number of his overly cautious Moderate colleagues had opposed the application.[184]

Wodrow and Kenrick espoused a 'rational piety' and scorned 'Bigots & Methodists or mere enthusiasts'.[185] Unhappy with the growing popularity of Evangelicalism, Wodrow and Kenrick nevertheless maintained good relations with some orthodox and Evangelical neighbours, and admired their charitable efforts. The Anglican preacher, John Wesley, passed through Bewdley each year as he promoted his Arminian version of Methodism throughout England. While Kenrick regarded him as a 'canting Methodist', he was impressed with how much the eighty-four-year-old did in the space of a four-hour visit: 'he gives them 2 prayers & a sermon— then takes a friendly repast w$^{th}$. them: & settles accounts towards supporting their stated teachers'; and noted that his followers 'consist of serious well disposed people of all denominations, who go under the name of Methodists'.[186] In turn, Wodrow provided Kenrick with a curious account of 'a new Sect of Enthusiasts', the Buchanites, that had started in Irvine. Their leader, Elspath Buchan, claimed to commune with the Holy Spirit. Accused of witchcraft and driven out of Irvine, she and around sixty followers lived communally and found shelter on an estate in Dumfries. Wodrow saw a letter by one of the leaders, which displayed 'an acquaintance with the Scriptures which almost astonished me'. He thought their ideas 'not so wild', as the letter contained 'the

---

[182] See Section IV.
[183] [John Mackenzie], *The Religious Establishment in Scotland Examined Upon Protestant Principles: A Tract, Occasioned by the Late Prosecution Against the Late Reverend Mr. Alexander Fergusson, Minister in Kilwinning* (1771). This publication has often been incorrectly attributed to John Graham. See the notes to Letter 84, SK to JW, 22 Oct. 1784.
[184] Letters 154 and 157. See also Section IV; and Sher, *Church and University*, pp. 189, 301–03.
[185] Letter 125, JW to SK, 23 Nov. 1786.
[186] W-K, I, p. 387; Letter 113, SK to JW, 20 March 1786.

strongest appeals to Scripture Authority & the boldest attacks imaginable on the high popular doctrines of all sects'.[187]

Despite having 'diametrically opposite sentiments', Kenrick developed a friendship with the 'agreeable lively good natured' Rev. William Jesse, rector of Dowles near Bewdley, who was a Methodist and 'orthodox to the highest pitch'.[188] Wodrow enjoyed hearing about Jesse, and noted that his 'methodistical enthusiasm & his narrow principles do not seem to sour his temper as is the case with many of his brethren' in Scotland.[189] But he wondered why this good nature had not prevented Jesse from displaying a 'vile spirit of bigotry & bitterness' in his publications. Wodrow contrasted this behaviour with that of his own friend, Rev. Robert Dow, who, though a Calvinist who preached in a 'high orthodox strain', had a good heart that 'corected & sweetened all the barbarism of his System' in both his sermons and behaviour.[190]

Kenrick found himself in the midst of a pamphlet battle between Jesse and one of his closest friends, Rev. Thomas Wigan, an Anglican Latitudinarian rector of Oldswinford. This provides a good example of how energetic religious debate could be at the local level in England.[191] Jesse preached a sermon at the opening of a charity school in Bewdley in which he complained that there were 'multitudes who shew no serious regard for God' because their 'education has been neglected by the parochial clergy', whose 'sermons are dwindled away into moral essays'.[192] When this was criticized by Wigan under the name 'Clericus', Jesse responded with a collection of letters that criticized '*Rational* Christianity' as 'nothing else than a proud affectation of philosophic wisdom', and he declared that the 'doctrine of THE ATONEMENT is the object of my zeal...for it is the foundation of all my hopes toward God'.[193] Kenrick considered Wigan superior

---

[187] Letter 88, JW to SK, 7 January 1785. See also Letter 84.
[188] Letter 100, SK to JW, 19 Sept. 1785; Letter 118, SK to JW, 3 July 1786.
[189] Letter 121, JW to SK, 28 Aug. 1786.
[190] Letter 125, JW to SK, 23 Nov. 1786.
[191] Nineteenth-century critics, both Evangelicals like Jesse and Radical Reformers, depicted the eighteenth-century Church of England and its widespread Latitudinarianism as complacent and corrupt. This has been challenged by revisionist scholarship, starting with Norman Sykes, *Church and State in England in the XVIIIth Century* (Cambridge, 1934); more recently, see Jeremy Gregory, ed., *The Oxford History of Anglicanism: Volume II, Establishment and Empire, 1662–1829* (Oxford, 2017).
[192] William Jesse, *The Importance of Education: A Discourse, Preached in Bewdley Chapel, on Sunday the 27th day of March, 1785. By William Jesse, Rector of Dowles, and Chaplain to the Right Honourable the Earl of Glasgow* (Kidderminster, 1785), pp. 15, 18.
[193] William Jesse, *Parochialia; Or Observations on the Discharge of Parochial Duties, in which Defects and Errors are Pointed out and Improvements Suggested and Recommended to The Parochial Clergy: in*

to his opponent in 'acuteness & abilities' but noted that this did not 'terrify M<sup>r</sup>. Jesse', who confessed that one of his letters, 'on moral preaching', was based on John Witherspoon's withering attack on the Moderate Scottish clergy.[194] Jesse was delighted to receive a 'congratulatory' letter from his bishop, Richard Hurd, who also advised him to adopt a 'philosophic calmness & silence' in the face of any further provocation by 'Clericus'.[195] Wigan visited Jesse to tell him that a reply was in the press and that his 'ideas and considerations were crude', and, 'pointing to his head', he accused Jesse of being mentally deficient.[196] Kenrick saw this 'petite guerre theologique' as 'hooked into' the broader issue of 'Who are Christians? or rather who are the Church? Whether those who litterally stick to her articles & rubricks, or those who w<sup>d</sup>. accommodate these to common sense & reason'.[197] Rather than skirmish further with his neighbour, however, Jesse proceeded to publish imaginary lectures dedicated to Edward Gibbon, in which he ridiculed 'philosophers, sceptics, Deists, and speculative professors of religion'; and then attacked England's most high-profile nonconformist Unitarian, Joseph Priestley, whom he 'should as soon expect to meet…in heaven as the devil'.[198]

In 1780 Joseph Priestley became minister of the New Meeting in Birmingham, and as an avowed Unitarian Kenrick was eager to meet the prolific polymath. This did not happen, however, until Wednesday 11 August 1784, around 9am, as Kenrick noted precisely in a short letter he dashed off to Wodrow. He had posted Priestley a 'curious little tract' on the body and blood of Jesus by a ninth-century monk, and in return received a friendly reply and invitation to visit. Kenrick

*Seventeen Letters to Clericus with Remarks on a Letter Containing Strictures on a Discourse Lately Preached in Bewdley Chapel* (Kidderminster, 1785), pp. 121, v.

[194] John Witherspoon's pamphlet, *Ecclesiastical Characteristics; Or, The Arcana of Church Policy: Being an Humble Attempt to Open Up the Mystery of Moderation; Wherein is Shewn a Plain and Easy Way of Attaining to the Character of a Moderate Man, as at Present in Repute in the Church of Scotland* (Glasgow, 1753).

[195] Letter 115, SK to JW, 15 April 1784.

[196] Clericus [Thomas Wigan], *A Defence of the Clergy of the Church of England; in a Letter to the Rev. William Jesse, Rector of Dowles, Occasioned by his Parochialia* (Gloucester, 1786); Letter 117, SK shorthand note.

[197] Letter 123, SK to JW, 7 Oct. 1786.

[198] The quotation is related by SK in Letter 118, SK to JW, 3 July 1786. The publications were William Jesse, *Lectures, Supposed to have been delivered, by the author of A View of the Internal Evidence of the Christian Religion to a Select Company of Friends: Dedicated to Edward Gibbon Esq* (1787); and *A Defence of the Established Church or, Letters to the Gentlemen of Oxford and Cambridge who are in the Course of Education for the Christian Ministry in which Dr Priestley's Arguments against Subscription, and the Peculiar Doctrines of Christianity, are Examined and their Futility are Exposed. By William Jesse, Rector of Dowles, and Chaplain to the Right Honourable the Earl of Glasgow* (1788).

wrote a short letter two days after the visit, describing his 'lively & cheerful' hero, who is also referred to as 'friend' from that point in the correspondence.[199] Kenrick was not an uncritical follower of Priestley, noting that 'sadly' he wanted to 'get rid of' the miraculous conception.[200] And he agreed with Wodrow and Wigan that Priestley's fiery *A Letter to the Right Honourable William Pitt... on the Subject of Toleration and Church Establishments; Occasioned by his Speech against Repeal of the Test and Corporation Acts* (1787) was probably 'too violent to do any good to the cause'.[201] But overwhelmingly, Kenrick regarded Priestley as an intellectual powerhouse who published fearlessly and was an instrument of providence in advancing the world towards religious and political liberty. Kenrick urged Wodrow to send him a miniature portrait of himself so that it could be placed next to 'a cast I have of D[r]. Priestley in my museum'.[202]

Wodrow was keen to hear about Priestley, and admired his 'amazing' knowledge and abilities, but had already labelled him as having a 'Bee in his Bonnet', with the influence of his writings being undermined by a lack of 'judgement or prudence'. He was too combative in pushing his version of Unitarianism, and he 'writes too much and consequently too carelessly'.[203] Priestley had provoked a storm of controversy with his 1782 *History of the Corruptions of Christianity*, and discussion of various theological points in relation to this and subsequent publications is a key feature of this volume of the correspondence. Despite his reservations, Wodrow reported reading a number of Priestley's works on religion and philosophy.[204]

Priestley's Unitarianism was linked to his 'necessarian' materialist philosophy.[205] He rejected the dualist philosophy of matter and spirit, which he saw as rooted in Greek philosophy, and which he viewed as responsible for many of the 'corruptions' of orthodox Christian doctrine. Priestley was heavily influenced by

---

[199] Kenrick describes Priestley in Letters 81 and 83 and provides anecdotes in Letter 123.
[200] Letter 122, SK to JW, 28 Sept. 1786.
[201] See Letters 129, 134, and 135.
[202] Letter 133, SK to JW, 28 Sept. 1787.
[203] Letter 79, JW to SK, 15 April 1784.
[204] In Oct. 1784 he was reading Priestley's *Doctrine of Philosophical Necessity Illustrated* (Letter 84); on a visit to Edinburgh in June 1785 he was reading Priestley's *History of the Corruptions of Christianity* (Letter 96); in Aug. 1786, as it would be a long time before he could see Priestley's *An History of Early Opinions Concerning Jesus Christ* (Birmingham, 1786), he asked Kenrick to summarize it for him (Letter 121); in June 1787 at Edinburgh he read a volume of Priestley's *Letters to a Philosophical Unbeliever* '& liked it much. Yet it is too Metaphysical for me, neither am I perfectly satisfyed of the soundness of his & Hartley's Philosophy' (Letter 130).
[205] On Priestley's monistic materialism, which initially 'shocked large numbers of readers', see Schofield, *The Enlightened Joseph Priestley*, pp. 59–76, quoted at 59.

David Hartley's *Observations on Man* (1749) and, after reading his 'Edition & abridgement' of this work, Kenrick observed that he was confident 'that mankind are daily' and determinedly 'improving in wisdom and virtue', and was 'still more confirmed in it from the writings of Hartley and Priestley'.[206] Wodrow was not convinced. He considered Priestley's *Doctrine of Philosophical Necessity* a 'very clear & strong book on that side of the Question', but could not see how his God differed in any way from the materialist Nature espoused by atheists: 'If there realy be an absolute invariable irresistible fatality what sort of Providence care or agency continues to be exercised about the universe by its maker?' Having created the universe and its laws, Priestley's God could be nothing more than an 'inactive spectator'.[207] Priestley had, in Kenrick's words, 'brandished his tawmahawk' in an attack on the Scottish 'common sense' philosophers in the 1770s.[208] Wodrow, however, was more persuaded by their approach, which allowed for a concept of free will. He praised Thomas Reid's philosophy as 'more intelligible more founded in fact & feeling & more likely to prevail even in this Sceptical age'.[209] Reid was 'a most Acute Metaphysician & sound Moralist', and in opposing Priestley on 'the subject of Liberty & Necessity', he 'states with great modesty & precision the bounds of human knowledge on these deep subjects'.[210]

When Kenrick asked for his thoughts on the question of Christ's pre-existence, Wodrow replied that it was 'one of the few theological points' on which he had 'formed no decided opinion'. While this was a key point that divided Socinians from Arians, for Wodrow it was 'like many other disputed points … of little consequence to $X^{ty}$'. He focussed on the fact that Jesus always 'spoke & acted' in the name of God the Father and 'never in his own'. He thought the 'general strain' of the New Testament was 'undoubtedly' in favour of the Socinians, though there are 'a few Passages in the Gospel of John' that would 'naturaly lead a Bible Xian' to believe that Christ had 'been with God before he appeared in this world'. Aside from that, the 'Arian scheme' was stronger 'in point of reason & Philosophy viz

---

[206] Letter 112, SK to JW, 11 Feb. 1786; Joseph Priestley, *Hartley's Theory of the Human Mind, on the Principle of the Association of Ideas; With Essays Relating to the Subject of It* (1775); for Hartley's philosophy and influence, see Richard C. Allen, *David Hartley on Human Nature* (New York, 1999).

[207] Letter 84, JW to SK, 22 Oct. 1784.

[208] Letter 72, W-K, I, p. 457; Joseph Priestley, *An Examination of Dr. Reid's Inquiry into the Human Mind, Dr. Beattie's Essay on the Nature and Immutability of Truth, and Dr. Oswald's Appeal to Common Sense in Behalf of Religion* (1775); Allan P. F. Sell, 'Priestley's Polemic against Reid', *The Price-Priestley Newsletter*, 3 (1979), pp. 41–52.

[209] Letter 130, JW to SK, 15 June 1787.

[210] Letter 137, JW to SK, 3 July 1788.

that it is much more congruous to our conceptions of our Lords Exaltation to the Supremacy of the Universe or of the Church of God in heaven & earth'.[211] The issue was debatable, and Priestley should show less attachment to his own 'nostrums or prejudices & more gentleness to those of others'; he did not show 'sufficient candour to see or feel the weight of what is advanced by his antagonists'.[212] Rational Christians should accept that the truth about Christ's pre-existence was not clear, and it did not affect Christ's essential status as the messiah who had been resurrected and exalted.

Wodrow was therefore an anti-trinitarian who saw Christ as subordinate to God, but he thought the messiah's exact nature remained debatable. When he visited Theophilus Lindsey's Essex street Unitarian chapel in 1788, Wodrow noted the pleasure he had of 'joining in the reformed English Service'.[213] Having started reading the early Socinians in the late 1760s, Wodrow thought they understood the New Testament better than any other commentators he had read, and declared that most of the learned and freethinking clergy in Protestant nations would 'soon become Socinians'.[214] He was keen to get a copy of Joshua Toulmin's *Memoirs of the Life, Character, Sentiments and Writings of Faustus Socinus* (1777).[215] However, he disliked the doctrinaire stance of the modern Unitarianism that developed in the last quarter of the eighteenth century. Wodrow observed that the 'old Socinians would have almost excommunicated' Priestley for his determinist philosophy and not allowing worship of Christ. If Priestley had read more deeply in the first Socinians, Wodrow declared, he would have seen that they worshipped Christ as a 'subordinate' being who was 'the immediate head of the Church of God'.[216] Combatively insisting upon his particular version of the Socinian 'hypothesis' was unjustified and divisive, causing conflict with the orthodox and alienating moderate and open-minded rational Christians.

Wodrow liked the term 'Bible Christian' and preferred scholarship that aimed to clarify and explain scripture.[217] He was fortunate that the 1780s saw a burst of philological publications as the British sought to catch up to Dutch and German

---

[211] Letter 79, JW to SK, 15 April 1784.
[212] Letter 79; and Letter 125, JW to SK, 23 November 1786.
[213] Letter 140, JW to SK, 15 October 1788.
[214] W-K, I, pp. 163, 293; see also Letter 87, JW to SK, 3 January 1785.
[215] Letter 79, JW to SK, 15 April 1784.
[216] Letter 96, JW to SK, 16 June 1785. Priestley was aware of this difference of opinion and thought the early Socinian practice of praying to Christ unjustified. Priestley, *History of the Corruptions of Christianity*, I, p. 134.
[217] Letter 79, JW to SK, 15 April 1784.

advances in biblical scholarship.[218] In the mid-eighteenth century some Anglicans associated with Archbishop Secker had urged the need to revise and update the language of the King James authorized version of the Bible. This scheme was dropped, however, in the context of the revolutionary era and the increasing association of critical scholarship with dissent and heterodoxy.[219] Along with Dissenters in England, Scots contributed to the individual late eighteenth-century efforts to revise translations of the scriptures. When visiting London, Wodrow dined with the radical Scottish Catholic priest Alexander Geddes, who was working on a new translation of the Bible.[220] Kenrick was impressed with James Macknight's *Translation of the Epistles to the Thessalonians* (1787).[221] Wodrow had read some of the translation in manuscript, and had several discussions about it with Macknight, a Moderate Edinburgh minister and an old friend—including during a long walk after 'Dinner & enough of Drink'. Wodrow had a high opinion of Macknight's originality and 'abilities as a Critick on the Scriptures' but thought he was 'too fanciful in some of his notions', which were 'not sufficiently founded in Scripture or fact'. 'I cannot help thinking', Wodrow wrote, 'that he loses in many places the real simple plain sense of the sacred writers by his over ingenuity & refinement in searching after it.' Their theological 'sentiments' differed, which Wodrow could judge by 'several specimens he has read to me', and he was surprised that Macknight had not read the sixteenth-century Socinians, who 'seem to understand the N.T. better than any who have attempted it'.[222] Macknight wanted to publish a full translation with commentaries of all of the epistles, but owing to the cost being more than £3 he had trouble obtaining subscriptions from the Scottish clergy. Commercial publication was not an option as, during his visit to London, Andrew Kippis told Wodrow that the major booksellers would 'not bite at the hook' for such a book; so he enlisted Kenrick's help in spreading the subscription request among both Anglican and Dissenting clergy in the west of England. Macknight had taken

---

[218] Jonathan Sheehan, *The Enlightenment Bible: Translation, Scholarship, Culture* (Princeton, NJ, 2005), p. 241.

[219] Scott Mandelbrote, 'The English Bible and Its Readers in the Eighteenth Century', in Isabel Rivers, ed., *Books and Their Readers in 18th Century England, Volume 2: New Essays* (2003), pp. 35–78, at 55–63; see also Neil W. Hitchin, 'The Politics of English Bible Translation in Georgian Britain: The Alexander Prize', *Transactions of the Royal Historical Society*, 9 (1999), pp. 67–92.

[220] Letter 139, JW to SK, 27 Sept. 1788.

[221] Letters 131 and 133.

[222] For these quotations see JW's Letters 87, 99, and 132.

'infinite pains' with this work, drafting the full four-volume manuscript in his own hand five times.[223]

Also putting his shoulder to the wheel of biblical philology was the respected George Campbell, principal and professor of divinity at Aberdeen's Marischal College, who published *The Four Gospels, Translated from the Greek, with Preliminary Dissertations, and Notes Critical and Explanatory* (1789). Campbell aimed to provide a translation that was more accurate and intelligible for his eighteenth-century readers than the dated and flawed King James Bible.[224] When Wodrow got hold of this more than 1,500-page book by a 'great & Masterly Genius', he read it eagerly but was disappointed. The translation was excellent, but there was too much textual criticism and not enough 'on the Spirit & sentiments of the Sacred Writers'.[225]

Wodrow and Kenrick were also interested in scholarship on the history and nature of the Jewish religion. Wodrow found two interesting discourses on the character and 'Grandeur of the Hebrew Nation' among the late William Leechman's papers,[226] and he also noted the publication *The History and Philosophy of Judaism* (1787), by Duncan Shaw of Aberdeen.[227] When in London, Wodrow twice visited the Portuguese Jewish synagogue to witness their prayers and 'chanting during their great fast of the Annual Attonement', and also visited a house where he was allowed to observe 'the circumcision of an Infant'.[228] In 1784 Wodrow said he would like to see 'the Jew's book' that Kenrick had mentioned in a missing letter, which was possibly David Levi's influential *Succinct Account of the Rites and Ceremonies of the Jews* (1782).[229] A few years later, Kenrick noted that he had seen the exchange of pamphlets between Joseph Priestley and David Levi, which 'promise in my opinion a great revolution'.[230] Priestley sought to convince the Jews to convert to Christianity and return to the Holy Land, as this would hasten

---

[223] See Letters 151, 152, and 153 in 1789. Macknight's *New Literal Translation from the Original Greek of All the Apostolic Epistles* was eventually published in 1795. Lionel Alexander Ritchie, 'Macknight, James (1721–1800)', *ODNB*.

[224] Jeffrey M. Suderman, *Orthodoxy and Enlightenment: George Campbell in the Eighteenth Century* (Montréal, 2001), p. 148.

[225] Letter 148, JW to SK, 23 May 1789.

[226] Letter 109, JW to SK, 9 January 1786.

[227] Letter 130, JW to SK, 15 June 1787.

[228] Letter 140, JW to SK, 15 Oct. 1788.

[229] Letter 79, JW to SK, 15 April 1784.

[230] Letter 131, SK to JW, 23 Aug. 1787; Joseph Priestley, *Letters to the Jews* (Birmingham, 1786); David Levi, *Letters to Dr Priestley, in Answer to those he Addressed to the Jews; Inviting them to an Amicable Discussion of the Evidences of Christianity* (Birmingham, 1787); Joseph Priestley, *Letters to the Jews, Part II. Occasioned by Mr David Levi's Reply to the Former Letters* (Birmingham, 1787).

the return of Christ and the start of the Millennium. He argued that they should have few objections to Unitarian Christianity, and could even retain many of their rituals and customs. This approach was rejected by Levi, however, who, as a Jewish traditionalist, was loyal to the established constitution in church and state, and did not accept Unitarianism as Christian.[231] The Wodrow–Kenrick letters testify to the philo-semitism that was a feature of British Protestantism since the seventeenth century.[232]

The prosecution of Wodrow's friend, William M'Gill, for heresy is a major theme in this volume of the correspondence.[233] M'Gill was minister of the second charge in Ayr and, as noted above, Wodrow helped him to publish *A Practical Essay on the Death of Jesus Christ* (Edinburgh, 1786). Focussed on explaining the nature and significance of the crucifixion by a careful reading of the New Testament texts, it was the type of 'Bible Christian' book that appealed to Wodrow. M'Gill disliked Priestley's militant approach and narrow definition of Unitarianism, but was influenced by his writings.[234] The book was implicitly Socinian and rejected the orthodox doctrine of Christ's atonement—it depicted the crucifixion as primarily evidence of resurrection to an afterlife and an inspiration to follow the teachings of Jesus, without which 'we can neither be reconciled to GOD by his death, nor saved by his life'.[235] 'The climate of Scotland', Wodrow feared, 'was too hot to bear such an open publication', but he thought the manuscript 'excellent & much superior to any thing I have ever seen on the subject'. It could only be accused of the 'Heresy of Ommission', as he had advised M'Gill to remove or soften some footnotes on atonement that would 'certainly irritate' the orthodox.[236] With the support of several hundred subscribers, Wodrow reported the book was in press in 1786 and 'the Orthodox at Edinburgh

---

[231] Jack Fruchtman, 'Joseph Priestley and Early English Zionism', *Enlightenment and Dissent*, 2 (1983), pp. 39–46; on David Levi's response to Priestley, see David B. Ruderman, *Jewish Enlightenment in an English Key: Anglo-Jewry's Construction of Modern Jewish Thought* (Princeton, NJ, 2018), pp. 170–79.

[232] Todd M. Endelman, *The Jews of Georgian England, 1714–1830: Tradition and Change in a Liberal Society* (Ann Arbor, MI, 1999), pp. 50–85.

[233] The following paragraphs draw from Martin Fitzpatrick, 'Varieties of Candour: English and Scottish Style', *Enlightenment and Dissent*, 7 (1988), pp. 35–56. See also Robert Richard, 'An Examination of the Life and Career of Rev William McGill (1732–1807): Controversial Ayr Theologian' (PhD thesis, University of Glasgow, 2010).

[234] Letter 87, JW to SK, 3 Jan. 1785; M'Gill approvingly cited Priestley's *Theological Repository* in *A Practical Essay on the Death of Christ* (Edinburgh, 1786), pp. 336, 542–43.

[235] M'Gill, *Death of Christ*, pp. 548–49.

[236] Letter 84, SK to JW, 22 Oct. 1784.

and Glasgow have taken the alarm already and are impatient to see it'.[237] Yet he was happy with the initial response. The book was well received among the Moderates, and he hoped there would be a second edition. It had been carefully crafted so as not to give grounds for a prosecution in the church courts. The 'zeal of young Bigots', Wodrow thought, would be restrained by wiser old heads among the orthodox, who would not risk failure and subsequent censure for being slanderous.[238]

M'Gill had received support from his Moderate friends on the understanding that he would prudently not respond to attacks. 'That he failed to do so', Martin Fitzpatrick has observed, 'is perhaps indicative of the breakdown of the Moderate consensus' in the revolutionary era.[239] 'A man of erect and commanding stature', in John R. McIntosh's words, 'M'Gill was highly and warmly regarded by his congregation', and a close friend of the young poet, Robert Burns.[240] Controversy flared, however, when sermons were delivered marking the centenary of the Revolution of 1688. William Peebles, the minister at neighbouring Newton-upon-Ayr, published a sermon in which, according to Wodrow, he 'bloodily' attacked M'Gill's book as anti-Christian and characterized 'the Moderate Clergy of Scotland as a set of base Parricides & perjured Traitors for supporting Patronage & preaching & writing directly contrary to their Subscription'.[241] M'Gill had ignored earlier attacks by those who had seceded from the church, but this provoked him to publish his own centenary sermon, with a lengthy appendix criticizing Peebles.[242] Wodrow had not been consulted about this publication and feared that it would prompt a prosecution of M'Gill's book.[243] He was right. In April 1789, Peebles and thirty 'Country Elders' who left their 'ploughing & harrowing'

---

[237] Letter 120, JW to SK, 15 Aug. 1786.
[238] Letter 126, JW to SK, 9 Jan. 1787.
[239] Fitzpatrick, 'Varieties of Candour', p. 42.
[240] John R. Mackintosh, 'M'Gill, William (1732–1807)', *ODNB*.
[241] Letter 146, JW to SK, 8 March 1789; for the passage to which JW refers, see William Peebles, *The Great Things Which the Lord Hath Done for This Nation, Illustrated and Improved; in Two Sermons Preached on the 5th of November, 1788* (Kilmarnock, 1788), pp. 34–36.
[242] William M'Gill, *The Benefits of the Revolution: A Sermon, Preached at Ayr, on the 5th of November, 1788, by William M'Gill, D. D. To which are Added, Remarks on a Sermon, Preached on the Same Day, at Newton upon Ayr; Very necessary for all the Readers of said Sermon* (Kilmarnock, 1789). For earlier attacks by dissenters from the Church of Scotland, see the evangelical Anti-Burgher, John Jamieson, *Socinianism Unmasked* (1787); and [Associate Synod of the Secession Church], *A Warning Against Socinianism: Drawn up and Published by a Committee of the Associate Synod. In which, Particular Notice is Taken of a Late Publication, Intituled, a Practical Essay upon the Death of Jesus Christ, by Dr. M'Gill* (Falkirk, 1788).
[243] Letter 146, JW to SK, 8 March 1789.

instigated a prosecution for heresy in the Synod of Glasgow and Ayr. With Peebles the only minister from Ayrshire in attendance, some Moderate Glasgow ministers protested, and the case was referred to the General Assembly. M'Gill's parish in Ayr published a declaration of support for their minister in opposition to the 'malignant' attack by the Synod.[244] Wodrow was confident the Synod's 'nonsensical fooling' would be overruled 'without entering upon the points of Heresy Subscription &c, which our political Leaders at Ed$^r$. never chuse to bring above board'.[245]

Wodrow's confidence was misplaced. At its June 1789 meeting the General Assembly's time was consumed by a heated contest over the election of a new Clerk.[246] When they reached M'Gill's case, a 'long & voilent Debate which lasted two days' resulted in the Synod's sentence being overruled, but it was also referred to the Presbytery of Ayr for resolution. Unfortunately, Wodrow noted, that presbytery was not as friendly to Moderates as Irvine had been in the 1760s at the time of the Fergusson prosecution—up to a third of the ministers opposed M'Gill and, along with the elders, 'the rotten part of our constitution', they had a majority. M'Gill spoke affectingly for two hours, but could not win over his opponents. A majority voted to prosecute, M'Gill's allies protested, and the case was referred to the Synod. Wodrow's thoughts on how to proceed illustrate his long experience and skill in using institutional church politics to protect Moderatism: to 'protract the matter somehow' until after the Synod met in Glasgow, then try to elect friendly elders in Ayr so as 'to terminate the matter' there. If that failed, the case could go to the subsequent meeting of the Synod, which was scheduled to gather in Ayr, where M'Gill's friends could 'by a proper Effort…carry a sentence in his favour'.[247] When a committee of the Ayr presbytery read out a fifty-page list of passages in M'Gill's publications that were alleged to be 'contrary to the word of God & Confession of Faith', M'Gill's allies argued that the document should lie on their table 'to be seen & answered' by him in due course. This was refused, however, and the list was submitted to the Synod, which met at Glasgow in October.

While the majority of the ministers at the Synod were Moderate, nearly all the elders were of the Evangelical Popular Party, along with 'the Mob of Glasgow

---

[244] *Caledonian Mercury*, 7 May 1789.
[245] Letter 148, JW to SK, 23 May 1789.
[246] See Letter 149, JW to SK, 5 Aug. 1789 for JW's detailed account of the competition between Alexander Carlyle and Andrew Dalzel for the post of principal clerk to the General Assembly of the Church of Scotland in May.
[247] Letter 149, JW to SK, 5 Aug. 1789.

raised to a pitch of Enthusiam by some of their speeches & a Sermon at the opening of the synod'. No business could be conducted in the courthouse on the first evening owing to 'the mob filling the house to the Exclusion of a part of the Synod'. The following day, soldiers stood guard and only allowed members of the Synod to enter. After a long and heated meeting, the Synod agreed 'for the sake of decency' to send the list back to lie on the presbytery's table for a few months so that M'Gill could study it. M'Gill had remained in Ayrshire, and Wodrow wrote letters stressing that much depended on his displaying the 'meekness & Gentleness of Christ' in his answers. Meanwhile, ahead of the next meeting of the Synod in Ayr, Wodrow encouraged the appointment of 'proper Elders' to outnumber the 'fools & bigots', but was frustrated by a 'lukewarmness & even a timidity' on the part of his fellow Moderates. As a consolation, however, he sent Kenrick a copy of Robert Burns's poem, 'The Tattered Garland', which satirized the prosecution of his friend.[248]

The prosecution was eventually stopped by a compromise. After M'Gill submitted his answers to the Presbytery in January 1790, they again referred him to the Synod, which met at Ayr in April. Wodrow was included on a committee appointed by Synod to help M'Gill draft an apology, which stated that he was 'extremely sorry' that his attempt at a 'wholly practical' study of Christ's death had caused offence. He noted that any large publication would contain some 'failures and blemishes', and that 'I may in some instances have omitted things which I hold to be true, when the practical use of them did not immediately occur to me'. What followed was a carefully worded response in which he affirmed the central role of Jesus as the 'Saviour of the World', and noted that the Westminster Confession states that 'repentance is of such necessity to sinners, that none may expect pardon without it'. M'Gill admitted that some ideas in his *Death of Christ* may 'appear improper' and certain expressions 'ambiguous and unguarded' on doctrinal points. For that he was 'heartily sorry', and declared his belief in the 'great articles, as they are laid down in the standards of this church'.[249] While Wodrow had preferred a clear ruling against the charge of heresy, politics was the art of the possible, and he clearly played an important role in crafting this act of damage control. He and other 'sensible men in both parties' were satisfied with the compromise, while 'the bigots and zealots' were outraged. The latter accused

---

[248] Letter 151, JW to SK, 9 Nov. 1789. The poem was also known as 'The Kirk's Alarm'.
[249] For William M'Gill's 'declaration and apology', see *Proceedings of the Very Reverend the Synod of Glasgow and Ayr, held at Ayr on the 13th & 14th April 1790, Relating to some Late Publications of the Rev. Dr. William M'Gill, with the Final Decisions in that Cause* ([Glasgow], 1790), cited at pp. 6–7, 10, 12.

the Synod of being 'Traitors' and 'basely betraying the cause of truth & orthodoxy by accepting an ambiguous Declaration'. While several 'Virulent' pamphlets were published in response, attempts to renew the prosecution were blocked.[250]

Having keenly followed the case, Kenrick's optimistic Rational Dissenting commitment to candour, liberty, and progress was offended by the outcome. He had cast M'Gill in the role of David standing up to the Philistines, and had seen the case as part of the broader movement whereby 'liberty and free enquiry' were inexorably overcoming error and superstition. He had confidently declared that

This contest will I foresee soon bring down your ragged remnant of the old harlot's petticoat, of creeds & subscriptions, & establish Christianity upon its only true solid basis– *the Bible*.[251]

Instead, Wodrow had helped engineer a backsliding compromise that disappointed Rational Dissenters. Kenrick drew his attention to a recent sermon by the young Unitarian Thomas Belsham, on *The Importance of Truth and the Duty of Making an Open Profession of It*, which included a note on M'Gill's apology: 'The Synod of Ayr have given recent proof that the worst part of the spirit of popery, *persecution*, is not limited to the members of the Romish communion.'[252] Wodrow replied that, while he was 'realy ashamed of my Country', M'Gill had not been forced to retract any 'single sentiment sentence or iota of his publication'. And he stressed that, without the apology, the case could have ended in M'Gill being convicted of heresy, given the 'fanaticism & madness' of the Popular Party and the 'political timidity & worldly spirit' of the Moderates.[253] Wodrow was still working to prevent a renewed prosecution in early 1791, and he noted the 'incredible load of scurrility & abuse poured upon' M'Gill and his allies by 'the bigotry & fanaticism of Glasgow & Paisley &c'. He also pointedly noted that, while in Scotland the Synod's decision was attacked as a providing 'an open Indemnity to Socinianism', Rational Dissenters in England thought it was 'an open and severe persecution of it'.[254]

[250] Letter 154, JW to SK, 2 June 1790. See, for example, James Moir, *A Distinct and Impartial Account of the Process for Socinian Heresy against William M'Gill, D.D., One of the Ministers of Ayr: With Observations on his Explanations and Apology; And on the Proceedings and Final Decision of the Reverend Synod of Glasgow and Ayr, in that Cause. Dedicated to the Members, Commonly called the Orthodox Party without their Permission* (Edinburgh, 1790).
[251] Letter 152, SK to JW, 16 Dec. 1789.
[252] Letter 155, SK to JW, 25 Sept. 1790.
[253] Letter 156, JW to SK, 10 Jan. 1791. See Volume 3.
[254] Letter 159, JW to SK, 28 March 1791. See Volume 3.

The M'Gill affair reveals the different contexts Wodrow and Kenrick inhabited near the end of the Enlightenment, as well as the strength of a friendship that persisted through serious disagreements. Kenrick was arguably in line with their revered mentor, William Leechman, who had taught that 'the spirit of Christianity' was one of 'courage and boldness, and not of fearfulness and timidity'.[255] But Leechman had written that back in the 1760s, and in his final years, he had said that the days of 'Heresy processes in Scotland was now over'.[256] As Leechman passed away, and M'Gill was prosecuted, Wodrow could see that the mid-century confidence in a Moderate future was failing to materialize. Evangelicalism was on the march, his colleagues' grip on power was slipping, and they were in a revolutionary era in which polarization and conflict were about to escalate dramatically.

## IV. Politics, 1784–90

Of the four volumes of *The Wodrow–Kenrick Correspondence*, this second volume contains the least discussion of politics. Our first volume ended with the American War of Independence, and they did not start to discuss the French Revolution in detail until after the publication of Edmund Burke's *Reflections on the Revolution in France* in November 1790. This second volume begins with the young William Pitt coming to power as prime minister. The mid-1780s was a period of relative political calm as economic ties were re-established with the former colonies that had become the United States of America, before George III descended into a period of 'madness' that threatened to cause a constitutional crisis. The late 1780s also saw Wodrow and Kenrick discussing some modest attempts at political and religious reform in Scotland, along with two petitioning campaigns. In England, Kenrick joined other Dissenters in petitioning for repeal of the Test and Corporation Acts in 1787 and 1790. At the same time, an innovative British campaign arose, petitioning Parliament to abolish the slave trade.

A constitutional crisis had arisen in 1783, with a coalition formed between former parliamentary foes, the wartime prime minister, Lord North, and the opposition Whigs, now headed by Charles James Fox. George III contemplated abdication rather than appoint a government that included the charismatic Fox,

---

[255] William Leechman, *The Excellency of the Spirit of Christianity: A Sermon, Preached before the Society in Scotland for Propagating Christian Knowledge, at their Anniversary Meeting, in the High Church of Edinburgh, on Friday, June 5. 1767* (Edinburgh, 1768), p. 5.

[256] Letter 120, JW to SK, 15 Aug. 1786.

who had long been an eloquent critic of the crown and its American war. Ultimately appointing the coalition in April, the king engineered its defeat in December when he let it be known that any member of the House of Lords who voted for Fox's East India bill would be considered his enemy. When the bill was defeated in the Lords, George dismissed the government and appointed one led by the twenty-four-year-old William Pitt. Lacking a majority in the House of Commons, the younger Pitt's government suffered multiple parliamentary defeats in the early months of 1784. Meanwhile, addresses of support came in from around the nation, Fox allowed money bills to pass, and the margins of defeat grew smaller as some independent MPs began to side with Pitt. With the year's finances secured, Parliament was dissolved on 24 March and an early general election called.[257]

Unfortunately, this period of political crisis coincided with a gap in the Wodrow–Kenrick correspondence. There are only two surviving letters from 1783, of which the second in October is the last in Volume 1. The first letter in this volume, however, was written by Wodrow in mid-April 1784, with the general election underway. Eighteenth-century elections took weeks to conduct, as constituencies of various shapes, size, and constitution elected their members. Only a small percentage of adult males were qualified to vote, and only some of those lived in a constituency that was contested—where the outcome was not predetermined by leading families. Voting was, however, very public, with the secret ballot not introduced until the late nineteenth century. Many men and women who did not qualify to vote nevertheless took an interest in politics, expressing their views in various ways via print, petitions, associations, and on the hustings.[258] The 1784 election was hotly contested.[259] Pitt showed himself friendly to moderate reforms and appealed to patriotism, while the Foxites lost the support of many Dissenters and others who were disgusted by their coalition with Lord North. While soundly beaten, in an age where faction was a dirty word, the Foxite

---

[257] John Ehrman, *The Younger Pitt*, 3 vols (1969–96), I, pp. 118–53; John Cannon, *The Fox-North Coalition: Crisis of the Constitution, 1782–4* (Cambridge, 1969).

[258] H. T. Dickinson, *The Politics of the People in Eighteenth-Century Britain* (New York, 1994), pp. 31–55; Frank O'Gorman, *Voters, Patrons, and Parties: The Unreformed Electoral System of Hanoverian England 1734–1832* (Oxford, 1989).

[259] Paul Kelly, 'Radicalism and Public Opinion in the General Election of 1784', *Historical Research*, 45 (1972), pp. 73–88; Amelia F. Rauser, 'The Butcher-Kissing Duchess of Devonshire: Between Caricature and Allegory in 1784', *Eighteenth-Century Studies*, 36 (2002), pp. 23–46; Renata Lana, 'Women and the Foxite Strategy in the Westminster Election of 1784', *Eighteenth-Century Life*, 26 (2002), pp. 46–69.

Whigs nevertheless continued to pioneer the concept of a modern, organized opposition party—a loyal opposition that provided an alternative government.[260] Charles James Fox only won in the large electorate of Westminster after a lengthy scrutiny of the votes, and in the interim was elected by three votes to two for the northern Scottish Tain burghs. Over the following two decades the contest between the cool and calculating Prime Minister Pitt and the gregarious and progressive Fox arguably became the high-point in the history of British parliamentary debate.[261]

Wodrow and Kenrick happily found themselves both Pittites in the 1780s. Wodrow observed that in Scotland 'the Elections will go against the Coalition yet not so much as in England', and wondered whether Kenrick might support Fox, like 'all the Republicans' in Scotland.[262] Kenrick replied that, while many of his friends remained Foxites, he could not forgive the coalition with Lord North, an 'old veteran in iniquity' who had lost America. The Foxites had become a 'disappointed desperate party' and were encouraging the debauched prince of Wales to oppose the king. In contrast, the king and queen were models of 'decency' and 'domestic happiness', and the king was 'never so popular'.[263]

Wodrow's and Kenrick's interest in national politics waned in the mid-1780s. While Pitt pursued administrative and economic reform, he was defeated in his attempt at moderate parliamentary reform.[264] They may have discussed more in some of their missing letters, but it is notable that the surviving letters for this period contain no mention of Edmund Burke's prosecution of Warren Hastings for 'high crimes and misdemeanours' and behaving like an 'oriental despot' as governor-general of the British East India Company.[265] When asked

---

[260] While the concept of a loyal opposition was 'slowly developing' during the eighteenth century, it 'did not come to its full realisation until the 1820s'. Frank O'Gorman, 'Ordering the Political World: The Pattern of Politics in Eighteenth-Century Britain (1660–1832)', in Diana Donald and Frank O'Gorman, eds, *Ordering the World in the Eighteenth Century* (Basingstoke, 2006), p. 103; see also Max Skjönsberg, *The Persistence of Party: Ideas of Harmonious Discord in Eighteenth-Century Britain* (Cambridge, 2021).

[261] For a popular account, see Dick Leonard and Mark Garnett, *Titans: Fox vs. Pitt* (2019).

[262] Letter 79, SK to JW, 15 April 1784.

[263] Letter 80, SK to JW, 2 June 1784.

[264] Paul Kelly, 'British Parliamentary Politics, 1784–1786', *Historical Journal*, 17 (1974), pp. 733–53.

[265] Chiara Rolli, *The Trial of Warren Hastings Classical Oratory and Reception in Eighteenth-Century England* (2019), especially ch. 5. For a brief outline, see Anthony Page, *Britain and the Seventy Years War, 1744–1815* (2015), pp. 201–03. In 1795, however, Wodrow noted that 'I did not think it possible to have comprehended the E Indian Transactions in such a clear & orderly Narrative' as provided in William Belsham, *Memoirs of the Reign of George III. To the Session of Parliament Ending A.D. 1793*, 4 vols (1795), pp. 102–47, 188–95, 288–92. See Letter 204, JW to SK, 9 Dec. 1795.

what he thought of Pitt's proposed constitutional and commercial regulations with the Irish Parliament, now legislatively independent, Kenrick's response was revealing:

> As to politics I never trouble my head about them. I was once as strenuous for the liberty and independency of Ireland as of America. But now I think no more about it. I go little out; or if I did, I have nobody to dispute with. I & my friends are all of one mind. I look upon the stocks as the barometer of the state: when they are high, as at present, I flatter myself everything goes on well! Tis true we have many complaints about the weight of taxes &c. but where people are frugal & industrious they live as comfortably as ever they did.[266]

It was in this climate that the London radical, John Jebb, complained of the 'general apathy' of the public with respect to political reform.[267] There are only passing mentions of America in this volume of correspondence, a topic that dominated the second half of Volume 1. Wodrow noted that 'notwithstanding the loss of America', Glasgow and Paisley continued to 'enlarge & thrive'.[268] He was surprised to learn from the Ayrshire MP, Sir Adam Fergusson, that Richard Oswald, who advised government and helped negotiate the peace treaty, had been privately opposed to the war from the start.[269] And at the end of 1784, Wodrow also noted that Dr John Witherspoon, on a return visit to Scotland, told him that 'popular influence' in American politics and culture was being 'carried too high even to an extreme'.[270] Yet while 'Friends of America' like the Rational Dissenting philosopher, Rev. Richard Price, anxiously observed and commented on the development of the federal constitution of the United States in the late 1780s, it is not discussed in this volume of correspondence.[271]

Political crisis flared again in late 1788, when George III became seriously mentally ill—with the Duke of York describing him in November as 'now a compleat

---

And in the context of opposing war with revolutionary France, SK condemned Britain for spreading 'war & famine' and a 'world of wretchedness' in India. Letter 188, SK to JW, 22 March 1794, W–K, III.

[266] Letter 110, SK to JW, 21 Jan. 1786.
[267] Cited in Page, *John Jebb*, p. 262.
[268] Letter 96, JW to SK, 16 June 1785.
[269] See his account of a conversation with the Ayrshire MP, Adam Fergusson, in Letter 86, JW to SK, 7 Dec. 1784.
[270] Letter 86, JW to SK, 7 Dec. 1784.
[271] Emma Macleod, 'A Proper Manner of Carrying on Controversies: Richard Price and the American Revolution', *Huntington Library Quarterly*, 82 (2019), pp. 277–302; D. O. Thomas, *The Honest Mind: The Thought and Work of Richard Price* (Oxford, 1977), pp. 260–83; for the range of British perceptions, see the first three chapters of Emma Macleod, *British Visions of America, 1775–1820: Republican Realities* (2013).

lunatick'.²⁷² The king was moved to Kew Palace where he could be secluded, restrained, and placed under the management of doctors. With the king incapacitated, the Foxites campaigned for their boozy friend and patron, the prince of Wales, to be made regent with full monarchical powers. Pitt stalled and argued that Parliament should place restraints on the regent, and was fortunate that the king recovered in mid-February 1789. George III probably suffered from manic-depressive psychosis, and repeat episodes in the early nineteenth century led to permanent insanity for the final decade of his life.²⁷³ The immediate political effect in 1789, however, was a growth in the popularity of 'Farmer George' as monarch and embodiment of Britishness.²⁷⁴ In light of his skilful and steadfast conduct, Pitt's position as prime minister was strengthened, and the Foxites lost seats at the general election in June 1790. Arguing for the prerogatives of the prince of Wales further damaged Fox's and Burke's reputations among reformers and made them generally appear as unreliable opportunists.²⁷⁵

Our correspondents were again in agreement on the Regency Crisis. Wodrow was 'entirely' supportive of Pitt and thought his position in line with the principles of the revolution of 1688–89.²⁷⁶ While he had been told by a physician friend that the king would probably not recover, Kenrick thought Pitt's Regency Bill had secured 'public liberty' and that 1788 should be commemorated like 1688.²⁷⁷ In early February, Wodrow thought Pitt's prime ministership was at an end but hoped to 'live to see him start anew'.²⁷⁸ Yet the king had recovered by the time Kenrick responded, after fortunately being removed from the care of his physicians and placed under a man 'they called a Quack!' There was 'universal rejoicing', and Pitt was honoured.²⁷⁹

Aside from the parliamentary contest between Pitt and Fox, there were two petitioning campaigns that arose towards the end of the decade that reflected the

---

²⁷² Duke of York to Prince Augustus, 3 Dec. 1788, *The Correspondence of George, Prince of Wales, 1770–1812: Volume I, 1770–1789*, ed. A. Aspinall (1965), p. 339.

²⁷³ See the 'Appendix: The Misdiagnosis of "The King's Malady" as Porphyria', in Andrew Roberts, *George III: The Life and Reign of Britain's Most Misunderstood Monarch* (2021).

²⁷⁴ Linda Colley, 'The Apotheosis of George III: Loyalty, Royalty and the British Nation 1760–1820', *Past and Present*, 102 (1984), pp. 94–129; on the nature of his reign, see G. M. Ditchfield, *George III: An Essay in Monarchy* (Basingstoke, 2002); Jeremy Black, *George III: America's Last King* (New Haven, CT, 2006).

²⁷⁵ John W. Derry, *Politics in the Age of Fox, Pitt, and Liverpool: Continuity and Transformation* (New York, 1990), pp. 66–68.

²⁷⁶ Letter 143, JW to SK, 25 Dec. 1788.

²⁷⁷ Letter 144, SK to JW, 16 and 20 Jan. 1789.

²⁷⁸ Letter 145, JW to SK, 5 Feb. 1789.

²⁷⁹ Letter 147, SK to JW, 20 March 1789.

growth of the public sphere and popular politics. In 1787 the Dissenters petitioned for repeal of the seventeenth-century Test and Corporation Acts, which limited various public offices to those who took communion in the Church of England. In the 1730s they had twice unsuccessfully petitioned for repeal. In the 1770s, despite initial defeats, they successfully petitioned for removal of the requirement that Dissenting ministers and schoolmasters subscribe to the theological doctrines contained in the Anglican Thirty-Nine Articles.[280] These petitioning campaigns were part of, and contributed to, the broader growth of the public sphere and popular political activism in the late eighteenth century.[281] In the late 1780s the Dissenters formed a committee tasked with organizing a renewed campaign for repeal.[282]

In March 1787, a motion to repeal the Test and Corporation Acts was debated in the House of Commons and defeated by 176 votes to 98. Wodrow was 'grieved' at the 'careless & illiberal' way the House of Commons had treated the Dissenting petitions, but agreed with Charles James Fox that they must persevere.[283] While Pitt had politely met with a delegation of Dissenters led by Rev. Andrew Kippis, there was little hope of him supporting a measure to which the monarch and nearly all bishops were hostile. As Grayson Ditchfield has argued, however, defeat was not inevitable—the Archbishop of Canterbury, for one, was very anxious and described the debate as an 'ugly thing' that had him in 'suspense'.[284] The ever-optimistic Kenrick was surprised at the defeat, thinking the bill would pass through the Commons and then face a 'hard struggle' in the Lords; but he was confident they would succeed in future as they had on the subscription issue in the 1770s. He praised a 'most spirited' *Letter to the Right Honourable William Pitt...on the Subjects of Toleration and Church Establishments* by Joseph Priestley, who had observed the debate—though he also noted that his Anglican friends thought it

---

[280] G. M. Ditchfield, 'The Subscription Issue in British Parliamentary Politics, 1772–79', *Parliamentary History*, 7 (2008), pp. 45–80.

[281] James E. Bradley, *Popular Politics and the American Revolution in England: Petitions, the Crown, and Public Opinion* (Macon, GA, 1986); idem., *Religion, Revolution and English Radicalism: Nonconformity in Eighteenth Century Politics and Society* (Cambridge, 1990); Henry Miller, *A Nation of Petitioners: Petitions and Petitioning in the United Kingdom, 1780–1918* (Cambridge, 2023).

[282] Thomas W. Davis, ed., *Committees for Repeal of the Test and Corporation Acts: Minutes 1786–90 and 1827–8* (1978).

[283] Letter 128, JW to SK, 26 April 1787.

[284] G. M. Ditchfield, 'The Parliamentary Struggle over the Repeal of the Test and Corporation Acts, 1787–1790', *English Historical Review*, 89 (1974), pp. 551–77; Archbishop John Moore cited at p. 552.

'too violent'.[285] Wodrow thought Priestley had hurt the prospects of a second attempt by 'irritating' Pitt, who was both very popular and 'sufficiently irritable'.[286] In the event, in a thin meeting of the Commons in May 1789 the second motion was narrowly defeated by 122 votes to 102. In early 1790, in the heady atmosphere of the early phase of the French Revolution, Dissenters held meetings and lobbied their local politicians ahead of a third attempt. Kenrick was appointed secretary of the Worcester Protestant Dissenters and sent Wodrow a printed copy of their resolutions. While the earlier motions had been presented by Henry Beaufoy, Kenrick was happy that Charles James Fox would introduce the bill on 2 March 1790, ensuring the support of the opposition, except for Edmund Burke, 'who never liked us nor our cause'.[287] With Pitt having called for the full house to meet, the motion for repeal was trounced by 294 votes to 105.[288] Kenrick had expected that the bill would be defeated given that the prime minister was opposed, but was happy that the Dissenters were organized and more united than in the past. He thought this boded well for the future, and he sent Wodrow the resolutions of the August meeting of the Worcester Protestant Dissenters.[289] The polarizing atmosphere of the debate over the French Revolution, however, saw the cause shelved and it was not until 1828 that repeal was enacted.[290]

Moves for reform in Scotland in the 1780s came from within the elite and were modest, restrained, and unsuccessful.[291] Keen to remove the taint of Jacobitism, the Scots had generally supported the government during the American Revolution, and periodic agitation for establishing a Scottish militia was arguably the hottest issue—a request not granted until 1797, when it was very unpopular with the general Scottish public.[292] Scottish politics was dominated by leading families, with Henry Dundas, a close confidant of the prime minister, in the

---

[285] Letter 129, SK to JW, 11 May 1787. Joseph Priestley, *A Letter to the Right Honourable William Pitt, ... on the Subjects of Toleration and Church Establishments; Occasioned by His Speech Against the Repeal of the Test and Corporation Acts, on Wednesday the 28th of March, 1787* (1787).

[286] Letter 134, JW to SK, 13 Dec. 1787.

[287] Letter 153, SK to JW, 24 Feb. 1790.

[288] J. C. D. Clark, *English Society, 1660–1832: Religion, Ideology, and Politics during the Ancien Regime* (Cambridge, 2000), pp. 413–17, provides a concise narrative of the repeal motions.

[289] Letter 155, SK to JW, 25 Sept. 1790.

[290] For a narrative of the repeal campaign and its failure in the early 1790s, see Richard B. Barlow, *Citizenship and Conscience* (Philadelphia, PA, 1962), pp. 221–99.

[291] For a detailed account of Scottish reform agitation in the 1780s, see the first two chapters of Henry W. Meikle, *Scotland and the French Revolution* (Glasgow, 1912); R. C. Primrose, 'The Scottish Burgh Reform Movement, 1783–93', *Aberdeen University Review*, 37 (1957), pp. 27–41.

[292] John Robertson, *The Scottish Enlightenment and the Militia Issue* (Edinburgh, 1985).

process of forging his 'despotism' through patronage.[293] A survey in 1788 found that there were only 2,668 voters in all of the Scottish county electorates combined.[294] The oligarchical nature of Scottish politics was reinforced by the spread of fictitious voting, and one critic complained that 'we might soon expect to see the meetings of elections for members of Parliament filled with the footman, postilions, cooks, pimps and parasites of these mighty superiors'.[295] A movement for reform of this nominal voting in county elections was only partially supported, faced strong opposition, and failed in the early 1780s. Prospects appeared better, however, for reform of the royal burghs—in which, for example, out of Glasgow's 100,000 residents only the thirty members of its town corporation had the right to vote. 'How absurd it is', wrote one reformer in the *Edinburgh Advertiser*, 'for a junto of twenty or thirty men to elect a member of parliament, when even this junto is not chosen by the people at large, but elect and re-elect themselves ad infinitum.'[296] After an initial meeting in 1784, an annual convention of delegates from forty-nine of the sixty-six burghs met at Edinburgh, and in 1787 issued a call for reform. Wodrow noted that some deputies had gone to London 'at their own private Expense to sollicit the Justice of the English Parliament'; yet he was not hopeful of success, and assumed the petition would be dismissed like the Dissenting motion for repeal of the Test Act.[297] After several MPs declined, Richard Brinsley Sheridan, an eloquent Foxite, agreed to lead the cause in Parliament. In the words of John Cannon, however, his 'parliamentary campaign had the impetuosity of a slow bicycle race'.[298] Despite being supported by petitions, Sheridan's annual motions were easily delayed and deflected by Dundas and eventually defeated in a thin house by sixty-seven to twenty-seven votes in 1792.

Wodrow had higher hopes for religious reform. Scottish clergy had watched the English Dissenting campaign for repeal with interest and concluded that a request to repeal the application of the Test Act with respect to Scotland might be looked upon more favourably.[299] The Test Act had been passed by the English

[293] Michael Fry, *The Dundas Despotism* (Edinburgh, 1992).
[294] David Allan, *Scotland in the Eighteenth Century: Union and Enlightenment* (2016), p. 16.
[295] *An Address to the Landed Gentlemen of Scotland* (27 March 1782), cited in John Cannon, *Parliamentary Reform 1640–1832* (Cambridge, 1973), p. 109.
[296] Cited in Cannon, *Parliamentary Reform*, p. 111.
[297] Letter 128, JW to SK, 26 April 1787.
[298] Cannon, *Parliamentary Reform*, p. 113. Nevertheless, party politics was heated in Scotland by this time: see Donald E. Ginter, ed., *Whig Organization in the General Election of 1790: Selections from the Blair Adam Papers* (1967).
[299] G. M. Ditchfield, 'The Scottish Campaign against the Test Act, 1790–1791', *Historical Journal*, 23 (1980), pp. 37–61.

Parliament in 1673 but continued to apply to offices in the British state following the 1707 Act of Union. It could be argued that it should not be applied to members of the established Church of Scotland, where there were no sacramental tests for public office. Initiated by Thomas Somerville, Moderate minister for Jedburgh, in April 1790 a movement began among the clergy in favour of repeal. His presbytery issued an overture to the forthcoming General Assembly, declaring that

> the Test Act, or the obligation imposed upon Members of the Church of Scotland in Office to receive Sacrament according to the form of the Church of England, is not only a profanation of sacred things, but inconsistent with the doctrines & worship of the Presbytery established in Scotland at the revolution & confirmed by the Union.[300]

Wodrow's letters are a valuable source for this campaign, and he reported that the nine-hour debate in the General Assembly on 27 May 1790 was 'incomparably the best & most interesting…I ever heard in our court'. The issue split the Moderate clergy. The Popular Party were all for repeal, and were joined by Wodrow and his fellow 'conscientious' Moderates.[301] They were opposed by the Moderate leadership and some prominent lay members, such as the Lord Advocate Robert Dundas, nephew of Henry Dundas. Allied to government and suspicious of any change, the Moderate leadership argued that repeal was divisive and was probably not possible under the Act of Union. With the numbers against them, however, 'after a little softening of the first resolutions' they agreed to establish a twenty-five-member committee to pursue repeal. Wodrow was appointed to the committee, which after much debate issued a *Memorial* in November 1790 that distinguished 'purely British' offices from those that were only English, and declared the Test Act 'derogatory to the Rights and Dignity of a high spirited people'.[302] However, when presented to Parliament in May 1791 by Sir Gilbert Elliot, their request for repeal was rejected.[303]

Of global significance, the 1780s also saw a national multi-denominational petitioning campaign arise to abolish the slave trade.[304] The European consumer revolution of the early eighteenth century saw a growing demand for sugar,

---

[300] Cited in Ditchfield, 'The Scottish Campaign against the Test Act', p. 39.
[301] Letter 154, JW to SK, 2 June 1790.
[302] Cited in Ditchfield, 'The Scottish Campaign against the Test Act', p. 42.
[303] This is discussed in Volume 3, which covers the years 1791–97.
[304] John Coffey, '"Tremble, Britannia!": Fear, Providence and the Abolition of the Slave Trade, 1758–1807', *English Historical Review*, 127 (2012), pp. 844–81; Anthony Page, 'Rational Dissent, Enlightenment and Abolition of the British Slave Trade', *Historical Journal*, 54 (2011), pp. 741–72.

coffee, tobacco, and other produce from plantations in the Americas worked by enslaved Africans, and Britain overtook Portugal as the leading nation in the transatlantic slave trade.[305] While modern scholarship has revealed the prominent role of chattel slavery in the economics and culture of Britain's Atlantic empire, until the American war this attracted limited critical comment.[306] Africans might be encountered as sailors in ports or servants of visiting or absentee plantation owners, or through literary representations. But those who did not venture beyond the shores of Britain had limited appreciation of the scale and violence of colonial slavery. It could be thought of as one of various systems of unfree labour in a world where servitude was widespread and 'English liberties' were exceptional. As the scale of chattel slavery grew in the eighteenth century, however, it attracted moral criticism as a peculiarly violent and degrading form of servitude—especially by clergy who had personal experience of the colonies and of planter hostility to the preaching of Christianity. The Somerset case of 1772, in which Lord Mansfield ruled that 'odious' slavery did not exist in England under common law, increased discussion and awareness. Inspired by the widely reported Somerset case, in 1778 *Knight v Wedderburn* led to a stronger ruling in Scotland that 'the state of slavery is not recognised by the laws of this Kingdom, and is inconsistent with the principles thereof'.[307] Wodrow boasted that

> L<sup>d</sup>. Mansfield<sup>s</sup> Decision was but partial compared to this [as it] only prevented the Slave from being forced on Shipboard. This is the first compleat sentence in favour of Liberty pronounced by any Court in Europe.[308]

Yet the Somerset and Knight cases also reinforced a distinction between Britain and the colonies. While antislavery ideas were circulating in the middle decades of the century, the political and economic power of merchants and planters appeared secure. 'The slave system', in the words of Christopher

---

[305] David Eltis and David Richardson, *Atlas of the Transatlantic Slave Trade* (New Haven, CT, 2015), pp. 21–36.

[306] On its economic value up to the eve of abolition of the slave trade, see Seymour Drescher, *Econocide: British Slavery in the Era of Abolition*, 2nd edn (Chapel Hill, NC, 2010); James Walvin, 'Why Did the British Abolish the Slave Trade? Econocide Revisited', *Slavery & Abolition*, 32 (2011), pp. 583–88; Maxine Berg and Pat Hudson, *Slavery, Capitalism and the Industrial Revolution* (Cambridge, 2023).

[307] Iain Whyte, *Scotland and the Abolition of Black Slavery, 1756–1838* (Edinburgh, 2006), pp. 16–18, cited at 18; see also John W. Cairns, 'Knight v Wedderburn', in David Dabydeen, John Gilmore, and Cecily Jones, eds, *The Oxford Companion to Black British History* (Oxford, 2007), pp. 244–46; John W. Cairns, 'After *Somerset*: The Scottish Experience', *Journal of Legal History*, 33 (2012), pp. 291–312.

[308] Letter 60, JW to SK, 16 March 1778.

Brown, 'enjoyed what looked like insurmountable political support before the Revolutionary era.'[309]

The American Revolution, with its heated debates about liberty and rights, saw the spread of antislavery sentiment—'How is it we hear the loudest yelps for liberty from the drivers of negroes?', Dr Johnson had pointedly asked.[310] Quakers in Pennsylvania established a Society for Promoting the Abolition of Slavery in 1775, and their counterparts in Britain petitioned Parliament in 1783 to abolish the slave trade.[311] Their petition was dismissed, with Lord North declaring that 'it was a trade which had, in some measure, become necessary to almost every nation in Europe'.[312] In the same year, the owners of the *Zong* confidently claimed compensation for enslaved Africans who had been thrown overboard owing to a shortage of drinking water. While they were awarded 'for the loss of 130-plus slaves at £30 each', many were shocked at how starkly this case illustrated the inherent and calculated brutality of the slave trade.[313] A pamphlet war developed in the mid-1780s, as apologists for slavery responded to tracts such as James Ramsay's *An Essay on the Treatment and Conversion of African Slaves in the British Sugar Colonies* (1784) and Thomas Clarkson's *An Essay on the Slavery and Commerce of the Human Species* (1786).[314]

The young Clarkson turned away from becoming an Anglican priest and, along with a group of Quakers, established a London Society for Abolition of the Slave Trade in May 1787, with the aim of transforming antislavery sentiment into abolitionist action.[315] Understanding that colonial slavery was an entrenched economic pillar of the British empire, the abolitionists decided to focus on

---

[309] The scholarship on slavery and abolition is vast. On mid-eighteenth-century antislavery sentiment, it is best to start with the insightful analysis in Christopher L. Brown, *Moral Capital: Foundations of British Abolitionism* (Chapel Hill, NC, 2006), ch. 1, 'Antislavery without Abolitionism', especially pp. 33–55, 98–101; quotation at p. 54.

[310] Samuel Johnson, *Taxation No Tyranny* (1775), p. 89.

[311] Judith Jennings, *The Business of Abolishing the British Slave Trade, 1783–1807* (1997), p. 41; Brycchan Carey and Geoffrey G. Plank, eds, *Quakers and Abolition* (Urbana, IL, 2014); Marcus Rediker, *The Fearless Benjamin Lay: The Quaker Dwarf Who Became the First Revolutionary Abolitionist* (Boston, MA, 2017).

[312] Cited in Paula E. Dumas, *Proslavery Britain: Fighting for Slavery in an Era of Abolition* (Basingstoke, 2016), p. 1.

[313] Verdict cited in James Walvin, *The Zong: A Massacre, the Law and the End of Slavery* (New Haven, CT, 2011), p. 106.

[314] Srividhya Swaminathan, *Debating the Slave Trade: Rhetoric of British National Identity, 1759–1815* (2009).

[315] J. R. Oldfield, *Popular Politics and British Anti-Slavery: The Mobilisation of Public Opinion against the Slave Trade, 1787–1807* (1998) emphasizes the leading role of the London committee.

petitioning and persuading politicians to end the transatlantic slave trade. They hoped that this might be politically achievable, would save many lives, would stop corrupting Africa and draining its population, and should encourage plantation owners to be more caring towards their enslaved workforce when unable to import replacements.[316] The campaign spread rapidly, especially in the industrializing north and Midlands, where Manchester generated a petition with over 10,000 signatures.[317] Following the loss of the American war, a campaign that aimed to restore some of Britain's 'moral capital' had wide appeal.[318] While drawing on established tactics of association meetings and lobbying MPs, the abolitionists were innovative. For example, Josiah Wedgwood produced 'Am I not a Man and Brother?' medallions, and the formerly enslaved Olaudah Equiano added his pioneering autobiography to a wave of antislavery publications.[319] Travelling thousands of miles, Thomas Clarkson led the agitation and, as James Walvin has noted, his at times dangerous research 'among slave captains, sailors, and slave ship rosters' provided 'hard evidence, culled from the belly of the slave ships, that both shocked and persuaded'.[320] With the prime minister's friend William Wilberforce, a recent Anglican Evangelical convert, leading the cause in Parliament, the Commons eventually voted for gradual abolition in 1792.[321] The bill then stalled in the Lords as the political climate became reactionary during the wars with revolutionary France. Eventually, however, the brief All the Talents ministry enacted abolition of the slave trade in 1807.[322] In the words of Seymour Drescher, the abolition campaign became the 'prototype of the modern social reform movement'.[323]

---

[316] David Brion Davis, *Inhuman Bondage: The Rise and Fall of Slavery in the New World* (Oxford, 2008), p. 235.

[317] Seymour Drescher, *Capitalism and Antislavery: British Mobilization in Comparative Perspective* (Oxford, 1987), pp. 71–73.

[318] Brown, *Moral Capital: Foundations of British Abolitionism*.

[319] Olaudah Equiano, *The Interesting Narrative and Other Writings*, ed. Vincent Carretta (New York, 2003); Vincent Carretta, *Equiano, the African: Biography of a Self-Made Man* (Athens, GA, 2005); Ryan Hanley, *Beyond Slavery and Abolition: Black British Writing, c. 1770–1830* (Cambridge, 2018).

[320] James Walvin, 'The Slave Trade, Quakers, and the Early Days of British Abolition', in Carey and Plank, *Quakers and Abolition*, p. 166.

[321] But see Stephen Mullen, 'Henry Dundas: A "Great Delayer" of the Abolition of the Transatlantic Slave Trade', *Scottish Historical Review*, 100 (2021), pp. 218–48.

[322] There is a very large scholarship on the relative roles of religion, social change, slave uprisings, identity crisis, and economics in causing the abolition of the British slave trade. For a concise survey, see Seymour Drescher, *Abolition: A History of Slavery and Antislavery* (Cambridge, 2009), ch. 8.

[323] Drescher, *Capitalism and Antislavery*, p. 67.

There is no mention of slavery in the early years of the Wodrow–Kenrick correspondence, despite Kenrick tutoring for the Milliken family. The family fortune had been made in the early eighteenth century by Major James Milliken (1669–1741), who rose from being a ruthless slave manager to marry the widow of a plantation owner on the West Indian island of Nevis.[324] Kenrick worked for the Major's son, James Milliken (1710–76), and his wife Jane *née* McDowall, whose father, William McDowall (1678–1748), was from a landed and mercantile family but also became a wealthy plantation owner in St Kitts and Nevis, and a friend of Major James Milliken. After he returned home in the 1720s, William McDowall also ordered that slaves be sent over to work as servants and tradesmen on his Scottish estates.[325] In addition, Elisabeth Kenrick had a brother in Jamaica who shipped her some mahogany timber.[326] And in 1765 Kenrick moved to Bewdley to join his brother in selling tobacco and snuff, placing him at the retail end of Britain's vast Atlantic slaving and trading system. In 1778 Wodrow expressed pride in the landmark judicial decision in *Knight v Wedderburn* outlawing slavery in Scotland, but the word 'slave' is generally used in their early correspondence in the context of debating colonial political rights.[327] There is, however, no discussion by them of the wealth that increasingly flowed into Glasgow and western Scotland from the slave trade and the West Indian plantations.[328] While Wodrow lived among what one historian has called the 'sugar plantocracy of Ayrshire', there is no discussion of it in the letters. For example, while he greatly admired Sir Adam Fergusson, MP for Ayrshire, there is no mention of his being an absentee co-owner of the Roselle estate in Jamaica, with around 200 enslaved Africans.[329] The estate had been established by Robert Hamilton (1698–1773), whose daughter married Wodrow's patron, Hugh Montgomerie, twelfth earl of Eglinton.[330] We can assume that Wodrow and Kenrick would have welcomed the

---

[324] Stuart Nisbet, 'Early Scottish Sugar Planters in the Leeward Islands, c. 1660–1740', in T. M. Devine, ed., *Recovering Scotland's Slavery Past: The Caribbean Connection* (Edinburgh, 2015), pp. 62–81.

[325] Nisbet, 'Early Scottish Sugar Planters in the Leeward Islands', pp. 73–74.

[326] Letter 61, SK to JW, 2 April 1778, W-K, I, p. 406.

[327] Letter 60, JW to SK, 16 March 1778, W-K, I, p. 153; John W. Cairns, 'After *Somerset*: The Scottish Experience', *Journal of Legal History*, 33 (2012), pp. 291–312.

[328] T. M. Devine, *The Tobacco Lords: A Study of the Tobacco Merchants of Glasgow and Their Trading Activities, c. 1740–90* (Edinburgh, 1975).

[329] Eric Graham, *Burns and the Sugar Plantocracy of Ayrshire* (2014), *passim*; see also Alex Renton, *Blood Legacy: Reckoning with a Family's Story of Slavery* (Edinburgh, 2021); Stephen Mullen, *Glasgow's Sugar Aristocracy in the British Atlantic World, 1776–1838* (2022).

[330] Eric J. Graham, 'The Scots Penetration of the Jamaican Plantation Business', in Devine, *Recovering Scotland's Slavery Past*, p. 92. Wodrow had been appointed to his parish by the tenth

outcome of the 1772 Somerset case, but unfortunately we cannot know that they were aware of it as it occurred during a gap in the correspondence.

The Wodrow–Kenrick letters illustrate the dramatic growth of the abolition movement in the late 1780s, and the wisdom of petitioning for an end to the slave trade rather than of colonial slavery. While pro- and antislavery books and pamphlets were being published in the mid-1780s, as Drescher has observed, 'a survey of London's newspapers in 1786–1787 shows a nation reveling in its prosperity, security and power'. It was the correspondence of the London committee, and Manchester's large petition in December 1787, that galvanized a wave of petitions in early 1788 in the name of 'humanity, religion and justice'.[331] At this time, in mid-February, Kenrick first raised the issue with his friend—though inaccurately describing the petitions as aiming to 'abolish slavery and the slave trade'. He noted that, as their MP, Pitt had presented a petition from Cambridge University, from where the 'plan seems to have originated' with Clarkson's prize-winning essay. In contrast, he expected only a faint contribution from Tory-dominated Oxford, where he heard a member of Christ Church College had declared it 'threatened the ruin of our West India settlements'.[332] With Pitt having motioned for Parliament to consider abolition in early May, Wodrow noted that Kenrick was correct in his forecast about the 'coolness' of Oxford. He confessed that Scotland had taken too long to join a cause 'which does honour to the age', and while the universities and clergy were organizing petitions, few towns had followed Edinburgh in doing so.[333] In total, Scotland submitted only sixteen petitions in 1788, with most coming from presbyteries and synods—the General Assembly noted its approval of the petitions, but did not submit one itself, which Wodrow thought 'foolish'.[334] Wodrow's short letter in late May 1789 does not mention the defeat of Wilberforce's motion for abolition earlier that month, as he was focussed on the publication of Leechman's sermons and the prosecution of M'Gill for heresy. The slave trade is not discussed again until the large abolition campaign of 1791, which culminated in the House of Commons voting to abolish the slave trade gradually in 1792.[335]

---

earl of Eglinton and posted letters franked by subsequent earls. W-K, I, pp. 47, 36n. Stevenston was only 4 miles west of the Eglinton estate near Kilwinning.

[331] Drescher, *Abolition*, pp. 212–15.
[332] Letter 135, SK to JW, 13 Feb. 1788.
[333] Letter 136, JW to SK, 28 May 1788.
[334] Letter 137, JW to SK, 3 July 1788; Edinburgh, Dundee, and Paisley were the only towns that petitioned. Whyte, *Scotland and the Abolition of Black Slavery*, p. 82.
[335] For which see Volume 3.

The French Revolution of 1789 overthrew absolute monarchy, and it was welcomed by our correspondents, as by many liberal-minded Britons. Wodrow had been in London in October 1788, and 'got a good deal of intelligence' from Richard Price, the leading Rational Dissenter, who had 'great hopes of the extension of Liberty from the present struggles in France'.[336] With the French state's finances a confusing mess, drowning in debt, and the nobility refusing to give up their privileged tax exemptions, Louis XVI reluctantly called for the election of an Estates-General for the first time since 1614.[337] A letter by Price to Thomas Jefferson, written a day after Wodrow's letter, describes his view:

what is now passing in France, is an object of my anxious attention. I am by no means properly informed about the nature and circumstances of the struggle; but as far as it is a struggle for a free constitution of government, and the recovery of their rights by the people I heartily wish it success whatever may be the consequence to this country, for I have learnt to consider myself more as a citizen of the world than of any particular country, and to such a person every advance that the cause of public liberty makes must be agreeable.[338]

Kenrick's November 1788 reply to Wodrow is unfortunately missing, but he no doubt shared Price's optimism.

Wodrow again raised the topic of France on 5 August 1789. A revolution had begun after the Estates-General met in May, and he was disappointed. Refusing to accept that votes should be determined by order, the Third Estate (representing the common people) declared itself a National Assembly and invited members of the aristocracy and nobility to join it in creating a constitution. A power struggle ensued during the summer, with crowds storming the Bastille on 14 July. With regiments being stationed on the outskirts of Paris, a 'Great Fear' of potential royalist counterrevolution swept across France, which saw peasants attacking châteaus and burning rent rolls. Wodrow had hoped that 'a grand & glorious revolution' that would make 'the Tyrants of Europe tremble on their Thrones' could occur without bloodshed, but instead violent mobs were rampaging throughout France and the Third Estate appeared to have lost control.[339] Unfortunately the

---

[336] Letter 141, JW to SK, 25 Oct. 1788.

[337] For a concise account, see William Doyle, *The French Revolution: A Very Short Introduction* (Oxford, 2001), ch. 2, 'Why It Happened'; and on the fiscal crisis as the key short-term cause, see Gail Bossenga, 'Financial Origins of the French Revolution', in Thomas E. Kaiser and Dale K. Van Kley, eds, *From Deficit to Deluge: The Origins of the French Revolution* (Stanford, CA, 2011), pp. 37–66.

[338] Richard Price to Thomas Jefferson, 26 Oct. 1788, in *The Correspondence of Richard Price*, eds Bernard Peach and D. O. Thomas, 3 vols (Durham, NC, 1983–94), III, p. 182.

[339] Letter 149, JW to SK, 5 Aug. 1789.

last part of Kenrick's reply on 10 August is missing, which may have included comment on the dramatic abolition of feudalism by the National Assembly on the day Wodrow posted his letter.[340]

The French Revolution arguably marks the beginning of modern politics, and is a central topic of the third volume of *The Wodrow–Kenrick Correspondence*. A widespread and heated debate ensued in Britain following Edmund Burke's condemnation of the revolution, and its Declaration of the Rights of Man and Citizen, in his November 1790 *Reflections on the Revolution in France: And on the Proceedings in Certain Societies in London Relative to that Event*.[341] Near the end of this second volume Kenrick noted Richard Price's sermon, preached on 4 November 1789 before the London society for commemorating Britain's revolution of 1688, and published as *A Discourse on the Love of Our Country*.[342] It was this tract that provoked Burke to attack the revolution in Parliament in February 1790 and write his book, with an eye to countering the spread of revolutionary ideas in Britain.[343] Without naming Burke, Kenrick observed that 'hellish invectives are now poured out upon' Price, but at the same time he was receiving new marks of 'respect & veneration from foreigners'.[344] In 1790, however, with France apparently peacefully crafting a constitutional monarchy, Wodrow and Kenrick were more focussed on religious issues such as the prosecution of M'Gill and the campaign to repeal the Test Act.

---

[340] Letter 150, SK to JW, 10 Aug. 1785. The August Degrees were being issued as JW posted Letter 149 on 5 Aug. In the words of one historian: 'On the night of 4 August 1789, the Assembly, spurred by the reports of rural insurrection arriving from around the country, held a special session at which one of the liberal nobles planned to propose abolishing some of his order's privileges.... The success of this motion launched a chain reaction of further renunciations.... By the time the exhausted deputies staggered out into the dawn on 5 August, they had gone far to "abolish the feudal regime entirely", as the preamble to their edicts promised'. Jeremy D. Popkin, *A Short History of the French Revolution*, 6th edn (Upper Saddle River, NJ, 2015), p. 32.

[341] The scholarship on this is large, but for a starting point see Emma Vincent Macleod, 'British Attitudes to the French Revolution', *Historical Journal*, 50 (2007), pp. 689–709.

[342] Letter 152, SK to JW, 16 Dec. 1789.

[343] F. P. Lock, *Edmund Burke: Volume II, 1784–1797* (Oxford, 2006), pp. 253–54. For an annotated edition that emphasizes the British religious context, see Edmund Burke, *Reflections on the Revolution in France*, ed. J. C. D. Clark (Stanford, CA, 2001).

[344] Letter 153, SK to JW, 24 Feb. 1790.

# WODROW–KENRICK CORRESPONDENCE
## Volume 2: 1784–1790
## Letters 79–155

### Letter 79: James Wodrow to Samuel Kenrick, 15 April 1784
Place: Stevenston
Note in Kenrick's hand: anw$^d$. June 5 SK & Mary

My Dear Friend

Yours of the 8th. of Oct$^{br}$.[1] did not reach me till towards the end of Nov$^r$. which is the usual and unacountable fate of all the Letters you send me by private hand's. It has however lain by me too long unacknowledged partly owing to what you so naturaly describe ~~of~~ in Yourself and is equaly a picture of me– a propensity to procrastination more especialy in all long Letters & also that I expected to hear from you soon after as you break off Your Letter abruptly.[2]

What you write about the poor rates surprized me for tho' I had often heard that Tax complained of I had no notion the burden was realy so heavy & such a check on Industry & improvement.[3] It woud look as if the Overseers or Managers had some power to increase it ad libitum[4] according to the real or apprehended increase of the poor. I see a<–> rational & most benevolent scheme for the application of it in a small book noticed in the Jan$^y$. Review[5] from that book it woud appear that a considerable part of it is sadly mismanaged. Our funds are so small as to exclude

---

[1] W-K, I, Letter 78, SK to JW, 8 Oct. 1783, pp. 489–92.

[2] Letter 78 is unsigned.

[3] In Letter 78, SK had written admiringly of the Scottish system of poor relief, administered wholly through local parish churches, which he thought both a more efficient and a more humane system than the English practice of levying poor rates, which both was felt as a heavy tax burden on ratepayers and resulted in the reluctance of parishes to admit new families to their numbers. W-K, I, p. 491.

[4] 'ad libitum', usually 'ad lib.', i.e. at one's pleasure or discretion.

[5] Possibly *The Means of Effectually Preventing Theft and Robbery; Together with Our Present Cruel Punishments of those and Other Crimes: The Means of Immediately Suppressing Vagrant Beggary: of Speedily Abolishing Our Poor's Rates: and of Relieving the Present Oppression of our Labouring Commonalty* (1783), reviewed in the *Monthly Review*, 70 (Feb. 1784), pp. 103–08.

the temptation to this & ^yet^ they accumulate in many country parishes.[6] In such populous & industrious places as this where I live from the constant influx of Strangers[7] I find it difficult enough to make tollerable provision for the numerous poor with all the assistance we get from the boxes of Sailours Coalhewers Weavers & some charitable Societies constituted on purpose<–> so that I have of late introduced the custom of collecting at all private Baptisms & Marriages which with a Guinea or two now & then put into my hands by the Gentl$^n$. of the parish makes a considerable addition to our Sundays Collections & raises our Funds to about £80 a year little enough for a parish of 1600 examinable persons.[8]

The Clergy of Scotland are not so much respected at least by their own people as when you were in the Country and I am inclined to think that the Number of Dissenters in the Western Counties & in Fife much exceeds the proportion of England.[9] Within this Presby consisting of 17 parishes we have about ten disenting

---

[6] Scottish poor relief was patchily organized before the imposition of the New Poor Law in 1845. It was managed by the Kirk Sessions of parish churches either on the basis of voluntary donations to the poor's fund via weekly collections at church services or, especially in the south and south-east of Scotland towards the later eighteenth century, on the basis of compulsory poor rates assessed on the heritors (landowners) of a parish. It appears that Stevenston, in the south-west of the country, was not such a parish, and that JW and his elders had to manage as well as they could on voluntary contributions. Rosalind Mitchison, 'The Making of the Old Scottish Poor Law', *Past and Present*, 63 (1974), pp. 58–93; Alistair Mutch, *Religion and National Identity: Governing Scottish Presbyterianism in the Eighteenth Century* (Edinburgh, 2015), pp. 106–30.

[7] The Scottish system did not, unlike the English poor law, ban vagrancy.

[8] James Wodrow, 'The Parish of Stevenston', in Sir John Sinclair, ed., *The Statistical Account of Scotland, Drawn Up from the Communications of the Ministers of the Different Parishes*, 13 vols (Edinburgh, 1791–99), VII (1793), pp. 26, 34–35 [hereafter OSA]. By 1793, JW estimated that there had been 1,884 souls in the parish of Stevenston in 1783 (rising to 2,425 by 1791). The account he wrote in his OSA article expands a little on what he tells SK here. The 'boxes' he refers to here seem to have been for particular collections for workers in these particular occupations. In OSA, however, he was less frank and perhaps more concerned to show Stevenston in a good light; he concluded that 'the private charity of the better sort…in a parish circumstanced like this, is very considerable and commendable, because the highest of them are well acquainted with the situation of the poor, and interest themselves in it' (pp. 34–35). There was often some tension between church ministers and local heritors in the raising of sufficient funds to help those who needed relief, particularly in the context of the growing population of the later eighteenth century.

[9] JW is here responding to SK's assertion in Letter 78 that 'there are more dissenters from the establishment, here than in Scotland– & that in general their religious sentiments are more liberal & rational, on some abstruse points'. He is also eliding the distinction sometimes made between Seceders (Presbyterian denominations outside the Church of Scotland) and Dissenters (non-Presbyterian denominations). Heterodox Dissent was almost certainly less common in Scotland than in England. Few national statistics are available for Scotland before the mid-nineteenth century. Some compilers of the *Statistical Accounts* in the 1790s tried to enumerate families attending different denominational churches in their parishes, but they were not asked to do so, and so the figures are incomplete—JW did not do so for Stevenston. The original

Houses most of them built since you was here. One of them just built within my parish a much neater & finer Church ^<in–>^ than my own belonging to the Relief Sect tho' there are fewer of my parishioners join them than from the neighbouring parishes.[10] That sect has encreased much of late.[11] ^The old Seceders[12] are declining.^ Our people are turned wild in their Sentiments about Patronage & the uniform decisions of the Gen[l]. Assembly in favour of the Law irritate them more & more.[13] Yet I believe the cheif cause is ^a^ difference in their Theological sentiments

Secession Church of 1734 left the Church of Scotland in Fife, and one of the first Relief Churches was established in Colinsburgh in Fife. JW will have been well versed, from reading his father's works, in the history of the Covenanters and Presbyterian Dissenters of the south-west of Scotland in the Restoration period. By the 1790s, however, Dissenters were 'comparatively thin on the ground in the south-west', while they reached around a quarter of the population elsewhere in the Lowlands and as many as 70 per cent of adults of Jedburgh in the eastern Scottish Borders. Callum G. Brown, *Religion and Society in Scotland since 1707* (Edinburgh, 1997), p. 20; *DSCHT*.

[10] In Wodrow, 'The parish of Stevenston', *OSA*, p. 27, he stated that it was built near Saltcoats in around 1783, and by 1793 there were 'about 80 families in this parish of that persuasion', together with '14 families of Burghers and Antiburghers, and a single Cameronian'.

[11] The Relief Church, another Presbyterian denomination, was established in 1761 in response to the Moderates' enforcement of the patronage laws in the Church of Scotland. It grew progressively over the next few decades both by attracting congregations seceding from the Church of Scotland and by evangelism. *DSCHT*; Gavin Struthers, *The History of the Rise, Progress and Principles of the Relief Church* (Glasgow, 1843).

[12] 'Old Seceders' were members of the group of churches which had departed from the Church of Scotland in 1733 over the patronage issue, or those congregations which later seceded from the Kirk and associated themselves with them. They split in 1747 into Burghers (Associate Synod) and Antiburghers (General Associate Synod) over the rectitude or not of taking the Burgess Oath. *DSCHT*; John M'Kerrow, *History of the Secession Church* (Glasgow, 1841).

[13] The dispute turned on the rights of local representatives, whether presbyteries and kirk sessions, or local landowners (heritors), in selecting parish ministers in the Church of Scotland, as opposed to their appointment by the Crown and other great landowners. Interference with ecclesiastical patronage had been contentious since the Reformation. Crown / great landowner patronage was abolished at the 'Glorious Revolution' in 1690 when Presbyterianism was restored as the established form of religion in Scotland, but it was re-established with the Patronage Act of 1712, in defiance of the terms of the Union of the Parliaments of 1707. It was not repealed until 1874, but the last great explosion of anti-patronage activity during the eighteenth century, before the 'Ten Years' Conflict' up to 1843, had burned out by 1785. Hence JW's remark. Broadly speaking, the eighteenth-century Moderate party in the Church, who were dominant in the General Assembly, came to defend the patronage laws, while many members of the Popular or Evangelical party opposed them for a range of reasons and with a variety of preferred alternatives. See Richard B. Sher and Alexander Murdoch, 'Patronage and Party in the Church of Scotland, 1750–1800' in Norman Macdougall, ed., *Church, Politics and Society: Scotland, 1408–1929* (Edinburgh, 1983), pp. 197–220; Martin Fitzpatrick, 'The Enlightenment, Politics and Providence', in Knud Haakonssen, ed., *Enlightenment and Religion: Rational Dissent in Eighteenth-Century Britain* (Cambridge, 1996), pp. 73–75.

with their Clergy they get Sermons more to their Tast <–>^i.e.^ more calvinistick in their turn, or suited to the books they are accustomed to read: at least this the case here where we have little disturbance with violent Settlements.[14]

You wish to know my Sentiments & M[r]. Magill's[15] on a particular point intimate as we are I scarce remember to have conversed with him ^directly^ on the subject yet have no doubt that his Sentiments are much the same with your own.[16] For myself it is one of the few theological points about which after sufficient enquiry I have formed no decided opinion. Like many other disputed points, It is of little consequence to X[ty]. The Credit of our Sav[rs]. religion and its Influence on Mankind stands on his Father['s] Authority. In his Name He ever spoke & acted & never in his own. This I think is acknowledged by all rational Xians. The S-c-ians[17]

---

[14] On the argument that ecclesiastical divisions in eighteenth-century Ayrshire were founded on theological divisions as much as on the patronage issue, see Luke Brekke, 'Heretics in the Pulpit, Inquisitors in the Pews: The Long Reformation and the Scottish Enlightenment', *Eighteenth-Century Studies*, 44 (2010), 79–98; Valerie Honeyman, '"That ye may judge for yourselves": The Contribution of Scottish Presbyterianism towards the Emergence of Political Awareness amongst Ordinary People in Scotland between 1746 and 1792' (PhD thesis, University of Stirling, 2012), especially chapter 6 on patronage riots and violent impositions of ministers on parishes, but also *passim* on the influence of popular Scottish Presbyterian theological reading; Colin Kidd, 'The Fergusson Affair: Calvinism and Dissimulation in the Scottish Enlightenment', *Intellectual History Review*, 26 (2016), pp. 339–54.

[15] Rev. William M'Gill (1732–1807) was minister of the second charge at Ayr (1761–1807), where he was the colleague of William Dalrymple (1723–1814) of the first charge in that parish, and married Dalrymple's niece, Elizabeth Dunlop. M'Gill had graduated MA at Glasgow University in 1753, and served in 1760 as assistant minister to Rev. Alexander Fergusson of Kilwinning, who had also acted in this role for JW, 1753–57. M'Gill was a Moderate, like Fergusson and JW, and he was awarded a DD by Glasgow University in 1785. He was also a friend of Robert Burns, and is the heretic 'Doctor Mac' in 'The Kirk's Alarm' (or 'The Tattered Garland') (1786). Influenced by Joseph Priestley's *Theological Repository* (1770–71), M'Gill's *A Practical Essay on the Death of Jesus Christ* (Edinburgh, 1786) was widely regarded as Socinian, and he was tried for heresy by the Presbytery of Ayr and the Synod of Glasgow and Ayr in 1789–90, a substantial topic of discussion in Letters 146–54 below. Martin Fitzpatrick, 'Varieties of Candour: English and Scottish Style', *Enlightenment and Dissent*, 7 (1988), pp. 35–56; Robert Richard, 'An Examination of the Life and Career of Rev. William McGill (1732–1807): Controversial Ayr Theologian' (PhD thesis, University of Glasgow, 2009), pp. 4–7.

[16] SK did not ask for JW's opinion on the pre-existence of Christ in the previous Letter 78, 8 Oct. 1783. It is possible JW is referring to a missing letter prior to that. SK had noted in Letter 77, 7 May 1783, that the atonement was the subject of the second chapter of Joseph Priestley's *An History of the Corruptions of Christianity*, 2 vols (Birmingham, 1782), and so the controversy occasioned by this book would ensure that M'Gill's forthcoming book, *A Practical Essay on the Death of Jesus Christ*, would 'be read ^& canvassed^ w[th]. great avidity'. *W-K*, I, p. 482.

[17] Socinians professed the unity of God, and rejected the orthodox doctrine of the Trinity. They held that Jesus was a human prophet who became exalted following his crucifixion, but remained subordinate in status to God. Joseph Priestley provided a concise twenty-eight-page case for Socinian Unitarianism in *A General View of the Arguments for the Unity of God; and Against the Divinity and Pre-existence of Christ, from Reason, from the Scriptures, and from History* (Birmingham, 1783).

appear to me to have a considerable advantage over ^<all>^ the other sects in urging the Example of X upon his followers as a motive to virtue & also in stating his Resurrection or future Life as ^a^ direct proof of ours. Yet on the other hand it may be said That whatever He was before he came into the World He emptied himself & became one of us[18] but I dont know if this is sufficient to place the above motives & proofs on the very same ground. The general strain of the new T. is undoubtedly in their favour– even the passages in the first of Col. & Heb. which the reviewers allude to are most naturaly explained in their way.[19] On the Other hand There are a few Passages in the Gospel of John which <—> ^will^ naturaly lead a Bible Xian (I like the term <—> greatly) to think that John believed that his Master <— —> had been with God before he appeared in this world <-> which it seems hard or unnatural to twist or turn into a different sense,[20] & which <—> ^forced even^ the first Socinians of all men in the world the most averse to systems & Hypotheses into a Hypothesis adverse to all their ~~former~~ ^usual^ principles even that our Sav$^r$. was taken up into heaven in the days of his flesh a Supposition for which there is scarce any ground at all in the Scripture–

I am perfectly of your mind ^that^ The Prexistence of X[21] if it is worth disputing at all can only be decided from Scripture for this reason I considered the dispute between Dr Priestly[22] and the Reviewer from the begin$^g$. as ^very^

---

[18] Cf. Philippians 2:5–8: '...Christ Jesus. Who, being in the form of God, thought it not robbery to be equal with God: But made himself of no reputation and took upon him the form of a servant, and was made in the likeness of men: And being found in fashion as a man, he humbled himself, and became obedient unto death, even the death of the cross.'

[19] The first chapters of the New Testament books of Colossians and Hebrews. As JW discusses Priestley's exchange with the *Monthly Review* in this letter (see below), he may have considered the following passage as alluding to these New Testament books: 'According to our present view of things, the PRE-EXISTENCE of Christ was a doctrine acknowledged, in terms the most explicit and unequivocal, by the earliest writers of the Christian church'. *Monthly Review*, 69 (Aug. 1783), p. 90. The only periodical review of Priestley's *History of the Corruptions of Christianity* (1782) explicitly to name Colossians and Hebrews was the *Edinburgh Weekly Magazine*, 58 (2 Oct. 1783), p. 22. It is notable that, in contrast to the reviewers, JW thought these passages were most 'naturally explained' by the Socinians.

[20] Reviewing Priestley's *Corruptions of Christianity*, the *Monthly Review* quoted John 16:28 as evidence of the pre-existence of Christ: he '"came from the Father into the world," as well as when he left the world, it was "to go unto the Father"'. *Monthly Review*, 69 (Aug. 1783), p. 90.

[21] Arians and Socinians both rejected the orthodox doctrine of the Trinity and saw Christ as a being who was subordinate to God. But while Socinians saw Jesus as human, Arians argued that he was a pre-existent divine being.

[22] Rev. Joseph Priestley (1733–1804), unitarian clergyman and natural philosopher. A polymath and polemicist, Priestley was arguably the most prolific and influential Rational Dissenting intellectual in the late eighteenth century. Kenrick enthusiastically embraced Priestley's Unitarianism, visited him in August 1784, and kept 'a cast...of Dr Priestley in my museum' (Letter 133, SK to JW, 28 Sept. 1787).

frivolous.[23] They seem to have departed from their Province by begin^g. the Dispute & they have also carried ^it^ on unhandsomely & tediously as if the ascertainin<g> the sense of two or three Passages in books[24] which not one in a thousand of their readers will ever open had been a matter of the same consequence to learning or Morality as their controversy about Polygamy for which they deserve the thanks of their readers.[25] They ought to have satisfyed themselves with a short Dissent from the D^r. ^if they thought him wrong^ & their reasons for it & let it sleep. They seem however to me to have ^much the^ better of the D^r. & our friend M^r. Cappe[26] in ascertaining the Historical fact yet this not of the least consequence in the decision of the Theological point. Their argument is quite inconclusive that because it was the opinion of Justin[27] and the Church therefore they learned it from the

---

[23] Joseph Priestley, *An History of the Corruptions of Christianity*, 2 vols (1782) was reviewed at length, very critically and anonymously by Samuel Badcock, a previous ally, in the *Monthly Review*, 68 (June 1783), pp. 515–26; ibid., 69 (Aug. 1783), pp. 89–105. Priestley replied with his *Reply to the Animadversions on the History of the Corruptions of Christianity in the Monthly Review* (Birmingham, 1783), and in the *Monthly Review*, 69 (Oct. 1783), p. 359. See Robert E. Schofield, *The Enlightened Joseph Priestley: A Study of His Life and Work from 1773 to 1804* (University Park, PA, 2004), pp. 223–24; Alison Kennedy, 'Historical Perspectives in the Mind of Joseph Priestley', in Isabel Rivers and David L. Wykes, eds, *Joseph Priestley: Scientist, Philosopher, and Theologian* (Oxford, 2008), pp. 190–3. As Kenrick did not ask about the pre-existence of Christ in the previous surviving letters, JW's reference to reviews published in June and July suggests that there may be a missing Kenrick letter from the period June to Sept.

[24] At issue was Priestley's interpretation of some passages in early Christian writings, and 'of my being charged with advancing that Justin Martyr was the first that started the notion of Christ's pre-existence'. Priestley summarized his position thus: 'The exaltation of the person of Jesus Christ began with the Gnostics, who maintained the doctrine of the pre-existence of all human souls, as independent created spirits, capable of animating human bodies. This error began in the time of the apostles, and is known to be referred to by John. When this notion was exploded, another, which I cannot trace any higher than Justin Martyr, was adopted, and this was the *personification of the Logos*, of the Father, which was a thing quite distinct from the doctrine of the Gnostics, so that the patrons of each were continually combating one another.' Priestley, *Reply to the Animadversions... in the Monthly Review*, p. 34.

[25] Rev. Samuel Badcock (1747–88), at that time a Dissenting minister in South Molton, Devon, had published a series of articles in the *Monthly Review* in response to a treatise on polygamy by Rev. Martin Madan: *Monthly Review*, 64 (1781), pp. 228–29, 234–36; *Monthly Review*, 65 (1781), pp. 57–65, 158, 161–82, 232–34; *Monthly Review*, 67 (1782), pp. 104–09.

[26] Rev. Newcome Cappe (1733–1800), Dissenting minister and unitarian theologian. He attended Glasgow University 1752–55 and met JW and SK during that time (*W-K*, I, p. 238). Cappe became minister at St Saviourgate, York, where he was visited by SK in 1759. JW is referring to his *Remarks in Vindication of Dr Priestley, on that Article of the Monthly Review for June, 1783, Which Relates to the First Part of Dr Priestley's History of the Corruptions of Christianity* (1783). Cappe's forty-page pamphlet sought to refute the 'serious charge' that Priestley had supported his 'own cause by a misrepresentation of Justin Martyr' (p. 4). See also Letter 80, and *W-K*, I, p. 238.

[27] Justin Martyr (100–165), who wrote two defences of the Christian faith in the second century AD, and was beheaded in Rome for his faith.

Appostles. Considering how familiar the conception of Angelick Orders were to the Jews & that of Subordinate Gods to the Heathens It woud have been marvellous indeed if the ^angelic or^ Divine nature of X had not been an early opinion in the Xian Ch. This was the very manner in which all the corruptions of X[ty]. were introduced whether this was a corruption or not must be decided on other data.[28] The Reviewer as you say must be a man of Learning & abilities. He touches upon the very strength of the Arian scheme in opposition to the Socinian I mean in point of reason & Philosophy viz that it is much more congruous to our conceptions of our Lords Exaltation to the Supremacy of the Universe or of the Church of God in heaven & earth.[29] Yet that Reviewer does not write like a Gentleman.[30] Neither does the D[r]. on some occasions perhaps on too many.[31] Yet I love & admire him for the honesty & integrity of his heart for the amazing variety & extent of his <—> knowledge and the ^almost^ equally amazing facility of comunicating it to others for the soundness of his Judgement in most points and for other qualities yet with all this excellence He has as we say something like a Bee in his Bonnet there is a certain want of Judgement or prudence in some things which hurts the influence & usefulness of his writings in the present age & will probably do it ~~with~~ to posterity. He writes too much and consequently too carelessly, considering the prodigious variety of things his mind

---

[28] i.e. scripture.

[29] SK later informed JW that the anonymous reviewer was Samuel Badcock, a 'dissenting minister & an Arian' (Letter 80). Badcock (1747–88) held ministries at Wimborne, Barnstaple, and South Molton. A controversial character, he was a regular and energetic *Monthly Reviewer*. A friend turned critic of Joseph Priestley, in 1786 he conformed to the Church of England. Surman Index; Benjamin Christie Nangle, *The Monthly Review, First Series, 1749–1789* (Oxford, 1934), pp. 2–3. Most of the review is devoted to critiquing Priestley's use of texts by early churchmen such as Justin Martyr and Eusebius. The following, however, may be the passage to which JW refers: 'With giving up the pre-existence of Christ, he must also give up the doctrine of his miraculous birth....If Christ was a mere man, and in no respect different from ourselves, why should he have been what Dr Priestley calls a *Unique* in the creation? Why might not every end of his coming into the world have been answered as well by a natural as by a miraculous conception? What had his conception to do with his qualifications as a Messiah? A higher nature was not, it seems, to be imparted. What gift did it convey? Was he made holier by it? Or wiser? Or any respect fitter for his office? We think a Jew could puzzle Dr Priestley with questions such as these; and a Christian could turn his own concessions against some of the leading principles of his scheme, and stagger him on his own *simple* and *rational* ground.' *Monthly Review*, 68 (June 1783), p. 523.

[30] Unknown to JW, Samuel Badcock was the son of a butcher. Priestley was the son of a cloth dresser.

[31] See JW's continuing criticisms of Priestley's over-aggressive style of argument in, for instance, Letter 125, JW to SK, 23 November 1786; Letter 134, JW to SK, 13 December 1787.

is engaged in; his depth of knowledge & accuracy is wonderful yet it is impossible for any one man to understand every thing.[32]

You blame him justly for calling himself a Socinian. The old Socinians would have almost excommunicated him for ^his^ sentiments about the worship of X[33] which I suppose are the same with ^the^ worthy & amiable Lindsay's[34] & yet more for his Calvinistick or necessitarian[35] principles which are opposite to theirs toto caelo.[36] Tho' he has successfully engaged the Arminians[37] of our day yet he has left their old & stronger bulwarks still standing. His book on the corruptions of X$^{ty}$. I have never seen & coud wish for a cheap copy of it if it coud be purchased from your Library. It is a grand subject of all the others most fit to check the infidelity of the present age and I coud have wished to have seen it treated by some writer of as much learning judgement & liberality of mind as D$^r$. Priestly <–> but with more leizure & more Candour i.e. less attachment to his own nostrums or prejudices & more gentleness to those of others. I have frequently thought of M$^r$. Fleming[38] or even M$^r$. Lang[39] for a work of that kind both of them are deep scholars in Ecclesiastical History & both men of high Abilities. There is a Life of Socinus[40] published some time ago in England & the two last vol$^s$. of Bourns Sermons[41]

---

[32] JW's friend, William M'Gill, shared similar concerns, for which see Letter 87.

[33] Priestley opposed the worship of Christ and argued that prayers could only be addressed to God. He thought it 'extraordinary' that the early Socinians prayed to Christ given they believed he was a 'mere man' and there was 'no authority whatever' in Scripture authorizing the practice. Priestley, *History of the Corruptions of Christianity*, I, p. 134.

[34] Rev. Theophilus Lindsey (1723–1808), unitarian minister in London. Priestley was indeed close to Lindsey, but he also wrote: 'Though a Socinian myself, I do not hold myself obliged to defend what has been advanced by any other Socinian. Like men who think for themselves we differ as much as others who go by the same common name.' Priestley, *Reply to the Animadversions on the History of the Corruptions of Christianity in the Monthly Review* (1783), p. 46.

[35] Determinist, as opposed to believing in free will. See Priestley's debate with Richard Price in their jointly authored pamphlet, *A Free Discussion of the Doctrines of Materialism, and Philosophical Necessity, in a Correspondence Between Dr. Price, and Dr. Priestley* (1778), in which Priestley argued for necessitarianism.

[36] 'toto caelo': by the extent of the whole heavens; diametrically.

[37] Arminianism denied that regeneration was the work of the Holy Spirit alone, and held that human beings could contribute to their own salvation; relatedly, some Moderates in eighteenth-century Scotland emphasized human ability at the expense of original sin. DSCHT.

[38] Rev. John Fleming, DD (1711–87), minister of Kilmacolm, near Paisley, Renfrewshire, 'a singularly able minister and a distinguished scholar', FES, III, p. 212. See W-K, I, pp. 296, 361, 404.

[39] Rev. Gilbert Lang (1725–91), minister of Largs, Ayrshire. FES, III, pp. 215–16.

[40] Joshua Toulmin, *Memoirs of the Life, Character, Sentiments and Writings of Faustus Socinus* (1777).

[41] Presumably *Twenty Sermons on the Most Serious and Practical Subjects of the Christian Religion, Fitted for the Use of Private Families Preached by the Late Revd Samuel Bourn, to which is Added Some Memoirs of the Life of the Author* (1755). These were the sermons of the English Presbyterian

neither of which I have seen & woud wish to have both but too much of Theology see separate paper.[42]

I long to hear your sentiments on Politicks & insist on a full Letter on that subject with all the Anecdotes you are master of. I make no doubt you are on the same side with me even for Mr. Pit & the Ministry[43] <&> ^yet^ there may be some reason to doubt it as I hear all the Republicans in this Country such as Proff{r}. Millar at Glasgow[44] Harry Erskine at Ed{r}.[45] lately Kings Advocate & many more are keen on Fox's side.[46] Jamie Boswell[47] has deserted them & joined the Adressers[48] both at York & Airshire with great eagerness I see. The Monthly Reviewers think him a man of ten times more figure & consequence in his own

---

Dissenter and Arian, Samuel Bourn (1689–1754), edited by his son, Samuel Bourn (1714–96), who was also an English Dissenting minister, educated at Glasgow under Francis Hutcheson and John Simson. He professed to teach only doctrines found in the New Testament, and in 1754 he became the colleague in Norwich of Rev. John Taylor, the influential Arian and correspondent of William Leechman. In Letter 45 Wodrow had declared: 'I dont reckon Roussau a Deist more than young Bourn & many more of the most freethinking Dissenters in England.'

[42] Follows the main text of Letter 79.

[43] Parliament had been dissolved on 25 March 1784, after the minority government of William Pitt the Younger (Dec. 1783–March 1784) had reduced its losses in House of Commons votes to single figures and felt sufficiently confident to call a general election. Pitt (1759–1806) was rewarded with a majority of 120 in a full House. HPO.

[44] John Millar (1735–1801), professor of civil law at Glasgow.

[45] Henry Erskine (1746–1817), lawyer and Whig politician in Edinburgh, middle brother of David Steuart Erskine (1742–1829), eleventh earl of Buchan, and Thomas Erskine (1750–1823). Popular and witty, he was Lord Advocate, Scotland's most senior law officer, from Aug.–Dec. 1783 during the Fox–North coalition, and Dean of the Faculty of Advocates from 1785 to 1796. He was ousted from the latter position in Jan. 1796 because of his membership of the Foxite Whig connection, his support for the peace petition of 1795, and his opposition to the 'Two Acts' of Dec. 1795, the Treasonable and Seditious Practices Act and the Seditious Meetings Act. He and Millar were hardly republicans, but they were supporters of Charles James Fox rather than William Pitt.

[46] Charles James Fox (1749–1806), Whig politician, co-leader of the Coalition government of Apr.–Dec. 1783 with Frederick, Lord North. The connection was defeated resoundingly in the election of 1784.

[47] James Boswell (1740–95), eldest son of Alexander Boswell (1706–82) and lawyer, diarist, and friend of Samuel Johnson. He wrote his *Letter to the People of Scotland: On the Present State of the Nation* (Edinburgh, 1783) in opposition to Fox's East India Bill, and he presented a loyal address for signature in Ayrshire in spring 1784. By then he had become a magistrate and president of the quarter sessions in Ayrshire, and he attempted to stand for election in May 1784 in the Earl of Eglinton's interest, but Eglinton continued to support the incumbent Sir Adam Fergusson.

[48] The supporters of Pitt at Yorkshire, led by Christopher Wyvill and the majority of the Yorkshire Association, proposed an address in Pitt's support on 25 March 1784, criticizing Fox's East India Bill of December 1783 and justifying King George III's ejection of the Fox–North ministry. Its success caused a major split among the members of the Association. John Brooke, 'Yorkshire', HPO.

Country than he realy is.[49] He figures only in our newspapers & uses every art in his power to make himself talked of. He has some Abilities not high an honest heart & is a warm friend to Liberty but has a little roughness & a bee in his Bonnet of a different kind from D[r]. Priestlys. I am in real hopes that the Westminster Poll will go against Fox– it will be a high Triumph to see some of the Chief of the Coalition Leaders thrown out of their seats altogether. Yet I suppose Burroughs will be bought for them. In this Country the <u>Elections will go</u> against the Coalition yet not so much as in <u>England. Crawford will lose the</u> Glasgow Burroughs[50] & the Kings Advocate Ilay Campbell carry them.[51] Andrew Stuart will also lose Lanarkshire & probably Cap[t]. Mure of Caldwell be ellected.[52] The Duke of Hamilton[53] for two months past has <-> taken a sort of lead in his Country & discovered more ability & spirit than we thought him capable of. The Marquis of Graham[54] M[r]. Pit's friend <-> in point of Ability integrity sobriety & love of his Country the most promising young Nobleman in Scotland——Sir Adam Fergusson[55] will probably lose

---

[49] We have not located this comment in the *Monthly Review*. There was a favourable review in the *Critical Review*, 57 (1784), p. 74; see also below, Letter 102, on the reception of Boswell's 1785 *Letter to the People of Scotland*.

[50] JW predicted this accurately. The seat was won by Ilay Campbell, but it was seized back by John 'Fish' Craufurd in February 1790 on the recommendation of John Campbell, fifth duke of Argyll. John Craufurd (c. 1742–1814) of Auchenames, MP for Old Sarum (1768–74); Renfrewshire (1774–80); Glasgow Burghs (1780–84); Glasgow Burghs (1790). A supporter of Charles James Fox, he was defeated in the 1784 election by Ilay Campbell, who had been sponsored by Henry Dundas. Following Campbell's appointment as lord president of the court of session, Craufurd was re-elected, only to lose the seat in the general election of 1790 some four months later. HPO.

[51] Sir Ilay Campbell (1734–1823), of Succoth, Argyll. A clever and eloquent lawyer, and Lord Advocate, Scotland's most senior law officer (1784–89), he represented the Glasgow Burghs from 1784 to Oct. 1789, after which he became president of the Court of Session on the recommendation of Henry Dundas, holding that position until 1808 when the Court of Session was reformed, splitting it into two divisions. HPO.

[52] Andrew Stuart (1725–1801), lawyer and politician, did lose the county of Lanarkshire, but he was beaten by Sir James Steuart Denham (1744–1839) rather than William Mure of Caldwell. HPO. Mure (d. 1831), son of William Mure of Caldwell (1718–76) whose tutor William Leechman had been, served as captain of the eighty-second regiment during the American War, and was present at the battle of Yorktown. He served as Rector of Glasgow University in 1793–94, and commanded militia regiments during the French Revolutionary Wars. William Mure, ed., *Selections from the Family Papers Preserved at Caldwell*, 2 vols (Glasgow, 1854), I, p. 45.

[53] Archibald Douglas-Hamilton (1740–1819), ninth duke of Hamilton. HPO.

[54] James Graham (1755–1836), marquess of Graham, and from 1790 third duke of Montrose. He had been appointed a Lord of the Treasury in Pitt's first, short administration, and in May 1784 was elected for the English constituency of Great Bedwyn, Wiltshire, a constituency in the gift of Lord Ailesbury, uncle of the duke of Buccleuch. HPO.

[55] Sir Adam Fergusson of Kilkerran (1733–1813), MP for the county of Ayrshire (1774–80, 1781–84, 1790–96) and for Edinburgh (1784–90). He was re-elected in 1781 against Hugh Montgomerie of Coilsfield, but at the general election of 1784 their supporters negotiated a settlement with

this county tho' he has got their thanks for his late conduct yet it is likely that Col. Montgomery who will succeed him[56] must take the same side & give some security of his being friendly to the Scheme of a Reform in Parliament. I hope Sir Adam will get in some how as he is a man of Ability & real worth. Dempster[57] will keep his seat & ought to do it for he is an honest man. I must conclude as I do not intend either to begin a new sheet or encroach on the Cover in case our blundering Postmasters shoud mark Postage & oblige you to send it so with my Love to you & yours I ever remain

your friend J$^s$. Wodrow

More upon reading over your Letter

I shoud like to see the Jew's book[58] which you speak of as I wish to hear the sentiments of every body who thinks for himself. We are accustomed to think X$^{ty}$. very imperfectly revealed in the O.T. Had it been otherwise the Jews woud have understood it better at the beginning. I do not recollect the conversation you mention to have passed in your room. My Difficulties about the first two Chap$^s$. of Math$^w$. woud probably arise from the number of Citations which they contain from the O.T. & the application of them rather than the single point you mention.

---

Henry Dundas allowing Montgomerie to represent Ayrshire in return for Fergusson to represent a safe seat (Edinburgh) and to return to represent Ayrshire in 1790. He was a friend of Dundas, whom he generally supported in Parliament, but also a close friend of the independent MP George Dempster. The eldest son of the judge Sir James Fergusson, Lord Kilkerran (c. 1688–1759), and brother of the judge George Fergusson, Lord Hermand (1743–1827), he too had been trained as a lawyer, and had been applauded for his abilities as an advocate for the Hamiltons in the Douglas case (1761–67). He also acted on behalf of the Countess of Sutherland (see Letter 84), who was his ward. He was a keen agricultural improver. *HPO; LBS*; see also Alex Renton, *Blood Legacy: Reckoning with a Family's Story of Slavery* (Edinburgh, 2021), *passim*; Eric J. Graham, *Burns and the Sugar Plantocracy of Ayrshire* (Edinburgh, 2014), pp. 28–29.

[56] Another accurate prediction, and Col. Hugh Montgomerie (1739–1819) of Coilsfield and Skelmorlie was indeed, like Fergusson (1733–1813), a Pittite. Hugh Montgomerie (1739–1819) was MP for Ayrshire (1780–81, 1784–89, and 1796), twelfth earl of Eglinton from 1796, and first baron Ardrossan from 1806. He served in the American War as captain of the seventy-eighth Highlanders and as captain of the first Royals. *HPO; W-K*, I, p. 435n; *ODNB*; Strawhorn, ed., *Ayrshire at the Time of Burns*, p. 292; Graham, *Burns and the Sugar Plantocracy of Ayrshire*, pp. 29, 30, 46, 90.

[57] George Dempster of Dunnichen (1732–1818) held the Forfar burghs continuously from 1761–90 except between 1768 and 1769. *HPO*.

[58] There is no reference to a 'Jew's book' in the previous surviving letters—so there may be a missing SK letter from June–Sept. 1783. This possibly refers to the recently published David Levi, *A Succinct Account of the Rites and Ceremonies of the Jews* (1782). A self-educated tradesman, Levi became an influential defender and expositor of Judaism in late eighteenth-century Britain. See Richard H. Popkin, 'David Levi, Anglo-Jewish Theologian', *The Jewish Quarterly Review*, 87 (1996), pp. 79–101.

I have a <book> ^Pamplet^ of Evansons about the Revelation (which I sent for from London when Lecturing on that deep book) against Bishop Hurd.[59] He gives the Bishop some deep thrusts has the better of him in my ^view^ in <giving> more liberal views of & and more accurate of the sense of the prophecy & yet in other points is very fanciful as ^such as^ the application of <-> it to the Athanasian Heresy.[60] I like however such conscientious & thinking Men as he is whether I enter into their views or not.[61] He rejects not only the first two chap$^{rs}$. but the whole Gospel of Mathew by the Lump on account of it's contradiction (as he thinks) <with> ^to^ the other Gospels in the circumstances of our Saviours resurection. I wonder the single point of the Miraculous conception shoud in the least startle M$^r$. Ev$^n$. the Jew, D$^r$. Priestly or any other man who admits the reality of Our Sav$^{rs}$. Miracles many of which were surely more miraculous so to speak than ^that^ single fact. But perhaps they have other reasons. Yet I once met with a Gentleman a believer in X$^{ty}$. who expressed his doubts to me in conversation on that single point alone. <He was> ^I thought it^ a curious Phænomenon as it was purely the Effect of his own thinking he having read nothing on the subject or on any other part of the Evidence of X$^{ty}$.

yours JW——

The Principal[62] has been very well in the Main this severe Winter. I cannot say spring for we had none yet even on this warm shore. I have been just now reading

---

[59] Edward Evanson, *A Letter to the Right Reverend the Lord Bishop of Litchfield and Coventry [Richard Hurd]; wherein the Importance of the Prophecies of the New Testament, and the Nature of the Grand Apostacy Predicted in Them, are Particularly and Impartially Considered* (1777). Richard Hurd (1720–1808) was bishop of Worcester (1781–1808), declining elevation to the archdiocese of Canterbury in 1783.

[60] Athanasius of Alexandria (c. 298–373) was a champion of the orthodox doctrine of the Trinity and leading opponent of Arians at the time of the Council of Nicaea. JW is being sarcastic in referring to the 'Athanasian Heresy', as Athanasius keenly attacked Arianism as heretical, and the Athanasian Creed became orthodox Christian doctrine. This phrase does not appear in the unitarian Evanson's book, though he did refer to the Athanasian Creed as 'this fatal contagion of Antichristian superstition' (p. 57). In a similar vein, John Goldie described the doctrine of original sin as 'this arch-heresy' in *Essays on Various Important Subjects, Moral and Divine. Moral and Divine. Being an Attempt to Distinguish True from False Religion* (Glasgow, 1779), p. 144.

[61] Rev. Edward Evanson (1731–1805), vicar of South Mimms (1766–69), Tewkesbury (1769–78), and Longdon (1770–78), Worcestershire. He held unitarian views. Although the defeat of the Feathers Tavern Petition (1771–74) ended the prospect of church reform, Evanson did not give up hope. The publication of his heterodox theology, however, only led to an attempt to prosecute him in the church courts, which failed on a technicality. Faced with an impossible situation, he resigned from the church in 1778. He thereafter established and taught at his school in Mitcham.

[62] Rev. William Leechman (1706–85), professor of divinity and principal of Glasgow University. JW later wrote a memoir of the life and teachings of his mentor for his two-volume edition of Leechman's sermons (1789). See W-K, I, *passim.*, for Leechman's significant influence on SK and JW.

Mason's English Garden.[63] Tho' one of the best Didactic Poems in the English ^Language^ & some fine pathetick touches in the fourth book, yet it appears to me ^too much^ loaded & embarassed with the affectation of Poetical Language & imagery. It does not suit my tast like Hayley's[64] clear elegant Classical Simplicity. The last I still think the superiour Poet & more fit for the Execution of the great design of an English Heroic Poem to which he endeavours to animate the Other.

## Letter 80: Samuel Kenrick to James Wodrow, 2 June 1784
Place: Bewdley
Addressed: The Rev$^d$. James Wodrow / near / Irvine
Note: 1785[1]

Dear Sir

I have so long delayed acknowledging your kind favour of 15th. of April, partly thro' my old increasing habit of procrastination, & indolence, but still more, by waiting for my daughter's setting out to see her native country– w$^{ch}$. she has been long projecting, & has at last fixed the time to a few days hence.[2] As she is resolved to see you, & your family if she can, before she returns, I must not miss that opportunity of saying something to you, whatever I may send by post afterwards.

I remember very well, when I finished my last, I broke it off abruptly,[3] w$^{th}$., as I thought, a fixt resolution, to write again in a post or two– & you see how it has turned out!–

---

[63] William Mason, *The English Garden: A Poem in Four Books* (1772–81). William Mason (1725–97), polymath, was a Cambridge graduate, ordained 1754, and appointed rector of Aston in the same year, an office which he held for the rest of his life to which he accumulated several other livings, holding five church offices in all. In 1768, a legacy on the death of his brother gave him independent means, enabling him to develop a range of interests: in garden design, music, political reform, and poetry. He was known for his satires, notably his *An Heroic Epistle to Sir William Chambers* (1773).

[64] William Hayley (1745–1820), poet and biographer. His *Triumphs of Temper: A Poem* (1781), advising women on how to attract and keep a husband, was a bestseller which ran through multiple editions. See *W-K*, I, p. 486n. For Kenrick's enthusiasm for him, see *W-K*, I, pp. 486–87.

[1] But the date 1784 is very clear at the head of the letter.
[2] Mary Kenrick (1754–1812).
[3] Kenrick's Letter 78 of 8 Oct. 1783, at the end of *W-K*, I, does not end particularly abruptly; this suggests there may be a missing letter in which he discussed 'the Jew's book', as noted near the end of Letter 79.

I cannot too often express to you, how happy your letters make me by their length & the variety of the matter they contain, which is entirely suited to my wish & taste. The idea of your postmaster, w^ch. in some measure abridgd your last, was not without foundation. For tho' it was folded ^in^ our representative's pass-port, he had the audacity to charge it 2/4– of w^ch. I did not pay one farth^g. because I looked upon it as an affront to our member.[4]

The prudent & frugal manner in w^ch. you provide for your poor has long been the favourite topic of my eloquence among my townsfolks here. It appears to them so extraordinary that I believe there is hardly one in ten of them that believes a word of it. For honest John Bull is very hard of belief, in whatever represents any part of the universe as in any respect superior ^to himself &^ to the spot where he dwells.

But the truth is that the poor here must always be poor, while they live in towns & villages, w^ch. are every where overstocked w^th. public houses.[5] Here they spend in an hour more than they can earn in a day; the longer they indulge they are the more unwilling to quit the enchanted ground; knowing that when the worst comes to the worst, the parish must at last support them & their families. Nor does a sense of decency restrain the weaker sex, in the lower walks of life, from partaking in the same excess. What inevitable ruin & wretchedness must ensue?– Here you have in general a great advantage over us. Your common liquor is not so strong, nor expensive: & drunkenness is rare & therefore disgraceful. For my part I hardly remember to have seen a drunken man among the common people in Scotland– nor ever to hear that riotous noise that is so common to our

---

[4] i.e. SK's MP: William Henry Lyttelton (1724–1808) of Hagley Hall, Worcestershire. Previously governor of South Carolina (1756–60) and Jamaica (1760–66), and ambassador to Portugal (1767–70), he represented the parliamentary borough of Bewdley, Worcestershire in 1748–55 and 1774–90. He was created Baron Westcote in 1776, and Baron Lyttelton in 1794, having succeeded his nephew Thomas, son of Lord Lyttelton (about whom JW had quizzed SK in 1774), both to the baronetcy and to the constituency of Bewdley. JW's letter had been franked, and therefore SK should not have had to pay postage.

[5] SK is expressing commonly held opinions amongst the Dissenting community, who to varying degrees had a 'puritan' disapproval of pubs. Carys Brown, *Friends, Neighbours, Sinners: Religious Difference and English Society, 1689–1750* (Cambridge, 2022), pp. 162–70. See also, for example, Richard Price, 25 July 1787, *The Correspondence of Richard Price*, eds D. O. Thomas and W. Bernard Peach, 3 vols (Durham, NC, 1983–94), III, p. 138. Kenneth Hobson has noted that 'As late as 1854 there were 87 licensed houses of one kind or another in Bewdley (excluding Wribbenhall). That is, roughly, one pub for every 42 persons…of the population'. See 'Every other house…Bewdley Inns', in Lawrence S. Snell, ed., *Essays towards the History of Bewdley* (Bewdley, 1972), pp. 115–22, at pp. 115–16.

pot-houses.[6] In manufacturing towns, even in proportion to their flourishing, I know it is otherwise w^th. you as well as with us. And consequently the poor & wretched are much more numerous in those places. Witness 2 manufacturing towns in this neighbourhood, Kidderminster & Birm^m. The poor's levy or rate in the latter is not less than £12,000 ⅌ ann.– & yet I suppose it is without exception the most busy industrious thriving spot in the world. Is this not a strong presumption, if not an infallible proof, that the happiness of mankind is not really promoted by the sedentary arts however ingenious & profitable to individuals & to the state in general?– For poverty ever follows close at the heels of this sort of riches. In a trading nation like Holland, there is hardly any appearance of poverty, as frugality is thoroughly established among the lower class of people. But in the most flourishing cantons of Switzerland, where none but the useful arts of agriculture are cultivated– there alone you see man in his natural happy state, enjoying health, competence & freedom.– You must manage well indeed, to support with £80 per ann. the poor of so numerous a parish as yours is. It would require near 10 times that sum here– the objects of it very wretched after all. At Glasgow & Paisley I should imagine the poor must multiply as they do here. ~~But~~ For as trade & manufactures increase, this evil will accompany them. A particular friend of mine is concerned in an Iron work,– ab^t. 35 miles north east of Glasgow. He has sent thither 5 or 6 work men out of Shropshire to carry it on, who can get from 20/to 30/per week– & they can get men to work there ^~~work there~~ under them^ for 5/or 6/per week. And this sav^g. is his great inducement to settle it in that country. But he now finds that his Shropshire men, not satisfied w^th. their high wages, must have english ale to drink, or they can't live. To obviate this difficulty he is obliged to send a Shropshire woman after them to brew their ale. Unless she can meet w^th. good stout hops, I suppose this ale of hers won't please them. And after all, to an unvitiated stomach what a nauseous beverage is this same ale? Your brisk sparkling twopenny is much more palatable; but your fine strong ale, which you drink in every private house in Scotland, is burgundy when compared to it. And yet the distant prospect of swallowing this mummy stuff gives force & elasticity to the brawny arms of the forge man, patience & perseverance to the fatigued labourer & new vigour to every human exertion in the more ingenious

---

[6] Drinking patterns had changed in the decades after SK left Scotland. The Presbyterian ministers who contributed to the *Statistical Account* in the 1790s criticized the growth of whisky drinking and drunkenness in Scotland. Anthony Cooke, *A History of Drinking: The Scottish Pub since 1700* (Edinburgh, 2015), p. 1.

arts. But when it foarms[7] upon the table amidst the social circle, what joy sparkles in every eye! At this period one would be ready to say that every tippling house was a temple dedicated to mirth & good humour– & that all who frequent such places were real philosophers, who had triumphed over all the vain cares & anxieties of this transitory mortal life.–

I am grieved as well as astonished at what you say about your clergy & the increase of dissenters among you. Not but that I am persuaded, that all these little dissentions, by appointment of an all wise & good Providence, will in due course of time produce the best effects:– but to think that the disciples of a Hutcheson[8] & Leechman[9] should degenerate so soon:– when 40 years ^ago^ they seemed eagerly to imbibe the most liberal sentiments in philosophy & in religion, at the fountainhead, w$^{ch}$. I expected long 'ere now, would have enriched w$^{th}$. its streams the most distant corners of the country.

I cannot however help thinking that to an enlightened & conscientious people– if such is to be found– patronage is a grievance: & contrary to the equal simplicity of our form of religion. But in the established church here, there is not the least murmur about ^it^, whether bishop or college or my Lord such a one, a hundred miles off, presents: or whether the person who is presented, officiate or reside in the parish or not– tho' they are to pay their tythes, easter-dues &c to him– they never troubled their heads. All they expect, is one to mount the desk & pulpit, once at least every Sunday, to bring them together to church: but whether he is sound & Orthodox or not, is never so much as imagined. Now your good folks are all criticks & can soon spy whether the preacher has the true unction & call to his office.

A propos– of Hutcheson, whom I have just mentioned– I find very honourable mention made of him in the illustrious Thomas Hollis' memoirs[10]– that most enthusiastic friend of liberty– where there is a good print of a well executed medallion, bearing a most striking resemblance, to that most excellent man's

---

[7] This appears to be an instance of Kenrick using a West Country accent: 'foarms' meaning 'foams'.

[8] Francis Hutcheson (1694–1746), professor of moral philosophy at Glasgow.

[9] William Leechman. See Letter 79.

[10] Francis Blackburne, *Memoirs of Thomas Hollis*, 2 vols (1780), II, p. 833. Thomas Hollis (1720–74) was a major publicist for radical politics in the mid-century, notable for his anti-Catholicism. See Caroline Robbins, *The Eighteenth-Century Commonwealthman: Studies in the Transition, Development, and Circumstance of English Liberal Thought from the Restoration of Charles II until the War with the Thirteen Colonies* (Cambridge, MA, 1959), pp. 257–62.

countenance, done at the expense of his honourable disciple L^d. Selkirk[11], w^th. his character verbatim, as drawn by D^r. Leechman for the Glasgow Paper– w^ch. I have by me copied in one of my memorial books of that time. This you may be sure gave me no small degree of pleasure– w^ch. was not lessened by finding a small niche, in that splendid monument ^in honour^ of the lovers of Freedom, appropriated to the memory of poor Rich^d. Barron[12] alias Norrab, who was well known at Glasgow 5 or 6 years before our time. Fortune seems to have frowned upon him to the last. But he found a most generous patron in M^r. Hollis– their principles were so much a-kin– joined to their bold enterprizing spirit.– that if Barron had been as steady & industrious as he was warm & zealous, he would have stood in need of no other protector. In short this M^r. Hollis was one of the greatest ornaments of this age & nation– whose beneficence was on the largest scale– it was extensive as it was disinterested.

I am exceedingly obliged to you for your usual frankness, in acquainting me w^th. your sentiments on theological subjects. Your generous sentiments with regard to D^r. Priestley & the harsh treatment he & his vindicator, our old friend Cappe,[13] has met with from the Reviewer– for he turns out to be only one, & that an intimate old crony & quondam extravagant admirer of the Doctor's– please me. To clear up this matter to you, I shall send you along with this, the D^r.'s answer to this same Reviewer by name.[14] In the last Review for May, they notice this pamphlet, & treat w^th. great disdain indeed– without denying the fact–but

---

[11] Dunbar Hamilton Douglas, fourth earl of Selkirk (1722–90). One side of the medal is a bust of Hutcheson based on a portrait by Allan Ramsay the younger, the other symbolizes the ascent of his soul or spirit. W. H. Bond, *Thomas Hollis of Lincoln's Inn: A Whig and His Books* (Cambridge, 1990), p. 70; Robbins, *Eighteenth-Century Commonwealthman*, p. 186.

[12] Blackburne, *Memoirs of Thomas Hollis*, II, pp. 573–86. Richard Baron (d. 1768), a Dissenter educated at Glasgow University (1737–40), became an energetic member of the circle of Thomas Hollis, sharing his anti-clerical views, exemplified in his *Pillars of Priestcraft and Orthodoxy Shaken* (1752, 2nd edn 1768). Hollis also published Baron's two-volume edition of Milton's *Prose Works* (1753–56). ODNB; G. M. Ditchfield, 'The Changing Nature of English Anticlericalism, c. 1750–c. 1800', in Nigel Aston and Matthew Cragoe, eds, *Anticlericalism in Britain c. 1500–1914* (Stroud, 2000), p. 90; see also Bond, *Thomas Hollis of Lincoln's Inn*.

[13] Newcome Cappe. See Letter 79.

[14] In the *Monthly Review*, 70 (January 1784), pp. 56–69, Samuel Badcock authored the anonymous review of Joseph Priestley's *Letters to Dr Horsley, in Answer to His Animadversions on the History of the Corruptions of Christianity: With Additional Evidence, that the Primitive Christian Church was Unitarian* (1783). Priestley responded to its 'gross ignorance, and evident malignity' by publishing *Remarks on the Monthly Review of the Letters to Dr. Horsley; In which the Rev. Mr. Samuel Badcock, the Writer of that Review, is Called upon to Defend what He has Advanced in It* (Birmingham, 1784), p. iii. Priestley felt justified by 'the almost unexampled insolence of the attack, in mentioning (what indeed is no secret) the name of the Reviewer' (p. 8).

only saying that the gentleman in question had no hand in the present article.[15] This M[r]. Badcock[16] is a dissenting minister & an Arian– two characters w[ch]. will never be relished by D[r]. Horsley[17] & the other Athenasian[18] dignitaries of our church, who have entered the lists w[th]. D[r]. Priestley: for as they are fond of forcing D[r]. Priestley whether he will or no into the company of Toland[19] the infidel, of Dan[l]. Zwicker,[20] the Socinian (whose Book it seems is not to be found in England–[21] nay now it appears that D[r]. Horsley never saw it– but found his name

---

[15] *Monthly Review*, 70 (May 1784), p. 399, observed an 'inviolable silence' regarding the name of the reviewer, and dismissed Priestley's *Remarks* as 'unimportant' and 'unwarranted'.

[16] Samuel Badcock. See Letter 79.

[17] Rev. Samuel Horsley (1733–1806), archdeacon of St Albans, bishop successively of St Davids (1788–93), and Rochester (1793–1802), concurrently with the Deanery of Westminster, and St Asaph (1802–06). An able scientist, elected a Fellow of the Royal Society in 1767, he first engaged Priestley in controversy over his metaphysics and subsequently in a heated dispute occasioned by Priestley's *An History of the Corruptions of Christianity* (1782). A passionate critic of the Dissenters' campaign for universal toleration, he was rewarded by government for his loyal support. He was also a first cousin of JW's wife Louisa (*née* Hamilton).

[18] The Athanasian Creed was a strong statement of orthodox Trinitarian Christian doctrine.

[19] John Toland (1670–1722), Irish philosopher and freethinker. Educated at Glasgow (1689) and Edinburgh (1690) Universities, and subsequently at Leiden and Utrecht. Notable for his *Christianity not Mysterious* (1695). His thesis that 'there is nothing in the Gospel contrary to reason, nor above it... And that no Christian Doctrine can be properly called a Mystery' was cited by Priestley in his *A General History of the Christian Church* (Northumberland, PA, 1802). He went on to note that Toland's ideas on authority of the Canon of Scripture had been 'abundantly refuted by many learned Christians'. *Works of Joseph Priestley*, X, p. 510.

[20] Daniel Zwicker (1612–78), born in Gdansk (Danzig), son of a Lutheran pastor. Educated at the Universities of Könisberg and Leiden, it appears that he practised as a physician in Gdansk. A controversial Socinian theologian and advocate of the community of goods, he proved to be a stormy petrel amongst the Polish brethren. Expelled from Gdansk, he eventually settled in Amsterdam in 1657, where he developed ideas for Christian reconciliation and his own utopian version of Christianity, and no longer associated himself with the Socinians. *Works of Joseph Priestley*, VI, p. 10; XVIII, p. 116; XIX, pp. 18–20; Stanislas Kot, *Socinianism in Poland: The Social and Political Ideas of the Polish Antitrinitarians in the Sixteenth and Seventeenth Centuries*, trans. Earl Morse Wilbur (Boston, MA, 1957). The most complete study of Zwicker's life and thought is Peter G. Pietenholz, *Daniel Zwicker 1612–1678: Peace, Tolerance and God—The One and Only* (Florence, 1998). See also his 'Daniel Zwicker's Views on Religious Peace and Unity', in C. Berkens-Stevenlinck, J. Israel, and G. H. Posthumus Meyjes, *The Emergence of Tolerance in the Dutch Republic* (Leiden, 1997), pp. 117–30.

[21] In his *Letters to Dr Horsley, in Answer to His Animadversions on the History of the Corruptions of Christianity: With Additional Evidence, that the Primitive Christian Church was Unitarian* (1783) and *An History of Early Opinions Concerning Jesus Christ* (Birmingham, 1786), Priestley denied Horsley's charge of borrowing from Zwicker, claiming that he only knew of Zwicker's work through his controversy with Bishop George Bull. He eventually devoted a separate *Letter to Horsley*, in which he distanced himself from Zwicker's views. *Works of Joseph Priestley*, VI, p. 10; XVIII, p. 116; XIX, pp. 18–20; Kot, *Socinianism in Poland*, pp. 157–63, 201. Piettenholz, *Daniel Zwicker 1612–1678*, pp. 110–14.

in B[p]. Bull[22]) of Huetius[23] the <u>papist</u>, Petavius[24] the <u>Jesuit</u>— nay they not only force him into the company of these learned men, but to deprecate his writings, will take it for granted that he borrowed his arguments from them— as fond I say as they are of this, they will ^be^ equally mortified to owe any assistance, in mawling the poor doctor, to the despicable harranguer of a conventicle & an impious Arian. When you see D[r]. Horsley's attack, you will be more sensible of this. The reviewers are too partial in the cause to give you any thing like a just idea of this supercilious champion. But he has fallen into good hands: & if he is true to his cause, he must expect to fight a long & tough battle w[th]. our spirited Doctor. For as he observes, "in a controversy so various & extensive as this will probably be, it must not be imagined that the question is absolutely decided, when any particular advantage is gained on either side. All men are liable to oversights; but a judicious reader will consider the extent & consequence of an oversight, & particularly whether it affects the question itself or the writer only".— He adds— "If you should think I have overlooked any thing material, & please to point it out to me, I will answer it as explicitly as I can, for I hope that this will only be the beginning of our correspondence on the subject, as I w[d]. gladly discuss it w[th]. you in the fullest manner".[25] What can be fairer or more handsome & this way of handling subject?— is not truth, the eternal truth of God, the sole object in view? But you do the D[r]. ample justice yourself, in the very elegant & handsome encomium you have paid him—therefore it were superfluous in me to add to it. Only you add that he has <u>a Bee in his bonnet</u>. Now tho' I cannot help laughing at this expression every time it comes a-cross me— yet I am not able fully to satisfy myself as to its precise meaning. The general meaning I take to be Something odd, outré, w[ch]. goes out of the common jog trot of life; & in this view it rather respects conduct & behaviour, than a mode of thinking & reasoning. This I take to be the patriotic Boswell's[26]

---

[22] Rev. George Bull (1634–1710), bishop of St David's (1705–10). His Latin works, edited by John Grabe, included his final work, a refutation of Zwicker's Unitarianism: *The Primitive and Apostolical Tradition of the Doctrine Received in the Catholic Church, Concerning the Divinity of our Saviour Jesus Christ* (1703).

[23] Pierre-Daniel Huet (Huetius) (1630–1721), French scholar and ecclesiastic, elected to the French Academy in 1674. Priestley refers to Huetius in his *Institutes of Natural and Revealed Religion*, 3 vols (1772–74) in which he discusses the prophecy of Ezekiel, during the time of the Babylonian captivity. *Works of Joseph Priestley*, II, p. 176; *Catholic Encyclopedia*.

[24] Denis Pétau (Dionysius Petavius) (1583–1652), French Jesuit philosopher and theologian of distinction. A prolific publicist for the Catholic faith. *Catholic Encyclopedia*.

[25] Joseph Priestley, *Letters to Dr Horsley, in Answer to His Animadversions on the History of the Corruptions of Christianity* (Birmingham, 1783), pp. xix, 109.

[26] James Boswell (1740–95). See Letter 79.

Bee– which you say is different from D[r]. Priestley's. For I take the former to be what he was when I knew him a youth of 17 or 18– vain & forward, w[th]. the best intentions: courting the applause of all around him, by some smart saying, genteel compliment, or generous proposal. You are right in supposing that the latter has nothing of this in his composition. I have not yet had the pleasure of seeing him[27]– but his friends all assure me that he is a man of the most unaffected simplicity in his demeanour & conversation. He most studiously avoids every disputable subject, whether in politics, religion, or philosophy. And if it were not for the distant respect, w[ch]. must unavoidably be paid him, by the company who know him, a stranger would be apt to take him for a person of little consequence. Had you not said that you <u>admired him for the soundness of his judgement–</u> I should take this be to be a certain want of judgement & prudence, w[ch]. you charge him w[th]. in some things– w[ch]. you add hurts the influence & usefulness &c it is true if he exposes folly, detects error & unmasks hypocrisy with a steady determined hand– he must infallibly incur unrelenting fury of fools knaves & hypocrites: & so has every reformer from the days of Socrates[28] to our time. But tho' he may offend many, it is to be presumed, he gives pleasure to many more; & that by means of his & other such free writings, the world will be enlightened– "it is happy, says he, for the cause of truth, as well as other valuable purposes, that man is mortal; & that while the species continues, the individuals go off the stage. For otherwise the whole species would soon arrive at its <u>maximum</u> in all improvements, as individuals now do."[29] With numberless such individuals vying with each other in the cause of truth & virtue, throughout Europe & the enlightened states of North America, what a glorious prospect, does it open before us.

But I hope to be able to send you his history & some of the principal of his opposers, with his answers, which to a mind like yours, so full of candour & open to conviction must I am persuaded ~~must~~ afford the most exquisite pleasure.

I wish as well as you (be it from a Bee or wasp to rouze them) that John Fleming[30] or Gilbert Lang[31]– or any such, w[th]. w[ch]. your Kirk abounds– would now step forth & strike out something decisive in this important controversy. What excellent materials must be found among the papers of our great master

---

[27] See Letter 81 for an account of SK's first meeting with Joseph Priestley in mid-1784.
[28] Socrates (d. 399 BC), Greek moral philosopher.
[29] Priestley, *Letters to Dr Horsley* (1783), p. iv.
[30] John Fleming. See Letter 79.
[31] Gilbert Lang. See Letter 79.

the judicious Leechman. These may probably some day come into your hands– & overcome your invincible modesty w^ch. tho' it makes you withhold your own, may giveaway to usher into the world, the important writings of that truly apostolic divine.

But you will be angry, if I leave you with out a little smack of politics– especially when I assure you that my sentiments now exactly accord w^th. yours & those of my other good friends with you. At the same time I must give you credit, for your hesitation in Determining this point, for I have left many of my quondam ^warm^ American friends in the minority w^th. Master Fox[32] & his cara sposa[33] Lord North[34]. This last old veteran in iniquity would never have joined Fox– if he could have accommodated matters w^th. Pitt[35]: but this young hero declared positively that he never would sit in the cabinet, w^th. the man who had brought this nation to the brink of the ruin, had lost America &c. But Fox it seems & Burke,[36] & many more of my old friends were not squeamish. And behold they are all left in the lurch– there I hope long to continue.

The King[37] was never so popular since he ascended the throne– nor never appeared more cheerful & satisfied– he has now his natural & true friends the good old Whigs to support him. And what gives him & still more his worthy Queen[38] the greatest uneasiness, still adds more disgrace to this disappointed desperate party, is their seducing young Hopeful the heir apparent[39] to patronize them, & raise an opposition to his father. Nothing can exceed the bad policy of such a step, for it cannot be attended w^th. any possible advantage to him or them. Then how shocking must it ^be^ to their Majesties, who had ever lived in a most exemplary manner, in this debauched age, for decency & regularity– in one word

---

[32] Charles James Fox. See Letter 79.

[33] SK's ironic use of the Italian for 'Dear wife' as a reflection on the unnatural coalition of political opponents, the Fox–North coalition. Formed on the downfall of the Shelburne ministry in 1783, it lasted less than a year. W-K, I, p. 76.

[34] Frederick North (1732–92), second earl of Guildford, prime minister (1770–82).

[35] Pitt the Younger had come to power with the support of George III at the end of 1783. Not expected to last the winter, Pitt called an election after only three months in office. He was returned with a majority of 120 MPs and remained in power for the next seventeen years.

[36] Edmund Burke (1730–97), Whig politician and political philosopher.

[37] King George III (1738–1820; r. 1760–1820).

[38] Queen Charlotte (1744–1818), née Princess Charlotte of Mecklenburg-Strelitz (m. 1761).

[39] George, Prince of Wales (1762–1830; r. as Prince Regent, 1810–20 and as King George IV, 1820–30). Hanoverian Princes of Wales regularly aligned themselves with the political opposition in Parliament during the lengthy reigns of their predecessors.

for matrimonial & domestic happiness:– to see their eldest son, who is probably to succeed them in the same high station, disgracing himself in the lower debaucheries, & ruining his constitution of mind & body, before they are arrived at their full growth?

It is generally imagined that our wishes will be gratified in seeing Fox ousted at Westminster– but how come your good folks all the way at John a Groat's house, to think of finding a hole for him.[40] If he has no property in the country, nor is free of the place,[41] I think he won't long represent that place. But his friend L$^d$. Surry[42] is ret$^d$. for 3 places– & will probably reserve one for his abandoned friend. I entirely agree w$^{th}$. you w$^{th}$. regard to the Marquis of Graham.[43] His noble speech on the qualifications & duties of a speaker, on the first opening of parliament does him great honour.– I know Crawfurd well. How a man of his want of consequence should represent Glasgow &c is astonish$^g$.[44] I remember Ilay Campbell[45] very well. I am very sorry Sir Adam Ferguson is turned out[46]– as he has abilities & virtues. Col. Montgomery I know too.[47]

Tho I am with difficulty brought to begin to write to you– yet there is no end of me when once well begun. I have been interrupted numberless times in the course of this letter– n'importe– I still return to the charge, the moment I have got rid of my interruption.

Our winter & spring have been much severer I imagine than yours. In the latter end of march I rode thro' snows, in Herefordshire Wales & Shropshire, tho' a flat country, in wreaths[48] 3 or 4 feet deep– & in Staffordshire to the eastward of these

---

[40] Fox was eventually returned for Westminster in the 1784 election, but only after a humiliating scrutiny of the result. Anticipating the possibility of defeat at Westminster, Fox arranged to be elected, three votes to two, and sat for the Tain burghs in northern Scotland (April 1784– March 1785). *HPO*.

[41] Meaning he had not been granted freedom of the borough.

[42] Charles Howard (1746–1815), earl of Surrey (1777–86), eleventh duke of Norfolk (1786–1815), MP for Carlisle (1780–86). He served as Lord of the Treasury in the Fox–North coalition. In the 1784 election he was returned for Carlisle, Arundel, and Hereford, and a candidate on his interest was elected for Gloucester. He succeeded as eleventh duke of Norfolk in 1786, and attended Theophilus Lindsey's Unitarian chapel in London. *HPO*.

[43] James Graham. See Letter 79.

[44] John Craufurd. See Letter 79.

[45] See Letter 79.

[46] See Letter 79.

[47] See Letter 79.

[48] 'wreath': 'A bank or drift of snow, a heaped-up snow-drift, prob. orig. an accumulation of swirls of snow'. *DSL*.

places, I met wth. snow above a month after, more than a foot deep– & everything else as winter like as usually in Jany. or Feby.

I entirely agree wth. you ab{t}. Mason[49]– who like Young[50] labours too hard to please, to please me.

But the sweet the elegant the enlightened Hayley is my favourite. I expect every moment his last publication, tragedies & comedies– of wch. we had an acct. in the April Review.[51] His Lord Russell must be excellent.[52] I have just recd. Professor Richardsons [n]ew Essays on Shakespeare– & Russian Anecdotes– & have just opened them.[53] I am glad to find he has dropped that ridiculous senseless title Esq– wch. your Scots Litterati are so fond of– your opinion of honest Evanson[54] pleases me– You guess right at the time & occasion of your remark alluded to– 'twas on Collins controversy on prophesy[55]– where Sykes's accommodation scheme[56]– & others where under consideration, wth. regard to those quotations in the beginning of Matthew without the most distant view of the other point. And

---

[49] William Mason. See Letter 79.

[50] Edward Young (c. 1683–1765), prolific poet, playwright, and satirist. Best known for his satires (1725–28), *Conjectures on Original Composition* (1759) and *The Complaints: Or, Night Thoughts on Life, Death and Immortality* (1742–46), which was translated into many languages.

[51] *Monthly Review*, 72 (1784), pp. 288–95.

[52] William Hayley, 'Lord Russel: A Tragedy, in Three Acts', in *Plays of Three Acts; Written for a Private Theatre* (1784), pp. 265–350.

[53] William Richardson (1743–1814), professor of humanity (Latin) at the University of Glasgow (1773–1814). SK had probably received Richardson's *Essays on Shakespeare's Dramatic Characters of Richard the Third, King Lear, and Timon of Athens* (1784), and his *Anecdotes of the Russian Empire; In a Series of Letters, Written, a Few Years Ago, from St. Petersburg* (1784). See W-K, I, p. 316n. SK's reference to Richardson's dropping the title 'Esq.' is to his *A Philosophical Analysis and Illustration of Some of Shakespeare's Remarkable Characters*, reissued by the London publisher John Murray in 1780 and in 1784, both of which recognized 'W. Richardson' as 'Esq.' on the title page, unlike its original edition in 1774 and unlike the two books SK had received. We are grateful to Richard B. Sher for this information.

[54] Edward Evanson. See Letter 79.

[55] Anthony Collins (1676–1729), philosopher and freethinker. Educated at Eton and King's College Cambridge, he was of independent means. The possessor of a magnificent library, he was able to pursue his philosophical and historical studies. In his most popular work, *A Discourse of Free-Thinking* (1713), he argued that 'Christianity has no solid foundation in the prophecies'. David Berman, 'Collins, Anthony (1676–1729)', *The Dictionary of Eighteenth-Century Philosophers*, I, pp. 222–6.

[56] Rev. Arthur Ashley Sykes (1684?–1756) clergyman, educated at Corpus Christi College, Cambridge. An energetic controversialist in the latitudinarian tradition, he defended Christianity against the scepticism of Anthony Collins. In his *Principles and Connexion of Natural and Revealed Religion* (1740) 'he denies that there is in Scripture any privileged access to moral truths not available to men by the exercise of reason'. David Oswald Thomas, 'Sykes, Arthur Ashley', in *The Dictionary of Eighteenth-Century Philosophers*, II, pp. 859–61.

now my dear friend I must release you w^th. my own & wife's[57] best regards– I hope Mary will have the pleasure of pay^g. hers in person.

Yours while<br>S. Kenrick.

## Letter 81: Samuel Kenrick to James Wodrow, 13 August 1784
Place: Bewdley
Addressed: Rev^d. M^r. Wodrow / Irvine / N. Britain
Postmarked: Bewdley
Franked: Free Westcote[1]

My dear friend

If it were any body else ~~than~~ ^but^ you, I should be afraid of humming you in this manner– But I know your honest benevolent soul so well– that I am sure it will not hurt you– Mary will let you know how desirous I have long been to be acquainted w^th. the gentleman w^th. the bee in his bonnet.– Last Wednesday the 11th inst. I had that pleasure. You must know I had picked up a curious little tract of Bertram the monk written in the end of the 8th or beginning of the 9th Century– de corpore & sanguine J.C.[2] in opposition to the doctrine of transubstantiation w^ch. you must have heard of. I sent it to the D^r.[3] who sent me a very friendly message ^back^ that he should be glad to see me. His first reception was introduced w^th. mention^g. that trifle: w^ch. he said was a curiosity. It was ab^t. 9 in the morn^g. He had been up from five. He was as lively & cheerful as some of our other friends w^d. be in an evening after the 3^d or 4th. glass. He is ab^t. the size of our late friend Andrews[4]– but rather lighter made. Walks very erect as he did, w^th.

---

[57] Elisabeth Kenrick, *née* Smith (c. 1726–1815), SK's wife. She grew up in Maybole, Ayrshire, and seems to have met SK when she was later living in Paisley. They married around 1754; Mary was born on 12 Oct. that year. W-K, I, pp. 19–20.

---

[1] William Henry Lyttelton, baron Westcote. See Letter 80.
[2] *The Book of Bertram, or, Rathram, Priest and Monk of Corbey, Concerning the Body and Blood of Jesus in the Sacrament* (Dublin, 1753). Authored by Ratramnus (d. c. 868), a monk in northern France, this tract argued against transubstantiation and was translated and published in many editions by Protestants since the sixteenth century. Justo L. Gonzalez, *A History of Christian Thought, Volume 2: From Augustine to the Eve of the Reformation* (Nashville, TN, 2010), pp. 119–23.
[3] This paragraph records SK's first meeting with Joseph Priestley.
[4] Rev. Robert Andrews (1723–66), presbyterian minister at Bridgnorth after 1755. He published *The Works of Virgil, Englished by Robert Andrews* (Birmingham, 1766). See W-K, I, p. 186n.

short steps & fast. He has dark lively eyes, & his countenance always sweetened w^th. a most benign smile: w^ch. you may remember Andrews had & his friend Cappe still more. In short nothing could be more prevenant[5] & easy than his whole demeanour. But ^I^ shall entertain you w^th. more of him when I have time– & am better acquainted w^th. him. I have only to say, that in mixed company he avoids every thing that is controversial. He mixes in conversation as a relaxation.

If Mary be n[ot now] w^th. you please forward the enclosed after reading them to her at [M^r. Bris]banes[6] Adams Court Glasgow.[7]

Our best respects to you & yours.<br>S.K.

## Letter 82: Samuel Kenrick to Mary Kenrick[1]
Addressed: Miss Kenrick / at Rob^t. Brisbane's of Milton Esq^r. / Glasgow
Stamp: 134 BEWDLEY
Note: Single Sheet

But[2] now I must leave my dear Mary,[3] to say a few words to my Good friend, who has been so kind to her– w^th. all his family.

Indeed my good friend you have been too good to this strolling daughter of ours– as you will yourself confess when I tell you that she is unwilling to leave your more than hospitable house, were it not for the pleasure she promises us & herself, in shewing England to Miss Wodrow,[4] & putting it in our power to make some return for the attention & kindness w^ch. you & yours have shewn her so affectionately. She has been more amused during her stay w^th. you than all the

---

[5] 'prévenant': 'obliging, polite'. OED.
[6] Robert Brisbane (d. 1807) of Milton, on the River Clyde, in the parish of Carluke, Lanarkshire. He was also a kinsman of SK and evidently had a residence at Adam's Court in Glasgow. See W-K, I, pp. 448n, 455; and Letter 84 below.
[7] Adam's Court was at the south-east corner of Argyle and Jamaica Streets, in what was then the western edge of Glasgow.

---

[1] This appears to be part of 'the enclosed' referred to at the end of Letter 81.
[2] Presumably there is a missing sheet which originally preceded this.
[3] This is written on the back of the cover sheet containing the address to Mary Kenrick. It appears that this letter contained one or more sheets written for Mary that have not been preserved.
[4] Helen ('Nell') Wodrow (c. 1763–95), JW's elder daughter.

time before. This I expected from the congeniality of her soul with you & your family: & the company you keep. The sea bathing you w[er]e so kind as recommend to her, must have added to it, by giving her new health & spirits. And the fine weather she has enjoyed ever since she has been w$^{th}$. you must have crowned all, by inviting her out to see your fine prospects, as well as visit your genteel neighbourhood. We cannot flatter Miss Wodrow w$^{th}$. all these advantages– but she may be sure of what you are so kind as [to] give us credit for– a most hearty welcome: not to m[ention] that the difference in customs, language, dress & face of the ^towns &^ country, will give her some amusement & enable her to entertain you & her other friends with her remarks thereon. I remember our late worthy friend M$^r$. H. Millar,[5] tho' he was in very low spirits, amused himself & his friends much this way. And tho' he was naturally averse to writing, yet he could ^not^ help scribbling large pacquets to the Abbot of Paisley,[6] full of his remarks.

You have quite raised my curiosity to see your worthy friend Campbell.[7] If he had only asked if there were any Scots people at Bewdley– he w$^d$. have soon found me out. I do not recollect him at all: but shall be most heartily glad to see him. Poor M$^r$. Haddow[8]– my wife remembers him perfectly well at Killwining– & his name quite familiar to me.– As you now acquiesce in these 2 young folks setting out immediately I will venture to assure you that it is much preferable to Jan$^y$. or even Feb$^y$. For they will have now the days longer, but the weather much milder & the roads infinitely better. After the long dry season w$^{ch}$. we have had– the weather will not probably change of a sudden– nor will the roads, be consequently much impaired. But in Jan$^y$. & Feb$^y$. we have always cold winds & often heavy snow, frost or rain.–So that if this l$^r$. should meet you at Glasgow– I w$^d$. beg the favour of you to hasten their departure– as they will probably stop 2 or 3 days at Ed$^r$. Adieu my dear friend. Never mind franks. I do not know where to buy real pleasure cheaper than at the post office.– Now you must allow me to take leave of my Mary.

God bless you & y$^{rs}$. SK.

---

[5] Rev. Henry 'Harry' Millar (d. 1771), minister at Neilston, Renfrewshire (1737–71), who was like a 'second father' to SK. His mother Elizabeth (d. 1759), wife of Rev. Robert Millar of Paisley (1672–1752), was a cousin of SK's mother. Henry's brother was Andrew Millar, the London bookseller. *W-K*, I, pp. 18, 23.

[6] Rev. James Hamilton (1721–82), minister of the Abbey Church, Paisley. *W-K*, I, p. 286.

[7] Unidentified. Perhaps it is the merchant father of the unidentified young divinity student in Letter 65, *W-K*, I, p. 427.

[8] For JW's account of the drowning of 'Mr Hadow', or Haddow, see Letter 84.

It is very kind of our good friend to take you[9] by Kilb[n]. & Mill[n]. You are right to give them a second call. My obligations are so great to that family– I always think of them with pleasure– & wish for nothing more than to make them every return in my power.– As to L[d]. Cassillis[10]– your mother says he can only take what is his due– & that he will have whether we will or no.– Every thing that has come from thence to me has been insidious. We granted them every thing the[y] asked– & got nothing– but abuse.– You have so many demands from your friends– I cannot mention Sally & Betsy. M[rs]. Hunt has been at Wchurch[11]– but never comes near us– tant mieux.[12]

God protect & bless you pray<br>yrs S&EK

Claud tells me that brown ^Tea^ Urns are from 40/to 50/. Jack I find pleases at last. But we have not got a place for Archy yet.[13] Jack Hayley is just married [to a] farmer's d[r]. in his parish 10 years older than himself.[14] Adieu [seal] write from Ed[r]. Turn at Ferry Bridge.

---

[9] Mary Kenrick.

[10] David Kennedy, tenth earl of Cassillis (1727–92), who had inherited the earldom when his brother Thomas, the ninth earl, died in 1775. He practised as an advocate, and was nominated for the joint chair in universal history and Greek and Roman antiquities at Edinburgh University, but he returned to Ayrshire in 1762 when his brother Thomas, the ninth earl, bought Newark Castle and its estate for him. He was MP for Ayrshire 1768–74; having succeeded to the earldom, he was elected a Scottish representative peer between 1776 and 1790. He supported Lord North in both houses of Parliament. He rebuilt Culzean Castle, the family seat on the Ayrshire coast, to the design of Robert Adam, and improved the estate, at the cost of accumulating large debts, and left it to wealthy cousins after his death. He died in substantial debt in December 1792, and was buried at Maybole Collegiate Church.

[11] Whitchurch. Mary Kenrick's friends, Sally and Betsy, and Mrs Hunt, are unidentified.

[12] 'Tant mieux': 'so much the better'.

[13] Claud, Jack, and Archy unidentified; possibly employees of the Kenrick family business.

[14] Possibly the Rev. John Hayley (c. 1757–95) who died at the age of thirty-six and was buried at Ribbesford in January 1795. The Hayleys appear to have been a prominent local family, with memorials to several of them on the wall of the Ribbesford Church. He was probably the John Hayley who was baptized in the Ribbesford Church in 1757, son of John and Sarah Hayley. There is no information on this John Hayley in the lists of Oxford and Cambridge alumni. However, he may have been a brother of William Burrell Hayley (c. 1756–96), son of John Hayley, a gentleman at Bewdley who matriculated in 1772 at the age of sixteen, and became a curate in the Bewdley chapel (1778–80) before moving to the parish of Brightling, East Sussex, where he died in 1796. *Clergy of the C of E*; *Alumni Oxonienses*, II, p. 634; *Ancestry*; J. R. Burton, *A History of Bewdley: With Concise Accounts of Some Neighbouring Parishes* (1883), pp. 26, 73.

## Letter 83: Samuel Kenrick to James Wodrow, 28 September 1784

Place: Bewdley
Addressed: The Rev[d]. M[r]. Wodrow / Irvine / N Britain
Postmarked: Stourbridge September the twenty ninth 1784–
Franked: Free Westcote
Stamp: STOURBRIDGE

My dearest Friend.

Your very kind l[r]. (of the 17th. inst. by Mary's date) reached us the 25th.– & I have delay'd answering it, 'till I have one more franked by Lord Westcote, w[th]. whom I am to dine to day at Hagley Park.[1] For you must know that members of Parliament make it a point of honour now, only to frank letter's on the spot, & to have them sent the same day to the post-office.[2] By the bye, this new regulation will bring a deal of money to government, though it may interrupt many an agreeable correspondence. Yet I cannot disapprove of it– when I consider its advantage & utility. For what pleasure is there, equal to that of conversing with a friend be the distance what it may? & by so quick a conveyance! When compared to any thing else it is certainly cheap. So that I shall never gr[um]ble at this tax or blame M[r]. Pitt for it. Ministers, I dare say, h[ave] long had it view. It is collected with so little trouble. But it was th[ought] that the members themselves would not have parted w[th]. a privilege, w[ch.] they could at no expense serve & please their friends. Therefore the minister was affraid of asking it. But it was found to be quite otherwise: for franking particularly in commercial places, was become so burdensome, that the members were glad to get shot of it. E.G. I used to send our representative 6 or 8 doz. at a time altho' one of the partners of our Banking house in London be in parliament, who furnished us w[th]. many more, by frank[g]. all the let l[ts]. addressed to their house: w[ch]. is now giveng up. For no l[r]. is free but what goes directly to him in person. This will make a great difference, you will say, in the expense of carrying on our business. Doubtless it will– but not so great as we at first imagined: because any number of bills (w[ch]. formerly paid single) under an ounce weight is only charged 3 ^single^ postages. The new additional postage, however, I can by no means relish. We pay 2[d]. from hence to Kidd[r].[3] w[ch].

---

[1] Hagley Hall, Hagley, Worcestershire, a Palladian Mansion, the family seat of the Lyttletons built by George, first Lord Lyttleton (1709–73). See W-K, I, p. 467 n.
[2] For a discussion of the postal system, see the 'General Introduction', W-K, I, pp. 34–36, and the Introduction to this volume.
[3] Kidderminster.

is only 3 miles off– & the same to Bridgnorth & Worcester w^(ch). are 15 miles. Neither can I see any good reason why l^(rs). from Glasgow should be dearer than those from Ed^(r).– for the same distance. But enough of posts. Your friendly reception, kind attention, & partial prepossesion in favour ^of^ our dear Mary– you may be sure is not thrown away upon us. When I say your– I mean that of your whole self, your family. And in particular to her I must say– that she is not undeserving of a share of it. For it was not her smallest motive to undertake such a long journey alone, to have the pleasure of seeing you & your family, who were become by means of our friendly intercourse of letters [in]timate together. None of you could be prevailed upon [to c]ome hither. She had therefore no alternative, but to do [as] she did. And the merit of it is entirely on her own. We have no other objection to her continuing longer under your hospitable & friendly roof– where she must be improved as well as made happy– but her time will not at present allow it. Winter is coming on w^(th). rapid steps– the days getting shorter– & the roads worse. So that as a prudent, as well as spirited traveller she will think it necessary to set out without delay. And why may not one of your daughters return along with her. My opinion is that honest Nell has no objection provided you have none. She would like to see her father's old fashioned friend– that plagues him so often w^(th). politics & nonsense. We shall make her as comfortable & happy as we can.

But I have not done w^(th). posts yet– I am affraid I overdid it, w^(th). my franks to you– & that you were obliged to pay for the last– w^(ch). I desired Mary in a former letter to reimburse you.

Your kind apology was entirely unnecessary. To instruct the ignorant, to improve & encourage the enlightened & good, & to comfort the dejected & disconsolate, are employments reserved for the happy few, whom providence hath blessed w^(th). superior talents, to carry on its benevolent purposes. Every other consideration must give way here.

I, like you, have not time to copy my letters. So that I do not recollect the particulars you are so kind as to allude to– in my late hasty scraps.– Only I always celebrate your good sense & wisdom, in the management of the poor– as well as many other parts of your civil & ecclesiastical po[licy]. But particularly that habit of sobriety & decent carriage [that] pervade your lowest ranks. John Bull may call it, as he [does] over his cups, mean tameness, & abject submission to tyran[nical] superiours, the ^consequence of the^ old rusty fetters of feudal servitude, w^(ch). you have not, like him, been able yet to shake off:– but you & I can remember, when the cause of liberty & religion were at stake in 1745–6, what a noble spirit appeared in the west of Scotland, to oppose the rebels:[4] & how many hundred brave hearty fellows, headed by their ministers flocked into Glasgow, when the enemy was expected every moment: & who w^d. certainly have given them battle & in all probability beat them, had they been properly commanded. I was enlisted one day as a volunteer in Capt^n. James M^cKnight's[5] comp^y. & was mustered in the grammar school on a Sunday ev^g. You were too young at least I do not remember you. But Witherspoon was the hero![6] My friend Brisbane[7] has been writ^g. me a deal about him & his reception & errand. I should like to know the particulars from you, as you probably must have seen him.

As to my friend w^th. the Bee in his bonnet, ^I^ shall never be tired in defending him– I love & admire him so much. Tho' I confess that there was a time that I highly blamed his furious attack on your harmless three old Doctors.[8] To treat the amiable Beattie[9] w^th. such severity shocked me– & I thought the modest industrious Reid[10] much too roughly handled. I am not sufficiently acquainted with my hero's character to account for it.– But you will perhaps be better

---

[4] In September 1745, the Jacobite army going south had raised from Glasgow a forcible levy of £5,500. No such sum was forthcoming when the army returned in December of the same year. See *W-K*, I, p. 53. On Presbyterian opposition to the Jacobite '45 in Glasgow and the south-west, see A. E. MacRobert, 'The Myths about the 1745 Jacobite Rebellion', *Historian*, 99 (2008), pp. 16–23; and MacRobert, *The 1745 Rebellion and the Southern Scottish Lowlands* (Ely, 2006).

[5] Perhaps Rev. James Macknight (1721–1800), biblical scholar and minister of the Old Church, Edinburgh, from 1778. A native of Irvine in North Ayrshire, he was JW's immediate predecessor as assistant minister at the Abbey Church of Kilwinning under the supervision of Rev. Alexander Fergusson between 1749 and 1753. Macknight moved from Kilwinning to the parish church of Maybole, Ayrshire (1753–69), where SK's wife Elisabeth grew up. He was awarded the degree of DD by the University of Edinburgh in 1759 in recognition of his *Harmony of the Four Gospels* (1756), which was very successful, reaching its fifth edition in 1819. *FES*, III, p. 408.

[6] Rev. John Witherspoon (1723–94), minister of Beith parish (1745–57), then at Laigh, Paisley (1757–68). He was a leading figure in the 'Popular Party' and critic of Moderatism. In 1745 he led a party of Volunteers against the Jacobite army. He was captured in January 1746 while observing the battle of Falkirk and was briefly imprisoned in Doune Castle. He emigrated to New Jersey in the summer of 1768 to become Principal of the College of New Jersey, later Princeton University. He was the only clergyman to be a signatory of the Declaration of Independence. See *W-K*, I, p. 396; Letter 84 below; Gideon Mailer, *John Witherspoon's American Revolution* (Chapel Hill, NC, 2017), pp. 62–64.

[7] Robert Brisbane. See Letters 81, 84.

[8] Joseph Priestley, *An Examination of Dr Reid's Inquiry into the Human Mind, Dr Beattie's Essay on the Nature and Immutability of Truth, and Dr Oswald's Appeal to Common Sense in Behalf of Religion* (1775).

[9] James Beattie (1735–1803), poet and professor of moral philosophy at Marischal College, Aberdeen.

[10] Thomas Reid (1710–96), philosopher and mathematician, professor and regent at King's College, Aberdeen (1752–64). In 1764 he succeeded Adam Smith as professor of moral philosophy at the University of Glasgow.

pleased, to hear how I was conducted to the Doctor's palace— for it is no less— by a common friend D[r]. Edw[d]. Johnstone.[11] Mary will give you the latter's character. It is ab[t]. a mile out of Birmingham. I chose to ride thither— but my conductor like parson Adams[12], whom he resembles in an honest warm heart & absence of [min]d, preferred walking— but at my pace: & as I had 4 legs to car[ry] me & he had but 2, he was obliged to make them run— while his [tou]ngue ran on still faster the whole way. We arrived at last [at] the stable to dispose of my horse in the first place. When behold it was converted in a chemical laboratory— full of retorts, receivers &c: w[ch]. the Doctor recollected the moment he saw it: & bursting out into a loud laugh, cried ^out^ bless me! I had quite forgot it: what shall we do now! I joined him in the laugh most heartily. But if it was fun to him & me— it was none to my poor horse. I made him however as happy as we ^could^ by turn[g]. him into an aftermath field adjoining, where he met with food as agreeable to his palate & in as great abundance as we did.— In the course of our conversation the Doctor who is well acquainted w[th]. Scotland & D[r]. Smith's Wealth of nations[13]— happened often to name the Ayr Bank[14] & its pernicious effects, adding that the Ayr bank w[d]. infallibly ruin some of the most opulent families in Scotland. D[r]. Priestly, who you know, is much conversant in air— hear[g]. the word[15]

---

[11] Edward Johnstone (1757–1851), physician, born at Kidderminster, Worcestershire. A graduate of Edinburgh University, he practised medicine for over fifty years in the Birmingham area. His patients included the famous actress Sarah Siddons and Samuel Johnson. A notable philanthropist, he played an energetic role in developing medical facilities in the Midlands, especially for the poor. See W-K, I, pp. 325–26n.

[12] Character in Henry Fielding's novel, *Joseph Andrews* (1742), who is well meaning, forgetful, and always looking on the bright side.

[13] Adam Smith (bap. 1723, d. 1790), moral philosopher and political economist, professor of logic (1751–52) and of moral philosophy (1751–64) at the University of Glasgow. Author of *The Theory of Moral Sentiments* (1759) and *An Inquiry into the Nature and Causes of the Wealth of Nations* (1776). Joseph Priestley shared the widespread admiration for *Wealth of Nations*. In the preface to his *Lectures on History, and General Policy* (Birmingham, 1788), p. vii, Priestley noted that 'I have enlarged the course since the syllabus of it was first printed [1765], with many valuable articles collected from works which have been published since, especially Dr Smith on *the Wealth of Nations* and Stuart's *Principles of Political Oeconomy*; and my wish is, that by the application of some general principles in such works as these, I may excite in youth a desire to become better acquainted with them'.

[14] The Ayr Bank collapsed in 1772, and amongst the losers was Elizabeth Dunlop, wife of Rev. William M'Gill. She lost her substantial dowry. See Letter 84; and the discussion in Smith, *Wealth of Nations*, eds R. H. Campbell and A. S. Skinner (Oxford, 1976), pp. 313–15.

[15] This is the end of a page, and the rest of the letter is missing.

## Letter 84: James Wodrow to Samuel Kenrick, 22 October 1784

Place: Stevenston
Addressed: Mr. Kenrick Bewdley
Notes: Octr. 24 1784 by Mary & Nell[1]
Answ{d}. all except the cover 3d. Decr. 84
84

My Dearest Friend

    I begin a long Letter to you which will not be finished for near a week as it is intended to accompany Your Daughter & mine to Bewdley & to contain various matter in the way of entertainment & bussiness which cannot be so conveniently transmitted to you by any other channel. I begin it just now because my time is liable to be broke in upon by necessary bussiness & company. I devote tomorrow sacredly to the bussiness of my parish i.e. to preparation for the Sundays work for I can neither yet lecture or preach extempore and I will not be able to command my time & pen when I get to Glasgow which will be G.W.[2] in the beginning of the week. For ~~yesterday~~ I received a Letter yesterday from your Daughter, to whom I am now almost as much attached by friendship as to yourself, calling upon her friend Nell & me to meet her at Glasgow as early as we can in the beginning of the week. Very happy shoud I be did time & money & other ~~things~~ circumstances put it in my power to accompany them the whole way to Bewdley: but that is impossible at present. I had the pleasure ^last week^ & a very real & sensible pleasure it was, of carrying Miss Kenrick on Horseback to Kibarchan[3] & Milliken[4] & next day to Paisley. The weather was fine which was some Compensation for my slow travelling. She saw Mr. Warner in one of his best situations, tho' looking miserably ill, yet was sensibly hurt & shocked once or twice & You woud have been infinitely more, from the recolection of his happier days.[5] Nothing almost in the World coud be more grating to your feelings and yet there ^is^ nothing dissagreable

---

  [1] i.e. carried by hand, by Mary Kenrick and 'Nell' (Helen) Wodrow.
  [2] 'G.W.', i.e. 'God Willing'.
  [3] Kilbarchan.
  [4] The estate of the wealthy Milliken family was in the parish of Kilbarchan, some six miles west of Paisley, Renfrewshire. In 1750 SK became tutor to the two sons of James Milliken (1710–76), employment which ended sadly with their premature deaths; James Jr (1741–63), and Alexander (1743–65). See 'General Introduction' and 'Introduction' to W-K, I, *passim*. LBS.
  [5] Rev. John Warner (1713–86), minister of Kilbarchan parish, JW's cousin on his mother's side, and SK's friend. He had suffered a debilitating stroke in 1775. See W-K, I, pp. 323–24.

about him, but what arises from the comparison of what he once was. His Memory is almost clean gone, yet he remembers you. His judgment remains, in so far as it can, to ^a^ man destitute of memory, & his old kindness to his friends remains, & breaks out in many instances troublesome to himself & them if kindness can be so. M^rs^. Milliken is a surprising old woman ^with^ the same sense & Cleverness as when you & I were at Milliken.[6] Before this last time I have not seen her in her own house since we were there together, but I shall now probably repeat my Visits. Your Relation M^rs^. Hamilton[7] is also much the same in the looks & every thing since I had the pleasure of spending some happy days with her & her worthy Abbot here at the Saltwater[8] but I leave these matters to the more fluent pen & conversation of your Daughter.

I mentioned to you in former Letters a treatise of my Friend Magill on the Death of Christ which is now lying ready for the Press, tho' perhaps it may not be published for years.[9] And I now send you the contents of the book wrote by his own hand at my desire this summer for the purpose of sending it to you. This will give you some Idea of the size & even the Matter of the book tho' a very slight one of the manner of or the Excution– which in my opinion is excellent & much supperior to any thing I have ever seen on the subject, yet I have only read part of it. The best way I can think of to give a stranger an Idea of M^r^. M. abilities for the Excution of such work is to send you some of the little things he has published. I will therefore cause Nell to put up with her Cloaths, a Speech on Patronage spoke by him at the Synod of Ayr Apr. last & printed at the desire of some of his

---

[6] Jean [Jane] Milliken, *née* McDowall of Garthland (d. 1791), daughter of William McDowall, and widow of James Milliken (1710–76), McDowall's business partner. Milliken and McDowall had owned sugar plantations in St Kitts and Nevis in the Leeward Islands. The Millikens employed SK as a tutor for their sons till 1765. *LBS*.

[7] Elizabeth Hamilton (d. 1798), wife (m. 1761) of Rev. James Hamilton of Paisley Abbey ('the worthy Abbot'), daughter of Hamilton's predecessor in the Abbey parish, Rev. Robert Millar. *FES*, III, p. 166.

[8] Presumably a name used for the stretch of the Scottish west coast in JW's parish of Stevenston, North Ayrshire, where salt had been harvested centuries previously, remembered in the name of the small seaside town of Saltcoats in the same parish. See James Wodrow, 'The Parish of Stevenston', *OSA*, VII, p. 2. Peter Fleming's town plan of Saltcoats in 1810, at https://maps.nls.uk/view/216443280, shows the salt pans and salt garnel (storehouse) still *in situ*.

[9] William M'Gill, *A Practical Essay on the Death of Jesus Christ, in Two Parts. Containing, I. The History, II. The Doctrine, of his Death* was 'printed for the author' in 1786 in Edinburgh, with between 700 and 800 subscribers for an edition of 1,000 copies (see Letter 120 below). According to John R. McIntosh, *ODNB*, it may have been influenced by Joseph Priestley's *Theological Repository* (1770–71). See also Martin Fitzpatrick, 'Varieties of Candour', p. 41.

Friends[10] particularly Sir A Fergusson[11] & I hope to be able to procure at Glasgow one or two of his printed Sermons for I can scarce think of parting with my own Copies sent as presents from the Author & marked with his own hand with some endearing Expression of regard to his friend.

With respect to the Manuscript Treatise, there was an attempt made during the Harvest & Winter last year to print it in Scotland & some correspondence between him & an Ed$^r$. Bookseller upon the terms. He then thought of setting his name to it publishing by Subscription, and after a sufficient number were ^to be^ sold to defray the Expense of the Impression. The bookseller I forget his name asked 20 or 25 ℔ Cent as his Share of the profits of the rest. I thought these terms high tho' a Stranger to these matters, but the Author himself seemed well enough satisfyed; when the Bookseller from some unaccountable causes drew off & declined the publication at present after he had seen a part of the Manuscript. I suspected he had been advised by some of the Orthodox at Ed$^r$. to decline ^it^ for fear of risking his own reputation. Yet I dare say there are booksellers enough in Scotland willing to publish it on the same terms. During last Winter & Spring Lord Hailes[12] an

---

[10] *A Speech, Addressed to the Provincial Synod of Glasgow and Ayr, Met at Ayr, 14th April 1784, by one of the Members of that Court, upon Patronage* (Edinburgh, 1784). M'Gill's speech was delivered at the meeting of the Synod of Glasgow and Ayr meeting at Ayr on 14 April 1784. National Records of Scotland [NRS], CH2/464/4 (Synod of Glasgow and Ayr Minutes [1761–1803]), f. 191; *Caledonian Mercury*, 26 Apr. 1784. In answer to a motion by William Peebles, proposing that the General Assembly should petition the king and Parliament for a repeal of the 1712 Act, M'Gill proposed a motion that the Synod should pass an overture to the General Assembly, to the effect 'That whereas the law of Patronage is never actually in force in this church, as it has been for upwards of 70 years last past, without being attended with any inconveniences to those parishes which have submitted peac[e]ably to it, and whereas unwarrantable & unusual endeavours have of late been made by divers members of this church to inflame the minds of the common people against it; Therefore the venerable Assembly would be pleased to take such measures, as to their wisdom shall seem meet for repressing the said disorders, and reconciling the people to the aforesaid law of Patronage as it at present stands, at least, untill a better law to supply its place, be framed & agreed to by its opposers, and till the same be got established in a legal & constitutional manner.'

[11] See Letter 79.

[12] Sir David Dalrymple (1726–92), third baronet, Lord Hailes, judge and historian, 'was widely esteemed as a literary critic', and it was common for authors of the stature of James Boswell, William Robertson, and James Beattie to submit their texts to him 'for his approval'. Patrick Cadell, 'Sir David Dalrymple, third baronet, Lord Hailes (1726–1792)', *ODNB*. His theological conservatism made him an interesting choice of reader for M'Gill, but, as JW observed, it may explain why Hailes refused, tactfully, to read the second, more heavily doctrinal, part of M'Gill's book. He had opposed the appointment of David Hume as Keeper of the Advocates' Library. Born in Edinburgh, the eldest of the sixteen children of Sir James Dalrymple, second baronet (1692–1751), Dalrymple was educated at Eton, the Middle Temple, London, and Utrecht before becoming a Scottish advocate in 1748. He joined the recently founded Edinburgh Revolution Society in November 1751 and, in July 1754, the Select Society. He became a judge in March 1766 with the title Lord Hailes.

Author himself was perswaded to read the first part of the book even the History of our Saviours ^Sufferings^ & to give his Corrections & remarks. My Friend & he tho' very little acquainted corresponded by Letter & his Lord^p^. sent him a few pages of short remarks or rather corrections on the stile & turns of ^some of^ the Expressions & Sentences they were sensible & modest & woud have pleased you much as a Critick they showed a much more accurate attention to the Structure of the English Language than I shoud have expected from his Lord^ps^. writings. But they were wholly verbal, except one single remark on Section I where the Author attempts at a rational & ingenious Account of the Agony in the Garden & the remarker dissaproves of this as a bold attempt because the inspired Writers have related the fact without presuming to give any account of the causes of it. His Lord^p^. absolutely refused to read & remark upon the 2^d^ main & Doctrinal part of the book from want of time & ability to judge of such matters. I apprehend ~~cheifly~~ however the cheif cause was the difference in their theological sentiments. But thus the correspondence ended.

I was ^of^ oppinion from the beginning that the Climate of Scotland especialy for two or three years past was too hot to bear such an ^open^ publication[13] & the Author himself from these two incidents[14] seems now to be of the same oppinion even that it woud be scarce prudent to do what he wished & intended at first, to set his name to the book & publish by Subscription. There is however little obnoxious in it but the Heresy of Ommission excepting indeed in some of the notes which picture the Absurdity and inhumanity of the common oppinion on the subject with too much severity & woud certainly irritate.[15] These I advised him either to suppress altogether or soften ^let him^ publish where he will because I realy dissaprove of the bitter spirit of controversy in all parties. But ~~tho there~~

---

[13] JW may be referring to the controversy over patronage in the early 1780s, or the Ayrshire controversy over John Goldie's *Essays* (1779) and second edition, as *The Gospel Recovered from its Captive State* (1785), or both. See Colin Kidd, 'Enlightenment and Anti-Enlightenment in Eighteenth-Century Scotland: an Ayrshire-Renfrewshire Microclimate', in Jean François Dunyachi and Ann Thomson, eds, *The Enlightenment in Scotland National and International Perspectives* (Oxford, 2015), pp. 76–77.

[14] That is, the refusal of the Edinburgh bookseller to pursue publication after having read part of the manuscript, and the refusal of Lord Hailes to read the second part of the book, containing the main doctrinal argument, perhaps due to differences in theology, as Wodrow surmised.

[15] M'Gill was accused of denying the divinity of Christ by emphasizing his weakness in anticipating his own death, in Gethsemane. In 1786 after the book's publication, JW noted that 'all the obnoxious Strictures against the common Oppinions about the Satisfaction' had been 'struck out by my advice', except that M'Gill kept 'one single note…as somewhat curious from the History of Carolina'. See Letter 125.

there is probably nothing in the book that woud ~~raise~~ give ground for a prosecution in our Church courts as every thing coud be easily defended on the common oppinion of the human nature of X yet as there is not the least hint of any thing else & the whole strain of the book calculated to raise the Suspicion perhaps the Hue & cry of S—c—n—sm.[16] It is not easy to say how far this might hurt our friends usefulness & Comfort as a Minister.

I write these things in confidence to you, for the intended publication is except insofar as I have mentioned an entire secret in this Country except to another friend or two of M^r. Magill. To my own friends here I was forbid to show the contents but allowed to send them to You. And I will be obliged to you for your Oppinion and Advice in so far as the lights I have given you enable you to Judge & also that you woud ^take^ the trouble to Show the Contents & a Sermon or two of the Authors to one or more of your friends ^Judges of such matters^ among the Literati in order to learn how far an anominous [sic] publication of this sort might be likely to answer at London & also the terms upon which it woud be undertaken. You will consider my Letter however as to yourself & communicate no more of it than You think needful it being cheifly intended for your own entertainment. It is very probable that an anonimous book of that sort would not be very saleable at present. The great reason why I woud prefer an open Publication by Subscription with the Authors name on the tittle page, which is the most honest & honourable way, is ^that^ the Sale is likely to be much greater in this Country as M^r. Magills name & character is known & much respected among one part of the Clergy as well as some of the Laity & His circumstances are such as to make the profits of this Effort of his Genius desireable to him & his Family. He unluckily threw his Wife's portion at her own ^most^ earnest desire into that distructive Ayr bank lost it all & some more.[17] Yet he has only paid up the Original stock of £500 which he considered himself as bound in Conscience to pay. He joined the party of the Proprietors who prosecuted the Managers & when they lost their cause before our courts he still refused to pay ^~~more~~^ tho' most of the rest have now paid to the amount of ^above^ £1500 ^the share^ pure loss & such is their regard to his character that He has never yet had any Legal Excicution issued against himself & his Effects & I hope never will for the rest.

[16] Socinianism.
[17] The Ayr Bank, or Douglas, Heron and Company, was established in 1769 and was initially exceptionally successful in attracting subscribed capital, but it collapsed in 1772, partly because of the inexperience of the partners, and partly due to the failure of the London Scottish banking house Neale, James, Fordyce and Downe. Richard Saville, *Bank of Scotland: A History, 1695–1995* (Edinburgh, 1996), pp. 156–66.

I believe I wrote you in my last of the very unfortunate Death of poor Haddow[18] and of the testimony of his friendship to me & my family in his Will. His friends in this corner who had the warmest regard to him that you can well conceive especially Mr. Cunninghame of Seabank[19] have prepared one of the largest & best stones which our Quaries can yeild to cover his grave. My Horse is assisting this day in carrying it to Irvine. They applyed to me among others for an Inscription descriptive of his character & fate & preferred the one I drew up tho too long but the stone easily contains it. I send you a copy of it it is quite ^a^ simple narration of the truth. Miss Kenrick has got from Peggy[20] a Copy of a poem incomparably more worth your attention which came to ~~my hand~~ ^me by post^ in a blank Cover in about a week after I had the melancholy Satisfaction of carrying his head to the grave in a printed disguised hand. Copies of it were soon taken by Mr. Haddows friends who were highly pleased with it. It was a long time before we discovered the Author at last her husband betrayed the secret. She is Mrs. Macreddie[21] a Lady in this neighbourhood whose poetical Talents nobody knew any thing of before. The cheif circumstances of the event & the distinguishing Strokes of Haddows character are touched with a masterly Pencil.

Did I ever write ^you^ any thing of the Buchanites a new Sect of Enthusiasts who started up in this neighbourhood last spring. It is surprising that none of our Periodical writers have taken the least notice of them, except an obscure Glasgow Newspaper.[22] Sir Adam Fergusson applied to me about a forthnight ago for some account of them. I mentioned that paper & promised to send ^it^ to him. Being unable to recover ^it^ here I luckily met with a written copy at Kilbarchan taken

---

[18] See Letter 82. The parish burial register records that a 'Mr Hadow' was buried in Irvine on 22 July 1784. Together with John McKenzie and Robert Stuart (both buried 20 July), Hugh Portuzon (also buried 22 July), and Dorothea Innes (buried 23 July), Hadow had been 'drowned going over the bar in a boat for Arran'. NRS, Old Parish Registers, Deaths 595/30 170 Irvine, f. 170.

[19] Robert Reid Cunninghame (1744–1814) of Seabank House, also known as Auchenharvie House in JW's parish of Stevenston. He took over management of his family estate in 1770 and, in partnership with Rev. Patrick Warner of Ardeer (1710–93), JW's cousin and Rev. John Warner's brother, formed the successful Stevenston Coal Company in 1774. Eric J. Graham, *Robert Reid Cunninghame of Seabank House, Entrepreneur and Life Time Manager of the Stevenson Coal Company 1770–1814*, Ayrshire Monographs, 19 (Ayrshire Archaeological and Natural History Society, 1997).

[20] Margaret ('Peggy') Wodrow (1767–1845), JW's younger daughter.

[21] There was a McReddie family in Irvine: Agnes Duff was married James McReddie, and gave birth to Janet (b. 1753), Jane and Mary (twins, b. 1758), as well as to James Jr (Apr. 1754). NRS, Old Parish Registers, Births 595/10 143, 162 Irvine. It is possible that Agnes was the Mrs Macreddie to whom JW refers here.

[22] *Glasgow Journal*, 17–24 June 1784. See also the *Scots Magazine*, vol. 46 (Nov. 1784), pp. 589–90.

by a friend for his own entertainment which I sent to the Knight a day or two ago. I will certainly be able to procure the printed ~~copy~~ ^Newspaper^ at Glasgow & inclose ^it^ to you to save myself the trouble of writing & I shall just now transcribe what I added in that letter but you must read the printed account first to make what follows intelligible.[23]

"The above Account[24] Sir I have no doubt was drawn by M[r] Millar mins[r]. of Cumnock,[25] the Stile & manner marks it to his friends as his. The representation he gives of their singular tenets agrees perfectly with all that we learned of them here from the Irvine people. I shall add some further particulars of their History in so far as I can recollect.

"M[rs]. Buchan[26] was said to have come originaly from Montrose or its neighbourhood to have lived for a while at Glasgow; Her Cha[r]. not good.[27] There & at Kilmarnock she made some converts but very few. She had been at Irvine occasionaly for a Year or two before, and had resided there constantly during the last winter & spring. She was a pretty old & ill looking Woman, but had something fascinating in her conversation & Manners, particularly the appearance of much gentleness & kindness, joined with a cheerful Piety & confidence in heaven. The converts were all made by herself; the Influence of her Enthusiasm being confined to those who were within the reach of her conversation; & cheifly tho' not

---

[23] Marginal note: 'read the seperate paper'. It is appended to the end of the letter.

[24] Quotation marks appear in the original in this paragraph but not on those that follow; the latter are added here to clarify which passages JW was quoting from his letter to Sir Adam Fergusson.

[25] Rev. Thomas Miller (1740–1819), minister of Old Cumnock parish church (1767–1819), East Ayrshire, married to Janet Stewart 1789, granddaughter of Professor Dugald Stewart of the University of Edinburgh. He was awarded the degree of DD by the University of Edinburgh in 1788. *FES*, III, p. 26.

[26] Elspeth Buchan, otherwise known as Elspeth Simpson, who was in fact a native of Banffshire. Jill Söderström, 'Elspeth Buchan (née Simpson) (c.1738–1791)', *ODNB*; *DSCHT*. Michael Riordan disputes the spelling of her name and prefers Elspath Simpson, following Joseph Train, *The Buchanites: From First to Last* (1846), an unsympathetic but early collection of papers regarding the sect. Michael D. Riordan, 'Mysticism and Prophecy in Scotland in the Long Eighteenth Century' (PhD thesis, University of Cambridge, 2015). The *Scots Magazine*, 46 (Nov. 1784), 589–90 spelled her name 'Elspeth'. JW's account here closely matches both one written by Robert Burns and quoted at length in *DSCHT*, and the report in the *Scots Magazine*. See also James Richmond, 'Parish of Irvine', *OSA*, VII, pp. 181–83; Joy Strong and Rowan Strong, 'Elspeth Buchan and the Buchanite Movement', in James Crossley and Alastair Lockhart, eds, *Critical Dictionary of Apocalyptic and Millenarian Movements*, 27 April 2021, www.cdamm.org/articles/buchanites.

[27] Simpson had married Robert Buchan, a potter from Ayrshire, and followed him to Glasgow to take up employment as a servant; they had had several children, but they later separated, reunited, and separated again, which may explain JW's remark about her character.

entirely to the relief congregation. It did not spread in the smallest degree in the neighbouring parishes. Mr. Whyte[28] was a chearful young man of no learning or talents of any kind except an easy flow of Language. He was married & had a young family. Mrs. Buchan lived in his house, and after she had in the course of a few weeks, infused her spirit into him & perhaps about a fourth part of his congregation, the rest were offended at him, diserted his ministry & lodged a complaint against him with the Presby of Relief. They met at Irvine & without the formality of a tryal gave Mr. Whyte five or six Queries relative to his obnoxious Tenets, which he answered in writing immediately & unequivocaly; and signed his Answer at their desire. Then, they condemned him upon his confession & suspended him from preaching sine die.[29] Upon this He gave up the Bond he had for his Stipend, and continued to preach to his little flock in his own house & garden.

"The people who became Mrs. Buchn's. Disciples had been mostly serious & well meaning people formerly; some of them people of good sense, and Education. They conceived themselves as quite new Creatures and indeed they were strang[e]ly changed both in their Principles and Habits. They rejected & abhorred the doctrines of particular Election & Reprobation & other high points for which they had been formally zealous; and some of them disputed against these things with considerable accuteness not from Script<sup>re</sup>. but from other Topicks. Their turn of mind was chearful not gloomy. They entered easily into conversation about their favourite religious points, and even attempted to turn every ordinary subject of discourse into that channel as if they had been wholly possessed by their Enthusiasm. And in common with all other Enthusiasts they neglected their ordinary bussiness & the care of their families & child<sup>n</sup>. There were more Women

---

[28] Rev. Hugh White, minister of the Relief congregation at Irvine, whom Buchan seems to have met at a communion in Glasgow in 1782 or 1783. According to John Strawhorn, he was born in Stirling, but had been in America before this time, where he was influenced by the Shakers. Although a licentiate of the Church of Scotland, he had been received into the Relief Church in 1781. Gavin Struthers, the historian of the Relief Church, assessed him similarly: 'though his talents and acquirements were not of the first order, he was pretty much esteemed as a preacher. He delighted, however, rather to speak from Sinai than from Zion. Like men of this stamp, he was vain of his own attainments while he was denouncing others with the terrors of the law. Being easily puffed up, he suffered himself to be cajoled and drawn aside by the flattery of Mrs Buchan, an artful fanatic, and thus gained to himself a notoriety which his slender talents, in the ordinary discharge of duty, would never have won'. Rev. Gavin Struthers, *The History of the Rise, Progress, and Principles of the Relief Church, Embracing Notices of the other Religious Denominations in Scotland* (Glasgow, 1843), p. 335. He was deposed by the Relief Church as described by JW on 8 Oct. 1783.

[29] *sine die*, indefinitely.

among them than Men; and they parted at last from their Relations their friends & some of them from their Lovers, without the least appearance of reluctance or regret.

"Besides the kind of inspiration which Mr. Millar mentions some of them such as Mrs. Buchan & Mr. White, laid claim to Visions & Revelations & lay for many hours & in a dark room covered with a Sheet in confident Expectation of them. One of these Visions, ~~fixing~~ Mrs. Buchan imprudently published, fixing the distruction of the town of Irvine to a particular short day. This exasperated the Mob who considered her as a Witch and drove her & Mr. Whyte from the town the rest immediately followed their leaders in the precipitate manner described in the Letter. Peter Hunter a Writer[30] was brought back by a warrand[31] on account of some Papers belonging to other people in his hands. He continued several days in Irvine sold his House which was a pretty good one; and the rest who had any property in furniture Cloaths or shop goods, took the opportunity of returning & selling off every thing by roup.[32] The money arising from this Sale was not put into a common purse and given to Mrs. Buchan as was expected, but retained by the individuals. It was still however a kind of common stock; for such is their mutual disinterested attachment, that every one was ready to part with whatever he had, to any other of the Fraternity who needed it. They had in truth a community of goods among them; and they were suspected by some & accused of having a community of a more criminal kind: yet I have never heard any thing amounting to a proof or presumption of that Licenciousness. They lived together like Brothers & Sisters; They asked & took provision from other people on the road, like those who were entitled to it, telling them that God woud repay them, and never offering any payment themselves except it was insisted on. Since they left Ayrshire I have heard little of them that can be depended on except that their numbers encreased at the beginning to about sixty– that not one of them ^had^ diserted Mrs. Buchan's Standard. That they are still somewhere between Closeburn[33] & Dumfries & had suffered in their health by living in the Open Air."[34]

So far my letter concluding with an appology for the Length of it & expressions of satisfaction in having it in my power to gratify his Curiousity about an object

---

[30] A Scots lawyer who is a member of the Society of Writers to the Signet.

[31] 'warrand': variant of 'warrant'. *DSL*.

[32] 'roup': 'A public auction; (also) the act of selling or letting by public auction', Scottish and Northern English. *OED*.

[33] Closeburn, a village near Thornhill, in central Dumfries and Galloway.

[34] See also Struthers, *Relief Church*, pp. 335–46, for a similar account of Hugh White and the Buchanites.

worthy of it ^for^ tho' sects of similar Enthusiasts ^have^ made their appearance in Holland & Germany about the begining of the Reformation & in America during the present Century yet the Phænomenon is new & singular in Scotland. But I must stop at present.

---

Mond^y morn^g 25th.

I am uncertain my good Friend whether ~~my Charge~~ Nell & I will set out for Glasgow about two after^n. this day & go the length of Dunlop or make our journey at once to-morrow. The Weather which was very unpromising in the end of the week has now turned fair & frosty & does not push us but having wrote so much about other matters I must now say a few words on a subject more nearly interesting to me even about my Daughter. I commit her in the first place to the care & conduct of divine providence & next to Miss Kenrick who seems to be perfectly acquainted with every thing relative to the roads & to travelling to which her companion is very much a stranger, & lastly upon her arrival at Bewdley I commit her to M^rs. Kenrick & you wishing you to take her under your direction & protection & to treat her in respect of Advice admonition & every thing else she may need, with all possible freedom just in the same Manner as you woud do your own daughter. I hope you will find her a good Girl in the main her greatest fault is too much sensibility or delicacy of feeling ^too much^ for her own happiness in life which her Mother[35] also has & I am much mistaken if Miss Kenrick ^and shall^ <shall> I add <——> her Father have not ^also^ an abundant portion of it. I dare say Nell will feel herself for a great while in an uneasy & awkward situation from the want of the English Language[36] & <-> I am much affraid that like your friend Brisbane she will ^not^ easily acquire a propriety in her manner of speaking whatever may be her ambition to do it yet there is no judging till She be tryed. Young Dunlop[37] had the same difficulty that she had to learn to read write & spell & yet very soon threw off his Scotch toungue & dialect. In other respects I hope you will not find her awkward at least more so than can be

---

[35] Louisa Wodrow, née Hamilton (1733–93). She was the daughter of the Edinburgh bookseller Gavin Hamilton (1704–67) and Helen, née Balfour (d. 1793), and she had married JW in 1759.

[36] Presumably the Wodrow children had grown up speaking a Scots dialect. Nell was around twenty-one years of age at this time.

[37] Probably Thomas Dunlop-Wallace (1750–1835), son of John Dunlop of Dunlop (1707–85) and Frances Anna Wallace (1730–1815) of Craigie House, Wallacetown, near Ayr. Thomas had been forced to sell the Wallace estate at Craigie in 1783 because of his poor management of it. See W-K, I, p. 457.

expected at her age ~~for~~ she having had rather more opportunities of Company &c, than her rank & station entitles her to.

As to musick which you mention I am perfectly indifferent. She has as much of it already as she shoud have. But I hope her mind will be oppened & improved by the opportunity of seeing the different customs tasts & manners of your people one of highest sources, or means of improvement that I know. She has had enough of curio~~u~~sity I wish she ^may^ also have enough of attention & observation to make a proper use of this opportunity. I am pretty sure her younger Sister woud, for, with a sufficient degree of sensibility she has an uncommon quickness of apprehension and a very penetrating eye or observation of persons & things when no body woud think she was <~~spending~~> giving any attention to them at all.

As to money matters I have, by Miss Kenrick advice, who is our informer & adviser in every thing of this sort, given Nell as much money as will easily carry her up to Bewdley and after this I must be obliged to my friend for supplying her with what more she may have use for. How much I cannot say, she must not be shabby in her appearance among strangers and at the same time manage matters with as much oeconomy as possible for her own sake & ours. Her little Legacy I am doubtful will not answer the expence of such an Expedition. Whatever money you advance intimate it to me & I will pay it instantly to your order either at Glasgow or Paisley where my friend I mean Mary K. informs me you have money transactions. If she shoud be mistaken as to the convenience of this Scheme I coud draw on her Uncle John Ham$^n$.[38] at London whether this may answer him I am not very certain but it can be no great matter the sum that will be needed can be given to his relations at Ed$^r$.

My Daughter will be your Guest for ~~some Months~~ ^months^ I realy cannot tell how long. It will depend on your liking one another which on her part I have no doubt of & perhaps as little on yours but we must not abuse the generosity of friendship for as I told your Daughter at Paisley when she was about to make some acknowledgment I conceive the Obligation to ly all ~~one~~ one side which she retorted upon me very cleverly but not quite <-> so agreable to truth or fact as might have been expected from such an honest Girl, Yes, so it does. I have not yet informed M$^r$. Hamilton at London of our design of sending his Neice so near him. I am told she can go as easily there as we can do ^to^ Ed$^r$. that is for a Guinea. It is probable therefore she will get an invitation from her Uncle to spend a few days or weeks with his family in the Spring tho' they have no great conveniency for

---

[38] John Hamilton (1740–92), merchant in London, brother of Louisa Wodrow.

Strangers. Miss Kenrick has already got a very warm invitation from M$^r$. Will$^m$. Fulton[39] but we will leave these matters to be determined as circumstances cast up. If any thing further occurs to me about Nell & her concerns I will acquaint your Daughter at meeting which will not now be till tomorrow night as the frost threatens to be so hard as to endanger some bolls[40] of Potatoes I have still in the ground & the digging of them cannot be managed without my Sev$^t$., I have determined to set out not till tomorrow morn$^g$. early which will only make a difference of three or four hours as to the time of our Arival at Glasgow.

I have been reading last week D$^r$. Priestly's book on Necessity[41] which is a very clear & strong book on that side of the Question & I am surprised nobody has answered it in England. Possibly the learned think the subject exhausted. Indeed I met with little new in it except the connecting this Oppinion with the material or mechanical structure of the human mind in which I think D$^r$. Pr. has added something to those who have gone before him & exhibited a more consistent & complete System than any other necessitarian. I was however much dissapointed in meeting with little or nothing of the History of the controversy. I still remember & you will also how very full Proffess$^r$. Hutcheson[42] was in his Lectures & have often wished since to be master of that History on which he spent two or three Lectures having never met with anything like it in the course of my reading.

---

[39] Letter 264, JW to SK, 13 July 1808, mentions a Mr William Fulton who was brother-in-law to 'young M$^r$. Kenrick', SK's nephew.
[40] Measure of dry weight 'varying according to commodity and locality'. DSL.
[41] Joseph Priestley, *The Doctrine of Philosophical Necessity Illustrated: Being an Appendix to the Disquisitions Relating to Matter and Spirit. To Which is Added, an Answer to the Letters on Materialism, and on Hartley's Theory of the Mind* (1777). It argued that human free will is constrained by divine omnipotence, and that the divine will is manifested in the material universe, including in the physicality of the brain inside the human body. Material necessity thus determined human perception and intellect. Most famously, Priestley debated the problem of free will and determinism in print with his close friend Richard Price, in *A Free Discussion of the Doctrines of Materialism and Philosophical Necessity. In a Correspondence between Dr Price and Dr Priestley* (1778). Schofield, *The Enlightened Joseph Priestley*, pp. 77–91; James Dybikowski, 'Joseph Priestley, Metaphysician and Philosopher of Religion', in Isabel Rivers and David L. Wykes, eds, *Joseph Priestley: Scientist, Philosopher, and Theologian* (Oxford, 2008), pp. 91–104; Alan Tapper, 'The Beginnings of Priestley's Materialism', *Enlightenment and Dissent*, 1 (1982), pp. 73–82.
[42] Francis Hutcheson argued that people were motivated not only by reason but also by their passions and desires. These could be uncontrolled, but they could also be calm. However, that was not the same thing as making rational choices. Therefore seeking moral development was as important as defending libertarian free will. Ruth Boeker discusses his teaching on this problem in 'Francis Hutcheson on Liberty', *Royal Institute of Philosophy Supplement*, 88 (2020), pp. 121–42. See also Francis Hutcheson, *An Essay on the Nature and Conduct of the Passions and Affections* (1728).

As D[r]. Pr. has changed his principles of Education on one side I believe I have changed mine on the opposite side which were once those of our worthy Master[43] for whom I have a greater veneration than for most men tho' I am apt sometimes to look upon it as a Metaphysical nicety about which both sides are agreed if they understood one another or a Question out of the reach of the human mind which can never be decided. You will not therefore wonder that I considered D[r]. Pr. arguments as a Petition principii[44] & perhaps I shoud consider the Dissertations of Prof[r]. Pap fagaras[45] & D[r]. Maclain[46] in the same light coud I have an opportunity of perusing them at full length. From the abstract in the Review[47] I see they are levelled at least part of them against the English D[r]. tho' he is not named. The Question between them if I mistake not is whether the Human mind acts or is acted upon. The Arguments of the Necessitarian appear to me most accute & metaphysical. Those of their antagonists more founded in fact or in consciousness which is realy a matter of experience or fact. D[r]. Pr. chap[r]. on Prescience & his connecting his necessity with religion & Piety pleased me better than ^perhaps^ any other part of the book. And yet this might be strongly retorted upon him. He considers his scheme as exhibiting the only just view of a Providence. The Divine being is not only the great but properly speaking the only agent in the Universe but is ^there^ any thing different in this view from the Natura about which the Atheists speak so much. If there realy be an absolute invariable irresistible fatality what sort of Providence care or agency continues to be ex^er^cised about the universe by its maker? His work ^of Providence^ is over & was over from all eternity. The machine once set a going can never go wrong & he seems to remain not as the supreme director & gover-

---

[43] i.e. Hutcheson.

[44] *Petitio principii*, the fallacy of begging the question, or a circular argument.

[45] Josephus Pap de Fagaras, *Dissertation sur la Force Primitive, qui a Remporté le Prix Proposé par L'Académie Royale des Sciences et Belles-Lettres pour l'année MDCCLXXIX* (Berlin, 1780). He was a minister and mathematician in Transylvania who had studied at Utrecht under Johann Friedrich Hennert. J. C. Boudri, *What Was Mechanical about Mechanics: The Concept of Force between Metaphysics and Mechanics from Newton to Lagrange* (Dordrecht, 2002), p. 190.

[46] Rev. Archibald Maclaine (1722–1804), the Glasgow-educated minister of the English church at The Hague 1747–96, and author of *A Series of Letters Addressed to Soame Jenyns, Esq., on Occasion of His View of the Internal Evidence of Christianity* (1777), which dismissed necessitarianism and predestination, pp. 76–79. Jenyns's pamphlet, *A View of the Internal Evidence of the Christian Religion* (1776), had emphasized the moral advantages of Christianity rather than supernatural demonstrations such as prophecies and miracles.

[47] See *Monthly Review*, 56 (June 1777), pp. 436–45, review of Maclaine's *Answer to Soame Jenyns*, which quotes Maclaine's dig at 'the *necessitarian* metaphysicians, from Zeno to Leibnitz' (Maclaine, p. 76) on p. 440.

nour but an <—> ^or ^inactive^ spectator of its invariable motions something like Divum Natura of Epicurus.

> Omnis enim per se Divum natura necessest
> Immortali ævo summa cum pace fruatur
> semota ab nostris rebus seiunctaque longe;
> Nam privata dolore omni, privata periclis,
> Ipsa suis pollens opibus, nihil indiga nostri
> Nec bene promeritis capitur nec tangitur ira.[48]

In the chapter of the Difference between his own Oppinion & Predestination I am affraid he scarce does justice to the poor Calvinists. Their oppinion about original sin and many others there introduced, having no connection with their oppinion on this point which they support I mean the rational Calvinists with ^the^ same arguments as he does besides the Scripture ones which he very wisely neglects or gives up. But I wonder what set me on this intricate subject you must blame your friend for it. The man with the bee in his Bonnet.[49]

I got last night a much more agreable & entertaining book even a very neat vol. of Hayleys plays price only 4/.[50] I had only time this afternoon to glance the last. It reads pleasantly but the entertainment is different from English Comedy nearer that of some of Priors poems[51] & the bath Guide.[52] But I must leave this Letter to be finished at Glasgow where I hope to be G.W.[53] tomorrow night. I was in hopes of a few lines from you by this post– perhaps they are lying for me at Glasgow.

Glasgow Oct<sup>r</sup>. 28 Thurs<sup>y</sup>. morn<sup>g</sup>.

---

[48] Few writings by the Greek philosopher Epicurus (341–270 BC) have survived, and, as in this case, his materialist philosophy was generally accessed through the writings of followers such as the Roman poet Lucretius, *De Rerum Natura*, Book 1, ll. 44–49. '[I pray to you for peace,] for the very nature of divinity must necessarily enjoy immortal life in the deepest peace, far removed and separated from our affairs; for without any pain, without danger, itself might by its own resources, needing us not at all, it is neither propitiated with services nor touched by wrath.' Lucretius, *De Rerum Natura, with an English Translation by W. H. D. Rouse*, revised by Martin Ferguson Smith (1975), p. 7.

[49] Joseph Priestley.

[50] William Hayley, *Plays of Three Acts; Written for a Private Theatre* (1784). See W-K, I, Letter 77, 14 May 1783, pp. 486–87; and above, Letter 79, JW to SK, 15 April 1784, Letter 80, SK to JW, 2 June 1784.

[51] Matthew Prior (1664–1721) published witty and satirical poems in the early eighteenth century, such as *Poems on Several Occasions* (1709).

[52] Christopher Anstey, *The New Bath Guide* (1766). See W-K, I, Letter 50, JW to SK, 5 April 1774, p. 318; Letter 53, SK to JW, 30 Aug. 1775, p. 329; Letter 77, SK to JW, 14 May 1783, p. 480.

[53] God willing.

<—> I have My Dear Sir at last brought my Daughter thus far in her progress to her friends at Bewdley. We had a pleasant Journey on Tues^y. bating[54] a little inconvenience from the hard frost in the morn^g. & came here about five at night found the worthy Princ^l. & M^rs. L. in their usual health. His frailty is visibly increased since I saw him last about eighteen months ago from attacks of a Gravelish kind joined to his Astmatick ones but his mind spirit & conversation is always the same. After Tea I had a happy meeting with Miss Kenrick ^in Adams Court^ and was kindly received by her two young Cousins.[55] Nell & I spent the greatest part of yesterday with them. They were both set upon keeping the travellers till monday & after much argument it is now settled that they are to leave this on Friday & the Tickets bought. M^rs. Leechman[56] & especialy <wished> the Principal wished to see your Daught^r. She waited on them before Dinner & both parties are very much pleased with one another. Miss Kenrick is to make a 2^d. call this day as her yesterdays visit was partly interupted by some of our people of Quality Lady Glasgow[57] & Lady Sutherland[58] &c, who came in after they had seen the Colledge. I was glad Miss Kenrick got a sight of that young Countess for it was little more. Lady Gl. good woman had forgot me tho' I had spent <days> several happy days & nights at Kelburn[59] in her husbands time & I had not the confidence to make myself known to her as nobody else did. But I will probably wait on her

---

[54] 'To bate': meaning 'to beat'. *DSL*. JW is saying that they were not beaten, but rather they overcame the inconvenience of the frost.

[55] Mary Kenrick was staying at Adam's Court, the Glasgow residence of Robert Brisbane, whose country estate was Milton on the Clyde, near Carluke in Lanarkshire (see the address for Letter 82). The cousins to which JW refers appear to be Brisbane and his sister (see the rest of this paragraph). Robert Brisbane was a relation of SK who had visited Bewdley in 1781. See Letter 72, *W-K*, I, p. 455.

[56] Bridget Leechman (d. 1792), née Balfour, wife of William Leechman and aunt of Louisa Wodrow.

[57] Elizabeth Boyle (d. 1791), née Ross, wife of John Boyle, third Earl of Glasgow (1714–75). Strawhorn, ed., *Ayrshire at the Time of Burns*, p. 298.

[58] Lady Elizabeth Sutherland (1765–1839), countess of Sutherland, who had inherited the estates of her father, William, eighteenth earl of Sutherland (1735–66), at the age of one year. With them she inherited enormous electoral power in the county of Sutherland: control of twenty-two of its thirty-four votes. Her interests, as an orphan, were placed in the care of tutors whose directives were executed by the general commissioner of the Sutherland estates. Between 1779 and 1782 Elizabeth Sutherland was educated in London, and she lived mainly there and in Edinburgh. She married George Granville Leveson-Gower, Viscount Trentham (1758–1833) on 4 Sept. 1785. A forceful personality, Lady Sutherland played a major part in the management of the extensive family estates, earning some notoriety for the policy of Highland clearance. Elaine Chalus, *Elite Women in English Political Life c. 1754–1790* (Oxford, 2005), p. 222.

[59] Kelburn Castle, near Fairlie, North Ayrshire, seat of the earl of Glasgow.

at Hacket[60] in my way home– Nell & I dined & drank tea in Adams Court. I like young Brisbane.[61] He has a plain good honest heart & is a kind hospitable Landlord tho his manner might have been better ^than it is^ from the opportunities he has had. I like his Sister still better she seems to be a pleasant sensible pretty Girl & hits my tast in her manner & behaviour better than any of the Glasgow Girls I know.[62] The Mother I have not seen enough of to form any oppinion about her.

I have only got one of M[r]. Magill's Sermons to send to you.[63] There is an excellent one on friendship preached at a Mason meeting which I wished to have got you also but I am afraid my search will be unsuccessful.[64] But I will try again today. Tait the printer of the newspaper[65] was very obliging & searched near an hour for the Paper I wanted but in vain. I luckily have in my Pocket book a short hand copy which I took to enable me to write to Sir A. Ferg[n]. This I must now copy ^on a separate paper^ out for you. I read to the honest Princ[l]. all the Literary part of this Letter last night. The account of the Buchanites was as new to him as it will be to you so little are they known in this Country. He is earnest to have My friends book published as he knows his abilitys says He has but a short time now to live but woud wish to see a book upon that plan published from this Country

---

[60] Lady Glasgow inherited Halkhead or 'Hawkhead', the seat of her father, George Ross, thirteenth Lord Ross, in 1777. 'Hacket' may be a local corruption.

[61] In 1781 SK described Robert as 'my kinsman Brisbane, who has been 4 years at College– & has a general knowledge of every thing! ... is grave, reserved & silent– & is very slow in shaking off his provincialisms: altho' he has ideas & language in plenty'. Letter 72, W-K, I, p. 458.

[62] Mary Brisbane. She later became the first wife of James Jeffray (1759–1848), professor of anatomy and botany at the University of Glasgow. In 1800, JW observed that she was the 'most sensible of the family', but 'thought to be unhappy in her marriage' (Letter 226, JW to SK, May 1800). In 1807 he noted that she 'had been dead years before & left one girl an infant now the Heir to the estate' at Milton (Letter 257, JW to SK, 3 Oct. 1807). See George Crawfurd, *A General Description of the Shire of Renfrew* (Paisley, 1818), p. 394; and W-K, I, p. 448n.

[63] Perhaps William M'Gill, *The Prayer of Our Saviour for the Union of His Followers Considered: A Sermon by William M'Gill, A.M. one of the Ministers of Ayr* (Glasgow, 1768), rather than M'Gill's 'A Humble Remonstrance Against Some Prevailing Vices of the Present Age: A Fast Sermon', published along with a sermon by William Dalrymple in *The Judgements of God Against Impiety, &c.: Illustrated and Improved, in Two Sermons, Preached at Ayr, December 24, 1772. On Occasion of a Fast Appointed by the Presbytery of Ayr* (Edinburgh, 1773).

[64] William M'Gill, *The Friends: A Sermon; Preached December 27, 1778 at the Annual Meeting of the Society of Free Masons at Ayr* (Edinburgh, 1779). See also Eugene Heath, 'Alexander Gillies and Adam Smith: Freemasonry and the Resonance of Self-Love', *Scottish Historical Review*, 103 (2024), pp. 289–317.

[65] Peter Tait (fl. 1768–95), merchant, bookseller, and printer of the *Glasgow Journal*. See John Tait, *Directory for the City of Glasgow, Villages of Anderston, Calton, and Gorbals; also for the Towns of Paisley, Greenock, Port-Glasgow, and Kilmarnock, from the 15th May 1783, to the 15th May 1784* (Glasgow, 1783), p. 65; Robert Hay Carnie, 'Scottish Printers and Booksellers 1668–1775: A Second Supplement (II)', *Studies in Bibliography*, 15 (1962), pp. 105–20 at p. 116.

before he die.[66] He hopes the Era of prosecution in Church courts is now over ^here^ yet he cannot answer for the zeal of some people even about Glasgow which is very high on that particular point. He is amazed at a man of Horsley's abilities appearing at this day as a defender of the Athanasian doctrines[67] & others of the same kind & is not sure but the best way of answering him, woud be in the way of ridicule, to contrast the depth & accuracy of his Mathematical knowledge with the childish weakness of his Theological Oppinions. He is equaly surprised that he should be encouraged or instigated to these things by such a man as Lowth[68] of whom he had a respectable oppinion as every body has. Yet your conjecture is fully confirmed by a paragraph of the last letter I had from J. Hamilton,[69] Horsleys cousin giving his connexion with the Bishop of London the preferments he has received & expects from ^him^ as the cause or rather an excuse or appology for His embarking in the present controversy against his own tast & inclination. I was very sorry I had brought none of your former letters about this matter to town as they woud have greatly entertained the worthy good man. He bids me enquire at you about this new Society for promoting Scripture knowledge[70] whether they are the same with the Publishers of the Th. repository.[71] But I shall never have done if I give way to my pen.

I have had so many things to say in this miscelaneous Letter that I have not ^had^ time to acknowledge the receipt of your kind one which Miss Kenrick tore

---

[66] M'Gill, *A Practical Essay on the Death of Jesus Christ*, which emphasized Christ's human weakness in the Garden of Gethsemane to the extent that it was accused of denying the deity of Christ.

[67] Samuel Horsley was nominated bishop of St David's in 1788 in recognition of his attack on Priestley's *History of the Corruptions of Christianity* (1782), in defence of orthodox Christian trinitarian doctrine. See Letter 80.

[68] Rev. Robert Lowth (1710–87), biblical critic, bishop of London, and Horsley's patron.

[69] Louisa Wodrow's brother John Hamilton. Horsley's mother, who died when he was two years old, was Anne Hamilton (d. 1736). She was the daughter of William Hamilton (1669–1732), professor of divinity and principal at Edinburgh University, and the sister of Gavin Hamilton (1704–67), John Hamilton's and Louisa Wodrow's father and partner in the prominent Edinburgh publishing and bookselling firm Hamilton and Balfour.

[70] John Jebb wrote 'A Sketch of the Plan of the Society for Promoting Knowledge of the Scriptures', established at the Essex Street Unitarian Chapel on 29 Sept. 1783. It published two volumes of undated *Commentaries and Essays*, sold by Joseph Johnson; and was a forerunner of the 'Unitarian Society' that was established in 1791. See John Jebb, *The Works Theological, Medical, Political, and Miscellaneous, of John Jebb*, ed. John Disney, 3 vols (1787), II, pp. 236–53.

[71] The *Theological Repository* was founded by Joseph Priestley, who was a member of the Society for Promoting the Knowledge of the Scriptures, but most of its contributors were not. Moreover, Priestley had intended it to discuss more than unitarian or Arian theology, but failed to attract contributors from other theological perspectives. He ran it from 1769 till 1771, and revived it from 1784 till 1788. Robert E. Schofield, *The Enlightenment of Joseph Priestley: A Study of His Life and Work from 1733 to 1773* (University Park, PA, 1997), pp. 193–201; Schofield, *The Enlightened Joseph Priestley*, pp. 202–07.

off from her own & gave me the first night I called on her. You are too grateful My Dear Sir for little for indeed I had it ^not^ in my power to show your amiable & accomplished Daughter so much attention as I wished to do, and as my esteem & affection to her dictated as it hapned to be the time of Harvest so that I had little command of my Serv$^t$. & Horses & allong with this an uncommon run of Company & visiting in our parish part of it attention & civility ^to her^ & also to M$^{rs}$. Balfour[72] who was in the parish at the time so that she wanted two rides which were planned for her one to the North to see Kelburn & the Fairlie[73] road as I think that part of the coast beautiful & romantick from the different appearances of the Islands & another to the South even Maybole & Kirkoswald. M$^{rs}$. Biggar[74] sent her a pressing invitation after she was gone, but neither ^she^ nor we woud have waited for any thing of this sort. Indeed she was not on horseback at all while at Stevenston. But I hope to live to see her in Scotland again & you also. I wonder that M$^{rs}$. Kenrick & you do<–> not think of it. She surely wishes to see her native Country once more– as Mary tells me she is much or more a Scotchwoman ^than^ ever that is enthusiasticaly fond of Scotland & it's honour. It woud <fold> [make me] very happy to see you both.

I have just now been looking at three pictures along with Mr Pearman (do you remember the Prin$^{ls}$. Nephew Willie Pearman now a Mins$^r$. in Fife)[75] & Nell. A fine one indeed of S$^t$. Kathrines Martyrdom. Another of Our Sav$^r$. taken down from the Cross & a Miniature Copy (tho' a large Picture) of the School of Athens ~~did~~ you have seen no doubt the Original by Raphael in the Vatican the copy by one of Foulis Scholars and also a book of coloured engravings which the Colledge has lately received in a present from M$^r$. Kennedy of Dunnure or Dalquarran[76]

---

[72] Presumably one of Louisa Wodrow's relatives through her mother, Helen Hamilton (d. 1793), née Balfour, who was one of sixteen siblings.

[73] Fairlie, previously a medieval estate, by this time a flourishing weaving and fishing village in the parish of Largs. NSA, V, 798, 802, 804. There was a turnpike road from Greenock on the north Renfrewshire coast to Stranraer in Galloway, which passed through the parish of Largs in north Ayrshire.

[74] JW's sister Margaret was married to Rev. Matthew Biggar (d. 1806), minister of Kirkoswald, Ayrshire.

[75] Rev. William Pairman (1735–98), minister of Elie (1761–98), in the presbytery of St Andrews, Fife. Leechman bequeathed his library to him. FES, V, 199.

[76] Thomas Kennedy (d. 1819) of Dunure in south Ayrshire, a member of a prominent Ayrshire legal dynasty. See National Galleries Scotland, 'Thomas Kennedy of Dunure' by Henry Raeburn (c. 1812), accessed 25 March 2023, www.nationalgalleries.org/art-and-artists/5332/thomas-francis-kennedy-dunure-1788-1879. Dunure is on the Firth of Clyde, five miles north-west of the town of Maybole, where Kenrick's wife Elisabeth had grown up and where their daughter Mary was born. Kennedy married the sister of the architect Robert Adam (1728–92), who had refashioned Culzean

(M^rs^. Kenrick will know him) engravings of the different views of Vesuvius & Mount Etna. I might have enough of entertainment here but my time will be short as I intend to leave this on Saturday by Paisley & Kilbarchan.

I hap'ned to enter into some conversation with Miss. K. on the road to Milliken about the distress of my Family three years ago & finding a ^short^ letter of the Princ^ls^. on Gavins death gave it her from my Pocketbook thinking some how it woud be agreable to you to read it in his own hand.[77] This you'll return me by Nell When she leaves Bewdley. I will now shut up this letter if I had made another attempt to find M^r^. Magills Sermon & inclose in it all the written scraps viz. M^r^. Magill Contents Haddows inscription the News paper Extract & give in ^a^ seperate Parcell to Miss Kenrick M^r^. Magills speech & sermon. She has also for you another little book ^for you^ we call the Scotch Confessional, by a friend of mine Makensie. I furnished him with the Material for the Preface but the Composition is his own.[78] You were out of Scotland during that Memorable Prosecution of the

---

Castle for David Kennedy, tenth earl of Cassillis (1727–92). Adam also designed Dalquharran Castle for Thomas Kennedy. It was completed in 1790.

[77] JW's son Gavin (c. 1761–81), who had lodged with the Leechmans as a student at Glasgow University, where he had died from a nervous disease, or possibly a brain tumour. See JW to SK, 31 July 1781, in W-K, I, pp. 451–52, where JW copied part of the letter from Leechman mentioned here, and told SK that Leechman had 'been a Father to Gavin who lived in his house many years'. Leechman was Gavin Wodrow's great-uncle through his wife Bridget, Louisa Wodrow's aunt.

[78] 'The Scotch Confessional' refers to John Mackenzie's anonymous *The Religious Establishment in Scotland Examined Upon Protestant Principles: A Tract, Occasioned by the Late Prosecution Against the Late Reverend Mr. Alexander Fergusson, Minister in Kilwinning* (1771), which was 'revised by some of the friends of Truth' (p. iv). It has a sixty-two-page preface, signed by 'Christianus', which provides a detailed account of the prosecution of Fergusson for heresy. JW was well placed to assist with this as he had managed the defence of Fergusson on behalf of the presbytery of Irvine, and had published an account of the proceedings in the *Scots Magazine*, 30 (Oct. 1768), pp. 556–58, and (Nov. 1768), pp. 610–12; W-K, I, pp. 158–62, 296–97. The publication of Francis Blackburne's *The Confessional* (1766) sparked a controversy over subscription to the Thirty-Nine Articles of the Church of England, which saw a couple of hundred Anglican clergy unsuccessfully petition Parliament to remove this requirement in the early 1770s. During this Feathers Tavern Petition campaign, the Cambridge unitarian, John Jebb, quoted from *The Religious Establishment in Scotland Examined*, and it is referred to as 'the Scots' confessional' in *The Works Theological, Medical, Political, and Miscellaneous, of John Jebb*, ed. John Disney, 3 vols (1787), III, p. 4n. Some give the author of *Religious Establishment in Scotland Examined* as John Graham (including Eighteenth Century Collections Online), but others as J. Mackenzie (FES, III, p. 118). In light of JW's letter, the latter is correct. In addition, 'Mr Mackenzie, of Portpatrick' is noted as the author of this 'very clever and lively book' in William C. Smith, 'Religious Freedom in Scotland', *The Theological Review*, 15 (1878), p. 457. This was John Mackenzie (1743–1836), licensed by the presbytery of Stranraer in 1771, and minister of Portpatrick 1773–1828. FES, II, p. 351. Mackenzie was around twenty-eight years old when the book was published, and at that time JW referred to the author as being 'a young friend of mine'; while John Graham (1732–1815), minister of Dunlop, was close

Abbot of Kilw^g.^79 & it was cheifly on account of the Preface I thought of sending ^it^. The first part of the book is also admirable & perhaps is the only part of that shoud have been published.

five at night

Not able to find any more of M^r. Magill^s I send you one of his Collegues who is a worthy man but has a stile & manner particular to himself. There is a much superiour one published by Fullarton one of the three Dissenters preached before the Synod of Aberdeen[80]– a very liberal spirit prevails ^there^ but such a sermon as scarce heard of in Glasg^w. Miss Kenrick astonished me by telling me that you have only one of the Princ^l. ^four printed^ Sermons she must be mistaken. I asked him just now if he had any of his two last public Sermons by him. One of them is long resembling a treatise the Wisdom of God in X^ty. He has none nor coud he direct me where they are to be had, but I will make Nell enquire [page torn] M^r. Balfour in Ed^r.[81] which is the only two you can want. Do you [know] this worthy

---

in age to Wodrow. Letter 49, JW to SK, 22 May 1771, W-K, I, p. 312. Mackenzie followed up with a short pamphlet titled *Subscription to Human Articles of Faith, Examined Particularly, in a Letter to the Reverend Mr Thomas Walker, Minister of Dundonald. By the Author of the Religious Establishment in Scotland, &c.* (1775). This focussed on the key point at issue: whether it is legitimate to require loyalty to a subordinate standard as well as scripture. Mackenzie argued that one could be an orthodox Calvinist, agreeing with the Westminster Confession of Faith in every article, and yet still hold that the only standard of truth should be scripture (e.g. pp. 6–7). It is notable that, in the same presbytery of Stranraer, Galloway, Andrew Ross, minister of Inch, asked to be relieved of the requirement of subscribing to the Confession of Faith in 1776. See Letter 150.

[79] Rev. Alexander Fergusson (1689–1770), minister of the Abbey Church, Kilwinning, Ayrshire, nicknamed by JW and SK 'the Abbot of Kilwinning'. JW had undertaken his probation as a newly ordained minister with him, and both he and SK treated him with esteem and affection. For the prosecution of Fergusson towards the end of his life, see W-K, I, pp. 294–97, 300–02.

[80] Alexander Fullerton, *The Measures of Toleration: A Sermon, Preached before the Synod of Aberdeen, at Aberdeen, October 8th, 1782* (Aberdeen, 1783). Rev. Alexander Fullerton (1737–87) was master at the Aberdeen Grammar School from 1760 until his death, and also ordained in 1774 as minister for St Clement's and the fishing village of Futtie on Aberdeen harbour. FES, VI, p. 28; OSA, vol. XIX (1797), p. 148. Fullerton declared that 'not only has every man a right to think and judge for himself, and to make choice of his own religious creed; but also…to make open and public profession of what he believes…There is much hazard of doing injustice by annexing civil penalties to mere opinions. It is actions, not opinions, that are directly mischievous to society…Certainly no person has a right to maintain with impunity the lawfulness of perjury, robbery, assassination, and other crimes pernicious to society: but the principles of morality are so deeply embedded in human nature, that there are but few men in their senses who would openly and avowedly plead the cause of such enormities'. Fullerton, *Measures of Toleration*, pp. 11, 14n.

[81] Louisa Wodrow's uncle, John Balfour (1715–95). He was the business partner of her father, Gavin Hamilton (1704–67), in the bookselling trade in Edinburgh till 1762, after which he imported European books and became printer to the Faculty of Advocates, the Bank of Scotland, and the University of Edinburgh. Warren McDougall, 'Gavin Hamilton, Bookseller in Edinburgh', *British Journal for Eighteenth-Century Studies*, 1 (1978), pp. 1–19; Iain Beaven and Warren

man has thoughts of adding two or three more <& publishing> to his four printed Sermons[82] & publishing a vol. which is most earnestly solicited by his friends but he is very doubtful himself if the state of his health will allow him & he has never been accustomed to write by an amanuensis but I must conclude. God bless you & M[rs]. Kenrick & your Daughter whom I just parted with from her to call here & am going down to drink tea with & to commit to her the care of this

                 Adieu
                 J Wodrow

Extract Glasgow News Paper[83]
Cumnock 29 May 84

The following piece of intelligence you may depend upon as a fact. Last week about 40 men Women & children passed thro' this place. These set off from Irvine on a pilgrimage to Jerusalem or to some place unknown. They represent themselves as the spiritual Offspring of a M[rs]. Buchan from Glasgow. Her firstborn is a M[r]. Whyte who lately was Mins[r]. of the Relief congregation at Irvine. <They> ^She^ professes to communicate the holy Ghost by the laying on of hands & breathing. Her disciples believe themselves to be filled with the Holy Ghost & that they neither <->do nor can commit sin. They believe themselves to be immortal, they believe that X is now about to make his appearance on earth & to reign a 1000 years & that they are to be the principal Members of his kingdom. They believe that their spiritual mother as they call M[rs]. Buch[n]. has bought forth children without the knowledge of man by the spiritual agency of the H. G.[84] When they are asked where they are going, they answer they are following the

---

McDougall, 'The Scottish Book Trade', in Michael F. Suarez and Michael L. Turner, eds, *The Cambridge History of the Book in Britain. Vol. 5, 1695–1830* (Cambridge, 2009), pp. 352–65; Stephen W. Brown and Warren McDougall, eds, *The Edinburgh History of the Book in Scotland: Vol. 2, Enlightenment and Expansion, 1707–1800* (Edinburgh, 2012). John Balfour had assisted JW in 1780–82 in his efforts to help SK recover a financial loan made to his wife's brother in Jamaica. *W-K*, vol. 1, pp. 438, 442, 447–50, 453–55, 460, 475.

[82] William Leechman, 'The Nature, Reasonableness, and Advantages, of Prayer; With an Attempt to Answer the Objections Against It', Sermon V, in *The Scotch Preacher: Or, A Collection of Sermons. By Some of the Most Eminent Clergymen of the Church of Scotland*, vol. I (Edinburgh and London, 1775), pp. 138–206; Leechman, 'The Temper, Character, and Duty of a Minister of the Gospel', Sermons VIII and IX, ibid., vol. II (London and Edinburgh, 1776), pp. 136–87; Leechman, 'The Wisdom of God in the Gospel-Revelation', Sermons XII and XIII, ibid., pp. 215–80; Leechman, 'The Excellency of the Spirit of Christianity', Sermons XV and XVI, ibid., vol. III (London and Edinburgh, 1779), pp. 287–338.

[83] *Glasgow Journal*, 17 June to 24 June 1784.

[84] i.e. the Holy Ghost.

lamb.[85] They do not pray for any thing as they look upon God as bound to give them all things without their asking.

Their ordinary duties are reading the N Testament and praising this they do upon the road as they are travelling. It is said they object to the O Testament and it is certain they reject all other books but the Scripture. Their flight from Irvine was so precip^it^ate that they left their Houses with goods in them: one had a washing[86] on the green which she did not stay to dry up neither did they stay to settle any other bussiness. One of them named Hunter[87] was by Warrant bought back to Irvine from Mauchline to settle his affairs and his Wife stayed some nights in this place. Several persons here conversed with her in order to learn her principles: & some endeavoured to prevail with her to go back but in vain. She is now gone to join her spiritual Mother & the other Members of the fraternity. M^r. Whyte preaches <to them> often as they go along the high way but will <take> ^receive^ no money from the people.

On the whole they seem to be a set of blinded people led by the Spirit of Enthusiasm. No person needs argue with them; for they still maintain themselves to be led by the Spirit– that they only know the right sense of the Script^re. that the Spirit shows it them in its true sense that all others are in a state of nature & cannot know the meaning of the Scripture. They allow that they themselves were in the same state before they were convicted & they pity the rest of the World as blind sinners. They now reside in a Wood near Dumfries where M^r. Whyte preaches to them.

## Letter 85: Samuel Kenrick to James Wodrow, 2–3 December 1784

Addressed: Rev^d. Ja^s. Wodrow / Irvine / Scotland
Postmarked: Bewdley December the third 1784
Franked: Free Westcote
Stamp: 134 BEWDLEY

My dear Friend

You may say what you will– but I cannot be brought to sit down & write to you till I see a frank to convey my letter– altho' I have thought of little else, ever since

---

[85] i.e. Jesus Christ, the Lamb of God (John 1:29, 35).
[86] 'a washing', i.e. 'a load of washed clothes', idiomatic Scottish expression.
[87] Peter Hunter, a writer (lawyer) in Irvine.

the 19th. Ult°. when I had the pleasure of receiving under my roof your gentle amiable daughter in company with my Mary– a most welcome sight you, have the feelings of a friend & father, will easily believe me. Your interesting packet was not long withheld from me. I will begin w$^{th}$. the agreeable task of reviewing your multifarious & entertaining epistle. Your hospitable entertainment & kind attention to my daughter, has not been thrown away upon her or us. She had before given us a minute description of her agreeable excursion with you to Kilbarchan, Milliken & Paisley.– To her amiable companion I leave the description of her journey from parting with you at Glasgow, to her arrival here.– Tho' they spent good part of a day at York, they did not call upon our friend Cappe[1]– the minster, or Cathedral, w$^{ch}$. was their principal inducement for going that way, took up all the time & attention while there.– Poor M$^r$. Warner![2]– what an awful example of him in the impenetrable ways– of a most wise just & good Providence! To whom I used to look up w$^{th}$. esteem & veneration as to a superior being– that all those powers & graces w$^{ch}$. shed such a lustre round them, should so suddenly be locked up & extinguished—while his strength & animal faculties continue hale & sound! M$^{rs}$. Milliken[3] is, on the other hand, a surprizing instance of a strong natural constitution. She has had her share of rubs & crosses to struggle with– & I am happy to hear she is daily surmounting them & likely to close a long life with peace honour & comfort.

 I am very much obliged to you for the interesting particulars you have favoured me w$^{th}$. an account of, respecting your worthy friend M$^r$. M$^c$Gill– & for his sermon & speech you were so kind as send me.[4] His sermon is a most excellent composition, in every respect– & must make every impartial reader impatient to see his other works– but more especially the treatise,[5] you mention, on w$^{ch}$. little any ways satisfactory, has ever fallen into my hands at least. Indeed all that I remember of this sort, are the hints our worthy Principal gave us long ago in his lectures. You may depend upon my doing all in my power to bring this valuable work to light– & shall give you freely every hint that falls in [my] way. I have shewn the sermon to my friend the clergyman[6]– who is quite in raptures w$^{th}$. it. But he has

---

  [1] Newcome Cappe. See Letter 79.
  [2] Rev. John Warner. See Letter 84.
  [3] Jean Milliken. See Letter 84.
  [4] William M'Gill. See Letter 84.
  [5] M'Gill's forthcoming *Practical Essay on the Death of Jesus Christ*.
  [6] Presumably the heterodox Rev. Thomas Wigan (c. 1744–1819), who became a close friend of Kenrick when living at Bewdley in the 1770s. See Letter 88.

not given me his opinion of the contents or analysis of the treatise. I shall take the first opportunity of sounding D^r. Priestley on the subject. But he is so much in engaged in a variety of pursuits of his own, that I feel no small reluctance, from our slight acquaintance, to intrude myself on him: w^ch. nothing but my firm persuasion that he loves ^truth^ above every other object, could make me conquer. If I should find the Doctor disposed to peruse the whole treatise, I suppose the author would have no objection to it: & you may easily convey it to me next feb^y by the Glasgow merchants to Wrexham fair. I have conceived a favourable opinion of L^d. Hailes' critical talents from the specimen of his strictures on Gibbon,[7] w^ch. the worthy Principal or you were so kind as to send me. But his objection to an attempt ~~to~~ at a rational account of the Agony,[8] as it is called, seems to me quite frivolous. Is not that the greatest excellency of the evangelical historians,[9] that they confine themselves to relate simply facts, as they occurred, without ever thinking of accounting for them?– I shall never forget D^r. Leechman's modest attempt to account for it– & ^to^ reconcile it to the real courage & intrepidity of that divine character.– Your conjecture ab^t. the Bookseller & his Lordship's shuffling conduct, is highly probable. Preconceived opinions like other habits, will warp the soundest understanding.

You are ^a^ much better judge than I can pretend to be, how far it may be consistant with prudence, to publish it in Scotland– or to put his name to it. I should prefer his putting his name to it, as I think ^as you do^ it would sell better, & turn out more to the author's advantage, both in fame & emolument. And as to printing I should be for its being done, where it can be well done & most convenient to the author to have it corrected.

I shall therefore trouble you no more on the subject till I can consult D^r. P. who is the only competetent judge of such matters, of my acquaintance hereabouts. I shall strictly observe the caution your confidence expects from me. If I should meet w^th. hints from any one else worth communicating, you shall be sure of them in due time. I am very sorry to find that his little fortune could not escape that devouring vortex, the Ayr Bank. The united testimony of regard to the memory of M^r. Haddow– is equally honourable to the deceased & his surviving friends.

---

[7] Edward Gibbon (1737–94), historian of ancient Rome, best known for his *History of the Decline and Fall of the Roman Empire*, 6 vols (1776–88). In 1786 Lord Hailes published a critique of his account of the role of Christianity in the decline of the Roman empire, his *An Inquiry into the Secondary Causes which Mr Gibbon has Assigned for the Rapid Growth of Christianity* (Edinburgh, 1786).

[8] One of the key purposes of M'Gill's *Practical Essay*. See Letter 84.

[9] i.e. the New Testament Gospel writers Matthew, Mark, Luke, and John.

As to inscriptions, it is impossible to say too little of great talents, or transcendent virtues. The simple name spreads such a lustre, as beggars the finest words. But characters w^ch. were adorned w^th. the more modest virtues & amiable graces, seem to lay a just claim to the partial description of a friendly hand, & I believe are always read w^th. pleasure by the friendly & humane. The excellent poem you mention, to be written by a Lady on the occasion, our giddy lasses have mislaid or left behind them.[10]

Many thanks to you for the numerous curious particulars you have collected for me, respecting this new set of enthusiasts, the Buchanites, who have just started up among you. Miss Wodrow has given me still more. But I have not time to trouble you with my reflections. I am come now to my friend on Monday morning the 25th. wherein we are both more interested. Be assured we received your daughter as the best pledge you could give us of your regard & affection for us, ^&^ that we shall be happy to make every ^thing^ agreeable to her & that she shall be treated in the same open hearty manner you treated our Mary. We are already all as much at home together as if we had been so all our lives. She is a great acquisition to our little circle– & will no doubt improve by the conversation of strangers, more than if she was always confined to the same company. Besides she is already engaged w^th. 2 or 3 young ladies our neighbours to read french together, along w^th. Mary. I leave to her to give an account of the company this little town affords. You will find they are all of the better sort– without any religious or political distinctions.

As to the English dialect it is soon acquired especially by the docile, gentle female sex, who are so chatty together. Very different was the case of our Glasgow friend R.B.[11]– who was what you call in Scotland a <u>spilt bairn</u>[12]– having no father, & soon becoming master of an indulgent mother & servants his humour was his law– & if he chose to talk or act childishly none durst laugh or contradict ^him^. Under such disadvantages, what could you expect, but a lingo of his own– & an untowardness to imitate the language of others. He had however a fund of good nature & good sense at bottom, w^ch. gained him the love & esteem of his acquaintance; w^ch. soon made him & them most sociable together. And tho' there remained a small shade of difference in their language, w^ch. every

---

[10] The poem was by 'M^rs. Macreddie a Lady in this neighbourhood' on the death by drowning of a 'Mr Haddow'. See Letter 84.
[11] Robert Brisbane. See Letter 84.
[12] 'spilt bairn': 'spoiled child'. *DSL*.

man in every country has from early habit, affectation, or immitation more or less, yet it no longer rose to be laughable, much less to be unintelligible. It is in this way that all englishmen, are supposed to speak alike– altho' to a discerning ear, there are as different shades (nuances) or specific differences, as in their characters or faces: arrising from the above mentioned or other accidental circumstances. But principally to people of the lower & midling ranks of life, their language but especially their pronunciation partakes of the vulgar dialect of the place of their birth. Thus D[r]. Priestley notwithstanding the variety of different & best company he has been long accustomed to, w[ch]. generally polishes & wears off these rough corners, still retains marks of the Yorkshire pronunciation both in familiar discourse & in the pulpit– & his lady a much stronger degree of the Westmoreland dialect, w[ch]. borders on the scotch. In Worcestershire, particularly hereabouts, they give a strong harsh aspiration (like the Tuscans) at the beginning of every word w[ch]. begins w[th]. a vowell & on the contrary if it begins w[th]. an h aspirated– they pronounce it without an aspiration. Thus <u>am, art, is</u> are pronounced <u>ham, hart, his</u>; & <u>ham, heart, his am, eart, is</u>. Thus our Bellman, begins– <u>I ham, to give notice, that a orse</u> &c. In Gloucestershire & Somersetshire s is pronounced z & f, v. Londoners pronounce w,– vee & vice versa. E.G. *Vine Wauts*– for Wine Vaults. In short there is vulgar pronunciation as well as a vulgar language, peculiar to every district in England (except Oxford) w[ch]. marks more or less the language of every individual who does not ^take^ great pains to guard against it. And perhaps it is most attended to & guarded against by people of the most superficial minds. At least my friend Harry Millar[13] used to say so. But Miss Nelly runs no risk of learning these vulgarisms– as her acquaintance are ashamed of them & avoid them w[th]. the greatest care.

As to dress & appearance, you may safely trust it to my wife & daughter, along w[th]. yours– who will do ^& advise^ everything for the best. And as to money matters, make yourself easy– I shall chearfully supply her with what she wants. As to the length of her stay, you judge as we do. The longer the more we shall be obliged to her & you. For it will be a strong presumption & it will be agreeable & of some advantage to her– w[ch]. is what we most wish: as to her excursion to London, & Mary's– we have time enough to think of those matters.

I have neither leisure nor inclination to enter into your profound dissertation on the difficult question of Liberty & necessity. I am happy, however, to find that

---

[13] Henry Millar. See Letter 82.

you, who have weighed this abstruse subject well, think that it is at bottom only a dispute about words.[14] My studies are on much lighter subjects.

I have read Blair's Rhetoric[15] w[th]. great pleasure. It is a Book universally admired in this country. His precepts are clear, & rationall. His criticisms on works & characters of authors are done w[th]. judgment, & shew that he has read & studied them w[th]. great care. His reading seems to be immense indeed; & to comprehend not only the classics of antiquity but also the modern french & italian authours from his personal knowledge & the spaniards & portugueeze upon the credit of others. His strictures on Addison[16] are ingenious & highly useful. In short it is a Book to my taste; w[ch]. calls back my attention to subjects I have formerly been conversant w[th]. & only demands that slight attention that I can spare in this way– from a daily laborious drudgery I am & have long been engaged in.

I have read Hayley's plays too– w[ch]. like every thing from his masterly hand & excellent heart, can't fail to entertain. But like you, I cannot relish them as comedy. The actors some how never seem to be in earnest– but to be only actors. The trajedy of Russell is truly good. Yet you find it will not do on the stage. The other trajedy is too deep– it harrows up the very soul. To me it was almost shocking. As a picture this is doubtless a high degree of merit: but as a moral lesson, it hurts one to think it possible– but shocks one to think it true.[17]

---

[14] See Letter 84.

[15] Rev. Hugh Blair (1718–80), *Lectures on Rhetoric and Belles Lettres* (1783; 2nd edn, 1785). Blair was professor of rhetoric at the University of Edinburgh and a leading Moderate in the Church of Scotland. His most famous publications were five volumes of his sermons (1777–1801) and his *Lectures on Rhetoric and Belles Lettres* (1783). He was awarded a specially created regius chair of rhetoric and belles lettres at the University of Edinburgh in 1762. The *Lectures* achieved fifty-six editions in America alone between 1805 and 1823. Andrew Hook, *Scotland and America: A Study of Cultural Relations, 1750–1835* (Glasgow, 1975), p. 81; W-K, I, p. 441n.

[16] Joseph Addison (1672–1719), essayist and politician. Blair admired Addison and his criticisms were mainly of Addison's attention to detail: 'though one of the most beautiful writers in the Language, he is not the most correct'; and 'Mr. Addison's chief excellency, as a writer, lay in describing and painting. There he is great; but in methodising and reasoning, he is not so eminent'. *Lectures on Rhetoric*, II, Lecture XX, p. 60; Lecture XXII, p. 107.

[17] Hayley's success as a dramatist was more mixed than as a poet and biographer; though perhaps his greatest influence was in his agency on behalf of other writers and artists. His tragedies included *Lord Russell* and *Marcella*, both published in his *Plays of Three Acts* (1784); *Eudora* was first performed in 1790. The comedies published in *Plays of Three Acts* were *The Happy Prescription*, *The Two Connoisseurs*, and *The Mausoleum*. See Letters 79 and 80 above; Daisy Hay, *Dinner with Joseph Johnson: Books and Friendship in a Revolutionary Age* (2022), pp. 297–303, 385–86.

3 Dec[r]. Now I find you at Glasgow– after having been often called away from you– w[th]. that venerable living saint[18] whom I never think of, without affection & respect. I am not surprized you should find a difference in his appearance after an absence of 18 months. I am greatly obliged to you for giving my daughter an opportunity of seeing him & his excellent lady– & to them for their kind reception of her. She is quite charmed with them both. Mary was fortunate in meeting w[th]. Lady Glasgow[19] at the Principals & still more so, for seeing the accomplished young Countess of Sutherland.[20] You have the advantage of me in know[g]. Miss Brisbane[21] & your high opinion of her, makes me still long more to see her. The honest mother I knew well above 40 years ago. At last I am come to your cousin Horsley– upon whom I intended to have bestowd one page at least. The principal's hint is a good one. But let him know that D[r]. Priestley has neither spared ridicule nor the harshest severity in his 2[d]. answer– w[ch]. I shall send you by the first opportunity– a jus talionis[22]– for the unprovoked insolence of M[r]. Archdeacon.[23] If he does not feel this attack to the quick– he must be pretty callous.[24] Your meek spirit perhaps will not relish this. Nor is it likely to make proselytes. At the same time I think it is a just & proper check to haughty pride & insolence.[25]– I have the first N[o]. published by the Society for promot[g]. Xtian knowledge– but do not know who the authors are.[26] When I do you shall be duly acquainted w[th]. it.

With best respects &c to yourself M[rs]. Wodrow & sweet Peggy. I ever am

yrs S.K.

I have not time to read over the inclosed nor to finish yours adieu my good friend the franks are dated & post going

---

[18] William Leechman.
[19] Elizabeth Boyle, Countess of Glasgow. See Letter 84.
[20] See Letter 84.
[21] See Letter 84; and W-K, I, p. 448n.
[22] i.e. the law of retaliation on the biblical basis of 'an eye for an eye'.
[23] Samuel Horsley. See Letter 81.
[24] Joseph Priestley, *Letters to Dr Horsley, Part II: Containing Further Evidence that the Primitive Church was Unitarian* (Birmingham, 1784).
[25] Horsley, an energetic and skilful episcopal administrator, was arrogant and intellectually vain. Schofield, *The Enlightened Joseph Priestley*, p. 225; F. C. Mather, *High Church Prophet: Bishop Samuel Horsley (1733–1806) and the Caroline Tradition in the Later Georgian Church* (Oxford, 1992), p. 248.
[26] The first volume of *Commentaries and Essays Published by the Society for Promoting the Knowledge of the Scriptures* [1784]. See Letter 84.

## Letter 86: James Wodrow to Samuel Kenrick, 7 December 1784

Addressed: M[r]. S. Kenrick Bewdley / W[cr]. Shire
Postmarked: Irvine December Eight 1784
Franked: Cassillis[1]

My Dear Freind

 I sympathise most sincerely with M[rs]. Kenrick & you in the joy you would feel in embracing your beloved Daughter ^after^ so long an absence– & shall I say, also, in receiving mine from her hand which woud increase your joy a little by reviving the tender Ideas of the friendship of our Youth more sensibly at least than any Letters can do. It woud have delighted me to have wittnessed the scene of her ^M.K.^ first meeting with her parents & their whole family. For few such scenes occur in the short & chequered period of our Lives. The next thing to the sight of it is a lively & faithful picture of it from her or your pen. Her talents for description I have an ~~very~~ ^exceeding^ good oppinion of but I know this ^is^ your fort.[2] You will find her not the worse for the Scotch Air & diet & her &lt;Short&gt; intercourse with the people. If her knowledge of the World is not much encreased for she had seen enough of it before; her kind & honest heart will retain the impressions made upon it by the intercourse with her Fathers old freinds wittness the parting we had with her at Glasgow which the joy of embracing her English friends will not yet have effaced the impression of. But I must confine my pen & my immagination within proper bounds as I have only a short letter to write for this frank will ^be^ overloaded with the Letters of Nells companions.

 I long to hear from you. I hope you have found before this time the Paper of M[r]. Magills hand writing which Nell tells me was a missing.[3] It will certainly be among the printed papers & if not I will procure you another copy.

 I have been riding about since harvest more than usual. The ride with your Daughter was but a prologue to it. I ^only^ returned last week from Tarlbolton[4] & Kirkoswald my Sister Mainy is in a very poor way.[5] Nell will read you the paragraph

---

[1] David Kennedy, tenth earl of Cassillis. See Letter 82.
[2] i.e. forte.
[3] See Letter 84. JW had sent SK a manuscript copy of the contents pages of M'Gill's *Practical Essay on the Death of Jesus Christ*, eventually published in Edinburgh in 1786.
[4] JW's brother Patrick (1713–93) was parish minister of Tarbolton, South Ayrshire.
[5] Marion ('Mainy') Wodrow (1719–85), JW's sister, of whom SK was fond. She did not marry, and latterly lived in Glasgow with, and cared for, three other unmarried sisters, whose health was frailer than her own and all of whom had predeceased her. She had then left Glasgow, at the end of 1781, and moved to Ayrshire to live alternately with the Wodrows in Stevenston and the Biggars in Kirkoswald. See *W-K*, I, pp. 129, 362–63, 431, 461.

in her Letter relative to this. I have been ^visiting^ the great, contrary to my custom & inclination. Lady Glasgow[6] Lord Cassils[7] & Sir Adam Fergusson[8]. Lord Cassils was quite by himself & I spent 24 hours with him more agreably than ever I did before. Sir Adam is a new acquaintance. I never was in ^his^ house before, but met with a very kind reception. He is perfectly frank & open on every subject. I admire him as one of the first rate men of our Country.[9] He remembers you.[10]

Old M$^r$. Oswald The American Ambassador[11] died at his House of Achincrue[12] about three Weeks ago & has left one of the greatest fortunes ever made by a Scotsman, yet I cannot tell precisely what it is.[13] The fortune of 30,000£ he got with M$^{rs}$. Oswald he has left at her own disposal together with a Liferent[14] or annuity of his Land rents in Ayrshire. She will not poor woman long survive him. His estates in Ayrshire Galloway & Nithsdale[15] with his whole vast fortune in Money (except some considerable annuities to his Nephews ^yet^ only for a term of years) He has left to George Oswald of Scotston the D$^r$. Son[16] & appointed the

---

[6] Probably at her Halkhead (or 'Hawkhead') estate near Paisley. See Letter 84.

[7] David Kennedy, tenth earl of Cassillis, who had franked this letter in his capacity as a Scottish representative peer. See Letter 82.

[8] See Letter 79.

[9] Probably JW used 'country' in a common eighteenth-century sense of 'county' here.

[10] Adam Fergusson attended Edinburgh University, so his memory of SK was an Ayrshire connection rather than educational. Kilkerran, his seat, is 5 miles south of Maybole, where Elisabeth Kenrick was born.

[11] Richard Oswald (1705–84), born in Caithness, a merchant in slaves, horses, tobacco, and sugar, and later a government contractor and land speculator in the Caribbean and North America. He was the earl of Shelburne's negotiator at the Peace of Paris with the United States of America in 1782–83. See David Hancock, *Citizens of the World: London Merchants and the Integration of the British Atlantic Community, 1735–1785* (Cambridge, 1995), passim. LBS.

[12] Auchincruive, designed by James Adam, Richard Oswald's mansion on the banks of the River Ayr. Also spelled 'Auchincrue' by the obituary for Richard Oswald in the *Scots Magazine*, 46 (Nov. 1784), p. 606. Hancock, *Citizens of the World*, pp. 321–47.

[13] Oswald left an estate of £500,000 in land, art, credit, stocks, annuities, and bank accounts. Hancock, *Citizens of the World*, p. 385.

[14] 'Liferent': 'a right to receive till death (or some other specified contingency) the revenue of a property, without the right to dispose of the capital'. DSL.

[15] Nithsdale, valley of the River Nith in Dumfries and Galloway.

[16] George Oswald of Scotstoun, Balshagray and Auchencruive (1735–1819), merchant, son of Richard Oswald's brother Rev. Dr James Oswald (1703–93), who was minister of Dunnet, Caithness, and an object of attack in Joseph Priestley's *Examination of Dr Reid's 'Inquiry into the Human Mind on the Principles of Common Sense', Dr Beattie's 'Essay on the Nature and Immutability of Truth', and Dr Oswald's 'Appeal to Common Sense in Behalf of Religion'* (1774). George Oswald established a firm trading tobacco from Virginia in the late 1760s, Oswald, Dennistoun & Co., and he was a partner in the Glasgow Ship's Bank. He was elected Rector of Glasgow University in 1797. LBS.

money to be laid out in purchasing more land <then> ^to be^ entailed on him & his family; a piece of vanity that I shoud not have expected from his plain good sense in all other matters but tho' a mischeif in the end, it will be a present advantage to this part of the Country by raising the price of land to several of the unfortunate proprietors of it who have been necessitated to bring their estates into the market & ^some of them^ to sell below the value.

Sir A.Ferg$^n$. seems to have been very intimate with M$^r$. Osw. & has the highest opinion you can conceive of the accuracy of his knowledge & the depth of his judgment in American matters tho' at the same time Sir A. does not approve of every part of the American treaty & if I am not mistaken he was with him in France during the transaction. He communicated several things in the course of conversation that struck me such as that M$^r$. Osw. was ^strongly^ against the American ^war^ from the begin$^g$. but was consulted by the Minstry in every important matter with respect to the plan of it at least during the three or four last years of it that he gave them long memorials[17] which passed thro' Sir A. hands which had but one fault that they were too minute & tedious but discovered a knowledge of the tempers resources & plans of the American Leaders quite astonishing in a man who was at a distance from the scene of action and a penetration into futurity that looked more like prophecy than anything else. That if he had his Letters & Papers now lying at London he coud show us some predictions of M$^r$. Osw. not general ones like those of the leaders of Opposition, but fortelling the very event almost in the very manner in which it happened several months before. Particularly as to L$^d$. Cornwallis if he pursued the plan laid down to him & entered Virginia (he rememembred the very expression) that He & his whole army woud with difficulty escape.

I was much pleased with this visit & woud have picked up a great deal more interesting information from a man that has been so much in the World as Sir A. had it not been for a Col$^l$. Hunter[18] a clattering eating & drinking man– who

---

[17] David Hancock notes that Oswald wrote 'memoranda on military strategy, drawing on years of experience in and with the colonies, and submitted them to friends in Whitehall' (ODNB). He was recommended to the Marquis of Rockingham by the earl of Shelburne, and was the chief negotiator of Shelburne's generous treaty of peace in Paris in 1783.

[18] William Hunter of Brownhill is listed (as Lieutenant) as an elector for Ayrshire at the Michaelmas Head Court in 1759: Strawhorn, *Ayrshire at the Time of Burns*, p. 107. He appears in the *Legacies of British Slave-Ownership Database* as Colonel William Hunter of Mainholm and Brownhill, joint owner from 1772 of the Roselle Estate, Jamaica, with Sir Adam Fergusson, 3rd Bart., of Kilkerran, to whom he seems to have sold his share in 1779. LBS; Graham, *Burns and the Sugar Plantocracy of Ayrshire*, pp. 21, 28–29.

happened to pay him a visit at the same time & which indeed he himself regreted when he took M[r]. Biggar[19] & me by the hand. This man from four in the After[n]. till near nine when we took a single rubber at Whist from ten till near two in the morn[g]. & next day at breakfast keept up an unceasing Lig lag[20] about the families & trifling incid[ents] in the neighbourhood which Sir A. entered into with much good humour & which indeed woud have been entertaining enough had nothing better than been in our power and as soon as I put a question or started a topick of conversation on any interesting subject of politicks Learning &c the Col[l]. sat quite dumb & left the whole discourse to his Landlord & me & I did not think myself entitled to draw ^much of^ his attention off from a man of the Col[s]. rank & otherwise connected with him for he is Brother to Hunter Blair.[21]

You put a questions to me in a former Letter about D[r]. Wootherspoon[22] which I never had time to Answer. I believe he had no other Errand here but to pay his debts & see his friends at least I never coud penetrate into any thing further from his conversations with his most intimate friends. His debts he payed punctualy & settled some intricate transactions in bussiness with a Company at Greenock this he did at London before he came down. One David Deal a noted Merch shopkeeper in Glasgow & Preacher at their congr[eg]ational meeting[23] was so

---

[19] Rev. Matthew Biggar (d. 1806), minister of Kirkoswald, Ayrshire, JW's brother-in-law.

[20] 'Lig Lag', 'chatter, idle talk', *DSL*, which interestingly attributes the term to the nineteenth- and early twentieth-century north-east of Scotland.

[21] Sir James Hunter Blair (1741–87), first baronet, banker. Born James Hunter, the son of a merchant banker, he was apprenticed to Coutts banking house in Edinburgh; at the age of twenty he received the interest in the firm together with his friend, Sir William Forbes. From 1773 it traded under the name Sir W. Forbes, J. Hunter & Co. He married Jane Blair of Dunskey House near Portpatrick, Wigtonshire in 1770. She inherited her father's estate in 1777, when Hunter added Blair to his name. He was MP for Edinburgh from 1781, releasing his seat in 1784 to Sir Adam Fergusson. He himself became Lord Provost of Edinburgh in that year, and was made a baronet in 1786 in recognition of his role in securing the reconstruction of the south bridge over the Cowgate in Edinburgh. *LBS*; Graham, *Burns and the Sugar Plantocracy of Ayrshire*, pp. 28–29, 40.

[22] Rev. John Witherspoon is mentioned by SK in Letter 83, 28 Sept. 1784, but no questions are put to JW there. There may be an unknown missing SK letter in the Nov. 1783–May 1784 gap in his surviving letters.

[23] David Dale (1739–1806), born in Stewarton, Ayrshire, textile merchant in Glasgow. He established in 1785 the cotton manufacturing business in New Lanark that his son-in-law, Robert Owen, later bought. Dale was known as the 'Benevolent Magistrate' who pastored the Old Scots Independents congregation in Greyfriars Wynd church, Glasgow, from 1769 till his death. The Old Scots Independents were one of the antecedents of the nineteenth-century Congregationalist churches. *DSCHT*. Ronald Lyndsay Crawford suggests that this large loan had been incurred in 1768, when Dale had paid Witherspoon's legal debts for his defence in the Court of Session against John Snodgrass and others for defamation. Ronald Lyndsay Crawford, *The Lost World of John Witherspoon: Unravelling the Snodgrass Affair, 1762 to 1776* (Aberdeen, 2014), *passim* and especially pp. 297–300.

pleased with the recovery of a debt of 1300£ which he did not expect that he presented the D^r. with one of the finest Carriages that coud be made in Scotland. The D^r. woud have come to Scotland sooner but was frightened by ^the^ aprehension of being mobbed on the Contrary he was well received every where except at Glasgow where some of his acquaintances declined speaking to him.[24] He preached to crowded audiences at Paisley & Beith.[25] I <—> did not get into his Company tho' I wished it much having once lived in habits of intimacy with him weakened tho' not broken by our different views & conduct in Ch courts. I had not the same unfavourable oppinion ^of him^ that M^r. Warner the abbott & most of my friends had. The D^r. showed an attachment to his old friends & neighbours went & visited old M^r. Brown of Kilbirny[26] who coud not come to him, was polite frank & communicative in his conversation. Tho' he is & always was a most excellent Preacher yet he retains the same calvinistick principles he had when he left this Country was surprized at the alteration in ^the^ theological sentiments of men in Britain—found them all either Socinians or Calvinists said there was not now such a man as D^r. Clark[27] to ^be^ met with or

---

[24] Possibly because of his support of American independence (he was a signatory to the Declaration of Independence), or because of his encouragement of Scottish emigration to the United States, for which he was criticized in the Scottish press. See Landsman, 'John Witherspoon (1723–94)', *ODNB*. As Crawford points out, Witherspoon had been advised against his trip home to Scotland for the purpose of raising funds for the College of New Jersey, as unlikely to succeed in this purpose, by friends in America and Scotland including Benjamin Franklin, John Jay, Ashbel Green, and John Erskine. Crawford, *The Lost World of John Witherspoon*, p. 297.

[25] Witherspoon had been minister of Beith parish (1745–57) and then the Laigh parish, Paisley (1757–68), before emigrating to become president of the College of New Jersey. As well as Crawford, *The Lost World of John Witherspoon*, see also Ronald Lyndsay Crawford, *The Chair of Verity: Political Preaching and Pulpit Censure in Eighteenth-Century Scotland* (Edinburgh, 2017), pp. 73–76; Ronald Lyndsay Crawford, *Scotland and America in the Age of Paine* (Aberdeen, 2022), pp. 318–19; Gideon Mailer, *John Witherspoon's American Revolution* (Chapel Hill, NC, 2017), pp. 43–100.

[26] Rev. Malcolm Brown of Kilbirnie (1694/5–1794), a small town about 10 miles north of Stevenston, north Ayrshire, whose parish church was associated with the Abbey of Kilwinning. Brown died 'Father of the Church' in 1794 at the age of ninety-nine. *FES*, III, pp. 101, 103.

[27] Rev. Samuel Clarke (1675–1729), Anglican clergyman, theologian, and Newtonian philosopher. Clarke's *Scripture Doctrine of the Trinity* (1712) proposed that Christ was pre-existent but not equal in divine status to God the Father, and this publication made him 'the fountainhead of what the eighteenth century understood as Arianism'. R. K. Webb, 'The Emergence of Rational Dissent', in Knud Haakonssen, *Enlightenment and Religion: Rational Dissent in Eighteenth-Century Britain* (Cambridge, 1996), p. 26. Robert Ingram has observed that 'while Clarke doggedly refused to align himself with a particular Christological camp and, indeed, rejected outright the appellation of *Arian*, nearly all his contemporaries and subsequent historians reckoned that his

Mr. Baxter[28] in which however he is much mistaken but I know he has a good Oppinion of both these men & his principles as to the Trinity not far from Clark's.[29] He has a rooted Aversion at your friend & Hero Dr. P{r}. & spoke of ^him^ in terms of contempt & detestation. Dr. W. carried four Preachers with him from Scotland & woud have got many more had he been able to give them any certain or probable hopes of providing for them but he told them their success depended on their pleasing the people. He seemed to think Popular influence in America carried too high even to an extreme & that it woud be difficult to conduct it in matters of Gov{t}. as well as other matters. He himself was upon the point of losing his Presidency of the College of N.J. & being thrown loose on the World about two years after he left Paisley. It was a mere accident of his being able to do some service to the revenue of the college which preserved to him his place.[30]

---

views embodied the Arian position…Facing prosecution from Convocation's lower house, Clarke accepted a settlement negotiated by some Whig bishops that allowed him to retract what he had earlier argued regarding Christ's subordinate nature in return for never again publicly discussing or writing about the subject. Clarke mostly kept to the letter of his end of the bargain, while violating its spirit by actively aiding surrogates'. Robert G. Ingram, *Reformation without End: Religion, Politics and the Past in Post-Revolutionary England* (Manchester, 2018), p. 51.

[28] Andrew Baxter (1686/7–1750), natural philosopher and metaphysician, who attacked the heterodox William Dudgeon and supported Samuel Clarke in his writings against atheism, deism, and materialism.

[29] JW's observation that the 'calvinistick' Witherspoon's views on the Trinity were 'not far from Clarke's' is intriguing. In contrast to Clarke, Witherspoon was clearly an orthodox trinitarian. In his 'Lectures on Divinity' (lectures 9–11), Witherspoon outlined the Trinity, with supporting passages from the Bible, and declared that in denying the divinity of Christ the Socinians were 'doing the utmost violence to scripture, and over throwing the whole doctrine of redemption'; while the Arians, who depicted Christ as a dependent 'creature', were not 'much better'. While 'the whole economy of our salvation teaches us the necessity of…believing this doctrine', Witherspoon argued that the nature of the Trinity was 'a mystery and above our comprehension [and] every attempt to explain it must be, if not criminal, yet unsuccessful'. Aside from his lectures on divinity, however, Witherspoon seldom mentioned the doctrine of the Trinity in his sermons, and encouraged his students to read widely, including works by Clarke, and by anti-trinitarians such as George Benson and John Taylor, among his recommended books. In declaring that the Trinity was 'beyond the power of reason to discover, and above the reach of reason to comprehend', he arguably did share some common ground with Clarke. John Witherspoon, *The Works of John Witherspoon*, 4 vols (Philadelphia, PA, 1802), IV, pp. 64–66; Gordon Tait, *The Piety of John Witherspoon: Pew, Pulpit and Public Forum* (Louisville, KY, 2001), pp. 37, 126–28, 135–36. Moreover, as Dafyyd Mills Daniel shows, Witherspoon and other Scottish Evangelicals appreciated Clarke's traditional use of biblical language, his defence of biblical values and immutable morality, and his accessibility, in opposition to Moderate elitism, relativism, and claims to be the arbiters of ethics and morality. Dafydd Mills Daniel, 'Modern Infidels, Conscientious Fools, and the *Douglas* Affair: The Orthodox Rhetoric of Conscience in the Scottish Enlightenment', *Journal of Religion*, 100 (2020), pp. 327–60.

[30] It is not clear that Witherspoon, despite the significant changes in teaching he introduced almost immediately, was ever under threat of losing his position at the College of New Jersey.

You may expect to hear from us again about a month hence as I have another frank of that date. But after sitting down of Parl^t. there can no franks come from Scotland but from the Lazy members that lag behind ^a month or two^ among whom is L^d. Eg^n.[31] but his hand shakes & he has an utter aversion at writing. My Wife & Peggy you join me in kindest wishes & Comp^s. to you & yours. I ever am

My Dear F^r.– most sincerely yours<br>J. Wodrow

Dec^r. 7th. Our winter has set in two days ago very hard.

## Letter 87: James Wodrow to Samuel Kenrick, 3 January 1785

Place: Stevenston
Addressed: M^r. S. Kenrick / Bewdly
Postmarked: Irvine, Jan^ry. Third 1785
Franked: Fergusson
Stamps: FREE/E; JA/6
Note in SK's hand: answ^d. 14 Jan^y.

Many Happy returns of this season to my old & very dear friends M^r. & M^rs. Kenrick to my young & dear friend Miss Kenrick & to my Daughter under their roof. May God make you all happy in this World ~~as well as~~ ^& especialy^ in a better. I thought to have begun this letter last night to you my good Sir but turned tired before I had finished my Scribble to Nell & now I have neither time nor room in the frank to write to you at much length nor to run over ~~any of~~ the

---

Mark Noll, *Princeton and the Republic, 1768–1822: The Search for a Christian Enlightenment in the Era of Samuel Stanhope Smith* (Princeton, NJ, 1989) notes that Witherspoon was indeed very successful in raising funds for the college, but that 'if anything, [he] underestimat[ed] the support of the board [of trustees], for he enjoyed its full confidence in almost every area of his activity. Minor matters aside, like concern for rabble-rousing at commencement, the trustees were pleased with his work and with the direction in which he was leading the college' (p. 55). See also Varnum Lansing Collins, *President Witherspoon*, 2 vols (New York, 1969), vol. 1, pp. 102–56.

[31] Archibald Montgomerie, eleventh earl of Eglinton (1726–96). He raised the seventy-seventh Regiment of Highlanders in 1757 and served in America, fighting at Fort Duquesne in 1758 and burning several Cherokee villages during an expedition in 1760. He returned to Scotland and was successively MP for Ayrshire (1761–68), eleventh earl of Eglinton from 1769, and one of the sixteen Scottish representative peers from 1774. The earls of Eglinton had been patrons of the Wodrows for centuries; this earl was also patron to Robert Burns.

particulars of your last agreable Letter which I received regularly.[1] My Wife has wrote to Nell, Peggy a joint letter to Miss K. & her, & there are two Letters lying here from two of her Companions one of which at least must be left to Saturday next when we will send you another Packet.

I thank^you^ for all the communications contained in your last & especialy for that part of it relative to my friend M^r^. Magill & his Mss. which is almost the only thing I will now write about. I transcribed the greatest part of it in a letter to him & in his answer he expresses a strong sense of his Obligations to you for your favourable Opinion ^of him^ & your assistance so frankly profered in this affair, and at the same time some doubts of the propriety of consulting D^r^. Priestly on the subject. For my own share I have none. I think it was both the most natural & proper step you coud take ^especialy to obtain information^ & I long to hear what has passed between you & the D^r^. on the subject. Yet I have some doubts in point of delicacy whether to communicate to you that part of his Letter, as it may perhaps lessen the very favourable oppinion you have of my friend. You will think his prejudices against the Worthy D^r^. still stronger than mine (for in that light I allow you to consider both) <—> but as there ought to be no reserves in the friendship between you & me I will fairly & frankly transcribe that part of his Letter & allow my friend to speak for himself.

"As to that Gentleman (meaning D^r^. P.) to tell you my thoughts freely I admire the variety & the vigour of his talents & believe with M^r^. Ken^k^. that he loves truth, but he does not seem to look at her with that respect & modesty which becomes one who sees but thro' a glass darkly; on the contrary he pushes boldly forward into her most secret recesses, & I fear often hugs an illusion in place of her. Many of his Nostrums both in Philosophy & Theology are too hastily taken up, and set forth in too peremptory & dogmatical a way; nor is he I think without pertinacity in maintaining what he has once asserted tho' realy unteneable. My great objection to him is, that he has used unwarrantable freedoms with the sacred authours of the N.T. & has betrayed marks of presumption if not of ignorance in attempting to show in diverse instances, the inconclusiveness of S^t^. Paul's reasonings, by all which he hath in my oppinion laid himself open and hurt the cause he means to serve;[2] not to mention the heat & bitterness of his controversial writings. Hence you will perceive that I would not chuse to submit the Mss. in question to

---

[1] Letter 85, SK to JW, 2–3 Dec. 1784.
[2] Priestley argued that Paul 'often reasons inconclusively, and therefore…he wrote as any other person, of his turn of mind and thinking, and in his situation, would have written,

his inspection tho' it were proper to part with it, nor woud desire his Imprimatur to any publication of mine, at the same time I am far from wishing to give him any Offence.

"Give me leave now to tell you, how I think M^r. Kenricks assistance might be useful. If he knows any Bookseller in London of the best credit & character (for at London I suspect it must be printed, if ever it be printed at all) and woud take the trouble to send the Analysis to him with the printed sermon & speech as specimens of the execution & enquire whether & on what terms he woud undertake such a publication".

So far M^r. Magill & I shall say no more of the publication as he expresses his wishes about it with sufficient precision. As to D^r. Priestley['s] writings he seems much better acquainted with them than I am. I have never ^seen^ that part of them he points at as having given ^him^ the great offence– is it in his last Publication[3] [or] even the Corruptions of X^ty.?[4] I have lectured thro' all the Epistles of Paul & studied them with as much care as I was able & have found indeed several arguments ad homines adapted to the sentiments & prejudices of the persons he is writing to, these perhaps the D^r. may consider as inconclusive reasoning but they appeared to me in a different light. One or two passages in the E^p. to the Heb.[5] I did not thro'ly understand but from what I did understand of the ^design &^ train of it it appeared to me the most masterly Epistle of them all.

Since I wrote you last I have read two little tracts of the D^rs. The appeals ^appeal^ to the serious & Candid Proff^rs. of X^ty. & familiar illustration of certain passages of Scripture.[6] The first I admire greatly as well adapted to the purpose & to the persons for whom it was written. The last I think much inferiour in point of

without any particular inspiration'. He noted that, 'though it was never doubted that Paul was an inspired apostle, and received the knowledge he had of the gospel from Jesus Christ himself, yet we find by his own writings, that there were violent factions against him all his life, and that his opinions were by no means implicitly received'. Similarly, Priestley observed that the gospel writers 'like other credible historians...agree in the main things, but they differ exceedingly in the order of their narrative, and with respect to incidents of little consequence; and to contend for any thing more than this is in effect to injure their credibility'. Priestley, *History of the Corruptions of Christianity*, II, pp. 370, 365, 369. Priestley's comment that Paul 'often reasons inconclusively' was noted in the *Monthly Review* 69 (Aug. 1783), p. 104.

[3] Probably a reference to Joseph Priestley, *Letters to Dr Horsley, Part II: Containing Farther Evidence that the Primitive Christian Church was Unitarian* (Birmingham, 1784).

[4] Priestley, *History of the Corruptions of Christianity*.

[5] Epistle to the Hebrews.

[6] Joseph Priestley, *An Appeal to the Serious and Candid Professors of Christianity* (1771); Joseph Priestley, *A Familiar Illustration of Certain Passages of Scripture Relating to the Power of Man to do the Will of God, Original Sin, Election and Reprobation, the Divinity of Christ and Atonement for Sin by the Death of Christ* (1772).

execution. I was dissapointed, having expected from him something in the way of Criticism both more neat & more accurate conceiving him to be more master both of the Ideas & conexion of the N.T. writings than he seems to be from that little but ^too^ extensive tract. D[r]. Taylour[7] Farmer[8] & perhaps more of the Dissenters appear to me much supperior to your friend in this particular branch. He refers to another little thing which I woud wish to see even the Triumph of truth.[9]

There are two or three publications of the Critical kind ready for the Press in this Country. A New Translation of the Gospels with notes by D[r]. Campbell of Aberdeen[10] which I long to see as I have heard a very favourable account of it from a good Judge. I mean my Br[r]. in Law who is one of the Proff[rs]. there[11] – a commentary on the Whole N.T. & part of the Old by the late Prin[l]. Tillydaff[12] of S[t]. Andrews & a large Commentary on all the Epistles of the N.T. by D[r]. Macnight.[13]

---

[7] Dr John Taylor (1694–1761) of Norwich, a presbyterian theologian with Arian leanings, who was admired by Scottish Moderates with liberal theological views and was awarded a DD by the University of Glasgow in 1756. His seminal work was *The Scripture Doctrine of Original Sin* (1740). See W-K, I, pp. 47, 159, 294.

[8] Hugh Farmer (1714/15–87), Dissenting minister in Walthamstow, Essex, preacher at Salters' Hall, London and theological writer.

[9] Joseph Priestley, *The Triumph of Truth; Being an Account of the Trial of Mr E. Elwall, for Heresy and Blasphemy, at Stafford Assizes, before Judge Denton. To Which are Added, Extracts from Some Other Pieces of Mr Elwall's, Concerning the Unity of God* (Leeds, 1771). It is not surprising that JW was interested in this tract, given his role in aiding defendants against charges of heresy in Scotland.

[10] Professor George Campbell (1719–96), principal of Marischal College, Aberdeen from 1759, and simultaneously both professor of divinity at Marischal College and minister of Greyfriars' Chapel, Aberdeen, from 1771. His long-awaited *The Four Gospels, Translated from the Greek, with Preliminary Dissertations, and Notes Critical and Explanatory* was eventually published in 1789.

[11] Louisa Wodrow's brother Robert Hamilton (1743–1829). He was a political economist and mathematician, and a co-founder of the Speculative Society in Edinburgh. He was rector of Perth Academy 1769–79, professor of natural philosophy at Marischal College, Aberdeen 1779–1817, and professor of mathematics there 1817–29. In fact, Hamilton had carried out the teaching of mathematics at the university since 1780, while the better-paid professor of that subject, Patrick Copland, had taught natural philosophy for Hamilton. R. E. Anderson, *rev.* Anita McConnell, 'Robert Hamilton, 1743–1829', *ODNB*. See Letter 99 below.

[12] Thomas Tullideph, *Enquiry Concerning the Intention of the Evangelists and the Writer of the Book of Acts of the Apostles in Quoting Passages from the Old Testament* (c. 1734)—a copy is held in the University of St Andrews Special Collections. Thomas Tullideph (1700–77), successively Church of Scotland minister at Dron (1727–31) and Markinch (1731–34), then professor of biblical criticism at St Mary's College, St Andrews (1734–39), principal of St Leonard's College, St Andrews (1739–47), and principal of the United College (1747–77). 'Thomas Tullideph "Oratio"', University of St Andrews, Special Collections.

[13] Macknight's *A New Literal Translation, from the Original, of the Apostle Paul's First and Second Epistles to the Thessalonians: With a Commentary and Notes* was published in 1787, followed by his

The D[r]. dined with me one day when Miss K. was here and I had some conversation & argument with him about particular passages.

There will be many curious & ingenious things in the D[rs]. Book[14] too much so, to be solid. He is fanciful in some of his notions but yet has not a spark of fancy in his stile & manner of writing to render it in the least agreable to an ordinary reader. There will be mixed with dry reasoning, much good criti^ci^sm & much uncommon learning & yet he had not read the set of Commentators who seem to understand the N.T. better than any who have attempted it. I mean the fratres Poloni.[15] The D[r]. spoke much of one Estius[16] a popish Commentator the father & founder as he represented him of D[r]. Taylours Scheme[17] & more master of it than he & seemed resolved to confute them both. It is not an easy attempt.

I have not read D[r]. Blairs Book which you speak so well of but intend it.[18] Arnot's history of Ed[r].[19] & [Ha]iles Annals[20] to make part of my reading this

---

*New Literal Translation from the Original Greek of All the Apostolic Epistles* in four volumes at Edinburgh in 1795. Macknight was engrossed in study 'for up to eleven hours a day and, even when he took his walks, it involved shuffling round the Meadows in Edinburgh with his nose in a book. Lord Cockburn remembered "his large, bony visage, his enormous white wig, girdled by many tiers of curls, his old snuffy black clothes, his broad flat feet, and his threadbare blue great-coat"'. Cited in Lionel Alexander Ritchie, 'Macknight, James (1721–1800)', *ODNB*. See Letter 83.

[14] i.e. Dr Macknight's commentary on the New Testament epistles.

[15] 'Faustus Socinus (Sozzini, 1539–1604) of Siena ... united and gave ideological direction to the most radical group in the Polish Reformation. Hence they came to be known in the seventeenth century in western Europe as Socinians. They preferred to style themselves *Fratres Poloni* or simply Christians (*chrystianie*) while their antagonists scornfully called them Arians.' H. Swiderska, 'Socinian Books with the Raków Imprint in the British Library', *The British Library Journal*, 8 (1982), p. 206. Wodrow may have read Joshua Toulmin's *Memoirs of the Life, Character, Sentiments and Writings of Faustus Socinus* (1777), which observes that 'there was by no means a perfect Uniformity in the sentiments of these UNITARIANS concerning the nature and character of CHRIST'. Some were Arians, others Budneians, and others became Socinians (pp. vi–vii). Toulmin declares that Poland had the 'honour of carrying the Reformation to a degree of perfection' not achieved anywhere else for two centuries, with 'their prayers directed to GOD the Father only, through Jesus Christ as the Mediator' (p. ix). See also *W-K*, I, pp. 43, 99, 163, 293–94, 317.

[16] Willem Hessels van Est (1542–1613), Dutch Roman Catholic commentator on the epistles of Paul. Elizabeth A. Livingstone and Frank Leslie Cross, eds, *Oxford Dictionary of the Christian Church*, 4th edn (Oxford, 2005), p. 567.

[17] John Taylor was an Arian, and according to a friend, 'if ever he expressed an uncommon warmth and honest indignation against anything, it was against Athanasianism, which he thought one of the greatest corruptions of pure and genuine Christianity, as this doctrine entirely subverts the unity of God'. Cited in Alan P. F. Sell, 'John Taylor (1694–1761)', *ODNB*.

[18] Hugh Blair (1718–80), *Lectures on Rhetoric and Belles Lettres* (1783, 2nd edn 1785). See Letter 85.

[19] Hugo Arnot, *The History of Edinburgh* (Edinburgh, 1779).

[20] David Dalrymple, Lord Hailes, *Annals of Scotland, From the Accession of Malcolm III, surnamed Canmore, to the Accession of Robert I* (Edinburgh, 1776).

winter & spring provided I can accomplish it for I read very little. But I will not detain you any longer with this chit chat intending if I can overtake it (for this a busy week in settling the poors funds) to write a few lines on Saturday. It is probable there may be a packet of yours on the road & that we may receive it before that time. I am ever

your sincere & aff<sup>te</sup>. Friend<br>J Wodrow

## Letter 88: James Wodrow to Samuel Kenrick, 7 January 1785

Place: Stevenston
Addressed: M<sup>r</sup>. S. Kenrick Bewdley / W<sup>cr</sup>Shire
Postmarked: Irvine Jan<sup>ry</sup>. the Eight 1785
Franked: Cassillis

My Dear Sir

I sit down to write you a few lines despairing almost of receiving the Letter or Packet from Bewdley which I expected. An Hour or two will put it out of doubt by the arival of our runner from Irvine. And as there have been formerly unlucky miscarriages & losses of our packets of Letters which however I am less afraid of now from the very particular directions yet I will distinctly inform you that I sent off one Pack<sup>t</sup>. L<sup>d</sup>. Cassilis[1] Frank on Dec<sup>r</sup>. the 8th filled cheifly with Letters to Nell & another of Sir Ad. Ferg<sup>ns</sup>. Jan<sup>r</sup>. the 3<sup>d</sup>.[2] In the last I transcribed M<sup>r</sup>. Magills answer to me relative to the concern you are so kind as to take about the Mss & shall say no more now on that head.

I have read over your letter of the 2<sup>d</sup> of Dec<sup>r</sup>. with a view to take notice of any other particulars that require it. Of J. Warner[3] I heard lately he had been very ill but is now in his usual health & state rather better than usual having lately written a long and very distinct letter to his Brother.[4] Miss Kenrick from what she saw of him woud not think him capable of this but in writing on common matters that interest him he blunders in nothing almost but the dates & names of particular

---

[1] Letter 86.
[2] Letter 87.
[3] See Letter 84.
[4] Patrick Warner (1710–93). See W-K, I, pp. 309, 325, 332–33, 343, 363, 431.

people for which his memory ^does not serve him^. It will add to your regret of the Catastrophe of this great & worthy man that almost all his valuable Papers are lost—dissipated by ^the^ cursed infidelity of a female Serv^t. (who is yet greatly attached to him & her care & attention to his person & health absolutely necessary) among some of her own relations who can read them, but cannot relish them. Among these are some setts of Sermons on the Spirit of Religion preached in the College Chapel at Glasgow which at the earnest desire of the Proffessors he had revised & written over more than once, & which I saw at the begin^g. of his illness <—> ^nearly^ ready for the press. I am affraid these & a 100 more never will be recovered. For your Satisfaction however The translation of the Theorie &c, is recoverable.[5] It is in M^r. Boyds hands whom I desired to take care of it if ever he shoud find it & he did find it.[6]

The Honest & venerable Prin^pl.[7] has had a good Winter so far according to all the accounts I have heard for I have had no Letter from himself which I expected having written lately allong with a Pamplet I sent him. His memory I believe begins to fail a little.

I return you my best thanks for all the kind things you write of my Daughter & for all the attention & affectionate treatment she has met from you M^rs. Kenrick & Miss Kenrick. She herself has & I hope ever will have a proper sense of it. If she keeps her health the cheif risk will be her growing too fond of England & of the place where she is, & feeling some reluctance to return to her own poor Country. I agree with you that it is time enough to speak of her Journey to London an event which has become more uncertain than it was in consequence of a Letter I lately received from her Uncle there.[8] As to her acquiring the English Accent & the facility of speaking the language with propriety I have no other wish than her acquiring so much of it as to prevent her from appearing awkward & enabling ^her^ to bear some ^decent^ share in conversation during the short time she is with you. She will soon lose it again & has indeed little use for it as it is scarce an object here.[9]

---

[5] While in London in 1759 SK had sought a publisher for John Warner's translation of Louis-Jean Lévesque de Pouilly, *Théorie des Sentimens Agréables* (Geneva, 1747). For more on this, see the notes on Thomas Christie's letter appended to Letter 143.

[6] Presumably Rev. William Boyd (1748–1828), minister of Fenwick, Ayrshire (1782–1828). *FES*, III, p. 95; *W-K*, I, p. 481n.

[7] Professor William Leechman.

[8] John Hamilton. See Letter 84.

[9] On Scots' nervous consciousness of their distinctive accents and language, see James G. Basker, 'Scotticisms and the Problem of Cultural Identity in Eighteenth-Century Britain', in

What is your friends name, the Clergyman to whom you showed the Analysis? Are not his Theological Sentiments toto cælo[10] opposite to M^r. Magills? If so, it ^is^ a wonder that he shoud be pleased even with the Sermon. It is an excellent sign of the goodness of his heart. Or is ^he^ a M^r. Wiggan[11] whom Nell mentions.

The Countess of Sutherland[12] is indeed an accomplished young Lady & her Grandmother Lady Ava[13] has much credit in the Education she has given her. I wish Miss Kenrick had had the opportunity of seeing as much of her as I saw on the Mond^y. following. Besides her accomplishments This young Countess seems to have not a small portion of public spirit. She is very intent on a Scheme for introducing the new invented Machines called the Jennies[14] for spinning Cotton warp yarn, into her town of Dornoch[15] & had taken some very proper judicious steps doubtless under the direction of her Grandmother to accomplish it, & laid

---

John Dwyer and Richard B. Sher, eds, *Sociability and Society in Eighteenth-Century Scotland* (Edinburgh, 1993), pp. 81–95; Colin Kidd, 'North Britishness and the Nature of Eighteenth-Century British Patriotisms', *Historical Journal*, 39 (1996), pp. 361–82, especially at pp. 366–67; Mark Towsey, *Reading the Scottish Enlightenment: Books and Their Readers in Provincial Scotland, 1750–1820* (Leiden, 2010), pp. 238–41.

[10] 'toto cælo': 'by the whole heaven', utterly, totally. OED.

[11] Rev. Thomas Wigan (c. 1744–1819), a close friend of SK's in Worcestershire. After serving as curate of Christchurch chapel in Wribbenhall, over the river opposite Bewdley, he became rector of Oldswinford, c. 1776–1819, 10 miles away near Stourbridge. Burton, *History of Bewdley*, pp. 84–85; *Alumni Oxonienses*, IV, p. 1549; W-K, I, pp. 120, 131, 422–23, 443; Letter 85.

[12] See Letter 84.

[13] Elizabeth Hairstanes Maxwell (b. 1717), Lady Alva, the countess's maternal grandmother. She brought the countess up after her parents (William Sutherland, eighteenth earl of Sutherland, and Mary) both died of putrid fever in 1766, when Lady Sutherland was about a year old.

[14] The spinning jenny, or engine, was invented by James Hargreaves in Lancashire in 1766, patented in 1770, and spread quickly in Scotland as well as England. Christopher A. Whatley, 'The Experience of Work', in T. M. Devine and Rosalind Mitchison, eds, *People and Society in Scotland, Vol. 1: 1760–1830* (Edinburgh, 1988), p. 234. See also R. H. Campbell, *The Rise and Fall of Scottish Industry, 1707–1930* (Edinburgh, 1980).

[15] Dornoch, a royal burgh in Sutherland, on the north side of the Dornoch Firth, which opens into the Moray Firth. The Countess of Sutherland was the principal landowner, though there were four other heritors in the parish in 1793. The population was estimated at around 500 by Rev. John Bethune in his report for the *Statistical Account of Scotland*, VIII, p. 7, when he noted that 'except two whisky distilleries, and some *flax* spun by the women, no branch of trade whatever is cultivated here', suggesting that the Countess's efforts to instigate mechanized cotton spinning had not borne fruit. She had contributed to the provision of food for the poor of the town during the severe dearth of 1782; but her greatest impact on the people of Sutherland was in her responsibility for the Clearances managed by the estates' administrator, James Loch. Her parents were memorialized in the parish church in Dornoch. Spinning jennies do seem to have been successfully introduced to the parish of Creich, Sutherland, but at the instigation of 'a company... consisting chiefly of Glasgow gentlemen'. Ibid., pp. 11, 14, 377; Eric Richards, 'Gower, Elizabeth Leveson-, duchess of Sutherland (1765–1839)'.

out money to a considerable extent on the Project. I had some curiosity to know whether she had invited any of the enthusiastick religious principles of her aunt Lady Glenorchy,[16] but coud discover nothing pro or con. She also, I am told, is a most agreable & accomplished woman but at the Head of the Methodists in Scotland.

I shall be glad to see D^r. Priestleys answer to D^r. Horsley but must read both sides to judge properly.[17] I wish M^r. Ha^n. woud send me his Cousins book.[18] I see the Rectors & dignified Clergy of the Diocese of Norwich have entered the lists against your Dissenting D^r. He has now a powerful Corps in the field, su^p^ported by the light troops of the Monthly Reviewers to encounter; but he is a bold & able Knight & will <——> ^doubtless^ think <——> it but a small thing to overthrow these united Chieftains, by the prowess of his single arm. Pray who is the Bishop of Norwich?[19] For I have not the honour of knowing ^him^ at least by that <——> title.

As to the honest Buchanites I happened last week to see a Letter giving an account of their present situation, wrote about the end of Oct^r from a M^r. James Stewart Monteath a Clergyman in the church of England who is about to resign a living of 500£ a year & to retire to the Estate of Closeburn[20] which he has lately purchased. It is a sensible good natured letter to his friend M^r. Boyle in Irvine

---

[16] Willielma Campbell (1741–86), Viscountess Glenorchy, who had married John Campbell, the son of John Campbell, third earl of Breadalbane and Holland (1689–1782) in 1761. Influenced by the Calvinist Methodism of Rev. Rowland Hill and his sister Jane, and by Selina, Countess of Huntingdon, Lady Glenorchy was active in promoting Evangelical Christianity in Edinburgh, Perthshire, and various towns in England.

[17] Samuel Horsley, *A Charge, Delivered to the Clergy of the Archdeaconry of St Albans, at a Visitation Holden May 22d 1783* (1783); Joseph Priestley, *Letters to Dr Horsley*; Samuel Horsley, *Letter from the Archdeacon of Saint Albans, in reply to Dr Priestley, with an appendix, containing Short Strictures on Dr Priestley's Letters by an unknown Hand* (1784). See Schofield, *The Enlightened Joseph Priestley*, pp. 229–32.

[18] John Hamilton.

[19] Rev. Lewis Bagot (1740–1802), dean of Christ Church, Oxford (1777–82), bishop of Bristol (1782–83), Norwich (1783–90), and St Asaph (1790–1802). Bagot was a prominent high churchman who contended against Rational Dissenters. His *A Sermon Preached at the Cathedral Church in Norwich, on Thursday August 21, 1783. On Occasion of the Anniversary meeting of the Governors of the Norfolk and Norwich Hospital. By Lewis Lord Bishop of Norwich* (Norwich, 1783) warned of the dangers of Enlightenment philosophy to the social and political order in general but did not refer to Priestley specifically.

[20] Closeburn, a parish in Dumfriesshire, about 12 miles north of Dumfries. Rev. James Stewart Monteath, previously Rector of Barrowby, Lincolnshire, had bought the estate from the ancient family of Osborne in 1783, and had 'built a very excellent house for himself, large, substantial, and commodious' as well as augmenting the stipend of the parish minister. *OSA*, vol. 8 (1794), pp. 232–34.

signifying that he had found them on a visit to his estate lo[d]ged mostly in a large barn belonging to one of his Tenants, the men & women seperated by a screen of blankets to the Number of 46 that they had been very useful in assisting this Tenant in Harvest & other ^work^ & woud take nothing for their Labour not even Victuals, such was their confidence in the protection & provision to be made for them by heaven. That They had built a much larger & more convenient house for themselves almost ready for them on his grounds that they had about 1200£ in stock part of it lodged in the bank of Dumfries & the rest went to people in that Neighbourhood on very bad security.——That he had protected them & was resolved to protect them from every insult as long as their moral conduct appeared to be good as it had hither to done &c&c.[21]

I have ^been^ also allowed the sight of a small part of a large & long correspondence by letter which has been carried on between a M$^r$. Hunter[22] one of their leaders & a religious man in Irvine who thought it his duty to convince Hunter of his Error & attack his Prinp$^{ls}$. as contrary to reason & Scripture, & I have been promised a sight of the whole. ^That part of^ Hunters long Letter that I saw is very curious & not ^at^ all the raving of a wild Enthusiast as I expected but a very able defense of the Principles of the Buchanites <—> in a stile & manner far above the common joined with an acquaintance with the Scriptures which almost astonished me. Their opinions are not so wild as they have been represented. There are the strongest appeals to Scripture Authority & the boldest attacks immaginable on the high popular doctrines of all sects which Hunter tells his Correspondent he lately believed as firmly as the Other &c, &c.

6 at night

I have [wax seal] no further correspondence with Sir A.F. about the Buchanites nor will except some thing particular happen to occasion it.[23] But I have been of late corresponding with him on another matter more in char$^r$. to him & less to me. The Proprietors of the Saltworks here & the inhabitants of Saltcoats had intended a petition to Parl$^t$. this Winter for enlarging & deepening their Harbour which at a small expense might easily be made more useful to themselves &

---

[21] In October 1784, when this letter had been written, JW had also written to SK, reporting that the Buchanites had been driven out of Irvine in Ayrshire and were living in the open air, 'somewhere between Closeburn and Dumfries' (Letter 84). By January 1785 they appear to have become established as 'a celibate community based on Apostolic precedent at the farm of New Cample, in the parish of Closeburn'. Riordan, 'Mysticism and Prophecy in Scotland in the Long Eighteenth Century', p. 202.

[22] Peter Hunter. See Letter 84.

[23] See Letter 84. JW had first looked into the Buchanites at Sir Adam Fergusson's request.

commodious to the whole coast[24] <—> ^as a^ fund for it they proposed to Petition not for any part of the present Revenue raised from the Salt there but to give Security for the continuance of this & to creat three new Saltpans provided the Revenue arising from these ^three^ was appropriated for a short term of years to this public & useful purpose after which it woud go to Gov[t]. Sir A. in conversing with ^me^ at his own house seemed to think it might be granted. I was employed by the People concerned to represent to him the public advantages of their Scheme, which I did to the utmost of my power in a long Letter. To This he gave an equaly long & very sensible ^answer^ signifying his reasons upon further consideration for thinking that the Parl[t]. coud not or woud not grant it. This has put an end to the project at least upon that footing. If it be tryed at all It must be by some taxes or burdens laid upon the shiping & trade which ^may^ perhaps be agreed to voluntarily without the Interposition of Authority.

The Post has brought no letters from England & it is needless to keep this open till tomorrow at noon or later which woud occasion my sending it Express to Irvine. The chance of hearing from you at any rate very small. I have been interrupted in this letter particularly by a visit from M[r]. Lauchlane[25] whom Nell knows. He tells me L[r]. Eg[n].[26] sets out in a forthnight. I shall scarce write ^again^ during that time but afterwards find means of sending single Letters to you or to Nell under his direction or some of our Members to London which ^will^ lessen the Postage of them I suppose about a half. In vain do <-> M[r]. Pit & others attempt to prevent Smugling & encrease the Revenue by new acts of Parliament.[27] The wit & ingenuity of men will battle the most effectual Laws than can well be framed.

[24] Saltcoats, 'the principal watering place in Ayrshire', attracted 300 to 500 people from Paisley, Glasgow and Hamilton 'in the Summer months, for sea-bathing', according to JW, *OSA*, iii. 8; but its harbour (built in 1684–1700), together with those at Ayr and Irvine, was too small for large vessels to enter, or even for smaller vessels in stormy weather, resulting in shipwrecks as well as the loss of trade that larger shipping might have conducted. JW, 'Stevenston, Ayrshire', *OSA*, iii (1793). 4, 8, 16–17, 38–41: Wodrow's article closed with three pages of argument for the improvement of the harbour, directed personally to the earl of Eglinton. David Landsborough, 'Stevenston, Ayrshire', *NSA*, v (1845), 440–41, 461–62, was still arguing for deepening the Saltcoats harbour.

[25] Possibly the earl of Eglinton's gardener. In February 1783, a 'Mr Lauchlan at Lord Eglinton' is listed among fifty-one recipients of Asafoetida seeds, a medicinal spice plant. See John H. Appleby, 'St Petersburg to Edinburgh: Matthew Guthrie's Introduction of Medicinal Plants in the Context of Scottish-Russian Natural History Exchange', *Archives of Natural History*, 14 (1987), p. 56.

[26] Presumably the earl planned to set out in late January for his parliamentary duties in London.

[27] Contrary to JW's view, beginning in 1784, Pitt's measures to crack down on smuggling were to a significant degree successful. John Ehrman, *The Younger Pitt: The Years of Acclaim* (1969), pp. 240–47.

I spent all yesterday with my Session[28] in going over the years accounts of the poors funds. Our Expenditure was near about 70£ our Income something more than £80 both of them larger than former years except the year 1783. We have ~~have~~ had already five weeks of ^continued^ frost before the time when our frosts commonly begin.[29] Who can tell when this one will end.

All comfort & Happiness to you & your family is my Dear Friend the sincere wish of

yours J Wodrow

## Letter 89: Samuel Kenrick to James Wodrow, 14 January 1785
Place: Bewdley

My most worthy friend's kind l$^r$. of the 3$^d$ inst. was duly rec$^d$. along w$^{th}$. your most acceptable packet to Miss Wodrow & Mary. You need make no apology for the shortness of it– My last did not deserve so much– as it was not a full answer to your former voluminous favour– for I was stinted as to the time by the date of the frank. I have too good reason to plead the same excuse now– & the hurry w$^{ch}$. my private affairs keep me– But I will wave them all, to bestow all the time I have on your letter.– I leave Nell & Mary to tell their own tale– they can do it much better than I can.

I have sent the Analysis[1] & printed sermon to D$^r$. Priestley– & am happy to find that you approved of that step, before you were sure I had taken it. But whom else could I consult. No one that was more able to give me proper information. I sent them to him by a private hand & next morning I rec$^d$. his answer by post– w$^{ch}$. I shall communicate to you with the same unreserved confidence that you use me with.

"I am obliged to you for the communication of M$^r$. M$^c$Gill's printed discourse[2] from w$^{ch}$. I expect much satisfaction. As to the work w$^{ch}$. he wishes to publish,

---

[28] Kirk Session, the ruling committee of elders in a parish church in presbyterian governance. See Letter 79 n. 6 on its role in dealing with poor relief in eighteenth-century Scotland.

[29] The Laki volcanic fissure in Iceland erupted in 1783 and caused harsh winters in Europe during the mid-1780s.

---

[1] See Letter 84. A manuscript summary of what was published as M'Gill's *Practical Essay on the Death of Jesus Christ* in 1786.

[2] Perhaps William M'Gill, *The Prayer of Our Saviour for the Union of His Followers Considered: A Sermon by William M'Gill, A.M. one of the Ministers of Ayr* (Glasgow, 1768). See Letter 84, n. 219.

I really cannot give you advice or assistance. The chance of such publications selling, in this country, is, at this <time> ^day^ very small; & perhaps the only way to indemnify the author is to print it by subscription. Certainly, however his own country & neighbourhood is the most proper place for the publication."

"M^r. M^cGill's sentiments, I perceive, & mine are considerably different from mine;[3] but this is one reason why I sincerely wish the work may be published– tho' I have little expectation of seeing any thing new on the subject."

Now you must know that I am so great a novice in these matters, that I was not aware of the great difference between these two worthy gentlemen's sentiments, from perusing the contents of M^r. M^cGill's treatise;[4] or else I should not have been so sanguine or forward in the affair; more especially if I had known M^r. M's aversion to it & particularly, as they appear to me, his violent prejudices against my prime favourite.– Here I have been interrupted for half an hour.–What I wish is that yourself, your friend & the Doctor were only personally acquainted & had an opportunity of canvassing these subjects in familiar conversation. D^r. Priestley is fond of such conversations & often meets his friends in that way, where each deliver their sentiments with calmness ease & freedom. I cannot help thinking you would both be surprized to find how near your sentiments coincided w^th. his. For candid & enlightened minds, cannot long or far disagree. Tho' in D^r. Horsley's turgid style,[5] I bow at a distance before your superior talents– yet I could wish both M^r. M & you would point out some of the most obnoxious things that you find in his writings. You mention his charge against the apostle Paul's reasoning. I think it is in the Hebrews & ^in^ his History on the article [on] attonement.[6] But I have not time to find it. Your distinction w^th. regard to this great & good man's reasoning pleases me much. I wish you w^d. some time or other send me a specimen. By the bye I am not satisfied w^th. your writing everything in short hand w^ch.

---

[3] While Priestley thought their opinions were 'considerably different', SK and JW thought there was much similarity between M'Gill and Priestley (Letter 91). After M'Gill published *The Death of Christ*, it was attacked as Socinian. John Newton said it alarmed him more than 'all the volumes of Priestley'. William C. Smith, 'Religious Freedom in Scotland', *The Theological Review*, 15 (1878), p. 457. For Priestley's enthusiasm for public access to books published in opposition to his own opinions, so that readers could make up their own minds, see also Letter 135.

[4] M'Gill's work was implicitly Socinian. Priestley's comment reflects his own narrow definition of Unitarianism which, in contrast to traditional Socinianism, denied the miraculous conception and did not allow the worship of Christ. Valerie Smith, *Rational Dissenters in Late Eighteenth-Century England* (Woodbridge, 2021), pp. 84–85, 88–89.

[5] See Letter 88.

[6] Priestley argued that Paul 'often reasons inconclusively' in *History of the Corruptions of Christianity*, II, p. 370. For more on this, see Letter 87.

none of your family besides, understands. What a number of valuable remarks, w^ch. you have been accumulating these 30 years, must be locked up from your friends & the world. You mention 2 of the D^rs. little treatises his appeal & Illustration.[7] You admire the first– but are not satisfied w^th. the last. But recollect for whose use it was intended– for the lower class of people; & read again his preface– is there ^is^ not modesty there tho' M^r. M seems unwill^g. to allow it any where. And this brings me back to what you & M^r. M have you been all this while expecting something more satisfactory about.– Let your friend know, after D^r. P.'s opinion, that I am willing to do anything in my power to serve him. I have no acquaintance w^th. any Bookseller in London; if I had I should most readily comply w^th. his request. And when I get the Analysis & Sermon from the D^r. I will do what I can to make them more known. Meanwhile if M^r. M. should take the more secure way, w^ch. the D^r. points out & send me his proposals, I shall chearfully get him all the subscriptions I can.

I am happy to hear we have the prospect of so much theological or rather Scriptural learning from your quarter. It would give me pleasure to see you figuring among them; w^ch. all the world know you are so well qualified to do. If D^r. P. has too little, M^r. M. will join me in saying you have too much of that same modesty. I wish I knew half as much as you do of those honest Fratres Poloni– w^ch. I remember you mentioned to me many years ago, w^th. warm admiration.[8] And yet D^r. M^cKnight to be a stranger to them.[9] We have a little pocket Lexicon, that I value for its dedication by the school of Bremen ^to^.– *Jesu xti filii Dei, piis scholis, qua sunt apud Ecclesias Reverend. Unit. Fratrum, puram doctrinam Evangelii per Bohem. Morav. & Polon servantes.*[10]

But I must leave my dear friend w^th. this abrupt farrago– being ever his most affec^te.

S. Kenrick

---

[7] See Letter 87. Joseph Priestley, *An Appeal to the Serious and Candid Professors of Christianity* (1771); Joseph Priestley, *A Familiar Illustration of Certain Passages of Scripture Relating to the Power of Man to do the Will of God, Original Sin, Election and Reprobation, the Divinity of Christ and Atonement for Sin by the Death of Christ* (1772).

[8] Letter 45, JW to SK, 25 Jan. 1769, and Letter 50, JW to SK, 5 April 1774, W-K, I, pp. 294, 317.

[9] James Macknight. See Letter 87.

[10] 'To the pious schools of Jesus Christ, son of God, which are among the Churches a Reverend Concord of Brothers, preserving the pure doctrine of the Gospel through Bohemia, Moravia and Poland' (translated by Graeme Miles, University of Tasmania).

## Letter 90: James Wodrow to Samuel Kenrick, 19 January 1785

Addressed: M`r`. S. Kenrick Bewdley, Worcester`e`.
Postmarked: Irvine January nineteenth 1785
Franked: E. Eglintoune
Note in JW's hand: M`r`. Kenrick Bewdley / By fav`r`. of Mess`rs`. Gordons / To the care of M`r`. Jas Finlay[1] / Head of the Stockwell[2] / Glasgow

Having nothing ~~very~~ at all material to say to you just now & very little time tho I had I ~~just~~ ^only^ make use of your name to convey two Letters to Nell from her Companions (which have lain here some time); in the last frank (in case I shall be able to procure it) you will receive from Scotland for four or five months to come.[3] We begin to be a little uneasy in having heard nothing from [page torn]f you since the last packet dated about the third of Dec`r`. [page torn]nd look as if some of the Harpies as you once called them, of Postmasters or Mistresses had laid their accursed paws on some Packet which we have been expecting every day for a fortnight past from you, & it will be well if they have not dared to commit the same Outrage on one or other of the three I have last sent you of Dec`r`. 8th. Jan`r`. 3`d`. and 8th. Strange! that the full & particular directions of our venerable Senators[4] shoud not make those profane creatures stand in Awe. In that of Jan`r`. 3`d`. I sent you a transcript of M`r`. Magills Answer. I have not heard from him since, there was also in that packet a Hair ring which Peggy sent to Miss Kenrick which I was very much affraid ~~woud~~ ^might^ tempt to a[n] Attempt on the whole. But I am weary of conjectures the next we receive from you must end them you will perceive the senseless Allusion. I have been reading two Novels one of them not so much to my tast as the Other reading also Arnots History of Ed`r`.[5] light & easy reading as you call Blairs last book. There is much curious knowledge

---

[1] James Finlay of Finlay, Robert & Co., Merchants. See *John Tait's Directory, for the City of Glasgow*... (Glasgow, 1783).

[2] A fashionable residential street in eighteenth-century Glasgow, which later degenerated into slum tenements. From 1757 the Custom House was located at its corner. Corner of Stockwell Street, Burrell Collection Photo Library, The Glasgow Story, accessed 23 July 2021, www.theglasgowstory.com/image/?inum=TGSE00526; tenement near the head of Stockwell Street, Mitchell Library, Glasgow Collection, The Glasgow Story, accessed 23 July 2021, www.theglasgowstory.com/image/?inum=TGSA01001&t=2.

[3] When MPs were in London to attend Parliament, they were unavailable to provide postage franks before returning again to Scotland for the summer.

[4] i.e. the franks of the Earls of Cassillis and Eglintoun who were 'Senators'—members of the House of Lords as Scottish Representative Peers.

[5] Hugo Arnot, *History of Edinburgh* (Edinburgh, 1779).

to be got from Arnot a considerable part of it however [ve]ry uninteresting to me & much less to an Englishman.⁶ Yet L.ᵈ Hales has muc[h] more of the spirit of mere antiquarian than Arnot.⁷ The last is a kind of Infidel body & yet writes both with ^some^ judgement & candour on these of obnoxious subjects of Religion & government.⁸ His pictures of the fanaticism of the Presbyterians are by much too strong. He betrays little of his Infidelity but a good deal of the Cloven foot of Jacobitism appears in his account of the last of Rebellion & the Partisans of it.⁹ I must conclude with my best wishes & comp.ˢ to M.ʳˢ & Miss Kenrick & ever am

most sincerely & affect.ˡʸ Yours
J Wodrow

## Letter 91: James Wodrow to Samuel Kenrick, 6 February 1785
Place: Stevenston
Notes in SK's hand: Feb. 6 1785/anw.ᵈ 22 Feb 85

My Dear friend

I had the pleasure of both your Letters the joint one with Nell by post of the 28th.¹ & the frank of the 14th of Jan.ʳ ² We must now drop all future censures on the Postmasters & M.ʳˢ ˢ for they have behaved most handsomely in the conveyance of the last mentioned packet & I must intreat my friend to get tougher & more

---

⁶ But a second edition was published in 1816.
⁷ Sir David Dalrymple (Lord Hailes), *Annals of Scotland: From the Accession of Malcolm III, surnamed Canmore, to the Accession of Robert I* (Edinburgh, 1776); Dalrymple, *Annals of Scotland: From the Accession of Robert I, surnamed Bruce, to the Accession of the House of Stewart* (Edinburgh, 1779).
⁸ Lord Hailes was a sincere churchman; apparently, Hugo Arnot (1749–86) was not.
⁹ Note the part played in the Killing Times by JW's Covenanting forebears, James Wodrow (1637–1707), William Guthrie (1620–65), and Patrick Warner (c. 1640–1724). If JW's theology was significantly different from theirs, it is not impossible that he also reserved the right to defend them. See Robert Wodrow, *The Life of James Wodrow, A.M., Professor of Divinity in the University of Glasgow from MDCXCII to MDCCVII. Written by his Son Robert Wodrow, A.M., Minister of the Gospel at Eastwood* (Edinburgh, 1828), p. 196; W-K, I, 4–6; and Christopher A. Whatley, 'Reformed Religion, Regime Change, Scottish Whigs and the Struggle for the 'Soul' of Scotland, c.1688–c.1788', *Scottish Historical Review*, 92 (2013), pp. 66–99, on the emotional depth of anti-Jacobitism among Scottish Presbyterians in the later eighteenth century.

---

¹ This SK letter of 28 Jan. 1785 is missing.
² Letter 89.

durable paper at least for the cover of his Letters. The frank without seeming to have suffered anything from the Weather or any other accident came to my ^hand^ quite open all round, & the direction worn ^off^ & separated from the rest. But some good friendly Postmaster or mistress had neatly tyed it up with a piece of twist & sealed it a second time at the knott & thus preserved the contents quite safe till they reached their owner. Was not this a very kind Office to an unknown person?

I have no time either this night or tomorrow ^morn$^g$.^ to take proper notice of the contents of your two short but most acceptable Letters only I approved & still continue to approve of all you have done relative to the Mss.[3] ~~My~~ I have been much occupied in my mind & otherwise by my Sisters Death you knew her well long ago & will very sincerely sympathise with us.[4] Tho' I passed thro' Ayr & returned about ten days after yet my time was so much curtailed by the shortness of the day & Nell bussiness on the road that I durst not trust myself even with a call on my friend who by the by I am told is now dignifyed by the letter of D$^r$. an unsolicited favour from the Colledge of Glasgow.[5] I will write him this week such a part of the contents of your first as ^it^ is necessary to communicate & will write you soon again if it be needful having in my Letter to Nell chaulked out a path by which we may correspond with little or no Expense only the letters will go round by Lond$^n$. & thus loiter a day or two longer on the road which they sometimes do as it is. But this path of correspondence must be seldom used on your part at least till we see more of it.

Mond$^y$. morn$^g$.

I am much of your oppinion as to a circumstance mentioned in yours of the 14th. viz that our two D$^{rs}$. do not differ materialy as to the great point which is the subject of the Mss. Your D$^r$. however best knows his own sentiments yet he has but ^very^ slight means of knowing D$^r$. M$^s$. from the Analysis & may easily mistake them. The cheif difference if there be any will ^be with^ respect to the Merit of JX[6] on which D$^r$. M. runs out at great length & it is the most beautiful & ingenious part of the treatise something of the same train of thought with the amiable

---

[3] See Letters 84–89.

[4] Marion ('Mainy' or 'Meny') Wodrow, often greeted by SK as he signed off letters to JW in the early decades of their correspondence. See Letter 86.

[5] William M'Gill, to whom the University of Glasgow awarded the degree of DD in 1785.

[6] Jesus Christ. JW and SK often shortened 'Christ' to 'X'.

Emlyn[7] but much more accurate & finished & yet Magill never read or heard of anything wrote by Emlyn on that point nor have I since I was at the Divinity hall. To a man of D^r. Pr. amazing learning nothing will appear new. The point Divines have laboured is to explain the connection between the Death of X & the forgiveness of sin both the Socinians & the Calvinists have run too much into theory & System about to this the ~~former~~ ^latter^ however infinitely more than the former. Tho the connexion is indubitable from numberless passages of the N.T. yet it is doubtful whether it is any other but the connexion or <—> ^chains^ of facts in the course of Providence—any other in the minds of the inspired writers. The Death ~~of there~~ of their Master led them by this chain to the Publication of pardon & Grace ^of God^ to the World. The best way for a candid & enquiring mind to satisfy itself about this is to read & consider carefully their short simple Sermons in the Acts & also 1 Cor. XV from the begin^g. to the middle.[8] M^r. Magill is surely much more read in D^r. P. writings than I am. You know my high opinion of him with a small deduction.

There is a most terrible stramash[9] at present in the Colledge of Gl. I know little of it only all the Proff^rs. seem resolved to humble Prof^r. And-n.[10] He for many years treated the worthy Prin^l. with an insolence & scurility that you cannot conceive. He has now quarrelled with all the rest of them but D^r. Reid[11] & has given them endless trouble.[12] They have deprived ^him^ of all Jur[is]d[ic]tion even over

---

[7] Rev. Thomas Emlyn (1663–1741), Dissenting minister and pioneer of Unitarianism in his published works (rather than in his preaching). JW is probably referring to his *An Humble Inquiry into the Scripture Account of Jesus Christ* (1702).

[8] The Acts of the Apostles and Paul's first letter to the Corinthians, chapter 15, in the New Testament.

[9] 'stramash': commotion, argument, excitement. *DSL*.

[10] John Anderson (1726–96), professor of natural philosophy at Glasgow since 1757. He was an enthusiastic and popular teacher but a combative colleague, as the relevant correspondence in this volume reinforces. He had been a slightly older contemporary and friend of SK and JW as a student, and had accompanied SK and his pupil James Milliken on their tour of England in 1759, which explains JW's and SK's astonishment at his behaviour in the 1780s. His will provided for the founding of an Institute in Glasgow in his name, which later became Strathclyde University.

[11] Thomas Reid. See Letter 83.

[12] On the natural philosopher John Anderson's dispute with Principal Leechman, see Paul Wood, 'John Anderson (1726–1796)' and 'Thomas Reid (1710–1796)', both in *ODNB*; John Butt, *John Anderson's Legacy: The University of Strathclyde and Its Antecedents, 1796–1996* (East Linton, 1996), pp. 12–17. Copies of correspondence relating to Anderson's years of strife with Leechman and others at the University are held at the University of Glasgow Archives and are listed in Julie Gardham and Lesley Richmond, 'Research Resources in the University of Glasgow for Adam Smith and the Scottish Enlightenment', University of Glasgow Library, 2009, rev. 2013,

his own students. He has put himself at the head of the Irish & a few others publishe[d state]ments in the N. Papers[13] holding the weekly meetings in the Tontine Tavern,[14] & taking strange methods to get subscriptions to a Petition to the King for a Royal Visitation.[15]

I enclose Nell's receipt having given her sufficient directions as to the signing & returning it which you will explain if she is at any loss. I have never said any thing further about supplying her with money let me know whether it is convenient for you to order me to pay it here or if I shall attempt to procure & send you a draught on Lond$^n$.

My kindest comps to M$^{rs}$. & Miss Kenrick. In hast aff$^y$. yours.

J. Wodrow

## Letter 92: Samuel Kenrick to James Wodrow, 22 February 1785
Place: Bewdley

My Dear Friend

Your kind favour of the 6th. inst. contributed its share w$^{th}$. the rest of the packet to make us happy. We all join most heartily in the just economium you pay to the Postmaster or mistress who behaved so generously to our last packet, in its shattered forlorn condition. Was it done by the sacrilegious hand, w$^{ch}$. formerly dared to violate the public faith, by repeatedly purloining our harmless letters, w$^{ch}$. could be of little value to any one, in comparison of what they were to ourselves– I should be happy– as it shews they are sensible to their fault & are therefore entitled to forgiveness. If it was done by one that never injured us they were kind

---

www.gla.ac.uk/media/Media_138989_smxx.pdf, pp. 8–13, especially the items listed on p. 12 for the 1785 'stramash'; and in the John Anderson Papers, Archives and Special Collections, University of Strathclyde, at GB 249 OA/6/26–28.

[13] E.g. *Glasgow Journal*, 3–10 Feb., 10–17 Feb., 24 Feb.–3 March 1785; *Caledonian Mercury*, 9, 16 and 21 Feb. 1785.

[14] The Tontine Tavern and Coffee-room, at Glasgow Cross on the Trongate, was one of the principal meeting-places for merchants, pressmen, and political men in late eighteenth-century Glasgow. See Alex Benchimol, 'The "Spirit of Liberal Reform": Representation, Slavery and Constitutional Liberty in the *Glasgow Advertiser*, 1789–94', *Scottish Historical Review*, 99 (2020), pp. 51–84, at pp. 56, 76. A tontine was a form of investment plan, and there were Tontine taverns and hotels in many British towns.

[15] Paul Wood, '"Jolly Jack Phosphorus" in the Venice of the North, or, Who Was John Anderson?', in Andrew Hook and Richard B. Sher, eds, *The Glasgow Enlightenment* (East Linton, 1995), pp. 111–32.

& generous indeed. The real fault was I know mine, in trusting such a valuable contents in such a slender rotten cover. You may depend upon my taking care it shall not happen again.

I am happy to find that the little I have done to serve your friend D$^r$. M. meets w$^{th}$. your approbation. I need not say what pleasure it w$^d$. give me for your sake as well as his, to do something to the purpose. And from your acc$^t$. of the work & of the author, I am impatient to see it, to be better acquainted with a subject of that importance, w$^{ch}$. I own I am too much a stranger to. The foundation w$^{ch}$. I laid under the tuition of that worthiest & best of men D$^r$. L.[1] assisted by your friendly conversation, & a long habit of intimacy w$^{th}$. the Saint of Kilbarchan[2]– without any regular superstructure, is all that I can boast of. For w$^{ch}$. reason I ought to be very cautious on these subjects before such as you.

I do most sincerely sympathise w$^{th}$. you on the loss of your excellent sister. It is easy to feel what your tender affectionate soul must suffer, from the breach of a connexion so intimate & of so long a standing. I know she was very ingenious & make no doubt of your having many pleasing remembrances of her, in her compositions in prose & verse. The sketch you have given of her amiable character & of your long uninterrupted friendly intimacy, charmed me– and does equal honour to your feelings & her memory.[3] Perhaps some time or other you will favour us w$^{th}$. a sight of some of her productions.

You bring me again back to the 2 Doctors.[4] But peace be to them– they are both good men. And if Paul & Peter differed, nay had a bit of a squabble together,[5] should I be surprized to find the same phenomenon at this day into equally zealous christians. While your gentle evangelical temper makes the most charitable allowances for each.[6] From the little that I know of the subject, I plainly see, that

---

[1] William Leechman.

[2] John Warner.

[3] See Letter 91, in which JW conveyed the news of Mainy Wodrow's death to SK, but which does not contain such a portrait of her; perhaps that memory was incorporated in a letter to Nell. But see W-K, I, p. 362, for his brief encomium on the life of his sister Jenny after her death in 1776.

[4] Joseph Priestley and William M'Gill.

[5] See Galatians 2:11–12 (which SK will probably have read in the original Greek rather than in the King James Version). Paul noted, of his confrontation with Peter at Antioch: 'I opposed him to his face, because he stood self-condemned; for until certain people came from James, he used to eat with the Gentiles. But after they came, he drew back and kept himself separate for fear of the circumcision faction'. *The Bible, New Revised Standard Version*.

[6] 'Evangelical' in the sense of 'the spirit of the gospel': both 'eirenical' and 'with biblical authority'. W-K, I, p. 100 n. 495. Linford D. Fisher, 'Evangelicals and Unevangelicals: The

most of our theological disputes, are too much founded, in idle quibbling– in using words in their natural or metaphorical senses, just as suit their purposes. Thus our Saviour calls bread his body & wine his blood– & that his disciples must eat his flesh & drink his blood: w^ch. figurative expressions were easily understood at the time, however they have been perverted since. But he says they must drink the cup, too: & there I believe no language will allow the natural & litteral sense– altho' more than the half of christendom admit it in the former expression. So we are said to [be] washed in the blood of X; & cleansed by it from all sin. Whereas blood can never wash out stains, being itself the greatest of stains. These & many such expressions were familiar & obvious in the hebrew & chaldee languages, but when translated into a different idiom, has become the grounds of endless ranglings. I intend to observe the judicious rule you have laid down & when I have more time, may probably trouble you again on the subject.

My friend M^r. Brisbane, gave me some acc^t. of the terrible stramash among the present family of our old Alma Mater– poor gentlewoman![7] How our quondam friend Anderson, who was such ^a^ divine & philosopher in his youth, should disgrace his gray hairs, with the works of the flesh, astonishes me: & particularly that he should harbour the least shadow of rancour against ^his^ old friend & venerable instructor D^r. L. When I enjoyed his company in a tour through England 25 years ago, I well remember, what jealousies & enmities prevailed among them. Adam Smith was the principal object at that time– who you know was as firey & choleric as Anderson himself.[8] Their high words frequently brought them very near to blows, by his account, at their Faculty meetings; when we poor souls tho^t. that all their attention was taken up in promoting the cause of litterature & the interests of the good old Lady. How much wiser are the lazy drones of our Universities; who pass the harmless hours, in the dull routine of

---

Contested History of a Word, 1500–1950', *Religion and American Culture*, 26 (2016), pp. 184–226, has shown that New England Unitarians used the word in this sense into the mid-nineteenth century. Thanks to David W. Bebbington for advice on this point.

[7] The University of Glasgow.

[8] For Anderson's place in the world of learning, see Wood, 'Jolly Jack Phosphorus'. Adam Smith (1723–90) was professor of moral philosophy at Glasgow University from 1751 to 1764. One of his students, James Boswell, observed that Adam Smith 'in his private character is realy amiable... [and] is extreamly fond of having his Students with him and treats them with all the easiness and affability imaginable'. Nicholas Phillipson adds that Anderson was 'the only recalcitrant colleague who made [Smith] lose his temper'. Nicholas Phillipson, *Adam Smith: An Enlightened Life* (2010), pp. 135, 301n. It is interesting that Kenrick viewed Smith as being as 'fiery and choleric' as Anderson.

college exercises, & in good eating & drinking– and exact no harder task of their obsequious pupils![9]

In the litterary way– I have only to tell you that there is just set up a 2nd. Book Society in this little place: not to rival ours which has now flourished 18 years,[10] but because we had not room for them. Ours consists of 20 Members– & 14 have already subscribed to the new one. In ours we have high Church & low-church & no church, catholics & presbyterians– D$^{rs}$. of divinity & Doctors of physic, gentlemen & tradesmen ^Foxites & Pittites.^[11]– Yet in all this medley, we have not the least dissension or animosity: & for the moderate expense of 7/6 annually, have 4 comfortable convivial meetings, & as many & whatever books we please. At Birmingham they have a noble institution of this sort under the direction of D$^r$. Priestley. Their books are not sold as in other Societies, but kept in a large room or Library, where a person constantly attends– & any member has access at any time or may have any book. The same is at Manchester. And some of our members wanted the same here. But our numbers are too few– & the subscriptions w$^d$. be too heavy.[12]

As to money matters w$^{th}$. Miss Wodrow– give yourself no concern about it. Remember she lives in the Bank & may have what she pleases.

But our l$^r$. must go today– tho' it happens not to be a post day– & we must part. Adieu My D$^r$. fr$^d$. w$^{th}$. our most affectionate regards to yrself M$^{rs}$. W. & dear Peggy.

S.K. E.K. & M.K.

---

[9] For a similar comment, see Edward Gibbon's description of Oxford, where he spent 'fourteen months the most idle and unprofitable of my whole life'. Edward Gibbon, *Memoirs of My Life*, ed. Betty Radice (1984), ch. 3.

[10] This figure is difficult to be certain of: possibly '10', but more likely '18'.

[11] i.e. supporters of Charles James Fox (1749–1806), leader of the opposition Whigs in the House of Commons, and, on the other hand, those of the prime minister, William Pitt the Younger (1759–1806).

[12] On subscription book societies, see the Introduction, p. 15, and Peter Clark, *British Clubs and Societies, 1580–1800; The Origins of an Associational World* (Oxford, 2000), pp. 109–10; Mark Towsey and Kyle B. Roberts, eds, *Before the Public Library: Reading, Community, and Identity in the Atlantic World, 1650–1850* (Leiden, 2018); James Raven, 'Libraries for Sociability: The Advance of the Subscription Library', in Giles Mandelbrote and Keith A. Manley, eds, *The Cambridge History of Libraries in Britain and Ireland, Volume II 1640–1850* (Cambridge, 2006), pp. 241–63; William St Clair, *The Reading Nation in the Romantic Period* (Cambridge, 2004). David Allan, *A Nation of Readers: The Lending Library in Georgian England* (2008), pp. 26, 172, suggests that there may have been between 600 and 2,000 book clubs in England by 1820. On the book societies at Birmingham and Manchester, see also Letter 135, SK to JW, 13 Feb. 1788.

## Letter 93: Samuel Kenrick to James Wodrow, 21 March 1785
Place: Bewdley
Addressed: The Rev^d. James Wodrow
Note: 1785

We have not had the pleasure of hearing from my dear & worthy friend since our pacquet of the 22^d Ult°. w^ch. we hope came safe to hand & that the recêt was properly executed. This goes by the merchant's conveyance from Wrexham fair[1] in company w^th. many more from your most amiable & sweet tempered daughter & Mary, to their numerous correspondents in & about Glasgow– & will probably linger longer on the road before it reach you. There will be no great loss– as you will soon find by the perusal.

I have just made a tour (on business) of 120 Miles thro' Shropshire & the skirts of Montgomeryshire. I hardly ever travelled more pleasantly, having neither met w^th. snow nor rain for 5 whole days. It was cold indeed– particularly in the mornings. But the roads were as smooth, dry & dusty as at midsummer. The face of the country was, however, far from being pleasing– for large fields of wheat w^ch. 3 months before were covered w^th. a promising verdure, were now as brown & bare in appearance as the most barren heath or mountain. But the frost is not yet gone so that all vegetation is at a stand. Our gardens as well as fields are one dreary desart. When the frost goes the farmer will roll his wheat & fall immediately to sowing his Lent grain– as they call oats & barley.

This has been here a tedious Siberian winter[2] w^ch. makes fodder & provisions excessively dear in the mean time: but the farmer & planter looks forward w^th. joyful expectation, to the probable prospect of large future crops. For short winters, w^th. transitory sudden gleams of heat bring on vegetation too soon; & expose the tender germ & bud & blossom, to a nipping cold w^ch. it cannot withstand: whereas, when kept back by a continued cold, it shoots forth w^th. new vigour, & fostered w^th. warm suns & long days, it grows to its natural maturity & perfection. We had a very great crop, (or <u>hit</u> as they call it ^of fruit^) last year of everything.

---

[1] Wrexham is a market town near the Welsh border with Cheshire.
[2] As with JW's account of the hard frost in Letter 88, this passage reflects the ongoing climate impact of the 1783 Laki volcanic eruption in Iceland.

1785, MARCH 21

The same is expected this year from the above circumstances. And this makes us patiently submit to the present temporary inconveniences.

My reading has been confined of late to tours & travels– particularly Coxe's most entertaining acc$^t$. of Poland Russia &c.[3] That gentleman is at present abroad at Petersburgh[4] accompanying a M$^r$. Whitbread[5]– son of an eminent Brewer & member of Parliament of that name– who shews his good sense as well as liberality of mind, in not grudging the expence of having such a Tutor & sending him first into those uncultivated countries, where they will meet w$^{th}$. more improvement than in the flirting gaiety of France or the delicious scenes of Italy. I remember Sir Joseph Yorke[6] mentioned this circumstance to M$^r$. M.[7] & me in 1760, in honour of the Lord Hope[8] of that time & particular of his Tutor M$^r$. Rouet:[9] w$^{ch}$. if I had had as much sense & experience as I now have, I should not have hesitated imitating.

---

[3] Rev. William Coxe (1748–1828), historian and Church of England clergyman. He became a fellow of King's College, Cambridge, 1768–71, and ordained deacon in 1771. After touring Europe with the eleventh earl of Pembroke, he published a three-volume *Travels into Poland, Russia, Sweden and Denmark* (1784). He also published several biographies, including one of Sir Robert Walpole.

[4] i.e. St Petersburg.

[5] Heir to England's largest porter brewery, and estates in Bedfordshire, Samuel Whitbread (1764–1815) was educated at Eton, Oxford, and Cambridge, where he graduated BA in 1785. After travelling to Europe in the mid-1780s, he socialized with Whig politicians and married Elizabeth, the sister of Charles Grey, in 1788. At the general election of 1790 Whitbread took over his father's seat at Bedford and represented the constituency during his lifetime. He became a leading Foxite Whig and an enthusiastic supporter of reform issues, including the abolition of the slave trade, universal toleration, and parliamentary reform. Of a rather unstable temperament, after several years of declining health, he committed suicide in 1815.

[6] Joseph Yorke (1724–92), baron Dover, soldier and diplomat, third son of the first earl of Hardwicke (1690–1764), minister-plenipotentiary (1751–61), and subsequently ambassador to the Hague (1761–68). Created Baron Dover in 1787. SK and James Milliken Jr were in the Hague for about a week in August 1760. SK's recollections were of that time. See W-K, I, pp. 273–77.

[7] Milliken.

[8] Charles, Lord Hope (1740–66), was the eldest son of the second earl of Hopetoun. Suffering ill-health, and accompanied by his brother James, he undertook the Grand Tour to Italy, and then travelled to Carolina and Jamaica, but died upon return at Portsmouth. D. M. Eddy, 'Johnston, James Hope-, third earl of Hopetoun and *de jure* fifth earl of Annandale and Hartfell (1741–1816)', *ODNB*. Nathaniel Dance painted *Charles, Lord Hope, The Honorable James Hope and William Rouett* (1762) on tour in Rome.

[9] William Rouet or Ruat (1714–85), professor of oriental languages at Glasgow 1751–52, then professor of ecclesiastical history at Glasgow University (1752–62), took unauthorized leave from the university to accompany the Hopes to Utrecht on their Grand Tour. James Boswell met them at Brunswick, and 'at night Rouet and I talked a good deal. He was a sensible, forward fellow'. James Boswell, *Boswell on the Grand Tour: Germany and Switzerland 1764*, ed. Frederick A. Pottle (1953), p. 16. He was removed from office after this excursion, but the University later settled the case by reinstating him and reimbursing his salary in return for his retirement. '[T]he ending of his tenure gave rise to one of the longest and keenest controversies in an age when long and keen controversies were far too common.' Coutts, *History of Glasgow University*, p. 240; see also

The tour is that of M^r. Pennant thro' Cheshire Shropshire & North Wales.[10] Most of my last journey was comprehended in this: w^ch. added greatly to its pleasantness. This gentleman is very well acquainted with our environs. I have had the pleasure of seeing him here & hearing his rapturous admiration of some of our prospects: & has given some hints of publishing an *Iter Sabrinense* or trip down the River Severn. His tours in Scotland I suppose you have seen.[11] He has ~~his~~ foibles– who is without them? But to me he is a pleasing writer– as he possesses an extensive practical knowledge, in natural philosophy & history– & a benevolent, chearful heart & soul.

With our joint best wishes & respects to you & yours I am my dear friend's most affect^te.

S. Kenrick

## Letter 94: James Wodrow to Samuel Kenrick, 25 March 1785

Place: Stevenston
Addressed: Mr Sam^l. Kenrick / Bewdley
Postmarked: Lond. April first 1785
Franked: E. Eglintoune
Stamps: FREE; AP/1
Note in SK's hand: answ^d. 29th Apr.

My Dear Friend

I have never had time & I have even now but little to acknowledge the receipt of your kind Letter Feb^r. 22^d. & to advert to the agreable matter contained in it. My

---

pp. 223, 230, 240–46. William Leechman and John Anderson were two of Ruat's defenders during the lengthy controversy: GUA27026, Reasons for protest by William Leechman, Robert Simson, James Clow and John Anderson, 1760, and GUA27027, Reply to GUA27026 by Hercules Lindsay, Dean of Faculty, James Moor and Adam Smith, 1760.

[10] Thomas Pennant (1726–98), naturalist, traveller, and writer. Born to a landed family in Flintshire, he was educated at Wrexham, Queen's College and Oriel College, Oxford. Pennant soon became a distinguished natural historian and corresponded with major Enlightenment figures. He undertook many tours, including two of Scotland (1769 and 1772). There are several editions of his tours in Wales. His *A Tour of Wales*, 2 vols (1784), I, 'The Tour in North Wales' outlines the route followed by SK. See Mary-Ann Constantine, Nigel Leask, Lisa Cardy et al., 'Curious Travellers: Thomas Pennant and the Welsh and Scottish Tour (1760–1820)', https://curioustravellers.ac.uk/en, accessed 1 Aug. 2023.

[11] Thomas Pennant, *A Tour in Scotland. MDCCLXIX [1769]* (Chester, 1771) and *A Tour in Scotland and Voyage to the Hebrides. MDCCLXXII [1772]* (Chester, 1774). See also Constantine et al., 'Curious Travellers', https://curioustravellers.ac.uk/en.

late dear Sisters Settlements have engrossed a great deal of my time & cost me a good deal of writing. She was the last of the four unmarried Sisters. She & my eldest Sister before her Death made a Settlement dividing what they had among their Heirs with much judgment & Equity & yet in unequal Legacies. The settlement or Testament quite formal & Legal but by the designed ommission of ^the^ Writer of it to get a little bussiness & money to the Commissary court[1] at Glasgow of which he is a member (at least I aprehend ^this to have been his design^) He has ommitted the usual clause of appointing an Executor to the will. I wish to have the matter managed so as to dissapoint him & save expenses to myself & all concerned & hope to be able to do so being in use to do their bussiness, & in habits of intimacy with the Gentlemen who have my sisters money in their hands but it has cost & will cost some trouble. I must not however trouble you any further with it at present.

I have had a short letter from D$^r$. Magill expressing a high sense of his Obligation both to you & me. He is very busy just now transcribing another copy of his Manu$^{pt}$. wishing to correct some things & to make it as fit as he can for the publics inspection. It is probable that he will come to the resolution of setting his name to it yet he wishes still to try the inclinations & terms of the London Booksellers by means of my Br$^r$. in law M$^r$. Hamilton,[2] to whom I have written—& if he undertakes to manage the business I will probably give you the trouble of sending the Analysis &c. to him which M$^r$. Magill will replace to you as soon as he has time by another copy & more of his printed sermons.

I see you have not forgot your theological learning you had indeed two of the best masters in Christendom[3] and with a little practise you woud ^still^ do as well as most of us in understanding & explaining the Scriptures which is the principal bussiness of a divine. I have often from the bottom of my heart regreted that we lost you as a preacher & only soothed myself with the hope of your being richer easyer & Happier in the line of Life you have chosen. I admire the contrivance & conduct of your book Societies & envy you not so much for the opportunity of reading many books but the time you can spare for doing it. For myself I have not the time to read the sixth part of the books I have it in my power & woud wish to read. In the younger part of Life I spent much time in writing Sermons &c, now

---

[1] The Commissary Courts dealt with marriage, divorce, and legitimacy. There were local commissary courts with a superior court in Edinburgh. David M. Walker, 'The Background of the Institutions', in David M. Walker, ed., *Stair Tercentenary Studies* (Edinburgh, 1981), p. 73.

[2] John Hamilton. See Letter 84.

[3] William Leechman and John Warner. See Letter 92.

I spend very little & yet from an extensive correspondence by Letters from doing my own & cheifly other people's bussiness which everyone will have too much of who has any ability integrity & disposition to oblige, from the Company & amusements of this neighbourhood & the increased populousness of the Parish & other causes I often cannot spend above five or six hours in a week in reading.

How justly do you mark our quondam friend[4] with disgracing his grey hairs with these works of the flesh according to the apostles sense,[5] besides others which are not to be named among saints. I am tempted to transcribe part of a Letter my Wife received from her Aunt[6] last night who by the by wishes to be particularly remembered to Miss K. "Mr. W (she says) will be much interested in what is going on here. It is a most vexatious shameful story, & wonderful how such a flame shoud be raised & how general the prejudice against us. Mr L. has got the lye in the rudest manner. They make him to say things that are false in his Protest (against the trades house of Glasgow published in the N Papers) knowing them to be so.[7] I am much more hurt with these things than he is. He rests in the Integrity of his heart without being disconcerted with all they can say. It is realy laughable to see the methods they have taken to get names to their Petition. Nine different parties were at Will[m]. Fergussons shop (an old Servant of the Princ[ls]. now married to his Neice) trying to get him to subscribe it. They stand at the doors of the places wherein the Petition lyes & take in all that will come from the street, many low people & many boys of ten years old have subscribed it. I hope it (the Petition) will soon go away, which will settle matters a little, till we see the end of it." Can you conceive anything like this? & yet Anderson will be quite in his Element & as happy as Ritchard III Lovelace[8] or the Devil himself can be in the

---

[4] Professor John Anderson.

[5] Galatians 5:19–21, 'Now the works of the flesh are manifest, which are these; Adultery, fornication, uncleanness, lasciviousness, idolatry, witchcraft, hatred, variance, emulations, wrath, strife, seditions, heresies, envyings, murders, drunkenness, revellings, and such like'.

[6] Bridget Leechman. See Letter 84.

[7] E.g. *Glasgow Journal*, 10–17 March 1785, though this report did not cast any personal aspersions on Leechman but only mentioned the petition for a royal visitation 'to settle the dissentions which at present prevail in this University'. The *Caledonian Mercury*, 14 March 1785, published a robust defence of the university's management by Professor Meek and Rev. William Taylor. This was followed on 16 March 1785 by a brief response from the trades and students promising a full complaint, which does not seem to have been published in the *Caledonian Mercury*.

[8] Perhaps John Lovelace (1640–93), third baron Lovelace, an outspoken Whig politician of the later seventeenth century: an 'intemperate whig partisan who almost certainly was an alcoholic as well as a compulsive gambler and given to sexual excess'. David Hosford, 'John Lovelace (c. 1640–1693), third baron Lovelace', *ODNB*.

success of his Projects. It woud amuse you to see <u>some of the Papers</u> published in the [page torn] news, one of them last week entitled the Anticipation on the side of the College gives a history of the Royal Visitation[9] as a past Event & the different Proffessorships & Professors turned to Secular purposes by the Chamber of Commerce at Glasgow with a great deal of fancy & <good> Humour.

I will enclose a Draft on London for Nell of £10 which will be much the safest way of remitting her any thing as I understand you are rather in the way of drawing money from Scotland than paying it, & I find it in my power without any trouble to get such drafts from two or three people in this neighbourhood. From the numerous Letters we have received from her we have no doubt that she has spent a happier Winter with you than ever she did in her Life. She speaks with gratitude of the attention & kindness she has met with & particularly of her obligation to Miss Kenrick. But my best friend We must not suffer Your kindness & her wandering humour to go too far. She has now made a long visit & it is high time she were thinking of her return to the bleak barren Mountains of the North & of the manner of accomplishing it. I mean not to fix a particular week but to leave this to herself. Her stay in England must be the shorter as there is little prospect of her going to London for tho' her Uncle be in town every day on his bussiness, Yet M$^{rs}$. Hamilton & he live in what they call a Hovel about six miles from town where she coud see nothing. M$^{rs}$. Leechman speaks in her Letter of a M$^{rs}$. Gibson[10] going up to London to do bussiness for her Husband. She is Louisa's cousin & a lovely woman– perhaps matters might be contrived so as that Nell might join her a few days before she leaves L$^o$. & return with her to Ed$^r$. but of this nothing can be said till we know her motions more certainly. My sincere love to you & yours.

J. Wodrow

---

[9] *Glasgow Journal*, 10–17 March 1785, p. 1. Also reprinted as a single sheet, printed on both sides, in the following year: 'Anticipation, Glasgow, 1st April 1786'. A campaign for a royal visitation of Glasgow was the current focus of Anderson's campaign against Leechman and his supporters at the University of Glasgow, but it did not materialize, this squib to the contrary. (The first recommendation from the claimed visitation, for instance, was 'That the Principal, in consideration of his age and infirmities, be allowed to retire from all kind of business, and for the remainder of his life, enjoy himself in *otium cum dignitate*.') See Letter 91.

[10] See Letter 106 for the Gibsons.

## Letter 95: Samuel Kenrick to James Wodrow, 27 April 1785

Place: Bewdley
Addressed: The Rev$^d$. James Wodrow
Note: 1795

I was duly fav$^d$. w$^{th}$. my dear Friend's of the 25th. Ult°. making a part of the most acceptable pacquet to your amiable daughter, & I am now called upon by her, to have my share of a conveyance of this to you under L$^{d.}$ Eglintoun's cover.

What a plague is law to us, when in the hands of crafty and designing men? I have had enough of it, to disgust me with it. Tho' I must say, that what you were so kind as to get done for me, gives me a more favourable opinion of the profession in Scotland than here[1]– added to what I experienced from a M$^r$. Nicoll Writer[2] in Aberdeen– w$^{th}$. whom I had not the slightest connection or acquaintance, who paid me a Legacy of £50 to a poor person in this town– & as I begged his indulgence on that acc$^t$. he remitted me the Fifty Pounds undiminished– & said that as he had had the money in his hands for some little time, that should go against the expences of postage &c attend$^g$. the transaction. I was used myself in a different way– but that was by a friend. And you know what signify friends if we cannot make some advantage of them?– By this time I hope you have got clear of these difficulties, & that the person who has given you all this trouble has met with his deserts– the contempt of all who know him.

I am glad to find D$^r$. M$^c$Gill persists in his resolution to give this work to the public– & I hope he will meet with due success. The cause of truth and Christianity must be gainers by every impartial inquiry of this sort– How much have they gained within your remembrance & mine, when subjects of this sort could not be so much as mentioned but in a whisper. The fears of ignorance, the interest of cunning & the pride of science are the main springs: every human passion has contributed its addition. I owe this last sentence to M$^r$. Mitford whose history of Greece I am just now reading– a most entertaining work indeed to every classical reader.[3] His

---

[1] Probably a reference to JW's protracted negotiations in 1778–81 for the recovery of money owed to SK in payment for a load of mahogany that had been sent to his wife by her brother in Jamaica some years previously. See W-K, I, Letters 60–77.

[2] Not identified; there is no Nicoll listed for this period in *A History of the Society of Writers to Her Majesty's Signet, With a List of the Members of the Society from 1594 to 1890 and an Abstract of the Minutes* (Edinburgh, 1890). SK may be using the term 'Writer' in a loose sense to mean a solicitor, rather than a solicitor who was also a WS (Writer to the Signet).

[3] William Mitford (1744–1827), historian. In 1784 he published the first volume of his ambitious *History of Greece*. The first volume covered events from early times to the end of the Persian wars (479 BC). The history was finally completed with volume five published in 1818.

style is far from being elegant or pleasing– but natural strong & nervous, such as we should expect from an original genius. He has all his greek authorities at his fingers ends. Hence honest Homer makes a great figure at the beginning. You cannot help having him in your hand two or three times in every page. This has the most agreeable effect of bringing one back into the company of an old entertaining acquaintance– & as I can still pick up the meaning of 20 or 30 lines without looking at the translation, it is with difficulty I can part with him– & often wish Bank & business were far enough, that I might indulge myself in the farther perusal of this divine bard. But what I admire & indeed injoy in this writer & still more in Gibbon is their collateral instruction with w$^{ch}$. their notes abound. These are like a constant comentary on the text as well as upon the authorities, where the author descends from his dictatorial chair & freely converses with his hearers upon what he has been saying. This is what I call learning– or it is the sort that pleases me best.[4] As to the rest it is amazing to see the immense information w$^{ch}$. he has drawn ^from^ this first painter & historian as well as poet.[5]

I am obliged to you my good friend for your good wishes & your favourable opinion of my talents as a divine. It certainly was my earliest wish, joined to a serious turn of mind from a strictly religious education, to have figured away in the pulpit. But I am affraid vanity had more to do here than solid talents– & glad I am that this same vanity dissuaded ^me^ from the pursuit, as I became better acquainted w$^{th}$. the business. For when I compared myself w$^{th}$. you & many others younger & older than myself, I felt my inferiority so much– that I found it would make me inferior to myself so to speak, to continue in it. And in that case I should have been much more troublesome to you & my other sympathizing friends w$^{th}$. my real or imaginary complaints, than in the road of life I have taken to. I own the advantages I was blessed w$^{th}$. in having my mind early impressed w$^{th}$. the instructions of two such eminent masters w$^{ch}$. must have given a tinge to every subsequent attainment.

And I am very thankful to a kind Providen[ce] that has directed me to a line of life, where if [I] have not been so useful as I might from my education otherwise

---

[4] Anthony Grafton begins his history of the footnote: 'In the eighteenth century, the historical footnote was a high form of literary art. No Enlightenment historian achieved a work of more epic scale or more classic style than Edward Gibbon's *History of the Decline and Fall of the Roman Empire*. And nothing in that work did more than its footnotes to amuse his friends or enrage his enemies.' Anthony Grafton, *The Footnote: A Curious History* (Cambridge, MA, 1999), p. 1.

[5] Presumably this refers to Homer.

have been, & where I have had rubs & crosses to encounter of a different sort— yet I am so far at liberty, as to enjoy the peace of my own mind, more than if I was tied down to the periodical labours of a public teacher. As to riches & ease in circumstances— I do not know if I have more. For we always live in the same frugal way. The pomp & shew of the world I never coveted. To me they are troublesome. They intrench too much on that ease & tranquility— the fallentis semita vitæ,[6] w$^{ch}$. I always wish to enjoy.

Poor Anderson— I do not know whether most to pity or detest him. To disturb, to attempt it I mean— the virtuous tranquility of that best of men, the venerable Principal, is really unaccountable. As my f$^{rd}$. D$^r$. P. says— every effect must have its cause— but how to account for this behaviour of Anderson & others at Glasgow— is beyond my comprehension. Your climax on the occasion is admirable— Richard, Lovelace & the Divil!

Miss Nelly has already acquainted you of the receipt of the £10— of w$^{ch}$. she is so kind as make me her Banker. But there was no occasion of your troubling yourself ab$^t$. it, 'till she wanted it.

Nothing can make all of us happier than to find that this most excellent girl is so happy with us. She has her share of merit in it— for we give ourselves no trouble about her— & she give us none. We every one go on in our usual way & she the same. Each on his own hobby horse as Sterne says, without ever shouldering or jostling his neighbour.[7] And we desire you not to disturb us w$^{th}$. your prancer— to hint at removing her. Why she has not seen a bit of the country.

Adieu my fr$^d$. May God bless you & y$^{rs}$. ever prays,<br>
Y$^r$. S. K.

---

[6] Horace, *Epistles*, I, xviii, line 103: 'the pathway of a life unnoticed'. Loeb Classical Library.

[7] See Laurence Sterne, *The Life and Opinions of Tristram Shandy* (1759–67), ed. Graham Petrie, intro. Christopher Ricks (1985), I, ch. 7, p. 43: 'Sir, have not the wisest of men in all ages, not excepting Solomon himself,— have they not had their HOBBY-HORSES; their running horses,— their coins and their cockle shells, their drums and their trumpets, their fiddles, their pallets,— their maggots and their butterflies?— and so long as a man rides his HOBBY-HORSE peaceably and quietly along the King's highway, and neither compels you or me to get up behind him,— pray Sir, what have either you or I to do with it?'

## Letter 96: James Wodrow to Samuel Kenrick, 16 June 1785
Place: Edinburgh
Addressed: M[r]. Kenrick.
Note in SK's hand: answ[d]. 30th June
Note in JW's hand: June 1785

My Dear Friend

I wrote you a few hurried lines about a month ago[1] when I was about to leave Stev[n]. Since that time I have had the pleasure of hearing of your wellfare by ^a^ letter from Nell which her Mother received about a fortnight ago. We spent four or five days very agreably at Glasgow with M[r]. & M[rs]. Leechman. He was better in his health and more able to converse with me than he had been at the Synod[2] & exceedingly interested in the Success of the College cause[3] (as he considered it) at the general Ass[ly]. which we began to have some apprehensions about, from the answers to our Letters & these were encreased on my arival here by finding

---

[1] Missing letter: JW to SK, 12 May 1785 (see Letter 97, SK to JW).
[2] 12–13 April 1785. See NRS, CH2/464/4, Minutes of the Synod of Glasgow and Ayr, 1761–1803, ff. 198–200, where the issue debated at the General Assembly in May, as reported here by JW, was previously discussed at Synod, with JW in attendance and playing an active part. The synod meeting was reported in the *Glasgow Journal*, 7–14 April 1785.
[3] For a full narrative of these events at Glasgow University, see James Coutts, *History of the University of Glasgow: From Its Foundation in 1451 to 1909* (Glasgow, 1909), pp. 268–69, 278–94; J. D. Mackie, *The University of Glasgow 1451–1951: A Short History* (Glasgow, 1954), pp. 206–09. Professor John Anderson and others, including Professor Thomas Reid, had carried on a dispute for ten years with Principal William Leechman and his supporters over the question of whether or not the University's accounts were kept accurately, and when the University's factor (manager), Matthew Morthland, retired in 1785, it was found that he indeed owed thousands of pounds to the University. Anderson, however, had become isolated by 1785 because of the number of rather heated and eccentric disputes he sustained with students and colleagues: he 'was almost always at variance with some his colleagues' (p. 286) and particularly with Leechman, against whom Anderson's complaints rumbled on till the time of the events related here by JW. Yet he was popular with students: Ronnie Young, 'Thomas Muir at Glasgow: John Millar and the University', in Gerard Carruthers and Don Martin, eds, *Thomas Muir of Huntershill: Essays for the Twenty-First Century* (Edinburgh, 2016), pp. 112–40, at pp. 129, 133. See also Gardham and Richmond, 'Research Resources in the University of Glasgow', pp. 8–13, for a listing of the manuscript documents relating to this and various others of Anderson's disputes in the University. For Anderson's side, see University of Strathclyde, Special Collections, GB 249 OA/6/26, John Anderson papers, Petitions to the King, from the Trades House of Glasgow, the merchants and other inhabitants, students, former students and Professor John Anderson, requesting a royal visitation to examine the conduct of the authorities at Glasgow College (Feb.–May 1785); ibid., GB 249 OA/6/28, John Anderson papers, Glasgow College dispute with Mathew Morthland, late Factor, concerning his claim and accounts (1787).

considerable prejudices conceived against the Colledge as having acted arbitrarly in the Expulsion of the Students,[4] by the apparent complexion of the Asembly ~~a majority~~ ^the majority of Mins^rs^.^ of the same religious sentiments with the Presby of Glasgow[5] & therefore expected to stick by them in this point & finding several of our own party[6] doubtful of the propriety of sustaining a Colledge sentence of Expulsion as a bar to admission into the Church.[7]

---

[4] Coutts, *History of the University of Glasgow*, pp. 287–94. By 1784 Anderson had determined to secure a Royal Commission to investigate the University's administration and, having lost support among his colleagues, attempted to rally support in the form of petitions by students and by Glasgow citizens, a request which was declined by the king, who made clear his support for the principal. Three students who had joined Anderson especially vigorously in his efforts to bring Leechman's administration into disrepute—David M'Indoe, Alexander Humphreys, and William Clydesdale—were expelled. M'Indoe appealed to the Presbytery of Glasgow and then the General Assembly of the Church of Scotland, which still retained considerable authority over the universities: Richard B. Sher, *Church and University in the Scottish Enlightenment* (Edinburgh, 1985), especially pp. 120–26. A minority from the Synod of Glasgow and Ayr, led by JW, also brought the case to the General Assembly, as a complaint against Glasgow Presbytery.

[5] i.e. Evangelical, or aligned with the Popular party. Leechman was a father of the Moderate party. Because the General Assembly was composed of an annually changing body of delegates from each Presbytery (clergy and lay elders) rather than the whole body of ministers, its doctrinal and ecclesiological leaning could vary from year to year, not least since many ministers did not identify with either party. It seems, however, that Anderson aligned himself with the Popular party in opposition to Leechman and his allies. Gerard Carruthers and Satinder Kaur, 'Thomas Muir and Staff and Student Politics at the University of Glasgow', in Gerard Carruthers and Don Martin, eds, *Thomas Muir of Huntershill: Essays for the Twenty-First Century* (Edinburgh, 2016), pp. 112–40, at pp. 99, 102, 109; Young, 'Thomas Muir at Glasgow', pp. 134–35.

[6] The Moderate party; see Ian D. L. Clark, 'Moderatism and the Moderate Party in the Church of Scotland, 1752–1805', unpublished PhD thesis (University of Cambridge, 1963); Ian D. L. Clark, 'From Protest to Reaction: The Moderate Regime in the Church of Scotland', in Phillipson and Mitchison, eds, *Scotland in the Age of Improvement*; Sher, *Church and University in the Scottish Enlightenment*; Friedhelm Voges, 'Moderate and Evangelical Thinking in the Later Eighteenth Century: Differences and Shared Attitudes', *Records of the Scottish Church History Society*, 22 (1985), pp. 141–57.

[7] NRS, CH2/464/4, ff. 198–200 provides details of the Synod debate over whether the Presbytery of Glasgow ought to be allowed to proceed with David M'Indoe's trials for licence as a minister of the Church of Scotland, or whether the case ought to be referred to the General Assembly, which JW evidently retailed to SK in the missing letter of 12 May 1785. The majority on 12 April was to remit the case back to the Presbytery and allow them to proceed. However, JW intervened by dissenting from and protesting the vote of the majority; he 'craved liberty to complain to the next Gen. Assembly', and he was supported by Rev. Alexander Hutchinson, Rev. James Scot, Rev. John M'Aulay, Rev. William Thom, Rev. John Allan, and Rev. Dr James Meek, Dean of Faculties at Glasgow University. The following morning, they were joined also by Rev. John Risk, Rev. George Laurie, Rev. James Couper, Rev. Robert Boog, Rev. James Miln, and Rev. Alexander M'Aulay.

This situation of matters obliged the Proff^rs. Jardine[8] and Macleod[9] M^r. Geo. Laurie[10] & myself to take inconceivable pains for eight or ten days to represent this cause properly to those who were either intirely ignorant of it which most of them were or had very partial views of it and as there was no printed case you cannot easily conceive of the trouble of this in a popular court consisting of about 160 members (i.e. present & voting members but not a half of the Legal number).[11] Our Success however was owing to this more than any thing else. When the cause came to be heard after Our Complaint and the Defense by the Presby of Glasgow the Court entered on a long Debate in which we had all the principal ^Lawyers &^ speakers in the Ass^ly on our side & one or two of the best Lawyers had not room to ~~appear~~ speak for the Other party gave it up at last & suffered a most compleat sentence to pass in our favour without a vote, reversing the Sentence of the Synod and finding it incompetent in the present cause for the Synod to allow ~~M^r. M'Indoe's tryals~~ the presby to proceed in M^r. M'Indoe's tryals till the Sentence of Expulsion passed on ^him^ by the Colledge for Contumacy was removed.[12] I understand tho' I have had a very indifferent Accounts of it that he has since Appeared before the Colledge Faculty but with so little sign of

---

[8] Rev. George Jardine (1742–1827), Church of Scotland minister and professor of logic at Glasgow University, who was a pedagogic and administrative reformer.

[9] Hugh Macleod (d. 1809), professor of ecclesiastical history at Glasgow University from 1778. He was involved in 'a furious quarrel' with Anderson in 1783: Coutts, *History of the University of Glasgow*, p. 286. He was not a minister of the Church but was presumably an elder and attending the Assembly in that capacity.

[10] Rev. George Lawrie or Laurie (d. 1799), minister of Loudoun parish church, Ayrshire. *FES*, III, p. 121.

[11] See Sher, *Church and University*, p. 124. Around 360 delegates could attend the General Assembly each year, from the 938 parishes, but it was rare that as many as 200 were present, and sometimes there were fewer than 150.

[12] David M'Indoe (d. 1826), matriculated at the University of Glasgow in 1773, expelled 1785 and his name scored through in the Matriculation Albums of the university. After preaching for some time at Borrowstouness (now Bo'ness) in West Lothian, he was ordained as minister to the Groat Market Meeting-House (Scotch Presbyterian) church in Newcastle on 29 Sept. 1790, where he remained till his death in 1826. 'At the commencement of his ministry here, he frequently expressed from the pulpit his political opinions in strong terms; but his fervour on such subjects gradually declined. He published "A Fast-day Sermon", a Missionary Sermon, and, in 1823, a volume of "Sermons on important Subjects", which were published for the benefit of the fund for superannuated ministers and their widows. His temper being irritable, and his pronunciation defective, his congregation yearly diminished. Latterly, he was obliged to engage assistants, with one of whom, the Rev. W. Newlands, A. M. he had a violent quarrel. Both parties appealed to the public through the press. Mr. M'Indoe was an active member of the committees of the Bible Society and the Royal Jubilee School.' *Historical Account of Newcastle-upon-Tyne, Including the Borough of Gateshead* (Newcastle-upon-Tyne, 1827), p. 387.

Submission that they have unanimously confirmed and continued their former Sentence.[13] They have in some sort already & are likely to have the same triumph over Poor Anderson at London.[14] When he arived there he anounced his arrival with his 15 Petitions[15] to the Marquiss of Graham[16] Chancelour to the University together with an appology for not waiting on him as he had been indisposed.[17] L$^d$. Graham in his answer expressed his regret for his indisposition & at the same time a high dissaprobation of his Errand and of the Petitions which he had bought with him and occasioned refused to see him at his own house or to meet & converse with him any where but at Lord Sydney's Office where I suppose he will present them.[18] L$^d$. Graham wrote at the same time to the Convener of the trades house at Glasgow signifying the receipt of his Letter relative to the Petitions presented by a few of the Corporations– that he was at a loss to conceive what connection they had with the College and what tittle they had to give their advice to his Majesty in the Matter,[19] that the Kings Mins$^{rs}$. & the Proff $^{rs}$. of the University woud unite in measures if any were necessary for restorin[g] peace & order & concluding with an expression of his regard to their House & inclination to pay ~~all possible~~ every attention [and] regard to their advice in matters where they

---

[13] Thomas Muir was also heavily involved, but left the university before he could be expelled, moving to the University of Edinburgh. Carruthers and Kaur, 'Thomas Muir and Staff and Student Politics', pp. 89–111; Young, 'Thomas Muir at Glasgow', pp. 131–33.

[14] Indeed. Anderson had been preceded in his visit to London by letters from Leechman to such powerful figures as Ilay Campbell, duke of Argyll, the Marquis of Graham, Edmund Burke, and Henry Dundas, asking them to throw their weight against Anderson's request for a royal visitation to the university, as well as a memorial and petition to Lord Sydney from Leechman and the professors of the university. University of Glasgow Library, Archive Services [GUA], GUA27346–27350, 27363.

[15] See the long note at the start of this letter. Anderson circulated a public letter detailing the petitions and concluding that 'a Royal Visitation was never asked by so many and such a variety of persons; and if it is not granted, the University must for many years fall into such contempt that it will not answer the end of its institution'. Coutts, *History of the University of Glasgow*, p. 291.

[16] James, marquess of Graham, was chancellor of the University of Glasgow from 1780 till 1836. See Letter 79. Anderson had unsuccessfully asked his help to secure a royal visitation to the university in 1784.

[17] As Coutts puts it, 'Anderson's valour remained, but his discretion had departed', *History of the University of Glasgow*, p. 290.

[18] Thomas 'Tommy' Townshend (1733–1800), first viscount Sydney, home secretary in Pitt's administration, 1783–89. MP for Whitchurch, Shropshire (1754–83) and member of the extensive Townshend connection of Whiggish complexion. His most lasting legacy is that the colony in Botany Bay was named Sydney after him.

[19] The Glasgow Trades had voted by a large majority in support of Anderson's campaign on 24 Feb. 1785, but this result was overturned after 'an impassioned appeal' from Leechman. Carruthers and Kaur, 'Thomas Muir and Staff and Student Politics', p. 93.

were competent judges. Of these Letters he has sent Copies to the Prin¹.²⁰ signifying at the same time ^the^ receipt of a Memorial on the part of the College which he approved of & woud present. It is not difficult from these things to predict the fate of the Petitions above. I saw the one signed by fifty or sixty students the ~~one~~ half of them Irish with M'Indoe's name at the Head of it for it comprehends all sorts of Students both Togati & not.[21] It is full of the same sorts of scurrility, falsehood & perversion of harmless facts with the anonimous publications, indeed I was astonished at the indecency of it. The Election of Burke as their Rector[22] is complained of as a factious measure carried in Opposition to Order & decency with insinuations of its being disloyal or disrespectful to his majesty, coud any ^thing^ be more illiberal & even more impolitick for it must irritate all his friends & at the same time be easily seen thro' by the opposite party. It is strange how the Irish shoud sign it but I have bored you with this Affair which I consider as now over with respect to any hurt it can do the College, tho' I am affraid & very sorry to think it may end in the ruin of Anderson himself.

There was no other cause of any public consequence before the Ass$^{ly}$. except the Overtures about Patronage[23] in which it was proposed that the Church shoud

---

[20] Glasgow University Archives, John Anderson Papers, GUA27352, Copy letter from Lord Sydney to Professor John Anderson turning down his official request for a Royal Visitation on the grounds that it would 'be much more likely to injure the discipline...than to promote the peace and good order of that respectable seat of learning', 17 June 1785.

[21] At the University of Glasgow, 'the students are divided into *togati* and *non-togati*; the former wear a gown of scarlet cloth, and belong to the Latin, Greek, logic, ethics, and natural philosophy classes. All these must attend the college chapel on Sunday, (where service is performed according to the rights of the Established church) unless they belong to another church or sect, when leave of absence is granted. The reminder of the students are the *non-togati*, and (except those who are students of divinity), are unrestricted in their address, order of attendance, or presence at worship in the chapel of the university'. James Pagan, *Sketch of the History of Glasgow* (Glasgow, 1847), p. 119.

[22] Edmund Burke was rector of the University of Glasgow in Nov. 1783, the first to be elected to that office who was not Scottish. In fact, by June 1785, when JW was writing, he was coming towards the end of his second year's tenure of the position, but he only made his second year's visit to Glasgow in August 1785, and there were inevitably some who thought it was a political appointment, implying support for the Foxite Whigs. That political grouping found some support in the Popular party of the Church of Scotland. Coutts, *History of the University of Glasgow*, p. 335; F. P. Lock, *Edmund Burke, Volume I: 1730–1784* (Oxford, 1998), pp. 536–38; Lock, *Edmund Burke, Volume II: 1784–1797* (Oxford, 2006), pp. 51–53; Emma Macleod, 'The Scottish Opposition Whigs and the French Revolution', in Bob Harris, ed., *Scotland in the Age of the French Revolution* (Edinburgh, 2005), pp. 81–82.

[23] Patronage, the power residing in the Crown and other great landowners in the appointment of parish ministers. It was abolished in 1649, restored in 1660, abolished in 1690, and restored again in 1712 against the terms of the Treaty of Union of 1707. The General Assembly

consult the Landed Interest of Scotland whether they wished Queen Annes[24] act repealed and King Williams[25] restored[26] which puts the Election of a Mins^r in ^the^ hands of the Heretors & Elders or whether they woud chuse the present Act continued with some restrictions on the unlimited power of Patrons. This Debate lasted from 11 to 8 at night & was indeed one of the most decent and sensible debates I ever saw in the Ass^ly. very different from one ^on the same subject^ I was wittness to about 15 years ago. The Candour Moderation and good sense exhibited in the Speeches of what we use to call the high party[27] was a very pleasing <—> Symptom of the improving spirit of the Age. Had they proposed any specifick plan of restriction of the Law of Patronage and specifick mode of Application to the Counties I & many more of my friends woud have joined them but in the loose general way in which it was proposed it seemed to me to have a tendency to revive a flame in the different parishes which was very high about two years ago and is now in some measure sopite.[28] The Overtures were rejected by 100 against 64. All the landed Gentleman & a great number of them were Members of the Court voted with the majority except Harry Erskine[29] whose speech was from beginning to end in a strain of the finest irony good humour & pleasantry that you can conceive.

My Wife has been very much troubled with a cold & sore throat ever since she left Stev^n. which has confined ^her^ to the house sometimes for two or three days together. There are such a number of her near relations here most of them I may say all of them good people that my time has been greatly taken up in visiting them & also an equal number of my own acquaintance from different places of the Country particularly Airshire who expect calls & visits that I have been disappointed in one prin^l. purpose of my coming here– the looking at some of the new

---

protested against it annually until 1784, although the Moderate party were less offended by it than the Popular party. It was not repealed till 1874. *DSCHT*.

[24] Queen Anne (1665–1714, r. 1702–14).

[25] King William III and II (1650–1702, r. 1689–1702).

[26] The Acts of 1712 and 1690, respectively. Under the 1690 Act, heritors (local landowners) and elders of a parish church nominated a minister to the congregation, and the presbytery had final approval. Under the 1712 Act the right of nomination rested with the Crown or other great landowners. See also Letter 79 above.

[27] The Evangelical or Popular party.

[28] 'Sopite': 'put to rest'. *OED*.

[29] Henry Erskine. See Letter 79. Although he was a leading member of the Scottish Foxite Whig connection, he was well liked by politicians and churchmen of all views.

publications so that except Priestleys Corruptions and Horsleys Answer[30] – I have had time to read nothing almost. Several new acquaintances I have picked ^up^ unavoidable in a scene of this kind, such as some of M^r. Haddows[31] intimate friends who made up to me purely on the Score of ^our^ mutual friendship to him an atraction which I found irresistible. From the same ^sort of^ atraction I was led last night to ^go &^ drink tea with M^rs. Stewart[32] & D^r. Spence[33] your friends & Miss Kenricks; & I sincerely regret that it was not in my power to cultivate their valuable acquaintance further, & accept the Invitation they gave me to dinner; for they seem both to be worthy people. I was obliged to introduce myself which was easily done but a perfect stranger to both, I felt myself restrained from saying one word on the too tender subject of the loss of his Son[34] and yet it was often at my toungue roots as we say, for I had spent a very happy night with Gremy at Milliken in my return home in winter– where there was a great deal of innocent pleasantry & romping between him & that lightheaded & lighthearted Girl Miss Campbell.[35] Had I found M^rs. Stewart by herself I had resolved to start this painful < > subject but in the presence of the Father and both of them apparently out of spirit I coud say nothing. Yourself Miss Kenrick M^rs. Milliken[36] and her Sons[37] made the cheif part of our Conversation. He desired me to tell you at parting that he wished & expected a Letter from you.

Were you to revisit Scotland you woud be surprized at the increase of this town which will soon be, if it is not already the second city in the Island. It has

---

[30] Joseph Priestley, *An History of the Corruptions of Christianity*, 2 vols (1782); Samuel Horsley, *A Charge Delivered to the Clergy of the Archdeaconry of St Albans at a Visitation Holden May 22nd 1783* (1783). See Letters 85 and 88 above.

[31] See Letter 84 above.

[32] Unidentified.

[33] Dr Nathaniel Spens (1728–1815), a noted Edinburgh physician and close friend of SK, who had married Mary Milliken (1746–74), the daughter of SK's first employer, James Milliken Sr.

[34] Died 'at Shrubhill, in his 15^th year, Mr Graham Spens, son of Dr Nathaniel Spens, physician in Edinburgh'. *Scots Magazine*, 47 (1 May 1785), pp. 257–58.

[35] 'Gremy' appears to be a nickname for Graham Spens. 'Miss Campbell' is possibly Ann Campbell, daughter of Robert Campbell of Downie, Argyllshire. In August 1786 she married Robert John Milliken Napier (1765–1808), the heir to the Milliken estate. John Burke, *A Genealogical and Heraldic Dictionary of the Peerage and Baronetage of the British Empire* (1869), p. 812. The young poet, Thomas Campbell (1777–1844), spent time at Downie in 1797, where he had heated debates over politics with his Tory grandfather. *The Life and Letters of Thomas Campbell*, ed. William Beattie, 2 vols (1850), I, pp. 136–63.

[36] Jean Milliken. See Letter 84.

[37] James Milliken (1741–63) and Alexander Milliken (1743–65), whose tutor SK had been from 1750–65.

doubled in the Extent of building within 12 or twenty years & is still going on at an amazing rate, so that since the short time Miss Kenrick was here there ^are^ 200 Houses ^to be^ added to the new town that is contracted for, and the foundations of ~~most~~ ^many^ of them laid.[38] You know it stands on the hill or ridge to the North of the Old town with a delightful prospect of the Firth the Fife Coast & hills; & runs parallel to the high street. It is connected with it by the new bridge on the East which runs in a line from the tron Church[39] & within this month it is connected with the High Street on the West by a Mound of ea[r]th of the same height with the bridge formed out of the rubish of the new buildings & pointing <nearly>[40] on the Weighhouse or those buildings that are nearest the Castle.[41] It is extending every year further & further to the West & will in a short time be contiguous to the West kirk[42] that is about double its present Extent. The buildings are grand beautiful & have every convenience. The streets and squares so perfectly regular that a stranger after looking for five minutes at the plan of it or walking two or three times thro' it may find any street square or house in it without any embarrassment.

---

[38] The building of Edinburgh's New Town had begun in 1768, and was still ongoing in 1785. St Andrew's Square was completed only in 1784, the George Street Assembly Rooms did not open till 1787, and Robert Adam was only commissioned to design the elevations for the frontage of Charlotte Square in 1791. A. J. Youngson, *The Making of Classical Edinburgh* (Edinburgh, 1966); James Buchan, *Capital of the Mind: How Edinburgh Changed the World* (2003), pp. 191–204; Christopher Fleet and Daniel MacCannell, *Edinburgh: Mapping the City* (Edinburgh, 2023), pp. 69–95. For the earlier development of Edinburgh, see Murray Pittock, *Enlightenment in a Smart City: Edinburgh, 1680–1750* (Edinburgh, 2018).

[39] The Tron Church, originally built between 1637 and 1647 on the model of contemporary Dutch ecclesiastical architecture, was reduced in size, and tenements around it destroyed, in the redevelopment of Edinburgh in the late eighteenth century. This created room for the North Bridge, to which JW refers here. The Tron Church sits in Hunter's Square, named after Rev. Andrew Hunter (1743–1827), who was translated to the Tron Parish from New Greyfriars in Edinburgh in 1786 after the death of Rev. George Wishart (d. 1785). A tron was a public weighing machine which stood in the marketplace of a town centre, and gave its name to the area around it; Glasgow also has a Tron Church. Scottish Historical Buildings Trust, The Tron, https://www.shbt.org.uk/our-projects/the-tron/, accessed 19 June 2024; *FES*, I, pp. 136–37; *DSL*.

[40] Ms is difficult to read. Probably 'nearly', but possibly 'neatly'.

[41] This eminence, created from some 1.5 million cartloads of earth from the levelling of the site of the New Town, is still known as 'The Mound' in Edinburgh. New College, University of Edinburgh, and the Assembly Hall of the Church of Scotland are located on Mound Place. Fleet and MacCannell, *Edinburgh: Mapping the City*, p. 90.

[42] St Cuthbert's parish church, also known as the West Kirk, on Lothian Road.

On the Southside of the town the same spirit for building is going on tho' not all with the same beautiful and singular regularity. They have already begun their operations in consequence of the Act of Parl$^t$.[43] for oppening that part of the Suburbs & connecting it with the High street by a bridge[44] over the Cowgate.[45] The street leading to this, will be a continuation of the one from the present bridge meeting the tron church on the high street with a large sweep on <every> each side of it which will prevent much confusion from the passing Carriages; going down Nidrys wind[46] & passing through the middle of D$^r$. Spence's house crossing the Cowgate & ascending the other hill a little to the east of the Colledge & passing thro' the Principals Garden & the City wall in which they have already made a breach to ascertain the proper line & levels. This will make it an easy & convenient entry to the City from the South & west which was much needed & there will be little occasion for the old & dangerous one by the Bow.[47] I am not sure if you remember so much of Ed$^r$. as perfectly to understand my description. According to the calculations which some people here have made two Millions have of late ^years^ been sunk in buildings on the South and North of the town. I give you this on D$^r$. Spence's authority, & you see how much more is still to be laid out. It is astonishing where it comes from in such a poor Country.[48] Instead of sending their child$^n$. to boarding schools it is now become customary for Country Gentlemen to come here with their families & live two or three years from all the different shires in Scotland, and I am told also from the North of

---

[43] An Act for Opening an Easy and Commodious Communication from the High Street of Edinburgh, to the Country Southward, or The South Bridge Act (25 Geo. III c. 28), was passed in 1785.

[44] The South Bridge was built between 1785 and 1788. It forms one long road with the North Bridge, through the Old Town of Edinburgh, 1,075 feet long and consisting of twenty-two stone arches. At its highest point it stood 31 feet above ground and had foundations which penetrated Edinburgh's bed rock as far down as 22 feet. Fleet and MacCannell, *Edinburgh: Mapping the City*, p. 93; E. C. Ruddock, 'The Building of the North Bridge, Edinburgh: 1763–1775', *Transactions of the Newcomen Society*, 47 (1974), pp. 9–33.

[45] The Cowgate is a long street running perpendicular to the Bridges, underneath the South Bridge and also (since 1825) George IV Bridge, which runs parallel to the Bridges some distance to the west of them.

[46] Niddry's Wynd, one of the many narrow alleys or closes between tenements, running from the High Street to the Cowgate. It had been widened in 1750, becoming Niddry Street.

[47] The West Bow (or arched gateway) in the Grassmarket, Edinburgh.

[48] See A. R. Lewis, 'The Builders of Edinburgh's New Town, 1767–1795' (PhD thesis, University of Edinburgh, 2006), pp. 216–37 for a discussion of the investors in Edinburgh's building projects in this period.

England. This may account tho' not fully for the increasing buildings & populousness of Ed[r]. beyond the Proportion of other parts of the kingdom without the same spirit of trade and Manufactures. Glasgow notwithstanding the loss of America seems still to enlarge & thrive & Paisley in a proportion perhaps greater than either.[49]

But I must draw to a conclusion as I am in danger of tiring both myself & you. I have had time to read only the first vol. of Priestley[50] & this in a cursory way have met with entertainment & instruction from the account of the Oppinions of the Fathers & Schoolmen tho' this is the dryest part of the book. The Article on the Atonement I liked best yet it confirmed me in the Oppinion that D[r]. Priestley and the English ^Socinians^ have never read the Writings of the old fratres Poloni at least with real ^any^ attention.[51] It is amusing to see how thinking men fall upon the same train of discovery if it can be called so from the unprejudiced search of the Scripture. It has much the cast of Originality in Dr Priestley and even more so in Socinus writings. Crellius has improved on his master & treated the points with more accuracy but less Agreably.[52] Dr Priestleys book woud have been more accurate & perfect especialy in the point of lucidus Ordo[53] had he dipt more into their Writings. Nor woud he have been in the least surprized at the Worship they pay to J Christ which I had almost called Apostolical for it is quite subordinate and founded on the power & knowledge they Ascribe to him as the immediate head of the Church of God.[54]

---

[49] For Glasgow, see Brad Jones, 'The American Revolution, Glasgow, and the Making of the Second City of the Empire', in Simon Newman, ed., *Europe's American Revolution* (2006), pp. 1–25; Richard B. Sher and Andrew Hook, 'Introduction: Glasgow and the Enlightenment', in Hook and Sher, eds, *Glasgow Enlightenment*, pp. 2–9; Irene Maver, *Glasgow* (Edinburgh, 2000), pp. 16–20; and the following essays in T. M. Devine and Gordon Jackson, eds, *Glasgow, Volume 1: Beginnings to 1830* (Manchester, 1995): Devine, 'The Golden Age of Tobacco', pp. 166–76; R. H. Campbell, 'The Making of the Industrial City', pp. 184–213; Gordon Jackson, 'New Horizons in Trade', pp. 214–38. For Paisley, see Derek Alexander and Gordon McCrae, *Renfrewshire: A Scottish County's Hidden Past* (Edinburgh, 2012).
[50] *History of the Corruptions of Christianity* (1782).
[51] See Letter 87.
[52] Johannes Crellius (1590–1633), a Polish-German Socinian, who wrote 'the central Socinian text', *De Uno Deo Patre* (Raków, 1631). Sarah Mortimer, 'Exile, Apostasy and Anglicanism in the English Revolution', in Philip Major, ed., *Literatures of Exile in the English Revolution and Its Aftermath, 1640–1690* (Farnham, 2010), pp. 93–94.
[53] Latin: clear arrangement.
[54] Socinians believed that Jesus was a major prophet and moral example, but not divine.

I have been a good deal with D^rs. Robertson[55] Blair[56] Erskine[57] & Macnight[58] all of them good and Social men in their way. I preached for the first & last. He is about to publish his Comentaries on the Epistles some passages of which he read to me which have the Air of Originality.[59] A vol of Sermons is about to be published by Sam^l. Charters[60] which of all the promised publications I wish most to see.

M^r. Ruats[61] Death & some ^other^ things which I have in my head I must take up in my Letter to Nell, lest I shoud swell this frank beyond the proper bulk. She & your good family must think of parting in six weeks or so as I have wrote a day or two ago to her Uncle who proposes to be in Scotland this Summer to contrive some means of bringing her down along with him. Yet I am loath to part such good friends and will not lay any absolute Commands upon her but leave her to her own Judgment & discretion. Only She will never get a fitter Companion on the road then her own ^uncle^ if it be consistent with his ~~own~~ Schemes to take her & this seems to be the cheif thing about which her Mother & herself are anxious. All here join in most affectionate Comp^s. to you and to M^rs. & Miss Kenrick. I ever am

My D^r. Sir
most sincerely yours
J. Wodrow

---

[55] Rev. Dr William Robertson (1721–93), historian, principal of the University of Edinburgh, minister of Old Greyfriars parish church in Edinburgh, and leader of the Moderate party in the Church of Scotland. He wrote *The History of Scotland during the Reigns of Queen Mary and James VI* (1759), *The History of the Reign of Charles V* (1769), and *The History of America* (1777), as well as *An Historical Disquisition Concerning the Knowledge which the Ancients had of India* (1791). His histories, which were internationally successful, were marked by his narrative skill, ability to survey major historical landscapes, and embrace of the stadial history approach.

[56] Hugh Blair. See Letter 85.

[57] Rev. Dr John Erskine (1721–1803), minister of the second charge of Old Greyfriars parish church in Edinburgh, writer, and leading member of the Popular party in the Church of Scotland.

[58] James Macknight. See Letter 83.

[59] See Letter 87. The closest extant publications to JW's description here and in Letter 87 are James Macknight, *Translation of the Epistles to the Thessalonians* (Edinburgh, 1787), followed by his *New Literal Translation from the Original Greek of All the Apostolic Epistles*, 4 vols (Edinburgh, 1795).

[60] Samuel Charters, *Sermons* (Edinburgh, 1786), advertised in the *Edinburgh Evening Courant* of 21 Jan. 1786, priced 4/6 in boards or 5/6 bound. Charters (1742–1825) matriculated from Glasgow University 1757, and was awarded a DD in 1789. He was minister of Wilton, near Hawick (1764–1825). *FES*, II, pp. 143–44; *ODNB*.

[61] William Ruat, Rouet or Rowat, Esq. of Belretiro, Ayrshire, d. 4 June 1785. *Scots Magazine*, 47 (June 1785), p. 312. See also Letter 93. Mrs Ruat was Mrs Leechman's niece and a sister of Louisa Wodrow, and so Nell's aunt (see Letter 108).

## Letter 97: Samuel Kenrick to James Wodrow, 29 June 1785

Place: Bewdley
Addressed: The Rev^d. James Wodrow / Irvine / Scotland
Postmarked: Stourbridge July the First 1785
Franked: Free Westcote
Stamp: 128 STOURBRIDGE

My dear Friend,

I have to acknowledge, w^th. most grateful thanks, your most entertaining & interesting favour of May 12th.[1] & June 16th. from Ed^r. The former, in w^ch. you gave me a particular account of the first rise of the business, & of your masterly manage^ment^ of matters before the synod, filled me w^th. impatience to hear the event au dernier resort before the General assembly. Your last letter has gratified it in the most compleat manner & affords me the unspeakable pleasure of congratulating you & your friends upon this signal triumph of Truth & Good sense, over their eternal enemies Ignorance & Bigotry.

Poor Anderson & his 15 petitions in his pocket. What a figure must he make in London among his Great as well as his Learned friends the *F.R.SS!*[2] how humiliating to his proud spirit! With you, however, I am really sorry for him– as I think, it must not only make him wretched, but prevent his usefulness as a teacher & hurt the interests of the respectable body to w^ch. he belongs. There was a time when neither of you nor I would have believed ^it^ possible. But his falling out w^th. his first & best friend & the most excellent of men D^r. Leechman is to me unaccountable. Miss Wodrow gives me the most probable solution of it– that his understanding is impaired. And in that case he is indeed to be pitied!

To my no small surprize about a fortnight ago, I met w^th. a strenuous defender of this gentleman, in a stranger, at an inn in Shrewsbury in a public company. He told me that Anderson was gone to London on a most important business, & would certainly bring about a royal visitation of the University– w^ch. was much wanted. For, he said, the professors had been very unfaithful stewards & w^d. by this spirited step of M^r. And^n's. be compelled to refund to a considerable amount.

---

[1] This JW letter of 12 May 1785 is unfortunately missing. However, the synod minutes are extant and record the part JW played in managing Leechman's and the University's cause against Anderson's allegations. See Letter 96 nn. 2, 7 above for details.

[2] The Fellows of the Royal Society in London, the final 'S' denoting the plural, i.e. FRSs. Anderson was elected a Fellow on 1 Feb. 1759.

As for And[n]. he trumpetted him ^forth^ as the most learned man of the age, particularly in hebrew & latin: & raising his voice and fist, he declared in a strong Irish brogue, with a violent thump on the table, By St Paul there was not such a man alive as his hero Anderson. This energetic apostrophe attracted the attention of the whole company for a moment– but being all strangers to each other & the subject of it only known to himself & me, the conversation was soon divided into parties, as is commonly the case in large companies, & I & my gentleman were left to enjoy our own tête ^à tete^ w[ch]. you will easily believe was on my part very interesting. He execrated the purse-proud Glasgow merchants & the presbyterians– w[ch]. w[th]. his brogue disposed me to think he was no caledonian. But as we stuck close together 'till all the company were gone to bed, He then told me in confidence that his name was Hamilton, that he was a Scotsman & ^a^ near relation of the Duke's– being son of a Lord Frederick Hamilton.[3] And to confirm this he produced his seal w[th]. the Hamilton arms & motto, neatly engraved on a large field. I told him that I remembered a M[r]. Frederick Hamilton[4], a student at Glasgow who was son of a Lord Arch[d]. Hamilton[5]– great uncle to the present Duke.[6] This he contradicted, asserting the person I mentioned not to be a legitimate descendent of that house.[7] This convinced me that I was not to take every thing for truth w[ch]. he averred to be so: as well as the great improbability of many of his asseverations.

For tho' he confirmed to me the acc[t]. you sent me in your last, of the prodigious increase & improvement of Ed[r]. & added, what pains were taking at present in that metropolis, by men of rank & learning to polish & perfect the English language– w[ch]. I know is very true: but when he assured us that the Scotch nobility

---

[3] Robert (d. 1809) was the only son of Rev. Frederick Hamilton (below), but this stranger appears to have denied that identity.

[4] Rev. Fredrick Hamilton (1728–1811), vicar of Wellingborough, Northamptonshire, was the second son of Lord Archibald Hamilton (see below). See 'Correspondence from the Reverend Frederick Hamilton to Mary Hamilton', University of Manchester Library GB 133 HAM/1/4/1.

[5] Lord Archibald Hamilton (1673–1754), youngest son of William Douglas Hamilton, third duke of Hamilton. Archibald became a naval officer, served as governor of Jamaica (1710–16) and Lord of the Admiralty (1729–37), and was a Whig MP (1708–10 and 1718–47). 'Hamilton, Lord Archibald (1673–1754), of Riccarton, nr. Linlithgow, and Motherwell, Lanark', HPO.

[6] Archibald (1740–1819), ninth duke of Hamilton and sixth duke of Brandon.

[7] According to Alumni Cantabrigienses, Rev. Fredrick Hamilton (1728–1811) was admitted to Clare Hall, Cambridge, May 1746, and was awarded MA in 1749, and ordained an Anglican priest at London in 1752. It is also recorded that Fredrick Hamilton, the son of Archibald Hamilton (son of the former Duke of Hamilton), matriculated at Glasgow University in 1749. Addison, Matriculation Albums, p. 42, no. 1372.

& gentry were now become so fond of the english idiom & pronunciation, that they admitted none but english servants about their persons & particularly w<sup>th</sup>. their children– not a scots servant to be seen– this I could not give credit to. Next we had a long history of a Russian princess, who resided 3 years in Ed<sup>r</sup>. & had a son born there christened Hamilton Edinburgh in honour of the surgeon who presided at her delivery & of the city where she was treated w<sup>th</sup>. so much respect[8]– & many other wonderful tales too tedious to mention. In confirmation of his saying he boarded w<sup>th</sup>. Anderson, Miss Nelly, says she recollects an Irish gentleman of that name at M<sup>r</sup>. Anderson's 9 or 10 years ago, who answered as far as she could remember the description I gave of him– a tall fair man, of a grave inanimated countenance, somewhat genteel & formal in his appearance, but tawdry in his dress. The first impression he gave me, ^was^ that he was a player, belonging to one of the strolling companies, of w<sup>ch</sup>. there were many at that time going about. And so strong was this conceit in my imagination that I thought I had recollected seeing him act in a barn near Bewdley. To try him however I ventured to talk of M<sup>rs</sup>. Bellamy,[9] whose history is in every body's hands, & of the stage & M<sup>rs</sup>. Siddons.[10] But the bait did not take. He seemed to be quite indifferent or an entire stranger to the subject. But as I have got into a garrulous tale telling humour, & indeed I am fit for little else, I must give you another trait of him. But first I must tell you, that the late M<sup>r</sup>. Speirs[11] of Glasgow, passes for one of the most extraordinary instances of a most rapid accumulation of a princely fortune

---

[8] Possibly an inaccurate account of Princess Dashkova (1743–1810). She had three children in Russia in the early 1760s, and then travelled in Europe after her husband died and she fell out with Catherine II. She lived in Edinburgh from December 1776 to June 1779 while her son Pavel attended the university. *The Memoirs of Princess Dashkova*, Kyril Fitzlyon, trans. and ed. (Durham, NC, 1995).

[9] George Anne Bellamy (c. 1731–88), actress. Her mother was a minor actress, and father Lord Tyrawley, a diplomat. Destined for the stage, she first appeared in Covent Garden as early as 1731; but her brilliant theatrical career was impacted by extravagance and a willingness to court controversy. In 1785 she published an autobiography titled *An Apology for the Life of George Anne Bellamy*.

[10] Sarah Siddons (1755–1831), née Kemble, actress. Born in the Shoulder of Mutton inn at Brecon, the eldest of twelve, she grew up in the travelling theatre of her father, Roger Kemble (1721–1802). She made her name with an appearance at Drury Lane in 1782, and went on to become Britain's leading actress until she retired in 1812 following a final performance of Macbeth.

[11] Alexander Speirs (1714–82) of Elderslie, Renfrewshire who had made a fortune in banking and the trade in tobacco and sugar with the Caribbean and North America, and headed one of the most substantial syndicates controlling the Clyde tobacco trade. By 1773 he was worth more than £153,000. He bought the Culcreuch estate in Renfrewshire from Colonel Napier at a cheap price according to JW. T. M. Devine, *The Tobacco Lords: A Study of the Tobacco Merchants of Glasgow*

in our days. This wonder is heightened, by looking back on the humble station from w^ch. he arose. A M^r. Bailey, who assured me he was son of the author of the English Dictionary of that name,[12] & who travelled thro' the principal towns of Scotland & England, to make what is called a Directory[13]– that is an alphabetical list of the names of Merchants, tradesmen, physicians, attorneys &c in every town. You have probably seen the one he has made for Glasgow & Paisley.[14] This M^r. Bayley told me he had received great civilities from M^r. Speirs at Glasgow, & had the honour of dining w^th. him– where every thing was carried on in the most magnificent style. Becoming pretty familiar with his land-lord over their bottle, from what motive I cannot pretend to say– but Speirs told his guest, that he had sat cross legged on the board a journeyman taylor to the age of 36– & commenced merchant afterwards. I wrote this piece of intelligence soon after to my friend M^r. Patterson of Craigton[15]– who wrote me back, that there was not the least shadow of truth in it.[16] By some means or other Speirs' name came on the carpet before Hamilton, who knew him & every shilling he was worth– or at least the

---

*and Their Trading Activities* c. 1740–90 (Edinburgh, 1975), pp. 4, 10, 11, 14, 30, 74; Lionel Alexander Ritchie, 'Speirs (Robert Cunningham) Graham (1797–1847)', *ODNB*. See W-K, I, pp. 57, 432; Alexander and McCrae, *Renfrewshire*, pp. 173–75.

[12] The father was Nathan Bailey (c. 1691–1742), lexicographer and schoolmaster. His first dictionary, *An Universal Etymological English Dictionary: Comprehending the Derivations of the Generality of Words in the English Tongue, Either Ancient or Modern*, was published in 1721, with a second volume in 1727, both in octavo. They were soon succeeded by the folio *Dictionarium Britannicum* (1730; 2nd edn 1736). These dictionaries went into many editions. Samuel Johnson used the second folio edition as a basis for developing his own dictionary, which formed a rival source of authority with Bailey's for decades.

[13] William Bailey of *Bailey's Western and Midland Directory…for the Year, 1783* (Birmingham, 1783).

[14] *Bailey's Northern Directory; or, Merchant's and Tradesman's Useful Companion for the Year 1781…in every principal town from the River Trent to Berwick upon Tweed; with the Cities of London and Westminster, Edinburgh and Glasgow* (Warrington, 1781) also included short lists of merchants and manufacturers in Paisley, Greenock, Port Glasgow, and various other Scottish towns. Speirs is not listed in the Directory, perhaps because he had retired from trading by 1781.

[15] In 1789 'John Paterson Craigton' paid £1 Horse and Carriage Tax in the parish of Erskine, south-west of Glasgow. NRS, Historical Tax Rolls, horse tax rolls, 1785–1798 horse tax, volume 13, E326/9/13/113. A possible relation was 'Miss Ann Patterson of Craigton', died aged ninety-seven at Paisley in 1817. *Scots Magazine* (1 Dec. 1817), p. 502. The Craigton estate, south-west of Glasgow city centre, was owned by the Glasgow merchant James Ritchie (1722–99), a leading tobacco merchant and banker. Thomas Annan, John Guthrie Smith, and John Oswald Mitchell, *The Old Country Houses of the Old Glasgow Gentry*, 2nd edn (Glasgow, 1878), 'Craigton'; Devine, *Tobacco Lords*, pp. 18, 183.

[16] Speirs was the son of an Edinburgh merchant, so his choice of career was indeed probably less haphazard than this tale suggested. T. M. Devine, 'A Glasgow Tobacco Merchant: Alexander Speirs of Elderslie, 1775 to 1781', *William and Mary Quarterly*, 33 (July 1976), pp. 501–13 at p. 502; Devine, *Tobacco Lords*, p. 6.

number of the estates he had purchased. He pronounced Baileys story to be a d–d lye– but to make the matter better, he assured the company, that Speirs had been transported to America for some crime he had committed in the early part of his life.[17]

[18] Dr McKnight's[19] Commentaries on the Epistles will be read. He is looked upon in a very favourable light by all parties here. You have raised my curiosity much about Sam Charters sermons[20]– by only expressing your own. But why did you not say something more, to give us the pleasure of guessing at their contents?

I sympathize w$^{th}$. M$^{rs}$. Ruatt[21] & her family for their sudden loss– tho' I am happy to think he has left them in such comfortable circumstances.

As to our friend Nelly. I am not surprized at you & her mother's desire to see her– neither must you be surprized at our unwillingness to part w$^{th}$. her. She seems to be quite satisfied & she makes us all happy with ^her^ agreeable company. Indeed to tell you the truth she is now so domesticated & become one of ourselves, that it will be like tearing off a limb ever to part with her. So far from gi[ving] us the least trouble or making any difference [page torn] menage, ~~that~~ we have made a comfortable acquisition in her w$^{ch}$. we & all our friends enjoy. Besides her uncle is not yet clear if he can take her– so that matter must be first settled.

We therefore beg you M$^{rs}$. Wodrow & eke[22] Miss Margaret to have a little [p]atience to see how things [t]urn out.

With our best & most affectionate wishes to you all we remain sincerely yours

S E & M Kenrick

P.S. We cannot part with Helen D$^r$. Sir veril[y] MK. June 30 1785 when Meg writes to me I will write to her.[23]

---

[17] Speirs was a resident tobacco plantation owner in Virginia before he returned to Glasgow in 1744.

[18] At this point we have corrected an error in the Dr Williams's Library collection (which has been preserved in the microfilm edition of the correspondence), whereby two pages from Letter 122 were accidentally included in Letter 97 as DWL 24.157(97)ii. We have moved that sheet to Letter 122. Letter 97 continues with this sentence at the start of the sheet archived as DWL 24.157(97)iii. As Macknight has been mentioned in Letters 87 and 89, it makes sense for SK to be commenting here in Letter 97. In addition, there is a reference to Nelly Wodrow as still at Bewdley, and a 30 June note at the end of the page.

[19] James Macknight. See Letter 83.

[20] See Letter 96.

[21] See Letter 96 for the death of William Ruat.

[22] 'eke': 'also'. Johnson's *Dictionary*.

[23] MK is Mary Kenrick, and Meg refers to Margaret 'Peggy' Wodrow. This final note appears to be written in Mary Kenrick's hand.

## Letter 98: James Wodrow to Samuel Kenrick, 21 July 1785

Addressed: M$^r$. Samuel Kenrick / Bewdley
Postmarked: Irvine July twenty second 1785
Franked: Casillis 85
Note: this & Aug$^t$. 5th. Answ$^d$. Aug$^t$. 22

My Dear Friend

Expecting a frank from L$^d$. Cassilis which I have wrote for to M$^r$. Biggar I sit down to answer your long entertaining & very acceptable letter of 29th of June which came to hand regularly. I am happy to find that you at such distance interest yourself so feelingly in the cause of Alma mater who was indeed <——> ^sometime^ in a disconsolate situation but has now lifted up her head in triumph over her enemies both in Church and state. I beg you to offer my Comp$^s$. & best thanks to your honest friend who Nell writes me has repeatedly drunk my health & who seems equaly jealous of the Honour of the University with you & me. Indeed it was a gross affront to her to attempt to open the way for the reception of her excommunicated Students into the Offices & Honours of our Church.[1]

I must give ^you^ the full sequel of this story since it interests you. About the beginning of June M'Indoe wrote a letter to the Faculty expressing his concern that any part of his conduct shoud have met with the disapprobation of the Gen$^l$. Ass$^{ly}$. of the Church & that he had deserved it by some improper things he had said before the Faculty requesting their forgiveness & having no doubt they woud replace him in the same situation he was in before &c. Their Clerk was desired to answer his letter ^in their name^ by signifying that they were ever ready to treat Offending students in the character of Parents upon proper submission & acknowledgment of Faults but found it necessary he shoud appear before them in person &c, this he did & their Preses after an introduction of the same mild strain with the Letter signifying their readyness to remove the sentence of Expulsion upon proper acknowledgments on his part, asked him two Questions 1. ^whether^ if he acknowledged the justice of the sentence of Expulsion for contumacy. 2. <u>whether</u> he was willing to renounce any reflexions he had uttered & published against that sentence as being unjust and Arbitrary. (In a printed case signed by himself about a fortnight after the Expulsion containing an account of

---

[1] See Letters 94 and 96 above. The sentence of expulsion from the university against David M'Indoe was withdrawn on 21 Nov. 1785, however. Coutts, *History of the University of Glasgow*, pp. 293–94.

his tryal before the Faculty & the Magistrates of Glasgow who ^had^ found him in the wrong in retaining the Subscriptions against <u>the consent</u> of the Subscribers & granted them Liberty to cancell them He had published some very gross and scandalous reflexions on the Proff$^{rs}$.) When these short Questions were put to him in the very words specyfied He returned to his former shuffling manner asking written copies of them upon which they were repeated & explained to refer merely to his contumacy & this <-> often till he said he understood them but declined answering them. Then he was informed no answer was desired sooner than he thought proper & when he intended to answer, it woud be necessary to make a new application to the Faculty meeting. & so the matter ended. The Faculty have been much blamed for their severity by M$^r$. M'Indoe's friends in Glasgow who consider him as a Saint & Martyr but I have given you a fair state of the matter abridged from their minutes that you may judge for yourself as it is possible he may complain of them by a petition to the Gen$^l$. Assl$^y$. for I <u>scarce think</u> he will adress that court in the more familiar mode of a Letter the impropriety of which the Faculty have a very wisely overlooked.

M$^r$. Anderson had a very full & Formal hearing of his cause at the Secretary of State's office.[2] ~~After~~ Not only all his 15 Petitions were read but long representations of the State of ^the^ Colledge explaining them and He himself was heard viva voce. The Colledge made no appearance on their side except by a very short Memorial to the Secretary of State.[3] Indeed, after the Sentence of the Gen$^l$. Assl$^y$. an Account of what passed there, was immediately transmitted by a private Letter to L$^d$. Graham[4] as an Evidence of the sense which some of the Nobility & Gentry & the princ$^l$. Lawyers & Clergy of this country had of the affair; M'Indoe being the cheif tool that Anderson had employed both among the Students & in the town. Before I left Glasgow the Princ$^l$. got the Account of the result of the whole affair in the following Letters which were sent by an Express & came to him the third day when we were sitting at Table by ourselves drinking a glass after dinner.

Rev D$^r$. W.L. Whitehall 17 June

---

[2] Viscount Sydney, home secretary. See Letter 96.

[3] GUA27363, Copy memorial and petition to Lord Sydney from the Principal and Professors of Glasgow College relating to Professor John Anderson's demand for a Royal Visitation [1785].

[4] James, Marquess of Graham, chancellor of Glasgow University. See Letter 96. GUA27349, Copy letter from Principal Leechman, College of Glasgow, to the Marquis of Grahame relating to the unauthorized visit of Professor John Anderson to London with a 'whole cargo' of petitions and calumnious allegations against the College, May 1785.

"Sir your Memorial & Petition in behalf of yourself and the principal Proff$^{rs}$. & other Masters in the University of Gl$^w$. have been received. Since that time M$^r$. Anderson has arrived in town & delivered to me sundry petitions which were intended to be presented to the King, desiring that his Majesty woud be graciously pleased to order a royal Visitation for the redress of Grievances & abuses, said to exist in that Colledge.

"Having called to my Assistance the L$^d$ Advocate of Scotland,[5] & the Heads of the Coll$^{ge}$ now in London" (The Chancelour The Rector M$^r$. Burke[6] & probably the former Rector M$^r$. Dundas)[7] "It has after a full discussion of the subject been judged adviseable that a Letter of which the inclosed is a copy, shoud be written to M$^r$. Anderson.

"The decision which you will see has taken place on this occasion will I hope tend to suppress any discontent or dissatisfaction, and to discourage applications to the Crown in future of a similar nature which ought not to be made while there remains an ordinary mode of redress.

"I have not failed to mention to his Majesty all the Steps which have been pursued by me in consequence of M$^r$. A's. representations. And I have his Maj's Commands to acquaint you, that he has no reason to be dissatisfyed with your conduct, or is, in any degree enclined, to entertain an Oppinion to your disadvantage or to the discredit of the University. I am Sir your most obed$^t$. hum$^{bl}$. Serv$^t$. (signed Sydney"

Follows a Copy of the Letter to M$^r$. A. Whitehall June 17th.[8]

"Sir your Letter to me of the 18$^{th}$. of last Month as also the Copies of the Petitions to his Maj$^y$. with w$^h$ you are charged, from the Trades House Merch$^s$, Traders &c, of the city of Gl$^w$., from the Students Masters of Arts &c, and sundry other papers that I have been furnished with, representing the state of the Uni$^y$. of Gl$^w$. & desiring

---

[5] The Lord Advocate was and is the chief legal officer in Scotland. For Sir Ilay Campbell of Succoth, Argyll, see Letter 79. He was rector of Glasgow University from 1799–1801.

[6] See Letter 96.

[7] Henry Dundas (1742–1811), first viscount Melville (1742–1811), was Burke's predecessor as rector of the university, serving from 1781–83. MP for Edinburghshire (1774–90), and for the city of Edinburgh (1790–1802) until he was elevated to the peerage, he held a multiplicity of offices during a long career including Lord Advocate of Scotland (1775–83), keeper of the signet (1782), keeper of the Great Seal of Scotland (1800–1810), treasurer to the navy (1782–83; 1784–1800), home secretary (1791–94), secretary of state for war (1794–1800), and first lord of the admiralty (1804–05).

[8] See also GUA27352, Copy letter from Lord Sydney to Professor John Anderson turning down his official request for a Royal Visitation, 17 June 1785.

a royal visitation, have had the fullest consideration. In answer to your Request for an Official Reply to your Letter on the subject, I am to acquaint you, that altho' there is every disposition to give effectual redress to grievances in every instance wherin they have been suffered to exist, yet it is not judged either necessary or expedient, in the present instance to appoint a royal Visitation. The Complaints seem to be of a nature which may be redressed by the ordinary Visitors; or in case their decision should not be satisfactory, there lyes an Appeal to a Court of Law (The Court of Session). Under these circumstances, the extraordinary interference of the Crown, by a royal visitation, seems, much more likely to injure the Discipline of the Univ$^y$. than to promote the peace & order of that respectable seat of Learning. I am Sir &c, (signed) Sydney".

As this affair has made so much noise, & the Colledge has been so shamefuly abused in print without any answer almost on their part I was of Oppinion that and signifyed it to the Princ$^l$. and the few Proff$^s$. who were in town, that these two Letters shoud be printed & published without any comment at all, & that They should <–> ^ask^ permission to do this, which they will probably obtain, as every word in the Letters seems to be weighed & intended for the public. What they have done I don't know. In the mean time I took a copy in shorthand you may read them to anybody you please but they must ^not^ appear in print till they come from themselves.

I was greatly amused with your account of your adventure and conversation with the chattering Irishman, I shoud suspect He has been at Glasgow later than nine years ago tho' perhaps And$^n$. may correspond with him as he is unwearied in his efforts to hurt the Society.[9] Most of Irish Students at Glasgow have the very same Ideas of the Patriotism of their Hero with Hamilton. I doubt much the truth both of Baillies[10] & his Anecdotes as to Speirs but shall enquire a little further into them the first time I see M$^r$. Bowman who was an intimate friend of his as well as ^a^ Partner in bussiness.[11] Speirs had very great judgment and abilities in mercantile

---

[9] Either the university, or possibly the Literary Society, of Glasgow. See Letter 108 for the Literary Society.

[10] William Bailey. See Letter 97.

[11] Alexander Speirs and John Bowman of Ashgrove, Ayrshire (1701–97) had been business partners since 1744, together with the Buchanan and Hopkirk families; that firm was renamed Speirs, Bowman & Co. in the 1760s, and both were founder members of the Glasgow Arms Bank in 1750. Both built large houses on Virginia Street, Glasgow. Speirs's will in 1782 listed Bowman as his brother-in-law. Bowman, a native of Ayrshire, was Dean of the Guild of the Merchants House of Glasgow in 1755 and 1756, a merchant councillor on Glasgow burgh council in 1762 and 1763, and Lord Provost in 1764–65 and 1765–66. Devine, 'A Glasgow Tobacco

matters, & seemed to have very mean talents in every thing else, in so far as I coud judge from being twice or thrice in his company, in circumstances where he could have no embarrassment or reserve. Yet I considered him as a good man he seemed to have a considerable dash of vanity without any pride, the purse pride of many of the Glasg^w. Merch^s. consious seemingly of ^the^ bounds of his own understanding he listened willingly to the opinions of other people in matters which they knew much more ^of^ than he.[12] Perhaps a certain embarrassment he had in his speech & manner ~~might~~ might mislead one into an oppinion of his apparent humility & want of talents.

Entre nous, you seem to be at a loss to account for A—n's present conduct, from not knowing him so thoroughly as I do and I am doubtful whether I ought to undeceive you by giving you any further oppening into his char^r. Yet perhaps justice to the honest Prin^l. & others who have suffered so much from his licentious toungue & pen, may require it yet take ^it^ in confidence of friendship & entirely to yourself. A^n. is indeed very wrongheaded in most things, as you judge, but in many things also I am affraid his heart is as wrong as his head. His ruling passions pervert his mind to a degree that you cannot well conceive. He is not indeed selfish or a lover of money & therefore has often done humane freindly & very generous things. But on the other hand his Vanity & love of Popularity of the lowest kind, his Ambition or desire of taking the lead, his party spirit, & revenge have often driven him to do such things as you & I & and every honest man woud shudder at on account of their meanness dishonesty & cruelty, in order to justify himself & <— —> blacken the char^r. of others. What think you of fals^if^ying Minutes, forging Letters, inventing falsehoods & perverting plain facts into a direct contrary appearance from truth & reality. To account for this, he has a certain intriguing turn of mind, which makes him take a pleasure in these things

---

Merchant', p. 503; Devine, *Tobacco Lords*, pp. 28, 72, 74, 178; Carolyn Marie Peters, 'Glasgow's Tobacco Lords: An Examination of Wealth Creators in the Eighteenth Century' (PhD thesis, University of Glasgow, 1990), pp. 45, 1, 146, 289, 308, 346 (n. 166 lists Speirs's will as held at Strathclyde Regional Archives, Glasgow: Glasgow Burgh Register of Deeds, B10/15/8435, Settlement Alexander Speirs, 16 December 1782); George Eyre-Todd, *History of Glasgow*, vol. 3 (1934), in Robert Renwick, John Lindsay, and George Eyre-Todd, *History of Glasgow*, 3 vols (Glasgow, 1921–34), pp. 242–43.

[12] 'Yet I considered him a good man': in 1785 it was still possible for one who would support the abolition of the slave trade by 1788 (Letter 136 below) to consider a major tobacco plantation owner to be a good man. See Christopher Leslie Brown, *Moral Capital: Foundations of British Abolitionism* (Williamsburg, VA, 2006), pp. 366–68; Anthony Page, 'Rational Dissent, Enlightenment, and Abolition of the British Slave Trade', *Historical Journal*, 54 (2011), pp. 741–72.

& a certain talent at composition, by which he can make the worst & the most absurd things appear plausible, especially to those who are inclined to listen only to one side, or who know little of the matter. His success in this arises, not merely from his taking more Liberty than others with truth and fact; but (I have often thought) from his power of misleading & deceiving his own mind & making himself believe palpable absurdities & falsehoods. I woud be inclined with you to impute this to a disordered immagination were it not for the deep art or the low cunning & adress that shines thro' it.

The first opening into his char$^r$. that I had ~~was~~ so far back as 32 years ago, was, his making love to ^a^ Girl much above his rank when I was applyed to by her friends to interpose & actually rode to Ed$^r$. on purpose to meet him there & prevent ^an intended^ duel between him & her Brother <———> which was done with some difficulty on both sides cheifly by preventing any meeting: tho' I was provoked at the airs of dignity or rather insolence that he affected, yet I pityed his folly & thought him a little disordered which might be the case as she was indeed one of the most beautiful Girls I ever saw, yet not 14 & a mere child in her appearance. Whatever I thought or said to her brother the disorder was probably more affected than real as A. has fallen into several scrapes of the same kind since, which were not managed with the same prudence & secrecy.

Anders$^n$. owed his present very lucrative place in the Colledge entirely to the Prin$^l$. & his friends, who carried their point with difficulty by M$^r$. Boyle the Rectors casting vote;[13] <—> even to delay the Election & thus prevented Smith[14] & the other party from filling up the Place till the arival of their Patron Arch$^d$. Duke of Argyle[15] whose presence & declaration in favour of Anderson, overawed & confounded Smith and his Freinds. Yet this Proff$^r$. forgetting past favours & obligations entered into a most indecent contest, with the honest Prin$^l$. Clow[16]

---

[13] Patrick Boyle (1717–98), Lord Shewalton, army chaplain and landowner, rector of Glasgow University 1757–59 and lord high commissioner to the General Assembly of the Church of Scotland in 1764–72. See W-K, I, p. 404 n. 8; Strawhorn, ed., *Ayrshire at the Time of Burns*, pp. 108, 312. Anderson was appointed professor of oriental languages in 1755, and successfully moved to the chair of natural philosophy 1757. Ilay Campbell, third duke of Argyll, opposed Anderson's election to the chair of natural philosophy in 1757, but Patrick Boyle had the casting vote. Roger Emerson, *Academic Patronage in the Scottish Enlightenment: Glasgow, Edinburgh and St Andrews Universities* (Edinburgh, 2008), pp. 137–38. Emerson points out that Anderson was victorious also only because he was prepared to vote for himself.

[14] Adam Smith.

[15] Archibald Campbell (1682–1761), third duke of Argyll. See Roger L. Emerson, *An Enlightened Duke: The Life of Archibald Campbell (1682–1761), Earl of Ilay, 3rd Duke of Argyll* (Edinburgh, 2013), p. 352.

[16] James Clow (d. 1787), professor of logic (1752–87), University of Glasgow.

&c, about the manner of keeping the Colledge books. He was joined by D^r. Reid[17] & others & sometimes had the majority of the Fac^y. on his side & found means to get inserted into the Minutes some ^Papers representations which ought not to have been there. Other^ violent Papers & Memorials ^were written^ full ^ of <———>^ personal reflections on the Prin^l as ~~if he~~ ^a man who^ had lost his judgment &c, the Prin^ls. Answers were calm & Masterly, yet Anderson triumphed by gaining the prin^l. point ^of contest^ by a Sentence of the Ordinary Visitors, to whose final Arbitration it was at last referred;[18] even that according to the very literal interpretation of a statute, the books that should be keept in the Italian way. ^Yet^ D^r. Leechman besides his humanity to Morthland their old Factor[19] which perhaps was his cheif motive, was so well founded in ^his judgment of^ the Colledge bussiness, that his prediction has come to pass. And^n. & Reid with the asistance of two writers ^attorneys^ & four of the best accountants in Glasgow have not been able to execute the Sentence to this day; tho' they have had to the books & every thing in their own hands or power. But I must not run into such a detail. After that matter was over And^n. without allowance collected all the Memorials &c, in the Faculty ^Books^ with many more still worse ^in the process^ Papers that had never been inserted & printed them in a Quatro vol & presented them to his friends & the Principals friends. Several of the last resented this Affront on the Worthy man and themselves so highly, that they tore the book from its boards & threw it into the fire & never spoke to And^n. after they had informed him of what they had done. The worthy ^man^ forbade me this & every other expression of my resentment of such a present & desired me to give the book to him (which I did) as he wanted <–> a collection of the scattered Papers to ly by him to consult if needful.

This happened several years ago & since that time the unhappy man, has Quarelled with all the Proff^rs. one after another treated some of ^them^ with scurility tho' not so much, as he poured on D^r. Leech^n. At last even D^r. Reid deserted

---

[17] Thomas Reid. See Letter 83.

[18] GUA34651, Manuscript memorial of John Anderson, professor of natural philosophy, to the Ordinary Visitors of Glasgow College, 13 Oct., and reply by Henry Dundas, Rector of the College, on behalf of the Visitors, 14 Oct. 1783.

[19] Matthew Morthland, the university's factor (manager), who, when he retired in 1785, was indeed found to owe enormous sums to the university, as Anderson, Reid, and others had claimed. See Letter 96; also University of Strathclyde, Special Collections, GB 249 OA/6/28, John Anderson papers, Glasgow College dispute with Mathew Morthland, late Factor, concerning his claim and accounts (1787).

him; so that for two or three years past, he has stood single by himself. Ritchardson[20] & others who had joined with him in that contest about the book [-k]eeping, became sensible that they were in the wrong, made Apollogies to the Prin^l. for any improper ^things^ they might have said in the heat of party debate (for they had not signed the worst Papers) & least his character like Prin^l. Stirling's should be transmitted to Posterity with any false stain upon it.[21] They drew up of themselves a full & Very honourable Attestation of his worth, his Fidelity in his Office the obligations of the Soceity to him &c, inserted it into their ^minutes^ & formaly subscribed it every Proff^r. ^of them^ except And^n. and another & that other vouched the truth of every thing in it yet declined the Subscription from some fancy that it was an improper way of gaining their purpose or vindicating D^r. Leechman.

In his single & solitary state he continued to Harrass & Plague ^them^ with endless Lawsuits, & interuptions of bussiness, taking advantage of every form, & carrying ^them^ for the least triffle, before the Lord[s] ordinary of the Court of Session, who refused his Bills of Advocation & remitted him back to them, & upon some Contumacy or gross insult to them I know not exactly what it was, they deprived him, by a sentence, of his Jurisdictio Ordinaria over the students, his Office of Elder in their chapel ^&c^ & confined him pretty much to the meer teaching of his class till he shoud ^give^ evidences of a better temper & behaviour.[22] This irritated him highly. He deserted their Faculties & began his intrigues among the students & especialy the Masters of Arts, attempted to form them into a sort of Corporation, independent of the Colledge under the Pretence of some Literary prizes he had put into their disposal: & play them ^off^ as an Engine against the Proffessors. The wisest of these young men saw thro' this designs, & got a numerous meeting, in consequence of one of his advertisements, in which he found himself & his party in the Minority. This did not stagger him in the least. ~~Having~~ ^Carrying^ the books ~~in his~~ away before they were aware, he withdrew

---

[20] William Richardson. See Letter 80.

[21] John Stirling (1654–1727) became principal of the University of Glasgow in 1701. He introduced new chairs, doubled the number of teaching staff, and tried to shield the professor of divinity, John Simson, when he was charged with heresy. With factional divisions among the professors, 'there was much strife and unrest in the University during his time'. Coutts, *History of the University of Glasgow*, pp. 185, 212.

[22] For evidence of Anderson's disputations regarding his authority in matters relating to his students and to the university chapel, see items listed in Gardham and Richmond, 'Research Resources in the University of Glasgow' (2009), pp. 8–13, *passim*.

with his adherents to the Tontine Coffee house,[23] & constituted them the sole Soceity of Masters of Arts: who met every week & published scurilous Papers in the news. This was the beginning of his Paper ^war^ last winter ^all however on one side^ which increased to a pitch that you cannot conceive, after M'Indoe's Expulsion; which gave him an opportunity of arousing the spirit off Fanaticism in the Mob of Glasgow, whom he plyed every week, with hand bills advertisments & other more laboured publications, stuffed with the meanest & grossest personal abuse, ever seen in print, against Proff[rs]. Ritchardson, Young,[24] Macleod,[25] Hamilton[26] & two or three more then most obnoxious to him, & Under feigned names however, but yet so marked as to be understood by every body.[27] Some of the better sort of people ^of the town^ seemed on his side at the beginning; but at last he was thoroly dispised by them & nobody in the dress of a Gentleman when he came in^to^ the Tontine spoke or looked at him. This was the consequence of his ^closer^ association with the Mob over whom in his Success was such as to procure, his friends say, some thousands of Subscriptions to his fifteen Petitions. But I weary you & myself with a tedious history of this Strange man, of whom I shall only say further that most of the scurilous stuff published last spring was the Efusion of his pen. After my appearance at the Synod[28] a great part ^of it^ was put into my hands. <—> I know his characteristic stile & manner, <—> so well, as to be certain of this point, having near a hundred of his Letters in my Cabinet. There are two prosecutions in dependance before the court of Session, one of them against a News Writer, for asserting without any salvo[29] that the Extract given in to ^the^ Synod was false & fabricated the other a very heavy one against M[r]. And[n]. himself for ^a^ printed Letter against D[r]. Taylour a Mins[r]. of Glasgow & Visitor[30] in which the damages are laid at £2,000. A dreadful letter of 18 quarto

---

[23] See Letter 91. John Mennons, publisher of the *Glasgow Advertiser* since 1783, had his printing office at Tontine Close.

[24] John Young (1747–1820), professor of Greek at the University of Glasgow, 1774–1820.

[25] Hugh Macleod (d. 1809), professor of ecclesiastical history at the University of Glasgow, 1779–1809. By 1797 his health had declined so far that William M'Turk was appointed his assistant and successor. Coutts, *History of Glasgow University*, pp. 286, 325, 354.

[26] This seems to have been Thomas Hamilton, professor of anatomy at the University of Glasgow (1757–81), according to Coutts, *History of Glasgow University*, pp. 284, 286.

[27] See, for example, printed items contained in the productions for William Taylor's suit against Anderson in the Court of Session, NRS, CS230/T/3/1.

[28] See Letter 96.

[29] 'salvo': 'an exception; a reservation; an excuse'. Johnson's *Dictionary*.

[30] Rev. Dr William Taylor (1744–1823), of the North or High Church, also known as St Mungo's, Glasgow, who was later moderator of the General Assembly of the Church of Scotland (1798)

pages, subscribed by Humphreys an Irishman[31] President of the Junto of Masters of arts & adressed to the D[rs]. Session in which their ^Minister^ is charged name & surname with Hypocrisie lying Vilainy & every thing black ^no other provocation given but a mild modest testimony of one page in favour of the Cole[ge]>^& how they will fix it by proof in a Court of Law on A. is more than I know, tho' it is as certainly his, as this Letter is mine.[32] Coud you ever have immagined that this Country had turned so licentious. I have done with this Subject for ever if I had again desired you not to give any body copies of L[d]. Sydneys Letters as I received a Letter last night from Wilson Clerk to the Faculty[33] cautioning me upon this point which looks as if they had been refused permission to print them, or wished to manage matters with a more than ordinary prudence till they know the full Effects of And[ns]. resentment. It is my oppinion tho' he wants not feeling that he will appear among them as if nothing had happened. You will have the prudence to keep a Page or two at the begin[g] of this history to yourself. I must glance ^at^ your letter again tho' I will not answer it fully having another frank at a forthnights distance. When convenor Lang[34] received L[d]. Grahams Letter He said the Marquess "was not blate[35] ^that^ but, for his four Quarters, he ^the Marquess^ had

---

and principal of Glasgow University (1803–23). Indicating his loyalties, he named one of his sons, born on 8 Dec.1785, William Leechman Taylor (d. 1812). *FES*, III, 458; Addison, *Matriculation Albums*, p. 190. The printed letter JW referred to was *A Letter by Students of Divinity, Law, Medicine, and Philosophy, in Glasgow College, to the Reverend William Taylor, D.D. Minister of the Inner High Church in Glasgow; Who, by Holding that Office, is appointed by the Foundation Charter of Glasgow College to be one of its Ordinary Visitors* (Glasgow: Printed by J. Mennons, Publisher of the GLASGOW ADVERTISER; And Sold by him, and P. Tait, Printers in the Saltmarket, 1785). The records of Taylor's Court of Session process against Anderson are held in NRS at CS230/T/3/1. Thanks to Professor Paul Wood for expert advice on this episode.

[31] Alexander Humphreys, MA 1777. 'Expelled when a student of Anatomy, and deprived of MA degree, for refusing to appear, unattended, before the Faculty on a charge of 'subscribing certain Publications injurious to this University' [Univ. Minute, 15th April 1785]': Addison, *Matriculation Albums*, p. 106.

[32] See Carruthers and Kaur, 'Thomas Muir and Staff and Student Politics at the University of Glasgow', pp. 102–08.

[33] Possibly John Wilson Sr, listed as one of the Faculty of Procurators in Glasgow, in *Jones's Directory; or Useful Pocket Companion for the Year 1789: containing an Alphabetical List of the Names and Places of Abode of the Merchants, Manufacturers, Traders and Shopkeepers in and about the City of Glasgow* (Glasgow, 1789), p. 76.

[34] The deacon convener led the craft incorporations of Glasgow and had a seat on the Town Council. Possibly James Lang, deacon of the Hammermen in Glasgow in 1787. See *Jones's Directory; or, Useful Pocket Companion for the year 1787* (Glasgow, 1787), p. 2; Robert Renwick, ed., *Extracts from the Records of the Burgh of Glasgow with Charters and Other Documents*, vol. viii: AD 1781–95 (Glasgow, 1913), p. 224.

[35] 'blate': 'dull, stupid, easily deceived'. *DSL*.

not been in the place or Office where he was," alluding to the petition of the trades house,[36] for the disolution of the late <–> Parliament which the Conveener, it seems, thought, had of itself done the bussiness.

I had it not in my power to pick up so many Anecdotes, among the literati at Ed$^r$. as you seem to immagine. Their conversation has less of that turn than you woud expect, especially during a Gen$^l$. Ass$^{ly}$. where they ask their friends in large mixed Companies & entertain with ^all^ the show of a table & the conversation turns cheifly on the topicks of the day ~~News Politicks~~ the bussiness & debates of the Ass$^{ly}$. or the Affairs & amusements of the town of Ed$^r$. Sometimes their Companies are more select, or ^the conversation^ takes a more select turn among a ^very^ few men of parts & Genius from distant parts of the kingdom, who have not seen one another for a great while then indeed it is a feast. Yet the cheif pleasure I had was to call upon them by themselves, & get a little tete a tete conversation on any subject literary, or not, in an unreserved way, which however one can do but sparingly, as they have so many Acquaintances; to know them as men rather than Scholars. If am able in some future Letter I will try to introduce you to them in that way as you did me to D$^r$. Priestly.[37] Samuel Chartres I have room to say nothing of. I am scarce acquainted with him as a friend tho' I have a high Idea of him from the accounts of other friends.[38] As an Author he is but just rising or <—> ^begin$^g$. to appear^ in this part of the Hemisphere. His turn is sentimental like Stern's but religious & devotional to a high degree; yet very rational or judicious not fanatical. He is the Author of that chapt$^r$. on Religion in L$^d$. Kaims Loose hints on Education[39] & it is perhaps worth all the rest of the book.

He preached a Sermon before the Society for propogating Xian knowledge a second Edition of which has been published at Ed$^r$. with a warning against the irreverent use of oaths ^Customhouse &c^ drawn up by him at the desire of his

---

[36] The letter of the marquess of Graham (chancellor of the University of Glasgow) to Anderson, disapproving of Anderson's attempt to persuade Lord Sydney to send a Royal Visitation to the university to investigate its accounts. See Letter 96.

[37] From Letter 72 on, *passim*.

[38] See Letter 96. Samuel Charters was married to Martha, cousin of Rev. Dr Thomas Somerville (1741–1830) of Jedburgh. Like Somerville, he was active in Moderate party politics in the Church of Scotland, and he campaigned for the abolition of the slave trade and for the dissociation of the Test Act from members of the Church of Scotland.

[39] Henry Home, Lord Kames, *Loose Hints upon Education, Chiefly Concerning the Culture of the Heart* (Edinburgh, 1781). In section VII, 'Education with Respect to Religion', Kames inserted a passage on revealed religion in education which he acknowledged had been written 'by another hand', and which he included despite reckoning upon his own work 'suffering by the comparison'. See pp. 174–81.

Presby & read in their Pulpits on a Public fast day.[40] This is all, I know of, that he has printed. The Subject of the Sermon is singular. Intercession or prayer for one another. His manner is equaly singular seemingly loose addressed entirely to the feelings of mens hearts. <—> I doubt if it ^his manner^ will take in the present Age. I find few that have such a high Idea of him as the honest Prin^l. whose tast on this point coincides with my own. A copy of the Sermon & warning I [page torn] ordered to be sent you from Ed^r. by a M^r. Dinwiddie[41] of Man[chester] who goes up soon I hope it will come to your hand as the best specimen I can give. Charters was a friend & great Admirer of our friend J. Warner & is said to have received his first religious impressions from hearing a Sermon of our friend's on the Love of X ^John XXI 15&c.^[42] He either ^had^ thought little or thought ill of revealed religion before; but was struck with that Sermon probably from some coincidence with the peculiar turn of his own mind, & from that time prosecuted his Theological Studies & bent his Attention & Genius that way. He went over & continued more than a Year in France merely for his improvement as a Preacher. His outward manner in company is cold & awkward. They say it is equaly so in the Pulpit but I never heard him.

I must write a line to Nell who I fancy will continue two or three weeks with you still & I have a Letter to write to her Uncle by a frank of the same date with this so must conclude in hast with my very affectionate Comp^s in which my Wife joins to M^rs. & Miss Kenrick.

My Dear friend very sincerly yours<br>J^s. Wodrow

When Nell leaves you Please give ^her^ as much money as she is likely to need in London & it will be settled & refunded in the Web Accounts between your wife & mine.

---

[40] Samuel Charters published *A Sermon Preached at the Anniversary Meeting of the Society in Scotland for Propagating Christian Knowledge, on Thursday, June 3. 1779* (Edinburgh, 1779) and its second edition, *A Sermon on Intercession* (Hawick, 1785), before his collected sermons were published in 1786.

[41] Unidentified, but see Letters 100 and 103.

[42] 'So when they had dined, Jesus saith to Simon Peter, Simon, son of Jonas, lovest thou me more than these? He saith unto him, Yea, Lord; thou knowest that I love thee. He saith unto him, Feed my lambs.' John 21:15.

## Letter 99: James Wodrow to Samuel Kenrick, 5 August 1785
Place: Stevenston
Addressed: M`r`. Samuel Kenrick / Bewdley
Postmarked: Irvin August the fifth 1785
Franked: Casillis
Note on cover: came torn to Chester S.K.

My Dear Friend

I wrote you a long perhaps a tedious Letter[1] about a fortnight ago relative to the intestine commotions of Alma Mater[2] a subject that has engrossed too much of our correspondence for some time past. I shoud be sorry if that Letter had fallen into any hands but your own as a page or two of it at least was only intended for your own eye. I now sit down to scribble something to fill up my other frank yet it will not be much just now as my time has been quite engrossed with D`r`. Hamilton my Brother in Law & his Wife[3] who came to us & have been our Guests since Sat`y`. last. Her We never saw before as he married her about three years ago in Aberdeenshire & this is the first visit she has paid to his friends in the South. She is a sensible, agreable, pleasant little woman with a good deal of the provincial brogue tho' she was a twelve month in London in the younger part of her Life. He <—> is one of the first men we have for ^<—>^ Genius <—> judgement & tast & this almost equaly in the lighter & more agreable walks of the Belle lettres Poetry ^&c,^ & in the deepest mines of Science Mathematicks astronomy Chimistry Natural history & Mechanicks. Yet his merit is little known but to his particular friends. His Genius or rather his Spirit was depressed in the earlier part of Life by his circumstances by being obliged to drudge on for many years ^unsuccessfuly^ first in the mercantile way & then in the management of a Paper Manufacture the only thing left for the subsistance of his fathers family <—>. He threw himself out of that tract & was resolved ^to try^ the tract more natural to him. Upon an advertisement in the news Papers he prepared himself in the space of two or three months for standing a Comparative tryal for the Mathematical Proffessorship at Aberdeen.[4] It was one of the severest that ever was made. Five

---

[1] Letter 98, 21 July 1785.
[2] The University of Glasgow.
[3] Robert Hamilton. See Letter 87. His first wife, Anne Mitchell of Ladath, had died *c*. 1778, and he was remarried in 1782 to Jane Morrison of Elsick. See *W-K*, I, pp. 12, 290, 417, 478n.
[4] The vacancy resulted from the death of Professor John 'Triangles' Stewart (1711–66). Paul Wood, 'Aberdeen Philosophical Society [Wise Club], *act*. 1758–1753', *ODNB*, 28 Sept. 2006.

Candidates entered the lists two of them soon gave up.[5] The other three continued above a fortnight for several hours every day under the tryal and judgment of the four best Mathematicians in Scotland & D[r]. Campbell their Clark.[6] The manner of ascertaining their respective Merits was curious. It was by numbers 5, 7, 10, or whatever was ^the^ decision of the judges at the end of every diet <—> ^about^ the demonstrations solutions of difficult problems &c, the number was added to the name of <—> ^each^ Candidate. At the end, the ^Total^ Number of a M[r]. Trail[7] who gained the Place was ^between 2 &^ 300. M[r]. Hamilton came within four or five of him & had certainly gained it had he had time for a longer preparation; for Trail had been in the life of teaching Mathematicks for several years.[8] The third a M[r]. Playfair[9] was thrown behind the first two by more than a hundred & even he was no dunce for he has been admitted to the Proff[rs]. of <Natl. Philosophy> ^Mathematicks^ at Ed[r]. this last summer.

Tho' M[r]. Hamilton at that time even about 17 years ago lost his Labour & his place yet he gained some reputation & Ecclat & was soon after chosen Rector of the Accademy at Perth after M[r]. Muirs death without any Competition.[10] The cheif part of his Scholars were in the Mercantile line for which he was well fitted to give them a compleat education tho' he taught Nat or experimental Philosophy & other branches. He continued 10 years in Perth & published his course on Arithmetick Bookkeeping &c, in two vol.[11] not so properly corrected in the press as it ought to have been which hurt the sale greatly yet he had no loss nor gain. He

---

[5] Paul Wood, 'William Trail (1746–1831)', *ODNB* (2006), notes a total of six candidates for this competition.

[6] On Campbell, see note 15 below. The four examiners were chosen from the Universities of St Andrews, Glasgow, King's College Aberdeen, and Marischal College, Aberdeen, which sent Thomas Reid. Wood, 'William Trail'. Betty Ponting, 'Mathematics at Aberdeen: Developments, Characters, Traits, 1717–1860', *Aberdeen University Review*, 48 (1979–80), pp. 166–67, 172.

[7] William Trail (1746–1831), mathematician and later Church of Ireland clergyman. Wood, 'William Trail' and Ponting, 'Mathematics at Aberdeen', supply further details of the competition for the chair (13–28 Aug. 1766) described here by JW. According to Ponting, poor Trail lost his salary payment until June 1767, the sum retained by the university being used to pay for the cost of the expensive appointment process.

[8] According to Ponting, Trail scored 126, Hamilton 119, and Playfair 90, but the lowest score was 16. 'Details of Hamilton's actual questions may be found in the University archives.' Ponting, 'Mathematics at Aberdeen', pp. 166–67.

[9] Professor John Playfair (1748–1819), mathematician and geologist.

[10] John Muir. Alexander Campbell, *A Journey from Edinburgh Through Parts of North Britain*, 2 vols (1802), II, p. 361.

[11] Robert Hamilton, *An Introduction to Merchandise* (Edinburgh, 1777). A second edition, in one volume, was published in Edinburgh in 1788.

was then chosen to his present place Proff^r. of Nat. Ph^y. at Aberdeen[12] but he ^has^ taught the Mathematical Classes ^for some time past^ that being his fort & the Mathematical Proff^r. Copland[13] being most eminently fitted (M^r. Ham^n. says) for nat ^Phy^ & experiments having a fine inventive mechanical turn.[14] The fees of this Class are less lucrative than the former one the Mathematical Class. I wish we had D^r. Hamilton at Glasgow where the Proff^rs. have double or triple the income. He coud only undertake the Mathem. or the Nat^l. Philosophy.

He has made me better acquainted with Campbell,[15] Gerard[16] & Beatie[17] than I was before all of them very studious & worthy men. Yet the last not so agreable in private Life at least to his old friends as the former; too much elevated with his literary reputation & with the attention that has been shown him by the great for instance the Dutchess of Gordon.[18] 18 & others. It is thought he is about to publish something on the Evidences of X^ty. the substance of Lectures he has given on that subject.[19] Yet it probably will not suit your wishes & mine as an Answer to Gibbon.[20] I doubt if he is thro'ly qualifyed for this by his Acquaintance with

---

[12] i.e. at Marischal College, Aberdeen. He was appointed to this position in 1779.

[13] Patrick Copland (1748–1822), who indeed taught natural philosophy while Hamilton taught mathematics, till his own retirement in 1817, when Hamilton was appointed to the chair of mathematics; this is explained by JW's comment below about the fees for each of these classes. Robert Anderson, 'Robert Hamilton (1743–1829)', *ODNB* (2004).

[14] Copland 'was acknowledged to be the best teacher in the university in his day', while Hamilton, whatever his other gifts, was not skilled in practical experimental teaching, and broke the glass apparatus he was using in one class, so the swap of subjects was appropriate. While noting Hamilton's intellectual gifts and public citizenship, Ponting, unlike JW, also admits his eccentricity and the ridicule he sometimes attracted. Ponting, 'Mathematics at Aberdeen', pp. 167–68; on Copland, see John S. Reid, 'Patrick Copland (1748–1822)', *ODNB* (2004).

[15] George Campbell. See Letter 87. His best-selling *Dissertation on Miracles* (1762) was a reply to Hume's essay 'Of miracles', in which Campbell deployed the principles of common-sense philosophy to defend the plausibility of the miracles recounted in the New Testament.

[16] Rev. Alexander Gerard (1728–95), Church of Scotland minister, the first professor of moral philosophy and logic at Marischal College, Aberdeen (1753–71), and professor of divinity at King's College, Aberdeen (1771–95). Like his friends Campbell and Reid, and his pupil, Beattie, Gerard was a common-sense philosopher. He also attacked Hume's ideas, in *The Influence of the Pastoral Office on the Character Examined* (Aberdeen, 1760) and, later, in *The Corruptions of Christianity Considered as Affecting its Truth: A Sermon, Preached before the Society in Scotland for Propagating Christian Knowledge* (Edinburgh, 1792).

[17] James Beattie. See Letter 83. As well as the individual biographies of Campbell, Gerard, and Beattie in the *ODNB*, see also Paul Wood, 'The Aberdeen Philosophical Society [Wise Club]', *ODNB*.

[18] Jane Gordon, *née* Maxwell, duchess of Gordon (1748/9–1812), political hostess and agricultural reformer.

[19] James Beattie, *Evidences of the Christian Religion* (Edinburgh, 1786), based on the argument from design and on Christian revelation, though anti-Calvinist in insisting on the basic goodness of human nature.

[20] Beattie did not directly address the scepticism towards Christianity in chapter 15 of Gibbon's first volume of *The Decline and Fall of the Roman Empire* (1776). For the controversy

history & Xian Antiquity yet this ^is^ the branch of the Evidence that I woud most wish to see well cleared up. You have men in your Country better qualified for the task than perhaps any of our literati (except Campbell) for instance Farmer.[21]

Did I not promise to say something further about the Ed[r]. D[rs]. with whom however except Dr. Erskine[22] I had very little literary conversation. Rob[n].[23] & Blair[24] are men of the World as well as Scholars & have a wonderful knack at turning the ^course of the^ conversation on subjects & especialy on men that you are better acquainted with than they, & thus drawing new information & intelligence to themselves from their Guests tho' I cannot say they are averse to give you any intelligence on their part you woud wish for. They are sufficiently comunicative at least to their friends only the respect one has for them makes him rather follow their lead than give a new one to the conversation. Rob[n]. tho' I am less intimate with him than the other three, is the man whom I like best as a Companion especialy in his own house. He is as much a *domestick* man as you can well conceive, easy, frank & pleasant in his conversation & manners so that ^what^ you said of Gibbon in his notes answers perfectly to him.[25] You forget the dignity of the historian he speaks his mind without the least apparent reserve upon books men & all the familiar topicks of conversation & you see running thro' every thing he says the same Accuracy good sense sound well informed judgement & almost the same elegance that You see in his Writings only on a lower & more familiar key. Then there is ^such^ a pleasing exhibition of family Affection to the three Child[n]. that live in his family <—> two young Gentlemen[26]

---

provoked by Gibbon, see J. G. A. Pocock, *Barbarism and Religion: Volume 5, Religion: The First Triumph* (Cambridge, 2011), pp. 313–71.

[21] Hugh Farmer. See Letter 87. Taught by Philip Doddridge at Northampton, he was best known as a writer for his *Inquiry into the Nature and Design of Christ's Temptation in the Wilderness* (1761), *A Dissertation on Miracles: Containing an Examination of the Principles Advanced by David Hume, Esq; in an Essay on Miracles* (Edinburgh, 1762), and *An Essay on Demoniacs* (1775). He defended miracles on rationalist grounds, but his strong adherence to the primacy of natural law 'eventually undermined the basis for his argument on miracles'. Alan Ruston, 'Hugh Farmer (1714/15–1787)', *ODNB*. JW had long admired Farmer's work: see *W-K*, I, p. 314.

[22] John Erskine. See Letter 96. Like JW himself, Erskine was friendly across church party boundaries. Famously, his colleague in ministry at Old Greyfriars was the leader of the Moderate party, William Robertson, with whom Erskine vigorously disagreed in the General Assembly, but whose funeral sermon he preached and whose tribute he paid in 1793.

[23] William Robertson. See Letter 96.

[24] Hugh Blair. See Letter 85.

[25] See Letter 95, SK to JW, 27 April 1785.

[26] The Robertsons had three sons: William (1753–1835), advocate and later a judge; James (1762–1845), army officer and later general of the ninety-second Gordon Highlanders; and David (1764–1845), another army officer, eventually lieutenant-colonel of the twenty-third regiment. Presumably James and David were still at home in 1785 and referred to by JW here.

& a fine young Girl[27] & of friendship between ^himself^ M^rs^. Robertson[28] so attentive to what they say & he speaks so easily & feelingly of those that are absent especialy Cap^t^. Bredune[29] as one of them that you can scarce help conceiving yourself a Member of the family or enjoying every thing that passes as if you was. He is deafish for some years past, at times considerably so, yet it does not much interupt the pleasure of his conversation as he catches your meaning from hearing half your words, & talks a good deal himself tho' no more than you woud wish him to do. He commonly set me down close by what he calls his hearing ear which is his left one. He has been much blamed for giving up our Gen^l^. Ass^ly^. ^in disgust^ after he got his eldest son a Lawyer[30] fixed in the prin^l^ Office we have to dispose of Procurator to the Church; yet this I believe without any foundation as it was probably owing to his deafness which unfitted him to be any longer the leader of a Popular Court. Yet I never heard him give that reason or any other but that the Court coud ^& woud^ do everything equaly well without him. He is still consulted in every Quisquous[31] point, and his Sons speeches very much listened to. Tho' they want the Dignity and eloquence of his Fathers, yet they are always well-timed, full of good sense, mixed with a surprising knowledge of our Church Laws & forms for one of his Years. The Father made one speech in the last Ass^ly^. not as a Member but as a Petitioner for a Collection for the Royal Infirmary & ^as^ his Voice had not been heard for five years there He met with all the attention & respect from the court which he justly deserved.

D^r^. Blair I have been long acquainted with tho' not very intimately even above 30 years I used to receive an Annual Letter from him when the Mod^r^. for the Gen^l^. Ass^ly^. was fixed upon ^tho' I once voted for another^. I corresponded with him on

---

[27] There were also three Robertson daughters: Mary (b. 1752), who married the traveller and writer Patrick Brydone in 1785; Eleanor (1755–1837), who became the wife of John Russell, WS in 1776; and Janet (1756–89).

[28] Mary Robertson (1723–1802), née Nisbet, Robertson's cousin, whom he had married in 1751.

[29] Patrick Brydone (1736–1818), Robertson's son-in-law, who lived at Lennel House, near Coldstream in Berwickshire; the Robertsons stayed with the Brydones for extended periods in the last few years of Robertson's life. Brydone published *A Tour through Sicily and Malta: In a Series of Letters to William Beckford, esq. of Somerly in Suffolk*, 2 vols (1773). It was very successful, achieving nine editions, and Brydone was elected FRS, FRSE (Fellow of the Royal Society of Edinburgh), and FSA (Fellow of the Society of Antiquaries) for his discussions of vulcanology and electricity in it. According to the ODNB: 'At some point after completing his education he must have served in the army, since he is occasionally referred to as Captain (for example in 1778 by James Boswell in his Life, 3.356)'. Jeffrey R. Smitten, 'William Robertson (1721–1793)', ODNB.

[30] William Robertson (1753–1835).

[31] 'Quisquous': 'perplexing, doubtful, debatable, dubious'. DSL.

M[r]. Fergusson's great cause[32] & also the Colledge cause[33] last year. He is judicious and solid in his ^his observations &^ his turn of conversation & even in some degree frank & communicative– yet he wants the familiar ease & pleasantry of Robertson the accomodating or sinking himself down to your level without losing any thing but perhaps gaining by it. I apprehend it to be owing cheifly to a greater natural gravity of temper yet it has something of the Appearance of statlyness or selfimportance. I speak however of the general appearance I never experienced any thing myself but the most friendly & condescending treatment. Tho' he speaks with sufficient ease in common conversation yet he never in his Life spoke a word in a Church court tho' equaly keen with any man of his party; nor ventured upon an Extempore speech in public, no doubt for fear of <—> losing something of his high reputation. Neither of these D[rs]. have the least turn for wit or Jocular humour. When it is started & pursued as it will be in all free Companies R enters into it more easily than Bl. & has a number of pat & pleasant stories. Neither of them are the theological Scholars nor if I am not mistaken have much scriptural knowledge.[34] From B. Sermons it appears that he is fully master of the Morality of the N.T. but I apprehend of no other part of it either as a Critick or a Divine. R. preaches much of late & is said to excell in Lecturing. The book of Proverbs is his present Subject. I dare say it is cheifly extempore. These two D[rs] are most intimate friends. They excell in different ways, & there is no rivalship nor jealousy between them.

M'knight is my Old Country friend[35] & Companion far less polished than either of the other two tho' he has been much in the World & perhaps ^is^ still more in mixed Companys I mean of Ladies &c than either of them, yet his manners are hurt & in some degree disagreable, from a certain wit & repartee which

---

[32] The heresy trial in 1769 of Rev. Alexander Fergusson of Kilwinning (1689–70), JW's and SK's great friend and mentor. See *W-K*, I, Letters 45 and 46.

[33] Occasioned by Professor John Anderson. See Letters 91–98 above.

[34] Robertson's reputation as a parish minister in his first charge (Gladsmuir) was mixed—'he was probably more engaged with the larger issues of church policy and literary culture than he was with daily parish demands'. Jeffrey R. Smitten, 'Robertson, William (1721–1793)', *ODNB*. Most of his sermons for which records are extant discussed texts from six of the sixty-six books of the Bible: Proverbs, 1 Corinthians, Galatians, Luke, Matthew, and Acts. Jeffrey R. Smitten, *The Life of William Robertson: Minister, Historian, and Principal* (Edinburgh, 2017), p. 66.

[35] James Macknight. See Letter 87. He was the son of Rev. William Macknight (1685–50) of Irvine, Ayrshire, and he had been brought up and educated at Irvine, followed by Glasgow University. Like JW, he had been licensed by the presbytery of Irvine and he was JW's immediate predecessor as Rev. Alexander Fergusson's assistant at Kilwinning before he was ordained to his own charge at Maybole, Ayrshire.

he affects not ^always^ of the finest & most delicate kind. Yet he is a very friendly respectable & Worthy Man <—> a most eminent Critical & Scriptural Scholar & has a considerable portion of Original Genius or ingenuity in striking out new uncommon views & arranging & supporting them with a systematical accuracy, & yet he has little tast & scarce a spark of immagination at all. Many of these ^new^ Views are Nostrums of his own <—> which like some of your friend D$^r$. Priestly's I apprehend are not sufficiently founded in Scripture or fact. Others of them deserve a better name & will perhaps be admitted as new discoveries. I regretted I coud not be more with him– The Sunday I preached for him before I was well seated in his house he put into my hands his ^MS^ <—> Commentary on the S[econd] Ep[istle] of the Thess$^{ns}$[36] two or three Chap$^{rs}$. of which I went over instead of my own Sermon. If all the rest are executed with the same judgement & accuracy not to say invention his book will be a very valuable acquisition to the Public. It will be prefaced with an Essay on the Epistolary Writings of the Ancients ^such as Horace^ as distinguished from their more regular treatises. After public worship, Dinner & enough of Drink we took a long walk into a place of Retirem[ent] where he read me a very curious Dissertation founded on S Thess IV at the end S Cor. XV[37] & other places on the Different manner & bodies with which the righteous & the Wicked will be raised. He seems to be fully perswaded that the lost will ^be^ raised with Corruptible Bodies of Flesh & blood which will be consumed in the gen$^l$. conflagration– & that this will ^constitute^ the cheif part of the ^distinction of the^ Day of Judgment.

But I must leave room for a word or two about honest D$^r$. Erskine who is more of a Theologian than any of them & notwithstanding his Calvinistick principles, mixed with a certain portion of fanaticism not of the most amiable kind,[38] is yet a liberal minded man in many points & has much learning & worth.[39] He is a

---

[36] JW also refers, in Letter 87, to what Macknight published in 1787 as a *Translation of the Epistles to the Thessalonians* as a commentary.

[37] 2 Thessalonians 4; 2 Corinthians 15.

[38] Erskine was a leading critic of the government's plan to repeal the penal laws against Roman Catholics in Scotland in 1778, though he disapproved of the popular rioting against the proposal in Glasgow and Edinburgh, and he was content for Catholic worship to be engaged in privately and discreetly. JW will also have objected to Erskine's opposition to patronage in the appointment of parish ministers.

[39] Erskine's preaching was widely admired, and he published many sermons, often defending Calvinist orthodoxy, yet he was respected for his intellectual rigour by theological opponents such as JW, and he was influenced by and engaged with Enlightenment thinking. He also published three pamphlets in opposition to the British government's policy towards the American colonists, and was a regular correspondent of leading Evangelicals in America such

most indefatigable student & his studious air gives him in Company the appearance of the Aukwardness & simplicity of a Child, tho' born to an estate, & connected with the best families in the Kingdom.[40] I breakfasted with him & spent a great part of the forenoon & much intelligence I got from him about Lavater[41] whom he highly admires, & many of the French & Swiss Divines of whom I had never heard before. He keeps up a Correspondence & gets many of the publications of that part of the Continent & has lately learned the German Language to enable him to read several valuable books in it which have never been translated. M[r]. Hamilton tells me that same thing of D[r]. Campbell[42] who is master of many of the Modern & all the ancient Languages. D[rs]. Robertson & Erskine are Colleagues & the family of the last are so fanatical in their Sentiments of Religion that they never come to Church during the Diet of the former by this they lost the opportunity of hearing me. D[r] Er. himself was however my hearer, came out of Church with me arm in arm & tho' he must have seen that my theological Sentiments (for it was a Xian Sermon)[43] were different from his own yet when he preached in the Afternoon, every reference he made to my discourses both in his Prayers & Sermon, was calculated to convey favourable impressions <—> to his congregation. He preached himself a highly moral Sermon tho' a little in the casuistical cast of the old Divines. The two D[rs]. behave decently to, & speak with respect of one another.

It is a very pleasing testimony you mention of the Attachment of [page torn] congregation [page torn] to him & [page torn] to his Colleague very noble on the occasion.

I enclose a small draught for Nell ^of £5^. I coud not procure ^one of^ <—> a shorter date. You will be obliged to advance as much more as she & you think needful; to be accounted for in M[rs]. Kenricks Webs; for Nell seems to have a fancy of being obliged to you for ready Money rather than her Uncle[44] on whom also I had given her Credit. He has had a sad [scene of][45] distress for a great while past

---

as Jonathan Edwards. As well as Ned Landsman, 'John Erskine (1721–1803)', *ODNB*, see Jonathan Yeager, *Enlightened Evangelicalism: The Life and Thought of John Erskine* (New York, 2011).

[40] Erskine's father was John Erskine of Carnock (1695–1768), professor of Scots law at the University of Edinburgh.

[41] Johann Caspar Lavater (1741–1801), Swiss theologian, and physiognomist, philosopher, and poet.

[42] George Campbell. See Letter 87.

[43] JW presumably means that it was a sermon that touched on theology, rather than a sermon addressing social or political issues.

[44] John Hamilton. See Letter 96 for JW's plan that he should bring Nell home to Stevenston.

[45] Partially obscured by wax seal.

with his B^r. in Law pe<wax seal> bussiness which I thought had been terminated by M^r. B. [page torn] of which he gave undoubted proofs about three months ago such as made a separation necessary but he retains as much cunning still as to plague & distress him and I am afraid to hurt him in business a little. This pre[ven]ted him from fixing the [page torn] of his journey to Scotland [page torn] that her ^Nell's^ Wishes as well [page torn]ours & your kind familie's [page torn] stay have been gratifyed for I see sufficiently from the Letters of both that neither of you are ^as^ yet tired of one another yet it ^is^ almost time for the honey moon to be over. Is there a danger of her losing her attachment & relish for her poor Country? D^r. Spence's & M^rs. Stewarts short visit would be a high Solace to you & your family.[46] Yet it woud be a pleasing melancholy meeting. It was kind to you as well as to themselves to go on so fa[r] <before> she parted with D^r. Spence.

My best & kindest comp^ts. to M^rs. & Miss Kenrick.
I have scarce time to write to Nell, I am ever
most sincerely yours
J^s. Wodrow

## Letter 100: Samuel Kenrick to James Wodrow, 19 September 1785
Place: Bewdley
Addressed: The Rev^d. James Wodrow / Stevenston
Note: 1785

My worthy friend.

Alas! this is a disagreeable letter, to announce to you our parting with your most amiable daughter– w^ch. not only we but all our friends here feel most tenderly. She flatters us, however, with one consolation to make up for our present loss, that she leaves us with so much regret, that she will not find any reluctance to pay us another visit. This is a great point gained. Before my daughter visited you there was a wide fathomless gulph between us w^ch. nothing w^d. tempt you to allow her ^i.e. Nelly^ to pass. But a few months have thrown a short, safe &

---

[46] See Letter 96. SK's letter of 22 Aug. 1785 was lost (see Letter 103). So possibly JW heard about this visit from Spens and Mrs Stewart rather than from SK.

commodious bridge over it– w^ch^. a child may ^now^ travel over without danger. Distance is now nothing. It is as easy to come to Bewdley, as to go to Glasgow or Ed^r^. when you once set out. This gives me a ray of hope that sometime I may see here my worthy friend. As to the young folks I make no doubt of their visiting & revisiting each other, with as much ease as if the distance were not more than 20 or 30 miles.

As a specimen of the turn of mind & abilities of some of my neighbours, I send you, two pieces w^ch^. are like to be the commencement of a petite guerre theologique.[1] You must begin w^th^. the sermon w^ch^. ^by the bye^ when composed & preached was not intended for the eye of the public. It was at the opening of our Sunday School, w^ch^. I think I gave you an account of in my last letter.[2] The novelty of the thing & the preacher's lively manner, had such an effect on the audience in general & the promoters of the institution, that they must needs have it printed.[3] The author is a strict calvenist; & what they call here a methodist; that is a warm zealous stickler for the tenets he has adopted. You will see by this that in deep theological matters we ~~have~~ ^are^ above half a century behind you. You will not therefore be surprised to hear, that works w^ch^. have long ago sunk into oblivion in their native soil, are now revived again here w^th^. new splendour. When I went first to Glasgow, just after Whitfield's visit,[4] the great debate was between religion & morality. Witherspoon's characteristics are I suppose long ago forgotten among you[5]– & his blacksmith's letter.[6] But not so here, as I am going to tell you.

---

[1] i.e. 'a little theological warfare'.

[2] SK letter of 22 Aug. 1785 is missing.

[3] William Jesse, *The Importance of Education: A Discourse, Preached in Bewdley Chapel, on Sunday the 27th day of March, 1785. By William Jesse, Rector of Dowles, and Chaplain to the Right Honourable the Earl of Glasgow* (Kidderminster, 1785).

[4] Rev. George Whitefield (1714–70), evangelist and, along with Howel Harris (1714–73), founder of Methodism of the Calvinistic variety. The Countess of Huntingdon (1707–91) appointed him as her chaplain and endowed many chapels for him. While he first visited Glasgow in 1741, Whitefield's biggest impact was made in the following year where his open-air evangelical preaching at Cambuslang attracted thousands, and 'far out-did all that I ever saw in America', with overwhelmed hearers 'carryd out by Scores as Dead people out of the fi[e]ld'. Boyd Stanley Schlenther, 'Whitefield, George (1714–1770)', *ODNB*. Kenrick started at Glasgow University in 1743.

[5] John Witherspoon's pamphlet, *Ecclesiastical Characteristics; Or, The Arcana of Church Policy: Being an Humble Attempt to Open Up the Mystery of Moderation; Wherein is Shewn a Plain and Easy Way of Attaining to the Character of a Moderate Man, as at Present in Repute in the Church of Scotland* (Glasgow, 1753). Far from having been forgotten in Scotland, this biting satire on the Moderate clergy remained popular and was echoed in late eighteenth-century Evangelical polemics. Its seventh edition was printed in Philadelphia and London in 1767.

[6] John Witherspoon was thought by some to be the author of a satire on revivalism that was printed in several editions across the late eighteenth century, *A Letter from a Blacksmith to the*

As to M^r. Jesse[7] he is a most worthy, honest good tempered man. But orthodox to the highest pitch— even to a popish narrowness of mind— that he shudders at the name of D^r. Priestley, & looks upon him as an outcast, doomed to eternal punishment. I have expostulated with him on this subject, & made no secret of my attachment to the D^r. & my ~~prejudice~~ ^partiality^ in favour of his ^religious^ sentiments. Yet strange to say he does not fall out with me— but courts my acquaintance & even trusts me w^th. his MSS. As to M^r. Wigan, he is the most intimate friend I have in England.[8] I leave to Miss Nelly to say the rest— she knows him, & his high esteem & regard for you.

You will soon see, in point of acuteness & abilities how much superior the latter is to his antagonist. Yet this does ^not^ terrify M^r. Jesse— he has already in the press in great forwardness 17 letters on a variety of topics, in defence of his tenets & those of his party.[9] I have seen some of them & the contents of the whole. One of w^ch. is on moral preaching— w^ch. he told was entirely from Wotherspoon's above pamphlet[10]— being an ironical panegyric on that mode of preaching. If I could think the work worthy your perusal, I sh^d. certainly send it you.— But I cannot leave you without mentioning, that as I find you have many of your late worthy father's old Books undisposed of, I should be glad to know if any of

---

*Ministers and Elders of the Church of Scotland: In which the Manner of Public Worship in that Church is Considered* (Dublin, 1759). But his authorship is doubtful. In Ned C. Landsman's view, 'there is no solid evidence to connect Witherspoon to that publication'. Landsman, 'Witherspoon and the Problem of Provincial Identity in Scottish Evangelical Culture,' in Richard B. Sher and Jeffrey R. Smitten, eds, *Scotland and America in the Age of the Enlightenment* (Edinburgh, 1990), p. 44, n. 14.

[7] Rev. William Jesse (c. 1739–1815), BA 1761 at Trinity College, Oxford. Rector of Dowles near Bewdley from 1779 to 1815, and rector of Ribbesford 1795–1815. He held other livings at the same time: the perpetual curacy of Kilnwick, Berwick Chapel 1765–99, and the perpetual curacy of West Bromwich 1790–1815. After 1801 he left a curate, Rev. John Cawood, an orthodox evangelical clergyman, in sole charge of Dowles and Ribbeford. From 1804–17 Cawood was headmaster of Bewdley Grammar School. *Clergy of the C of E*; *Alumni Oxonienses*, II, p. 753; Joan Hobson, 'A Short History of the "Free Grammar School of King James in Bewdley"', in Lawrence S. Snell, ed., *Essays towards a History of Bewdley* (Bewdley, 1972), p. 107.

[8] Thomas Wigan. See Letter 88.

[9] William Jesse, *Parochialia; Or Observations on the Discharge of Parochial Duties, in which Defects and Errors are Pointed out and Improvements Suggested and Recommended to The Parochial Clergy: in Seventeen Letters to Clericus with Remarks on a Letter Containing Strictures on a Discourse Lately Preached in Bewdley Chapel* (Kidderminster, 1785). In his short review of the book, Samuel Badcock ridiculed Jesse for being one of those Methodist preachers who are fond of listening 'to their own *sweet* eloquence; and are humbly content to be *all ear*, provided they can be *all tongue* at the same time'. *Monthly Review*, 76 (May 1787), pp. 426–27.

[10] Probably a reference to Witherspoon's *Ecclesiastical Characteristics*.

the following be among them. Vigilii Tapsensis Opera.[11] Ruffini[12] D[r]. Gregorii Turonensis[13] D[r]. Dan[l]. Zwicker's Irenicum[14] & other pieces in defence of it. It is owing to an advertisement of D[r]. P. in the last N[o]. of the Theological Repository,[15] where he offers a fair price for them. With all our united love & affection to you & yours I ever am My worthy friend's sincerely

S. Kenrick

This goes w[th]. our dear Nell to Manchester, where I hope she will meet w[th]. much amusement & information. It is certainly one of the most enlightened spots in this Kingdom and she will be there at the celebrated Music Meeting w[ch]. it is thought will not be in[fer]iour to the 2 exhibitions at Westminster Abbey. It has been advertised in the London papers for 2 months past.

Adieu my D[r] friend.
I intend to send you something by [post] before this reach you.
S. K.

---

[11] Pierre-François Chifflet, ed., *Victoris Vitensis, et Vigilii Tapsensis, Provinciae Bizacenae Episcoporum Opera* (Dijon, 1664), which included writings against Arianism by the fifth-century Vigilius, bishop of Thapsus.

[12] Tyrannius Rufinus (*c.* 345–411) was a Roman theologian who translated earlier theological works from Greek into Latin, at a time when knowledge of Greek was in decline, particularly those of Origen and Eusebius. He engaged in a controversy with Jerome, and being accused of introducing heresy in his translation of Origen, Rufinus addressed an *Apologia* to Pope Anastasius. For a modern edition of his writings, see *The Sacred Writings of Rufinus*, ed. Johann Peter Kirsch (Altenmunster, 2012). According to Priestley, 'the *descent of Christ into hell*, in what we call the *apostles creed*, is not mentioned by any writer before Ruffinus, who found it in his own church at Aquileia'; and he noted that Rufinus espoused the 'Pelagian heresy' that rejected the doctrine of original sin. Priestley, *Corruptions of Christianity*, I, pp. 298. 410. He later observed that thanks to Rufinus, 'we now have several of the works of Origen…but he is not thought to have translated exactly or faithfully'. Joseph Priestley, *A General History of the Christian Church, to the Fall of the Western Empire*, 2 vols (1790), II, p. 492.

[13] Gregory of Tours (538–94), bishop of Tours. Theologically orthodox, he wrote an influential *History of the Franks*.

[14] Daniel Zwicker. See Letter 80. The *Irenicum Irenicoram* (Amsterdam, 1658) was published anonymously and was an argument for both unitarian heterodoxy and Christian unity.

[15] See also Letter 105 below.

## Letter 101: Samuel Kenrick to James Wodrow, 23 September 1785
Place: Bewdley

My worthy Friend

As this will reach you before you have the pleasure of seeing again your dear Nelly– I must acquaint you that she tore herself away from us & many more reluctant friends in this place on Monday last the 19th. & went to Birm^m. that day accompanied by her affectionate Mary– How they parted I will leave you to imagine– All I can say is that she was seen safe with all her luggage in a Manchester coach at 12 of the clock that night by a good friend of ours, by w^ch. conveyance she was I hope deliverd safe into the hands of M^rs. Dunwiddy[1] at Manchester the following evening. We expect to day or Sunday to have this confirmed to us under her own hand. It is a most fortunate circumstance for her, that she could not see Manchester to so much advantage, & to gratify our own curiosity & taste than at this particular time– when next to the ^late^ grand exhibition at Westminster Abby,[2] she will have the pleasure of assisting w^th. a numerous concourse of the most polite & intelligent people of the kingdom, at one of the most splendid musical entertainments ever yet attempted.

Under the protection of such kind & respectable friends I know what a feast this will be to Miss Nelly who is so fond of music & good company– & will abundantly make amends, for the disappointment of not seeing London– w^ch. had it succeeded would have fallen far short of her expectations– taken her near 150 miles farther from home & given her the less chance of a commodious conveyance to Glasgow than she will now have. Meanwhile we have the comfort now of flattering ourselves w^th. the practicability of a closer intercourse between our two families, w^ch. both you & I have long wished for. Miss Nelly was often so kind as to press me to pay one visit at least to your family & my other good friends: w^ch. she said w^d. very probably prevail upon you to return the compliment. For this price I do not know what I might not do. Otherwise, such is my aversion to long journies, that I am glad with the approach of winter to be sheltered w^th. an excuse to enjoy myself & lie snug at home. Besides Mary & Nelly are

---

[1] Unidentified; but the name is Dinwiddie, and she resided with her husband at Redvale. See Letters 98 and 103.

[2] Probably a reference to Charles Burney, *An Account of the Musical Performances in Westminster Abbey and the Pantheon, May 26th, 27th, 29th; And June the 3d and 5th, 1784* (1785).

such travellers now they will save me the trouble: they will soon teach Miss Peggy the same knack, if she dare venture with them: & w[th]. this additional attraction, I may perhaps have yet the happiness to see your whole family in Worcestershire. Without this prospect before us we should have been very unwilling to part w[th]. Miss Nelly, being so justly endeared not only to <us> but to all our best friends: who remember her with the warmest affection & esteem. We therefore all beg you will favour w[th]. the earliest notice of her safe arrival at home. Unless a very favourable opportunity offer, I should not be surprized at her making the stay of some days or weeks at Manchester, not for her friends sake only, but to gratify her own laudable curiosity. For we look upon Manchester (as I believe I mentioned to you before) as one of the most respectable places in England, for ingenuity & improvement of every sort. Our neighbour her sister Birm[m]. is perhaps as industrious & plodding in pursuit of wealth, but she is a grimy dirty drab; & has not yet arrived at the genteel & elegant form of her elder more polite Sister.

Of this I doubt not you will hear more fully from Miss Nelly when she sees you.

To some of my ^best^ friends, ^(who are very few in number)^ are so much enamoured w[th]. your pencil, in some admirable portraits you have been so kind as send me– that I should be happy to be favour'd w[th]. a few more.– When you have time I should like to hear or rather see your sketches of the other professors at Glasgow– & some of her ministers.[3]

But the post is going & I must leave my worthy friend w[th]. my own familys best wishes & most affectionate regards

Y[rs] while S. Kenrick

---

[3] See the verbal 'portraits' of various Edinburgh literati JW sketched for SK in Letter 99.

## Letter 102: James Wodrow to Samuel Kenrick, 27 September 1785

Place: Stevenston
Addressed: M<sup>r</sup>. Samuel Kenrick Mercht<sup>t</sup>. / in Bewdley / Worcestershire
Postmarked: 27 Sept<sup>r</sup>. 1785
Stamped: SE/29
Note in JW's hand: turn at Ferrybridge
Note in SK's hand: answ<sup>d</sup>. Oct<sup>r</sup> 5.

My very Dear Friend

Tho' I have sent to my L<sup>d</sup>. Eglington for franks yet as they are long of coming I must in consequence of my own anxiety & my Wife's still greater anxiety, write a few lines to you without them. Coud you have believed it that is now between five ^5^ & ^7^ seven weeks since we have had the scrap of a pen from Bewdley? And considering that Nelly in consequence of Our last Letters to her, must either be on the Eve of setting out or actualy gone to Manchester this circumstance considerably encreases my Wifes anxiety, & makes her figure something bad to have happened during that journey, notwithstanding she does every thing in her power to check such troublesome Phantoms of the Immagination. I am persuaded & she also, that one or more of your Packets are lost in their Way hither. I can conjecture nothing else to account for the present Phaenomenon except that you have wrote by some private hand & that I think unlikely, or at least that you woud trust to that alone, after repeated experience of the uncertainty of such a way of conveyance.

To give you some Idea as far as my recollection will serve, of the Number of Letters & Packets lying at Bewdley since we heard from you: After my return from Ed<sup>r</sup>. & the receipt of a long one from you I wrote you in July at Equal length all on College Characters & incidents, I wrote a second time a fortnight after attempting a scketch of the 4 Ed<sup>r</sup>. D<sup>rs</sup>. In which I believe I enclosed a 5£ Drafft on London. After receiving Nells Letter relative to her Uncles Invitation– I wrote her ^an^ answer about the Middle ^or more^ of Aug<sup>st</sup>. without a frank I sent off a 4th Packet filled with Letters to Nelly & one from myself to Miss Kenrick expressive of my Gratitude to her & her Parents & containing a warm yet hopeless wish that she coud accompany her friend down & spend the Winter in Scotland. This ^Frank^ was sent the first of Sept<sup>r</sup>. 5<sup>ly</sup>. My Wife wrote a single Letter to Miss Kenrick on Sab<sup>th</sup>. Sennight expressive of her anxiety ^to^ which I hope We will have an immediate return in a few days which will put an end to this Anxiety. The receipt of none of these has been acknowledged except the first in Nells Letter Aug$^{st}$. 7th. & besides there were Letters sent with the Lawn[1] which was to leave Glasg$^w$ Sept$^r$ 16 & can only be on the road.

In the course of correspondence with M$^r$. Hamilton at London[2] on a very accidental piece of bussiness in the Mercantile way There was a Paragraph in his Letter dated Sept$^r$ 20th & received yesterday about Nell which has lessened my anxiety tho' not her mothers about her. Tho my principal Letters to him have been lost from the wrong direction of the franks yet from a hint in one of the Letters on bussiness he sees that there has been some misaprehension of his conduct and as I wish him to stand well in ^the^ Oppinion of your family as well as Nells I transcribe the paragraph which you will read to her if she is still with you. "I had a letter from my Niece mentioning that she was going to Manch$^r$. from whence she might probably have company home. I am sorry that it has not been in my power to have the Pleasure of a visit from her, without a chance of it's being as uncomfortable to her as it woud have been inconvenient to me, but this is a matter which I cannot sufficiently explain to you on Paper, and will therefore wait in expectation of meeting as I see plainly some explanation is necessary to prevent misaprehension. I shall probably in ten days know whether I am to be in Scotland this Season; and if I go, and can by any means contrive it, I shall take Manchest$^r$. in going down & if your Daugh$^r$. finds no earlier opportunity bring her with me."

It runs strongly in my mind that Nelly will be in Manchester before this can reach you. I shall not again express my Obligations to you M$^{rs}$. Kenrick & Miss Kenrick for all ^the^ kindnesses & numberless attentions she has met with during her long continued stay under your friendly roof. We have all a <strong> ^real^ sense of them. M$^{rs}$. Roberts[3] is also entitled to the best thanks of this family for the uncommon attention & civility ^I know^ she has shown a young stranger tho' a friend & Guest of your family.

---

[1] i.e. fine linen (as in a bishop's sleeves—Johnson's *Dictionary*).

[2] John Hamilton.

[3] Betty Carolina Roberts (1745–1817), the wife of Wilson Aylesbury Roberts (1736–1819), SK's banking partner. See *W-K*, I, p. 478n. They married on 11 April 1763 at Ribbesford. Baptized Betty Carolina Crane at Ribbesford 29 Dec. 1745, she was buried at Packwood, Warwickshire, 1 April 1817 aged seventy-one years, with her abode listed as Bewdley. *Ancestry*; Warwickshire County Record Office; Warwickshire Anglican Registers; Roll: PG 3320; Document Reference: DRB 25.

I have been reading lately M^r. Boswells Letter to the People of Scotland.[4] It will entertain you highly if you can get a sight of it & you will need no explication of what I said of the Bee in His bonnet. With some Genius, ^&^ fire, & muc[h] [page torn] public spirit. He is a ten times greater oddity than your worthy friend[5] who is indeed d[e]based by the Comparison. I think Boswells argument when he does argue is good & carries conviction but such farrago of stories picked up in private Companys, & Scraps of Latin Poets English plays & Scots ballads dashed with such a mixture of family & personal vanity, of whig & Tory principles, fine Liberal sentiments, & weak narrow prejudices I never indeed saw in print. It must hurt his chance of preferrment who can trust a man that has so little regard to decency as [to] expose the nakedness of his Country his Mother? so little command of himself as to come out with every thing that is uppermost in his strange head. Some body asked Harry Erskine[6] your favourite who is happy in his Puns Have ^you^ seen Boswells Pamplet? what think ye of his half Crown's worth? I think, said he, no body woud ^have^ ventured to write it who had a Whole Crown.

I beg to hear from you on receipt of this every thing you know of Nell as I am involved with the Sacr^t.[7] & other business it will probably not be in my power to write you again for some time. All here join in kindest wishes & Comp^s. to your family yours most sincerly.

J^s Wodrow

---

[4] James Boswell. For his first *Letter to the People of Scotland*, see Letter 79. His second pamphlet of the same title, to which JW refers here, was published on 26 May 1785, to oppose the government's reforms of the Court of Session in Edinburgh and to expostulate against the power of Henry Dundas in Scotland generally. James Boswell, *Letter to the People of Scotland on the Alarming Attempt to Infringe the Articles of Union and Introduce a Most Pernicious Innovation by Diminishing the Number of Lords of Session* (Edinburgh, 1785). See *Boswell: The Applause of the Jury, 1782–1785*, eds I. S. Lustig and F. A. Pottle (1981), p. 302; Frank Brady, *Boswell's Political Career* (New Haven, CT, 1965), pp. 119–29; Frank Brady, *James Boswell: The Later Years, 1769–1795* (New York, 1984), pp. 274–81.

[5] Joseph Priestley. JW referred to him having a bee in his bonnet in Letter 79, and there are several subsequent similar references.

[6] Henry Erskine. See Letter 79. He printed this *bon mot* in his review of Boswell's pamphlet, signed 'Ximenes', in the *Gentleman's Magazine*, 55 (1785), p. 682. Nevertheless, reviews of the pamphlet in the *Scots Magazine*, the *Critical Review*, the *Monthly Review*, and the *English Review*, as well as the *Gentleman's Magazine*, complimented Boswell's patriotism, his arguments, and his humour. See *Boswell: The Applause of the Jury*, eds Lustig and Pottle, p. 302n.

[7] i.e. the sacrament of the Lord's Supper, which entailed a communion season of several days. See Letter 104.

## Letter 103: Samuel Kenrick to James Wodrow, 5 October 1785
Place: Bewdley
Addressed: The Rev[d]. James Wodrow / Irvine / Scotland
Stamped: 148 BRIDGE NORTH/IRELAND[1]

My very worthy friend

Remember all your most entertaining packets to us came safe– tho' thro' perils– being wofully mawled on the out side.

Tho' I have the same reason for delaying to answer your favour of the 27th. Ult[o]. that Mary had & submitted to, ^for^ not acknowledging M[rs]. Wodrow's of the 18th– namely, that our franked packet of the 23rd. must have anticipated all we could have said, to remove your groundless alarm on Miss Wodrow's account as well as cleared up the mystery of our seemingly long silence & neglect of you.– But as this second frank may have miscarried by the same malignant power that intercepted our first franked packet of the 22nd. of Aug[t]– the sad cause of all the succeeding disappointments. (This frank was put into Stourbridge post office that day, by a person I sent it by on purpose, to comply w[th]. Lord Westcote's[2] scrupulous exactness in those matters, that being his post town– & upon my complaint of the miscarriage of it, the post master assured me, he recollected it & had forwarded it to Birmingham the next office.)– I say on the possibility of the repetition of the same mischief & to take the most certain way to set your mind & M[rs]. Wodrow's at rest, I now send this by first post without a frank– to inform you of the above particulars, & that we were robbed of our most agreeable guest on monday the 19th Sept[r]. when her affectionate Mary accompanied her to Birmingham & parted w[th]. her that night at 12 of the clock, to set out for Manchester, where she arrived the following evening (as we have had the pleasure of hearing from herself since) & was there met by M[r]. Dinwiddie who conveyed her that night in his own carriage to his house at Redvale.[3] The £5– bill you sent, came safe & was placed to the credit of your account, as you will find in a note of it I gave Miss Wodrow.

We observe w[th]. concern what you copied from Mr. Hamilton's letters & think he is much to be pitied. All that hurt us in the matter was Miss Wodrow's

---

[1] The first stamp probably refers to Bridgenorth, on the Severn River 15 miles north of Bewdley. The 'Ireland' stamp appears on the back of the letter.

[2] See Letter 83, SK to JW, 28 Sept. 1784. For Lord Westcote, see Letter 80.

[3] Redvale is a district in the southern area of the town of Bury, near Manchester.

6. Seal on Letter 103.

disappointment who seemed to have set her heart on seeing London; while at the same time we were sensible of the great additional travelling expence it must have been attended with, by making such a circuitous journey home. But I trust she will yet meet with a more favourable opportunity the next visit she will be so kind as make us, when matters of this sort may be more easily accommodated. In short I repeat it again, the hideous unsurmountable obstacle that was between your family & mine is removed– we see we can visit each other w$^{th}$. no great inconveniency, & I hope yet to see it accomplished before I leave this vale of tears.– As to any attention & kindness & all that to dear honest Nell– say no more of it– we were indebted to you & yours before for as much– & tho' we had not, we had too much pleasure in doing any little thing we did, to wish or expect to hear any thing more of the matter. And indeed the favour, were it to be considered fairly, was conferred upon us– her friendship, her kindness, her goodness to venture so far to see us justly entitled her to every kind return in our power– w$^{ch}$. was still heightened by her agreeable manners & behaviour– w$^{ch}$. made her equally beloved by all our friends. Your kind remembrance of our best of friends M$^{rs}$. Roberts on that score, shall be communicated to her the first time we see her.

If I had time, I hardly know what to say to you on account of what I have already written, & of w$^{ch}$. I am uncertain what has reached your hands. Your next letter will put me in the train.

I am much diverted w$^{th}$. your acct. of Boswell's pamphlet[4] & Erskine's[5] pun upon it. But the News papers announce another work of his viz Johnsoniana:– w$^{ch}$. from a short specimen, frittered in one of those papers, seem to be very trifling indeed– the shreds, dust & cobwebs of his slovenly bed chamber: w$^{ch}$. I should imagine from his dress & appearance was not kept very neat.[6] Not to say, that the public has been long ago tired w$^{th}$. lives, bons mots & anecdotes of this hero of his.[7]

Thirty years ago, I thought Boswell a promising genius, who w$^{d}$. soon be a credit & honour to his family & country. His printed voyage to Corsica,[8] his enthusiastic love of Liberty– charmed & confirmed my first expectations. But it seems that plaguy Bee in the Bonnet, will blast all these fine prospects.

Our best wishes love &c ever attend you.

Y$^{rs}$. S. E & M K

---

[4] See Letter 102 for Boswell's *Letter to the People of Scotland* (1785).

[5] Henry Erskine. See Letter 102.

[6] This is a reference to James Boswell's *Journal of a Tour to the Hebrides*, which was advertised as published in the *Morning Chronicle*, 1 Oct. 1785. For the 'short specimen', see 'The Character of the Late Dr. Johnson. By James Boswell, Esq.', *London Chronicle*, 8 Oct. 1785. Boswell's full *Life of Samuel Johnson* was not published until 1791.

[7] Notwithstanding SK's view, shared with others, the *Journal of a Tour to the Hebrides* was 'an instant bestseller'. 'Some reviewers were inevitably baffled by its novelty and personal candour, and hostile to its attention to minute quotidian detail, but its success increased Boswell's confidence in his closely personal and anecdotal approach to biography.' Gordon Turnbull, 'James Boswell (1740–1795)', *ODNB* (10 Oct. 2019).

[8] James Boswell, *An Account of Corsica: The Journal of a Tour to that Island; and Memoirs of Pascal Paoli* (1768).

## Letter 104: James Wodrow to Samuel Kenrick, 31 October 1785

Place: Stevenston
Addressed: M^r. Samuel Kenrick Merch^t. / in Bewdley / Worcestershire
Stamped: IRVINE
Notes: 85 / turn at Ferrybridge / a single sheet
Note in SK's hand: answ^d. 11 Nov^r. 85

My Dear Friend

Do not be allarmed at seeing my hand write so soon again & without a frank. It is only a Commission for Hops in way of your bussiness or your beloved Daughter's.[1] I don't know which of you manages this branch but It was forgot by me in the hurry of my last wrote about ten days ago & it can now no longer be delayed. There is a Brewery near Saltcoats[2] carried on by two very honest & industrious & worthy Parishioners of mine– whom I lately nominated as Elders among others, & nothing but their own Modesty hindered them from accepting the Office. They have but lately begun the bussiness & propose to prosecute it pretty extensively by brewing both Ale & Porter & they wish to take all their hops from you if you can serve them as no doubt you will as easily & cheap as another. The principal branch of their sale at present & always must be is small beer or ale for the table which they sell at 14^d. ℔ Scots Gallon ^about 17 or 18 bottles^.[3] They are in terms with a Porter brewer but have not yet begun that branch. Now they wish you <u>to send them two bags or Pockets of Hops immediately</u> directed to M^r. Hugh Wat ~~at the~~ & Comp^y. at the Brewery Saltcoats and <-> ^will^ follow your advice as to ^the^ kind of Hops that will best answer their different branches having themselves but newly begun the bussiness the time of buying them & every other direction you may think it necessary to give them. You will know the cheapest & speediest method of sending them to Saltcoats under the above direction & write to me as soon as you can after receipt of this, how soon they may expect the above small Quantity for a tryal & tho' they are almost out they will

---

[1] Mary Kenrick seems to have participated in some aspects of the family economy, including trade in hops as here; see also Letters 145 and 256.
[2] In his parish account of 1793 JW noted that 'Some time after [the American war], a considerable brewery was built near Saltcoats, which continues to supply the towns and the country for several miles round with small-beer.' Wodrow, 'Parish of Stevenston', *OSA*, VII, p. 22.
[3] A Scots gallon was approximately three times the volume of an English gallon, at 840 English cubic inches to 282 in an English ale gallon. Strawhorn, ed., *Ayrshire at the Time of Burns*, pp. 134–35.

commission no more from Glasgow till they hear from you. The money you may depend upon to be paid accordingly to your Order.

I wrote you on Sat[y]. sennight[4] under a cover of Col[l]. Montgomery[5] in the greatest hurry I ever did before. The Sacr[t]. was given here the day after with much order & comfort. We had the same number of Communicants as usual & rather a greater Crowd of other people than we commonly have at a Winter Sacr[t].[6] The Weather was fine and the parish & neighbourhood seemed to make it a point of honour to attend us. The Collection was greater than we ever had at any Sacr[t]. above £10.[7] My honest but too zealous & Enthusiastick Collegue[8] made but a poor figure as to numbers & will probably not attempt anything of this kind again.

Nelly has not yet made her appearance. I had a letter from her last week & from a letter last night from my Nephew at London[9] to one of his ~~Partners~~ Employers at Saltcoats I understand her uncle was to set out in a few days after the 23[d]. was resolved to take Manchester in his way & bring her down to Glasgow where it is likely they may be about the middle of this week. She has been dispointed in several Schemes that M[r]. Dinwiddie had formed of getting her properly escorted down which has protracted her to stay from time to time.

This County had a very full meeting last week[10] upon the bill before the Parliament for diminishing the number of Judges in the Court of Session.[11]

---

[4] Missing letter: JW to SK, 22 Oct. 1785.

[5] One of the Ayrshire MPs 1784–89. See *W-K*, vol. I, p. 435n.; Letters 79 and 80.

[6] See Mutch, *Religion and National Identity*, pp. 100–04 on the substantial organization entailed by a Scottish parish communion season, including the previous evaluation of who was and who was not considered to be in a spiritual state fit to receive the sacrament as well as to worship and hear the sermons, which everyone was entitled to do.

[7] See Mutch, *Religion and National Identity*, pp. 106–30 on parish finances, especially in connection with poor relief.

[8] A relief church was built in Saltcoats in 1782, which comprised around eighty families by the time JW wrote his parish account in 1793. Perhaps its minister, Rev. David Ewing (ordained on 28 April 1784), held its sacrament on the same Sunday as the parish church, in unsuccessful competition. Wodrow, 'The Parish of Stevenston', p. 27; Strawhorn, ed., *Ayrshire at the Time of Burns*, p. 128.

[9] Presumably a son of John Hamilton (1740–92), Louisa Wodrow's brother.

[10] On the political importance of the annual Scottish Michaelmas Head Court meeting of the freeholders in each county, see William Ferguson, 'Electoral Law and Procedure in Eighteenth and Early Nineteenth Century Scotland', 2 vols (PhD thesis, University of Glasgow, 1957), I, pp. 31–36.

[11] The Judges Bill, 1785, proposed by Henry Dundas, MP, and Ilay Campbell (1734–1823), Lord Advocate, would have reduced the size of the Inner House of the Court of Session in Edinburgh from fifteen judges to ten or eleven by means of not replacing seats left vacant. The purposes were to increase the efficiency of collective decision-making, to exclude political patronage in favour of legal ability as the qualification for admission to the bench, and to raise judicial salaries without spending more public money. Nicholas T. Phillipson, *The Scottish Whigs and the Reform of the Court of Session 1785–1830* (Edinburgh, 1990), pp. 62–64.

The members of Parl$^t$. belonging to the County viz the Lord$^s$. Eglinton & Cassillis & Sir Ad$^m$. Fergusson did not chuse to appear. Col. Montg$^y$. was there & was put into the Chair. M$^r$. Boswell carried his point yet not to the extent that he wished.[12] The Resolutions which he proposed in very strong terms were softened.[13] They however ~~found~~ resolved that the Attempt of the L$^d$. Advocate[14] to introduce the bill without the consent of the people of Scotland was improper & disrespectful to his Country.[15] That it ought not to be insisted on & carried except some proper compensation was made to them either by giving them Juries in matters of property according to the English form, or by some regulation which woud render processes before the court of Session less tedious & expensive than they are. This last alternative was carried by a single vote against M$^r$. Boswell & his friends & indeed I think very improperly, as it is too vague & insignificant in comparison with the other. I shoud have mentioned a previous resolution which introduced all the rest viz that the Articles of the Union are unalterable by Parliament without the consent of the people in both kingdoms particularly the one struck at by the bill. Hunter Blair[16] the Provost of Ed$^r$. & Sir A. Fergusson's friend was the principal Speaker against M$^r$. Boswell who spoke ^himself^ a great deal, & was said to be well supported by several Gentlemen.[17] The cheif point in Dispute between

---

[12] Ayrshire was one of nine Scottish counties whose electoral meetings in October 1785 passed resolutions opposing or at least questioning the legitimacy of the Judges Bill, which was enough, together with the likely silent disapproval of the other counties, to cause the government to withdraw it. Boswell's *Letter to the People of Scotland* (1785), discussed in Letter 102 above, described Ayrshire as 'the Yorkshire of Scotland' for the robust independence of spirit of its many independent country gentlemen. He and others across several of the counties argued for the introduction of civil jury trials (as operated in England), instead of the reduction of the number of judges, as the most necessary reform to be pursued. Boswell, *Letter to the People of Scotland*, pp. 12–13, 15, 56; Phillipson, *Scottish Whigs and the Reform of the Court of Session*, pp. 68–69, 73–74, 76–77.

[13] Boswell changed the original words 'unwise, rash, and insolent' to describe the Diminishing Bill to 'most improper and disrespectful', in which form the Bill was overwhelmingly supported at the meeting. Brady, *Boswell's Political Career*, p. 126; Brady, *James Boswell: The Later Years, 1769–1795*, p. 280.

[14] Ilay Campbell. See Letters 79 and 80.

[15] A common ground for rejecting the Bill in the nine Scottish counties was that Parliament was not sufficient to change the constitution of the Court of Session; the Scottish people, in the form of the county meetings, must be consulted. Another account of the Ayrshire meeting and its resolutions was published by the *Caledonian Mercury*, 29 Oct. 1785. Phillipson, *Scottish Whigs and the Reform of the Court of Session*, pp. 69–71.

[16] James Hunter Blair. See Letter 86; also the discussion in Letters 134–35 below on Robert Burns's 'Elegy on Sir James Hunter Blair'.

[17] See Brady, *Boswell's Political Career*, p. 126, for this meeting on 25 Oct. 1785, and pp. 119–29 for Boswell's pamphlet on the subject and its reception. See also Frank Brady, *James Boswell: The Later Years, 1769–1795* (1984), pp. 279–80.

these Gentlemen & which occasioned a great deal of Argument was the point touched upon some time ago in our correspondence the Propriety of Juries in Scotland whether ~~Our~~ ^our^ people <–> wished ~~for~~ ^to have^ them & woud submit to the trouble of them; & whether our property woud be rendered more secure by them than it is. On the first point Hunter Blair took your side of the Question & his Antagonists mine.[18] It was allowed by all that We once had them & how we came to lose them nobody seems to know. We have them still in criminal causes & in Exchequer causes ^all matters of Revenue^ & I never heard any body complain of the trouble of them. I see advertisements in the newspapers for meetings of the <~~rest of the~~> ^other^ Counties of Scotland for the same purpose.

D$^r$. Leechman has been ^ill^ of late of a Rose as they call it in his face.[19] Louisa ^has^ written to her Aunt[20] for more <certain> account<s> than we have had as he is not without danger. Miss Dunlop daughter to our old Greek Proff$^r$.[21] had called to ask for him lately, when he was confined to his bed. When he heard her named he sent for her to his bed^side^ & accosted her in this Manner. "Sally! I wished to see you & talk with you a little, for I hope very soon to see your Father &c." I hope however this meeting of the two ^very^ dear & worthy friends will be put off for some little time if it be the will of heaven.

I have heard nothing further of the Prosecution to be carried on before the court of Session against the Colledge.– I think it probable the grounds of it are quite frivolous & that ^it^ is no more than a vain attempt to awaken the attention of the World which has been asleep since the Secretary of the state's Letters.[22]

---

[18] See Kenrick's discussion in 1783 of the libertarian merits of the English jury system, *W-K*, I, pp. 150–51, 484–85, 490. Wodrow's letter of 10 Sept. 1783, which seems to have put his 'side of the Question', is missing.

[19] A synonym for erysipelas, a skin inflammation of a deep-red colour. *OED*.

[20] Louisa Wodrow was Bridget Leechman's niece; her mother, Helen Hamilton (d. 1793), *née* Balfour, was Bridget Leechman's sister.

[21] Alexander Dunlop (1684–1747), 'perhaps the most distinguished professor of Greek in Scotland, and the leader of the progressive party in the faculty' at Glasgow University, where he taught from 1704 till 1746. His students included Francis Hutcheson as well as, later, JW and SK. His own uncle was William Carstares (1649–1715), principal of Edinburgh University, and his brother was William Dunlop (1692–1720), professor of ecclesiastical history, also at Edinburgh. Alexander Dunlop had supported Leechman in his early struggles at Glasgow, and it was therefore natural for his daughter to have called to see Leechman in his illness. H. L. Fulton, 'John Moore, the Medical Profession and the Glasgow Enlightenment', in Hook and Sher, eds, *Glasgow Enlightenment*, p. 177; Thomas D. Kennedy, 'William Leechman, Pulpit Eloquence and the Glasgow Enlightenment', in Hook and Sher, eds, *Glasgow Enlightenment*, p. 57.

[22] In connection with John Anderson's failed attempt several months earlier to secure a Royal Visitation to inspect Glasgow University's financial accounts. See Letter 98.

I saw when I was last in Glasgow a Letter from the Marquiss of Graham to D$^r$. Leechman & another (indeed one of the most polite & Gentlemanny Letters I ever read) from L$^d$. Sydney to M$^r$. Burke the purport of both was to decline the request of the Prin$^l$. to give Liberty to print the Letters & make any further appeal to the Public as the measure best calculated to answer ^the intention^ of the king & min$^{rs}$ of putting an end to their differences & most suitable to the Dignity or honour of the University. I had not time to copy these Letters. My Wife Peggy & I join in most affectionate comp$^s$. to M$^{rs.}$ Kenrick & you & Miss Kenrick.

My Dear Friend most sincerely yours<br>J. Wodrow

## Letter 105: Samuel Kenrick to James Wodrow, 11 November 1785
Place: Bewdley
Addressed: The Rev$^d$. James Wodrow / Irvine / Scotland
Stamped: CARLISLE
Note: One Single Sheet

My worthy Friend

I have been duly favoured w$^{th}$. both your kind letters of the 21$^{st}$. & 31$^{st}$. Ult.– & begin w$^{th}$. business. We are much obliged to you for your kind order of Hops. We can supply your friends w$^{th}$. new or old– that is this year's or last. They will probably prefer the latter– w$^{ch}$. they may have from 70/to 80/℔ C$^t$ deliverd either at Liverpool or Bristol. We should be glad to know w$^{ch}$. of these seaports they prefer– & upon their advising us, shall immediately forward them 2 Pockets as a sample. Good, stout strong, brown hops we suppose they prefer to those of a finer colour & less condition as the dealers call it. They will please direct– *To Kenrick & Bennett Bewdley.*[1] Turn at Ferry Bridge.

---

[1] Probably Richard Bennett, tobacco merchant, unitarian, and one of the 'friends' whom Elisabeth Kenrick nominated as an executor of her will. B. W. E. Alford, *W.D. & H.O. Wills and the Development of the UK Tobacco Industry, 1786–1965* (1973), p. 29; he is recorded as a tobacconist who mortgaged Warley Hall to William Prattinton of Bewdley in 1788, Birmingham Archives, Galton Papers, Deeds relating to Warley Hall farm, MS3101/A/B/7/7; Richard Bennett of Bewdley is listed as a member of 'The Society of Unitarian Christians, in the West of England', in Thomas Belsham, *Freedom of Enquiry, and Zeal in the Diffusion of Christian Truth, Asserted and Recommended in a Discourse Delivered at Bristol, July 9, 1800, Before the Society of Unitarian Christians, Established in the West of England, for Promoting Christian Knowledge and the Practice of Virtue, by the Distribution of Books* (1800), p. 38.

And now for your first favour– w[ch]. you found time to write amidst such a multiplicity of serious business. How happy would this little family have been to have joined you & your friends on that late solemn occasion you were then preparing for![2] We have nothing of the sort here. Opportunities are to be sure frequent but they are dull languid solitary & formal. Our kind Nelly will confirm this to you– & how often we have lamented the difference to our friends here & wished to have been again in Scotland on such occasions. We hope she is safe arrived at her dear home before this time. She has left a great blank at our fire side, by breaking our partie quarree[3] w[ch]. was so comfortable last winter. Let her know that we expect Lord Westcote here very soon, when Mary will take an opportunity of sending her all our news in one of his franks– tho' I find she has already sent a pretty voluminous packet from Chester fair. The Lawn is come safe & gives great satisfaction.[4]

It was I suppose in the unfortunate packet of the 22[d] of Aug[t].[5] that I wrote you an advertisement of Dr. Priestley's from the last number of the Theological Repository– viz. for the follow[g]. Books at a reasonable price –

Vigilii Tapsensis Opera

Ruffini opera

Gregorii Turonensis D[o].

D. Zwicker's Irenicon & his other pieces in defence of it. As it is probable some if not most of the above, must have been in your late learned Father's collection many of w[ch]. I understand lie useless in chests at Glasgow; I suppose you or your brother will have no objection to liberate them from their close confinement & give them a chance of doing some good once more, before they sink into oblivion.

I hope Anderson is at last tired of doing mischief & disturbing the world to no purpose– particularly that best of men D[r]. Leechman. What a pity is it that his repose, after a life of so much honour & usefulness, should be interrupted by the madness of this firebrand!– I am glad to hear there is a stop put to it from above. You have already sent me Ld. Sydneys L[rs]. to D[r]. L. & M[r]. And[n].[6]

It gives me the greatest pleasure to find so liberal a spirit gaining ground thro' Scotland. If a real reform in civil or religious matters should take place, it must come from you or our northern counties.

---

[2] Presumably the sacrament, or communion, which JW mentioned in Letter 104, 31 Oct. 1785.
[3] 'Partie carrée'; party of four people. *OED*.
[4] See Letter 102 above.
[5] In fact, in Letter 100, 19 Sept. 1785.
[6] See Letter 98 above.

I am just reading D$^r$. Fordyce's <u>Addresses to the Deity</u>.[7] Like every thing of his, they are elegant and sensible but not so direct or pathetic as I could wish. They run too much into meditation and talking to ^rather^ than addressing the Supreme Being. But this is perhaps more my fault than the author's. I was spoiled at first by hearing the warm pious elevated effusions of our worthy professors, to relish anything of the sort since. My imagination too is cooled & my feelings of heart become callous with years– so that I can find nothing that entirely pleases me, amidst the numerous devotional pieces w$^{ch}$. I daily peruse: nothing to be compared w$^{th}$. what came so naturally viva voce from our worthy professor.

As the 6th. & last address pleased me for its singularity as well as excellence, I will transcribe part of it to you.[8] 'Tis on the death of the late celebrated Sam$^l$. Johnson, w$^{th}$. whom it seems the D$^r$. had for some years lived in habits of intimacy & as a true friend attended him in his last moments.[9] By w$^{ch}$. means the world is now made acquainted w$^{th}$. some traits in his character hitherto unknown– In enumerating his shining abilities, he says, "In his presence the infidel was awed, the profane stood corrected, & the mouth of the swearer was stopped. In his discourse, the majesty of genius impressed & the attentive & unprejudiced with a reverence for wisdom; the virtuous & the pious were encouraged, by the approbation of superiour discernment; & truths, that had lost the allurement of novelty recovered their influence from the native but peculiar force with w$^{ch}$. they were proposed."– Such is the picture drawn by the partial friendly hand of an admirer, when the original was in health & spirits. See him next when adversity comes upon him; "Then he communed with his own heart upon his bed, & examined himself in the view of his last & great account, he saw wherein he had offended. Then it was that I heard him condemn, with holy self-abasement, the pride of understanding by w$^{ch}$. he had often trespassed against the laws of courteous demeanour & forgotten the fallible condition of his nature. Then it was, that I heard him w$^{th}$. ingenuous freedom commend the virtues of forbearance & moderation in matters of belief, as more conformable to ~~the~~ reason, & to the

---

[7] *Addresses to the Deity* (1785), by Rev. James Fordyce (1720–96), Scottish minister and moralist. Educated at Marischal College, Aberdeen, he served as minister at Monkwell Street Presbyterian chapel, London (1760–82). He had already acquired a reputation as a preacher before going to London, and was awarded a DD by Glasgow University in 1760. Regarded as one of the best Dissenting preachers, his religious sentiments have been described as liberal, and 'this liberality increased with his age'. The tone of his *Addresses to the Deity* (1785) was one of cheerful devotion. Wilson, *Dissenting Churches*, III, pp. 209–14; Surman Index.

[8] 'Address VI: On the Death of Dr Samuel Jonson', in Fordyce, *Addresses to the Deity*, pp. 209–32.

[9] Samuel Johnson had died on 13 Dec. 1784.

Gospel of thy son, than he had long conceived. \_ \_ \_ Let not such as were strangers to the piety & benevolence of thy departed servant, censure too severely the [par]tial or prejudiced opinions that sometimes contracted & unhappily obscured a mind otherwise comprehensive & enlightened. Teach them, O Lord more charitable allowance for mistakes hastily imbibed in the days of youth, & afterwards from the power of early prepossession without consciousness of evil, fondly retained & vehemently defended. It may be that in Him they were permitted by thy unnerring Providence, to manifest more clearly the frailty of the wisest men, & to raise our minds from the defective patterns of excellence here below, to thyself, the only standard of [p]erfection."– # #.[10] But how comes it to pass, that this man who made no great noise when alive, should now have so many panegyrics heaped on his tomb.[11] One w$^d$. think that Genius, Piety & Virtue were no more. His industry was great witness his dictionary. But I do not think that Ainsworth's was short of it[12]– or that of Chamber's and Hill,[13] & yet their names are forgot. His critical abilities were great, but sullied w$^{th}$. partial prejudice– which indeed tainted all his writings. How cheap did Adam Smith hold him thirty years ago, in his strictures on the Rambler,[14] when he pronounced ^him^ only fit to compose such a laborious work as a dictionary.[15] We have certainly many superiour to him still in every walk of literature.

I cannot help mentioning a striking Episode in D$^r$. Fordyce's first address on a view of the Ocean, where he introduces his brother who was swallowed by the merciless waves, on his return from foreign lands, rich in accumulated treasures

[10] Fordyce, 'Address VI: On the Death of Dr Samuel Jonson'. In a heavy hand, SK quotes accurately from pp. 213–15 and 222–23.

[11] It may appear surprising that SK thought Samuel Johnson made 'no great noise' when alive!

[12] *Thesaurus Linguae Latinae Compendiarius: Or, A Compendious Dictionary of the Latin Tongue: Designed for the Use of the British Nations*, 2 vols (1736), by Robert Ainsworth (1660–1743).

[13] The *Cyclopaedia; or, An Universal Dictionary of Arts and Sciences ... Compiled from the Best Authors*, 2 vols (1728), by Ephraim Chambers (1680?–1740) influenced Samuel Johnson. After Chambers died, Dr John Hill used Chambers's voluminous manuscripts to publish a supplement in 1753.

[14] A twice-weekly journal of essays by Samuel Johnson which began on 20 March 1750 and lasted until 14 March 1752. In all, Johnson had written 208 essays on a whole range of contemporary issues.

[15] For Smith's critical view of Johnson's *Dictionary*, see *Edinburgh Review*, 1 (July 1755), pp. 61–73. On Johnson's *Rambler*, an article in the *Bee, or Literary Weekly Intelligencer*, 11 May 1791, following Smith's death, on 'Anecdotes tending to throw light on the character and opinions of the late Adam Smith, LLD', noted that, 'Of the late Dr. Samuel Johnson, Dr. Smith had a very contemptuous opinion. ... He was no admirer of the Rambler or the Idler, and hinted, that he had never been able to read them.' Printed in Adam Smith, *Lectures on Rhetoric and Belles Lettres*, ed. J. C. Bryce (Indianapolis, IN, 1985), p. 228.

of learning, eloquence & wisdom.[16] So it seemed good in thy sight mysterious unnerring Ruler &c. –

In a late excursion I made to Birmingham, I had the curiosity to go to see what is called a Shew– w$^{ch}$. I had not done before for many years. The company consisted of about a dozen gentlemen. The Shewman was a modest old gentleman, who only spoke french– a native of Lyons. In one corner of the room, in a small recess about 1½ foot deep & ab$^t$. 4 foot square, where there had probably been a cupboard or press, we found suspended by ribbons from each side a little wax figure like a child's doll, w$^{th}$. a tin trumpet about 4 foot long, pointing horizontally from its mouth & between 4 & five foot from the floor. We were desired to ask any question aloud at the mouth of this trumpet in English, French, Italian, Spanish or Portugueze, & then apply our ear to the same place, when we heard a distinct answer in the same language, in a low whisper like a human voice at a great distance, but pronounced articulately.

I asked it several questions in english & french, & heard the sound of its answers, distinctly & some of the words– but either from the noise of the company or my hearing not being quick enough, I confess I could not hear it so intelligibly as I could wish. But there were younger persons in the room, who carried on a lively dialogue in w$^{ch}$. it made several smart repartees– I suspect there was a ventriloquist in the room who conveyed the sounds, but how I do not know.

There is another automoton in London of a different sort, in the shape of a man w$^{th}$. a chess-board & men before ^him^– who challenges & is hitherto superiour to the best player of that game, that can be found.

But friends must part– as some wise sage observed– My wife & daughter join me in our most affectionate regards to yourself M$^{rs}$. Wodrow & Nelly & Peggy. I ever am

Yours &c S. Kenrick

---

[16] In the first of his *Addresses to the Deity* (1785), 'On a View of the Sea', Fordyce referred to his 'much loved and long lamented brother', and looked forward to the day when 'the plans of all providence will be fulfilled' and he would meet his brother in 'perfect glory'. The brother was David Fordyce (bap. 1711–51), who became professor of moral philosophy at Marischal College, Aberdeen, in 1742 and published on education, moral philosophy, and the art of preaching. In 1750 he went on a Grand Tour to Italy, but on his return drowned in a shipwreck off the Dutch coast.

## Letter 106: James Wodrow to Samuel Kenrick, 1 December 1785

Place: Stevenston
Addressed: M$^r$. Samuel Kenrick Merch$^t$. / Bewdley / Worcestershire
Stamped: IRVINE
Note in JW's hand: Turn at Ferrybridge/a single sheet
Notes in SK's hand: Dec$^r$. 1st 1785 / Answ$^d$. 21$^{st}$. & 22$^{nd}$. Jan$^y$. / NB D$^r$. Leechman / died 3$^d$. Dec$^r$. 1785 / Came to Glasgow Dec$^r$. 1743 / Profess$^r$. of Divinity

My Dear & beloved Friend

 I write you a few hurried lines (which will put you to the Expense of Postage) lest you shoud blame me for neglect as I have one of your Letters lying by me of Nov$^r$. 11th. and another of an old ^date^ brought me by Nelly. I went <-> to Glasgow near three weeks ago to meet <u>her Uncle & her as</u> well <u>as to see the Worthy Prin$^l$</u>. once more for the time of his Departure is now at hand. I expected her in Glasgow near a week before she Arived, as her Uncle & her Cousin M$^r$. Gibson[1] had carried her round by Ed$^r$. I at last brought her about a week ^ago^ to her old habitation here where her Mother & Sister received her with much joy. She looks thinner since she left Scotland but is otherwise greatly improved by her long stay in England, not merely in her Language <—> which she will soon lose, but in other more material & durable Qualifications which I hope she will never lose. So that her Mother & I have great Satisfaction in having yeilded to her own desire & Miss Kenricks kind invitation & woud not have ^grudged^ the extraordinary expense this Excursion has cost, had it been much greater than it realy is. She has loaded her Mother with presents who says she never received so many at once except at her Marriage & has brought me some likewise for which I return my best thanks to you & your beloved Daughter tell her I will wear the seal as long as I live for her sake & the Inkhorn will be a very convenient traveling companion.

 I must ^neglect^ <overlook> the contents of the above mentioned letters however acceptable & worthy of notice, & hasten to a subject more interesting to you,

---

[1] See Letter 214, addressed by SK to 'The Rev$^d$. D$^r$. Wodrow, at Mr Gibson's, South Bridge Street, Edinburgh'; and Letter 94, where JW refers to 'Mrs Gibson going up to London to do bussiness for her Husband. She is Louisa's cousin & a lovely woman'. Thomas Aitchison, *The Edinburgh Directory, From July 1797 to July 1798* (Edinburgh, 1797), p. 98, lists a 'Peter Gibson, haberdasher, no. 9 south bridge, west side'; and the same listing is found in Peter Williamson, *Williamson's Directory for the City of Edinburgh, Canongate, Leith, and Suburbs, From June, 1784, to June, 1785* (Edinburgh, 1784), p. 42, while 'Peter Gibson, merchant, South Bridge Street', is found in Peter Williamson, *Williamson's Directory for the City of Edinburgh, Canongate, Leith, and Suburbs, From June, 1788, to June, 1789* (Edinburgh, 1788), p. 39.

melancholy but yet pleas[ing] even the last scene of D[r]. Leechman's life for it is now draw[ing] to a close if not actualy closed. After recovering ^from^ what we call a Rose[2] and swelling in his face & other complaints he was ^about five weeks ago^ seized suddenly when drinking a dish of Tea in his Dining ^room^ in his usual health & conversing with his friends in a more lively way than usual, with a shaking all over his body ^& <panting>^ resembling as M[rs]. Leechman wrote, the last pangs of nature. He lost the power of his left side. Physicians & asistance were got in five minutes. He was carried to his bed & in a short time recovered his speech & took the Medicines given him. When M[rs]. Leechman told him she was glad to find him so easy he said it was too soft a term he was in a state of joy & exultation. In that happy state ^of mind^, he ^has^ continued ^almost^ ever since <— —> amidst extreme bodily weakness unable to turn himself in his bed & various turns of his disease. That first letter of M[rs]. L. to her niece[3] in a manner forbad our going to Glasgow. She & her Servants were so constantly occupied night & day in their attendance upon him she wished no assistance from her friends but their prayers. In ten days or a fortnight however he was seized with a violent flux[4] which it was thought woud soon carry him off. She then desired D[r]. Irvine[5] who allong with Your friend D[r]. Stevenston[6] attended him to write for

[2] Erysipelas: see Letter 104.
[3] Louisa Wodrow.
[4] Flux: 'an abnormally copious flowing of blood, excrement, etc. from the bowels or other organs; a morbid or excessive discharge' (*OED*).
[5] Dr William Irvine (1743–87), lecturer in *materia medica* (1766–87) and, concurrently, chemistry (1769–87) at Glasgow University. He matriculated at Glasgow University (1756) and graduated MD (1766). He was a member of the Faculty of Physicians and Surgeons of Glasgow, and president of the Faculty in 1775–77 and 1783–85. His research examined heat, water, and light, and at the time of his death he had been invited by the Spanish government to direct a large glassworks and saltworks there; he was also notable, with various Glasgow colleagues such as John Robison, William Cullen, and William Trail, for developing a quantitative approach to his research. Andrew Kent, 'William Irvine, M.D.', in Andrew Kent, ed., *An Eighteenth-Century Lectureship in Chemistry* (Glasgow, 1950), pp. 140–50; Roger Emerson and Paul Wood, 'Science and Enlightenment in Glasgow, 1690–1802', in Charles W. J. Withers and Paul Wood, eds, *Science and Medicine in the Scottish Enlightenment* (East Linton, 2002), p. 103.
[6] Dr Alexander Stevenson (*c.* 1725–91), graduated MD from Glasgow University (1749). He was a member of the Faculty of Physicians and Surgeons of Glasgow (1756) and president of the Faculty (1757–58 and 1773–75). He was professor of the Practice of Medicine in the University of Glasgow (1766–88). He resigned because of ill-health, but was reappointed with his nephew, Thomas Charles Hope, as his assistant. He had resided in Edinburgh from the early 1750s and was a member of the Royal College of Physicians of Edinburgh. He was also a member of the Select Society and the Philosophical Society of Edinburgh, as well as the Literary Society and the Hodge-Podge Club in Glasgow. He was First Physician to the Prince of Wales for the Principality of Scotland. Addison, *Matriculation Albums*, p. 81; Roger L. Emerson, 'Select Society (act. 1754–64)', *ODNB*; Coutts, pp. 249, 496–97 and elsewhere, *passim*.

me. I was in Glasgow before the letter coud reach me, & found him indeed very weak unable to speak but at times, & then his mind as firm composed & acute as ever & for the most ^part^ easy & free of pain at other times restless & his posture <—ed>[7] uneasy to him so that it was necessary to move ^him^ & alter it every minute almost, which however he bore with great patience, longing for his dissolution & triumphing in the prospect of it, repeating <u>at times to himself the finest passages in the new testament. This</u> ~~mortal shall~~ <u>corruptible</u> shall put on incorruption & this Mortal put on immortality. O Death where is thy sting &c,[8] Even so come Lord Jesus[9] & many others to the same purpose. When he ^once^ complained of his bodily weakness I congratulated ^him^ on the distinctness ease and vigour of his mind. He said the promises of the Gospel were so plain that it required no stretch of mind to recollect or apply them. He confessed he was sometimes a Coward for pain but never ~~in his Life~~ was afraid of Death.

It woud far exceed the bounds of a Letter to tell you everything worthy of admiration in ^the behaviour of^ this Saint as you once with great propriety called him, who has appeared as dignifyed and venerable in his later end as his best friends could wish. Most of the things I allude to happened before I came such as his sending for Prof^r^. Anderson & giving him as a Xian a full & formal forgiveness. He spoke about 10 minutes to him but M^rs^. Leechman not quite pleased with And^ns^. behaviour woud not tell me fully what passed. On a Sund^y^. the day before I went in/Expecting it woud be his last day from the violence of the flux & finding himself revive a little, He sent for all his Servants & family gave proper advices ^first^ to M^r^. Pearman his Nephew a Minis^r^.[10] Then to each of the Servants seperately, thanked ^them^ for their concern attention & toil; ^shook hands with each of them &^ gave them his blessing. Then prayed, & part of this was a most fervent & excellent prayer for the Colledge, both Proffessors & students. In all this he spoke near half an hour with astonishing vigour & fervour. Next day he sent for D^r^. Finlay[11] told him he was sorry he was now so weak that he coud ^not^ see each of the Proff^rs^. seperately as he ^had^ intended but sent them by him his best wishes & blessing & advice to continue to exert themselves <—> in their several

---

[7] Blot.
[8] 1 Corinthians 15: 53–55.
[9] Revelation 22:20.
[10] William Pairman. See Letter 84.
[11] Rev. Dr Robert Findlay (1721–1814), dean of the Faculty of Divinity, Glasgow University, and minister successively of JW's parish of Stevenston (1744–45), Galston, Paisley (Laigh), and Glasgow (St David's). He received a DD from the University of Glasgow in 1776, and was appointed to the chair of divinity in Sept. 1782.

departments &c, A very affecting Interview he had with a M[r]. Cathcart[12] youngest son of the late L[d]. Cathcart[13] an intimate friend of the Prin[l]. The young man a Student at Oxford for the Church had called & was denied admittance by the Serv[ts]. The Prin[l]. sent for him & gave him his Advice & his blessing in such a manner as <-> is likely to leave an indelible impression on him. M[r]. Ritchardson,[14] ^who was present^ told me the Substance of what the Prin[l]. said & that M[r]. C. was greatly affected. Other things I coud write of the same kind had I time & room some of which I was wittness to but he was so weak before I saw him that he spoke little <—>. I saw him only two or three times every ^day^ sometimes drank Tea ^by Him^ chatted with my Brother[15] M[rs]. Leechman M[r]. Pearman ^&c,^ at his bedside unable to speak himself he liked to hear us chatt about what was passing in ^the^ Colledge books &c, now & then ^He^ spoke a sentence for his mind at perfect ease was susceptible of entertainment & amusement & entered into ^it^ with ^much^ good humour.

They found means to stop his flux & for two days at the end of the first week I stayed in Glasgow ^when^ he took more nourishment ^than before^ & had gained some more strength to speak, recovered the use of his left hand &c. I had some faint hope he might still recover. But the begin[g]. of last week he fell ^again^ into a sleepy dozing way yet perfectly sensible when roused & began again to lose, every day the last day I was in town he spoke <u>none at all. After taking some</u> drink I asked him how he was? He answered distressed but not miserable and this in such a faint voice that I coud not understand it till M[rs]. L. repeated it. Good Woman she is wonderfuly composed & resigned night & day she continues at his bedside & it is perfectly astonishing how her delicate frame has stood the anxiety watching & fatigue of her attendance. I left Glasg[w]. on Thurs[y]. had a letter from

---

[12] Rev. Archibald Hamilton Cathcart (1764–1841), matriculated at the University of Glasgow 1774, attended Oxford as Snell exhibitioner in 1782, and graduated from Oxford with a BA in 1786 and an MA in 1788. He became rector of Methley, Vicar of Kippax, Yorkshire, and Prebendary of York. Addison, *Matriculation Albums*, p. 108.

[13] Charles Schaw Cathcart, ninth Lord Cathcart (1721–76), army officer and diplomat and rector to the university (1773–75). As rector of the university, Cathcart helped to secure the appointment of William Richardson to the chair of humanity.

[14] William Richardson. See Letter 80. He was tutor to the two eldest sons of the ninth Lord Cathcart and Jane Hamilton, sister of Sir William Hamilton, and his lordship's secretary when Cathcart was ambassador-extraordinary at St Petersburg (1768–72). Following the death of Lady Cathcart in childbirth, Richardson returned to Scotland and was appointed to his chair at Glasgow University.

[15] Rev. Patrick Wodrow (1713–93), minister of Tarbolton, Ayrshire. He was married to Elizabeth, *née* Balfour, sister of Mrs Leechman.

D[r]. Irvine on Sunday signifying that he had fevered that day I left Gl[w]. & was growing worse & worse. This determined me to return to Gl[w]. as yestersd[y]. but on Tues[y]. I had a second letter from the D[r]. describing the progress of his disease that the fever had taken his head that he was in great pain on Sund[y]. & Mond[y]. but that night he had slept well his skin cooled his pulse become regular on Tuesday morn[g]. so that the D[r]. apprehended he might live some days still yet he was subject to such sudden turns that nothing coud be promised on him. Upon this I returned from Irvine where my Serv[t]. & horses were ready to go forward that I may preach another sabath at home determined to go ^again^ in the begin[g]. of the next week. I will be keeped at Glasgow perhaps for three weeks as the Worthy man has appointed me one of the Trustees for the Excecution of his will and only another acting one M[r]. Jardine.[16] I expect still to see him in Life on Mon[y].

Nell joins us all ^in^ grateful & affectionate wishes to her friends at Bewdley. She has received Miss Kenricks Packet & will write her when she gets a frank. L[d]. Eg[n]. is not at home.

Yours very sincerly
J. Wodrow

I shall remember your books when at Glasgow tho' every thing is in confusion & the search will not be easy. I was so fortunate as to see Lunardi's ascencion from St ^Andrews^ Church yard Glasgow Nov[r]. 23.[17] The spectacle was astonishing & affecting. The day most favourable. After a flight of near three hours he alighted six miles beyond Hawick[18] about sixty miles from Glasgow. If you write direct to <D[r]. L> at D[r]. Irvine's Glasgow.[19]

---

[16] George Jardine (1742–1827). See Letter 96; and *W-K*, I, p. 426.

[17] Vincenzo Lunardi (1754–1806), who followed and then overshadowed James Tytler's first successful flight by balloon in Edinburgh in August 1784 with his own flights in London in summer 1785 and then five spectacular flights in Scotland that autumn and winter. At least two of these flights were from Glasgow. Lunardi published *An Account of Five Aerial Voyages in Scotland in a Series of Letters to his Guardian, Chevalier Gerardo Compagni* (1786). The account of the first Glasgow flight on 23 Nov. from St Andrews Church-Yard includes extracts from the report in the *Glasgow Advertiser* for 28 Nov.: 'Many were amazingly affected. Some shed tears, and some fainted; while others insisted he was in compact with the Devil, and ought be looked upon as a man reprobated by the Almighty.' See also Paul Keen, 'The "Balloonomania": Science and Spectacle in 1780s England', *Eighteenth-Century Studies*, 39 (2006), pp. 507–35.

[18] Hawick, an ancient textile town in Roxburghshire, in the eastern Scottish Borders. It was a burgh of barony, whose population was estimated to be 2,320 at the time of the composition of its *Statistical Account* in 1793. OSA, VIII, p. 531.

[19] This paragraph is written on the left-side margin, from bottom to top, on the first page of the letter.

## Letter 107: Samuel Kenrick to James Wodrow, 1 December 1785

Place: Bewdley
Addressed: The Rev. James Wodrow / Irvine / Scotland
Postmarked: Bewdley December the First 1785
Franked: Free Westcote
Stamped: CARLISLE 302 / BEWDLEY

My Dear Friend

As my daughter has [page torn]red the inside of this packet w$^{th}$. entertaining her dear Nelly & Peggy, to its legal weight, I have only the envelope left me for you–

By Mess$^{rs}$. Hugh Watt & C$^{o}$'s. l$^{r}$. of the 22$^{nd}$. Ult$^{o}$. (to w$^{ch}$. please to tell them that Kenrick & Bennett will pay due attention) I find you were then gone to Glasgow to meet our dear Nell. I trust you found her in good health & spirits & [in] no respect worse for the visit she was so kind as to [m]ake us. You had another call too, (we were informed by the same channel,) of a more awful, I cannot call it melancholy, nature; to attend the last moments of that most excellent of men D$^{r}$. Leechman. In your last l$^{r}$. you dropt us some hints, in what he said to Miss Dunlop,[1] as if he thought his end was not far off– I mean his release from mortality, & his joyful entrance into an eternal state of bliss & happiness. When [you] have time I should be [page torn] to hear more from you on this most interesting subject to every thinking mind.

I am now reading Cicero de Senectate, a subject nearly akin to this in Melmoth's most elegant translation w$^{th}$. most instructive & entertaining notes– w$^{th}$. the original under my eye. I admire & love the author & revere the memory of honest old Cato.[2] M$^{r}$. Hutcheson inspired you & me w$^{th}$. this affectionate attachment, more than 40 years ago. I am reading also Ferguson's Roman History– w$^{ch}$. I like much.[3]

---

[1] See Letter 104.

[2] William Melmoth, the younger (c. 1710–99), was well respected for his Latin translations and commentaries. Cicero's essay, *Cato Maior de Senectute* was written in 44 BC, and Melmoth published a translation as *Cato; An Essay on Old-Age. By Marcus Tullius Cicero: With Remarks*, ed. William Melmoth (1773). SK was probably reading it as the first volume of *Cato and Laelius: Or, Essays on Old-Age and Friendship. By Marcus Tullius Cicero: With remarks by William Melmoth* (1785).

[3] *The History of the Progress and Termination of the Roman Republic* (Edinburgh, 1783), a three-volume work tracing the rise and fall of republican civic virtue, by Adam Ferguson (1723–1816), Scottish philosopher, historian, and army chaplain; educated at St Andrews and Edinburgh Universities. Born in Logierait, Perthshire, he grew up in the borderland between the Lowlands and Highlands and developed some familiarity with Gaelic. Fascinated by the martial spirit, Ferguson served as chaplain to the Black Watch regiment (1745–54). In 1759 he was appointed

We shall soon have that important History compleated to the middle of the 15th. Century by Gibbon, who has pitched upon Geneva, as a proper retirement to arrange his materials & finish the work.[4]

I have been interrupted by a gentleman just come from Windsor– who has been entertaining me w^th. a sketch of his Majesty's present plain mode of living. His ^annual^ houshold expences do not exceed £5000– in short is not more grand than a gentleman's of that income. He walks about unattended & only one footman behind his carriage. He hunts 3 days a week, with no more parade than any other gentleman & walks about the other 3 either in the town or neighbourhood, calling sans ceremonie at different houses or shops. He wears a close short wig & round hat, in a plain coat except the star.[5]– Seeing a lubberly[6] fellow one day standing centinel, he says to one of the young princes he was leading by the hand, shall we shoot that crow, pointing to one at no great distance. Yes says the child eagerly– but we have never a gun. Go says his Maj. & bring me the gun from that man who has it on his shoulder there. The child obeyd– & begged the soldier to let his papa have the gun for a moment. The other replied in a sur'ly manner, you shan't have it nor your father neither. The child was shocked & came whimpering back to his father with his complaint. Aye, Aye does he say so says the K– & search^g. his pocket, then here take this half crown to him.– He has turned his dear park, into a dairy field & the Q. makes cheese & butter.

You see I am driven to my last legs & have only room to repeat what you know already, that I & mine are most affectionately you & family's

S.K.

---

professor of natural philosophy at Edinburgh University, and subsequently of moral philosophy and pneumatics (1764–85). A leading figure in the Edinburgh literati, his major works included *An Essay on the History of Civil Society* (Edinburgh, 1767).

[4] Edward Gibbon returned to his beloved Lausanne, Switzerland, in late 1783, where he completed the last three volumes of his *Decline and Fall of the Roman Empire*, writing the last lines in his garden summer-house on 27 June 1787.

[5] While he was satirized as 'Farmer George', the king's 'domestication of the monarchy and his lack of ostentatious grandeur made a valuable contribution to a revival in the popularity of the monarchy'. Jeremy Black, *George III: America's Last King* (New Haven, CT, 2006), p. 148. See also Linda Colley, 'The Apotheosis of George III: Loyalty, Royalty and the British Nation 1760–1820', *Past and Present*, 102 (1984), pp. 94–129; G. M. Ditchfield, *George III: An Essay in Monarchy* (Houndmills, 2002). The star referred to here is the star of the Order of the Garter. See, for instance, Peter Edward Stroehling, 'King George III at Windsor Castle', oil on copper (1807), Royal Collection Trust, RCIN 404865.

[6] 'Lazy and bulky': Johnson's *Dictionary*.

## Letter 108: James Wodrow to Samuel Kenrick, 27 December 1785

Place: Stevenston
Addressed: M$^r$ Sam$^l$. Kenrick / Bewdly / Worcesters$^e$.
Postmarked: Irvine December twenty ninth 1785
Franked: E. Eglintoune
Stamped: FREE E/DE/30
Notes in SK's hand: 85 / answ$^d$. 22$^d$. Jan$^y$. 86

My Dear Freind,

Upon my return from Glasgow on Thurs$^y$. night, I found your short but acceptable Letter on the cover wrote nearly about the ^same^ time with my last to you,[1] which I hope you have received long ere now. In it I gave you (& you seem to have expected it from me by some strange presage) an account of the last illness of our much esteemed friend, till within a few days of his Death– which happened sooner than I expected. And I ^now^ regret that I was prevented by a flattering letter from D$^r$. Irvine from prosecuting my journey on the Wed$^y$ & being Wittness to the last moments of this great & good man. He recovered on the Thurs$^y$. to a degree that astonished the Physicians & his friends, conversed with them easily & chearfuly, & was thought better than he had been for many weeks. But this gleam of hope was soon extinguished by a sudden attack of his first Disease; not only on his extremities as formerly, but on his whole body, it convulsed his breast & face in a terrible manner; so that ^as^ the D$^r$. wrote he never dreamed he coud have got out of it. He did however recover it perfectly in an hour or two, seemed quite sensible & free of Pain tho' he spoke none but *yes* or *no* in answer to their questions: his countenance resumed it's wonted placid serenity & sensibility & even exhibited a higher degree of elevation of mind than ever it had done before: yet his eyes were shut for the most part, sometimes opened, but only to lift them up to heaven regardless of every thing around him, except M$^{rs}$. Leechman who repeated some of the passages of Scripture ^which^ he had often done before & a hymn that he was fond of. In this manner he continued thro the evening & night till between twelve & one on Sat$^y$. morn$^g$ he expired & this in so easy & insensible a way that they judged it might have happened a quarter of an hour before they observed it. May You & I & our good friend M$^r$. Wiggan have the like happy Death every the smallest circumstance about this Saint I doubt not will be interesting to You.

[1] Letters 106 and 107, both written on 1 Dec. 1785.

MS 24157 (108)

On Saturday, the 3d current, died the Reverend WILLIAM LEECHMAN, D.D. Principal of the College of Glasgow. He was born in the parish of Dolphington, in Lanarkshire, in the year 1706, ordained a minister of the gospel at Beith in 1736, elected Professor of Divinity by the University in 1743, and presented by the King to the office of Principal in 1761. In the several stations which he occupied, during a long, laborious, and useful life, he thought and acted with the liberality and candour which are inseparable from an enlightened and elevated mind. His learning, especially in Theology and Ethics, and in the sciences connected with them, was extensive: And his inquiries after valuable knowledge were prosecuted, with unremitting ardour, even in the last period of his life. His taste was elegant, and had been early formed by a diligent attention to the writings of the best Poets, Historians, and Philosophers of antiquity. Animated with the spirit of true and rational religion, and familiarly acquainted with its principles, he explained and enforced its doctrines and precepts, both in the theological chair, and in the pulpit, with a nervous and commanding eloquence. His publications were few, but they are generally known and admired, and will remain lasting monuments of a devout and benevolent heart, as well as of an enlarged and highly cultivated understanding. The numerous scholars trained up under his care, many of whom are at present an ornament to literature and religion, are the most honourable testimony to the utility of his labours. During the declining period of his life, when attacked by many bodily disorders, his soul, in the full possession of its faculties, retained its former vigour; and, rejoicing in the hopes presented by the gospel, rose above affliction with invincible magnanimity; and looked forward to the approaching day of dissolution, not merely with resignation, but with triumph. In the society over which he presided he was loved and revered. The loss which that seminary has sustained by the death of so eminent a person, whose unwearied study and constant delight it has been, for more than forty years, to promote its most valuable interests, will be long and sincerely regretted.

GLASGOW, December 8th, 1785.

7. Archibald Arthur's obituary for William Leechman, Glasgow, 8 December 1785, published in the *Caledonian Mercury*, 12 December 1785 (printed enclosure, Letter 108).

I got two Letters from D<sup>r</sup>. Irvine anouncing the Event & the resolutions about the funeral on Sat<sup>y</sup>. night. I preached <all day> on Sund<sup>y</sup>. & went on part of the way that night got to Glasgow on Mond<sup>y</sup>. by two & found M<sup>rs</sup>. Leechman behaving with all the composure & fortitude I expected she has indeed thro the whole of this Scene shown herself to be a Wife worthy of such a husband she was so thankful for the continuance of that comfortable elevated state of mind he was in to the very last; for her being enabled to ^do^ her duty to him on his deathbed; (having often figured something very bad had she dyed first) & for the long enjoyment she has of his company & friendship that she seems to forget her own loss. Nay she sometimes intimated that she thought it almost impious even to murmur & indulge wishes for his continuing longer in a state of pain & weakness here detained from the glorious state that was before him. Her ^favourite^ niece M<sup>rs</sup>. Ruat & her sister in law M<sup>rs</sup>. Balfour both of ^them^ sensible good women came to her that night with ^her^ Br. the Major.[2] I assisted with other friends in laying the Principal in his Coffin & had an inclination to have taken a last farewell look of him but was restrained by the apprehension that his countenance might be changed from the happy appearance it had at his Death. The funeral was on Wed<sup>y</sup>. The Company consisting of the Magistrates & Mini<sup>rs</sup>. of Glasgow & near 70 Gentl<sup>n</sup>. from the town & Country; assembled in the great hall next to the Prin<sup>ls</sup>. house. All the Colledge Servants were put into Mourn<sup>s</sup>. after a Glass or two of wine & a biscuit. The Company walked before the Corps[e] attended by nine or ten of his & her Relations & followed by the whole Colledge each class led by its respective Proff<sup>rs</sup>. to the Colledge churchyard where he was interred. The Procession was too long for the short length of street they had to walk, but by taking in the College area they made the most of it.

A character of him was put into the Glasgow and Ed<sup>r</sup>. news papers on Thurs<sup>y</sup>. drawn up by M<sup>r</sup>. Arthur.[3] The printer was desired to throw off twenty separate

---

[2] See Letter 96. Mrs Ruat, Mrs Balfour and the Major all seem to have been members of the large Balfour/Hamilton family, as were Mrs Leechman and Louisa Wodrow.

[3] Rev. Archibald Arthur (1744–97), a Renfrewshire farmer's son, was a Church of Scotland minister, Glasgow University librarian (1774–94), and later professor of moral philosophy. He was appointed assistant to Thomas Reid in 1780, whom he succeeded to the chair of moral philosophy in 1796 on Reid's death, having variously taught logic, botany, Latin, and church history, and having catalogued some 20,000 books of Glasgow University Library. He was one of the first members of the Royal Society of Edinburgh on its foundation in 1783. Coutts, *History of the University of Glasgow*, pp. 316–18, 327–28. See Letter 114. In fact, this tribute to Leechman, enclosed in this letter and reprinted here, dated 8 Dec. 1785, was published in the *Caledonian Mercury*, on Monday 12 Dec. 1785 rather than Thursday 22 Dec. as implied by JW here.

copies for friends, one of which I send you. I dare say you will admire it as modest simple & elegant & perfectly just. M^rs. Leech^n. had expressed a desire to some of the Faculty in consequence of which they intimated to me their own desire & hers, that I shoud preach the after^n. of the sab^th. following in their chapel a Sermon suited to the occasion. This she had done without giving me any intimation beforehand [blot] excuseable from her situation. I wished M^r. Arthur to have preached who had once some thoughts of doing it & I had on purpose ^to avoid it^ engaged myself at Cathcart, but he happened to be uncommonly hurried that week with the blackstone Examination[4] & a discourse promised to their literary Society.[5] And he grasped at the invitation given me & sent a preacher to Cathcart in my place. I had luckily brought a Sermon with me only with an intention to have read it as I afterwards did to M^rs. Leechman herself. This ^old action sermon^[6] I was obliged to shorten near a third tho' even then it much exceeded M^r. Wigans 25 minutes, & draw up a short ^& too^ hurried application suited to the recent Event. I delivered it in better spirits than I expected in their little chapel crowded beyond what it coud hold; for the curiosity & concern of the town was awakened. The Text was Amen! even so come Lord Jesus![7] And the purport of the

---

[4] An oral examination held in public by the Arts Faculty at the University of Glasgow, held in the autumn term to determine whether a student might progress to the next class (Latin in the first year was followed by Greek in the second year, logic in the third year, ethics in the fourth year, and natural philosophy in the final year). Coutts, *History of the University of Glasgow*, pp. 343–44.

[5] The Glasgow Literary Society, established in 1752, of which Arthur and Leechman were members, as were, at various times, scholars such as Robert and Andrew Foulis, John Anderson, Joseph Black, Adam Smith, Robert Simson, Thomas Reid, and David Hume. It met weekly on Friday evenings from November till May for the discussion of academic papers dealing with a wide range of scientific, philosophical, theological, and literary subjects, and it was one of the most important literary societies of the Scottish Enlightenment. Coutts, *History of the University of Glasgow*, pp. 216, 227, 316–17; Davis D. McElroy, *Scotland's Age of Improvement: A Survey of Eighteenth-Century Literary Clubs and Societies* ([Pullman], WA, [1969]), pp. 41–44; Ralph McLean, 'Professors, Merchants, and Ministers in the Clubs of Eighteenth-Century Glasgow', in Mark C. Wallace and Jane Rendall, eds, *Association and Enlightenment: Scottish Clubs and Societies, 1700–1830* (Lewisburg, PA, 2020), pp. 92–96; Richard B. Sher, 'Commerce, Religion and the Enlightenment', in Devine and Jackson, eds, *Glasgow, Volume 1*, pp. 335–37, 342; Emerson and Wood, 'Science and Enlightenment in Glasgow, 1690–1802', in *Science and Medicine in the Scottish Enlightenment*, pp. 101–04; Kathleen Holcomb, 'Thomas Reid in the Glasgow Literary Society', in Hook and Sher, eds, *Glasgow Enlightenment*, pp. 95–110. A typed transcript made in 1892 of the minutes of the Literary Society, 1764–79 is held in Glasgow University Archives and Special Collections, at GB 247 MS Murray 505, as is the original manuscript of the minutes 1790–1800, at GB 247 MS Gen 4/1. We are grateful to Zubin Meer for sharing his expertise in relation to these minutes.

[6] 'action sermon': the sermon preceding the celebration of the Lord's Supper. *DSL*.

[7] Revelation 22:21.

Discourse was to lead the Hearers ^from the Scripture^ to contemplate the 2ᵈ. Coming of X as an Object of delightful Desire and hope by calling their attention to some circumstances of it respecting JX himself that headᵍ. consisted cheifly in the Scripture contrast between his first & second coming.– To the circumstances & consequences of it respecting the world in general. <&> where some view was given of the grand purposes of providence from the New T. prophesies particulary the Visions of John the happy change on the state of the World previous to it, the scene closed & crowned by the coming of JX the Resurrection the General Judgment as an event most desireable to Mankind to have such a Judge appointed ^them^ who had given such proofs & pledges of his equity & mercy while in this World & the Issue of the judgement in the extermination of wickedness & misery from this part of the kingdom of God & the establishment of eternal order & felicity. The last object of contemplation was the consequences to the good Xian himself in the happiness of heaven the longest branch of the Sermon tho' I cannot abrige it <—> consisting cheifly in Illustrations of the previous passages of Johns visions ^views of it^ as a mansion in ^the^ house or universe of God filled for their reception under the immediate Govᵗ. of JX their sheperd & King a freedom from from Death & all the miseries of this world a state of bussiness & action a City or Co^m^munity consisting entirely of the wise & good in perfect order & placed in the most favourable circumstances for their endless improvement.

Shall I give you the conclusion which for want of time & leizure was not finished in point of Language & composition equaly with the Sermon & suffers by the Comparison of Mʳ. Arthurs more classical composition. Take it however as delivered "The subject of this Discourse will I apprehend be deemed seasonable after a late mournful Event, the Death of a worthy Member & Head of this Society, whose loss is deeply felt– not only by yourselves but by all the friends of Religion & Learning who were acquainted with him. You see the abundant consolation suggested by the Faith & hopes of the Gospel under this & such like distressing events. Some Testimony is due from this place to the distinguished Talents & Virtues of the deceased. These tho' veiled with an amiable modesty, were yet vigourously exerted on every proper Occasion which called them forth. They contributed for a considerable space of time to increase the rising reputation of this University,[8] & they have done eminent Service to the Church: particularly, by inspiring young minds with an Ardour for truth, cherishing a Spirit of Enquiry

---

[8] On Glasgow University in the eighteenth century, see the General Introduction in W-K, I, pp. 53–56.

after it, and diffusing rational & Liberal sentiments of Religion in this corner of the kingdom."

"But I mean not to enlarge on these & other parts of his usefulness & Worth. I speak to those who are no strangers to it. I shall only say further that those grand & delightful views of X$^{ty}$. which I have attempted to set before you in the Discourse were ever familiar to his thoughts: he felt the consolation & joy flowing from them, more perhaps than most men, in a stream that ran calm evenly & deep in his Soul, that gave a new spur to the native vigour & ardour of his mind in the pursuit of valuable knowledge, & the exertion of active virtue thro the whole course of his public & private Life. Especialy in the last the trying scene of Life– He felt the supporting power of the faith of the Gospel, he breathed the Spirit of it, even that <u>warm desire to do good, that setled meekness</u> & patience, that generous forgiveness of injuries received, and that serene fortitude which it inspires. He saw Death full before him; but he saw it disarmed of all its terrors, ready to introduce him into the presence of his God & his Saviour & into the midst of the glorious Community of enlightened & purifyed Spirits in the celestial World. He longed for this happy introduction: He waited for it in a state of mind humble, indeed, but calm, firm, elevated, and Triumphant."

"He has now my Xian Brethren finished his course; he has fought a good fight, He has kept the faith; henceforth there is laid up for him a Crown of righteousness which the Lord the righteous Judge will give ^to^ him at that day & not to him only but to all them also that love his appearance.[9] Do you as He did study to live under the faith and impression of this interesting event and hold yourselves in readiness for it by the vigourous and faithful Discharge of your duty in the very important stations in which providence has placed you. Do you as he did follow the direction of the heavenly wisdom of Jesus Christ, ask the succours of his Grace which will be made sufficient for you,[10] to assist you in every duty, support you under every tryal and guard you amidst all the temptations & dangers that are yet before you in the World. Yet a little while and this present passing scene will be over & issue in that glorious scene we have been speaking of– yet a little while & He who is to come will come & will not tarry.[11] He will come to receive you, & all the wise &

---

[9] 'I have fought a good fight, I have finished my course, I have kept the faith: Henceforth there is laid up for me a crown of righteousness, which the Lord, the righteous judge, shall give me at that day: and not to me only, but unto all them also that love his appearing.' 2 Timothy 4:7–8.

[10] 'And he said unto me, My grace is sufficient for thee: for my strength is made perfect in weakness.' 2 Corinthians 12:9.

[11] 'For yet a little while, and he that shall come will come, and will not tarry.' Hebrews 10:37.

good into that Mansion in the House of God all ready fitted up for your reception & where he is you shall be also.[12] Amen! <u>Even so come Lord</u> Jesus."[13]

The <—> marked expression about forgiveness of Injuries was applyed to the single Proff$^r$. who had experienced it[14] & it was lucky perhaps both for himself & me that he was not ^present^ sitting ^in^ the bench among the rest as undoubtedly it woud have drawn the eyes of the crowded Audience upon him. Yet be the consequence what it would I coud not think of supressing it, in a representation of the worthy mans deathbed behaviour. The Advices given them M$^{rs}$. Leech$^n$. said coincided with those he himself sent them by D$^r$. Findlay of the particulars of which I was ignorant of. I am sorry for the length of this Extract. I must shorten the rest of the letter.

The Prin$^l$. has thrown all his estate into the hands of five Trustees. M$^r$. Jardine & I are the only two who have ^no^ particular concern in it. M$^{rs}$. Leech$^n$. with M$^r$. Peerman[15] & M$^r$. Fergusson ^<->^ his Brother in Law[16] are the other three. We had sufficient bussiness the time I was in Glasg$^w$. as nothing coud be done without us but we have now appointed a Factor to act under direction & advertised the Sale of Achinairn.[17] Land sells high at present in this Country & I expect it will bring above £2000 perhaps £2500. Of this there will be a deduction of 100£ or 2 for a debt contracted in the Original purchase of the last part of the lands. M$^{rs}$. Leechman has an annuity of 75£ besides <&> £25 more from our Widows fund[18] <-> and also the Disposal of 200£ and all the furniture of both houses and at her Death[19] ^The estate^ is to be divided in diferent proportions among <—> ^his^ nearest Relations viz two families of Sisters child$^n$. These are all good people <-> to whom he was kind during his Life but never raised any of them above their

---

[12] 'In my Father's house are many mansions: if it were not so, I would have told you. I go to prepare a place for you.... that where I am, there ye may be also.' John 14:2–3.

[13] Revelation 22:21.

[14] i.e. John Anderson.

[15] William Pairman.

[16] Presumably the husband of one of Leechman's sisters mentioned by JW below.

[17] The Leechmans' small farm near Glasgow. See James Wodrow, 'The Life of Dr. Leechman, with some Account of his Lectures', in *Sermons, by William Leechman, D.D., Late Principal of the College of Glasgow. To which is prefixed some account of the author's life, and of his lectures, by James Wodrow, D.D., minister at Stevenston*, 2 vols (1789), I, p. 85.

[18] The Church of Scotland Ministers' and Scottish University Professors' Widows' Fund, which JW was personally involved in administering. See Richard Price to [James Wodrow], 20 Jan. 1790, in W. Bernard Peach and D. O. Thomas, eds, *The Correspondence of Richard Price*, 3 vols (Durham, NC and Cardiff, 1994), III, pp. 269–71; cf. ibid., I, p. 104 n. 1.

[19] Bridget Leechman, *née* Balfour, died in early Oct. 1792, reported by JW in Letter 179, 7 March 1793.

rank except his Nephew M[r]. Peerman. To him & his family he has appointed rather more than the rest & he has given ^him^ his Library or rather the remains of it for some years ago he made a most magnificent present of several hundred vol[s]. to the Theological Library especialy many vols of Pamplets now rare & before his Death he gave them also an interleafved English Bible <^two^ > 4[to]. vols <-> the white leaves marked with many references to the vol[s]. & pages of these books for the illustration of almost all the Difficult passages of the Scripture.[20]

His Manuscript papers he left to M[rs]. Leechman & she <-> a day or two before I left Glasgow <-> put them into my hands. I have not had time to examine & know the contents of this treasure which consists of five or six bundles put up by himself & marked in the outside with his own hand, they are cheifly Sermons, such as a bundle of those preached in the Colledge Chapel. Another entitled Sacramental Sermons. Another Sermons that may be used with a small change. A small bundle of Discourses delivered to the Literary Society.[21] These I have begun to read on General Subjects of learning & History many of them however connected with his own Profession. The particular bundles are put together without any order– few dates. And I am affraid there is nothing in the whole papers any way finished or fit for the public eye as he himself often told me–. Even the Sermons are incompleat any of them I have looked at mixed more or less with scraps of written paper loose or pinned to them– but I shall be able to give you a better Account of them some time hence.

Your friend M[r]. Ar[d]. Davidson Mins[r]. of Inchinnan[22] is fixed upon for Successor to the Prin[l]. a promise was given for the place to his Brother some years ago.

---

[20] Still held by Glasgow University Library. Leechman's Bible was printed in two volumes by Robert Freebairn in 1734. Sp Coll T.C.L. q86 and q87.

[21] The Minutes of the Glasgow Literary Society, 1764–79, show that Leechman delivered a discourse annually in mid-November, as the second most senior member after Robert Foulis, between 1764 and 1771. Four of these concerned education, two discussed aspects of David Hume's *History of England*, and one explored the life and character of the emperor Julian 'the apostat'. He also posed questions for discussion on eight occasions in this period: three on education, two on social improvement, one on civil liberty, and one on ancient Greek and Roman religion. There are no minutes extant for the years 1772, 1774, or 1775; Leechman was absent from the one meeting recorded in 1773, and he no longer seems to have been a member of the Society from 1776. Glasgow University Archives and Special Collections, GB 247 MS Murray 505.

[22] Rev. Archibald Davidson (c. 1732–1803), minister of Inchinnan, principal of Glasgow University from 1786 until his death in 1803. Coutts, *History of Glasgow University*, p. 338. His appointment as principal was announced in newspapers as far from Glasgow as the *Kentish Gazette* (29 Dec. 1785), the *Oxford and Bristol Post-Coach* (31 Dec. 1785), the *Norfolk Chronicle* (31 Dec. 1785), the *Sussex Advertiser* (2 Jan. 1786), and the *Chester Courant* (3 Jan. 1786), as well as in the

The Faculty applyed for another.[23] Anderson is still continuing his evil practises but they do no mischief. He prints a squib every week & encloses it ^in^ a letter to each of the Proff^rs^. put into the Posthouse sometimes at Ed^r^. & sometimes at Glasgow they often return them unopened. As a Specimen of his low scurilous wit I send you one of them[24] that was enclosed last week in Letters to all the Ladies of the Colledge even to M^rs^. Leechman among the rest relative to a little pickeering[25] that happened between a M^rs^. Robertson & M^rs^. Young wife to the Greek Proff^r^. The Nickname given ^him^ last year by Anderson in the sqibs he published in the News papers is Cockey Bung because his Father was a Cooper.[26] M^r^. Rose an English Gentleman is the Boarder not however of M^r^. Young but Ritchardson.[27] The Dialogue <of> ^is^ of his own Invention. I begin to think with you that his head is turned. I conjecture he has raised & spread prejudices against the College in England & Ireland. I saw a Letter among the Prin^ls^. papers ^dated^ Oct^r^. last from a M^r^. Simson[28] near Leeds desiring his name to be erased from the Matriculation Subscription in the 1766 &c, from a<-> ^false^ apprehension that he had at that time subscribed the Articles of the Ch of Scotland without knowing it. I beg you will contradict these groundless calumnies. So far from requiring subscription to Articles of faith from Students[29] that they are on a more Liberal

---

*Caledonian Mercury* (31 Dec. 1785). Emerson, *Academic Patronage in the Scottish Enlightenment*, pp. 183–84, confirms JW's assertion that Davidson's elder brother John had originally been promised the principalship (by Henry Dundas), and explains that John Davidson had become too frail for the position by 1785.

[23] Rev. Dr William Taylor. See Letter 98. He succeeded Davidson as principal in 1803.

[24] Not extant in the manuscript correspondence.

[25] 'Pickeering': 'Wordy, playful, or amorous skirmishing; wrangling, bickering, petty quarrelling; an instance of this'. OED.

[26] Professor John Young. See Letter 98. A good-humoured and popular lecturer, students nicknamed him 'Cocky Bung' because his father was a cooper in the city. Coopers make or repair barrels; and the cork stopper used to close a barrel's hole is called a bung. OED.

[27] Samuel Rose (1767–1804), lawyer, born at Chiswick, to Dr William Rose (1719–86) and Sarah *née* Clark (1730–1805). After beginning his education at his father's school in Chiswick, he studied at Glasgow University (1784–87), where he boarded with Professor William Richardson. He was friendly with Adam Smith and Henry Mackenzie in Edinburgh, but he was particularly close to the English poet William Cowper, after whom he named his second son. ODNB; Nangle, *Monthly Review*, p. 37.

[28] There is no Simson recorded as having matriculated in the 1760s or 1770s. Addison, *Matriculation Albums*.

[29] Professors, however, were obliged to subscribe the Westminster Confession, a condition protested by Leechman in 1744: Coutts, *History of the University of Glasgow*, p. 238; Mackie, *The University of Glasgow*, p. 133; William C. Lehmann, *John Millar of Glasgow* (Cambridge, 1960), p. 19; Roger Emerson, 'Politics and the Glasgow Professors, 1690–1800', in Hook and Sher, eds, *Glasgow Enlightenment*, p. 25; Nicholas Phillipson, *Adam Smith: An Enlightened Life* (2010), p. 31.

footing in this respect than any university in Britain being at Liberty from their constitution & having sometimes given Degrees for instance of D<sup>r</sup>. of Medicine to Papists.[30] Among the Proff<sup>rs</sup>. there is a diligence in teaching which you can scarce conceive their Holydays are abridged not a teaching ^hour^ is ommitted even from Want of health except they are in bed. & the Proff<sup>r</sup>. I lodged with Irvine was twice or thrice in his class when he ought to have been in his bed.[31] On the part of the Students I believe there is more sobriety attention & emulation than in most places. Prejudices have also been spread against them about the extravagant board in the Proff<sup>rs</sup>. Houses. I cannot state this exactly but it is no higher than usual. M<sup>r</sup>. Ritchardson told me he intended to write to you on this point and state the different boards accurately & give you at the same time every thing he coud recollect relative to the Prin<sup>l</sup>. I wish you woud send me a Copy or the substance of that ^last^ part of his Letter.

It was not in my power to make any search at Glasgow for the books D<sup>r</sup>. Priestly wants those that were in my Sisters house are all lying in confusion but are soon to be catalogued & I was busy almost every hour. I thank you for the entertainment afforded by your last Letters <u>& the two Pamplets</u> which I have read. As the Jockies[32]

---

[30] Carruthers and Kaur point out that the Roman Catholic priest and biblical scholar Alexander Geddes (see Letter 138 below) was given access to Glasgow University Library at Thomas Reid's behest. Young notes the high proportion of Ulster Presbyterians among the Glasgow student body in the later eighteenth century. Glasgow was clearly also a congenial university for those such as SK with liberal Dissenting tendencies. Carruthers and Kaur, 'Thomas Muir and Staff and Student Politics at the University of Glasgow', p. 99; Young, 'Thomas Muir and Glasgow', p. 118. Phillipson observes the paradox that in Glasgow, 'this most strictly Presbyterian of cities', the university 'became the intellectual powerhouse of a highly successful attempt by moderate Presbyterian professors to develop an alternative Presbyterian academic culture, which would be more in tune with the demands of a Whig regime and the polite manners demanded by a commercial age'. The Crown favoured the appointment of professors who would teach moderate over radical Presbyterianism. Phillipson, *Adam Smith*, p. 32; Roger Emerson, 'Politics and the Glasgow Professors', in Sher and Hook, eds, *Glasgow Enlightenment*, pp. 27, 30–33.

[31] i.e. JW lodged with William Irvine on various occasions, notably during Leechman's final illness; this cannot refer to JW's period as a student, since Irvine was younger than he. See Introduction, pp. 29–30 for Adam Smith's estimation in 1774 of the academic excellence and good management of the Scottish universities by contrast with others in Europe. He went on to acknowledge that formal visitations were the only way to cause them to keep improving, but only if both the visitors appointed, and the reforms they might propose, were known and wise. Adam Smith to William Cullen, 20 Sept. 1774, *The Correspondence of Adam Smith*, eds Ernest Campbell Mossner and Ian Simpson Ross, in *The Glasgow Edition of the Works and Correspondence of Adam Smith*, vol. 6 (Indianapolis, IN, 1987), pp. 173–74. See also Ronald Lyndsay Crawford, *Scotland and America in the Age of Paine: Ideas of Liberty and the Making of Four Americans* (Aberdeen, 2022), p. 193.

[32] 'Jockie': 'a vagrant or Gypsy'. *DSL*.

say It is no Match. Your friend and mine has too much superiority not only in point of argument but wit & talents. M[r]. Jesse will however carry it with the people and that will satisfy him. The controversy about moral preaching[33] is by no means over in Scotland tho' now only verbal. I will be glad to see the sequel of it. Sir Ad[m]. Ferg[n]. had seen the two automatons you describe at London & was astonished at the last. Is it true that Fordyce is diserted by his Parish & has given over preaching?[34] I will be obliged to ask two franks if I can get them as the Girls are writing & I will enclose this in a Copy of Dr. Magill's Proposals which are now published or circulated tho' not printed.[35] We have got near 150 subscribers at Glasgow & the invirons but will not be equaly successful in other places of the kingdom. My kindest Comp[s]. to M[rs]. & Miss Kenrick & to our Friend

most sincerely yours<br>J Wodrow

I have weighed the contents not above what will do for a single frank

Wed[y]. morn[g].

I thought to have enclosed the whole in M[r]. Magill's Proposals but it wont do. You will be obliged to take the trouble of copying them over & sending one or two ~~as~~ if you find it needful to a friend at a distance. I thank You for your extracts from Fordyce's book & will take an opportunity when I get it to read the whole tho' they do not please my tast as specimens of Devotion.[36] I hope to find something in that way among the Prin[ls]. papers. In one period of his Life even when he was

---

[33] JW perhaps refers to the difference of emphasis in Moderate and Popular Party preaching, the former tending to see moral reform as the purpose of doctrinal orthodoxy, and the latter emphasizing the saving work of Christ, with moral reform the consequence, but salvation the priority. See John R. McIntosh, *Church and Theology in Enlightenment Scotland: The Popular Party, 1740–1800* (East Linton, 1998), pp. 63–68; Thomas Ahnert, *The Moral Culture of the Scottish Enlightenment 1690–1805* (New Haven, CT, 2014), pp. 137–40.

[34] See Letter 105. James Fordyce, who had served as minister at the Presbyterian church in Monkwell Street, London (1760–82), had resigned the charge and retired at the end of 1782. He had been a highly popular Dissenting preacher, but he fell out of favour from the early 1770s, whether due to fashion, because of the effects of the bankruptcy of his brother Alexander, or because Fordyce's dispute with the second preacher at Monkwell Street split the congregation. Alan Ruston, 'James Fordyce (1720–1796)', ODNB.

[35] Presumably for printing M'Gill's *Practical Essay on the Death of Jesus Christ*, which was published in 1786.

[36] James Fordyce, *Addresses to the Deity* (1785). See Letter 105, n. 615.

Mins$^r$. of Beith[37] he took more pains in studying his Prayers than his Sermons so that his Excellence in that way, superiour to any other man I ever heard pray, tho' in a manner extempore when you & I heard him was yet the Effect of acquired habit. I wish much to have a Life of him composed either to be prefixed to a vol of Sermons if we can find two or three fit to be joined to a new edition of the rest or put into the Biographica Britanica.[38] Ritchardson read me a Life of D$^r$. Craig[39] intended for that Dictionary. But I must give over as I will weary myself & you. For a week past we have here all the severity of Winter. Adieu.

Printed enclosure:[40]

On Saturday, the 3d current, died the Reverend WILLIAM LEECHMAN, D.D. Principal of the College of Glasgow. He was born in the parish of Dolphington, in Lanarkshire, in the year 1706, ordained a minister of the gospel at Beith in 1736, elected Professor of Divinity by the University in 1743, and presented by the King to the office of Principal in 1761. In the several stations which he occupied, during a long, laborious, and useful life, he thought and acted with the liberality and candour which are inseparable from an enlightened and elevated mind. His learning, especially in Theology and Ethics, and in the sciences connected with them, was extensive: and his inquiries after valuable knowledge were prosecuted, with unremitting ardour, even in the last period of his life. His taste was elegant, and had been early formed by a diligent attention to the writings of the best Poets, Historians, and Philosophers of antiquity. Animated with the spirit of true and rational religion, and familiarly acquainted with its principles, he explained and enforced its doctrines and precepts, both in the theological chair, and in the pulpit, with a nervous and commanding eloquence. His publications were few, but they are generally known and admired, and will remain

---

[37] 1736–43, before his appointment to the Glasgow chair of divinity.

[38] A reference to the *Biographia Britannica*, edited by Rev. Andrew Kippis (1725–95). A biography of Leechman would not have appeared in it as it only reached the sixth volume, ending in 'Foster' in 1795, the year of Kippis's death, and his enterprise died with him.

[39] Dr William Craig (1709–84), friend of Leechman and minister of St Andrew's Church, Glasgow. William Richardson, 'Craig, William', in Andrew Kippis, ed., *Biographica Britannica: Or, the Lives of the Most Eminent Persons Who have Flourished in Great-Britain and Ireland, From the Earliest Ages, to the Present Times*, 5 vols, 2nd edn (1778–93), IV, pp. 414–18. A protégé of Francis Hutcheson, Craig was in 1743 a candidate for the chair of Divinity but withdrew in favour of his friend William Leechman. See *W-K*, I, p. 206, n. 7.

[40] It was this tribute by Archibald Arthur which was published on 12 Dec. 1785 in the *Caledonian Mercury*.

lasting monuments of a devout and benevolent heart, as well as of an enlarged and highly cultivated understanding. The numerous scholars trained up under his care, many of whom are at present an ornament to literature and religion, are the most honourable testimony to the utility of his labours. During the declining period of his life, when attacked by many bodily disorders, his soul, in the full possession of its faculties, retained its former vigour; and, rejoicing in the hopes presented by the gospel, rose above affliction with invincible magnanimity; and looked forward to the approaching day of dissolution, not merely with resignation, but with triumph. In the society over which he presided he was loved and revered. The loss which that seminary has sustained by the death of so eminent a person, whose unwearied study and constant delight it has been,[41] for more than forty years, to promote its valuable interests, will be long and sincerely regretted.

GLASGOW, December 8, 1785.

## Letter 109: James Wodrow to Samuel Kenrick, 9 January 1786.

Place: Stevenston
Addressed: Mr. Samuel Kenrick / Bewdley
Postmarked: Irvine January the tenth 1786
Franked: Cassillis
Stamped: Free E/JA/12
Note in SK's hand: Answ$^d$ 22 Jan. 1786.

My Dear Friend

Having unexpectedly got two franks sent me by L$^d$ Cassils <—> for the 10th. & 24th. of this month I write you a few lines were it for no more than to wish M$^{rs}$. & Miss Kenrick & you many happy returns of the Season. You are now two packets in our debt, the last sent about ten or twelve days ago directed by L$^d$. Eglinton containing several things that I thought you woud wish to know relative to the late worthy Principals Death &c. This was wrote after my return from Glasgow & I had wrote without a frank about the begin$^g$. of Dec$^r$.[1] Your Members of Parliament like ours will now soon hasten to London but let not that circumstance

---

[41] Corrected in ink in the right-hand margin to 'was', in JW's hand.

[1] A reference to JW's Letters 106 and 108. It appears he had not yet received SK's Letter 107 of 1 Dec. 1785—though he had by the time he wrote his next letter on 23 Jan. (Letter 111).

prevent your regular correspondence with us as it will not prevent our writing to you.²

We have been all ill of the Cold especialy Peggy who was so hoarse for a day or two that we coud not hear her speak but we are all better since the change of the weather a sudden change it was from the severest cold I have felt for several years to the mildness of spring or Summer.

I mentioned in my last that M^rs. Leechman had put into my Hands her Husband's literary Papers. I have not got half thro^g one of the smallest bundles entitled Discourses read at the Profess^rs. Club.³ It is doubtful to me whether they have ^been^ all read or only intended to be read some of them look like old Essays on Literary subjects that struck him. The best paper among them that I have yet perused is an Essay on Education or rather on the most proper & successful method of conducting it, contained in <one entitled> 3 Lectures the first wrote in 1766 & the two last in the 1769 each of the three as long or rather considerably longer than an ordinary Sermon.⁴ Nothing coud more be more proper ^than this^ to deliver to a Society of Colledge Masters and I conjecture from the time & date of it that they have actualy profited by some of the hints thrown out some of the Advices given & strongly supported in the Discourse, for ^the Masters of^ all the five public Classes especialy the three Philosophical ones⁵ have since that time made a great change in their manner of teaching by prescribing to the Students more Excercises & giving them more to do themselves, than is done I believe in any other Seminary in Britain.⁶

---

² In other words, they would not have ready access to franks as they did outside the parliamentary season.

³ The Glasgow Literary Society. See Letter 108.

⁴ According to the Minutes of the Glasgow Literary Society, 1764–79, Leechman delivered discourses on 15 Nov. 1765, on the subject of conducting education; on 17 Nov. 1769, on the proper method of cultivating human faculties, especially the moral faculty; and on 15 Nov. 1771, on moral education. University of Glasgow Archives and Special Collections, GB 247 MS Murray 205, Minutes, Literary Society in Glasgow College, 1764–79, pp. 14, 32, 39. He also opened discussions on whether it was wise to make young people study Greek and Latin for so long (8 May 1767), whether teaching different theories of morality actually made any difference to educating young minds in the practice of virtue (30 Dec. 1768), and whether there was any useful distinction between true and false learning (1 Nov. 1771). Ibid., pp. 23, 29, 39.

⁵ i.e. the professors of natural philosophy, logic, and moral philosophy.

⁶ See Wodrow, 'Life of Leechman', p. 29: 'The Professor gave a lecture of a full hour's length regularly four days every week, during a six months session; and besides this, spent an hour on Friday, and sometimes another on Saturday, in hearing the discourses composed by the students on particular texts or portions of Scripture prescribed to them. After these were delivered, he made his *observations* on each of them in a manner that showed the most accurate attention; commending with judgment, or censuring with delicacy. When a stronger censure was required, it was reserved to a private conference with the student.'

These Discourses on ^Educat^n.^ like all the others of D^r. Leechman are full of just & most ^important^ observations drawn from his knowledge of the human mind and of human Life, some of them new or at least illustrated in a new manner & little attended ^to^ by the generality of teachers; <and> ranged in a very proper order, expressed in ^a^ simple clear Nervuous[7] stile & the Composition of them tho' far from being such as it would have been if polished with his own hand & wrote twice or thrice ^over^ yet with all ^his^ little peculiarities of stile It is obvious to observe &c &c,[8] it is such as I believe woud bear the eye of the public as a posthumous work, & in my apprehension woud be most a useful Publication.

After a short introduction relative to the importance of the Subject & discussing, the Question what is the end of Education to form a young mind not <—> merely to be a citizen but to be a Man– a rational and moral creature– He proceeds to enquire into the best means of cultivating his rational & moral powers. 1st watching & marking the original Discriminations in Genius & Dispos^it^ion prior to all education & assisting them or checking them if faulty. Then he lays down the Capital rule, of which all others are only the particular Application, viz. "to observe the natural progress of the young mind & adapt all instructions & assistances to the natural stages of this progression". The natural progress ^of the mind he states^ 1st. the Notices of the senses 2^ly. the powers of Immagination begin to unfold themselves 3^ly. the intellectual & moral powers begin to opperate in a more extensive & vigorous manner than in the prior stages of Life. He drops the 2 first entirely ^& takes up the cultivation of the^ <The> intellectual powers in what remains of the first Discourse and of the Moral powers in the two subsequent Discourses, in other words the most proper & successful method of forming a young mind to the sense and practise of Virtue; & supposes these two branches of Education carried on together.

I cannot descend into a detail on either of these branches. The first is levelled cheifly against the common fault of Education storing and stuffing the mind with knowledge before it can clearly comprehend it & properly exert its own judgment ^upon it^.– He considers the mind as passive in receiving knowledge & active in comparing & judging & "Education as nothing else than placing the Materials for thinking before the mind on which its intellectual powers may freely go to work; & perhaps furnishing it with some proper scaffolding by the

---

[7] 'Nervous': 'Well-strung; strong; vigorous'. Johnson's *Dictionary*.
[8] These words are underlined in the original, and seem to be intended as a quotation of Leechman's characteristic style.

help of which it may raise itself on some Occasions. It is thus the mind may be led thro' its several stages of natural progression in such a gradual <u>manner</u> that by the <u>exertions</u> of its own native energy it <~~may~~> will form & instruct itself." He <u>wishes of his</u> Pupil to form the Man of judgment & not the man of mere Erudition to form Talents for Original Composition, & not such compositions as are drawn from the storehouse of Memory & express only the thoughts of Others.

I cannot enter upon the Other branches which takes up the 2$^d$. & 3$^d$. Lectures the means of guarding a young mind from vice, & forming it to the love and practise of virtue; the cautions & corrections of the common methods, the rules, directions, means & motives he suggests are so various. He <u>warms</u> upon this part of the Subject which you know was his fort[e] & every thing He throws out is just, & ^highly^ important.

I have read two Discourses relative to the Jews.[9] One on their national Character with an intention to vindicate <—> ^it^ from the contempt thrown on it by the greek & Roman writers to account for this, from their ignorance & prejudices as to this singular people. It is learned, in the usual sense of the word, full of citations from the Classicks relative to the Jews. I did not think it possible to collect such a number of them, & the National Char$^r$. of the people rather in my judgement carried too high. The other is On the Grandeur of the Hebrew Nation in its most flourishing times compared with the other Nations of the World in the same Age. This is a very sensible ^curious^ well composed Discourse founded cheifly on Scripture. It has no coincidence with the other.

I have perused also, An Enquiry into the Origin of the Heathen Mysteries.[10] Curious & ingenious, at least it appeared so to me, who had read ^nothing^ very particular on the Subject. ^It^ refutes the Oppinion of Warburton & others, that just notions of the true God the origin of the Universe &c. we^re^ there^by^ communicated to the initiated.[11] Shows at least <—> ^<—>^ very probable. Arguments

---

[9] Not noted in the Society's minutes for 1764–79, so Leechman may have delivered these between 1752 and 1763, or between 1772 and 1775. On Protestant philosemitism, see Todd M. Endelman, *The Jews of Georgian England, 1714–1830: Tradition and Change in a Liberal Society* (Ann Arbor, MI, 1999), pp. 50–85; and more generally Gertrude Himmelfarb, *The People of the Book: Philosemitism in England, from Cromwell to Churchill* (2011).

[10] Also not noted in the Society's minutes for 1764–79, so presumably read in another year.

[11] Rev. William Warburton (1698–1779) *The Divine Legation of Moses Demonstrated* (1738–41). Warburton was a fierce religious controversialist and became bishop of Gloucester in 1760. See Robert G. Ingram, 'William Warburton, Divine Action, and Enlightened Christianity', in William Gibson and Robert G. Ingram, eds, *Religious Identities in Britain, 1660–1832* (Aldershot, 2005), pp. 97–118.

that the knowledge of them ^the Mysteries^ or the rites practiced in them, were conceald from the Vulgar for a Contrary purpose, because these rites were disgraceful to Paganism in enlightened ages & Countries not ^so much merely^ on account of their impurity but because, however agreable to the last of the rude & barbarous ages in which they were first introduced, they woud have exposed ^even^ to the ^contempt of the^ Vulgar in after ages, the history & human origin of the Gods in whose Honour, they were celebrated.

Also another essay on the Importance of Moral Philosophy among the Sciences & in After Life which probably might be an introductory Lecture– when he taught that Class the begin$^g$. of a Session[12] the last of them I have read is a Discourse at the Club[13] "Considerations on the Principles of Human knowledge according to some Philosophers [Hume &c.] with a view to the influence ^which^ the embracing these principles may have on young Minds" leveled against Metaphysical Disquisitions & their tendency to lead to Scepticism, showing that as the judgments of other men are often a dupe to their immaginations or their Passions; so the Judgements of these Philosophers are Dupe to their own Subtilety.

There are as many more Discourses or Essays in that Bundle. One On the Life & Character of Julian.[14] Several that seem to have been occasioned by his reading Humes History;[15] controverting the Ideas & reasonings of that Historian but I have not looked into them.[16] You see something of the way in which our Worthy friend spent his time after he was made Prin$^l$. besides much Occasional preaching in the Chapel for D$^r$. Craig[17] &c. He begun a Theological Lecture to the Stud$^s$. of Divinity on the Sund$^y$. nights & continued it a great part of a Session but Trail[18] was so hurt & fretted with it, that he gave it up, which he ought not to have done.

---

[12] Leechman contributed to the teaching of moral philosophy at Glasgow between Thomas Craigie's leave of absence on grounds of ill-health in April 1751 and April 1752, when Adam Smith was appointed to that chair following Craigie's death at Lisbon on 27 Nov. 1751. Coutts, *History of the University of Glasgow*, pp. 220–21.

[13] This was read at the Glasgow Literary Society on 21 Nov. 1766. Minutes, Literary Society in Glasgow College, 1764–79, p. 19.

[14] Flavius Claudius Julianus (332–63), Roman emperor Julian (r. 361–63), nephew of Constantine the Great. Otherwise known as 'Julian the Apostate', a philosopher who tried to reestablish paganism as the official imperial religion. Leechman read this paper at the Glasgow Literary Society on 25 Nov. 1768. Minutes, Literary Society in Glasgow College, 1764–79, p. 28.

[15] David Hume, *The History of England from the Invasion of Julius Caesar to the Revolution in 1688*, 6 vols (1754–61).

[16] 16 Nov. 1764, 20 Nov. 1767. Minutes, Literary Society in Glasgow College, 1764–79, pp. 10, 24.

[17] See Letter 108.

[18] Rev. Dr Robert Trail (1720–75), professor of ecclesiastical history at the University of Glasgow, and a key ally of Leechman's during the trouble caused by Professor John Anderson. Coutts, *History of the University of Glasgow*, pp. 228, 240, 272–73, 286, 325.

We have given up all political & other inteligence, what think you of our Taxes?[19] of our Situation with respect to Ireland[20] & to the Schemes of the Other nations of Europe?[21] I have another letter to write to night interesting to the peace of a family so I must bid you

Adieu

J. Wodrow

## Letter 110: Samuel Kenrick to James Wodrow, 21 January, 2 March 1786

Place: Bewdley
Addressed: Rev[d]. James Wodrow / Irvine / Scotland
Postmarked: Stourbridge January the Twenty third 1786
Franked: Free Westcote
Stamped: CARLISLE / STOURBRIDGE

I have been made unspeakably happy w[th]. all my worthy & dear Friends pacquets– viz 1st. & 29th. Dec[r]. & 10th. Jan[y].[1]– w[ch]. have thrown me so far in

---

[19] William Pitt the Younger, First Lord of the Treasury as well as prime minister, was engaged in trying to reduce the national debt in the 1780s. As well as attempting to increase the efficiency of gathering existing taxes, he imposed duties on new objects including, in 1785, post horses (which will have interested JW and SK), retail shops (the most unpopular of these new taxes, repealed in 1789), gloves, employers of female servants, pawnbrokers' licences, gundogs and sporting guns, attorneys, the servants of bachelors, coachmakers' licences, and new carriages. John Ehrman, *The Younger Pitt: The Years of Acclaim* (1969), p. 250.

[20] The Pitt administration's Irish Propositions, seeking to regulate commercial, defence, and constitutional relations between Britain and Ireland in the new era of Irish legislative independence, had passed the Westminster Parliament in July 1785 but were defeated in Dublin in August because of objections to the proposals not having to do with trade. This failure substantially coloured Pitt's view of the Anglo-Irish relationship. Ehrman, *Younger Pitt: The Years of Acclaim*, p. 211; Thomas Bartlett, 'Ireland: From Legislative Independence to Legislative Union, 1782–1800', in H. T. Dickinson and Michael Lynch, eds, *The Challenge to Westminster: Sovereignty, Devolution and Independence* (East Linton, 2000), pp. 64–66.

[21] In 1785 the Pitt government had attempted to restore amity between itself and various European powers after the American war, which resulted eventually in a commercial treaty between itself and France in 1786 and, later still, in the Triple Alliance in 1788 with Prussia and the Dutch Republic, but which, in the early days of 1786, had only produced 'Isolation and irritation', as Black puts it. Jeremy Black, *British Foreign Policy in an Age of Revolutions, 1783–1793* (Cambridge, 1994), p. 97; Anthony Page, *Britain and the Seventy Years War, 1774–1815: Enlightenment, Revolution and Empire* (2015), pp. 40–42.

---

[1] Letters 106, 108, and 109, dated by their postmarks.

arrears, that like other poor debtors I am beginning almost to grow averse to undertake the discharge of them.– And yet how pleasing is the task when I once sit down to it– could I but secure undisturbed one hour or two to myself!

I will begin w$^{th}$. the first, w$^{ch}$. announces us the good news of Miss Wodrow's safe arrival at her dear home after so many tedious delays. We are happy to find that you & M$^{rs}$. Wodrow do not think her journey was thrown away: w$^{ch}$. gives us hopes that she may soon again favour her Bewdley friends with another visit. She has left a great blank at our little fireside this winter– where she knows we were all so much at home: w$^{ch}$. she seemed to enjoy as much as we did. She has not however a little contributed to make up the loss by her easy entertaining letters since she left us. There is so much good humour, good sense & good nature in her observations & descriptions, w$^{ch}$. cannot fail to please, & must make her a most agreeable correspondent. I say thus much to encourage her to persist in it as it will be an agreeable amusement to herself & be a valuable fund of entertainment to her absent friends. Nor am I unmindful of the merit of her chearful sister: but I must reserve what I could say about it 'till we are better acquainted w$^{ch}$. I hope will be soon.

The many interesting particulars you have been so kind to favour me w$^{th}$., ^even^ in this first letter, respecting the last moments of that most excellent man D$^r$. Leechman, I have read over & over with increasing pleasure. What a consolation, amidst his bodily pains & sufferings, to be surrounded w$^{th}$. so many & such friends! & above all to have the wife of his bosom, w$^{th}$. whom he had lived so many ^happy^ years, always near him! & that her tender affection & strength of mind should enable her delicate frame of body to go through so much fatigue! What comfort & satisfaction must it now give to her heart, to recollect the numberless little aids she was able to afford him! But above all how joyful must the prospect be of soon meeting again with this best of friends never more to part! He has shown himself ^in this trying scene^, as you justly observe, as dignified & venerable as his best friends could wish. What a truly manly & Christian spirit was he possessed of to send for Prof$^r$. Anderson, & giveng him his forgiveness! How solemn, how tender, how endearing must his parting addresses have been, to the different characters to whom they were made– where his humble friends, his servants were not forgot– & what I am sure they will with pleasure remember as long as they live.

I am happy to find that the invalluable treasure of his papers are fallen into such hands as yours, whose soul seems to be so congenial with his, & who had the happiness of living from your earliest youth in the strictest habits of friendship and intimacy.– After congratulating you on the pleasure of seeing Lunardi's ascension– in w$^{ch}$. you have got the start of me, owing to the shortness of my sight. For you must know that one of these aeronauts passed near this town when Miss Wodrow was here, & was clearly discerned by her & many more. But that must be far short of the pleasure of seeing him begin his flight– I say, I come now to your 2nd l$^t$. of the 29 ult$^o$.[2] w$^{ch}$. is a most valuable repository of various articles.

But here I have neither time nor room to specify to you half of what I could wish. Besides to tell you the truth my dear friend I am overwhelmed w$^{th}$. joy & pleasure in perusing the several particulars, & above all w$^{th}$. the just character you have drawn of this best of men,[3] that I can only thank you ten thousand times for it. I agree with you that M$^r$. Arthur's sketch is neat and elegant!– But pray who is M$^r$. Arthur?[4]– but your's is much fuller, warmer & more compleat. I much admire your spirit in setting forth in the strongest colours that leading Xtian virtue– forgiveness of injuries– w$^{ch}$. was so well exemplified in this eminent character. Poor Anderson how pitiable must his case be thus to shun the light & the day– & to love darkness rather &c.[5]

I do not find that you mention his Theological lectures, namely those in composition & on the Evidences of Christianity of w$^{ch}$. you & I & many more ~~of~~ ^scribbled^ transcripts. I should imagine that these having been so often delivered ex cathedra (as D$^r$. Horsley[6] says) must be in a pretty correct state.

It gives me great pleasure to hear M$^{rs}$. Leechman is so comfortably provided for: & that after her, his fortune is to be fairly divided among his relations.

It surprized me not a little to see Davidson appointed his successor. The Faculty, I presume, applied for a very different person– the same whom I expected & long wished to see in that important station.

2$^d$ March

You have given me such a sovereign contempt & disgust at Anderson that I wish never more to think or say a word of him. I thank you for the Baloon Squib– w$^{ch}$. is to be sure the lowest & most malicious scurrility. ^I see no fun in it.^

---

[2] Ultimo—i.e. reference to last month.
[3] i.e. Professor William Leechman.
[4] Archibald Arthur: see Letters 108 and 114. It appears that SK had forgotten about him, as he mentions Arthur in Letter 61, 2 April 1778, W-K, I, p. 410.
[5] John 3:19–20: 'And this is the condemnation, that light is come into the world, and men loved darkness rather than light, because their deeds were evil. For every one that doeth evil hateth the light, neither cometh to the light, lest his deeds should be reproved.'
[6] Samuel Horsley, archdeacon of St Albans at this stage in his career.

But to spread groundless reports, against the university of w^ch. he is himself a member– is without example. As to M^r. Simpson's charge I could have contradicted it;[7] for I knew the contrary to be fact from my own Father, when he took me to Glasgow above 40 years ago, who told me then, in the true spirit of a Dissenter, that they imposed no shackles of any sort on young minds, or if they had no son of his should ever go near them.[8] But the expence, I must own, has given me pain, as it put it out of my power to serve the interests of learning & of my venerable alma mater as I could wish. The very plan M^r. Richardson[9] sent me, appeared too high here. I believe I signified it to himself. By what you say, I hope he has not forgot it: & when he has time that he will give me a fair state of the matter: whatever he favours me w^th. respecting our late worthy friend & instructor, you may depend upon my sending you. I wish you could prevail upon him, jointly w^th. your self, ^to write his life^, for this reason that none can do it better– & few could do it w^th. more pleasure. I join w^th. you in wishing to see it done in either of the ways you mention: either prefixed to a volume of discourses, or prepared for the Biographia.[10] If it could be easier done in the former manner, it would soon find its way afterwards into the latter: & hand down his name & character, in company with so many Worthies, to the latest posterity.– You gave me reason to expect to meet with some devotional pieces, among his papers. If you do I should be glad to hear of what sort they are. He certainly had acquired a most powerful talent in this way, ^I mean extempore prayer^– far superior indeed to any I have ever heard.

---

[7] See Letter 108. The charges were that Glasgow students were required to sign a statement at matriculation that somehow tricked them into subscribing to the 'Articles of [Faith] of the Church of Scotland', presumably the 1647 Westminster Confession of Faith; that Glasgow professors were less than diligent in their teaching; and that they charged unreasonably high rates for the bed and board with which they provided their students. Professor William Richardson had sent SK a tariff of their rates in an attempt to disprove the last of these.

[8] SK's father John Kenrick was educated at Attercliffe Dissenting Academy in Sheffield (1702–04) so one may surmise that he did not have to subscribe to any articles of faith. The most important academy of the mid-century was Philip Doddridge's Northampton Academy (1729–51), which, after his death, continued at Daventry (1751–98). It was known for its liberal teaching and rejection of subscription for its students, amongst whom, in its Daventry phase, was the young Joseph Priestley who would have refused to subscribe to any subscription test for entry. It remains true, however, that some academies did have a subscription test, usually Calvinistic, and sometimes demanded a personal testimony of faith. Martin Fitzpatrick, 'Dissenting Academies', in Anthony Grayling, Andrew Pyle, and Naomi Goulder, eds, *The Continuum Encyclopedia of British Philosophy* (2006), II, pp. 862–64; see also Schofield, *The Enlightenment of Joseph Priestley*, pp. 32–36.

[9] See Letter 80.

[10] A reference to the *Biographia Britannica*, edited by Rev. Andrew Kippis (1725–95).

As to Fordyce's Addresses,[11] they seem to me to be a sort of poetical effusions, in the style of Harvey,[12] & composed on particular occasions. We have some of his actual prayers taken down in short hand from his mouth, & three sacramental exhortations– where tho' the language is flowery as all his compositions are, yet there runs thro' them a scriptural phraseology, & familiar devotional language very different from the Addresses.– It is certain he has resigned his charge, but upon what grounds, I cannot exactly say– It only appears from part of his farewell ~~address~~ ^sermon^ to the congregation; that some difference had arisen between him & some of his young friends– of whom he once thought well, but whom now alas! he wishes to forget; may he that of the very stones could raise up children to Abraham, create in them clean hearts & renew right spirits within them.[13] But he there mentions his declining health, as the cause of his resigning his public ministry. Upon the whole there seems to run a vein of melancholy thro' all his devotional pieces, w$^{ch}$. indicate a mind depressed with severe tryals.

I shall take care of D$^r$. M$^c$Gill's Proposals[14] & do all in my power to encourage the publication. When I have any thing worth sending you on that head, you may expect the first notice of it.

I am now come to your 3$^d$ fav$^r$. of the 9th. inst.– w$^{ch}$. I am obliged to my old school-fellow Lord Cassilis[15] for giving a helping hand to. ~~it~~ For form's sake, I must begin w$^{th}$. the compliments of the season to you & yours & that you may long enjoy many, many happy returns of the same– is the sincere wish of me & mine.

As to franks & members of Parliament, they are all good things in their way– but never let their names be mentioned, when the least part of friendly intercourse is in question.

We have experienced the same sudden change in the atmosphere that you did– & had the same repeated, within these 3 or 4 days, by a most severe frost w$^{ch}$. is now going off in the gentlest thaw.

I give you joy on the opening of your valuable budget.[16] The discourses on Education, of w$^{ch}$. you have given me the analysis seem to be most seasonable at

---

[11] James Fordyce, *Addresses to the Deity* (1785). See Letter 105.

[12] James Hervey (1714–58), an Evangelical Church of England clergyman whose *Meditations and Contemplations*, 2 vols (1746–47), were composed to appeal to a wealthy audience to attract them to the gospel, and had been written in a style execrated by the young JW. See W-K, I, Letter 2.

[13] Matthew 3:9; Psalm 51:10.

[14] See Letter 108.

[15] This must refer to Glasgow University rather than a school: Cassillis was educated there between 1742 and 1744, though Kenrick's attendance ran from 1745 till 1747.

[16] 'A bag, such as may be easily carried'. Johnson's *Dictionary*. This must refer to the bundle of papers given to JW by Mrs Leechman.

this time: & I make no doubt, it would be well received by the public.[17] Witness Knox's treatise on the initiatory part of it[18]– what a run has it already had– 5 or 6 editions within a few months! The other two discourses on the Jews, must be curious, from the new light w^ch. he throws on every subject he handles. His enquiry into the heathen Mysteries seems to be equally curious. It seems to coincide, with Geddes' opinion, whose book on the Composition of the Ancients,[19] was printed by Foulis,[20] as you may well remember & the author was said to have been a pupil of the late Principal.– His attack on Warburton who was ~~then~~ at the zenith of his glory, was thought at that time very bold.[21] In short how must your curiosity be gratified for years to come– considering the numberless avocations & interruptions your connections & station must make you liable to– in having this treasure at any leisure hour, to resort to: w^ch. I know you will be so kind, meanwhile, as to share with your friends & perhaps in a future day, communicate some of them to the world at large.

M^r. Jesse's 17 l^rs. are come out[22] & shall be sent you w^th. M^r. Wigan's answer.[23] The latter is in London, we suppose getting it printed.

As to politics I never trouble my head about them. I was once as strenuous for the liberty and independency of Ireland as of America. But now I think no more about it. I go little out; or if I did, I have nobody to dispute with. I & my friends are all of one mind. I look upon the stocks as the barometer of the state: when they are high, as at present, I flatter myself everything goes on well! Tis true we have

---

[17] In this paragraph SK comments on the Leechman manuscripts that JW described in the previous letter (109).

[18] Vicesimus Knox (1752–1821), priest and writer who graduated from St John's College, Oxford, in 1771 and succeeded his father as headmaster of Tonbridge School, Kent, in 1778. Published in 1781, his *Liberal Education: or a Practical Treatise on the Methods of Acquiring Useful Knowledge and Polite Learning* had gone into seven editions, and two volumes by 1785.

[19] James Geddes, *An Essay on the Composition and Manner of Writing of the Antients, Particularly Plato* (Glasgow, 1748). James Geddes (1710–45), after being privately tutored by William Leechman, attended the University of Edinburgh and worked as a lawyer. After Geddes died of consumption, Leechman edited and published the *Essay*. According to JW, the book 'deserves to be better known', as 'that young gentleman ventured to attack Warburton, then in the zenith of his glory, and to expose some of his fanciful opinions respecting Plato, by many just criticisms, mixed with a pleasant vein of good humour'. Wodrow, 'Account of the Author's Life', in Leechman, *Sermons*, I, pp. 4–6, 71.

[20] The Foulis press were the printers to the University of Glasgow, established by the brothers Andrew Foulis, the elder (d. 1775) and Robert Foulis (1707–76). See I, especially pp. 113, 379 n. 26–27.

[21] See Letter 109.

[22] William Jesse, *Parochialia*. See Letter 100.

[23] See Letter 115.

many complaints about the weight of taxes &c. but where people are frugal & industrious they live as comfortably as ever they did.

The only new thing I have seen lately is Dr. Priestley's Edition ^& abridgement^ of Dr. Hartley's Theory of the ^Human^ Mind published in 1775.[24]

I remember the original work when it came first out made a great noise ^in England on account of^ <―――> the novel ^or rather unpopular^ doctrine of the finite duration of future punishments w$^{ch}$. it inculcated, & that of necessity. I remember too how angry I was since w$^{th}$. D$^r$. P. for his harsh treatment of D$^r$. Reid, in his rude [page torn] on your 3 Co[mmon sense D]octors,[25] merely for [not] having seen or read this book. At present [I c]annot help being surprized that a work [of t]his sort should be so little known.

The first hint was suggested by Sir Isaac [New]ton in his Principia & Optics[26]– & has been [page torn]ed by this ingenious author in the most can[did] diligent experimental manner– so different [from] the flimsy cobweb metaphysics of the [page torn]ols– that I should imagine there was nothing [page torn] but attention [to make] the whole as [page torn] conclusive as the [page torn]nts of Euclid.

At the same time I must confess my great difficulty to arise from want of those habits of abstraction w$^{ch}$. are familiar to you– & therefore I could wish you could see it.

Adieu my dear Friend w$^{th}$. compliments &c to you & yours
S.K.

---

[24] Joseph Priestley, *Hartley's Theory of the Human Mind, on the Principle of the Association of Ideas; With Essays Relating to the Subject of It* (1775). David Hartley (bap. 1705, d. 1757), philosopher and physician. His *Observations on Man, His Frame, His Duties, and His Expectations* (1749) was a key influence on Priestley, second only to the Bible. His abridged version popularized Hartley's associationist psychology, which exerted a profound influence on British thought in the late eighteenth century and remains significant to this day. See Richard C. Allen, *David Hartley on Human Nature* (New York, 1999); and Schofield, *The Enlightened Joseph Priestley*, pp. 51–57.

[25] The reference is to Priestley's *An Examination of Dr Reid's Inquiry into the Human Mind on the Principles of Common Sense, Dr Beattie's Essay on the Nature and Immutability of Truth, and Dr Oswald's Appeal to Common Sense in Behalf of Religion* (1775). See the end of Letter 72 where SK observed that Priestley had 'brandished his tawmahawk against the celebrated Oswald, Reid & Beattie'. W-K, I, p. 495.

[26] Sir Isaac Newton (1642–1727), natural philosopher and mathematician. SK refers to his *Philosophiae Naturalis Principia Mathematica* (1687); Newton, *Opticks: Or, A Treatise of the Reflexions, Refractions, Inflexions and Colours of Light* (1704).

## Letter 111: James Wodrow to Samuel Kenrick, 23 January 1786
Place: Stevenston

I am much affraid My good Friend that some Packet from Bewdley has been lost by the carelessness or criminal curiosity of some Postmaster or Mistress. You know what happened not long ago,[1] & our good Scots Proverb ^says^ "burn't bairns dread the fire". The fact is We have not had a Scrap of a pen from your friendly habitation since the frank of Dec[r]. first & this is the fourth Letter I have wrote ^to you^ since that time, including the one as an Irishman woud say, which was wrote a day or two before[2] <-> the receipt of which however (for there is always some good sense at the bottom or as the foundation of their foolish Bulls) you have never acknowledged.

Having a frank by me I write a short Epistle & have desired Nell to write also, warning you before hand that there will be nothing much worth your Notice in either of our Letters & this indeed is my fault for I might go on with some Account of the other Papers of the wise & Worthy Princ[l]. which I have been reading last week which I know will always be agreable to you & yet it is not my fault because I have not time just now from the Arival of my Nephew[3] after a years absence as well as other Company in the House yet having started the subject it will be great pity to dissapoint you altogether with the Materials at hand.

The next Essay (to continue the tract of my Letter about a fortnight ago). The next Essay which pleased me most was "On the spirit of Popery and Protestantism and its Effects on Literature Liberty and other great interests of human Society". It is exceeding short not above 4 Qu[a]rto leaves small paper. I only transcribe his stricture on a single Passage from David ^Humes^ History which seems to have led his thoughts to the Subject. "From the Admiration of ancient Literature (says M[r]. Hume) from the Enquiry after new discoveries; the minds of the Studious were every where turned, to Polemical Science, and in all Schools & Accademies, the furious controversies of Theology took place of the calm disquisitions of Learning".[4] It is not necessary (says the Prin[l].) "to enter into an examination of all

---

[1] SK expressed frustration in 1782 that a 'malignant fiend' in the post office must have 'intercepted' two packets he had sent to JW. Letter 76, 6 Dec. 1782, W-K, I, pp. 474–76.

[2] i.e. Letters 106, 108, 109, and 111.

[3] Unidentified. Possibly the same mentioned in Letter 104, but possibly not, given the number of LW's relatives.

[4] David Hume, *The History of Great Britain, Volume I: Containing the Reigns of James I and Charles I* (Edinburgh, 1754), p. 26. See John Seed, *Dissenting Histories: Religious Division and the Politics of Memory in Eighteenth-Century England* (Edinburgh, 2008), p. 77 and chapter 3 in general.

these contemptuous stroaks: what the important Disquisitions of Philos^y^. & what the new Discoveries were, in which the Schools & Accademies were intently & calmly employed, ought to have ^been^ mentioned for the instruction of <the> ^his^ more ignorant Readers. The Controversies in Theology agitated at that time, were so important & so intimately connected, with civil and Relig^s^. Liberty with all the great Interests of mankind & Society, that in the eye of every Lover of truth of Virtue & of human happiness, they will justify a very considerable degree of zeal. The Discussion of such Questions, as, Whether, the Rom^n^. Pontiff received his plenitude of power from the Apos^le^. Peter or from the Murderer & Usurper Phocas;[5] whether the Clerical claim of the Pope & his associates to convert a Wafer into a Deity, took it's rise in the 8th. or in the 1st. Century, whether the Pope has a real power to give plenary indulgence, and a thousand other Quest.^ns^ seemingly trivial in the eye of our Historian; The Discussion of them I say was in its consequences at that time more important more beneficial to Europe many thousand times, than all the voluminous Philosophical Political or Historical ^Productions^ of this learned & elegant Author either have been, or ever can be."

"The Determination of these & such like Questions of the Theological kind, made the triple Crown[6] to shake on the head of its grand Usurper, & quickly rent from him a considerable part of his extensive dominions. No wonder that Controversies were carried on with kee[n]ness, which aimed at delivering Mankind from the most absolute Despotism that ever was established over them: No wonder that Controversies which aimed at the restoration of the most invaluable & unalienable rights of the Human race, shoud be decided by the sword, when the toungue & the Pen were found ineffectual for the purpose. For surely if there can be any just causes of War, the deliverance of Mankind from an enormous tyrannical power which oppressed their minds & souls, must be one of that Number."

"As to the contempt shown by our Historian to the Characters of the Reformers as enraged, furious, Rustick Appostles[7] & such like opprobrious

---

[5] Phocas (547–610), Byzantine emperor (602–10), a centurion who capitalized on an army rebellion against the emperor Maurice to succeed and execute Maurice and his son. He established good relations with the papacy in the person of Gregory I.

[6] The papal crown or tiara.

[7] Hume had criticized the 'gross rusticity' of the Reformers. Hume, *The History of Great Britain, Vol. I* (1754), p. 27. See also Seed, *Dissenting Histories*, p. 77; John Seed, 'The Spectre of Puritanism: Forgetting the Seventeenth Century in David Hume's "History of England"', *Social History*, 30 (2005), pp. 444–62.

epithets, let it be observed; that whatever may be said as to their Genius tast & erudition compared with that of our Author; surely their Spirit, their Aim, their Magnanimity will not suffer by the comparison. A Luther, and even a John Knox, were instruments in bringing about great & happy revolutions, for which all succeeding Ages will bless them; and they must stand among the <first> ^foremost^, in the noble list, of determined & magnanimous champions for truth & Liberty. However inferiour, in parts, in Literature in tast & politeness, they may be to our elegant & discerning Historian, their Character, & the part they acted was of unspeakably greater consequence to the age in which they lived, and will be to all succeeding generations than all that has ^yet^ been wrote & yet done by this celebrated Author."

He touches on other more incidental & occasional advantages to Truth & Learning produced by the Reformation. He allows the Popish Writers their due share of praise & gives a long list of them in different Orders who have laboured with great industry in the Vineyard of Literature ^& well cultivated such <spots> of it^ as did not interfere with the Interests of their particular Societies or those of the Mother Church. He seems to acknowledge that the Rom. Cath$^k$. countries <even> ^may have^ produced a greater number of truely elegant & finished Compositions than the Protestant ones. But observes on the other hand "that full freedom of Enquiry unrestrained investigation of all Subjects is an advantage on the side of Protestants that can never be too highly valued or too cautiously secured. It gives me pain" adds he "to read a Montesquieu who seems to have felt an Enthusiasm for Liberty and Human happiness, and to find him not daring to express himself plainly on the most obvious & important points" and concludes with showing the importance of impressing the minds of youth with a proper sentiment, on this subject, in an age when indifference about Religion seems to be the prevailing & fashionable turn. All his Essays are unfinished. Hints observations &c, are added to every one of them almost, with a view to a second Edition of them.

He has another still shorter Essay on the difficult Question whether religious Oppinions & practises different from those of the State were tolerated in Greece & Rome. He decides it in the Negative & accounts for the small number of Persecutions before the Appearance of $X^{ty}$. Another very beautiful & ingenious one on this Question on which I have often conversed with him. "Whether there are inherent principles in human society by which it constantly tends towards improvement, at least till it arives at a certain point of acme or point of Perfection from which it begins to decline." He decides this in my opinion with great

Candour & justice against Millar, Smith, & most of the late Theories, (without naming any body) from[8]

## Letter 112: Samuel Kenrick to James Wodrow, 11 February 1786.
Place: Bewdley

I am in the same predicament, as my dear Friend was the 23$^d$ Ult$^o$.[1]– with a frank hanging over my head, with only an hour or so to run– like a dagger by a hair, telling me I must write, & that I must dispatch it, or it will be too late.– But why like other foolish things, you are every day guilty of, did you let it run to this pass? To answer this puzzling question, would take up more time than I can spare at present– & perhaps spare me some blushes to boot: & therefore I had better rest quiet if I consult my own credit– & proceed to review your last kind favour– w$^{ch}$ came in due time to hand. Ah! You recall the doleful tale of those sad fiends the postmasters & mistresses, whose unhallowed hands have more than once committed depredations on our friendly correspondence– tho' like detraction, it added nothing to their store, while it deprived us of an invaluable treasure.

I have been just reading the great Euler's Eloque[2] in the App. to the Mo. Rev$^w$.– I think I see many similar strokes of character with ^the^ deceased saint[3]– at least coincidencies that pleased ^me^. They were nearly of the same age– they had an universal genius, for every part of litterature– but pure devotion & the study & admiration of natural & revealed religion, were their favourite occupations.

I am obliged to you for the hints you have picked me out, from the short Essay on Hume's Hist$^y$.– Had this great man[4] had time & inclina^tion^ to pursue that

---

[8] This is the end of the sheet and the rest of the letter is missing. Fortunately, however, JW again describes Leechman's arguments against the Scottish Enlightenment's stadial theories of historical development in Letter 116. According to JW, Leechman argued that social progress was not 'natural, gradual & uniform but owing to some great & unforseen causes under the direction of Providence, particularly the raising up a few men of a more excellent spirit than the rest of an almost divine Genius & invention'.

[1] Letter 111.
[2] Though it is not an appendix: see '*Eloge de M. Leonard Euler*: i.e. The Eulogy of M. *L. Euler*. By M. Nicholas Fuss, Member of the Imperial Academy at Petersburgh. Berlin. 4to. 1784', Art. VI, *Monthly Review*, 73 (Dec. 1785), pp. 496–504. Leonard Euler (1707–83), Swiss mathematician and physicist.
[3] A reference to the recently deceased William Leechman, whose essay on Hume's *History* SK proceeds to discuss in the next paragraph.
[4] William Leechman.

subject, how acceptable would such a work have been to the judicious public who are justly offended w^th. many exceptionable hints in that celebrated <work> ^historian^.– I should hope from your notice that his essay on the improvement of mankind, had been twice written– that that piece & ma^n^y others you may find in the like finished state, may be offered to the public eye. It has always been my opinion as well as wish, that mankind are daily improving in wisdom and virtue. I am still more confirmed in it from the writings of Hartley and Priestley: & was not a little pleased to find the same benevolent sentiments warmly espoused by a venerable writer near the beginning of the last century– by Hakewell in his apology for the providence of God in the government of the World:[5] a work full of accumulated learning <according> ^suitable^ to the taste of those times; but abounding also with good sound sense and an e^n^larged view of the moral government of God. But I am not sure if I meet your idea on this subject– because I have no distinct notion of what you call Millar, & Smith's theories.[6] And therefore I am affraid I am out– & so drop it.– As to the character of Julian,[7] from what I heard drop from our worthy Professor in consequence of Montesquieu's[8] warm expressions in fav^r. of this singular character,[9] I had conceived a very high idea of him. And will you believe it I was greatly disappointed in Gibbon's pourtraiture of him. For however I might be led to admire his abilities &

---

[5] Rev. George Hakewill (1578–1649), clergyman and author. His *An Apologie of the Power and Providence of God in the Government of the World* was first published in 1627 (3rd edn revised 1635).

[6] This comment illustrates the differing intellectual contexts of Kenrick and Wodrow. As he noted above and at the end of Letter 110, Kenrick was familiar with David Hartley's influential combination of determinist philosophy and Christianity in England, as developed and promoted by Joseph Priestley. Here he confesses limited knowledge of John Millar and Adam Smith's Scottish stadial theories of historical development. Smith began lecturing at Glasgow in 1751, while Kenrick had graduated in 1747. See also Letters 111 and 116; and on the four-stage theory of history, see Christopher J. Berry, *The Social Theory of the Scottish Enlightenment* (Edinburgh, 1997), pp. 93–99.

[7] Julian the Apostate. See Letter 109. The view that, after abandoning Christianity at about the age of twenty, he continued to lead an exemplary life was challenged by Gibbon. See below.

[8] Charles-Louis de Secondat (1689–1755), baron de la Brède and de Montesquieu, was a major Enlightenment philosopher. His *De l'Esprit des Lois* was published in 1748, and Nugent's English translation in 1750.

[9] In his chapter on 'Of the Sect of Stoics', Montesquieu wrote, 'It was this sect alone that made citizens; this alone that made great men; this alone great emperors. // Laying aside for a moment revealed truths, let us search through all nature, and we shall not find a nobler object than the Antoninus's; even Julian himself, Julian (a commendation thus wrested from me, will not render me an accomplice of his apostasy), no, there has not been a prince since his reign more worthy to govern mankind.' *The Spirit of Laws by Baron De Montesquieu*, trans. Thomas Nugent, 2nd edn, 2 vols (1752), II, bk. XXIV, ch. X.

splendid virtues I was quite disgusted w*th*. his minute description of his filth & nastiness.[10] I would venture to assert that there are now living in the numerous convents of the order of St Francis, a thousand capuchins who never had a shirt to their back, or felt a razor on their face, or ever suffered a hat or cap to cover their heads from the cold, who will match him in patience, abstinence, & all those hardy virtues of the Stoic school, as well as in personal uncleanliness. In the litterary way I grant you, he was far superior to these idle Franciscans.– I am sorry you stop at so critical a part– namely the essay on Liberty– & without giving me the french quotation with w.*ch* it begins.– I should be glad to hear how Achinairn was sold. I hope your fears will be disappointed & that it will bring more than you expect– as my friend Brisbane writes me that the price of land has risen amazingly for some months past.

The account you give me of Ireland is shocking indeed. There are certainly remains of barbarism and barbarity in that Island, of wh*ch*. there seems to be little or none in this of ours. If we except our sea coasts when a wreck appears. I have got a sermon & Charge[11] at the ordination of my nephew at Exeter,[12] w*ch*. will I think please you. The author of the Charge M*r*. Belsham,[13] whose assistant tutor my nephew was many years at Daventry (removed by D*r*. Ashworth[14] from

---

[10] Gibbon explains how Julian's 'powers of an enlightened understanding were betrayed and corrupted by the influence of superstitious prejudice' and goes on to give the gory details of Julian's personal participation in the making of blood sacrifices to the Gods. Gibbon, *History of the Decline and Fall of the Roman Empire*, IV, pp. 356, 373.

[11] *A Sermon Preached by the Rev. Thomas Jervis; and a Charge Delivered by the Rev. Thomas Belsham; at the Ordination of the Rev. Timothy Kenrick; in the New Meeting, Exeter, on Thursday the 28th of July, 1785*. Thomas Jervis (1748–1833) was a tutor at Exeter academy (1769–72) before his appointment as tutor to the sons of the earl of Shelburne. At the time of Timothy Kenrick's ordination Jervis was minister at St Thomas's Southwark. He would succeed Andrew Kippis at Princess Street Westminster in 1796, and William Wood at Mill-Hill, Leeds, in 1808. The topic of his sermon was 'The Blessing of Christ's Mission', Wilson, *Dissenting Churches*, IV, pp. 317–18. Brockett, *Nonconformity in Exeter, 1650–1875* (1962), p. 140.

[12] Rev. Timothy Kenrick (1759–1804) was assistant tutor at Daventry Academy (1778–84) and minister of George's Meeting, Exeter, from 1784 until his sudden death on 22 Aug. 1804 after a serious fall crossing a stile. He shared SK's unitarian views and in 1792 was a founder of, and then secretary to, the Western Unitarian Society. Allan Brockett, *Nonconformity in Exeter* (Manchester, 1962), especially pp. 140–49, 153–59.

[13] Rev. Thomas Belsham (1750–1829), Independent minister and divinity tutor at Daventry, was Timothy Kenrick's future father-in-law. Timothy's first wife died in 1792 after giving birth to their fifth child. He married Elizabeth Belsham in 1794.

[14] Rev. Caleb Ashworth (1722–75) was tutor at Daventry Academy, the successor to the Northampton Academy (*c.* 1729–51) of Philip Doddridge (1702–51). He had been a Dissenting minister at Daventry since 1746. DAO.

Northampton after D`r`. Doddridge's death)[15] is a most excellent young man. He shines particularly like our late worthy friend in the devotional parts of religious worship, & is moreover the gentleman & scholar. If I had any thing to say at Glasgow; I should like to sound the professors ab`t`. conferring the degrees of DD or LLD on so worthy a man. But at present I have not the front to do it. If they were acquainted w`th`. him I do not doubt of their readiness to distinguish him w`th`. this mark of their approbation. I shall have an opportunity of sending you the above, by way of Wrexham next month.

D`r`. Priestley has just published a sermon preached the 5th. of Nov`r`. on the importance & extent of free Inquiry in matters of religion[16] in his usual animated way– followed w`th`. reflections on the same subject, w`th`. several hard blows on a M`r`. White who gave the D`r`. a slap in the face, in his sermons at the Bampton Lecture,[17] w`ch`. the Rev`rs`.[18] I think & M`r`. W. too make too much fuss about– a second parting blow to D`r`. Horsley and we are acquainted that the new work is in great forwardness.[19]

---

[15] Rev. Philip Doddridge (1702–51), Independent minister, writer, and founder of the Northampton Dissenting Academy.

[16] Joseph Priestley, *The Importance and Extent of Free Inquiry in Matters of Religion: A Sermon, Preached Before the Congregations of the Old and New Meeting of Protestant Dissenters at Birmingham, November 5, 1785. To which are added, Reflections on the Present State of Free Enquiry in this Country*… (Birmingham, 1785). This sermon earned Priestley notoriety, as he suggested that the unitarians were 'laying gunpowder, grain by grain, under the old building of error and superstition [the established church], which a single spark may hereafter inflame, so as to produce an instantaneous explosion, in consequence of which that edifice, the erection of which has been the work of ages, may be overturned in a moment and so effectually as that the same foundation can never be built upon again' (p. 40). This passage was cited by Sir William Dolben in the debate on the Repeal of the Test and Corporation Acts, on 28 March 1787 as evidence of the subversive aims of the Dissenters, and it would continue to be used against Dissenting aspirations. *Works of Joseph Priestley*, XVII, appendix XI, p. 544.

[17] The Bampton Lectureship was established at Oxford University in 1779. The holder of the lectureship is required to give a series of eight lecture sermons on divinity. In 1784 the lecturer was Joseph White (bap. 1746, d. 1814), BD, Fellow of Wadham College, Archbishop Laud's professor of Arabic and one of His Majesty's Preachers at Whitehall; rector of Melton, Suffolk from 1787, and prebend in Gloucester Cathedral from 1788. In the published version of the lectures (1785), he added a sermon preached on 4 July 1784, 'On the Duty of Attempting the Propagation of the Gospel among our Mahometan and Gentoo Subjects in India'. Rutt points out that in Sermon VIII of the Bampton Lectures, 'there is a long note, on that favourite topic, the "agreement of the Koran of Mahomet and the Creed of Socinus" in rejecting "the doctrines of the Divinity and Atonement of Christ"'. *Works of Joseph Priestley*, XVIII, p. 276, n. 2.

[18] i.e. the *Monthly Reviewers*.

[19] Part II of Priestley's *Letters to Horsley* was completed in September 1784, and part III on 1 June 1786. *Works of Priestley*, XVIII, pp. 274, 277.

A propos of academies– there is only one now in England for the education of dissent<sup>g</sup>. ministers viz. at Daventry– whereas there were formerly at London, Exeter, Taunton, Derby, Warrington, Kendall– now no more– but more of this again.[20] My time & paper stop me.

Adieu my worthy fr<sup>d</sup>.<br>S.K.

## Letter 113: Samuel Kenrick to James Wodrow, 20 March 1786
Place: Bewdley
Addressed: The Rev<sup>d</sup>. M<sup>r</sup>. Wodrow / Stevenston
Note: 1786

My dear Friend

Tho' I have nothing worth communicating to you– yet I cannot let this opportunity pass, without reminding you of me.

You must often have heard of honest John Westley,[1] the travelling arminian preacher & zealous rival of the ^late^ as zealous calvinist, George Whitfield.[2] John has a little flock in this town whom he statedly visits in his regular excursions. Sometimes he comes accompanied w<sup>th</sup>. the noise & parade of half a score horsemen, preceding his chariot, who set our whole streets in a gaze: at other times, with only a single companion in his post chaise. He has just been here in this private manner. His apostolic visits are very short: being all the time probably he can spare in such an extensive undertaking. Yet I find there is a good deal done in this short space of time. For he gives them 2 prayers & a sermon– then takes a friendly repast w<sup>th</sup>. them: & settles accounts towards supporting their stated teachers, who instruct them in his absence. And tho' in his 84 year, his friends assure me, he is as lively & brisk as a young man of 30. He came here from Worcester ab<sup>t</sup>. 11 & returned again ab<sup>t</sup>. 3 in the afternoon. His friends consist of serious well disposed people of all denominations, who go under the name of

---

[20] These academies were those which SK considered significant; that is, they were broadly liberal in their teachings.

---

[1] Rev. John Wesley (1703–91), evangelist and founder of Arminian Methodism. He visited Bewdley annually. Described by SK as 'the canting Methodist'. See *W-K*, I, p. 68 and Letter 59, 13 Feb. 1778, p. 387.

[2] George Whitefield. See Letter 100.

Methodists.– who are patronized by many of the established church laymen & clergy: of whom the former take a part of the work; that is they pray extempore & exhort: but never I believe to far intrude on the clerical department as to read the common prayer Book.

This name of Methodist, tho' intended as a mark of reproach, is bestowed promiscuously on the best of characters. Thus both my friends Jesse & Wigan, at present antagonists, are called so:– tho' both strict churchmen & utter strangers to conventicles. So is M$^r$. Raikes of Gloucester;[3] who tho' little known at present, will probably appear to posterity, what he really is, without a Pope to celebrate his virtues, an ornament to the cause of virtue & religion. M$^r$. Raikes is a Printer, Bookseller & publisher of a Newspaper at Gloucester. Being blessed w$^{th}$. a serious & benevolent turn of mind, like generous Howard,[4] he visited the prisoners, in the Goal of that city– conversed & prayed w$^{th}$. them, & administered every comfort he could, to these pitiable wretches. From conversing w$^{th}$. them he probably discovered, that want of education, idleness & early bad example, are the great sources of vice & misery. He was particularly struck w$^{th}$. the appearance of many idle boys strolling along the streets on Sundays. Upon enquiring he found that tho' they were employed on week days, to enable them to get a livelyhood; yet having nothing to do on Sunday they spent their time in this idle way, being too ragged to go to church. This he immediately saw was the prolific nursery of human woe. To counteract it, he <imediately> ^directly^ set on foot a subscription for Sunday schools: by w$^{ch}$. means at a trifling expense, boys & girls might be decently clothed & instructed every sunday & learn the early habit of going regularly to church.

---

[3] Robert Raikes (1736–1811), businessman, editor of the *Gloucester Journal*, and founder of Sunday schools in Gloucester. On becoming aware of children with nothing to do on Sundays and of a movement particularly amongst Dissenters towards the creation of Sunday Schools, he founded several in Gloucestershire. Raikes used the journal to publicize his efforts and succeeded spectacularly in popularizing the Sunday school movement which soon developed its own momentum across the denominations. It has been estimated that at the time of his death half a million British children were attending Sunday schools and the movement had spread abroad. Raikes's philanthropic activity was not confined to Sunday schools—he was interested in prison reform and the creation of an infirmary in Gloucester, but his fame, which led to an audience with Queen Charlotte in 1787, came from his enthusiastic encouragement of the Sunday school movement. This passage by SK on Raikes was later published by George Kenrick in *The Christian Reformer*, 93 (Sept. 1841), pp. 533–34.

[4] John Howard (c. 1726–90), philanthropist and penal reformer. On his philanthropy, prison reforms, and influence, see chapters 4 and 5 in Hugh Cunningham, *The Reputation of Philanthropy since 1750: Britain and Beyond* (Manchester, 2020).

The event answered his most sanguine expectations– not only at Gloucester– but is now gaining ground in most populous towns in England– particularly in manufacturing towns, where institutions of this sort are most wanted. So that thousands & thousands to come will have reason to bless the name of Raikes in future generations. I wish you could meet w$^{th}$. his own acc$^t$. of this matter in some of our periodical repositories– as his elegant manner of relating it w$^d$. charm you little less than the noble object he had in view. I accidentally met w$^{th}$. it in a country newspaper about a year ago– but have never seen it since, else I should have copied it. It gave me great pleasure to see the matter taken up by the Dean of Lincoln, lately, in a visitation address to the clergy of his diocese.[5]– I look upon these sunday schools to be of more real use– because more extensively so, than established charity schools: indeed the latter like all free schools, with length of time are much abused. But these depending upon the annual contributions of those that support them, will probably be closer looked into.

And yet what an age of profligacy do we live in! Altho' our civil & political priviledges are infinitely superiour– yet our internal police is certainly worse managed than that of any other country in Europe: w$^{ch}$. is owing to the corruption of our manners. Would you believe it, that at our last county assizes (w$^{ch}$. happens half yearly) we had 90 felons tried: of whom 7 were capitally convicted– & ours is but a small county. These Sunday schools bid fair to lessen this alarming evil.

How do you relish the clandestine marriage of the Heir apparent w$^{th}$. you![6] Is it not astonishing that so little notice should be taken of it. In another age Wales, Cornwall, Chester, Carrick & Rothsay, w$^d$. have been rouzed to arms by such an event. The Lady's maiden name is Smith, she was ^I believe^, born & ^certainly^ lived in this neighbourhood since I came to Bewdley.[7] Her father & mother are Roman Catholics. She was married when very young to a gentleman of the same religion of the name of Weld, who died in a few weeks after. She was next married to

---

[5] The dean of Lincoln Cathedral at this time was Rev. Sir Richard Kaye (1736–1809), who published *A Sermon Preached at the Anniversary Meeting of the Sons of the Clergy, in the Cathedral Church of St Paul, on Thursday, May 22, 1783* (1784). While addressed to the charitable needs of the sons of the clergy, the sentiments expressed had wider significance regarding the need for charity towards those suffering 'orphan-distress' (p. 8).

[6] George, Prince of Wales (see Letter 80), married the widow Mrs Maria Fitzherbert, née Smythe (1756–1837), in secret on 15 Dec. 1785. The wedding was unlawful because the Act of Settlement 1701 and the Act of Union 1707 banned anyone married to a Roman Catholic from succeeding to the throne, and the Royal Marriages Act 1772 required members of the royal family to obtain the monarch's consent to their marriages.

[7] According to the *ODNB*, she was born in Shropshire, though it is not known exactly where, and grew up in Hampshire before being educated in Paris.

M$^r$. Fitzherbert of Somerton⁸ in Staffordshire, ^of the same persuasion^ with whom she lived ab$^t$. a year & half & brought him one child– but are both since dead. She is said to be about five & twenty– very handsome– & that they were married by a romish priest (no protestant clergyman daring to do it, as it w$^d$. incur that highest of penalties, a præmunire)⁹ in the most regular form. If this be true he ipso facto¹⁰ forfeits his title to the crown, by marrying a Roman Catholic: & by the late marriage ^act^,¹¹ the marriage is null & void, as he is under age. Two or three centuries ago what fine fun would all this have been at the court of Rome! What fulminations, eternal damnations &c w$^d$. have been preparing: & what submissions & evasions, to ward them off! In a later period, we should have had wars & rumours of wars.

We have great complaints of the badness of trade; particularly from Birmingham & Manchester– owing to the Emperor of Germany's late prohibition.¹² It will probably extend to you.

But what do you think of a report that is current in London, that there are arrived these deputies from Five of the American States to make a tender of offer of re-union, w$^{th}$. their good old lady mother, who in a fit of childish peevishness, they had spurned away from them & renouncing all the authority of Congress w$^{ch}$. they had so eagerly submitted to in a fit of foolish fondness. This report is I find eagerly listened to by our anti-americans– but in my opinion it is too good to be true.¹³

---

⁸ Thomas Fitzherbert (1746–81) of Swynnerton, Staffordshire. Somerton is in Somerset.

⁹ 'Praemunire': a legal accusation of allegiance to papal above monarchical jurisdiction. OED. In fact, the priest seems to have been an Anglican—Rev. Robert Burt, one of the Prince of Wales's own chaplains in ordinary, who was then imprisoned for debt in Fleet prison. Prince George paid £500 to have him released to perform the ceremony.

¹⁰ 'ipso facto', by that very act.

¹¹ The Royal Marriages Act (1772) required the consent of the monarch to the marriage of a member of the royal family under the age of twenty-five. The Prince of Wales was twenty-three.

¹² SK's reference is to Joseph II, the Holy Roman Emperor (1765–90) and head of the house of Habsburg (1780–90). He introduced a programme of economic modernization which involved a protectionist system of tariffs. T. C. W. Blanning, *Joseph II* (1994), pp. 76–79. The authoritative biography is Derek Beales, *Joseph II*, 2 vols (Cambridge, 1987 and 2009).

¹³ It is not clear to what SK is referring: possibly the ongoing reunion campaign of William Smith, a New York loyalist politician, who had worked for Sir Guy Carleton, emigrated to Britain in 1783, and went to Quebec in 1786 as Chief Justice, still campaigning for reunion, when Carleton, now Lord Dorchester, became governor of Quebec. P. J. Marshall, *Remaking the British Atlantic: The United States and the British Empire after American Independence* (Oxford, 2012), pp. 87–89. Or SK may be reporting a confused rumour inspired by Virginia's call in early 1786 for states to appoint delegates to discuss improvement of trade relations. Only five states (New Jersey, New York, Pennsylvania, Delaware, and Virginia) sent delegates to the meeting at Annapolis in September. This meeting in turn called for a convention that met at Philadelphia in May 1787 and drafted the new Federal Constitution. Michael, J. Llarman, *The Framers Coup: The Making of the United States Constitution* (Oxford, 2016), pp. 104–08.

In spite of the badness of trade just mentioned– what would you think of near £200,000 being actualy subscribed, within a circle of 25 miles from this place, for the purpose of promoting water-carriage in the river Severn & a new inland navigation from this river at Worcester, towards the coal mines & manufacturing countries to the north east. We have one navigation already, extending Liverpool in the north west & Hull & the Humber to the north east. But as a comunication with the same river will be soon effected w$^{th}$. the Thames at Oxford, this will make such an opening to the metropolis, as it is expected, will answer their most sanguine wishes.[14]

But such is the power of jealousy in trade, & of the jarring interests of selfish individuals, that great opposition is raised in parliament against these plans. So that it is expected the 2 parties will bring together as full a House (some day this week for the 2nd. reading of the Bills, in w$^{ch}$. their fate is supposed to depend) as if the most important interests of the Empire were at stake. Several thousand pounds it is supposed will be spent on the occasion– But my paper stops my carreer. Accept our best love & wishes to yourself & every one of yours & every ^friend that^ remembers D$^r$. Sir

Yours in the strictest bonds of affect.$^n$

S. Kenrick

P.S. I have not been able to procure you a copy of the sermon I promised yet– but have written to my bro$^r$. at Wrexham to forward one if he can get it.

---

[14] See *W-K*, I, Introduction, p. 66. Canal development occurred at a bewildering rate. The most important engineer, James Brindley (1717–72), planned a 'grand cross' linking the Mersey, the Humber, the Severn, and the Thames and was remarkably successful in originating at least twenty-three schemes, only five of which were left on the drawing board. These developments, clearly noted by SK, did Bewdley no favours. Its decline as a major Severn port can be dated from the opening of Brindley's Staffordshire and Worcester canal at Stourport in 1771. The canal completed in 1772 would eventually link up with the Grand Trunk canal which opened in 1777, linking the Trent and Mersey. In the same year another link—to the Birmingham canal—gave the West Midlands access to the sea via the Severn, while in 1783 the Birmingham Fazeley canal opened, giving the West Midlands a new and shorter route to Hull and the European ports. For Bewdley, it was a gradual decline. SK himself had continued trading in tobacco on the Severn at least for a while after his brother Edward's death in 1779. A diary entry of one Richard Wintle for 26 July 1783 refers to a delivery up the Severn from Worcester to 'Mr. Kenrick's Warehouse'. K. R. Fairclough, 'Brindley, James (1716–1772)' *ODNB*; Peter M. Jones, *Industrial Enlightenment: Science, Technology, and Culture in Birmingham and the West Midlands, 1760–1820* (Manchester, 2008), pp. 25–26; R. N. Fisher and C. M. Pagett, 'A Brief History of Transportation in Bewdley', in Snell, ed., *Essays towards a History of Bewdley*, pp. 75–76; and, for Bewdley's interest in having its own canal terminal, see C. W. F. Garrett, 'Bewdley and the Stinking Ditch: An Exposition', also in Snell, ed., *History of Bewdley*, pp. 1–14. See also Letter 119 below.

## Letter 114: James Wodrow to Samuel Kenrick, 11 April 1786

Place: Stevenston
Addressed: M^r Samuel Kenrick / Bewdley / Worcestershire
Notes: 86/11 Apr. 1786
Notes in SK's hand: Rec^d. the 16th. tho' sent by London/ans.^d 29th.[1]

My Dear & worthy friend

I write you a short letter which I intend to send by London as it will give some ease to my own feelings to say nothing of yours for I have felt some compunction for a fortnight ~~night~~ past at my long silence having ^never^ acknowledged the receipt of your two last very acceptable letters of Jan.^y & Feb.^y. Whether I write or not I hope you will never suffer any immagination to enter into your mind that my gratitude & warm friendship to you & your family is any how cooled. It has continued uninterrupted for a very long time & I hope it will till we meet in the regions of eternal friendship & join many of our worthy friends there whom we have now lost for a time. Among the rest the Minister of Kilbarchan John Warner[2] who had the kindest & warmest heart joined with the finest immagination & Genius of any man I was ever intimately acquainted with. About a month ago he got a final release from all his troubles a happy one for himself & a relief to his friends for his stupefying disease had rather encreased & was accompanied with fits of the Gravel.[3] His ^Death^ was sudden at least unexpected by us at some distance from him and as to the circumstances of it it is enough to say that he suffered no pain more than ^he did^ usualy till within a few hours of his Death.

I was realy so much engaged about his burrial at the time & have been with his Papers since &lt;that and&gt; with other things, that I have scarce had a leizure ^hour^ to intimate ^it^ to you so that [it] is possible from the newspapers or some other channel the accounts of it may reach you before this letter. I was obliged to ride there directly & give the necessary orders such was his Brothers state of health.[4] He followed me however soon with M^rs. Warner.[5] The Interrment was conducted with great decency & something more. All the neighbouring Gentlemen most of whom were his Relations six or eight Clergymen his friends & neighbours & a great body of his own parish attended him to the grave. His Brother applyed to

---

[1] In fact answered on 25 April 1786 (Letter 115).
[2] JW's cousin and SK's friend. He had suffered a debilitating stroke in 1775. See Letter 84.
[3] Kidney stones.
[4] Patrick Warner. See Letter 88.
[5] Patrick Warner's wife. See W-K, I, p. 325.

M[r]. Cunningham of Craigends[6] <–> as a Relation for a place within their family Aile but it had been so much occupied of late by their own family that it was not convenient so that our friend lyes burried in the open ch.yard near the west end of the Church. We have not yet thought of any inscription for the stone which ^is^ to cover him. His brother is against any thing but the bare name– coud you help us to a single sentence or two in Latin or English? I ~~supply~~ signifyed his death to M[r]. Arthur by a letter & also a wish that he woud draw up a short Character of him & insert it in one of the Glasgow papers which he did. From that it was copied into the Ed[r]. ones & possibly may get into some of the London ones.[7] I will inclose a Copy of it in this Letter.

You asked in one of your Letters who M[r]. Arthur was? I thought you had known Bauldy Arthur[8] one of the two young men patronised by M[r]. Warner when they passed tryals in the Presby of Paisley & successfully carried thro by him & his brethren in opposition to ^an^ invidious charge of heresy lodged against their discourses by Dr. Wootherspoon & his Collegue M[r]. Moor.[9] He continued long a preacher especialy in the Colledge Chapel & is now Proffessor of Moral Philosophy & teaches that class D[r]. Reid retaining his ^own^ place in the Faculty & Sallary as <–> emeritus Professor: Arthur is in my oppinion the best Scholar in Scotland and has a masterly & original Genius like M[r]. Warners with far greater advantages from study & Education. He has published some anonimous things[10]

---

[6] Alexander Cunningham, eleventh laird of Craigends (1756–90), who married Anne, daughter of William McDowall of Garthland and Castle Semple (1719–84), the son of the business partner of James Milliken (1669–1741). The Cunninghams of Craigends were a major landowning family in Renfrewshire, whose possessions included property in Kilbarchan village, and whose coat of arms could be seen in Kilbarchan church. Their money, like that of the Millikens and the McDowalls, was made on Caribbean slave plantations—in their case, the Grandville plantation on Jamaica, where nearly 300 Africans were working by the 1770s. As Stuart Nisbet notes: 'There is a deep conflict between the church connections of Renfrewshire's landed elite and their ownership of Africans.' Stuart Nisbet, 'Renfrewshire's Slave Legacy 3: The Cunninghams of Craigends', Renfrewshire Local History Forum, 2019, https://rlhf.info/renfrewshires-slave-legacy-3-the-cunninghams-of-craigends. LBS.

[7] Warner's death was noted in the *Scots Magazine* (March 1786), p. 155, and Arthur's obituary of him was published in the *Caledonian Mercury*, 18 March 1786.

[8] Archibald Arthur. See Letter 108.

[9] Rev. George Muir (1723–71), minister of the High Kirk, Paisley 1766–71, and therefore Witherspoon's colleague in ministry in Paisley till Witherspoon demitted the St George's/Laigh Kirk charge in that town to sail for New Jersey in 1768. *FES*, III, p. 172.

[10] Paul Wood notes that three papers delivered by Arthur at the Glasgow Literary Society, on religion, languages, and fine arts, were published in an anonymous collection titled *Original Essays and Translations* (Edinburgh, 1780), edited by George Chapman. The discourse 'On the arrangement of ancient and Modern Languages' was proposed on 27 Dec. 1776 and presumably read on 3 Jan. 1777, but this is not recorded. Paul Woods, 'Archibald Arthur (1744–1797)', *ODNB*; Minutes, Literary Society of Glasgow College, 1764–79, p. 44.

& is sufficiently known in Scotland <--> notwithstanding his uncommon modesty & reserve which hurts his appearance in Company. He preached before Burk their Rector who was perfectly struck with him.[11] He is the first man without exception both for Learning & Genius in that university & will if he lives be known all over Europe.

M[r]. Warners Papers are all in my hands but in the greatest confusion you can immagine & many of his best sermons those of them which he had wrote twice or thrice over carried away & the rest of the mutilated parts of them lost. I am attempting to arrange them & put them in some order which is a Herculean Labour on the whole. However there are many of them much fitter for publication than the worthy Principals. His Lectures which you mention on the Evidence of X.[ty] &c, are in such a confused state that he attempted himself to burn them but was prevented by M[rs]. Leechman.

I write in a hurry being about to set out this morning to pay a visit to M[r]. Boyle[12] who is on the eve of setting out for Glasgow. One of his sons a fine boy <--> is soon to have his Leg cut off. A neice of mine here a Sister of the Capt[n]. has had a tedious fever for six weeks past but is now on the recovery. I was obliged to leave ^her^ when at the worst & spend a week at Kilbarchan hapily our young folks have escaped it they left the house for some time.[13] I am not able nor have room to take

---

[11] Edmund Burke (see Letter 80) was rector of Glasgow University (an honorary post elected by students) in 1783–85. There is no known record of Burke commending a sermon by Arthur. However, the high esteem in which Arthur held Burke is clear from Arthur's discourse to the Glasgow Literary Society titled 'Concerning Mr. Burke's Theory of Beauty', which concludes: 'It must, however, be acknowledged, if we except Dr. Hutcheson, that Mr. Burke has done more to explain the nature of beauty distinctly, than any of his predecessors who have pursued such investigations.' *Discourses on Theological and Literary Subjects. By the Late Rev. Archibald Arthur, M.A...with an Account of Some Particulars in His Life and Character by William Richardson* (Glasgow, 1803), pp. 208–30. We are indebted to Richard B. Sher for this information.

[12] Presumably Patrick Boyle of Shewalton. See Letter 98.

[13] The niece was Mary Ann Wodrow (1762–1841), daughter of JW's older brother Rev. Robert Wodrow, and his second wife, Anne Ruthven (1718/19–1814). They lived on the Isle of Little Cumbrae, on the Firth of Clyde, off the north Ayrshire coast, where Robert had died in 1784. Mary Ann developed a very close friendship with her cousin, Margaret 'Peggy' Wodrow. Visiting Stevenston in early 1786 with her mother, Mary Ann became gravely ill with a 'high fever'. She stayed at JW's house and left an account of the episode in her journal: 'I shall never forget the Paternal tenderness with which my unkle traited me sitting whole hours by my bedside with the solicitude of a Parent who watched an only child.' Mary Ann was close to death, and JW calls it a 'tedious & dangerous fever' in Letter 116. Diaries of Mary Ann Wodrow Archbald, I, March 1786, f. 116. The captain was Andrew Wodrow (b. 1752), a son from Robert Wodrow's first marriage, who served as an officer in America during the War of Independence. W-K, I, pp. 420, 429. Thanks to members of the Ayrshire Archaeological & Natural History Society who made us aware of Mary Ann Wodrow's journal.

any notice of the contents of your two last Letters. I have not yet received the Ordination Sermon you mention nor heard from you ^at all^ since the middle of Feb^y. Nelly will write the first frank she can get she longs also to hear from you. Tell Miss Kenrick that Miss Jack Hamilton was married Thurs^y. last to a M^r. M^c cormick a Lawyer & Brother of M^rs. Macnights.[14] It is & will be a very happy Marriage. Accept of our Love & best wishes to you & yours. I ever am

most sincerely yours<br>J Wodrow

I have ^of M^r. Warn^rs.^ got one or two Italian books with your name on them. The greek interleaved NT. has not above a written page in it. The clean copy of the translation of Theorie &c, is not in my hands but safe in a friends.[15]

### Letter 115: Samuel Kenrick to James Wodrow, 25 April 1786

Place: Bewdley
Addressed: The Rev^d. James Wodrow / Stevenston
Notes: 1786 / Letters from the 1780 to 1790 [probably JW's hand]

My worthy friend

Your very kind favour of the 11th inst. was bro^t. hither the 16th. tho' it made the circuit of London– w^ch. is ab^t. 600 miles in less than 5 days– owing to M^r. Palmer's[1]

---

[14] Edward McCormick (1745–1814), advocate (from 28 July 1772), who was later appointed sheriff of Ayr on 15 Feb. 1793. He married Miss John Hamilton on 6 April 1786. McCormick seems to have married again, in the year before his death, an Agnes Nielsen, suggesting that perhaps his first marriage had indeed been long as well as happy. His sister Elizabeth (d. 1813) married the biblical scholar Dr James Macknight (1721–1800) on 30 April 1754. Strawhorn, *Ayrshire at the Time of Burns*, p. 96; University of Virginia Law Library, Scottish Court of Session Digital Archive, https://scos.law.virginia.edu/explore/people-organizations/edward-mccormick, accessed 30 Sep. 2022; NRS, Old Parish Registers, Marriages 615/20 52 Stevenston, record of the banns having been read on 5 Jan. and the wedding conducted on 6 April 1786.

[15] John Warner's translation of Louis-Jean Lévesque de Pouilly, *Théorie des Sentimens Agréables* (Geneva, 1747). For more on this, see the notes on Thomas Christie's letter appended to Letter 143, and Letter 144.

---

[1] John Palmer (1742–1818), theatre proprietor and postal reformer. He proposed a scheme of mail coaches, protected by armed guards and given priority over other coaches and vehicles. With Pitt the Younger's enthusiastic support, the plan had been implemented on most major roads in England and Wales by the end of 1785, and Palmer visited Scotland in 1786 with a view to extending its operation there.

late improvements in the conveyance of letters– if your date be right. By the same means we have now our London letters & evening newspapers on the next evenings– that is thro' the space of 127 miles. When his plan extends farther northward, we may expect the business to be done in still a shorter time– as by his advertisements it only extends to Leeds in Yorkshire on the East & to Carlisle on the West road.

Altho' I believe few souls are more intimately united than your's & mine, yet how comes it to pass that we see the same object in such different lights! You seem disposed to blame yourself for not writing to me oftner. But however fond I am of your letters, I never find the smallest propensity to blame you for it. On the contrary I am more & more surprized, how, amidst the multiplicity of your important engagements, you can find time– your kind inclination I never questioned– to be so much more than punctual in our correspondence. I wish therefore to hear no more apologies on this score. Yes, my dearest friend, I trust too that our correspondence here will hold out 'till we meet in the regions of eternal friendship & join many of our worthy friends there whom we have lost for a time.

We all rejoice to hear that it has pleased the will of Heaven to release our worthy friends M[r]. Warner to go before us. I do join you in declaring that he was the greatest & best of men I ever was acquainted with. Blest w[th]. the first rate talents to command admiration, he had every thing amiable & endearing to attract love & esteem. I am much obliged to you for the well drawn character of our late friend by M[r]. Arthur[2] & for your making me better acquainted with the latter. If nothing occurs to yourself I should think he was the lik[el]iest to furnish you w[th]. a proper inscription. I dare not offer anything. *Non nostrum*.[3]

I am happy to find our worthy friends' papers are fallen into your hands also. Then, they are all in long hand– & tho' small & without stops, as he used generally to write– yet I hope you will be able to pick out something worthy of notice, for the benefit of posterity. What pity that so many should be lost & the rest mutilated, as well as left in confusion! And yet that these sh[d]. be in a more perfect state than D[r] L's– astonishes me beyond measure– particularly the latter's Lectures on the Truth of Xy.– w[ch]. I am surprized have not already found their way into the world after the numberless transcripts w[ch]. must have been taken from them, when delivered vivâ voce.– To say nothing of his lectures on Eloquence; of w[ch]. a friend of mine, transcribed a fair copy so long ago as 1747, 8. I believe you were

---

[2] See Letter 108.
[3] Latin: 'Not for us'.

not acquainted with him. His name was Benj. Yate[4] the first friend I ever knew. He was bred to the bar, but cut of in his youth. D^r. Cullen,[5] I remember, took a good deal of notice of him.

I sympathize w^th. poor M^r. Boyle & yourself on the melancholy occasion you mention– & w^th. your family on the late sickness you have had there. We most heartily rejoice that M^rs. Wodrow, yourself & your dear girls have escaped it.– I desired my Bro^r. to send you a copy of the ordination sermon from Wrexham,[6] with our last packet by Mess^rs. Gordon to Glasgow. The reason was, that it was not to be had here. If it be not sent I shall be sure to send you one at midsummer to Chester, along w^th. M^r Jesse's answ^r to M^r. Wigan[7]– the latter's rejoinder[8] is not yet come to hand, altho' he is returned after a 3 mo^n^ths stay from London– & begs me to offer you & yours his best respects. M^r. Jesse is not a little elevated w^th. a congratulatory l^r. from D^r. Hurd[9] Bishop of Worcester, who after expressing his warmest approbation of his conduct in this petite guerre theologique, advises him to proceed no farther, what steps soever his antagonist may take:– but to hear it with a philosophic calmness & silence as D^r. Horsley does the heavy charges of D^r. Priestley.[10]– But I ask the Archdeacon's pardon– For I find by a paper of the 22^d.

---

[4] Benjamin Yate came from Whitchurch, Shropshire. He matriculated at Glasgow University in 1746. See W-K, I, pp. 175, 181, 191, 266. SK wrote about him on these earlier occasions, so, if JW did not know him directly, he certainly knew who he was.

[5] William Cullen (1710–90), chemist and physician. He graduated MD at Glasgow in 1740 and began lecturing in medicine there in 1744/5. He subsequently expanded the range of subjects taught to include materia medica, botany, and physic. He was awarded a chair in chemistry in 1751, but in 1755 he moved to Edinburgh as professor in chemistry, becoming sole occupant of that chair in 1756. In 1766 he was awarded a chair in the theory of medicine, and in 1773 he took over the more prestigious professorship in the practice of medicine. *ODNB*; Coutts, *History of the University of Glasgow*, pp. 487–91.

[6] Rev. Thomas Browne (1761–1820) minister of Chester Street, Wrexham (1783–1820), educated at Daventry Academy. The charge given at his ordination was substantially the same as that delivered for Timothy Kenrick, and was given by his former tutor, Thomas Belsham: *A Charge Delivered by the Rev. Thomas Belsham; at the Ordination of the Rev. Timothy Kenrick ... And the Substance of which was afterwards Repeated at the Ordination at Wrexham, August 24th, 1785* (1785). Surman Index; and DAO.

[7] William Jesse, *Parochialia*. See Letter 100.

[8] Clericus [Thomas Wigan], *A Defence of the Clergy of the Church of England; in a Letter to the Rev. William Jesse, Rector of Dowles, Occasioned by his Parochialia* (Gloucester, printed by R. Raikes for the author, 1786). A detailed, not to say tedious, refutation of Jesse's accusation that the clergy were guilty of heresy and infidelity, and that their sermons 'were dwindled away into *Moral Essays*', pp. 9–10.

[9] Richard Hurd. See Letter 79.

[10] *Letters to Dr Horsley, Part III: Containing an Answer to His Remarks on Letters, Part II* (Birmingham, 1786). See *Works of Joseph Priestley*, XVIII, pp. 275–309.

## 1786, APRIL 25

his answer ^advertised^ to D^r. P.'s last Vol. of l^rs. pr. 3/- & at the bottom of D^r. P's new publication of 4 Vol^s. of fresh authorities to prove the Unitarianism of the early X^tian. church[11]— in his true original invincible spirit— he says, he has seen it & pledges himself to prove ^the A's^ (his) deficiency in argument & temper.

Since writing the above I find it asserted in one of the London papers, that a new work is now preparing for the press, wherein it is proved that Luther & Melancton in Germany, Viret & Calvin at Geneva,^Latimer & Rydley in England^ & John Knox in Scotland, were Unitarians: w^ch. may be called a History of the corruptions of Christianity since the Reformation.[12] That the leading English Reformers were so in the reign of Edw^d. VI. is clearly evinced ^in my opinion^ by a latin catechism, w^ch. was appointed by the King's authority to be taught in all the public schools. It was printed in 1551 addressed to the King. In conformity to the first mode ^of^ public instruction then introduced, of rehearsing in English the Lord's prayer the ten commandments & the apostles Creed, it contains a minute explication by way of question & answer, of these three formulas in plain elegant latin. The supreme soveraignty & unity of God is established in the clearest & most unequivocal manner ^on the words Our Father^: & the word trinity is but once mentioned & that in the slightest manner. So that when I first read it I was astonished to see how ^much^ nearer to Socinianism the church of England was above 200 years ago than it is now.[13]

---

[11] Priestley's *History of the Corruptions of Christianity* was published in 1782; in 1786 he published a four-volume extrapolation of part 1, entitled *An History of Early Opinions Concerning Jesus Christ*.

[12] See the news from Cambridge, 26 April, printed in the *Stamford Mercury*, 28 April 1786: 'We hear that a new work is preparing for the press, and in considerable forwardness, entitled, *An History of the Corruptions of Christianity, since the Reformation*; in which will be clearly proved, among other things, that Luther and Melanchthon in Germany, Cranmer, Latimer and Ridley in England; and John Knox in Scotland, were *Unitarians*; ant that they held precisely the same principles, opinions and tenets, respecting the *trinity*, with the Unitarians of the present day, commonly called *Socinians*. It is said the work, which is the fruit of much reading, reflection, and anxiety, for the improvement of religion, may be considered a proper supplement to the learned, pious, and illustrious, Dr Priestley's *Corruptions of Christianity*. It is expected this work will be translated into Latin, for the use of the learned seminaries abroad, as well as all the European languages, as a standard of a new system of modern education.' It appears that this intended book was not published. Those mentioned in this passage were all key figures in the Protestant Reformation: Martin Luther (1483–1546), Philip Melanchthon (1497–1560), Pierre Viret (1511–71), Jean Calvin (1509–64), Hugh Latimer (c. 1485–1555), Nicholas Ridley (c. 1500–55), and John Knox (c. 1513–72).

[13] Edward VI (1537–53) reigned from 1547 to 1553. SK may be referring to *A Short Catechisme, or Playne Instruction, Conteynynge the Sume of Christian Learninge, Sett Fourth by the Kings Maiesties Authoritie, for all Scholemaisters to Teache… Published by the Kinges Maiesties Authoritie* (1553), which was published in both Latin and English. It was controversial as, despite appearances, it had not been formally agreed by the Convocation of Canterbury. Diarmaid MacCulloch, *The Boy King Edward VI and the Protestant Reformation* (Chapel Hill, NC, 2002), p. 164.

I am just returned from my 100 mile excursion– w$^{ch}$. Miss Wodrow can explain to you– and having fine weather, I enjoyed it beyond expression. In the first place the roads are good, & the country in general thro' w$^{ch}$. I passed is in high cultivation. The weather was not hot nor the roads dusty. The banks & sides of the roads are in many places adorned w$^{th}$. profusion of primroses, scattered with the easy negligence of nature. The hedges above are just beginning to grow green, & here & there are just powdered w$^{th}$. infant blossoms.

The fields beyond are clothed in the richest verdure, whether covered w$^{th}$. grass or corn– with here & there a brown fallow– to give variety to the prospect. Sometimes the road was skirted w$^{th}$. woods just sprouting up green & enlivened w$^{th}$. the numberless tuneful notes of their feathered inhabitants. Nor to a feeling mind is the landscape a little heightened by the contentment w$^{ch}$. prevails among the flocks & herds after a scanty winter, to wallow in plenty, w$^{th}$. the frisky Colts & skipping lambs around them.– But I must stop– w$^{th}$. the resolution of writing you again very soon.

With our best wishes &c I am ever yours<br>
S. K.

## Letter 116: James Wodrow to Samuel Kenrick, 2 May 1786

Place: Stevenston
Addressed: M$^r$. S. Kenrick
Notes: 86 / May 2. 1786 / Prov. III. 17. Her ways are ways of pleasantness and all her paths are peace. / Rom. XIV.4 Who art thou that judgest another's servant? to his own master shall he stand or fall.[1]

My Dear friend

I wrote you by London two or three weeks ago[2] after a long silence on my part occasioned by my absence sometime at Kilbarchan doing the last duty to John Warner, by a tedious & dangerous fever my niece had here, & other matters that engrossed my time & attention. This goes to England by M$^r$. Rose[3] who has been ^studying^ at Glasgow three or four Sessions, a member of Proff$^r$. Ritchardsons

---

[1] Both verses noted by SK in Rich's Doddridge's shorthand (translated by Tony Rail). See the closing lines of this letter.
[2] Letter 114, 11 April 1786.
[3] Samuel Rose. See Letter 108.

family. Possibly it may not reach you for a month– If he delivers it to you with his own hand I beg leave to introduce him to you as a Young friend and a very valuable one both for his temper & his uncommon abilities. It is likely you may know something of his Father[4] who left Scotland about 40 years ago as master of an Accademy near London, lives in that neighbourhood still, & is much esteemed as a man of Learning & worth. He has given his son a very Liberal Education and I dare say never will repent it. For the Young Gentleman has applyed to his Studies with great ardour, was represented to me as among the best– perhaps the very best Scholar of his age at that University, & appears to me from the little acquaintance I have of him to be one of the most promising young men I have seen.

Soon after I wrote I received yours of the 20th of March containing much agreable & valuable intelligence together with a Copy of the Sermon & charge delivered at your Nephews Ordination for which I thank you. I like the Sermon very well for the Symplicity & Scriptural strain of it & the charge extremely well. The Author must be a man of Abilities deserving the Character you give him & the Honour you wish for him.

I have neither time nor room to advert to many things in your three last letters so much as they deserve as I am on the Wing, that is about to set out for Glasgow to spend four or five days with M$^{rs}$. Leech$^n$. before she gives up her house & woud have ^been^ there today but for a sore throat which has confined me a day or two perhaps I may write another Letter by M$^r$. Rose if I meet him there for he is in this neighbourhood at present or by some other channel before this reach you. I dare say Prin$^l$. Leechman & you coincide in sentiment as to the grand & comfortable fact of the progressive improvement of Mankind.[5] Smith Millar, &c, improving upon the more original Ideas or hints of Montesqueu, attempt to account for this at least for the civilization of men & their improvement in the arts of Life from something natural and uniform in the state of Society, to trace a progress from the Savage Life to the Pastural from that to Agriculture– then Manufactures trade & all the Arts & Sciences. Pr. Leechman controverts their principles by taking a very extensive view of the History of Mankind from which it appears that many

---

[4] Dr William Rose (1719–86), Dissenting schoolmaster, editor, translator, and co-founder of the *Monthly Review* with his brother-in-law Ralph Griffiths. He was born in Birse, Aberdeenshire, to Hugh Rose, and educated at Marischal College, Aberdeen. Before establishing his own school in Chiswick, he assisted Dr Philip Doddridge at the Dissenting academy in Northampton. He taught Dr Charles Burney Jr, Samuel Johnson admired him, and his estate was executed by the publishers Cadell and Strahan.

[5] See Letter 112.

nations & tracts of the Globe have continued ^nearly^ in the same state for ages & that the <-> high improv^m^ent of others has not been natural, gradual & uniform but owing to some great & unforseen causes under the direction of Providence, particularly the raising up a few men of a more excellent spirit than the rest of an almost divine Genius & invention in particular Arts & branches of knowledge– and that the sudden & wonderful discoveries of these superior men <-> com^m^unicated first to their own country men ^& thence^ & spreading gradualy wider & wider have given a new spur to human improvement, & kindled the latent seeds of Genius <-> invention & industry ^in thousands^ which woud never had otherwise appeared. I leave you to judge & decide on the two theories if the last can be called so, for there is certainly a material difference.

If by M[r]. W. in that Letter[6] you mean your friend[7] he never saw M[r] White[s] Sermons at the Bampton Lectures[8] & he thinks that Article of the June Monthly Review a fulsom Panagyric upon them not justifyed by any Extracts they have given. By the by that Corps of Criticks have strangely altered their theological sentiments for two or three years past & seem verging to an alteration in their Political sentiments. You once promised me some history of them. They <-> are surely a different set of men than when M[r]. Rose[9] was among them.[10]

I am obliged to you for your account of John Westley. I have heard he is a kind of Pope among his people & has a very great annual revenue at his Disposal.[11] M[r]. Raikes of Glocester is a Heroe. He is one of Prin[l]. Leechmans heavenborn men[12]

---

[6] Letter 112.

[7] JW may be referring to himself in the description 'your friend', as he does elsewhere in the correspondence (e.g. at Letter 117, n. 879). SK later clarifies that he was referring to his Worcestershire friend, Thomas Wigan (see Letter 119), but notes that Wigan's 'sentiments accord entirely with yours on that head'.

[8] See Letter 112.

[9] William Rose was still reviewing in 1781, when he wrote for the Monthly on Gibbon's second and third volumes of his Decline and Fall of the Roman Empire. He died in 1786. Derek Roper, Reviewing before the Edinburgh, 1788–1802 (1978), pp. 21, 228, 262 n. 10; Sher, Enlightenment and the Book, p. 368.

[10] Roper identifies a movement towards the Foxite Whigs in the Monthly Review from 1784 or 1785. The periodical was generally reflective of moderate Dissenting views, although latitudinarian Anglicans also wrote for it. It supported the American revolutionaries, parliamentary reformers, and the campaign to repeal the Test Acts. By the early 1790s unitarians such as Thomas Pearne were reviewing for it. Roper, Reviewing before the Edinburgh, pp. 174–76, 203.

[11] After a financial crisis in the 1760s, the Wesleyans developed an 'adaptable and resilient business model', in which preachers were largely funded by local communities, while national income fluctuated but became increasingly reliant on wealthy supporters. Clive Murray Norris, The Financing of John Wesley's Methodism c.1740–1800 (Oxford, 2017), pp. 222–44.

[12] OED: 'of such great ability in a particular field as to appear divinely ordained to it'.

& I hope is raised up to give a check to the natural progress of the Profligacy of the Age. The Princes marriage has passed unheeded here[13]– nobody is surprised at any thing he does. Let me hear more of your public Spirited scheme of the Water carriage. I have read little of late have slightly run over Boswells Tour[14]– it is a strange book yet there are many entertaining things in it. I have got Charteris Sermons[15] you will be delighted with them I am perswaded, especialy with the three or four on the payment of Debts & will see in all of them marks of an original Genius. Let me know what Subscribers you have got for D$^r$. Magills book as it is now going to the press.[16] You must not stand on ceremony with me in writing during my present situation as I have been & will be uncommonly busy more perhaps than is consistent with my health. John Warners papers interrupted my attention to the Prin$^{ls}$. The former were ^in^ inconceivable confusion hudled together in one drawer to be collected in different leaves & pieces ~~some~~ ^most^ of them without pages or any key to put them in order but the connexion of the discourse which coud not be come at without reading. Now that I have arranged them a little tho' I have read few of them– I have a better Idea of them than what I signified in my former Letter they are ^in^ general ^many of them^ much fitter for Publication than the Prin$^{ls}$. & perhaps more suited to the tast of an inquisitive age yet not intirely so. I think of carrying in about 8 sermons preached to the Colledge chapel 5 of them on Prov. III 17.[17] Three of them of Rom. XIV 4.[18] The last tho less finished than the first woud be highly acceptable to the English Dissenters. I wish to have M$^r$. Arthurs oppinion about the Publication of them & the drawing up some Life of him in which you must assist having more materials than we but I must stop adieu

J. Wodrow

---

[13] See Letter 113.

[14] James Boswell, *Journey of a Tour to the Hebrides* (1785).

[15] Samuel Charters, *Sermons* (Edinburgh, 1786). See Letters 96–98. The collection included three sermons (XVI, XVII, and XVIII, pp. 249–315) on Romans 13:8, 'Owe no man any thing'.

[16] M'Gill, *Practical Essay on the Death of Jesus Christ* (1786).

[17] '[Wisdom's] ways are ways of pleasantness, and all her paths are peace.' Proverbs 3:17. See Letter 117 below.

[18] 'Who art thou that judgest another man's servant? to his own master he standeth or falleth. Yea, he shall be holden up: for God is able to make him stand.' Romans 14:4.

## Letter 117: James Wodrow to Samuel Kenrick, 17 May 1786

Place: Glasgow
Addressed: M[r]. Kenrick Bewdley / Worcestershire / by the favour / of M[r]. Rose
Note in SK's hand: Wrote to M[r]. Wodrow 21st July 86
Note: 86

My Dear friend,

I have been here for near a forthnight. M[rs]. Leechman wished to see ^me^ before she gave up her house to assist her in ~~reading~~ ^looking^ over a mass of old Papers Letters &c, which she wished to destroy & at the same to preserve such of them as might be of any use to the College or to anybody else. In this kind of Melancholy Labour I have been employed for several ^days^ & yet it was but the gleanings of what was done in the same way by her Nephew M[r]. Peerman[1] & herself during some weeks when he was with her in the spring but she complains of him as having destroyed too much. The Literary reputation of the Prin[l]. drew upon him a very extensive correspondence ~~from~~ with several men of Learning whom he never <-> saw in ~~America~~ England as well as this country but little of this has come under my View. I have asked a few Letters & will carry them with me rather from veneration for the writers than any thing valuable in the contents of them— One from D[r]. John Taylour[2] when he received his Degree from this University two or three from D[r]. Price[3] who sent him ^all^ his books & writes with a strain of Piety & all intimacy of friendship & others which I have not time to mention. I also carry to Stevenston the Lectures on Composition— some Critical Lectures on the Old Testament & part of the New— On the Excellence of the Scriptures pointing out their beauties as compositions on purpose to incite young people to study them & many old Sermons composed in the early part of his Life some of them scarce legible.[4]

---

[1] William Pairman. See Letter 84.

[2] Dr John Taylor of Norwich. See Letter 87.

[3] Rev. Dr Richard Price (1723–91), philosopher, demographer, political reformer, and presbyterian minister. Over the course of his career he ministered to several congregations in the London area: Newington Green (1758–83), the Old Jewry (1762–70), Poor Jewry Lane (1762–70), and the Gravel Pit, Hackney (1770–91). There are no Leechman letters in the published *Correspondence of Richard Price*, but in a letter *c.* 1772 to Thomas Reid, Price observed: 'Your respect for Dr Leechman is well founded. He is a Man of great Worth and Respects you highly. I am sorry to acquaint you that he has been very valetudinary this Winter.' *Correspondence of Richard Price*, I, p. 154.

[4] It does not appear that any of these sermons were included in Wodrow's two-volume edition, no doubt at least in some cases for the reason he mentions here.

The Letters from me & Nelly which are inclosed in this were wrote about three weeks ago to have gone with M^r. Rose[5] who has since by his worthy Fathers advice altered his intention of returning immediately to England. He continues in Scotland for two or three months longer goes tomorrow to Ed^r. to see the Gen^l. Ass^ly. & to attend the court of Session for a month or so ^under the countenance of Lord Ancerville^[6] as he himself is designed for the English Law & to be introduced to the Literati at Ed^r. Rose if I am not much mistaken will one day make a figure. It is pity his health is so delicate. I expect to see him in the Country again in the month of July & may possibly write to you all that time by him.

You asked the price at which Achinairn[7] sold. It was £2140 the stock in it woud raise it to above £2200 I remonstrated by letter against setting it up so low as they did, & they are all now sensible that had my advice been taken it woud have brought two or three hund^d. more. But M^r. Peerman & those immediately concerned were too delicate in saving the rest of the Trustees any further trouble which none of us woud have grudged our trouble now will be very little. M^rs. Leechman ^is in^ <—> remarkably good health at present considering the delicacy of her constitution. She goes in about three weeks to Tarbolton[8] stays some time there then some time at Stevenston then spends the rest of the summer with her Neice M^rs. Ruat[9] goes to Ed^r. with her about the end of Oct^r. continues her Guest during the Winter & renews her acquaintance with her very numerous & valuable relations at Ed^r. returns to Glasgow about a year hence & is resolved to end her days here.

I have put some of M^r. Warners papers into M^r. Arthurs hands that some judgment may be formed as to the publication of them. The Prin^ls. friends wish for two or three Sermons[10] to be printed along [with] the four already published & a short Life prefixed to the vol^me. I wish this scheme may be practicable as I have not met

---

[5] See Letter 116.

[6] David Ross, Lord Ankerville of Tarlogie (1727–1805), steward-depute of Kirkcudbright (1756–63), principal clerk of session (1763–76), and Senator of the College of Justice (1776–1805). 'He sat on the bench for twenty-nine years, during which long period we are not aware that he was distinguished for any thing very extraordinary, either in the line of his profession or out of it.' John Kay, *A Series of Original Portraits and Caricature Etchings by the Late John Kay, with Biographical Sketches and Illustrative Anecdotes* [by Hugh Paton], 2 vols (Edinburgh, 1877), I, p. 248.

[7] The Leechmans' farm outside Glasgow. See Letter 108.

[8] Tarbolton, an Ayrshire parish about 20 miles south-east and inland from JW's parish of Stevenston. His older brother Patrick (1713–93) was minister there, and was married to Mrs Leechman's sister Elizabeth, *née* Balfour (d. 1812).

[9] See Letter 96.

[10] i.e. two or three further sermons by Leechman, not by Warner.

with a single sermon twice wrote over & none but what are more or less unfinished & mixed with scraps of loose paper containing additions & alterations.

This University about three weeks ago had resolved to confer on your old friend[11] a degree of D.D. & have now unanimously executed their purpose. It was an honour unasked on his part as well as undeserved nay it was refused by ^him^ about a year ago when ^the fancy^ first struck them, because he was to make an appearance in their cause at the bar of the Gen^l. Ass^ly.[12] But now when that matter is out of peoples mouths & heads it woud have looked like affectation to refuse it any longer. Poor Anderson is loosing all his processes before the court of Session & the Process against himself by D^r. Taylour for reparation of Char^r. & damages sustained by the Scandalous Letter adressed to the D^rs. ˆSession^[13] will not only disgrace Anderson but I am afraid ruin him. The proof[14] has been taken here & every thing seems to come out against him surprizingly strong. That he dictated the Letter to his Amanuensis ordered it to be printed; published by dispersing 28 copies at Glasgow several at Ed^r. S^t. Andrews & Aberdeen & that he was the Authour of the Scandalous Advertisement in the News papers which preceeded & announced the publication.[15] Yet he is still continuing every week to pester the Professors with anonimous billingsgate[16] Letters & incendiary Letters from Ireland[17] at least they pay postage for the last as if they had come from that country. I have not met with him in town. Surely his head is wrong.

I leave this[18] tomorrow morn^g. & have scrawled the above in so much hurry that I am afraid some of it will scarce be legible. I have been reading in the Country

---

[11] i.e. JW. Addison, *Matriculation Albums*, p. 27.

[12] In the John Anderson affair. See Letters 91–98.

[13] See Letter 98. This is a reference to Dr William Taylor of the North or High Church, Glasgow.

[14] Evidence. See *DSL*.

[15] e.g. see the *Glasgow Advertiser*, 4 April 1785.

[16] Billingsgate, the London fish-market, whose name had come by the early eighteenth century to connote scurrilous, abusive language. Some of the ephemeral printed handbills circulated by Anderson's supporters are included in the bundle of papers associated with Dr Taylor's suit against Anderson, in NRS, CS230/T/3/1.

[17] Anderson had many Irish students among his supporters. Significant numbers had signed his petition to the king to send a Royal Visitation to investigate the university's accounts, and an Irish anatomy student, Alexander Humphreys, had joined the controversy in print, replying to a pamphlet written by Taylor and the dean of faculties, Dr James Meek (1739–1810), defending the university.

[18] i.e. 'this place', a Scots idiom. *DSL*.

Boswells book about Johnson[19] & since I came here Madam Piozzi[20] which I like still better & Beaties <-> book on the Evidences of X[ty].[21] The last tho' it contains little new yet some things are set in a new light the stile & manner is something different from a Clergymans everything is said cleverly and strikingly bating one or two exceptionable passages upon the Whole it will be a most useful book for young people.

I offer my Love & best wishes to M[rs]. & Miss Kenrick & ever am

> My Dear Sir yours most sincerely
> J Wodrow

[The following is written in SK's shorthand on the cover of JW's letter—translated by Tony Rail].

12 July '86

M[r]. Jesse called upon me and told me that M[r]. Wigan had paid him a visit and told him that his Answer was now in the press and would be soon published.[22]

He charged M[r]. J. with deficiency here (pointing to his head) that his ideas and considerations were crude and his expressions vague and indistinct, that he could have made a volume out of these inaccuracies from his small publications; he had once a mind to have put them into an appendix; that Knox also was inaccurate.[23]

---

[19] James Boswell's *Journal of a Tour to the Hebrides* was published in 1785. It was an immediate success, selling out in less than three weeks (and 1,500 copies in the first month after publication), and widely extracted and serialized. His *Life of Johnson* was not published till 1791.

[20] Hester Lynch Piozzi (1741–1821), previously Thrale, writer and a friend of Samuel Johnson (1709–84) till her marriage to the Italian musician Gabriel Mario Piozzi. Her first book, *Anecdotes of the Late Samuel Johnson*, was published in 1786. If anything, it was even more successful than Boswell's *Tour*, selling out on the first day of publication.

[21] James Beattie, *Evidences of the Christian Religion* (Edinburgh, 1786). See also JW's discussion in Letter 99.

[22] Clericus [Thomas Wigan], *A Defence of the Clergy of the Church of England; in a Letter to the Rev. William Jesse, Rector of Dowles, Occasioned by his Parochialia* (Gloucester, 1786).

[23] Rev. Vicesimus Knox (1752–1821), Anglican clergyman and writer who graduated from St John's College, Oxford, in 1771 and succeeded his father as headmaster of Tonbridge School, Kent, in 1778. In his published letter, Wigan criticized Knox as one of those who 'throw Obscurity on the Gospel, or Aspersions on its Teachers'. Clericus [Thomas Wigan], *Defence of the Clergy*, p. 48. Theophilus Lindsey reported that in a sermon Knox had 'turned himself to the doctrine of the Trinity, deplored the defection of many from it, to the loss of their own souls, and great danger of infecting others'. Theophilus Lindsey to William Tayleur, 2 April 1791, in Ditchfield, *Letters of Lindsey*, II, p. 109.

~~And our~~ His friend Stillingfleet[24] had written to him that he hears that a double ram'd[25] charge by Clericus[26] would soon fall upon him.

M[r]. Loder[27] had told him that a sensible clergyman at Bristol could not understand how he could be scholar in that expression where he says he was a teacher by choice and a scholar by necessity.[28] Now, M[r]. J thought that teacher being put there in opposition, would clearly show the meaning, *viz.* a learner or schoolboy, and not a man of learning as it seems it was supposed to be, by those who thought the expression absurd.

That the Bishop of Worcester[29] had <-----> told Dr Johnstone he was with an < > comes < >, <William L> asked [page torn]. The witness [page torn] exist, how cautious said the Bishop should we be in popular disco[page torn] not know [page torn] word is not understood. Mr J. asked a poor woman in Yorkshire how she expected to be saved [page torn] familiar [page torn] him by the merits of Christ, and yet it appears upon his farther questioning her, that it was to her own endeavours and good works, and so to understand the meaning of [page torn].

He added, with the greatest good nature, to be so we are partial to ourselves and do not judge of our own abilities with justice, and perhaps think ourselves understood where we are not; but this I deny, though I take all the pains I can to speak plain and I think I am understood, and I particularly avoid all hard words, and those derived from the latin.

Eunapius, lived in the time of Julian, has written in his *Life* that he calls Plutarch, $\theta\epsilon\iota\acute{o}\tau\alpha\tau os$.[30] ^or $\Theta\epsilon o\pi\acute{\epsilon}\sigma\iota os$.^[31] $\dot{\eta}\ \varphi\iota\lambda o\sigma o\varphi\acute{\iota}as\ \dot{a}\pi\acute{a}\sigma\eta s\ \dot{a}\varphi\rho o\delta\acute{\iota}\tau\eta\ \kappa a\grave{\iota}\ \lambda\acute{\upsilon}\rho a$.[32] But

---

[24] Not mentioned elsewhere in the Wodrow–Kenrick correspondence. Possibly Rev. Edward Stillingfleet (d. 1795), who was curate at West Bromwich near Birmingham 1758–82, and then rector of How Caple and Sollershope south-west of Worcester; alternatively, it might be Rev. James Stillingfleet, vicar of St Martin, Worcester, 1772–1817. *Alumni Oxonienses*, IV, p. 1355.

[25] i.e. *rammed*, as a bullet rammed into a muzzle-loaded musket.

[26] SK's friend Thomas Wigan.

[27] Unidentified, and does not appear elsewhere in the W–K correspondence.

[28] In the dedication, dated 9 Sep. 1785, to his *Parochialia*, William Jesse writes, 'I am a teacher, by my profession; but, a scholar, through necessity.'

[29] Richard Hurd. See Letter 79.

[30] 'Divine'. SK is making a note here of a variation in the original manuscripts. Recent editions have opted for $\theta\epsilon\iota\acute{o}\tau a\tau os$. (This and the following notes on Greek translation are by Graeme Miles, University of Tasmania.)

[31] This also means 'divine' but is applied to different sorts of things. It is mostly a difference of usage, with $\theta\epsilon\sigma\pi\acute{\epsilon}\sigma\iota os$ generally applied, for instance, to utterances and weather (i.e. as divinely decreed). It is less apt for a person, so that is another reason that $\theta\epsilon\iota\acute{o}\tau a\tau os$ is more likely to be the correct reading. SK's use of Greek accents is a bit sloppy: sometimes he has written them, at other times not. These have been corrected in the transcription.

[32] 'The loveliness and lyre of all philosophy'. See Flavius Philostratus and Eunapius, *Philostratus, Lives of the Sophists; Eunapius, Lives of Philosophers and Sophists*, ed. and trans. Graeme Miles and Han Baltussen (Cambridge, MA, 2023).

Apolonius Tyaneus[33] οὐκέτι ^"less so than"^[34] φιλοσοφος αλλα ἦν τι θεῶν τε και ανθρώπου μέσον;[35] that Philòstratus' Life of Apolonius ought rather to have been entitled επιδημιαν ετς ανθρωπους θεοῦ[36]—The sojourning of God among men.[37]

M[r]. Raikes I am now told, does not pretend to be a religious man in the sense of his ever attending any place of worship, but his benevolence is boundless, and like Howard, he is indefatigable. I will give you an instance of it. After the parent of an urchin, a girl explained to him that they could not prevail upon her to go to school, he went to the house, bade the girl to be brought, he asked her if it was true, she owned it; he used every argument to persuade, but in vain. Very well, he says, and turning to the parents he adds, you have nothing more to do with her, but you must look away as your child. He dropped down on his knees, and holding up both his hands in a supliant posture and hushing his voice into the most

---

[33] Apollonius of Tyana (c. 3 BC–c. 97 AD).

[34] It is a stretch to make οὐκέτι mean 'less so than', though it is understandable that SK has been tempted to fudge the phrase. It is more accurately 'not yet' or 'no longer'. Eunapius is alluding to a fragment of Empedocles, which is quoted in Philostratus's *Life of Apollonius of Tyana* in the discussion of Apollonius's nature (between human and divine) in the Pythagorean tradition, in which he includes Empedocles. Empedocles famously said: 'Greetings, I am an immortal god, no longer mortal'. SK has interpreted the 'no longer' of Empedocles's phrase as 'less so than', perhaps missing its role in the original context. See Flavius Philostratus, *Vita Apollonii Tyanei*, ed. Gerard Boter (Berlin, 2022).

[35] 'Rather he was something in-between gods and humans.'

[36] 'Visit of a God Among Mortals'.

[37] In these notes Kenrick is transcribing and interpreting from Eunapius, *Lives of the Philosophers and Sophists*, line 454. This is towards the beginning of the work, where Eunapius is positioning his own work in relation to predecessors and reflecting on the possibility of certain people rising above the normal limits of humanity. SK has picked out the parts which talk about Plutarch, as a 'divine' figure, and about Apollonius of Tyana. Plutarch (c. 46–c. 120 AD, Greek historian, biographer, and philosopher) is important to Eunapius in several senses: as an eminent Platonist of the past (Eunapius is a Platonist too) and as a writer of biographies. Eunapius's work is a kind of history of the philosophers of the relatively recent past, presented as a series of brief, biographical sketches. Apollonius is, for Eunapius and for many other pagans/non-Christians, the pagan answer to Christ. The work which Eunapius says should have been called *Visit of a God to Mortals* (or similar) is the *Life of Apollonius of Tyana* by Philostratus. The part that Eunapius is looking at here is one of many which grapples inconclusively with the question of where Apollonius sits in relation to humanity and divinity. Eunapius places him confidently in the 'between god and mortal' category, and closer to the divine. It appears that SK had the book open in front of him while making this note, as he corrects a word in the last line of Greek, changing εἰς to ἐς (i.e. he crosses out the iota). There is no difference of meaning—the change is only an orthographic one—but SK alters it to the less familiar form, which is the correct one in this case. The note as a whole reflects his scholarly and theological attention to detail, and his interest in the idea of intermediate figures, between humanity and divinity. There followed a long nineteenth-century debate about Apollonius and what the sources on him (primarily Philostratus) can tell us in relation to the Gospels. The discussion was still going in the twentieth century, especially in Ludwig Bieler's *Theios Anēr: Das Bild des 'göttlichen Menschen' Spätantike und Frühchristentum* (Vienna, 1935).

plaintive tone, he cried out ^< >^ flog flog me my dear parents, I will cheerfully submit to a chastisement for I desire it; inflict it on me without mercy. The parents stood astonished, the child could not resist it any longer, but dropping on her knees along with her personifier, she cried out he shan't, he shan't suf'er 'tis < > begun.[38]

## Letter 118: Samuel Kenrick to James Wodrow, 3 July 1786
Place: Bewdley

My dearest Friend

As L$^d$. Westcote was in town I took that opportunity of writing you the 30th. Ult°. by post.[1]

I can easily imagine how busy you must have been for some time past, not only with your usual avocations, but in examining the curious papers of our two worthy friends. M$^r$. Wigan joins me in begging you to allow your friends & the world, to come in for a share of the pleasure you have enjoyed in the perusal of ^them^. We think you might easily make a decent little volume of the pieces you have already announced & given us some sketch of from the Principal's papers. Not that we wish any thing of the sort to be done in a hurry– to the injury of ^either of^ their reputations: on the contrary we wish to see it done with the utmost care; & introduced w$^{th}$. a sketch of the life & character of that worthy man. I find M$^r$. Richardson has drawn up a life of D$^r$. Craig,[2] w$^{ch}$. he tells me, D$^r$. Kippis is to insert in the next volume of the Biographia Britanica.[3] I wish you had time to attempt the same of the principal. It affords a much wider field. A delineation of the character of the times, particularly of that spirit of bigotry w$^{ch}$. infested Scotland so late as 1743 when he was called to the theological Chair at Glasgow, would be a useful & curious lesson to posterity.[4] A particular account of his course of critical, rhetorical & theological

---

[38] See the equivalent but not identical passage in Letter 119.

[1] Missing SK letter of 30 June 1786.
[2] William Craig. See Letter 109.
[3] Rev. Dr Andrew Kippis (1725–95), the Presbyterian minister at Princes Street, Westminster, writer, activist in the campaign for Dissenting rights, and biographer. He was awarded a DD by Edinburgh University (1767), Fellowship of the Society of Antiquaries (1778), and Fellowship of the Royal Society (1779). He was the founder and editor of the six-volume *Biographica Britannica* (1778–95), a substantial scholarly achievement.
[4] Leechman was elected to the chair of divinity on 13 Dec. 1743 in succession to Michael Potter, who had died on 29 Nov. 1743. Popular party members of the Presbytery of Glasgow, led

lectures; & of the manner in w^ch. students of divinity are educated– where occasion might be taken to mention the form & discipline of the other classes– w^d. be highly acceptable at this time & of advantage to the university when contrasted with the indolence & slovenly negligence w^ch. prevail at the two English universities– as published by M^r. Knox,[5] & never contradicted. On the contrary, it is daily confirmed by almost every one that has had the misfortune to be educated there. And the still greater improvements wc^h. have been lately made during his principalship deserve still more to be made universally known.[6]

I have already told you that there is a new academical Institution forming in London for the education of ministers & others, among what are called rational Dissenters, upon a very noble plan.[7] At the very first meeting, about 2 months ago,

---

by Rev. James Robe of Kilsyth, brought a heresy process against him, producing Leechman's sermon, *On the Nature, Reasonableness, and Advantages of Prayer* (Glasgow, 1743) as evidence of heresy by omission. (This sermon was republished in 1775 and again in Wodrow, ed., *Sermons, by William Leechman* (1789), I, pp. 172–239. See Letter 140.) The Synod of Glasgow and Ayr were 'almost unanimously' satisfied by Leechman's answers to the eight charges, a judgment later supported by the General Assembly, which forbade Glasgow presbytery from reopening the proceedings against Leechman. Wodrow, 'Life of Leechman', pp. 20–27; Coutts, *History of the University of Glasgow*, pp. 238–39; James Robe, *The Remarks of the Committee of the Presbytery of Glasgow, upon Mr Leechman's Sermon on Prayer, with His Replies Thereunto* (Edinburgh, 1744); Kennedy, 'William Leechman, Pulpit Eloquence and the Glasgow Enlightenment', pp. 56–58.

[5] In the essay LXXVII, 'On Some Parts of Discipline in our English Universities', Vicesimus Knox launched a devastating critique of Oxbridge education which he described as 'silly and obsolete' (p. 336). In contrast he asserted: 'That populous university, London, and that region of literary labour, Scotland, have seized every palm of literary honour, and left the sons of Oxford and Cambridge to enjoy every substantial comfort, in the smoke of the common or combination room.' *Essays, Moral and Literary*, 2 vols (1782), II, pp. 331–37, at p. 332.

[6] During his tenure as principal (1761–85) and, previously, as vice-rector, Leechman presided over a period when the university flourished splendidly, not least in terms of its eminent professoriate—as the earl of Buchan later put it, 'a Groupe not equalled in their Departments at that time in any University in the world'. Mitchell Library, Glasgow, Baillie 32,225, ff. 61–62, Buchan to JW, 9 May 1808. He also instituted reform of administrative processes which removed financial decision-making out of the hands of academic staff; whether this led to improvement in practice was disputed, and was at the root of John Anderson's complaints against him and his factor, Mr Morthland. Coutts, *History of the University of Glasgow*, pp. 239, 268–94, *passim*. Kenrick probably sympathized with the former view, expressed by another supporter of Leechman and a friend of both JW and SK, William Richardson, that Leechman's appointment as principal 'contributed to promote the interests of religion, learning, and classical taste, among the Students in that Seminary'. Richardson thought this opinion was 'very generally known, and will be long remembered'. Richardson, 'Craig, William', in Kippis, *Biographica Britannica*, IV, p. 415. For discussion of both views, see Richard B. Sher, 'Commerce, Religion and Enlightenment', in T. M. Devine and Gordon Jackson, eds, *Glasgow: Volume I: Beginnings to 1830* (Manchester, 1995), pp. 344–48.

[7] New College, Hackney, or Hackney Academy, which Andrew Kippis joined as a tutor in 1786, the year of its establishment. Stephen Burley, 'New College, Hackney (1786–96)', *DAO*.

there was £10,000 subscribed in benefactions & annual subscriptions– w^ch. I dare say is much increased since: notwithstanding that there is one much of the same sort just started at Manchester,[8] in place of that at Warrington,[9] poor Seddon's[10] favourite hobbyhorse– w^ch. flourished amazingly as long as he lived: but declined soon after, thro' want of strict discipline, & sumptuary restrictions over young gentlemen of fortune. You may be sure the term rational dissenters, would not pass long unnoticed.[11] It has alarmed the jealousy of their own brethren, of the orthodox or calvinistical cast, who carry their opposition so far as to circulate printed anonymous letters, addressed to the heads of different congregations, through the country, ^charging them^ with Socinianism, Deism & Worldlymindedness. The success with w^ch. it is attended seems to hurt them most.[12]

I have thrown in my mite towards it[s] support, not merely as a proof of my approbation, but as a ~~retribution~~ ^restitution^ of what I owe to the cause, being indebted for my education to a generous aid of the same sort– I mean D^r. Williams' exhibition to English students at Glasgow, w^ch. I enjoyed several years.[13]– For your amusement I will send you a copy of their papers, w^ch. M^r. Rogers[14] the Chairman of the comittee transmitted to me. This gentleman is from this country– his

---

[8] New College, Manchester (1786–1803). David L. Wykes, 'New College, Manchester (1786 to 1803)', *DAO*.

[9] Warrington Academy (1757–86). Simon Mills, 'Warrington Academy (1757-1786)', *DAO*.

[10] Rev. John Seddon (1724–69), Dissenting minister and tutor, matriculated at Glasgow University in 1744. In 1747 he became minister at Cairo Street, Warrington. He played a major role in the creation of and teaching at the Warrington Academy. See *W-K*, I, p. 330n.

[11] See Webb, 'Emergence of Rational Dissent', in Haakonssen, *Enlightenment and Religion*.

[12] See Smith, *Rational Dissenters in Late Eighteenth-Century England*, at pp. 29–51 for orthodox hostility towards Rational Dissent, and *passim* on the Dissenting academies.

[13] New College was located at Dr Williams's Library in Cripplegate during the first year of its life, before it moved to its grander building in Hackney, 3 miles outside London. For SK's benefit from a Dr Williams scholarship, see *W-K*, I, p. 17. See also David L. Wykes, 'Daniel Williams (*c.* 1643–1716), Presbyterian minister and benefactor', *ODNB*.

[14] Thomas Rogers (d. 1793) was chairman of the committee for establishing the college. The son of a glass manufacturer at Stourbridge, he moved to London to work for the firm and married Mary, the daughter of his father's partner, Samuel Radford. Their son was Samuel Rogers, a celebrated poet. In 1765, Thomas entered into a banking partnership with George and Thomas Welch, which proved to be the foundation of a considerable fortune. He settled at Newington Green, where he became treasurer of the Dissenting Meeting House. Rev. Richard Price was the minister and his neighbour. Of reformist views, he was a member of the Society for Constitutional Information and was a considerable figure among the Dissenters. He was a Protestant Dissenting Deputy, a Trustee of Dr Williams's Library, and an active member of the Committee for the Repeal of the Test and Corporation Acts (1786–90). See Thomas W. Davis, ed., *Committees for Repeal of the Test and Corporation Acts* (1978), especially p. 109.

family are church people– rather strictly so: but he married a Lady of fortune in London, one of Dʳ. Price's Meeting[15]– & is become a dissenter– & presides with great propriety over this noble undertaking. He ~~is heir to~~ ^inherits^ a handsome paternal estate, but resides principally in London where ^he^ is a Banker. To gratify your curiosity, I will send you the names of the rest of the subscribers when they come to hand: as I know, like myself, you would like to see them– & also the names of the masters. I find by my nephew that they have not lost sight of reviving their academy at Exeter[16]– at wᶜʰ. place & its neighbourhood many eminent dissenters have been educated: but this has not prevented many opulent gentlemen from becoming subscribers in support of this larger undertaking.

I intend to send you Mʳ. Jesse's Lʳˢ. so often promised. You will find him, my nephew says, no contemptible antagonist. Our friend has not yet finished his answer. But you shall have it as soon as it comes out. Mʳ. Jesse is not a little elated wᵗʰ. Bᵖ. Hurd's[17] approbation as well as the warm congratulations of his methodist friends. The Bᵖ. you will find is handsomely complimented & our frᵈ. beside his supposed heretical taint has never so much as paid the least court to his Diocesan.

As to Mʳ. Jesse, he is one of the most agreeable lively good natured companions you could wish to be with. He even reckons me among his friends, altho' he says, we only agree in one thing, in having the most diametrically opposite sentiments with each other. & as to Dʳ. Priestley, whom I have assured him, he wᵈ. most affectionately love, was he but acquainted with him– he declared to a friend of mine, he should as soon expect to meet ^him^ in ^heaven^ as the devil. I mean ὕστερον πρότερον.[18] Nay he gave me several of these letters in MS to correct or alter & condescended to adopt some of my alterations. As a minister, he reads the prayers of the church, wᵗʰ. the most solemn seriousness & warmest fervour: & delivers his

---

[15] After moving from Worcestershire to Stoke Newington, Thomas Rodgers married Mary Radford in 1760; she was the only daughter of his father's business partner, Daniel Radford. P. W. Clayden, *The Early Life of Samuel Rogers* (1887), p. 6.

[16] A Dissenting academy existed at Exeter from 1760 to 1771. A plan to re-establish one in 1785 did not proceed, but an academy briefly flourished again in 1799–1805 under the leadership of Timothy Kenrick, SK's nephew (see Letter 112). See David A. Reid, 'Rational Dissent and the Rhetoric of Educational Philanthropy in the Dissenting Academies of Lancashire, Hackney and Exeter', *Northern History*, 47 (2010), pp. 97–116, at 99, 106. See also *DAO*.

[17] Richard Hurd. See Letter 79.

[18] 'Hysteron proteron' meaning 'putting the latter earlier'. It is a common rhetorical term meaning the kind of expression where the sequentially first and more important action is placed second; for example, asking children to go to bed and put their pyjamas on (Graeme Miles, University of Tasmania).

discourses with much earnestness & action. So that he is much followed by the lower sort of people, both of the church & dissenters. Indeed he has carried off many of our good folks. He is what is called an Hutchinsonian,[19] & can adapt all the abstruse fanciful notions of that sect, founded upon verbal hebrew criticisms, to the palate of his enthusiastic hearers: altho' he knows little of either greek or hebrew.[20] But what compleats his popular character in the pulpit, is his warm extemporaneous effusions both in his sermons & prayers. This is uncommon here, except w[th]. our itinerant preachers of Lady Huntington[21] & Westley's[22] school, & is sure to meet with great applause among what are called serious & well disposed people. In short he now devotes a day or two every week to catechize poor children of both sexes at his own house– where I found him once in his <-> great hall surrounded w[th]. 50 of them all in tatters– haranguing them like another Demosthenes[23] & when he had finished his instructions he made them join him in singing one of Watts[24] hymns. But like the good natured masters in Horace's days— qui pueris olim dant crustala blandi doctores[25]– he entices these little elves w[th]. pecuniary rewards– & feasts– & does not withhold his charitable donations to the parents of such as behave well. For being in easy circumstances

---

[19] Followers of the somewhat eccentric Hebraist, John Hutchinson (d. 1737), author of *Moses's Principia. Of the Invisible Parts of Matter; Of Motion: Of Visible Forms; And of their Dissolution, and Reformation* (1724). Closely associated with the University of Oxford, the Hutchinsonians were anti-Newtonian and anti-rationalist. Despite their high church credentials, their emphasis on spirituality appealed strongly to Evangelicals within the church, including the Methodists. See Peter B. Nockles, 'Church Parties in the Pre-Tractarian Church of England, 1750–1833: The "Orthodox"—Some Problems of Definition and Identity', in Walsh, Haydon, and Taylor, eds, *Church of England c. 1689–c. 1833*, especially pp. 344–45. Peter B. Nockles, *The Oxford Movement in Context: Anglican High Churchmanship, 1760–1857* (Cambridge, 1994)

[20] In the words of David Katz, 'in their understanding of the literal validity of the Old Testament, the Hutchinsonians provided the link between the millenarianism of the seventeenth century, and the beginnings of Fundamentalism in the nineteenth'. David S. Katz, 'Hutchinsonians and Hebraic Fundamentalism in Eighteenth-Century England', in D. S. Katz and J. I. Israel, eds, *Sceptics, Millenarians and Jews* (Leiden, 1990), p. 237.

[21] Selina Hastings (*née* Shirley), countess of Huntingdon (1707–91), created her own network of Calvinistic Methodist chapels. See Letter 59 in *W-K*, I, p. 400.

[22] John Wesley's Methodists.

[23] Demosthenes (384–322 BC), Athenian statesman and the greatest of the Greek orators.

[24] Rev. Dr Isaac Watts (1674–1748), Independent minister and writer, whose hymns have widespread appeal to this day. The Universities of Edinburgh and Aberdeen awarded him DD degrees in 1728 in recognition of his theological works.

[25] Horace, *Satires*, I, i, line 25: 'as teachers sometimes give cookies to children to coax them into learning'. Loeb Classical Library.

he is generous. In short he w^d. make no contemptible figure in your country,[26] among the admirers of your Bains,[27] Adams[28] &c.

I have just seen D^r. Priestley's larger work in 4 Vol^s. but that is all.[29] The D^r. has adorned his name in the title page w^th. a long string of titles from numerous foreign Societies or Academys, in the abbreviated latin form of inscriptions– & dedicates this collection of greek & latin authorities to– a lady– M^rs. Rayner[30]– a name entirely unknown to me. So that I think D^r. Horsley– besides he has a long quotation in pure greek– who is so fond of titles & dignities, will be obliged to treat his antagonist, with a little more respect. But I have seen his answer to D^r. Horsley's 2^d. reply[31] w^ch. is short & pithy.[32] In 4 letters he overturns the Dr.'s 4 Arguments

---

[26] See SK's praise for the practice of parish poor relief in Scotland in Letters 78 (W-K, I, p. 491), 122, and 125.

[27] Rev. James Baines (1710–90), minister of the Relief Church. He studied at Edinburgh and Glasgow Universities and was awarded his MA by Glasgow in 1755. In 1740 he married Margaret Potter, daughter of the Glasgow professor of divinity. An opponent of patronage and with evangelical sympathies, he was a supporter of the Popular party in the church. In 1756 he became minister of the High Kirk, Paisley. In 1766 he left the Church of Scotland and was inducted minister to the Relief congregation caused by a breakaway from Lady Yester's church, Edinburgh. He became the most effective champion of the Relief Church cause in its early years. ODNB.

[28] Presumably Rev. Dr John Adam (1719–92). Matriculated Glasgow University in 1734. Minister, West Kilbride 1751–70, then of Middle Church, Greenock (1770–92). He was a critic of Moderatism. See W-K, I, pp. 159, 295.

[29] Joseph Priestley, *An History of Early Opinions Concerning Jesus Christ: Compiled from Original Writers; Proving that the Christian Church was at First Unitarian*, 4 vols (Birmingham, 1786).

[30] A wealthy widow, Elizabeth Rayner (1714–1800), of Sunbury on Thames, then in Middlesex (now in Surrey), was related to the duchess of Northumberland and Lord Gwydir, and had married John Rayner, a gentleman of 'large fortune'. She was one of Joseph Priestley's main patrons. He dedicated his *History of Early Opinions Concerning Jesus Christ* to 'Mrs Rayner of Sunbury, Middlesex', whom he praised for her 'enlarged views' and 'Noble intrepidity in following truth' (p. vi). She was one of the most generous supporters of Theophilus Lindsey's Essex Street Unitarian Chapel, London, where Priestley first met her. F. W. Gibbs, *Joseph Priestley: Adventurer in Science and Champion of Truth* (1965), p. 24; Ditchfield, *Letters of Lindsey*, I, p. 336; II, pp. 155, 498–503; *Works of Joseph Priestley*, I, p. 93; ibid., VI, pp. 3–4; Thomas Belsham, *Memoirs of the Late Theophilus Lindsey* (1812), pp. 119–21, 156.

[31] Samuel Horsley, *Remarks upon Dr Priestley's Second Letters to the Archdeacon of St Albans with Proofs of Certain Facts Asserted by the Archdeacon* (1786).

[32] Joseph Priestley, *Letters to Dr Horsley, Part III: Containing an Answer to His Remarks on Letters, Part II* (Birmingham, 1786).

respect[g]. Origen,[33] a greek orthodox church in the time of Adrian,[34] Epiphanius[35] & St Jerom.[36]

He next attacks the D[r].'s curious sermon on the incarnation,[37] w[ch]. is to be sure one of the strangest rhapsodies– not to say shock[g]. & indecent– that ever was penned.[38] He has a 6th letter on Miscellanious subjects, where he gives his antagonist some rare raps over the knuckles– & concludes w[th].[39] an attack on a M[r]. Howes of Norwich[40]– whom he calls more learned than the D[r].

But I shall tire you–

With my own & family's best wishes & respects to you & yours
I ever am Y[rs]. Sincerely
S. Kenrick

---

[33] Origen (c. 185–254), early church father. Born in Alexandria, the son of a Christian martyr, he would also die a martyr. A distinguished scholar and teacher, he combined Greek philosophy and Christian theology, and was influential in Arian thought. For Priestley, Origen provided evidence of the Unitarianism of the Jewish Christians *'in his time... and consequently of the Christian Church in general, in the time of the apostles'*. *Works of Joseph Priestley*, XVIII, pp. 278–79; Maurice Wiles, *Archetypal Heresy: Arianism through the Centuries* (Oxford, 2001), pp. 21–22.

[34] The emperor Adrian (b. 76 AD) ruled from 117–38 AD. Priestley denied Horsley's argument that Adrian looked favourably on the Christians, and asserted that the Christian church in Jerusalem after Adrian's death was Greek Orthodox, not Jewish. *Works of Joseph Priestley*, XVIII, pp. 285–88.

[35] St Epiphanius (c. 315–403), early church father. Born in Palestine, from 367 until his death he was bishop of Constantia. He was a critic of Origen and of Arianism. Priestley examined the evidence from Epiphanius in favour of the 'existence of a Church of Orthodox Jewish Christians at Jerusalem, after the Time of Adrian' and found it wanting. *Works of Joseph Priestley*, XVIII, pp. 288–90.

[36] St Jerome (c. 342–420), Italian scholar. He settled in Jerusalem in 386 where he worked on the Vulgate Bible, the first Latin translation of the Hebrew Bible. He was a fierce controversialist. Priestley asked the same question as of Epiphanius and came to a similar conclusion. *Works of Joseph Priestley*, XVIII, pp. 291–96.

[37] Samuel Horsley, *On the Incarnation: A Sermon, Preached in the Parish Church of St Mary Newington, in Surrey, Dec. 25, 1785* (1786).

[38] Joseph Priestley, *Letters to Dr Horsley, Part III*, Letter V, 'Of the Miraculous Conception', pp. 35–39.

[39] *Strictures on Mr Howes's Ninth Number of Observations on Books, Ancient and Modern*. These were annexed to his *Letters to Dr Horsley, Part III*, letter VI, and appendix XIII, *Works of Joseph Priestley*, XVIII, pp. 310–14, 562–64. Thomas Howes (1724–1814) was rector of Thorndon (1771–1814). Priestley's *History of the Corruptions of Christianity* (1782) led Howes to set aside his work on ancient chronology to defend trinitarianism.

[40] Thomas Howes, *A Discourse on the Abuse of the Talent of Disputation in Religion, Particularly as Practiced by Dr Priestley, Mr Gibbon, and Others of the Modern Sect of Philosophic Christians. Preached in the Cathedral Church, Norwich... on June 23, 1784* (Norwich, 1784). This was published separately and also as part of his *Ninth Number of Observations on Books, Ancient and Modern*.

# Letter 119: Samuel Kenrick to James Wodrow, 20 July 1786
Place: Bewdley

My Dear Friend

You must blame L$^d$. Westcote & not me, for my intruding upon you so soon again. About 3 weeks ago, he set me a scribbling before– & soon after I sent you a scrawl by way of Chester: from whence I received your 2 kind favours of the 2$^d$. & 17th. of May.[1] The first was intended to be sent me by M$^r$. Rose[2]– whom I should have been very happy to have seen. I have heard a great deal of this young gentleman, & have not the least doubt of his answering the expectations of his friends, & doing credit to Professor Richardson & his colleagues. His late Father[3]– who I see by the newspapers is lately dead– I was long acquainted with. He was the gentleman, & the scholar, & the most agreeable companion. He was one of those open ingenuous characters whom you get intimate with at the first interview– who always retain their primitive candour & warmth of heart, tho' hackney'd in the ways of men. Our first acquaintance commenced in 1759. He told me he was then only occasionally a Reviewer to assist now & then a friend who was a stated one; I should suppose that as his school increased, he w$^d$. find less leisure for this business. About the year 1745 or 6 I find he was at D$^r$. Dodderidge's Academy[4] at Northampton, as private tutor to the present L$^d$. Dunmore.[5] He told me he tramped on foot from Aberdeen to London. That his first Work was a translation of Sallust,[6] w$^{ch}$. he principally undertook w$^{th}$. the view of being enabled thereby to send his affectionate mother a small present. When I went first abroad in the year 1760, he gave me some excellent advice & directions– w$^{ch}$. I did not follow so exactly as I have often since wished I had done.[7] He married Miss Clarke daughter of a dissenting Minister at Albans,[8] whose brother was probably his fellow student at

---

[1] Letters 116 and 117.
[2] Samuel Rose. See Letter 108.
[3] William Rose. See Letter 109.
[4] Philip Doddridge. See Letter 112.
[5] John Murray (1732–1809), fourth earl of Dunmore, son of William Murray and Catherine Nairn. The record of his period at the Northampton Academy is incomplete, but he was there in 1749. He was a Scottish representative peer (1761–74; 1776–90). He was governor of New York (1769–70) and of Virginia (1771–75) and governor of the Bahamas (1786–96). *DAO*; *ODNB*.
[6] William Rose, *The History of Catiline's Conspiracy, and the Jugurthine War. By C. C. Sallust. With a New Translation of Cicero's Four Orations against Catiline. To which is Prefixed, the Life of Sallust* (1751).
[7] For SK's European tour with James Milliken (1741–63) in 1760–63, see W-K, I, Letter 41.
[8] Rev. Dr Samuel Clarke Sr (1684–1750), minister at Dagnall Lane Meeting-house, St Albans (1712–50). He was awarded a DD by Glasgow University in 1744. Surman Index, id: 5888; *DAO*.

Northampton;[9] who was also a dissenting minister of great eminence of the old meeting at Birm^m. – ~~who~~^&^ was unfortunately killed by a fall from his horse some years ago.

I am glad you have got the sermon & charge & that they please you. M^r. Belsham, the author of the latter, is now during the vacation, on a tour thro' Ireland, with the intention of taking the west of Scotland in his way home. He has a sister married to an Irish Dean, whom he is gone to see.

I do entirely agree w^th. Principal Leechman respecting the progressive improvement of mankind; & the means by w^ch. Providence carries it on: namely by the successive interposition of great & good men from time ^to time^ in different departments & in different parts of this little spot of ours: to say nothing of other parts of our system; much less of the myriad of worlds w^ch. form the immense universe. To him probably I am indebted for the thought at first, as I am for many more, w^ch. are the great comforts of my life. I consider you my friend in the same line– not merely for your own abilities & virtues– but as the depository of the valuable papers of your 2 departed friends, w^ch. when made public will contribute their share to that great end, in establishing & confirming the great truths of virtue & religion & thus promoting the highest temporal & eternal interests of mankind. May nothing interrupt you in this noble enterprize!– But I must follow your l^r.

<u>By M^r. W. respecting White's Sermons</u>,[10] I meant my friend Mr. Wigan, whose sentiments accord entirely w^th. yours on that head, & particularly as to the article in the Review for June. And I agree w^th. you that corps of critics are greatly degenerating from their predecessors in most of the walks of litterature. To me it is amazing that that Journal should have stood so long with any thing like consistency, considering how it is carried on. I am far from being au fait as to its history. By what I have learned from different quarters, it was first projected by the present proprietor R^d. Griffiths[11] a Bookseller. At his first outset he was greatly

---

[9] He married Sarah, daughter of Dr Samuel Clarke Jr (1728–69), and they moved first to Kew and then, in 1758, to Chiswick, where he ran a successful boarding-school until his death. Samuel Clarke had been Doddridge's assistant tutor (1745–c. 1750). After Doddridge's death, he, along with Caleb Ashworth, continued the academy at Daventry (1752). He left in 1757 to become minister of the Old Meeting Birmingham. DAO.

[10] See Letter 112.

[11] A slip of the pen: this was Ralph Griffiths (1720?–1803), bookseller, editor of the *Monthly Review*, and publisher of various other periodicals. Griffiths denied that Isabella, his first wife (d. 1764), had written for the *Monthly Review*. His second wife was Elizabeth Clark (d. 1812). For the history of the *Monthly Review*, see Derek Roper, *Reviewing before the Edinburgh, 1788–1802* (1978), pp. 20–21.

assisted by his wife, who was not only a person of letters but had a great fund of wit, w$^{ch}$. she displayed to great advantage in striking off the characters of the minor productions towards the close of the Review in a few words or sentences & generally of a satirical cast: w$^{ch}$. were sure to give pleasure to the reader & vogue to the work– however it might hurt the poor author.– I remember your showing me instances of this sort at Kilwinning, & I believe at Glasgow: w$^{ch}$. was the first time I ever saw it. When this lady died, this witty part of the Review sunk w$^{th}$. her– w$^{ch}$. naturally led people to think she was the author. He married again a literatta, who is probably his coadjutor in the work. His general mode is to pay well, w$^{ch}$. tempts ^ingenious^ people at a great distance to supply him with contributions. And as interest is his as well as the ruling motive of others, he certainly finds it at present in the sacrifices he makes to the powers that be in church & state. His writers are indeed different men from what they were when M$^r$. Rose was among them.

I am glad you are amused w$^{th}$. my account of Mr. Raikes of Gloucester. You shall have a farther account of him. So far from being what is called a methodist, I am ^now^ told, that he pretends to no religion & never attends any place of worship. But his benevolence is boundless, &, like Howard,[12] he is indefatiguable in the exercise of it. I will give you one instance, w$^{ch}$. shows his steadiness as well as goodness of heart. The parents of an obstinate girl complained to him, that they c$^d$. not prevail upon her to go to school; intreaties, threats & chastisement had no effect. He went immediately himself to their house– he called for the girl. Asked her if it was possible she could be so much an enemy to her own happiness as to disobey her parents in what they could have nothing ^in^ view, but her good. He used every argument he could think of in a most pathetic strain– but all in vain– she persisted obstinately in her first purpose. Upon w$^{ch}$. he turned suddenly to the parents & told them, since it is so, you have nothing more to do w$^{th}$. this child but you must look upon me as your child. He dropped down on his knees before them & holding both his hands in a suppliant manner, he cried out in a plaintive tone of voice– forgive my disobedience my dear parents & inflict on me the punishment I justly deserve for it; I will not stir from hence till you do it. The parents stood equally amazed & affected. The child not able to resist any longer dropp'd down on her knees by his side– & sobbed out– No– No– You shan't punish him– but me– & so he gained his point.

---

[12] John Howard. See Letter 113.

But to your letter—

We had near ^£^200,000 subscribed in this neighbourhood in support of 2 water carriage schemes. One was to render the river Severn perpetually navigable for ab^t. 50 miles: whereas in a dry season, it is not above 3 months in the year so for heavy vessels, from 10 to 80 tons burden. This was to be effected by locks in the bed of the river. Ab^t. £60,000 was subscribed for this, principally by the Shropshire iron-masters as they are called– that is the proprietors of furnaces, forges, slitting-mills[13] &c. The other was for a new inland navigation from ^the river Severn at^ Worcester to the N.E. about 30 miles– into a coal country, towards the great manufacturing towns of Birm^m. Wolverhampton &c– w^ch. would not only bring those heavy articles sooner & cheaper to the great outlet at Bristol, but also, to communicate ^sooner^ w^th. the new cut w^ch. will soon be compleated from the Severn to London, thro' Gloucestershire, Oxfordshire &c. This was in opposition to an inland navigation w^ch. has lately been made, w^ch. communicates w^th. Severn 3 miles south of Bewdley & 12 miles N. of Worcester & extends to the N.E. to the ^Trent &^ Humber & East Sea & to the N.W. to the Mersey & Liverpool. For this there was £140,000 subscribed. The first of these was lost in the House of Commons– & the last in the House of Lords, chiefly, what is pretty extraordinary by the influence of the bench of bishops– & what is more so, these spiritual lords were gained over by an orthodox dissenter an inhabitant of Kidderminster. But tho' foiled this time both parties threaten to make a fresh attempt next sessions. They have sunk 2 or ^£^3000 in the attempt– & like losing gamesters, they want to have another chance for their money.[14]

I have not seen Boswell's Book yet[15] & what pleased me most in Piozzi, was Johnson's translation of that beautiful ode of Anacreaon[16] to his travelling dove,

---

[13] 'slitting-mill': 'A mill or machine by which iron bars or plates are slit into nail-rods, etc.'. *OED*.

[14] Something like canal mania occurred as the economy recovered from the American War of Independence. Pitt's government found that more and more time was being taken up by new canal schemes. As profits grew, rival companies sprang up to challenge existing ones. The Midlands was at the heart of such struggles. The Birmingham Canal Company was challenged by a new company. After lively public disputation, a compromise was reached. This was better than no result at all which was often the outcome of the squabbles of rival promoters. Parliament introduced a special set of standing orders in 1792 to try to bring order to the chaos of schemes; 1793 was the peak year. Parliament had to deal with lengthy petitions, and listen to scores of witnesses, taking up more and more parliamentary time. In that year the debate in the committee of the House of Lords on the Dudley (Staffordshire) bill took twenty-three days. SK's account provides a microcosm of the canal building mania. Anthony Burton, *The Canal Builders: The Men Who Constructed Britain's Canals* (Barnsley, 1972), especially pp. 49–51.

[15] Boswell, *Journal of a Tour to the Hebrides*.

[16] Piozzi, *Anecdotes of the Late Samuel Johnson*, pp. 46–47; Anacreon (b. c. 570 BC), Greek lyric poet.

w[ch]. I have copied. As to the rest, this seems to be an awkward apology for discarding her husband's bosom friend after his death, being by that time heartily tired of him.[17] There is a letter from the Shades to both of them from their indignant hero, w[ch]. charges both of these panegyrists w[th]."rien moins que de l'amitie," in their minute details of every thing he said or did. The witty Peter Pindar[18] does not spare them & Soame Jennings has tickled them off in a most excellent Epitaph.[19] Your acc[t]. of Charteris charms me— as does that of Beattie, w[ch]. I shall certainly read as soon as I can get it out of M[r]. Wigan's hands. I have already sent you my poor pittance of subscribers to D[r]. Magills book— but lest it sh[d]. miscarry shall give them again in the cover.

How fortunate are you to have found so many of Mr. Warner's papers! What hair-breadth escapes do books & papers as well as men meet with! Not to mention the splendid MS of Justinian's Institutes[20]— w[ch]. I have seen— found under ground at Amalphi— a friend has been just telling me how narrowly he recovered some curious MS. Notes on the old & new testament, by the late worthy & old friend of mine Mr. Orton[21] of Salop. These papers were first entrusted by Mr. O's executors to the rev[d]. Mr. Palmer[22] of Hackney an intimate friend of the deceased. M[r]. P. finding it encroached too much on his other

---

[17] After Henry Thrale died in 1781, his widow and Thrale's close friend and demanding house-guest, Samuel Johnson, were immediately the subject of London gossip, not least from the mischievous James Boswell. Johnson was extremely displeased when Hester Thrale found happiness in marriage to the Italian singer Gabriel Mario Piozzi (1740–1809) in 1784.

[18] *Bozzy and Piozzi: Or the British Biographers, a Town Eclogue by Peter Pindar Esq.* (1786). Pindar was a pseudonym for John Walcot (1738–1819), the author of popular satirical verse commentaries on personalities and issues of the day. This satire went into seven editions within the year.

[19] Soame Jenyns, 'Epitaph on Dr. Samuel Johnson' is as follows: 'Here lies SAM JOHNSON:– Reader, have a care, / Tread lightly, lest you wake a sleeping Beare: / Religious, moral, generous, and humane / He was; but self-sufficient, proud, and vain, / Fond of, and overbearing in dispute, / A Christian, and a Scholar– but a Brute.' *The Works of Soame Jenyns, Esq.*, ed. Charles Nason Cole, 4 vols (1790), I, p. 222.

[20] The Institutes is the textbook of Roman Law commissioned by Emperor Justinian (r. 527–65). The manuscript was discovered in Amalfi in 1135. SK must have visited Amalfi after the death of James Milliken in April 1763.

[21] Rev. Job Orton (1717–83), Minister of High Street Chapel Shrewsbury (1742–65). See W-K, I, Letter 43, p. 285n, Letter 44, p. 287n.

[22] Rev. Samuel Palmer (1741–1813), minister of Mare Street Congregation, Hackney, 1762–1813. He was the author of *The Protestant Dissenter's Catechism… Designed to Instruct and Establish Young Persons among the Dissenters, in the Principles of Nonconformity* (1772) which went into many editions through to the end of the nineteenth century. He eventually edited several of Orton's works: *Letters to Dissenting Ministers* (1806); *Memoirs… of Matthew Henry* (1809); and *Dr Watts, no Socinian* (1813). E. D. Priestley Evans, *A History of the New Meeting House Kidderminster* (Kidderminster, 1990), p. 289.

business, to bestow the time he c^d. wish in arranging these papers, applied to the rev^d. M^r. Warburton of Worcester,[23] as having more leisure for it: w^ch. the latter chearfully undertook. But alas death put a stop to his career before he had made any progress in it: & these papers with his other property fell into the hands of a worthless dissolute son. Upon hearing of his death M^r. Palmer, began to enquire after these papers, w^ch. were for a long time given over for lost. As he found that the son had seized the father's effects & converted them into money, he applied to him for these papers: but to little purpose as he knew nothing of them: all he could learn was, that he had sold all his father's papers, to a little huc[k]ster in some obscure street of the metropolis, to be employed as usual– vendentum rhus & odores.

Et piper & quicquid chartis amicitur ineptis.[24] No doubt he lost no time in flying to the Huckster's: where after tumbling & tossing about numberless little bundles, many of w^ch. equally valuable ^perhaps^ in the estimation of somebody or other were they known.– (For who w^d. believe that I once found in a pitiful little snuff-shop at Paisley ^a book^ w^ch. Dictionary Bayle,[25] c^d. never find, although it was printed in France, & ^he^ has written many pages in folio concerning its author, & of w^ch. the late great Hollis[26] makes particular mention– & is now in the hands of principal Davidson[27]– its title is Vindiciæ contra tyrannos.)[28]– he found the lost sheep who delivered it up to my friend, who is now preparing it for the press. I am impatient to hear the result of your consultation w^th. M^r. Arthur & still more to see our worthy friend's discourses. In an acc.^t of his life it would ^not^ be unentertaining– or useless– to many here, to know the business, or in other words the stated employment of a Scots

---

[23] Unidentified. There is only one Warburton in the Dissenting database: William Warburton, educated at Northampton Academy (1742–c. 47), assistant minister at Northampton and Creaton (1753–60), minister at Creaton (1760–73) and Lowestoft (1773–74). *DAO*.

[24] Horace, *Epistles*, II, i, lines 269–70: 'vicum vendentem tus et odores / et piper et quidquid chartis amicitur ineptis'; translated as 'they sell frankincense and perfumes and pepper and everything else that is wrapped in sheets of useless paper'. Loeb Classical Library.

[25] Pierre Bayle (1647–1706), Huguenot philosopher, theologian, and historian. His *Dictionnaire Historique et Critique* (Rotterdam, 1697) was a key work in the early Enlightenment.

[26] Thomas Hollis. See Letter 80.

[27] Archibald Davidson. See Letter 108.

[28] This was an anonymous pamphlet of the late sixteenth century justifying tyrannicide, published under the pseudonym 'Stephen Junius Brutus'. For a modern translation, see Brutus, *Vindiciae, Contra Tyrannos: Or, Concerning the Legitimate Power of a Prince over the People, and of the People over a Prince*, trans. and ed. George Garnett (Cambridge, 2003).

minister. To give 3 regular discourses every sunday– at least for 6 mo. in the year– to visit & examine his parish once– to hold a sessions w$^{th}$. his elders almost every sunday & 20 things more w$^{ch}$. I need not inumerate to you: add to all our friend was carnal as well as spiritual doctor– judge umpire, friend Father to every one of his parishioners. How w$^d$. this appear here, where some never see their parson & others only to wrangle & dispute w$^{th}$. him about his tythes!– Y$^r$. 2nd· letter–

The melancholy labour you were engaged in was not without its own gloomy pleasure– in reviewing the extensive correspondence of this great good man. I am sorry to find M$^r$. Peerman[29] had got before you– & from his natural want of a laudable curiosity may have overlooked what you or I w$^d$. have relished & cherished. I am glad to find you have got so many of his lectures into your hands– as well as his other compositions. How every friend must rejoice to find M$^{rs}$. Leechman enjoys such a stock of health & strength after the long fatigue she has gone through!– I was already apprized from Glasgow as you will find by my two last letters, of the honour the university conferred upon you:[30] w$^{ch}$. whatever your modesty may think, your friends unanimously think you were justly entitled to at their hands.– What poor wretch must Anderson be, to involve himself in such difficulties & distresses, to gratify the meanest & vilest of passions! Are there not crosses & disappointments enough in life, without wilfully seeking for them, as this poor infatuated wretch seems to do! Good heavens! What a mind & heart must that man have, whose only pleasure ^at his time of life the <—> of you <—>^ is raking into the foibles, follies & vices of his neighbours & stabbing them in the dark! A I am sorry to have interrupted you so long– but remember I do not expect to hear from you 'till you & M$^r$. Arthur have done something. With our united good wishes & love to you & yours I ever am D$^r$. Sir Yours affectly

S. Kenrick.

---

[29] William Pairman. See Letter 84.
[30] James Wodrow was awarded DD in 1786. See Letter 117. Addison, *Graduates of Glasgow*, p. 656. SK is probably referring to a missing letter of 30 June 1786.

## Letter 120: James Wodrow to Samuel Kenrick, 15 August 1786

Place: Stevenston; Tarbolton; Kirkoswald
Addressed: M[r]. Kenrick / Bewdley
Postmarked: Maybole / fifteenth August 1786
Franked: H. Mongomery[1]
Stamped: AU/17
Notes in SK's hand: ans[d]. 29 Sept[r]. 86

My Dear Freind,

Tho' I have no frank at present I expect to procure one next week from Col.[l] Montgomery or L[d]. Cassils[2] in a journey I intend to that side of the County next week, and cannot therefore ^avoid^ <—> taking up the Pen to thank you for the various & most agreable entertainment I have received from your last three packets. Your Modesty tends you to consider them as interruptions or intrusions on my more serious or useful Occupations but in truth during the bussiest moment I ever had a Packet from Bewdley gives new fillip to my spirits & makes me go on with more alacrity. And alas I have not been much engaged of late in the manner which you figure– The visiting my parish too long neglected & not yet finished took some days a week every week after my return from Glasgow & when I gave up that, the examination & instruction of young Communicants in the view of giving the Sacr.[t] engrossed me a little, & then I happned to fall on a Sacramental subject for preaching on, & my thoughts once engaged instead of two Sermons I had intended when I begun it produced five long ones. It was rather unfortunate when I have so many Papers in my hands more valuable than any thing I am capable to produce. Yet I coud not resist the temptation. The subject if you have any curiosity to know it was a connected Scripture view of the Sufferings & Glory of X from the predictions of the Old Test[t]. & the facts of the New. Test Luke XXIV 25, 26, 27.[3]

Tarbolton Thur[sy]. 10th.

I have looked over some more of the worthy Prin[ls]. Sermons & am hopeful a sufficient number may be got to make up a vol[me]. that will not need great polishing

---

[1] Col. Hugh Montgomerie. See Letter 79.
[2] David Kennedy, tenth earl of Cassillis. See Letter 86.
[3] 'Then he said unto them, O fools, and slow of heart to believe all that the prophets have spoken: Ought not Christ to have suffered these things, and to enter into his glory? And beginning at Moses and all the prophets, he expounded unto them in all the scriptures the things concerning himself.' Luke 24: 25–27.

or other alterations. The mischief is that all I have perused are some way incompleat or unfinished either on one branch of the subject or generaly at the conclusion where only perhaps two or three hints are given on the ground of what was delivered viva voce and the Principal's stile was so nervuous & so much his own that is will be difficult & dangerous for any other person to attempt to imitate it. I have wrote ^last week^ to several persons for materials as to the earlier part of his Life about which I scarce know any thing: such as Miss or M$^{rs}$. El. Mure at Caldwell[4] M$^r$. John Bradfoot Mins$^r$. of Dunsyre[5] whose Father was a friend & Patron of M$^r$. Leech$^n$. when he was a Student of Divinity also to his Sister & Brother in Law still alive sensible good worthy people tho still in the rank of Farmers. I am obliged to you for the hints in one of your last as ^to^ this Account of his Life & perfectly agree with you that it must cheifly exhibit him in the Pulpit and the theological chair. I wish you woud sett at greater length your Idea of what it ought to be it will be more of more use to me than you can well immagine & also take care of those scraps of my Letters relative to his Deathbed appearance & that anecdote sent you by M$^r$. Ritchardson. Insignificant & hurried as the former were they may bring things to my remembrance which will not otherwise occur for except to yourself & to Louisa I have never put pen to paper on the subject ^not^ having had the least thought at the time that ever his Papers woud be put into my hands or any thing expected from me relative to this great & good man.

M$^{rs}$. Leechman was upon the point of following him to heaven sooner than her friends wished. Selfish creatures we are to grudge her what I have reason to think woud have given very great pleasure to herself. About a forthnight after she left Glasgow that is about the Middle of June, when she was at her Sisters house Tarbolton[6] she was seized suddenly with a spitting of blood during the night which she concealed (strange to think) & even made an intended visit next day of 8 or nine miles & continued two or three days in a friends house. When she

---

[4] Elizabeth Mure (c. 1714–95), sister of William Mure of Caldwell (1718–76), politician and friend of David Hume. 'Miss Elizabeth Mure' was 'a lady of literary taste and intimate in her youth with Hume'. She died at Caldwell aged eighty-one in 1795, and left a valuable manuscript essay titled 'Some remarks on the change of manners in my own time, 1700–1790'. William Mure, ed., *Selections from the Family Papers Preserved at Caldwell*, 2 vols (Glasgow, 1854), I, pp. 41, 258, and the essay pp. 259–72; Wodrow, 'Life of Leechman', pp. 4–8, 13–14.

[5] Rev. John Bradfute (1725–93), minister of Dunsyre, South Lanarkshire. His son John (1763–1820) was a co-founder with his uncle, John Bell (1735–1806), of the Edinburgh bookselling firm Bell & Bradfute. See *FES*, I, p. 253; Wodrow, 'Life of Leechman', pp. 4–5. Dunsyre is 3 miles north-west of Dolphinton, where Leechman was born.

[6] See Letter 117.

returned to Tarbolton it recurred on her but not in the same Quantity as at first. Then the Medical people were sent for she was bleeded & blistered pretty severely for one of her very delicate constitution & happily she has scarce any appearance of bloody spitting since but she was left in a very weak state for some time which she has now gradually recovered & come nearly to her usual strength. But We are dissapointed of the pleasure of her company at Stevenston which she had promised us for three weeks or a month. My wife went over soon after the first alarm & spent a week with her. I came here to Tarbolton on Tues. still in hopes of getting her to Stevenston but after trying her strength & feeling herself the better of two rides in a chaise she had taken the resolution before I saw her of returning to Glasgow & going from thence in a few days to her favorite Neice M$^{rs}$. Ruat[7] & accordingly she did set out on Wed$^y$. forenoon with her sister M$^{rs}$. Wodrow for Glasgow.[8] I shoud not have easily forgiven myself had I missed her as she wished to see me & give me two orders but I woud have followed her soon & will probably still follow her to Bellretiro.[9] I had no conception that she was able for such a journey. She looks very pale & yet has more flesh than when I saw her at Glasgow. But I think & she thinks, her own Life very uncertain the principal reason I immagine of her leaving Airshire. She is equaly composed tho' not so high spirited & triumphant as her husband was <—> under the near view of Death.

You will forgive me that I have scarce left myself room for taking notice of the various entertaining contents of your three letters. The first of the 30th. of June[10] gave us much pleasure as it notifyed the health & welfare of you all at Bewdley after a long Silence. The presents alas they do not deserve the name but I am glad they came safe to hand & were acceptable to our good friends. Dr. Magill's book is in the press & will soon be published. I hear the Orthodox at Ed$^r$. & Glasgow have taken the alarm already and are impatient to see it. They will surely not be so mad at this hour of the day as to meddle at least with the Author but there is ^no^ foretelling what may happen whether D$^r$. Leechman or L$^d$. Hailes will be the truest prophet. The former said he hoped or thought the season of Heresy

---

[7] See Letters 96, 108, and 117.

[8] Elizabeth Wodrow (d. 1812), née Balfour, the wife of JW's brother Patrick, minister of Tarbolton, and, like Bridget Leechman, the aunt of JW's wife Louisa.

[9] The house in Dunbartonshire owned by the Ruat family, to which Mrs Leechman retired in her widowhood. William and Robert Chambers, *Chambers's Information for the People: A Popular Encyclopedia* (Edinburgh, 1849), described Belretiro, near Dumbarton at the south end of Loch Lomond, as 'a fine modern mansion', II, p. 648.

[10] Missing SK letter of 30 June 1786.

processes in Scotland was now over. The lat[t]er wrote that the Sparks of fiery zeal thought to be extinguished were only suppositos cinere doloso[11], and might flame out as high as ever. I shall see my friend to morrow G. w.[12] being keept here today along with Peggy my fellow traveler by a heavy rain & taking the opportunity which I may not easily find at Kirkoswald where the Sacrament is to be given Sab^th. next of scribbling a little to my English friend. I rejoice with him in the happiness of his Clerical Nephew[13] happy in his people and in his family connexions. I will be glad to have further accounts of him from time to time. Hirtzell[14] I had heard of at Glasgow & of his wonderful discoveries but there are some particulars in your Nephews Account as to his pension &c., which I was a stranger to. This is an Age of Discovery beyond any other particularly in Mechanical invention. We have been amused for some time with an Account of a family at Leadhills who have invented a carriage to be moved by a little steam Engine which will go in any direction ^up or down hill^ at the rate of ten miles an hour & carry 1600 weight at the triffling expense of five pence worth of coals consumed every twelve hours.[15] This was actualy announced in the Glasgow news papers, the Inventor named who is applying for a Patent. If the fact coud be depended on it ~~might~~ may well cool the spirit of all your projectors & Subscribers for Canals for it will render these utterly useless & with them all the Carriage & draught horses in the Kingdom Ploughs Balloons &c, &c, for surely such a self moving Machine may easily [be] applied to the purposes of tillage of mounting in the air as it goes in every direction sailing on the sea & what not. But Seriously they have actualy begun in this Country to apply the new Cotton spinning machines to the spinning of wool & it is said the spinning of a mixture of a mixture of cotton and

---

[11] Horace, *Odes*, II, i, lines 7–8: 'Incedis per ignes / Suppositos cineri doloso', translated as: 'walking, as it were, over fires hidden beneath treacherous ashes'. Loeb Classical Library. SK also quotes this line in Letter 152.

[12] God willing.

[13] Timothy Kenrick. See Letter 112.

[14] William Herschel (1738–1822), discoverer of the planet Uranus in 1781 and astronomer to George III.

[15] Leadhills, South Lanarkshire, a lead miners' community famous for the first subscription library in Britain, founded in 1741. William Symington, a student at Edinburgh University in 1786, demonstrated a model carriage driven by a steam engine both on a turnpike road near Leadhills and in Edinburgh. The vehicle was sponsored by Gilbert Meason, the managing partner in the mines at Wanlockhead, a mile south of Leadhills, and noted in the *Edinburgh Evening Courant*, 12 July 1786. Graeme Symington, 'William Symington's Steam Carriage 1786, with notes on the origins of steam carriages in Great Britain', in 'William Symington 1764-1831: Engineer, Inventor and Steamboat Pioneer', revised 3 Nov. 2022, https://sites.google.com/view/william-symington/introduction-and-contents/steam-carriage-1786?authuser=0&pli=1.

tow.[16] As to Hirtzell D[r]. Reid (who with M[rs]. Reid gave us the pleasure of their company for a day lately at Stev[n].) told me that he is just now finishing a most wonderful reflecting Telescope between three & four feet in Diameter from which considerable discoveries are expected particularly in the moon.[17] Much success to him & all these uncommon men whom God raises up from time to time <-> ^or^ endows with some portion of a divine spirit for the improvement or even entertainment of the rest of Mankind.

Your second Letter nearly of the same date[18] I received some time after, together with the printed papers of that very noble Accademical institution to which I wish all success.[19] You have a spirit in your part of the Island I mean a generosity of Spirit which animates such undertaking which we are strangers to in this part of the Island for I reckon nothing either in the Ed[r]. schemes[20] or that of our Fisheries[21] compared with the Subscription of £10,000 in a single day. But I must leave the contents of that & of your 3[d] Pack[t]. July 21[22] which I received about the time of our Sac[r]. to another Cover. I dined with Col. Montg[y]. yesterday the first time I have been in his house since his Fathers Death[23] & got two Covers one for

---

[16] Flax or hemp fibre. The cotton industry increased dramatically in the years after the American War of Independence, supplied by raw cotton from the United States as well as from India, and transformed by the rise of spinning machines, powered first by water and, from 1792, by steam. The New Lanark mills, to which JW refers here, were established by David Dale and Robert Arkwright in 1786. Hand-powered spinning jennies were still widespread in Ayrshire. William Ferguson, *Scotland: 1689 to the Present* (Edinburgh, 1968), pp. 185–86; Christopher A. Whatley, *Scottish Society, 1707–1830: Beyond Jacobitism, towards Industrialisation* (Manchester, 2000), pp. 223–88.

[17] This refers to the mirror of the telescope. In 1781 Herschel tried himself unsuccessfully to cast such a mirror. At this time, he was using a 20-foot reflector telescope with 18-inch mirrors, but in 1785 he had been awarded funds to build his cherished project of a monster telescope with 4-foot mirrors. This was eventually completed in 1789 but was not a great success. Michael Hoskin, *ODNB*.

[18] Letter 118, 3 July 1786.

[19] Hackney Academy. See Letter 118.

[20] In June 1785 JW had provided SK with a glowing account of the development of Edinburgh's New Town (Letter 96).

[21] The British Fisheries Society was founded in 1786, a joint stock company on semi-charitable principles, to establish fishing villages round the northern coasts of Scotland from Oban to Dornoch. This scheme was framed by a committee of the House of Commons, but bore similarities to the proposals drafted by the Highland Society of London in 1785, a committee of which became the British Fisheries Society. In May 1786, £7,000 was raised when subscriptions were first invited, rather less than the £150,000 maximum envisaged by the parliamentary committee, though by 1798 the Society had raised £36,475 in shares. Jean Dunlop, *The British Fisheries Society 1786–1803* (Edinburgh, 1978), pp. 18–32, 108.

[22] Letter 119.

[23] Col. Hugh Montgomerie (see Letter 79) was the son of Alexander Montgomerie (d. 1783) of Coilsfield, Ayrshire.

the 15th. another for the 29th. of this Month. The next time I have that honour I shall take less of his Drink. Peggy & I go on to Carick[24] G. w. tomorrow. If I have some time I shall add a few lines in the Cover in the meantime Adieu

Kirkoswald Tues$^y$. 15th.

I found all my relations here in their usual health. My Sister[25] now very aged & infirm yet able to manage her house as well as ever but not able to attend public worship except on the Sund$^y$ forenoon. She remembers M$^{rs}$. Kenrick & you affectionately & wishes to be remembered by you. M$^r$. Biggar has been quite blind for two or three years but continues to preach with wonderful spirit & I think with more distinctness than ever he did in his Life. We had an agreable meeting of friends & good Sermons but a continued rain which obliged them to meet in the kirk Sat$^y$. Sabath & Mond$^y$ a thing I never remember to have seen in this place. Yet even this did not keep back the Crowd on Sab$^{th}$. A fair morn$^g$. flattered them & brought together several hundreds more than the large Church coud contain. These serious ^people^ sat patiently under the rain for five or six hours & heard us preach to them with seeming pleasure but we dismissed ^them^ before the Evening Service.– This woud have been a strange Phaenomenon to M$^r$. Wigan.[26] M$^r$. Wright of Maybole one of Mr. Biggars Assistants is an Author. He published a treatise lately on Brotherly Love with a History of Masonry subjoined to it a 5/8$^{vo}$.[27] The main part of the book on Xian Love is an excellent composition the substance of some sermons, but the book does not sell tho recomended by the Grand Lodge at Ed$^r$ to the rest. Prefixed to it is a Dedication of above 14 pages to your Class fellow Ld Cassils the half of which contains a Char$^r$. & account of the

---

[24] Carrick, the southern district of Ayrshire, of which Maybole was the main town.

[25] Margaret Biggar (b. 1717, d. after 1786), *née* Wodrow, wife of Rev. Matthew Biggar, parish minister of Kirkoswald.

[26] On the scale of organization of Scottish presbyterian communion seasons, see Mutch, *Religion and National Identity*, pp. 100–04, in which the consideration of the presbytery of Ayr in 1750 of holding more than one communion season each year is noted. The proposal was rejected on grounds of practicality. The Scottish communion season was one significant reason for the minister's annual visitation of all his parishioners, discussed by SK and JW in Letters 119 and 120. He was expected to discern which of them was in a fit spiritual state to receive communion at the Lord's Table.

[27] Rev. James Wright (d. 1812), minister of Maybole, was one of the local ministers assisting Matthew Biggar in this communion season, as were JW and William M'Gill. James Wright, *A Recommendation of Brotherly Love, Upon the Principles of Christianity. To which is Subjoined, an Inquiry into the True Design of the Institution of Masonry.... By James Wright, A.M., Minister of the Gospel at Maybole* (Edinburgh, 1786).

Death of the late L^d Cassils[28] broth^r. to the former. The impropriety of this & several things about Masonry has hurt the reputation of the Author & the book so that not a word passed about it at least in Mr. Wrights presence. I spent the greater part of frid^y. with Dr. Magill who also gave the Sacr^t. on Sab^th. last only about 150 pages of his book are printed it will consist of above 500. He has between 700 & 800 subscribers in Scotland so that he runs no risk having printed only 1,000 Copies. You will soon have a deluge of Theological publications from this Country but I must stop with my best wishes to you and yours

J. Wodrow

## Letter 121: James Wodrow to Samuel Kenrick, 28 August 1786
Place: Stevenston
Addressed: M^r Kenrick / Bewdley
Postmarked: Irvine Twenty ninth August 1786
Franked: H. Montgomery
Note in SK's hand: answd 29th Sept.

Near a fortnight ago I sent a packet to my best & dearest friend from Kirkoswald including besides my own, Letters from Nelly & Peggy to Miss Kenrick. I weighted it before I sealed it it was within the 2 oz^s. so that I hope bulkly as it was it would reach you without any challenge. I now take up the pen to fill up the other cover I got from the Col^l. & shall follow the thread of your two last received Letters. M^r. Wiggan & you speak of a decent little vol^me. of ^the^ Prinl^s. Papers read at the Proff^rs. Club some sketch of which I sent you but upon mentioning the contents of these to some of the Proff^rs. at Glasgow they seemed to think that nothing coud appear with dignity under his Name but Sermons indeed I believe they are right in their judgment. There is a solemnity and strength in his manner that ^just^ suits the Pulpit & does not so well suit any other thing. Besides there is scarce ^any^ of

---

[28] Thomas Kennedy, ninth earl of Cassillis (1726–75), a 'smuggler and landowner…full of contradictory passions'. As a Jacobite, his father had used the caves under Culzean Castle, on the coast south of Ayr, for smuggling. After enlisting in the British army and fighting at Fontenoy, and against the Jacobite '45, Thomas Kennedy settled on his 250,000-acre estate in 1755, and became the ninth earl of Cassillis in 1762. While improving his lands, gardens, and library, he continued to smuggle goods such as 'soap, port, burgundy, genever, claret, and green and black tea'. He also built a Palladian villa near Maybole, the home-town of Elisabeth Kenrick. Michael S. Moss, 'Kennedy, Thomas, ninth earl of Cassillis (1726–1775)', *ODNB*. W-K, I, p. 431.

these things fit for the public eye except the essay on Education & even that unfinished. But in these things I am not an Actor but an Adviser & assister. The Papers are M$^{rs}$. Leechmans property she has put them into my hands for a time. Other nearer connexions of the Prin$^l$. & hers have rather taken it amiss. She persists however in her too partial attachment to me– & is resolved I shall take the lead yet I will do nothing without the Advice of better judges. A vol$^{me}$. of Sermons including the printed ones is resolved on at least almost so with some Account of his Life. She intends this as a present to her Brother the bookseller[1] that is the profits of it if any are to be made so that both she and I are disinterested in the matter. I have not yet put pen to paper as to the Life but am collecting materials from every quarter I can think of and am <— —> very diffident not so much of my judgement in the choice of a few proper sermons but of my Abilities to execute the preliminary part even the Life & character of such an amiable eminent & worthy man & will therefore be obliged to you & every other friend for any hints on the Subject.

M$^{rs}$. Leechman stood her journey to Glasgow very well at first. Sleeped well for two nights after her arival, but the third day her spitting of blood attacked her, yet slightly. She was blooded then & other Medicines given her she went on to Bellretiro on ^the^ Mond$^y$. & my Wife had the pleasure of a Letter from her own hand two days ago signifying that she was better than she had been for a great while before tho' the slight pain or soreness in her left side still continues.

I was much amused with your account of M$^r$. Jesse. He must be a pleasant man notwithstanding his Oddities. No wonder he is popular. His methodistical enthusiasm & his narrow principles do not seem to sour his temper as is the case with many of his brethren in this part of the world.

It will be a long time before I can have an opportunity of seeing D$^r$. Priestleys larger work.[2] I will therefore be obliged to you for further accounts of it.

Now to your last long various entertaining Letter July 20th. In the beginning of it you make me acquainted with the deceased M$^r$. Rose of Chiswick[3] at least better <—> or more intimately than I was before for I have heard M$^r$. Ritchardson and D$^r$. Reid speak of him in terms of high esteem & affection. The last was acquainted with his relations in the North country, to whom his behaviour has been ever uniformly kind & amiable; & with himself, only however, in the chan$^l$. of a literary

---

[1] John Balfour. See Letter 84.
[2] Joseph Priestley, *An History of Early Opinions Concerning Jesus Christ: Compiled From Original Writers, Proving That the Christian Church was at First Unitarian*, 4 vols (Birmingham, 1786).
[3] William Rose. See Letter 116.

correspondence. His Death I apprehend will be a considerable loss to the Dissenting Interest. His Son in Law Burney[4] I understand carrys on the bussiness of the Academy ^or School^ but I should be afraid non passibus æquis[5] tho educated by the old Gentleman for the very purpose. He once intended his own son for that employment but his Daughters Marriage made him alter his scheme.

I had a visit from Young Rose[6] two days ago during a short start that he had made to take farewell of his numerous friends in this part of the Country. He received the Accounts of his Fathers death at Ed$^r$. where he has been for near two months on purpose to attend our Courts of Law, as he is designed for that walk ^in his own country^. He had been in bad health for some time before & has been still worse since so that I am afraid poor fellow he will not live long which indeed he seems to be apprehensive of himself. He has met with a very flatering attention from many of the literati at Ed$^r$. particularly Adam Smith also from some people of rank in the Country such as Lady Glasgow[7] & her family. Her Lady$^p$. was well acquainted with the Father & has indeed acted a motherly part to the Son. I am not surprised at the uncommon attention & regard that has been shown him, by every set of people to whom he has been introduced as besides his vivacity & cleverness he has realy much solid knowledge & judgment yet it is enough to turn the head of a young Lad of 19 & indeed <—> along with the English honesty & frankness he has a little too much vanity or inclination to talk; & a little too much wit neither of which I ever saw offensive, yet I understand they have made him some enemies while he has innumerable friends. He seems strongly attached to Scotland. He set out as this day for England and is to continue about York and the neighbourhood till Oct$^r$. among his Mothers relations. I think it very probable he will give you a call in his way to London. I showed him your printed Letters about the Grand

---

[4] Charles Burney (1757–1817), a schoolmaster and book collector, was a son of Dr Charles Burney (1726–1814), the music historian. He attended Gonville and Caius College, Cambridge, where his hedonistic lifestyle led him to steal books from the university library and sell them to pay debts. This led to his dismissal from Cambridge in disgrace, and he eventually continued to drink, gamble, and study classics at King's College Aberdeen, where he obtained an MA in 1781. He returned to London and became an assistant teacher in Dr William Rose's private school at Chiswick, and married his daughter Sarah (1759–1821). Burney became a respected scholar of classics and a friend of Samuel Parr. Contrary to Wodrow's fears, he was a successful schoolmaster. He moved the school to Greenwich in 1793, and in 1813 it was inherited by his son Charles Parr Burney (1785–1864). *ODNB*.

[5] 'With unequal steps'. Virgil, *Aeneid*, II, line 725, referring to the vulnerability of Aeneas's young son as he fled Troy with his father.

[6] Samuel Rose. See Letter 108.

[7] Elizabeth Boyle, Lady Glasgow. See Letter 84.

Accademy. He was acquainted with a number of the Subscribers & managers at least he knew something of them by their names. I know very few of them.

I thank you for your information relative to the monthly Review. If it goes on at the rate it has done I believe I will change it for some other when this year is out. What is your oppinion of the Critical and the English Reviews?

M[r]. Raikes of Glocester! worthy man! It is a beautiful picture you have given me of him in the Anecdote. It shows his ^deep^ knowledge of human nature as well as his uncommon quickness ^of mind^ to attempt such a strange expedient. The success has justified him, but indeed I shoud not have expected it before hand. You do M[r]. Raikes the Honour ^& he deserves it^ to join him with Howard the Glory of England who is now they say at Constantinople. A public statue of him has been talked of: No Patriot ancient or Modern was ever better entitled to it. The Glasgow people have caught the enthusiasm & resolving to stand foremost in the train of his Admirers they opened a Subscription last week for this Statue & in an hour got a considerable sum subscribed.[8]

It will be strange if ^the^ vast public spirited schemes of enlarging the inland Navigation in your part of the kingdom be dissapointed by the refusal of Parliament to concur with them. I see that the Managers of our Scotch Canal between Forth & Clyde are now taking steps to compleat it.[9] It has been at ^a^ stand for several years & the Proprietors have never drawn a farthing of Interest of the great sum of money advanced at the beginning. The reason I believe is that it had been under the Management of a set of people at Edr. who made a ^Job^[10] of it for their friends and connexions, like too many other public schemes to the reproach of our Country. By some Accident the Management for two or three years past has been ^partly or^ cheifly ^in the hands^ of Provost Colqhoon[11] at Glasgow & a few more honester men ^than the former Managers^. The Provost especialy has exerted himself not only in detecting the past villainy, but in recovering some large sums of money on the point of being lost to ^the^ Company & sunk in the same bottomless Gulf. This spirited & dissinterested conduct has struck the English Proprietors & managers who I believe are pretty numerous & made them resolve to take it out of

---

[8] No statue of Raikes appears to have been erected until 1880 in London, with copies in Gloucester and Toronto.

[9] The Forth and Clyde canal, the first in Scotland to be sanctioned by Parliament, was opened in 1775, but it was not finished until 1790. Whatley, *Scottish Society 1707–1830*, p. 75.

[10] 'job', i.e. the arrangement of a lucrative public position or contract for personal gain.

[11] Patrick Colquhoun (1745–1820), statistician, merchant, lord provost of Glasgow (Feb. 1782– Oct. 1784), a founder and first chairman of the Glasgow Chamber of Commerce, and a founder of the Thames police in London. *LBS*.

the hands of the Ed[r]. people altogether two parties are formed the largest consisting of those at London joined with the Glasgow ^people^ & the other of Ed[r]. folks by themselves.[12] I have ^seen^ ~~the~~ two Draughts of ~~the~~ an Act of Parl[t]. for which they were to apply next winter printed & distributed by each of the Parties among the Subscribers or Proprietors. According to one the whole Meetings and management are to go on at London and according to the Other at Ed[r]. I hope & think that the first must prevail & measures be settled for preventing the like abuses & embezlements for the future. The west part of the Canal not yet begun is to take a new direction & join the Clyde in deep water about 11 or twelve miles below Glasgow & the Canal to be so large & deep as to admit Vessels that can sail to any port in Britain or Ireland.[13] I see that Colqhoon & his party who seem to be in the management at present have put advertisements into the news papers for beginning the Work immediately.

Mr. Dempster[14] & Sir A. Ferg[n]. instead of return[g]. to their Country seats went on from Ed[r]. to the North & I see that they have last week gone aboard a ship at Fort William & are to spend six weeks in viewing the Western coast of the Highlands in order to ascertain the proper stations for the fishing towns & other prospected improvements.

Another public scheme is going in Scotland with some spirit, even a reform of the Burroughs & in the management of the funds belonging to these corporations.[15] But I have neither time nor room to enter on this as I must take some

---

[12] John Dwyer and Alexander Murdoch, 'Paradigms and Politics: Manners, Morals and the Rise of Henry Dundas, 1770–1784', in John Dwyer, R. A. Mason, and Alexander Murdoch, eds, *New Perspectives on the Politics and Culture of Early Modern Scotland* (Edinburgh, 1983), pp. 219–20. There seems to have been a competition between Edinburgh merchants and bankers and the Scottish landed elite, who favoured an ambitious scheme for the canal to contribute to the national honour of Scotland, and the more pragmatic Glasgow mercantile and financial community, who supported a more modest, shallower canal construction.

[13] The last section of the canal to be completed joined Grangemouth in central Scotland to Stockingfield on the river Kelvin, near Glasgow. Whatley, *Scottish Society 1707–1830*, pp. 75, 118.

[14] George Dempster (Letter 79) was a determined campaigner for the development of Scottish fisheries.

[15] The campaign for the reform of the closed political constitutions of the Scottish burghs emerged at the end of the American War of Independence via the *Letters of Zeno*, written by Thomas McGrugar, an Edinburgh burgess, and published in the *Caledonian Mercury* in Dec. 1782 and Jan. 1783. The choice of burgh councillors was significant not only in itself but also because they alone had the privilege of voting for the burgh MPs in Scotland (one MP to five burghs, except that Edinburgh had two MPs of its own). A convention of delegates from the royal burghs, representing thirty-three of the sixty-six royal burghs, was held in Edinburgh in 1784 and elected a committee to draft legislation for burgh reform. They produced two Bills in April 1785, one regarding internal mismanagement of the burghs and the other regarding the election

Notice of what you say of M[r]. Warners Papers. To these I have payed no attention for some time past six or seven of the most ingenious of his Sermons preached in the College Chapel are in the hands of M[r]. Arthur also the Translation of the Theorie &c.[16] It may be long enough before I get any Answer from M[r]. Arthur who I understand has now left Glasgow to spend some weeks as he usualy does with a Pupil one Brown who has now bought an Estate in the east Country nor do I hurry M[r]. Arthur having the other bussiness so much at heart. The translation I sent him only some weeks ago, after reading it carefully myself, I think it more finished than anything I have of M[r]. Warners. I mean the Notes which are judicious ingenious & curious. But this Work is not only His but yours all wrote with your own Hand. Perhaps I shoud have asked your consent before I even gave M[r]. Arthur the perusal of it. I wish ^now^ to hear from you about ^it^– the history of it for I do not now distinctly recollect it– M[r]. Warners share of it & yours in the book & in the Notes for I cannot distinguish them. & what is your oppinion and inclination about printing it in case it shoud be thought a right measure to begin with it by Mess[rs]. Arthur & Ritchardson for I allowed it to be shown to the last who eagerly desired it & to none but him.

I cannot encroach further on the cover without deforming it. So God bless you & yours the sinc[e]re wish & Prayer of James Wodrow.

## Letter 122: Samuel Kenrick to James Wodrow, 28 September 1786.

Place: Bewdley
Notes: James Wodrow / D[r]. Wodrow from M[r]. Kenrick / Oct[r]. 1786

My worthy Friend

Your 2 most welcome packets of the 15th. & 29th. Aug[t]. came duly free to hand. I am happy to find that any thing I can send you, should afford you least amusement, amidst your daily serious & important occupations.

---

of the MPs. The first was adopted by the convention in Oct. 1786, and an accompanying report was published in 1787 detailing the abuses and their results in the burghs. Richard Brinsley Sheridan proposed it to Parliament on behalf of the reformers, but the opposition of Henry Dundas, combined with the resistance of other burgh councils, defeated it. Henry W. Meikle, *Scotland and the French Revolution* (Glasgow, 1912), pp. 16–26. See also Letters 128 and 129.

[16] John Warner's translation of Louis-Jean Lévesque de Pouilly, *Théorie des Sentimens Agréables* (Geneva, 1747). For more on this, see the notes on Thomas Christie's letter appended to Letters 143 and 144.

We are all happy to find you have already collected among the Principal's papers, what with life will make up one decent volume– If it should be printed by subscription be so kind as to put M[r]. Wigan's name & mine. You may depend upon my keeping sacredly all the particulars you & M[r]. Richardson[1] sent me respecting that worthy man's last moments– w[ch]. I shall copy off & transmit you whenever you please. When you have collected together your materials, I trust you will set about it in good earnest. Give yourself no concern as to the event: your modesty w[ch]. discourages you, is the surest pledge to every body else of the merit of the performance. Remember my good friend there is not another person alive so well qualified for doing it: for your qualities apart– Who is there that was so well & so long acquainted with him? You remember his first coming to Glasgow & the generous stand that was made in his favour by the Synod so far back as 1743.[2] The real excellence of his character was then known & acknowledged. In 1747 you knew him as a teacher– & can give the best, because you can give the truest, account of him in this character. The nature, the variety & utility of his different lectures. How far superior to the dry latin harrangues w[ch]. were formerly pronounced in that chair under the name of theological erudition![3] The last remains of w[ch]. in that Seminary you & I were witness to under poor Mess John Loudon.[4] Good heavens how unfit ^was^ my mind ~~was~~ then to comprehend those new & abstruse subjects in the plainest dress– much more when made on purpose more unintelligible in a foreign garb– w[ch]. I was then very imperfectly acquainted with! M[r]. Hutcheson was I think the first who introduced ^english^ lectures:[5] & few understood latin or spoke it more fluently than he did. It was to him too, we were in a great measure indebted, as I well remember we were then told, for our worthy Professor: & that very circumstance made him unpopular with many at that time of day.[6] But his transcendent excellence & dignity of

---

[1] William Richardson, professor of humanity (Latin). See Letter 80.

[2] When Leechman was elected to the chair of divinity at Glasgow University in 1743, there was a sustained attempt to unseat him on the grounds of suspected unorthodoxy. Leechman was eventually cleared in 1745. See Martin Fitzpatrick, 'The Enlightenment, Politics and Providence: Some Scottish and English Comparisons', in Haakonssen, ed., *Enlightenment and Religion*, pp. 78–79.

[3] Leechman succeeded the brief tenure of Michael Potter, professor of divinity from 1740 to 1743. But SK probably refers to the much longer tradition of teaching in Latin pre-Leechman.

[4] John Loudon, regent (1699–1727), professor of logic and rhetoric at the University of Glasgow (1727–50).

[5] On Hutcheson's innovative and engaging lectures in English, see William Robert Scott, *Francis Hutcheson: His Life, Teaching and Position in the History of Philosophy* (Cambridge, 1900), pp. 63–65.

[6] For Hutcheson's support of Leechman during the campaign against him, see Kennedy, 'William Leechman, Pulpit Eloquence and the Glasgow Enlightenment', in Hook and Sher, eds, *Glasgow Enlightenment*, pp. 56–62.

character, soon gained him universal respect. No one can explain better than you his manner of treating critical, theological & Scriptural subjects– in w$^{ch}$. candour & liberality kept pace with penetration & sound judgment: w$^{ch}$. was all heightened by a spirit of manly devotion whenever occasion offered, w$^{ch}$. tho' in some measure evanescent, yet left on the minds & hearts of his ingenuous auditors, such impressions as will be cherished to their latest moments.

When he comes to be Principal of that respectable Society[7] you have a new field laid open to you, to expatiate on the duties of that office, & the manner in w$^{ch}$. he executed it. Might not their private litterary Society be mentioned here & the part he took in it?[8] were it only to rouze those gentlemen to make it more public, & to make the world the wiser for their labours. What specimens we have had from Mess$^{rs}$. Moore[9] & Richardson[10] have been well received; & have raised a curiosity to expect many more good things. Ed$^r$. as the Metropolis ought to begin first: there must be many more men of abilities there; the first volume of the Transactions of their Royal Society[11] is to be published this winter– It will be no disgrace to Glasgow to be the second. I hope I shall live to see it. I could not help observing without the greatest satisfaction so many names of laymen, subscribers to D$^r$. Kippis's new edition of D$^r$. Lardner's Works, in Eleven Volumes large 8vo.[12] This is to me a convincing proof of the advancement of knowledge & liberality of mind in that favourite spot. In England most of the subscribers are dissenters– as he was one– tho' I see some of the dignified clergy have honoured him w$^{th}$. their names. But this worthy man enjoy'd a felicity, w$^{ch}$. few of those who dare to differ from the world do; he was respected by all parties.[13] For tho' a

---

[7] i.e. Glasgow University.

[8] For the Glasgow Literary Society, see Letter 108.

[9] James Moor (c. 1712–79), professor of Greek from 1747. According to Richard Sher (ODNB): 'In 1752 he was among the twelve founding members of the Glasgow Literary Society, a university club at which scholarly discourses were read and discussed; there he subsequently presented discourses on a range of classical and modern literary topics. In 1759 he published three of his discourses as *Essays; Read to a Literary Society; at their Weekly Meetings within the College, at Glasgow*, in which he argued various Hutchesonian themes about the importance of classically defined notions of aesthetics for the cultivation of virtue and culture.'

[10] William Richardson, *Anecdotes of the Russian Empire; In a Series of Letters, Written, a Few Years Ago, from St. Petersburg* (1784).

[11] The Royal Society of Edinburgh gained its charter in 1783, and the first transactions were published in 1788. Clark, *British Clubs and Societies*, pp. 97, 264.

[12] 'Proposals for publishing by subscription, the entire works of Nathaniel Lardner' were issued on 10 Aug. 1786. Andrew Kippis, ed., *The Works of Nathaniel Lardner*, 11 vols (1788).

[13] Nathaniel Lardner (1684–1768), presbyterian minister in London and patristic scholar. His *Letter on the Logos* (1768) converted Joseph Priestley to Socinian Unitarianism. Anthony Page, *John Jebb and the Enlightenment Origins of British Radicalism* (Westport, CT, 2003), p. 69.

heretic of the most obnoxious sort, a Socinian, yet I never remember to ^have^ seen any sarcasm, or angry epithet thrown out against him: but when quoted he was generally termed the learned Lardner– he is to be excepted, as Jortin says, out of the number of those, who by following Truth too close at the heels, have had their teeth knocked out for their pains.[14]– But I am running away from my subject.– I still think, what I already mentioned to you that a minute description of the business of a Scots clergiman– w[ch]. might be introduced into the first part of this great & good man's life– would be highly acceptable in this country as it is so little known. The misfortune is, it is so familiar to you, that cannot enter into its minutiæ & real merits, so particularly as it deserves. But in this enlightened age it is high time it sh[d]. be done by a skilful hand– not only to do justice to so many deserving people, but to hold up a mirrour to others, who are so well paid for doing what they might do & have so shamefully neglected. This is one of my Hobbyhorses w[ch]. I c[d]. wish to see well mounted before I quit this mortal scene. The effect I know will in due time be brought about by that unerring wisdom & boundless goodness that pervades the immensity of space– but I cannot help wishing to have a glimpse of it during my transitory existence!

[15]But to go on w[th]. your first letter.– I am happy to find poor M[rs]. Leechman has got the better of her alarming complaints. I can easily believe the heavenly serenity that possesses her mind in every situation.– I am glad to hear that D[r]. Magill's work is in such forwardness & that he is encouraged & suported by so numerous a subscription. I sh[d]. fain hope that D[r]. Leechman's prophecy is true w[th]. regard to the persecution of heretics– tho' I pay the greatest defference to the judgment & penetration of the learned L[d]. Hailes. Be that as it may– All this noise & ferment be it ever so violent will terminate in the author's honour, & in the establishment of truth, as far as his views & arguments are founded in truth. It is astonishing

---

[14] Rev. John Jortin (1698–1770), of Huguenot descent, became a distinguished ecclesiastical historian and literary critic. An Anglican cleric of latitudinarian complexion, he ceased saying the Athanasian creed in the 1730s. For the quotation, see John Jortin, *Remarks on Ecclesiastical History*, 5 vols (1751), I, p. 179. See also B. W. Young, 'John Jortin, Ecclesiastical History, and the Christian Republic of Letters', *The Historical Journal*, 55 (2012), pp. 961–81.

[15] At this point we have corrected an error in the Dr Williams Library collection (which has been preserved in the microfilm edition of the correspondence), whereby a sheet from this Letter 122 was accidentally archived as part of Letter 97, and numbered DWL 24.157(97)ii. The following paragraphs appear to post-date June 1785, the date of Letter 97, referring to the New College, Hackney, which was established in early 1786. At the same time, SK refers to 'your favour of 28 August' and to 'Wright's book', which is mentioned in JW's 28 August 1785 Letter 120; and the 'College club' and Mrs Leechman's journey to Glasgow, which are mentioned in Letter 121.

that men will quarrel & fall out about what they cannot help– their seeing objects differently from each other: & are generous where no one thanks them for their generosity.– Your Leadhills philosophic family exceeds every improvement yet made in this improving age. Like Miss Wodrow's story of the infant Doctor– it only wants one trifling circumstance– its being really a fact.– I am wrong if I asserted that £10,000 was subscribed *in one day* for the establishing of a new academical Institution[16]– it amounts to that sum according to the first published acc$^t$. of the institution– & is since considerably increased. M$^r$. Rogers[17] the principal promoter of it called upon ^me^ some days ago & gave the most favourable report of the continuance of their success unanimity & spirit. I will send you a Copy of the printed acc$^t$. along w$^{th}$. the Wigan & Jesse controversy & an acc$^t$. of the Mo. Review in the course of next month to Chester fair– to be taken thither by Mess$^{rs}$. Gordon of Glasgow.– I cannot recommend any other Rev$^w$. altho I am tired of this as well as you. The English, considering it is carried on by a single person– M$^r$. Matty[18]– late secretary of the Royal Society– & who like M$^r$. Lindsey[19] resigned some good church preferment for conscience sake– I say the English Rev.[20] has been recomended to me for foreign publications particularly. For my own part I am pretty well satisfied w$^{th}$. the New Annual Register[21] w$^{ch}$. comenced 5 years ago– in w$^{ch}$. the article of litterature is very ably handled both foreign & domestic– tho' in a brief manner. You will easily believe his sentiments on these subjects coincide w$^{th}$. my own– w$^{ch}$. is no small recommendation. In this respect

---

[16] This was for the creation of a new Dissenting Academy at Hackney. New College, Hackney was formally established on 13 Jan. 1786 and closed in 1796. 'New College, Hackney (1786–1796)', *DAO*.

[17] Thomas Rogers. See Letter 118.

[18] Rev. Paul Henry Maty (1744–87), attended Trinity College, Cambridge (BA 1767 and MA 1770). The possibility of preferment in the Church ended when he publicized anti-trinitarian views (see the *Gentleman's Magazine*, October 1777). On his father's death in July 1776, he became a librarian in the British Museum, and also a secretary of the Royal Society. He resigned the latter in 1784 after a controversy with the president, Sir Joseph Banks. For the rest of his career, Maty made an inadequate living through writing, editing (*The New Review*, 1782–86), and teaching classical and modern languages. Thomas Seccombe, revis. Rebecca Mills, 'Maty, Paul Henry (1744–87)', *ODNB*.

[19] Theophilus Lindsey. See Letter 79.

[20] *The English Review, or An Abstract of English and Foreign Literature* (1783–96) was predominantly a Scottish enterprise, founded by John Murray (1737–93) and edited by Gilbert Stuart (1743–86). Roper, *Reviewing before the* Edinburgh, p. 22.

[21] The *New Annual Register or General Repository of History, Politics, Arts, Science, and Literature* (1780–1826) was founded by the influential Dissenting minister Dr Andrew Kippis (1725–95). As the title suggests, it was deliberately intended as a rival to the *Annual Register* (1758–), edited by Edmund Burke.

it is much more entertaining than the old Annual Register published by D[r]. Campbell.[22]

I have now accompanied you to Kirk Oswald where I am happy to find you w[th]. M[r]. & M[rs]. Biggar & so many other friends so comfortable.– I think I have seen an acc[t]. of M[r]. Wright's book – & am sorry the ingenious author should fail in meeting w[th]. the reward of his labours. I am now come to your favour of 28 August– M[r]. Wigan & I have nothing to say against the members of the College club– they are certainly much more competent to judge of the propriety of what of this great man's ought to be published than we can be– not to mention the weight of your own judgment. All we want is to see them. These winter nights I hope you will find time to arrange your materials & produce such a memorial of our worthy friend as he deserves & w[ch]. is so eagerly wished for by so many of his friends & admirers.– I am glad to have another glance of M[rs]. Leechman & that her journey to Glasgow was so comfortable. I intended to have given you a sketch as you desire me of D[r]. Priestleys 4 Vo[s][23]– & to begin w[th]. the miraculous conception w[ch]. he wants sadly to get rid of– but I have not time. I will only say that M[r]. Wigan is much disappointed in this performance & thinks his arguments very insufficient. With him it is parturiunt montes[24]– But from the little I have seen I think otherwise. We are both partial remember I for & he against the D[r]. So allowances must be made on both sides. Thank you for the sketch you have given me of the young cou[n]siller. I need not say what an excellent hand you have in striking off a character. One is master of it at the glance. I sh[d]. be very happy to see him however.

As to M[r]. Raikes of Gloucester– who is M[r]. Wigan's intimate friend & printer[25]– the latter I say scouts my story of the poor girl & his not being a Christian– as entirely

---

[22] The *Annual Register* was published by James and Robert Dodsley, and largely composed by Edmund Burke during its early years (1758–65). He was succeeded as editor by Thomas English, whose 'first assistant (1773–1775) was probably Dr John Campbell'. Bertram D. Sarason, 'Edmund Burke and the Two Registers', *PMLA*, 68 (1953), p. 507. Dr John Campbell (1708–75), writer and historian, held regular Sunday literary gatherings at his house in Bloomsbury, and according to Samuel Johnson he became 'the richest author that ever grazed the common of literature'. Francis Espinasse, revised by M. J. Mercer, 'Campbell, John (1708–1775)', *ODNB*. In Letter 59, SK referred to him as 'the late learned & laborious Dr Campbell', *W-K*, I, p. 391.

[23] Joseph Priestley, *An History of Early Opinions Concerning Jesus Christ*, 4 vols (Birmingham, 1786).

[24] Horace, *Ars Poetica*, line 139: 'Parturient montes, nascetur ridiculus mus'; translated as: 'Mountains will labour, to birth will come a laughter-rousing mouse.' Loeb Classical Library.

[25] Robert Raikes (1736–1811), businessman and philanthropist, and editor of the *Gloucester Journal* which his father had founded in 1722. See Letter 113. Raikes published Thomas Wigan's anonymous *Defence of the Clergy of the Church of England* (1786). See Letter 115.

fabulous & absurd. All I can say is, that I did not make it– but had it from the mouth of a reverend Divine who brought [it] directly here from Gloucester– As to the Translation[26] w[ch]. you have found– the notes are certainly M[r]. Warner's– as you will plainly see by his style & manner– & if any of the Translation is mine I should doubt its fidelity to the original from my not understant[g]. French so well as I do now– & even now I should be fond[27] of venturing to translate such a Book.[28] I have written to the same purpose to M[r]. Richardson.

Adieu my worthiest friend & expect to hear again soon. SK

[29]Excuse my hurry– I believe I wrote you some of these particulars before. Did I ever tell you any thing of the D[r]'s correspondence w[th]. Gibbon.[30]

Yrs S.K.

## Letter 123: Samuel Kenrick to James Wodrow, 7 October 1786
Place: Bewdley

Dear Sir,

I wrote you by the post the 29th Ult[o].,[1] an acknowledgement of your two last fav[rs]. of the 15th. & 29th August.[2]– This will introduce to you the farther progress of the controversy between my 2 rev[d]. neighbours. You will see a little of aigreur[3] in both parties, w[ch]. promises to keep up the contest– to the mutual discomfort

---

[26] This refers to John Warner's unpublished annotated translation of Louis-Jean Lévesque de Pouilly's *Théorie des Sentimens Agréables* (Geneva, 1747). For details about this, see Thomas Christie's letter appended to Letter 143, and also Letter 144.

[27] 'fond': 'foolish, silly, indiscreet, imprudent, injudicious'. Johnson's *Dictionary*, suggesting a Scottish etymology, supported by *DSL*.

[28] See Letter 88.

[29] These two lines are on a separate sheet (DWL 24 157(122) ii) that appears at the end of Letter 122 in both the paper Mss and microfilm copy of the correspondence.

[30] SK must have heard about this from Priestley. In his *History of the Corruptions of Christianity*, Priestley called upon Edward Gibbon to debate the evidence for Christianity publicly. Gibbon declined via a private correspondence in 1783 which, after Gibbon died, Priestley published as an appendix to his *Discourses on the Evidence of Revealed Religion* (1794), pp. 412–20. See Paul Turnbull, 'Gibbon's Exchange with Joseph Priestley', *British Journal for Eighteenth-Century Studies*, 14 (1991), pp. 139–58.

[1] Letter 122.
[2] Letters 120 and 121.
[3] i.e. bitterness.

of two worthy men, & in w^ch. the world in general seems to take little or no part. Even here upon the spot, it is almost already forgot.– However, I should like to hear your impartial sentiments on the subject. As to myself I cannot help seeing much truth and justice in the *Parochialia*:[4] so large an establishment as the church in its present form, must be liable to many imperfections– must have many unqualified and improper ministers, who do their duty in a slovenly not to say indecent manner– others affected & foppish. But our friend Wigan comes under neither of these descriptions. The only charges against him are, his zealous attachment to the cause of Civil & Religious liberty– in common w^th. many other fools & idiots, as we were deemed some years ago: w^ch. in reality is a Terra incognita to poor M^r. Jesse: & his preferring honey to butter (p. 121) on his bread for breakfast.[5] So that our friend might have been quiet, & the church have rec^d. no injury. But now a more serious matter is hooked into the dispute. Who are Christians? or rather who are the Church? Whether those who litterally stick to her articles & rubricks, or those who w^d. accommodate these to common sense & reason. Our friend has made the matter still more serious by committing his Diocesan in their dispute; who resides within four miles of him: & calling in question the language of a learned Prelate, whom his Majesty usually terms the Seraphic Hurd & whom our friend acknowledges to be distinguished by his virtues, Genius & Learning.[6] I told you already that the Bishop had taken M^r. Jesse's part.

I promised you a slight view of Dr. Priestley's last 4 Vo^s.[7] It must be slight as I am far from being master of the subject.

---

[4] SK is referring to William Jesse, *Parochialia; or Observations on the Discharge of Parochial Duties* (Kidderminster, 1785). See Letter 100.

[5] Jesse wrote: 'And what is there, which disgusts you, in the epithet *Sweet?* "Sweet Jesus."... The Psalmist tells us, that the word of God was sweeter to his soul, than the honey on which you breakfast, is to the taste;... So afraid are we grown of enthusiasm, that religious affections are regarded with a jealous eye: as if reason alone were baptized, and our *passions* to remain in a Pagan state. *Rational* Christianity, as it is called, which is nothing else than a proud affectation of philosophic wisdom, has almost thrust out of the Church that faith which worketh by love.' Jesse, *Parochialia*, pp. 120–21.

[6] Richard Hurd. See Letters 79 and 118. He had a genuine friendship with King George III, who appointed him tutor to his two eldest sons in 1776, and whose own choice he was for the diocese of Worcester five years later. 'In many ways George III's favourite bishop', Hurd was 'urbane, polished, with a distinguished record of literary as well as theological learning', and 'possessed some courtier-like qualities'. G. M. Ditchfield, *George III: An Essay in Monarchy* (Basingstoke, 2002), p. 97. A follower of William Warburton, Hurd was a leading polemicist against the spread of both heterodox rational Christianity and evangelical dissent. Wigan accused Jesse of selectively quoting from Hurd's *A Charge Delivered to the Clergy of the Diocese of Lichfield and Coventry, at the Bishop's Primary Visitation in 1775 and 1776* (1776), p. 15. At length, and 'with much Freedom', Wigan provided his own interpretation of the passage in question in *A Defence of the Clergy of the Church of England*, pp. 48–58.

[7] *An History of Early Opinions Concerning Jesus Christ, Compiled from Original Writers: Proving that the Christian Church was at First Unitarian*, 4 vols (Birmingham, 1786).

At the beginning is a biographical Chart presenting at one view, for the course of 600 years, the names of the principal personages concerned in this work & the time in w^ch. they lived. And at the end of the Work, you have not only an alphabetical list of the authors, but also a catalogue of their works and the editions the D^r. made use of– of which he collected all he could for love or money.

He has mottos in the title page of each vol.– the first has from Virgil– Antiquam exquirite matrem[8]– followed by a greek one from Eusebius– intimating that all the angry disputes among christians were owing to the neglect of the Scriptures & making use of αγραφαις φωναις,[9] unscriptural words. In w^ch. quotation one word is misprinted, having a syllable left out: w^ch. I expect to find a fresh matter of triumph w^th. D^r. Horsley or some other of the Doctor's antagonists, who are so happy to catch at the most trivial inaccuracy.–

The work is dedicated to a M^rs. Rayner,[10] whose zeal in the cause he here defends, is the motive of this public address, & that posterity may know that there are many warm & able advocates for ^it^ besides the Writers, of the present age. These silent advocates, he observes, have their influence in spurring on the activity of the others, & when united, however few, do not fear combined hosts. He continues in the same exulting strain of confidence of success in so good a Cause, w^ch. therefore ought to be made a matter of general discussion. He commends this Lady's greatness of mind, her extensive knowledge & her intrepidity in the cause of truth w^ch. he hopes will increase his firmness in the same cause. That the greatest happiness of his life is derived from such society as her's & M^r. Lindsey's as well as of many other's who think differently from them w^th. respect to the object of this work, whom it is his warmest wish to rejoin hereafter in the same noble pursuits– in that happy World where truth & virtue will reign triumphant.– But as I have not time to go through the whole I will stop here at present– to communicate to you some particulars w^ch. I have lately picked up concerning this worthy man– w^ch. I rec^d. from the son of one of the most intimate friends the D^r. has in Birm^m.– viz his predecessor in the pulpit where he now preaches.[11]

---

[8] Virgil, *Aeneid*, III, line 96: 'Seek out your ancient mother'. Loeb Classical Library.

[9] αγραφαις φωναις (agraphais phōnais), which translates as 'words which are not written' (in a particular text). As on Priestley's title page, SK has left out the accents and breathings, which should be written as follows: ἀγράφοις φωναῖς. The original text is in Eusebius, *Epistula ad Caeserienses*, 15.3: ἀγράφοις χρῆσθαι φωναῖς, διὸ σχεδὸν ἡ πᾶσα γέγονε σύγχυσις καὶ ἀκαταστασία τῆς ἐκκλησίας (Graeme Miles, University of Tasmania).

[10] Elizabeth Rayner. See Letter 118.

[11] Priestley succeeded Rev. William Hawkes (1732–96), who resigned as minister of the New Meeting, Birmingham, at the end of 1780. Together they published *Psalms and Hymns for the Use of the New Meeting in Birmingham* (Birmingham, 1790). SK probably refers to the son, William Hawkes

Every one knows the D[r].'s indefatigable industry. By this means he might have amassed a large fortune, had he persisted in his philosophical Works alone. But he preferred his Theological Repository,[12] w[ch]. he still supports tho' he loses money by it. That he has sunk a great deal of money in purchasing necessary Books for his History of the Corruptions of Christianity & the present work written in support of the first article.

It is incredible the quantity he reads. He does it in reality by <u>rapid glances</u>. He reads every book litterally thro' in the original. As he goes along he marks every passage ^on the margin^ to his purpose w[th]. a particular mark for the head or topic it belongs to. And when he has thus perused the Volume he gives it to his ammanuensis to transcribe. These transcriptions are then arranged for their different purposes– & he proceeds to the next book. But what a clear distinct head he must have to carry on as one may say so many different works [a]t one & the same time! & how exact must he be in keeping these different elements or materials in the[ir] proper places!

As D[r]. Priestley writes & composes w[th]. vast rapidity– dictating when he has once digested his subject as fast as his amanuensis can write– so he cannot so much as alter or improve what he has written. He is an entire stranger to Plato's[13] and Isocrates'[14] polishing & Horace's[15] tedious file.– Another fact I must tell you on the credit of the gentleman who told me the story of M[r]. Raikes. He assured me he heard a friend of D[r]. Priestley's ask him "are you sure that D[r]. Horsley is a Deist?" The D[r]. answered <u>"I have the most undoubted evidence that D[r]. Horsley is an unbeliever."</u>[16]– When the D[r]. knows this to be the case, what indignation must his honest heart feel in arguing w[th]. so disingenuous ^a^ mind. One anecdote

---

(1759–1820), who served as minister at Minister at Dob Lane, Failsworth, Lancashire, 1781–85; Bank Street, Bolton, 1785–89; and Moseley Street, Manchester, 1789–1820. *DAO*.

[12] The *Theological Repository: Consisting of Original Essays, Hints, Queries, &c. Calculated to Promote Religious Knowledge* was founded by Priestley in 1769 to encourage advanced theological thinking. He published three volumes. Despite support from his friends, they made a loss estimated at 'something less than £30 by the last volume'. He gave up the enterprise late in 1771, hoping that it might be renewed at some time in the future. He revived the journal at the end of 1784; another three volumes were published before it was discontinued in 1788, again for financial reasons. Schofield, *The Enlightenment of Joseph Priestley*, pp. 194–95; *The Enlightened Joseph Priestley*, pp. 202–03.

[13] Plato (c. 428–348 BC), Athenian philosopher.
[14] Isocrates (d. 338 BC), Athenian orator.
[15] Quintus Horatius Flaccus (65–8 BC), Roman lyric poet.
[16] Samuel Horsley, archdeacon of St Albans, was a leading critic of religious and political radicalism. In 1794 Samuel Taylor Coleridge also observed that Horsley was considered to be a deist. Duncan Wu, *30 Great Myths about the Romantics* (2015), pp. 233, 239n.

more. When the D[r]. was at Paris in company w[th]. some of the first rate French litterati, he found they ~~more~~ ^were^ generally unbelievers (as he calls them) & surprized they w[d]. not believe but he was the same. The D[r]. could not submit to such a surmise. But argued most strenuously on the side of revelation. Upon w[ch]. an ecclesiastic, who had been silent all the while, started up, flew to the D[r]., catch'd him in his arms & said, excuse my ardour, I cannot help it; for you are the first philosopher I ever met w[th]. that was a Christian. But hold said the D[r].– You may not perhaps think my notions of Christianity, may come up to your idea of a Christian. Your acknowledging yourself to be one is sufficient for me rejoined the other & embraced him again.[17]

*[The first sheet of the letter ends here, and there is no other sheet with it. It is unsigned and it appears that the rest of the letter is missing.]*

## Letter 124: Samuel Kenrick to James Wodrow, 16 October 1786
Place: Bewdley

My worthy Friend,

I wrote you lately[1] by post & via Chester by the Glasgow merchants[2]– in one of w[ch]. I promised to send you a history of the Monthly Review,[3] w[ch]. fell into my hands sometime ago– ^when^ by some accident it was left behind. But it shall go now.

To go on with D[r]. Priestley's History of the Early Opinions Concerning X– the first Vol. begins with an introduction of 84 pages,[4] in w[ch]. he gives a short view of the principal arguments against the doctrines of the divinity & pre-existence of Christ. (1) From the general tenour of the Scriptures; where the Unity of God is the leading characteristic from beginning to end, w[ch]. must at first sight strike every reader. This is well known to have been the great object of the religion of

---

[17] Priestley's encounters with unbelievers, both at home and abroad, led him to publish *Letters to Philosophical Unbelievers, Part 1* (1780). Schofield, *The Enlightened Joseph Priestley*, pp. 36–37.

[1] Letters 122 and 123.

[2] Probably 'Messrs. Gordon' of Glasgow, who at times carried letters between SK and JW via North Wales. See Letters 90, 115, and 122.

[3] See Letter 122, in which SK promised to send 'an acc[t]. of the Mo. Review in the course of next month to Chester fair– to be taken thither by Mess[rs]. Gordon of Glasgow'.

[4] Also printed in the *Works of Joseph Priestley*, VI, pp. 1–52. SK provides, as he says, a summary of the 'Introduction: Containing a View of the Principal Arguments Against the Doctrines of the Divinity and Pre-existence of Christ'.

the Jews by w^ch. they were distinguished from other nations who worshipped more Gods than one. No Jew of ancient or modern times had ever the most distant idea of a trinity. The same doctrine is as clearly & directly taught in the N.T. Our Saviour himself says that the first of all the commandments is Here O Israel the Lord thy God is one Lord; w^ch. is confirmed by the Scribe's answer. So also the apostles. Peter calls our Saviour Jesus of Nazareth a man approved of God: & Paul says there is one God &c. In consequence of this the first christians, for whose use these books were written saw nothing of the doctrine of the divinity ^& pre-existence^ of Christ (as will be shewn in this history) w^ch. so many christians at this day are so confident they see in them. (2) From the difficulty of tracing the time in w^ch. these doctrines were first divulged. John the baptist preached no such doctrines: & his own disciples considered him as being such a Messiah as the rest of the Jews expected– a man & a king. His being the Messiah was at first published w^th. great caution. The high priest was even so shocked, that he rent his clothes when he heard it. If he had made any higher pretensions they must have transpired. Nor was any such discovery made on the day of pentecost or in any subsequent time. Paul assures his fellow Christians A.D. 58 that he had declared to them the whole counsel of God. In a word in all the histories & copious writings of the apostles, we perceive no traces of their own surprize or doubts or objections of others. (3) from our Saviour being never represented in Scripture as the object of prayer. In the Clementine Liturgy, the oldest extant, contained in the Apostolical Constitutions & composed about the 4th. century, there are no traces of it. In Origen's time, who wrote on the subject of prayer, petitions addressed to any being but the supreme God, were entirely unknown. And such hold have early established customs on the minds of men, that excepting the Moravians only, whose prayers are always addressed to Christ, the general practice of trinitarians themselves is to pray to the Father only. He adds, w^th. his peculiar candour & honesty– *When I was myself a trinitarian, I remember praying conscientiously to all the three persons without distinction, only beginning with the Father; & what I myself did in the serious simplicity of my heart, when young, would, I doubt not, have been done by all christians from the beginning, if their minds had then been impressed, as mine was, with the firm persuasion that all the three persons were fully equal in power, wisdom, goodness, omnipresence & all divine attributes.*[5] This is farther confirmed by the precepts, practices & express example of the apostles– & by Polycarp's dying

---

[5] Priestley, *History of Early Opinions Concerning Jesus Christ*, I, p. 41.

prayer.[6] (4) From its implying an absolute contradiction w$^{ch}$. no miracles can prove. That they are three & yet they are not three.

He next touches on the Arian hypothesis, w$^{ch}$. tho' not an absolute contradiction or mathematical impossibility, as the former is– yet it appears to him highly improbable.[7] (1) There is something in the doctrine itself, w$^{ch}$. if we were not accustomed to it, would appear exceedingly revolting. A Being in human form who was born, grew up & died like other men; requiring the refreshments of food rest & sleep &c having been the maker, & while he was on earth & asleep the supporter & Governour of the world. In the present state of philosophy such an opinion at this day w$^d$. have been rejected without farther examination. That Christ emptied himself of his former glory & power & did not sustain the world during his abode on earth is quite a modern opinion, & on that account can never be rec$^d$. as the original and genuine doctrine of Christianity.– A contradiction is hardly more revolting to the mind than the improbabilities attending such a scheme as this. (2). This hypothesis is no where clearly expressed in the scriptures. The O.T. contains no such doctrine. (3) Christ having made the world hath no connection w$^{th}$. the great & obvious design of the mission of any of the prophets in general or that of Christ & the apostles in particular. The great object is to teach us how to live here so as to be happy hereafter– connected w$^{th}$. w$^{ch}$. is the unity of God, his universal presence & inspection, his placability to repenting sinners, & the certainty of a life of retribution after death. (4) It is not expressed by any of the apostles in a manner so definite & clear or so repeatedly as its magnitude naturally required. He then examines the 4 passages on w$^{ch}$. it is founded viz. Ephes. III.9 Coloss. I.15. Heb.I.8. & John I.1 &c. (5). It will be shewn that it was the natural consequence of other false principles, springing naturally from the philosophy of the times in w$^{ch}$. Christianity was promulgated. As these supports are now tottering he prognosticates the speedy downfal of this edifice, altho' he seems to have many very respectable friends among its still staunch adherents. He next proceeds to shew that arianism implies Idolatry ^& polytheism^ as well as trinitarianism. Lastly he disproves the pre-existence of X from the materiality of

---

[6] Polycarp lived between 70 and 155 AD. A pupil of the apostle John, he became bishop of Smyrna, and was martyred at a time when the Christians were suffering from Roman persecution. Before being burned alive, Polycarp prayed: 'O Lord God Almighty, the Father of thy well-beloved and blessed Son Jesus Christ; by whom we have received the knowledge of thee, the God of angels and powers, and of every creature, and especially of the whole race of men, &c.' Priestley, *History of Early Opinions Concerning Jesus Christ*, I, p. 46.

[7] Priestley, *History of Early Opinions Concerning Jesus Christ*, I, pp. 57–83.

man: & here we are referred to his <u>Disquisitions on Matter & Spirit</u>.[8]– And then we come to the four apostolic Fathers of the first age. But as I am not allowed to stay much longer with you I will release you from hearing any more of it till another opp.^y

I have read Boswell's Tour[9] as well as you & think it as you do a strange Hotchpotch– tho' I must own it is entertaining. But the numberless whims & conceits of himself & hero, ushered w^th. all the imposing solemnity of D^r. Horsley are quite disgusting.[10] You I dare say will cast a smile of pity on his theological notions, as I suppose every tanner & brewer w^d. burst out in a laugh of contempt on hearing of Doctor Johnson discant on their respective crafts:– while the greatest novice in the study of religious liberty must despise Johnson's sophistical reasoning on church establishments– & lastly how must an Oxonian a Cantabridgian or Glasguan be shocked at the author's modesty when he compares his loose crudities with the profound wisdom of Plutarch[11] & attic elegance of Xenophon[12]– In short I can hardly believe the tameness of your litterati before this surly giant. A gentleman told me who was present in London at a conversation between D^r. J & L^d. Montboddo,[13] when the subject was the cross breed between a dog & a fox when the former said it was impossible & therefore he did not believe it. When the other replied w^th. true Caledonian bluntness– *I know it to be a fact & therefore don't care a fig whether Dr. Johnson believes it or no.*

With our best wishes & respects to you & yours<br>
Adieu my dear friend<br>
S.K.

---

[8] Priestley, *History of Early Opinions Concerning Jesus Christ*, I, pp. 84–90. In 1777, Priestley published his *Disquisitions Relating to Matter and Spirit. To Which is added, the History of the Philosophical Doctrine Concerning the Origin of the Soul, and the Nature of Matter; with its Influence on Christianity, Especially with Respect to the Doctrine of the Pre-Existence of Christ*. For a discussion of his monistic materialism, see Schofield, *The Enlightened Joseph Priestley*, pp. 59–76.

[9] James Boswell, *The Journal of a Tour to the Hebrides, with Samuel Johnson* (1785).

[10] On Horsley, see Letters 118 and 123.

[11] See Letter 117.

[12] Xenophon (*c.* 435–354 BC), Greek historian, essayist, and military commander.

[13] James Burnett, Lord Monboddo (1714–99), Scottish judge, philosopher, and anthropologist, who earned some notoriety by claiming a close relationship between humans and chimpanzees. See W-K, I, p. 320n.

## Letter 125: James Wodrow to Samuel Kenrick, 23 November 1786

Place: Stevenston
Addressed: M[r]. Kenrick / of Bewdley / Worcestershire
Postmarked: Ayr Twenty ninth November 1786
Franked: H. Montgomery
Stamped: NO/30; DE/1; FREE E
Note in SK's hand: See that of 9 Jan[y].

My Dearest Friend,

I am now very deep in your debt having received all your three packets safe of Sept 29th. Oct[r]. the 17th. & the one Oct[r]. 7th by the private conveyance, which only, however, reached me about three days ago.[1] I return you my best thanks for all the various entertainment they have afforded; and am much obliged to our friend M[r]. Wigan for the present he ^has^ sent me of his Defense &c.[2] You ask my Oppinion of the whole which I shall give you when I have given a more ^careful^ perusal to both ^sides^ than I have yet done. In the meantime I think M[r]. Wigan's defense one of the ablest that coud be penned on the subject tho' at the same time it must be fruitless or have no effect on the Rector of Dowles[3] & those who think in the same manner with him. The Difference of sentiment is too wide to ^be^ ever accomodated. M[r]. J. & his friends think the tenets of Calvinism and Methodism the very truth & Cream of the Gospel & M[r]. Wigan thinks many of these are nonsensical, that the truths or facts of the Gospel are few & simple and that the grand purpose of it is moral improvement to which indeed every ^thing^ in it is subservient. Yet I have had good entertainment & perhaps some instruction from the Parochialia[4] & expect a little more, ~~having~~ (for I have only slightly read about the half of it having put the whole controversy just now into the hands of M[r]. Boyle[5] who was once a Clergyman in the Church of E. himself for a little intertainment ^to him^). But however well pleased I am with Mr. Jesse's Sincerity & a certain native goodness of heart I am surprised it has not had more influence in correcting that vile spirit of bigotry & bitterness ^he shows^ against his brethren (many

---

[1] Letters 122, 123, and 124 were carried to JW via 'the merchants of Glasgow', probably Messrs Gordon.

[2] Clericus [Thomas Wigan], *A Defence of the Clergy of the Church of England; in a Letter to the Rev. William Jesse, Rector of Dowles, Occasioned by his Parochialia* (Gloucester, 1786).

[3] William Jesse, who was rector of Dowles parish from 1779 to 1815. See Letter 100.

[4] William Jesse, *Parochialia; or Observations on the Discharge of Parochial Duties* (Kidderminster, 1785).

[5] Patrick Boyle. See Letter 98.

of Whom <-> ^he ought to consider as,^ as honest if not so useful as himself). How different is he in this respect from my worthy old friend & neighbour as sincere a Calvinist as himself <-> (yet not a methodist) I mean M^r. Dow of whom I once said, defending him when he was blamed for preaching in ^a^ very high orthodox strain, that the innate goodness of his heart corected & sweetened all the barbarism of his System which indeed it does in both in his Sermons & his temper & behaviour to his friends.[6] He & I have ^since^ lived in the strictest intimacy for 29 years. I believe he thinks me the best friend he has in the World & one of the best preachers. Yet our Articles of Faith are very different, but we happen to set the same value on the Morality of the Gospel & I have heard him often say that no heresy gives him any disturbance but Antinomianism.

I thank you for the encouragement you give me in your Letter Sep^t. 29 to go on with Our Worthy friends Life. Coud I follow your advice to divest myself of all anxiety about the success I am sensible I woud write with more ease & better promote the Success of the publication; but it is almost impossible. At the very time I received yours I was going ^on^ with a rough scetch much in the strain you sugest & you woud be surprised at the coincidence of our Ideas of him as a teacher. Not having sufficiently collected materials ^for the early part of his Life I had begun at His Election to the Theological chair the subsequent persecution he experienced, his method of teaching Polemick Divinity & his Lectures on the truth of X^ty. In the middle of which I am just now, but have been stopped for a month by another interruption one of the Parochialia that M^r. Jesse knows nothing of and it is possible he & his friend, the Attick Hurd[7] whom I not a little esteem from his writings may think of introducing it into the Diocese of W^r.[8] M^r. J. woud be admirably cut out for it by means of his warmth of heart & extempore talents. You will guess I mean the Scotch culture of visiting our parishes exhorting <—> & preaching from house to house. What woud your friend think of going in to every family under his charge giving ^them^ a few short & warm advices to a Xian

---

[6] Rev. Robert Dow (1707–87), parish minister of Ardrossan, north Ayrshire. *FES*, III, p. 79; *W-K*, I, pp. 161, 163, 301n.

[7] Bishop Richard Hurd. In his *Defence of the Clergy*, p. 49, Wigan quoted the following lines acknowledging Hurd's stature as a translator of classical poetry: 'deem infallible no Critic's Word, / Not e'en the Dictates of thy Attic Hurd', in William Hayley, *An Essay on Epic Poetry; in Five Epistles to the Revd Mr Mason* (1782), epistle I, lines 301–02, p. 17. 'Attic': 'Having characteristics peculiarly Athenian; hence, of literary style, etc.: Marked by simple and refined elegance, pure, classical.' *OED*.

[8] Worcester.

temper & behaviour to one another as Husbands & wives parents & child[n]. Masters & Servants &c, & then joining with them in a short prayer. Tell him every scotch clergyman almost, does this annualy besides catechising his Parish in the Church cheifly the Young people. As my parish is very numerous I now satisfy myself with catechising one year & visiting the next. & having neglected the last rather too long I took the advantage of the fine Weather we have had, to do it in the town of Saltcoats one half of which is my parish. It is an easier matter to me than to most of my brethren for tho I go in fact into every house it is only to chatt a few minutes about their temporal affairs, their daughters married or their sons gone to sea or to such & such a bussiness since I saw them ^last^ after which four or five or six families follow me into any house I name & get a little serious exhortation. I am sure this will catch your friends fancy and I expect to hear that is introduced into Bewdley <–> ^or^ the neighbour hood but where am I going— I perfectly agree with you that it woud be a useful & agreeable picture to exhibit a conscientious scots Minister doing his duty in his parish & that I have a fair opportunity in the intended Life of D[r]. L. Yet I cannot do it for the very reason you assign that the scene is too familiar to me & indeed to everybody in this country. It woud not strike or make any impression.[9] Try a few characteristick strokes yourself for you have a good <–> ^hand^ at this sort of painting & I shall see what I can make of it. I will also be much at a loss in drawing D[r]. L. as Prin[l]. I realy know little of the nature of the Office & his manner of discharging the duties of it. Mess[rs]. Arthur & Jardine[10] must scketch out this. Having now got all the materials I expect & little to interrupt me for some time to come except our flitting i.e. removal to our temporary habitation I will now claim your promised favour even the extracts from M[r]. ^Ritchardson's^ Letter to you & any thing from my own Letters memorable or material.

M[rs]. Leechman is now at Ed[r]. I hope well tho' we had a slight alarm about her lately. I must touch briefly on the rest of your Letters. You have forgot the printed Account of the new accademical institution or Project– ^Thank you for the History of the M. Review^. Poor Rose,[11] I had a letter from him in melancholy but pleasing strain from Chiswick about three weeks ago; which I answered immediately, & obtruded upon him my best advice & consolation, which I have no doubt he will take well. His health is not mended.–

---

[9] In fact, JW changed his mind on this question: see Wodrow, 'Account of the Author's Life', in Leechman, *Sermons*, I, pp. 14–15.
[10] George Jardine. See Letter 96.
[11] William Rose. See Letter 116.

I wonder what ails your friend D$^r$. Pr. at the miracoulous conception more than any other miracle. He has in this fulfilled the Prophesy of the M. R$^{rs}$.[12] & given his adversaries an advantage nor can I see how he can ever make good his point without giving up both the Gospels of Mathew & Luke <-> conceiving part of them as spurious or these historians as very credulous & innacurate, & thus shaking the whole fabrick of the Evidence of X$^{ty}$. even to the very foundation. I thank you for the Anecdotes you have sent me of this extraordinary man & also the view you have given me of his late large publication begging you woud go on if it is not very troublesome as it is all I am likely to see & know of that book at least for a great while to come. As to the first I can scarce believe Horsley to be a Deist except I knew the grounds on which D$^r$. P positive oppinion (supposing your friends acc$^t$ of it quite accurate) is founded. It is perfectly natural for D$^r$. Priestley to think <-> so I have often thought so as to the high people in this Country <-> to see a man of sense defending & supporting Nonsense with all his might & ingenuity looks strange & creates a suspicion of Hypocrisy yet you must have something further to establish the fact & if D$^r$. P. has, he woud do well, do a service to the cause of truth to expose its hypocritical Adversaries to the World after the example of his great master, & doubtless he will if it be in his power. For he is not over delicate in these matters. I respect him highly for his Genius, his various & prodigious Learn$^g$. his Ardour for what he thinks truth & his amazing industry in his search after her but I still see (you must forgive me) something of the Bee in his Bonnet something outree something extravagant & fanciful in some of his Oppinions which mightily hurts the Success of his writings & detracts from the weight of the solid arguments with which he supports the rest, I mean in the eyes of the World for as a lover of truth who weights evidence this is or ought to be nothing. Besides the D$^r$. is equaly zealous for every new discovery he makes & in his disputes has not I am afraid sufficient candour to see or feel the weight of what is advanced by his antagonists. He will be much more successful I apprehend in supporting the Socinian Hypothesis from reason & Scripture than from history. On the former point much has been advanced with equal ingenuity by the ancient Socinians & yet there are difficulties <-> on that Hyp$^s$. or arguments not for Arianism but ^for^ the prexistence of X both from reason & Scripture not easy to be surmounted. And <—> as to history ^tho'^ I am almost an entire stranger to the proper sources I suspect that the Historical point in dispute between him & his Adversaries is still more doubtful. You will think me as much prejudiced

---

[12] i.e. *Monthly Reviewers*.

against this good man as our friend Wiggan. It may be so, but I have another friend One John Allan[13] a preacher (a subscriber for Lardner)[14] now in M^r. Warners family who is as much prejudiced in favour of D^r. P. as you are, to whom I read the literary parts of your Letters. Allan tells me the D^r. has a few & but a few Admirers among the Students at Glasgow who go every length with him.

I must not follow the track of your letters any further that I may leave time & room to inform you that I have about a week ago got D^r. Magills book[15] & had read two thirds of it when I was interrupted by your Bewdley controversy. I am perswaded you will like the book tho' it is as he himself says wrote cheifly for the unlearned. The strain of rational piety ^in it^ & the Admirable adress he shows in turning every thing in the Xian scheme to support <-> morality & guarding against the Abuses of it must recommend it to all readers except Bigots & Methodists or mere enthusiasts. Yet I am almost perswaded M^r. Jesse will like it as he has scarce the penetration to see very deep into the Authors sentiments yet ~~doubtless~~ ^probably^ he will but give it him as soon as you can as a Specimen of Gospel preaching in Scotland for it is the Substance of ~~his~~ Sermons ^on these points^ & let me hear his jud[g]ment of it. It is not unlikely he may send the Author to hell as he does D^r. Pr. who is an excellent Practical Writer tho' not so warm & nervuous a one as D^r. M. & does ^not^ manage the Gospel motives to so much advantage. I shall be curious to hear D^r. Pr. sentiments of the book. He will find the Author of the same sentiments with himself as to the person of X except in the <—> point above mentioned but yet the book is harmless & innoffensive all the obnoxious Strictures against the common <-> Opinions about the Satisfaction[16] are struck out by my advice except one single note which he kept in as somewhat curious from the History of Carolina.[17]

---

[13] Rev. John Allan (1737–1812) was minister of Row (1761–1812) in Dunbartonshire, northwest of Glasgow. He married Elizabeth Colquhoun in 1771, and she may have had a family connection to Warner. In Letter 61, when discussing a transaction of mahogany timber, SK referred to both John Warner and a Humphrey Colquhoun, merchant at Port Glasgow. W-K, I, p. 407. 'J. Allen, Glasgow' is listed among the subscribers to Andrew Kippis, ed., *The Works of Nathaniel Lardner*, 11 vols (1788). There is no 'Allen' in the record of ministers in the Synod of Glasgow and Ayr, but it is probably a variant spelling. *FES*, III.

[14] See Letter 122 above.

[15] M'Gill, *Practical Essay on the Death of Jesus Christ*.

[16] i.e. Christ's atonement for the sins of humankind.

[17] See M'Gill, *Practical Essay on the Death of Jesus Christ*, pp. 339–40, citing Alexander Hewat, *An Historical Account of the Rise and Progress of the Colonies of South Carolina and Georgia*, 2 vols (1779), I, pp. 177–78.

Please write me immediately how I am to send the five Copies to you in the quickest & cheapest way. I think of sending you six as they will pack more neatly in a square parcel. & you can easily dispose of the Other to your friend D[r]. Priestley or any body else. If I find M[r]. Finlay[18] at Glasgow willing to undertake sending them I shall not wait for your Answer to this. My friend wishes to have my <—> sentiments of the whole when I have read it which I shall give ^him^ freely. In the meantime I have marked a few innaccuracies in the Language cheifly Scotticisms you will be able to see many more which I wish you woud mark as well as give your sentiments <-> of the whole & those of your friends.[19] The former may be easily corrected in a second Edition if it is demanded but nothwithstanding my repeated hints he has taken no measures to raise any attention to it in England and encourage an English sale without which the book will be in a manner lost notwithstanding his seven or 800 subscribers in this country.[20] I wish you can give any hints on this point. I am sure the book will suit the last of the rational Dissenters among you if it were known & any curiosity raised about it as well as many more of the Clergy in the Church of M[r]. Wigans turn. The Author has expressed [blot] [reg]ard to several of his friends in his notes[21] & paid [me] a Comp[t]. in a very short note above my deserts.[22] There is one note containing I believe one of the severest cuts that ever was given to M[r]. Gibbon at the same time it is ^a^ cut of a polished weapon not like the blunt Cudgels of the English Polemics he complains of. As it may be a while before you see the book I shall transcribe it page 492. It is on these words "Example it is commonly said & very justly is better than Precept". In the Note he says "Here the Ancient Philosophers were for the most part extremely defective. Thus their char[r]. is drawn by one who

---

[18] Probably James Finlay, of Finlay, Robert & Co., merchants in Glasgow. See Letters 90 and 153.
[19] See JW's similar concerns about his own prose in his biography of William Leechman, in Letter 130, and SK's robust reply in Letter 131. Moreover, SK was much less concerned than JW about the limitations that Scots language might place on the appeal of some of Robert Burns's poetry beyond Scotland: see Letters 134, 135, 151, and 152. SK did not reply to JW's concerns about M'Gill's book here until Sept. 1787 (Letter 133), but again, he was more optimistic: 'It is a good book. For it cannot be read, without our being made better thereby. We forget the author & style & think of nothing but the subject & our own feelings.'
[20] See Letter 84 for the financial losses M'Gill and his family had recently suffered, which, together with his high estimation of its quality, explains why JW was so keen to ensure that the *Practical Essay on the Death of Jesus Christ* sold as well as possible.
[21] e.g. Thomas Somerville, William Craig, James Macknight, and William Leechman.
[22] M'Gill, *Practical Essay on the Death of Jesus Christ*, p. 378. On the point that Christ's martyrdom was more perfect than any other martyr's, the note reads: 'These are the remarks of a very dear and valuable friend, the Rev. Dr James Woddrow, who, if he had undertaken this whole subject, would have rendered it unnecessary for me to attempt it.'

will not be suspected of having changed the picture beyond the truth. "In their writing & conversation" says M[r]. Gibbon "they asserted the dignity of reason, but they resigned their actions to the commands of law or of custom.... They concealed the sentiments of an Atheist under the sacerdotal robes... and they approached with the same inward contempt & the same external reverence, the altars of the Lybian, the Olympian & the capitoline Jupiter", which is as much as to say cont[inues] D[r]. M. that these Philos[rs]. were a set of despicable hy[po]cri[tes] who contradicted by their actions the plainest principles of reason, while they professed in their words & writings to assert its dignity; and that they had more knowledge than [the] Vulgar only to be more worthless & crim[page torn]. It is to be hoped our Modern Philos[rs]. who deny revelation, such of them at least as live in the British dominions, are of a very different char[r]., they not being under the same necessity to save appearances as the ancient sages were. They have no occasion to profess any regard to X[ty]. unless when they think the Mask of friendship will ennable them to give it a deeper Wound." He ends the note properly in point of sentiment Having the very force of ^the^ thought being left in ^the^ mind with not a word added to weaken it. But is not the sentence incompleat by <u>an omission which we Scotsmen are most</u> of all apt to fall into? Shoud it not be a deeper wound than an open ennemy or something equivalent. The Book is dedicated to his Collegue.[23]

But I must take my leave of you for the present & write a line to Col. Montgomery to forward this under his directions for L[d]. & Lady Eglinton left this neighbourhood yesterday she is six or seven months gone with child an heir to an estate of £14000 a year if a boy, & to the half of it if a Girl.[24] In the first case both the Col[l]. &

---

[23] i.e. Rev. William Dalrymple (1723–1814), minister of the first charge in Ayr (1756–1814), as M'Gill was minister of the second charge (1761–1807). They co-wrote the account of the parish of Ayr published in OSA, I (1799), pp. 89–96. Dalrymple baptized Robert Burns and was treated with affection in the poet's satire, 'The Kirk's Alarm' or 'The Tattered Garland'. Letters 151 and 152; FES, III, p. 10.

[24] Archibald Montgomerie, eleventh earl of Eglinton (1726–96). His first wife died in 1778, and in 1783 he married Frances Twysden (b. 1762, at Roydon Hall, Kent). Their first child, Mary Montgomerie, was born on 6 March 1787 at Kilwinning, Ayrshire. They divorced in 1788, when Frances was pregnant with a second child who was alleged to have been fathered by Douglas Hamilton (1756–99). Young Frances from Kent probably found it hard being married to an old earl who was, according to James Boswell, a 'violent Scotsman' who had a contempt for the English. 'Hard-drinking, hot-tempered, without intellectual interests, Eglinton was a man of limited ability in all his roles', according to John D. Grainger in his ODNB entry. See also Leah Leneman, *Alienated Affections: Divorce and Separation in Scotland 1684–1830* (Edinburgh, 2019), p. 119; HPO; NRS, Old Parish Registers, Births 599/20/249: Kilwinning, Mary Montgomerie, 6 March 1787, to Archibald Earl of Eglintoun and Frances Twisden Montgomerie.

Keith Stewart[25] will be cut out of their prospects. In the last case only K. Stewart. Nelly has been more than a month at Greenock & seems happy in the Amusements & civilities she has met in that town. I inclose a letter of hers of an old date & a Poem lately copied by Peggy both to Miss Kenrick. ^will^ My affectionate Comp[s]. to her & her Mother.

I ever am yours most sincerely<br>J. Wodrow

## Letter 126: James Wodrow to Samuel Kenrick, 9 January 1787
Place: Stevenston
Addressed: M[r]. Kenrick Bewdley / Worcestershire.
Stamped: JA/<->
Note: answ[d]. this & that of Nov[r]. <-> Jan[y]. 19th

My Dear Sir

I begin to be a little uneasy from not hearing from you. I wrote to you a very long Letter about six weeks or two months ago relative to M[r]. Jesse to D[rs]. Priestley Magill &c, &c, according to the train into which your former Letters led me. I enclosed it in a few lines to Col Montgomery by the post with a desire to direct & forward it with his ^own^ Letters which I do not think he woud refuse me, tho' He has not signified that He had done ^it^ nor did I expect this. I am now apprehensive that either that bulky Letter has been lost which I shall be sorry for, or yours in return, which will vex me still more; cheifly because I asked the promised favour of the extracts from my own letters relative to the Principals illness & death & especialy M[r]. Ritchardson's anecdote relative to M[r]. C.[1] And in case my suspicions be well founded, I am under the necessity of repeating my request & causing you [to] repeat your trouble at least of copying the last: for probably any thing I wrote you may be of little consequence. I also desired you to try your hand at the picture of a scots Country Clergyman.

---

[25] Keith Stewart (1739–95) was a cousin of Archibald Montgomerie, earl of Eglinton. In 1762 he succeeded Montgomerie as MP for Wigtown Burghs and was also promoted to captain in the Royal Navy, and then to admiral in 1790. *HPO.*

---

[1] Cathcart. See Letters 106 and 127.

## 1787, JANUARY 9

I am now thinking of putting in order or drawing out a regular account of the Life & Lectures of our valuable master from the scetches I have jotted down my self & two or three Letters I have sollicited & received from other people relative to the early part of his Life. It will be much too long as it stands at present a fault I am sensible that I am very apt to fall into and which increases with the infirmities of age & which therefore must be corrected if possible. The account I have scetched of his Lectures especialy on the Moral Doctrines & Life of J.X. & the presumptive argument thence arising for the truth of X$^{ty}$. with the principal rules he delivered in the Lectures on Composition makes up about a third or fourth part of the whole. This (with the account of the Heresy process) will need most to be shortned, yet it is calculated to give a stranger to him a distinct Idea of the spirit & even the stile & manner of his Lecturing & may be valuable as a scetch or skeleton of what never will be published. I have sometimes thought of seperating it & subjoining it to the account of his Life yet perhaps it may do as well where it is to give a proper Idea of his Genius talents & usefulness as a teacher.

The length of this preface or preliminary part will I find draw on the publication of two vol$^{ms}$. of his Sermons instead of a single vol. which was the only thing at first intended. And I wish I coud be in readiness to go in with them to Ed$^{r}$. this spring which however I am afraid will ^be^ impossible. They will not be published by subscription. His name ought to secure the success of the publication & the specimen may perhaps <raise> a desire for more.

I sent you by the Manchester Carriers from Glasgow about three weeks ago six copies of D$^{r}$. Magill's book merely because five woud ^did^ not make a convenient bundle. I have not heard from him for some time tho' I wrote ^sent him^ two sheets of paper of my observations or censures on his book (at his own desire) just after I had read it & this with a view to a 2$^{d}$. Edition which I hope will soon be called for. Any of the laity in this corner who have read it are much pleased with it, & also the moderate Clergy yet I see few at this season but I hear it begins to make a noise in other places of the country. They have been thundering anathemas against it, in the pulpits of Kilmarnock particularly a very young & very popular Brother lately ordained there a M$^{r}$. Makinley[2] one of my ^<list> of^

---

[2] Rev. James MacKinlay (1756–1841), ordained minister of the Laigh Kirk, Kilmarnock (second charge) on 6 April 1786. An 'Auld Licht conservative', his presentation in December 1785 by James Cunningham, earl of Glencairn was criticized by Moderates, and he was not ordained until April 1786; Burns condemned the appointment in 'The Ordination' (1786), and referred to him as 'Simper James'. Alan Bold, *A Burns Companion* (Basingstoke, 1991), 240–41; J. Walter McGinty, *Robert Burns and Religion* (Aldershot, 2003), pp. 160–62; *FES*, III, pp. 106, 108. Both

Subscribers, who called ^it^ from the Pulpit a refuge of Lies said, the Author represented our Sav^r^. as a fool & I know not what more stuff. Upon which a Club of his hearers next day, sent him a card, signifying that since he had so poor an oppinion of the book they woud be obliged to him for i[t] & woud thankfuly return him the price he had paid, not being able to find a Copy in town. He scratched his head, thought about it a little, & returned them an answer that he coud not part with the ^Book^ as yet. At Glasgow ^it is said^ the orthodox Clergy are highly offended, scheming a prosecution, & even drawing up a Libel against the Authour. The Language of the D^rs^. Friends is, "Go on, go on, you zealous fools! and you will soon propagate the Heresy <— —> sufficiently, & put some hundred pounds into the Pocket of the Author of it.["] The Book tho' wrote with that honest and decent freedom becoming the cause of truth, is yet as inoffensive as you can well immagine. It is impossible the Gen^l^. Assembly can find fault with it whatever the inferiour courts may do; & notwithstanding the zeal of young Bigots, the old leaders of the high party are too wise to risk a check, perhaps a stigma from that court, even the censure of being found slanderers usualy pronounced on those who fail in the prosecution of a Clergyman.

I have spoke to your customers Wat & Gray about the Hops they said the reason of their not repeating their commission was that yours tho' much cheaper than any they ever got did not answer their purpose & that they ^now^ find their account in getting the finest Kentish hopes from London at a much higher price.[3] They expected you woud have drawn on them for what they are indebted to you. And as soon as they can find your Account they are ready to settle with me that is to give my Wife about £1"12 & me £1"16 for M^rs^. ^Magill^ & remit you the ballance by a bill on London which shall be done.– Nelly is lately returned from Greenock in good health. We are on the eve of going into another house which will be troublesome.[4] I am also plagued with <the> a nigardly scheme of one of my Heritors[5] about the new manse. I expect he will soon be made sheriff by L^d^.

---

Burns and Wodrow emphasized Mackinlay's youth, but he was nearly thirty years old when he was presented to the charge. Wodrow had been only twenty-six when he was presented to the charge of Dunlop; but perhaps he did not take part in presbytery controversies at so early a point in his career.

[3] See Letters 104 and 105.

[4] A new manse (minister's house) was built for Wodrow and his family in 1787, which was still in use as the manse of Stevenston Church of Scotland in the early twenty-first century.

[5] Local landowners, who, as the principal financial contributors, had powerful voices in decision-making regarding the material fabric of a parish church and any associated buildings. Mutch, *Religion and National Identity*, pp. 93, 121, 128–30. See Letter 128.

Eglin^ns. Int^t. & that the adition of £200 a year will open his heart. As I am anxious to hear from you I will send this by post directly.

God bless you & yours<br>J Wodrow

## Letter 127: Samuel Kenrick to James Wodrow, 19 January 1787
Place: Bewdley
Addressed: D^r. Woodrow / Irvine / Scotland
Postmarked: Birmingham January the twenty third 1787
Franked: Free Westcote
Stamped: [B]IRMI[NG]HAM/[C]ARLISLE
Note: Please send the enclosed, if convenient by a private hand to Maybole, if not by post.

My dearest Friend,

Be assured your friend Col. Montgomery[1] was punctual in franking to me your very kind favour of 23^d Nov^r.– that I, & I alone, am to blame for not doing what I ought to do.– But first to the business in hand– & if I have room, shall notice other particulars in that & your last kind l^r. of the 9th. inst. at the close of this packet.

M^r. Richardson[2] in his l^r. of the 13th. May 1786– <u>says</u>, "That he had long intended to have given me some acc^t. of the last scenes of the life of <u>my</u> worthy friend D^r. Leechman. What I can remember, he continues, ^I will^ even at this late period, set before you; for it deserves to be known. His health declined gradually. He was attacked by no violent illness; but became almost a shadow. The feeble corporeal frame was quite disabled & rendered incapable of performing any vigorous function. But the spirit was entire: his understanding firm; his affections ardent. In his last days the contrast between debility of body & strength of mind was indeed remarkable: in so much that the difference was almost visible. For several weeks before his death he was quite sensible of his situation. And employed his remaining exertions in conversation with his friends. His topics were the truths & joys of religion; consolation to such of

---

[1] Hugh Montgomerie. See Letter 80.
[2] William Richardson. See Letters 80, 106, and 122.

his friends as needed it; affectionate exhortation to others; & warm wishes for the prosperity of our Society. I called for him one evening, about three weeks before he died, along with M$^r$. Cathcart,[3] formerly a pupil of mine, now at Oxford & intended for the church of England. The young gentleman's father had been intimate w$^{th}$. D$^r$. Leechman, & himself well known to him. The conversation between them was interesting: & as near as I can recollect, our good friend lying on his deathbed, a mere skeleton, but with a placid aspect, an animated eye, a distinct tho' feeble articulation, said to him, taking him by the hand,–

"'I am always happy to see you, particularly so at present. You see the situation in which I am. I have not many days to live, & am glad you have had an opportunity of witnessing the tranquility of my last moments. But it is not tranquility & composure alone. It is joy & triumph. It is complete exultation.'– his features kindled, his voice rose as he spoke– 'And whence' continued he, 'does this exultation spring? From that book'– pointing to a bible that lay on a little table by his bedside.– 'from that book, too much neglected indeed, but w$^{ch}$. contains invaluable treasures; treasures of joy & rejoicing; for it teaches us, that this mortal shall put on immortality. You have chosen the church for your profession. I am a Presbyterian; you are of the church of England. The difference between us is not great. I will therefore assure you, that if you enter with a just & proper spirit into the discharge of your duty, you will find it a source of the highest enjoyment, in all periods of your life, but especially at the last. If happiness be connected with the contemplation of the grandest & most elevating objects, what can be grander or more sublime than the views exhibited by Christianity! Your father was my friend; I have always been interested in your welfare, & am happy on my deathbed to give you an old man's blessing.'– He shook hands with him again.– But this scene affecting as it was, was not singular. It was in this manner, that, retaining his reason & affections till the last, he conversed with all his friends: & then easily fell asleep: so easily that for sometime those who were in the room with him were not sure of the exact minute of his death."–

The first mention that you make of this interesting subject, is at the end of your l$^r$. of the 31$^{st}$ Oct$^r$. 85.[4]

"D$^r$. Leechman has been ill of late of a Rose, as they call it, in his face. Louisa has written to her aunt for more certain acct$^{ts}$. than we have had as he is not without danger. Miss Dunlop daughter of our old Greek Professor had called to ask for

---

[3] See Letter 106.
[4] Letter 104. See that letter for footnotes.

him lately when he was confined to his bed. When he heard her named he sent for her to his bedside & accosted her in this manner. 'Sally I wished to see you & talk with you a little; for I hope very soon to see your father'" &c you add– "I hope however this meeting of the two very dear & worthy friends will be put off for some little time, if it be the will of heaven".– Next in your kind l$^r$. of 1st Dec$^r$. 85[5] you tell me you went to Glasgow 3 weeks ago to meet Nelly & to see the worthy Principal once more, for the time of his departure is now at hand.– After mentioning Miss Nelly's agreeable & safe arrival at home, you proceed– "But I must hasten to a subject more interesting to you– melancholy but yet pleasing– even the last scene of D$^r$. Leechman's life. For it is now drawing to a close, if not entirely closed. After recovering from what we call a Rose & swelling in his face & other complaints, he was ab$^t$. 5 weeks ago seized suddenly when drinking a dish of tea in his dining room in his usual health & conversing with his friends in a more lively way than usual, with a shaking all over his body, resembling as M$^{rs}$. Leechman wrote the last pangs of nature. He lost the power of his left side. Physicians & assistance were got in five minutes. He was carried to bed & in a short time recovered his speech & took the medicines given him. When M$^{rs}$. Leechman told him she was glad to find him so easy, he said it was too soft a term, he was in a state of joy & exultation. In that happy state of mind he has continued almost ever since, amidst extreme bodily weakness, unable to turn himself in his bed, & various turns of his disease. # # In ten days or a fortnight, however, he was seized w$^{th}$. a violent flux, w$^{ch}$. it was thought w$^d$. soon carry him off. M$^{rs}$. L (who hitherto had declined having the aid or assistance of any of her friends except their prayers) desired D$^r$. Irvine, ^who along^ w$^{th}$. D$^r$. Stevenston attended him, to write to me. I was in Glasgow before the letter could reach me & found him indeed very weak, unable to speak but at times, & then his mind as firm composed & acute as ever, & for the most part easy & free of pain; at other times restless & his posture uneasy to him, so that it was necessary to move him & alter it every minute almost w$^{ch}$. however he bore with great patience, longing for his dissolution & triumphing in the prospect of it, repeating at times to himself the finest passages in the N. Testament. This corruptible shall put on incorruption & this mortal put on imortality. O death where is thy sting &c Even so come Lord Jesus. And many others to the same purpose. When he once complained of his bodily weakness, I congratulated him on the distinctness, ease & vigour of his mind. He said the promises of the Gospel were so plain that it

---

[5] Letter 106, JW to SK, 1 Dec. 1785. See that letter for footnotes.

required no stretch of mind to recollect or apply them. He confessed he was sometimes a coward for pain but never was of death.

"It w$^d$. far exceed the bounds of a l$^r$. to tell you every thing worthy of admiration in the behaviour of this Saint, as you once with great propriety called him, who has appeard as dignified & venerable in his latter end as his best friends could wish. Most of the things I alluded to happened before I came such as his sending for Professor Anderson & giving him as a Xtian a full & formal forgiveness. He spoke about 10 minutes to him: but M$^{rs}$. L not quite pleased with Andersons behaviour w$^d$. not tell me fully what passed. On a Sunday, the day before I went in expecting it w$^d$. be his last day from the violence of the flux, & finding himself revive a little, he sent for all his servants & family, gave proper advices first to M$^r$. Pearman his nephew a minister, then to each of the servants separately, thank them for their concern attention & toil, shook hands w$^{th}$. each of them & gave them his blessing– then prayed & part of this was a most fervent & excellent prayer for the College, both Professors & students– in all this he spoke near half an hour with astonishing vigour & fervour. Next day he sent for D$^r$. Finlay, told him he was sorry he was now so weak that he could not see each of the Professors, & separately as he had intended, but sent them by him his best wishes & blessings & advice to continue to exert themselves in their several departments &c. A very affecting interview he had w$^{th}$. a M$^r$. Cathcart, youngest son of the late L$^d$. Cathcart, an intimate friend of the Principal's. The young man a student at Oxford for the church had called & was denied admittance by the servants. The Principal sent for him & gave him his advice & his blessing in such a manner as is likely to leave an indelible impression on him. M$^r$. Richardson who was present told the substance of what the Principal said & that M$^r$. C. was greatly affected. Other things I c$^d$. write of the same kind had I time or room, some of which I was witness to. But he was so weak before I saw him that he spoke little. I saw him only 2 or 3 times every day– sometimes drank tea by him, chatted w$^{th}$. my Brother, M$^{rs}$. L. M$^r$. Pearman at his bedside, unable to speak himself he liked to hear us chat about what was passing in the College, books &c. Now & then he spoke a sentence, for his mind at perfect ease was susceptible of entertainment & amusement, & entered into it w$^{th}$. much good humour. They found means to stop his flux & for 2 days at the end of the first week I staid in Glasgow when he took more nourishment & had gained some more strength to speak recovered the use of his left hand & I had some faint hope that he might still recover. But the beginning of last week he fell again into a sleepy dozing way yet perfectly sensible when roused, & began again to lose every day. The last day I was in town he spoke none at all. After taking some drink I asked him how he was? He answered distressed, but not miserable & this in such a faint voice that I could not understand it, till M^rs. L. repeated it. Good woman she is wonderfully composed & resigned, night & day she continues at his bedside. And it is perfectly astonishing how her delicate frame has stood the anxiety watching & fatigue of her attendance. I left Glasg. on Thursday had a l^r. from D^r. Irvine Sunday signifying that he had fevered that day I left Glasg. as & was growing worse & worse, this determin'd me to return to Glasg. as yesterday: but on Tuesday I had a second l^r. from the D^r. describing the progress of his disease. That the fever had taken his head, that he was in great pain on ~~Satur~~^un^day & Monday. But that night he had slept well, his skin cooled, his pulse became regular on Tuesday morning; so that the D^r. apprehended he might live some days still. Yet he was subject to such sudden turns that nothing c^d. be promised on him. Upon this I returned from Irvine # # & expect still to see him in life on Monday."–

Now I come to your last l^r. of the 27th Dec^r.[6] in w^ch. you regret your not proceeding from Irvine to Glasgow, to have seen & enjoyed more of the last moments of this truly great & good man. You say "The next day, thursday, he recovered to a degree that astonished the physicians & his friends: conversed w^th. them easily & chearfully & was thought better than he had been for many weeks. But this gleam of hope was soon extinguished by a sudden attack of his first disease; not only on his extremities as formerly, but on his whole body. It convulsed his breast & face in a terrible manner, so that as the D^r. wrote he never dreamed he could have got out of it. He did however recover it perfectly in an hour or two; seemed quite sensible & free of pain, tho' he spoke none, but <u>yes</u> or <u>no</u> in answer to their questions: his countenance resumed its wonted placid serenity & sensibility & even exhibited a higher degree of elevation of mind than ever it had done before: yet his eyes were shut for the most part, sometimes opened, but only to lift them up to heaven regardless of everything around him, except M^rs. L. who repeated some of the passages of Scripture w^ch. she had often done before & a hymn that he was fond of. In this manner he continued thro' the evening & night till between 12 & one on Saturd^y. morn^g. he expired & this in so easy & insensible a ~~manner~~ ^way^ that they judged it might have happened a quarter of an hour before they observed it." (I cannot resist the pleasure of adding your kind apostrophe) "May you & I & our good friend M^r. Wigan have the like happy death! Every the smallest circumstance about this Saint I doubt not will be interesting to you."– You

---

[6] Letter 108, JW to SK, 27 Dec. 1785. See that letter for footnotes.

then mention your journey to Glasgow the Monday following, where you found his most amiable consort behaving w[th]. her usual composure & fortitude, having shewn herself thro' the whole of this scene a wife worthy of such a husband.– Several other handsome things are said of this worthy lady, w[ch]. shew how well she is entitled to have her virtues recorded along with those of her excellent husband, in your intended memoirs.

This I will forward you immediately under my good friend Lord Westcote's cover– in return you will tell me if you are satisfied with these extracts– & let nothing cool your ardour in rendering justice to a Character, revered by many still alive who have been blessed w[th]. the benefit of these instructions & who will read w[th]. pleasure every particular tending to illustrate his memory.– while those who only knew him by the voice of fame & utter strangers will read w[th]. pleasure the history of so good & great a man. I shall not therefore detain you at present w[th]. my remarks w[ch]. I know you expect upon your warm attack on my favourite hero[7]– I know your view of doing it is only to provoke your friend to say all the good he can of the person in question, whose virtues & talents you love & admire as much as I do– much less, in giving you any farther acc[t]. of his late publication. But I make haste, to thank you for sending so many copies of D[r]. Magill's book;[8] w[ch]. I hope will put it into my power to extend his fame & promote as inter[ests] hereabouts. Therefore he may depend o[n my] presenting D[r]. Priestley w[th]. a copy & begging his [sentim]ents on it, w[ch]. I shall not delay forwarding to you.

Your last favour of the 9th inst. overwhelms me w[th]. shame & sorrow– that I should be the means of hindering in any respect progress of your work. I am happy to find you are so far advanced in it & have met w[th]. such encouragement. You must find the highest pleasure in it: & be assured that whatever pleasure you find in composing it, will be felt by me & thousands more in perusing it. As to the episode you are so kind as to assign to my feeble hands, I only wish I could do it: but w[d]. it not come more naturally in your intended sketch of the life of the late Saint of Kilbarchan?[9]

We are happy to hear you have a prospect soon of having a new & more comfortable manse. I hope you will prevail on your more niggardly Heritor– who I dare say is as rich as a Jew[10]– to withdraw his opposition. We are glad to hear

[7] Joseph Priestley.
[8] M'Gill, *Practical Essay on the Death of Jesus Christ.*
[9] John Warner. See Letters 84 and 114–21 inclusive.
[10] Edward I expelled Jewish people from his kingdom in 1290, and Oliver Cromwell readmitted them to Britain in the 1650s. While in the broader European context eighteenth-century

Miss Nelly is come home in such health & spirits. She & you may depend upon hearing from us soon again.

I much approve of your deducting what was due to M[rs]. Wodrow & for D[r]. Magill from Watt & C[o].'s[11] Acc[t]. & their sending us a draft on London for the Balance of their acc[t]. My wife & Mary unite in our most affect[te]. regards to you & yours. I ever remain

My dearest fr[d].,<br>S.K.

## Letter 128: James Wodrow to Samuel Kenrick, 26 April 1787

Place: Stevenston
Address: M[r]. Samuel Kenrick / Bewdley / Worcesters[el][1]
Postmark: Lond[n]. May fourth 1787
Frank: E. Eglintoune
Stamp: 4/MA/87
Note in SK's hand: answ[d]. to Ed[r]. 11th. May 87
Note: 87

The generous heart of my worthy friend has already anticipated my excuse for a silence of several months & made every allowance I coud wish for the occupation of my mind & my time with the intended Publication. I cannot any longer deny myself the pleasure of <——> writing a few lines to thank him for this and for the assistance he has given me, by his letter of Jan[r]. 19th. by reviving the impressions I had of the Princl[l's] Death at the time it happened & communicating M[r]. Ritchardsons Anecdote, which is an affecting and a capital one. I have now the Satisfaction to inform him that the Account of D[r]. L. Life & Lectures is finished excepting a few sentences relative to his Will & to the Sermons which may be

---

Britain was relatively tolerant, derogatory antisemitic stereotypes were common. Todd M. Endelman, 'The Jews of Great Britain (1650–1815)', in Jonathan Karp and Adam Sutcliffe, eds, *The Cambridge History of Judaism: Volume 7, The Early Modern World, 1500–1815* (Cambridge, 2017), ch. 35.
[11] Hugh Watt. See Letter 104.

[1] This letter is addressed more simply in JW's hand on an address panel on its final page, to M[r]. Samuel Kenrick / Bewdley / Worcestershire / Worcestershire. It is addressed as noted above in a different hand, and postmarked, franked, and stamped on a separate wrapper.

better added afterwards. And I am happy that it is so far advanced as to be put out of the reach of any accidents that may happen to myself. It has cost me more time & Labour than I expected for I have not the same facility in arranging & expressing my thoughts which I had in the prime of Life. The Labour has been pleasant as a grateful tribute of respect to the Memory of a man whom I loved & revered above all others. It has run out to a great length even 60 pages ~~the~~ ^the^ paper indeed a little smaller than this is. Perhaps ^it^ may be chargeable– with the common fault of Old Age. But the Account of the Lectures particularly those of the internal Evidences of X$^{ty}$. make ^up^ about a 3$^d$. part of it & the few friends to whom I have read it, say this is the best part of it as these Lectures never will be published. His Life has more variety than that of many Literary men. Of the private & retired part of it I have picked up something memorable from M$^r$. Bradfoot[1] of Dunsyre & Miss Mure of Caldwell[2] his Pupils Sister. A long extract from one of her letters I have inserted without naming her an admirably exact picture of him, before he appeared in public Life.[3] You will be struck with the likeness. I read the whole Life to her on Tuesday forenoon except a part of the lectures. She said it was long yet she woud not wish to ^have^ wantd[4] a sentence of it. She had wrote down something that ^He^ had said to her on his Deathbed which she made a search for, to have shown me but coud not lay her hand on it. And I was limited in time obliged to leave Caldwell before Dinner.

I have now began to read & revise some more of the Sermons. This will be a work of time & Labour tho' not accompanied with the same anxiety that I felt in the former branch & that was unavoidable in an effort to do justice to the memory of such a venerable man. The Sermons will speak for themselves even tho' they want the last polish of his hand. None of them are wrote a 2$^d$. time but several of them improved by additions on seperate scraps of Paper by Interlineations such as render them in some places almost illegible. These passages must be wrote over on a seperate Paper & the whole put into the hands of somebody to make out a fair Copy for the Printer for none of them can be printed from his own Copy intended only for himself. It is lucky he was a stranger to every kind of shorthand. I think there must be two vol$^s$. of Sermons printed & I wish it may be in my power engaged as I am with other necessary things before this, to have every thing ready for the press before next winter.–

[1] John Bradfute. See Letter 120.
[2] Elizabeth Mure. See Letter 120.
[3] Wodrow, 'Life of Leechman', pp. 10–13.
[4] 'wanted', i.e. 'missed, lacked'.

# 1787, APRIL 26

Nelly begs her excuse may be made to Miss Kenrick for her not writing but promises to do it ^in^ the first frank we can procure. I brought her home this week from Neilston where she had been some time with her friend M^rs^. Monteith Annie Cunn^m^.[5] Miss Kenrick knows her.

Your last Packet[6] came safe to my hand not long ago with all the Printed Papers. I have neither time nor room to advert to the contents of this & your former Letter. It grieved me to see the careless & illiberal spirit of a British house of Commons apparent in their treatment of the Dissenters Petitions.[7] It will be an indelible reproach on the good sense of the Age. But the honest & worthy men must persevere as Charles Fox directed them.[8] I suppose the H of C will treat in the very same manner our Petition from Scotland for a reformation of another kind even in the Constitution of our Royal Burghs,[9] a vile auttocracy founded on the Dutch plan: The Magistrates having it ^in^ their power to apply the revenues of the Burghs as they please. For [page torn] found that there is no court in Scotland have any power to call them to an account or controul them. The Courts of Session & of Exchequer have one after another ^declined^ to redress the complaints of the Inhabitants against the Magistrates confessing the justice of <—> the complaints & regreting their want of Power to help them directing ^them^ to apply to Parliament: and now the Deputies from the Inhabitants after expending a considerable part of the money subscribed ^for^ in their own Country, have set out for London, at their own private Expense to sollicit the Justice of the English House of C. ^Parliament^ & obtain if possible a better constitution but I am affraid with little chance of Success.[10]

---

[5] Ann Cunningham (c. 1762–1848), daughter and heiress of George Cunningham of Monkredding (approximately 2 miles north-east of Kilwinning). In August 1786 she married Rev. John Monteath (1752–1843), minister of Neilston (1785–97). He also served as minister of Houston and Killellan from 1781 until his death. *FES*, III, pp. 140, 158.

[6] Missing letter. Probably sent after 28 March 1787 (see next note).

[7] The motion to repeal the Test and Corporation Acts was defeated by 176 votes to 98 in the House of Commons on 28 March 1787. G. M. Ditchfield, 'The Parliamentary Struggle over the Repeal of the Test and Corporation Acts, 1787–1790', *English Historical Review*, 89 (1974), pp. 551–77, at 552.

[8] On Charles James Fox's support for the 1787 motion, see Theophilus Lindsey to William Tayleur, 5 April 1787, in Ditchfield, *Letters of Lindsey*, I, p. 505.

[9] See Letter 121. JW was correct, or even over-optimistic: Sheridan presented the Glasgow petition for the reform of the Scottish burghs to the House of Commons on 28 May 1787, which debated it briefly before dismissing it without a vote. *The Parliamentary History of England, From the Earliest Period to the Year 1803*, ed. William Cobbett, 36 vols (1812–20), XXVI, cols 1214–17.

[10] See Meikle, *Scotland and the French Revolution*, pp. 16–26. Two cases at the Courts of Session and Exchequer brought by the burgesses of Nairn and Dumbarton respectively in 1784–87 had tested the power of those Courts to reform the Scottish royal burghs. Failure in both cases

I do not remember if I wrote to you that M\(^r\). Ham\(^n\).[11] has at last gone into a very liberal scheme of rebuilding my manse. They have given me £260 besides the materials of the Old Manse & £13 more as 1½ years rent of the house I am in.[12] M\(^r\). Ham\(^{ns}\). share comes near £100 & M\(^r\). Warners not much less.[13] In consequence of this the building is begun & in a week will be up at the Joists that is 13 feet from the foundation but the floor is raised 1½ feet above the ground. It will be both a handsome & convenient house compared with the former. I cannot expect many years enjoyment of it but hope for a better & eternal House.– M\(^r\). Ham\(^n\). has lost the Sherrifship which M\(^r\). Craig has obtained.[14]

I think of going in a fortnight to Glasgow & forward to Ed\(^r\). where M\(^{rs}\). Leechman has been for seven or eight months & and has recovered her health. Our members of the Ass\(^{ly}\). are chosen.[15] If one of them declines I shall take his place. If not I am very indifferent having sufficient bussiness of diff\(^t\). kinds at Ed\(^r\). without the trouble of attending that Court. I hope D\(^r\). Magills books are now in your hands. Please signify if the bill was duely answered & if any thing further be necessary to be cleared between Wat & you.

We all join in affectionate Comp\(^s\). to all with you. I am ever sincerely yours

J. Wodrow

---

resulted in the parliamentary petition, but it proved difficult to persuade any MP to propose the motion in the House of Commons. George Dempster, William Pitt, William Wilberforce, and Charles James Fox all declined before Sheridan agreed.

[11] See Letter 126. Alexander Hamilton of Grange, a second cousin of the founding father of the USA of the same name, who inherited the Grange estate in 1774. In 1787 he also built or Kerelaw or Grange House as a family residence in place of Kerelaw (or Kerrylaw) Castle, which then fell into disrepair. He was also an advocate, and was thus eligible to stand for the sheriff-deputyship of Ayrshire; later, he was Lt. Col. of the second Regiment of Ayrshire Local Militia. He sold the Grange estate in 1792. Strawhorn, *Ayrshire at the Time of Burns*, p. 296.

[12] NRS, CH2/197/6 (Irvine presbytery minutes, 1759–94), ff. 519–20, 13 Feb. 1787 confirms JW's report here in detail and supplies the names of the heritors. See Appendix A.

[13] Patrick Warner, presumably JW's cousin, brother of John Warner (Letter 88). See *W-K*, I, pp. 325, 363, 431: JW blamed him for failing to settle the family portions of his father's bequest until 1776, when JW persuaded him to work through the accounts, which produced annuities for JW's unmarried sisters. Perhaps Warner's generosity in bearing two-fifths of the cost of the new manse at Stevenston repaired some of the irritation he had caused previously.

[14] William Craig, advocate, afterwards Lord Craig, son of Rev. Dr William Craig (see Letters 108 and 118) was appointed sheriff-depute of Ayr on 26 March 1787 after William Wallace of Cairnhill died on 28 Dec. 1786.

[15] i.e. the General Assembly of the Church of Scotland. In May 1787 the members from the Presbytery of Irvine were Rev. John Fullarton (1735–1802) of Dalry, Rev. Arthur Oughterson (1736–1822) of West Kilbride, Rev. James Mackinlay of Kilmarnock (see Letter 126), and the Hon. Patrick Boyle of Shewalton (see Letter 98). NRS, CH2/197/6 (Irvine presbytery minutes, 1759–94), f. 522. However, Wodrow did in fact attend this sitting of the Assembly: see Letter 130 below.

## Letter 129: Samuel Kenrick to James Wodrow, 11 May 1787
Place: Bewdley
Addressed: The Revd. Dr. Wodrow / at Mr. James Balfour's[1] / Writer to the Signet[2] / Edr.
Postmarked: May 11th. 1787
Notes: 83–7

My dear Friend,

Your welcome favour of the 26th. ult°. came duly to hand under the E. of Eglintoune's frank, written in a more legible hand than usual. His lordship seems to be getting young again in more things than one.[3] It gives me the greatest pleasure to find that you have finished the first part of your business; wch. I long to see. I can easily believe the labour & anxiety it must have cost you; from your desire of doing justice to the worthy character, wch. you have handed down to posterity– & from the awe wch. every ingenuous mind must feel, at its first appearance, at least, at the bar of the public. You think your toil & labour amply repaid, by finding yourself able to pay this grateful tribute of respect to the memory of the man whom you loved & revered above all others. Your pleasure must be still greater, when you reflect how many living friends & admirers of that great & good man, you will oblige by this work as well as the world at large. As the Life will be first printed off, you will excuse my impatience, in wishing to see it as soon as possible– if you could by any means spare me a copy of it. The circumstances you mention shew numberless difficulties you must necessarily meet wth. in preparing the Sermons for the press. Your long intimacy, however, wth. him & the congeniality, as I may say, of your minds & hearts, must point you out as the most proper person to undertake this arduous work. You will be so kind as to let me know from time ^to time^ how it goes on. And whether I live to see it finished or not, it gives me pleasure to see this monument preparing for the memory of the worthy Principal. Mary will be happy to hear from her friend Nelly & will not fail to acknowledge it.

---

[1] James Balfour, WS (1741–1806), was the son of George Balfour, WS (1711–51), and a cousin of Louisa Wodrow. Barbara Balfour-Melville, *The Balfours of Pilrig: A History for the Family* (Edinburgh, 1907), p. 256.

[2] A Scots lawyer who is a member of the Society of Writers to the Signet.

[3] See JW's report at the end of Letter 125.

I must own, I did not expect the Dissenters petition w^d. have met w^th. such a rebuff in the house of commons[4]– tho' I did not ~~expect~~ ^think^ it w^d. pass thro' the other house, without a hard struggle. If they persist, however, I make no doubt they will carry it thro' both, as they did their former petition to relieve their ministers from subscription to the 39 Articles.[5] You have probably seen that D^r. Priestley was present at the debate the 28th.– & the 31^st. published a most spirited letter, to M^r. Pitt[6] on the occasion, charging him pretty home w^th. versatility & want of sound policy.[7] The good Doctor in his usual way speaks out his mind without reserve upon this & other topics, not forgetting his favourite theme of unitarianism & anathemitizing trinitarianism ^w^th. a back stroke at the Arians^ whom he represents as the most timorous & contemptible beings.[8] He pays Lord North compliments for his consistency[9] & M^r. Fox, for his superiority in argument to the chancellor of the exchequer.[10]– But M^r. Wigan & my other church friends do not go along w^th. the Doctor at all– in D^r. Smith's style.[11] They think him too violent to do any good to the cause– nay some of them do not hesitate to say he is mad– or acts like ~~one~~ ^a madman^: So did Festus judge of Paul when he

---

[4] In early 1787 the Protestant Dissenters campaigned for the repeal of the Test and Corporations Acts insofar as they affected them. Their application to Parliament was defeated in the House of Commons on 28 March by 176 to 98 votes. See Letter 128.

[5] The Dissenters in 1772 and 1773 petitioned Parliament for relief from subscription to the Thirty-Nine Articles for ministers, tutors, and schoolmasters, and failed, only to succeed in 1779. G. M. Ditchfield, '"How Narrow Will the Limits of This Toleration Appear?": Dissenting Petitions to Parliament, 1772–1773', *Parliamentary History*, 24 (2005), pp. 91–106.

[6] Joseph Priestley, *A Letter to the Right Hon. William Pitt…on the Subject of Toleration and Church Establishments; Occasioned by his Speech against Repeal of the Test and Corporation Acts* (1787).

[7] 'Versatility': *OED*, 1: 'The condition or quality in persons, their conduct, etc., of being changeable, fickle, or inconstant; tendency or liability to vary in opinion or action; variableness, inconstancy.' Priestley claimed, 'all I ask of you [Pitt], as one of our governors, is to lay no undue bias on the minds of men'. *Works of Joseph Priestley*, XIX, p. 32.

[8] Priestley does not mention the Arians as such, but he does suggest that many clergymen did not believe in the Thirty-Nine Articles, 'notwithstanding their subscription of the same'. Priestley, *Letter to William Pitt*, in *Works of Joseph Priestley*, XIX, pp. 124–29.

[9] *Works of Joseph Priestley*, XIX, pp. 114, 122.

[10] *Works of Joseph Priestley*, XIX, pp. 116, 118.

[11] Adam Smith expressed common Enlightenment criticisms of 'superstition' and 'enthusiasm', but he was 'reticent about religious matters, as he was about most matters likely to arouse controversy…Smith was above all keen to avoid controversy about religious matters'. Paul Oslington, ed., *Adam Smith as Theologian* (2011), pp. 4–5. See also Ryan Patrick Hanley, 'Adam Smith on the "Natural Principles of Religion"', *The Journal of Scottish Philosophy*, 13 (2015), pp. 37–53; Michele Bee, 'The Nurse of Fanaticism: Adam Smith on the Origin of Anti-establishment Movements', *History of Political Thought*, 44 (2023), pp. 92–115.

spoke the words of truth & of a sound mind.[12] But it has produced another pamphlet, of w^ch. you will see a short acc^t. in the last Review, w^ch. has placed this subject in the clearest light and in the most temperate language.[13] This is applauded by every candid & impartial churchman. But will you believe it that many of the dissenters– & those who have their cause most at heart, do not wish this barbarous restraint to be taken off. For the moment it is done, ^they say^ then farewell to the distinction– the dissenters ^will^ melt down & mingle in one body w^th. the church. The moment persicution ceases & moderation takes place, mankind ^will^ shake hands & become friends– & ~~are~~ ^will be^ the happier & therefore the wiser for their pains. Is this not better than quarrelling & falling out about trifles? If the church was as willing to give up a few trifles & some palpable absurdities, as the dissenters are to conform– many of them at least: the business w^d. soon be closed. But this I am affraid will not be soon done.

I expect greater success in your petition as there is no one in this country affected by it.[14] Any reform, any the least alteration in church or state ^here^ causes a most dreadful alarm, & rouzes all the world to arms. Nobody knows where it will end, is the cry– it is like the letting out of water, w^ch. will deluge a whole country.

But I have lately read 2 other publications of D^r. Priestley's w^ch. have given me a great deal of pleasure viz his l^rs. to a philosophic unbeliever Part II[15]– & to D^r. Horne,[16] D^r. Price &c.[17]

---

[12] Porcius Festus was procurator of Judaea, c. AD 60–62. His predecessor, Felix, had kept the apostle Paul in prison for two years. Festus went to hear his case but brought the interrogation to a sudden close, declaring: 'Paul, thou art mad; thy much learning is turning thee mad'. Acts 26:24.

[13] SK is probably referring to Samuel Heywood, *The Right of Protestant Dissenters to a Compleat Toleration Asserted* (1787). It was given a short notice alongside Priestley's *Letter* in the *Monthly Review*, 76 (April 1787), p. 348: 'Considering the short time allowed for the writing and publishing of a work produced on the spur of the occasion, we think the Author has acquitted himself with reputation.—Whoever wishes for a complete view of the arguments, particularly those that have been urged in favour of the Dissenters, may be referred to this pamphlet.'

[14] See Letters 121 and 128 for the Glasgow petition for Scottish burgh reform, which failed in the House of Commons on 28 May 1787.

[15] Joseph Priestley, *Letters to a Philosophic Unbeliever. Part II. Containing a State of the Evidence of Revealed Religion, with Animadversions on the Two Last Chapters of the First Volume of Mr Gibbon's History of the Decline and Fall of the Roman Empire* (Birmingham, 1787).

[16] Rev. George Horne (1730–92), dean of Canterbury. He defended Anglicanism and trinitarian orthodoxy, for instance in *A Letter to the Reverend Doctor Priestley, by an Undergraduate* (Oxford, 1787), in response to Priestley's pamphlet listed in the following note.

[17] Joseph Priestley, *Letters to Dr Horne, Dean of Canterbury; To the Young Men who are in the Course of Education for the Christian Ministry at the Universities of Oxford and Cambridge; to Dr Price; and to Mr Parkhurst, on the Subject of the Person of Christ* (Birmingham, 1787).

But I must pass by these & many other things.

D[r]. Magill's Books are come at last & are much liked indeed.[18] But more of this when I have read it thorough.

We give you joy on the alteration in rebuilding your manse.[19] We never heard of it before. I hope you & yours will long enjoy it.

Finding your intention of being soon in Ed[r]. I enclose this one to my worthy friend D[r]. Spens[20]– from whence I expect the pleasure of hearing from you– don't mind a frank. We have no farther claim on Mess[rs]. Watt–[21] With our united affectionate regards to you & yours,

I ever am D[r] Sir Yours most affect[ly].
S. Kenrick.

## Letter 130: James Wodrow to Samuel Kenrick, 15 June 1787

Place: Stevenston
Addressed: M[r]. Kenrick / Bewdley / Worcestershire
Postmarked: Lond[n]. June twenty Second 1787
Franked: E Eglintoune
Stamped: FREE/JU/22/87
Notes: answered 23[d]. Aug[t]. 87

My Dear Friend,

Tho' I received yours of the 11th. regularly at Ed[r]. I could not command a leizure hour to answer it so much hurried as I was with attendance on the Gen[l]. Ass[ly]. at least the first dyets of it,[1] with some bussiness I had to do as a Curator or Trustee for an insane young man–[2] who has unluckily within this half year together with his Estate fallen under my sole care– and also with frequent visits & calls on

---

[18] JW had sent six copies of M'Gill, *Practical Essay on the Death of Jesus Christ* to SK.
[19] Though see Letters 126 and 127 as well as 128.
[20] Nathaniel Spens. See Letter 96.
[21] Hugh Watt & Co. See Letter 104.

---

[1] The General Assembly sat from 17 till 28 May 1787. The first major deliberation of the Assembly took place on Monday 21 May, and concerned the disputed settlement of Kilbarchan parish after the death of JW's cousin John Warner. See JW's report on this debate at the end of this letter. *Scots Magazine*, 49 (May 1787), p. 253.
[2] Unidentified.

M$^{rs}$. Leechman & many of the rest of my Wife's very numerous Relations at Ed$^r$. I have the pleasure to inform you that I found that worthy Woman in better health than I have seen her in for many years; the alarming Complaint she had in Ayrshire quite gone ^away^ & her looks & spirits remarkably good.[3] And yet she has had a tedious distressing attendance for three months closs, on her favourite Neice Mrs Rouet,[4] confined to her room, & in a great measure to her bed, during that time, with the care of her two Girls and her family matters, entirely devolved on M$^{rs}$. Leechman as the only ostensible person in it. M$^{rs}$. Rouet was recovering but so weak that they took three days to go between Ed$^r$. & Glasgow. I hope her recovery will go faster on at Bell retiro.[5]

Your Letter gives me much encouragement to go on, which I have also had from the few friends here & at Ed$^r$. to whom I showed the Life. I wish it were in my power to send it to you before it be printed which I am affraid it will not from the length of it. You woud be better able than they to correct the Scottisisms perhaps Vulgarisms in it which one unavoidably runs into, by aiming at an easy simple familiar stile which I have done– especially in the narative part & which is more natural to me than any other.[6] My friends have marked out a few phrazes which I shall correct which is all the censure they have ^past^ except one friend who thought it too minute which I am sensible is a just censure & yet I know not how to mend it in this respect or to give the world a just Idea of our venerable friend not only in public but private Life without descending into minutiae.

My Stay at Glasgow was curtailed by having two young Ladies as fellow travellers who were coming to this parish, so that I had only time & opportunity to show the M$^p$. to Proff$^r$. Jardine[7] there who promised me a Letter containing some further information which I wished to have about D$^r$. Leechman after he was Prin$^l$. I have taken no notice of his Difference with J.A.[8] nor of the party work in the Colledge– more than if it had never happened which Jardine much approved

---

[3] See Letters 120, 121, and 125.

[4] See Letter 96. JW variously spelled this name 'Ruat', 'Ruet', and 'Rouet'.

[5] The house in Dunbartonshire owned by the Ruat family, to which Mrs Leechman retired in her widowhood. See Letters 93 and 120.

[6] JW was frequently concerned about the use of Scots language and dialect by himself and others, fearing that it would limit understanding by potential readers and hearers, while SK tended not to accept that it was very problematic. See Letters 131 (on Wodrow's 'Life of Leechman'), 134 and 135 (on the poetry of Robert Burns), 125 and 133 (on M'Gill's *Death of Christ*), and 84 and 85 (on Nell Wodrow's visit to England).

[7] George Jardine, another trustee of Leechman's estate. See Letters 96 and 106.

[8] Professor John Anderson. See Letters 91–98 above.

of. I spoke to a proper man at Glasgow marked out by M^rs. Leechman for copying over the Sermons but there are none of them as yet ready for this and I know not when they will. Tho' I have given up whist entirely and all amusements of that sort for a long time– yet my time is more engrossed in Summer with Company & a thousand other avocations & calls than in Winter, not to mention the new house which is a sort of amusement that I can ^not^ resist; My mind has been in a state of dissipation for a month past with the variety of persons & scenes I have been engaged with & it is it difficult to shake those out of it which however I intend to do & begin to revise these sermons with as much attention & care as I can bestow. I am sensible the sooner they are got ready for the press so much the better. I hope his name will secure the success of the publication so far as to prevent any risk for we do not intend any subscription. Yet I wish I were better acquainted with the useful manoeuveres practised in a publication of that kind & the means of spreading it in London & in England which have been totally neglected by my friend D^r. Magill. We think of prefixing a print of him & getting it engraved from a very faithful & agreable picture of him which M^rs. Leech^n. has presented to the Theological Library at Glasgow along with the books he left ^them^.[9] I wish a proper engraver may be found at Ed^r. as it will be expensive to have it executed at London.[10] Can you assist any how by your advice and suggestions about these things.

I read at Edinburgh one of the vol^s. of Priestly's Letters that you mention to the Philosophical Unbeliever & liked it much.[11] Yet it is too Metaphysical for me, neither am I perfectly satisfyed of the soundness of his & Hartley's Philosophy.[12] I think D^r. Reids[13] more intelligible more founded in fact & feeling & more likely to prevail even in this Sceptical age. But I have given up in a great measure that kind of study & am realy no judge.

---

[9] See Plate 10, William Millar, 'Reverend William Leechman, Professor of Divinity and Principal at the University of Glasgow' (c. 1774/75). © The Hunterian, University of Glasgow.

[10] The engraving was made by James Caldwall (1739–1822) in London, who was particularly known for his engravings of portraits, although he also produced military scenes and worked on the plates for Cook's Voyages. National Portrait Gallery, 'James Caldwall (1739–1822), Engraver', www.npg.org.uk/collections/search/person/mp14135/james-caldwall-caldwell, accessed 5 Jan. 2023; British Museum, 'James Caldwall', www.britishmuseum.org/collection/term/BIOG21700, accessed 5 Jan. 2023. Wodrow was right to be concerned about the expense: see Letters 143 and 144, and Sher, *Enlightenment and the Book*, p. 249.

[11] See Letter 129.

[12] David Hartley. See Letters 110 and 112.

[13] Thomas Reid. See Letter 83.

There have been a number of publications from this Country on Theological Subjects which perhaps will make the present period unfavourable for D[r]. Leechmans. A D[r]. Shaw of Aberdeen Moderator to the Gen[l]. Ass[ly]. last year, has published a 6/book on the Jewish Religion which is commended.[14] I got acquainted with him at Ed[r]. & found him a very sensible man. He showed me a Manusc[p]. History of his Fathers of the Ch. of Scotland from the reformation to the year 1757 in four thin vol[s]. 4[to]. the most beautiful hand I ever saw very curious exact & impartial according to the acc[ts]. of those who had read part of it & a short civil history carried on & intermixed with it. Yet he cannot venture to publish it as the printing would cost £500.[15] D[rs]. Campbell and Beatie have gone to London with a view to publish a long expected work of the former an entire New Translation of the Gospels with critical and explanatory notes & observations 2 vols 4[to].[16] I should scarce think that such a voluminous work woud suit the tast of the age—yet every thing wrote by Campbell must be valuable <—>.[17] It is said there are many new and original Hints in it, with a thro' discussion of the sentiments of Writers of established reputation. The D[r]. has a contempt of all Systematick or controversial Divinity, and agreeing with no party will (it is said) give offense to all. D[r]. Macnight returned from London about the time I left Ed[r]. His ~~Commentary~~ ^Paraphrase^ on the two Epistles to the Thess[ns]. is now published with a new Translation & notes price 7/6 & many Dissertations.[18] D[r]. Dalrymple has published a 6/book at Ed[r]. on the Life of Jesus Christ with heathen & Jewish Testimonies for the truth of X[ty]. designed cheifly for young people.[19]

---

[14] Duncan Shaw, *The History and Philosophy of Judaism: Or, A Critical and Philosophical Analysis of the Jewish Religion. From which is Offered a Vindication of its Genius, Origin, and Authority, and of its Connection with the Christian, against the Objections and Misrepresentations of Modern Infidels* (Edinburgh, 1787). Duncan Shaw (1727–94) was, from 1783, a minister at St Nicholas's Church, Aberdeen, and served as moderator of the general assembly of the Church of Scotland in 1786. The book appeared while the General Assembly was meeting in Edinburgh, advertised in the *Edinburgh Evening Courant* on 21 May, for the price of 5s. in boards. Thanks to Richard B. Sher for this information.

[15] It appears this work was never published. On the difficulties of authors and publication, see Sher, *Enlightenment and the Book*, especially pp. 240–55, 344–52.

[16] Professor George Campbell's *The Four Gospels, Translated from the Greek, with Preliminary Dissertations, and Notes Critical and Explanatory* was eventually published in 1789. See Letter 87.

[17] JW's doubts were justified. Sher, *Enlightenment and the Book*, pp. 238–40.

[18] James Macknight, *A New Literal Translation from the Original, of the Apostle Paul's First and Second Epistles to the Thessalonians: With a Commentary and Notes* (1787).

[19] William Dalrymple, *A History of Christ, for the Use of the Unlearned: With Short Explanatory Notes and Practical Reflections. Humbly Recommended to Parents, and Teachers of Youth in Schools* (Edinburgh, 1787). It was followed by *A Sequel to the Life of Christ, Lately Published, For the Use of the Unlearned; Containing Practical Reflexions, Suited to Each Section* (Ayr, 1791). On Dalrymple, see Letter 125.

Tho' he has the same candid spirit & sentiments in Theology with his colleague[20] yet I am afraid his book will not have the same success as he is much inferiour as a Writer. I have commissioned both these last books but they are not come to hand. I read part of Macnights in Manuscript with approbation.

I had a Manusc$^p$.[21] put into my hands at Ed$^r$. wrote by a M$^r$. Christie[22] of Dundee now a <—> Physician a young man but the fruit of his Theological Studies in the early part of his Life. The Design of it is to show that the Xian Fathers during ^the^ three or four first Centuries were no enemies to <-> Learning & Philosophy & had their full share of any valuable kind of ^it^ that prevailed in that age. I think he clearly & unquestionably proves his point in opposition to Voltaire[23] & Gibbon.

---

[20] William M'Gill. See Letter 79. Not only were he and Dalrymple colleagues in ministry in Ayr; Dalrymple was also uncle of M'Gill's wife Elizabeth, *née* Dunlop.

[21] Published as 'Observations on the Literature of The Primitive Christian Writers. Being an attempt to vindicate them from the imputation of M. Rousseau and Mr. Gibbon, (that they were enemies to philosophy and human learning)', in [Thomas Christie], *Miscellanies: Literary, Philosophical and Moral*, 4 vols (1788), I, pp. 1–151.

[22] Thomas Christie (1761–96), political writer, was born at Montrose, 38 miles up the east coast from Dundee. His father, Alexander Christie (d. 1795), was a wealthy merchant who promoted the building of a bridge over the Esk, an infirmary, and Scotland's first mental asylum. Clashing with the kirk, Alexander Christie defended his unitarian views in *The Holy Scriptures the Only Rule of Faith, and Religious Liberty* (Montrose, 1790). Unitarianism was very much in the family, and perhaps this context represents the 'early theological studies' to which JW refers—Alexander's brother was the unitarian writer William Christie (1748–1823). Thomas Christie was educated at Montrose Grammar School. On leaving school Thomas took up a position in banking, but he inherited his father's wide range of interests and soon gave it up for a career in medicine. In 1784 he travelled to London and enrolled as a pupil at the Westminster General Dispensary. After further study of medicine at Edinburgh University (1785–86) and the Dispensary (1787–88), he abandoned medicine to devote himself exclusively to his literary interests. In May 1788, with the support of Joseph Johnson, he founded the *Analytical Review*. Christie wrote the preface and many of the articles in the earlier volumes. He attracted contributors eminent in the literary world, particularly those associated with radicalism, Dissent, and Joseph Johnson's circle: John Aikin, James Currie, Joshua Toulmin, Alexander Geddes, Mary Hays, Mary Wollstonecraft, Henry Fuseli, and William Cowper. In 1788 he published *Miscellanies: Philosophical, Medical, and Moral*, which he dedicated to Dr Thomas Percival (1740–1804). Christie probably met Percival while visiting Manchester on his extensive tour of Britain in 1787. Percival was the founder of the Manchester Literary and Philosophical society (1781) and, in the preface to *Miscellanies*, Christie praised eminent physicians of the day who were 'not only physicians, but also poets, moralists, classical scholars, and theologians' (p. xiv). In the early years of the French Revolution, he spent time in Paris and defended the revolution from its critics. By then Johnson was the main editor of the *Analytical Review*. Thomas Christie died in October 1796 on a business trip to Surinam. Roper, *Reviewing before the* Edinburgh, *1788–1802*, pp. 22–23; John W. Bugg, *The Joseph Johnson Letter Book* (Oxford, 2016), p. xxxv; Hay, *Dinner with Joseph Johnson*, pp. 168–70; *ODNB*; for the Christies and Unitarianism, see L. Baker Short, *Pioneers of Scottish Unitarianism* (Narbeth, 1963), pp. 42–48. LBS.

[23] François-Marie Arouet Voltaire (1694–1778), French Enlightenment philosopher and satirist. He and Edward Gibbon (see Letter 85) were prominent critics of Christianity.

The book is dry from the unavoidable citations, but candid sensible and enlivened by notes, full as large as the text, & sometimes digressing considerably from it, very entertaining ^notes^ intermixed with criticisms on Modern writers & some short ingenious disquisitions. The whole is short not above two or three hours reading, & I shoud wish to see it published. L^d. Hales has now published his Answer to Gibbons five reasons.[24] It was too dear for my purchasing of it but I have the promise of a reading of it.

I bought a shill^g. Pamphlet at Ed^r. entittled Socinianism unmasked in four Letters to the Lay Members of the Ch. of Scotland & especialy the Collegiate church of Air occasioned by D^r. Magill's Essay, proving that he denies the great Doctrines of the attonement and the Deity of X to which are added a Letter to the Doct^r. & a humble Adress to the Members of the Gen^l. Ass^ly. by a friend to truth.[25] Motto's Prov^r. XXVI 25 when he speaketh fair believe him not, for there are seven abominations in his Heart. Luke XXII Judas? betrayest thou the son of man with a kiss? &c, It is in large 8^vo. 148 pages of the very small & closs print: highly inflamatory as you may well conceive from such a tittle page. I take it to be the production of some of our Sectarian Mins^rs. The Author is a high Calvinist in every point, & seems to consider D^r. M. and all other Arian Socinian & even Arminian ^Writers^ as in the road to damnation. Yet the composition is not contemptible. He is sufficiently accute & smart in supporting his own tenets & is not a stranger to Scripture Criticism tho' still better acquainted with Polemical Divinity. His notes are crouded with mangled citations from the fratres Poloni,[26] which I suppose he has got from the writings of their opponents. There are advertisements in our news papers & proposals for printing by Subscription Other Answers to

---

[24] Sir David Dalrymple, Lord Hailes, *An Inquiry into the Secondary Causes which Mr. Gibbon has Assigned for the Rapid Growth of Christianity* (Edinburgh, 1786). It was advertised for sale at 7s. 6d. in quarto size in boards, in the *Caledonian Mercury*, 16 July 1787.

[25] [John Jamieson], *Socinianism Unmasked: In Four Letters to the Lay-Members of the Church of Scotland, and Especially to those of the Collegiate Church of Ayr: Occasioned by Dr M'Gill's Practical Essay on the Death of Jesus Christ. Proving that he Denies the Great Doctrines of the Atonement, and of the Deity of our Lord. To which are added, a Letter to the Doctor, and an Humble Address to the Members of the General Assembly of the Church of Scotland. By a Friend to Truth* (Edinburgh, 1787). It was published on 28 May 1787, price 1 shilling, stitched in blue paper (*Caledonian Mercury*, Mon. 28 May 1787). In the first letter, Socinianism is described as 'a gangrene which diffuses its fatal influence through almost every member of divine truth and contaminates the whole mass' (p. 2). The author was John Jamieson (1759–1838), antiquary, philologist, and minister at Forfar. His evangelical and polemical publications saw him appointed minister to the congregation of Anti-Burghers at Nicolson Street, Edinburgh, in 1797.

[26] When in exile in Poland the original sixteenth-century Socinians called themselves 'Fratres Poloni'.

the D[r]. by Seceding Mins[rs]. who will ^probably^ be much inferiour [to] this first Anonimous Adventurer. The Mod[r]. of the Gen[l]. Ass[ly].[27] was pestered with anonimous Letters almost every day relative to this ^obnoxious^ book some of them in the stile of Irony & poor wit, others of them serious, all attempting to rouse the zeal of the Lukewarm leaders of that court. But the time seems now to be past for this sort of Persecution. Yet I have reason to think the Ed[r]. D[rs]. ~~were~~ ^are^ by no means pleased with the freedom of it– that the Honour of the Mod[rs]. chair was intended for D[r]. Magill this year but the publication prevented their offering it. Indeed it woud have been imprudent in the present circumstances. These things will I hope soon occasion a demand for a 2[d]. Edition.[28]

As to the Gen[l]. Assembly nothing passed in it likely to be, to you, entertaining or interesting. The court were unanimous in their whole procedure a singular circumstance– at least I remember nothing like it before. There was ^only^ one difficult Settlement & that was the parish of Kilbarchan[29] before them. Sir Adam Ferguson M[rs]. Milliken & the rest of the Trustees had presented Mr Pat[k]. Maxwell, whom you probably know, in August last. The Presby had examined the rights of the family & of the Deed of trust & moderated in a call to the presentee which by M[rs]. M. influence turned out a Legal or good one signed by ^almost^ the whole valuation of the parish ^i.e. Heritors^ & the Elders & acceded to by 55 Heads of families nevertheless the great bulk of the parish were violently against him. The Presby[30] kept the call before them for eight months delaying from time to time without taking a single step and at last discovering what was thought some informality in ^other^ trustees' right to present recurred back to the presentation which they had formerly received & began to raise a civil process before the Court of Session on purpose to obtain a Declaratur[31] that ^the^ Patron's had lost their right by neglecting to use ^it^ within the six months & that it had consequently devolved on the Presby. The Ass[ly]. passed a severe censure on this conduct by finding ^it^ highly blameable & were on the point of going further even <the> bringing the Presby to their Bar & rebuking them publickly but this was given up in order to obtain an unanimous sentence, which was severe enough. They sus-

---

[27] Rev. Robert Liston (1730–96), minister of Aberdour. *Scots Magazine*, 49 (May 1787), p. 253; *FES*, VI, p. 3.
[28] No second edition of M'Gill's *Practical Essay* was ever published.
[29] Vacated by the death of John Warner on 6 March 1786.
[30] The presbytery of Paisley.
[31] A declarator, i.e. the legal declaration of a right or status.

tained the call appointed all the intermediate steps & the day of M^r. Maxwells admission for he is an ordained Mins^r.[32]— We deposed a poor old man for fornication a thing that has not happened for 19 years before.[33] The process had lasted six years, as every possible advantage had been taken & granted from the forms of the court. They delayed pronouncing the sentence to the last day of their meeting i.e till after Whitsunday & thus gave him another half years stipend & and then a Subscription ^Paper^ was handed thro the house & about £40 more instantly given him from the pockets of his Judges. He had a family of 4 or five young children. But I must conclude— The new Manse is in great forwardness. The Mason work will soon be finished & I hope the plastering & every thing [page torn] Winter but we do ^not^ intend entering it till next summer.[34] My best & kindest wishes to M^rs. & Miss [Kenrick].

I am ever my D^r sir
aff^ly. & sinc^y.
J. Wodrow

[32] The report in the *Scots Magazine* offered a slightly different view of events (though JW's is borne out by Robert Dunbar Mackenzie, *Kilbarchan: A Parish History* (Paisley, 1902), pp. 147–48). According to the *Scots Magazine*, the trustees of James Milliken (1710–76), the previous patron of the parish, had stated their intention to present Rev. Patrick Maxwell (1747–1806) to the parish, with the approval of many of the heritors, since Maxwell had long lived in the parish. According to FES, Maxwell had been employed as a tutor in the Milliken family, presumably for Robert Napier (1758–1808), James Milliken's grandson. (SK had been employed as tutor to the previous generation of Millikens, from 1750–65.) However, 'many' other heritors and heads of families opposed Maxwell's presentation to the parish. They argued that due process had not been followed, which would have recognized the inheritance of Capt. Robert Napier of the position of patron in the parish, who had come of age between the death of his grandfather and the death of Warner, thus rendering the trustees' position obsolete. The trustees' argument, that the call to the parish had been made and accepted and was now fait accompli, was accepted by the Assembly against the previous decision of the presbytery of Paisley in favour of the Napiers. The *Caledonian Mercury* pointed out the disparity in wealth between those supporting Maxwell and his patrons (£5,688 in total), and those opposing him (£430). *Scots Magazine*, 49 (May 1787), pp. 254–55; FES, III, p. 150; *Caledonian Mercury*, Mon. 21 May 1787, Thurs. 24 May 1787.
[33] Rev. James Macintosh or Mackintosh (1727–99), parish minister of Moy and Dalarossie, FES, VI, p. 476; *Scots Magazine*, 49 (May 1787), pp. 255, 257; *Caledonian Mercury*, Thurs. 24 May 1787, Mon. 28 May 1787.
[34] On the rebuilding of the manse, JW explained in his report on Stevenston in the *Statistical Account* that 'The manse, after undergoing several expensive reparations, was at last pulled down, and rebuilt about four years ago, and is now a very good one.' JW, 'The Parish of Stevenston', OSA, vol. 7 (1793), p. 34.

## Letter 131: Samuel Kenrick to James Wodrow, 23 August 1787
Place: Bewdley
Addressed: D[r]. Wodrow / Stevenson / Irvine / N. Britain
Postmarked: Birmingham August the Twenty fourth, 1787.
Franked: Free Westcote
Stamped: BIRMING/CARLISLE <303>/AU/29
Note: [recto] Rob[t]. Hamilton Weaver in Stevenston/Jean Crawford <-> in Dalry
    [verso]10½ days work    8[s] 9
    Barley - - -            5[s] 9
3 bolls Grasseeds    19- 6
                     [£]1 14
                        14
                         1

I duly rec[d]. my worthy Friend's favour of the 15th. June[1]– for w[ch]. I thank you most heartily– that amidst so many numberless avocations, you can find time to remember me.

We are happy to hear M[rs]. Leechman is getting better of all her complaints, w[th]. the prospect of being restored to perfect health; may she, & her friends long enjoy it!

I long impatiently to see your work published, as I have no chance to see it before. Little do you think, that what you call scoticisms & vulgarisms, will perhaps soon be as admired for their naïvete & true old sterling English, as they are now studiously avoided by your late & present litterati. I am led to think ^so^ from M[r]. Horne Tooke's ἔπεα πτερόεντα,[2] w[ch]. I am now reading, w[ch]. my knowledge of the scots dialect enables to me to understand & relish much more than I should otherwise have done. You have seen a pretty full acc[t]. of this curious work in a late review– w[ch]. will save me the trouble of saying more of it than I otherwise should.[3] In short he shews that we are all in the wrong– that from Aristotle down to Sam. Johnson we have been upon a wrong scent, & hunting after fancies & shadows, instead of truth & realities. There are the two parts of speech Nouns & Verbs & all the others invented by grammarians will be found to be easily resolved into these. This he is enabled to illustrate by his knowledge of the Northern ^&

---

[1] Letter 130.
[2] John Horne Tooke, *Epea Pteroenta. Or, The Diversions of Purley*, 2 vols (1786).
[3] *Monthly Review*, 76 (Jan. 1787), pp. 1–13.

Eastern^ modern languages of Europe of w^ch. the English is originally a dialect. All these languages he says might be easily learned at school in the same time as is now taken up (in England) in learning Latin & Greek.

He has nothing of the heavy lead of a grammarian, but is full of wit & satyr from beginning to end. You must know, tho' originally a clergiman, he is one of our sort– a zealous whig– & friend to the people. He attempted to change his profession & turn lawyer– but L^d. Mansfield,[4] L^d. Thurloe[5] & the rest of our dignified sages of the law opposed– & as He says by means of a conjunction (*That*) & two prepositions (*of* & *concerning*) have brought about his civil extinction.[6] This circumstance led him to examine these minute parts of language– & will possibly produce a great revolution in the system of grammar, as well as the course of education. So that we shall see professors of modern languages in as high repute as those of ancient ones have long been– & the ancient English or scottish dialect as much admired & studied as the old doric of Theocritus.[7] Gavin Douglas' Virgil[8] is the oldest authority he quotes– who tho' near 2 centuries later than Chaucer,[9] writes in a purer english style, not being corrupted w^th. the gallicisms introduced into our language by our norman kings & their courtiers. If this scheme takes place, how many other works will it call forth, that are now lying dispised a prey to worms. That there [are] many works of this sort cannot be doubted– when we consider how long the Romans resided in this Island– at least 500 years– & that it

---

[4] William Murray (1705–93), first earl of Mansfield, Lord Chief Justice of the King's Bench (1756–88).

[5] Edward Thurlow, first baron Thurlow (1731–1806), lord chancellor (1778–83; 1783–92).

[6] John Horne Tooke (1736–1812) was the third son of a wealthy London poulterer, whose education included Westminster school and Eton and then St John's College, Cambridge. Family pressure prevented him from pursuing a career in law, and in 1760 he was ordained a priest in the Church of England. He was drawn into politics by the 'Wilkes and Liberty' cause of the 1760s. Although he became disenchanted with Wilkes, he was set for a political career marked by a considerable wit. Convicted and imprisoned for libel in 1777, in his *Diversions of Purley* he claimed that he had been betrayed not by the forces of arbitrary tyranny but also by 'two prepositions and a conjunction'. A. V. Beedell and A. D. Harvey, *The Prison Diary (16 May–22 November 1794) of John Horne Tooke* (Leeds, 1995), pp. 18–20.

[7] Theocritus (b. c. 300 BC, d. after 260 BC), a Greek poet of Syracuse, creator of pastoral poetry whose verse was imitated by Virgil. Doric is the broad rustic dialect of the natives of Doris in Greece which came to be associated generally with poetry in that mode—in Scotland notably that of Burns.

[8] Gavin Douglas (1476–1522), bishop of Dunkeld, poet and translator of Virgil's *Aeneid*. His highly regarded *Eneados* was the first translation into English, which was of a vernacular sort. It was composed 'in the langage of the Scottis natioun', as he said in the prologue. *Eneados*, Buik 1, Prolog, line 103.

[9] Geoffrey Chaucer (c. 1345–1400), poet and author of *The Canterbury Tales*.

is the opinion of some of the wisest men of this age that England in the time of the Saxons was much more populous than it is at present– I mention the late D[r]. Campbell whose name is equall to an host.[10] According to M[r]. Tooke, M[r]. Locke is our first grammarian, who by a lucky mistake substituted the pompous words of Human Understanding, instead of the contemptible one Grammar, of w[ch]. it really treats & thus gave it celebrity in the world– otherwise it w[d]. probably have lain unnoticed consigned long ago to oblivion.[11] I could not help being hurt at [h]is rough treatment of the ingenious & amiable & as I hitherto thought learned M[r]. Harris of Salisbury[12]– & was glad he was out of the way & reach of every attack. But the more I think of it, I am now more reconciled to the justice & truth of his system. D[r]. Lowth is still alive & notwithstanding of his high & well earned fame, must feel a little mortified[13]– altho' he is hanged on the same gibbet– to use a rather too harsh figure– w[th]. his friend Harris. As to Johnson[14] I feel nothing for him, as his overbearing vanity rendered him invulnerable– & very little for Lord Montboddo,[15] as he posesses a good share of the same overbearing character. But they are all treated here w[th]. the unmerciful lash of Juvenal,[16] w[ch]. ought only to be inflicted on the immoral whose intentions were bad. The poet laureate Warton[17] does not escape him, for a stab at the cause of Whiggism thro' Milton's[18]

---

[10] John Campbell. See Letter 122.

[11] John Locke, *An Essay Concerning Human Understanding* (1690), a foundational text for an empiricist theory of knowledge.

[12] James Harris (1709–80), philosopher, author of *Hermes: Or, A Philosophical Inquiry Concerning Language and Universal Grammar* (1751). SK admired 'this acute philosopher.' Letter 19, *W-K*, I, p. 214. See *Diversions of Purley*, pp. 75–76, 166, for two examples among a number of critical references to Harris.

[13] Robert Lowth (1710–87), poet, critic, biblical scholar, and bishop of London. See Letter 84. In June 1741 Lowth was elected professor of poetry at Oxford. Re-elected in 1746, he served for a total of ten years. He made a name for himself as a young man through his composition of verses in both English and Latin. His poem, *The Judgment of Hercules*, printed in 1743, was frequently anthologized later in his life. In 1762 Lowth published his immensely successful *A Short Introduction to English Grammar*, in which, according to Scott Mandelbrote, 'he extolled the simplicity of the form and construction of the English language while remarking that it could still not rival the most ancient of languages, Hebrew, in this respect'. Mandelbrote, 'Lowth, Robert (1780–1787)', *ODNB*.

[14] Samuel Johnson. See Letter 117.

[15] James Burnett, Lord Monboddo. See Letter 124; *W-K*, I, p. 320n.

[16] Juvenal, Roman satirical poet, active in the years around 100 AD.

[17] Thomas Warton (1728–90), poet and historian. Professor of poetry at Oxford, 1757–67, and author of *The History of English Poetry from the Close of the Eleventh to the Commencement of the Eighteenth Century*, 3 vols (1774, 1778, 1781). Elected Camden Professor of History, Oxford, in 1785 and appointed poet laureate in the same year.

[18] John Milton (1608–74), Puritan poet and polemicist. He supported the Puritan cause during the English Civil War, openly favouring the trial and execution of Charles I.

sides— I intended to give you a specimen of his new system— but have not time— I only mention one instance, w[ch]. the author does not know is obvious to everyone in Scotland. His great principle is that every word is significant or has a real meaning. As to interjections— they are no more words than coughing, sneezing laughing &c. The words I mean are butt & benn— w[ch]. you w[d]. call particles or adverbs or conjunctions. While in reality the[y] are verbs— viz bi–utan & bi–innen. To be out & to be in— in the imperative mood: w[ch]. he shows to be the case w[th]. all prepositions & conjunctions.—[19]

I have got D[r]. McKnight[20] & am highly pleased w[th]. him— and if I had time could w[th]. pleasure devote it in study the epistles w[th]. his assistance. I wish he w[d]. take in the Acts— and publish it by subscription. I think he w[d]. not fail in meeting w[th]. great encouragement from a generous public. I for one will gladly subscribe.

But alas I must leave you— I am scribbling this by Lord Westcote— just to send you something. I have seen D[r]. Priestley's letter to the Jews. Levi's answer[21] & the D[r]'s. reply[22]— w[ch]. promise in my opinion a great revolution.

I have also seen Madan's Attack on the D[r]. by means of my friend Jesse— nothing but virulence & enthusiasm.[23] Our friend Wigan is going into the tutor

---

[19] OED, 'particle, n.', meaning 6.b: 'The adverb or preposition used with, and in certain constructions separated from, the verb in a phrasal verb.'

[20] James Macknight, *A New Literal Translation, from the Original, of the Apostle Paul's First and Second Epistles to the Thessalonians: With a Commentary and Notes* (1787). It was published on 7 June 1787, for 7 shillings and sixpence (*Caledonian Mercury*, 7 June 1787). See Letter 130.

[21] David Levi, *Letters to Dr Priestley, in Answer to those he Addressed to the Jews; Inviting them to an Amicable Discussion of the Evidences of Christianity* (1787). David Levi (1742–1801) was a writer on Judaism. In his early career he acted as an expositor of the Jewish faith, as in his *A Succinct Account of the Rites and Ceremonies of the Jews* (1782). When Joseph Priestley published his *Letter to the Jews* (1786), urging them to convert, Levi replied in defence of the Jewish faith. Others besides Priestley joined the controversy which eventually led Levi to explain the Jewish understanding of biblical prophecy in his three-volume *Dissertation on the Prophecies of the Old Testament*, 2 vols (1793–1800). He especially sought to refute Christian millenarian interpretations of various prophecies, principally those concerning the punishment and later redemption of the Jews.

[22] Joseph Priestley, *Letters to the Jews, Part II: Occasioned by Mr David Levi's Reply to the Former Letters* (Birmingham, 1787).

[23] Spencer Madan, *Letters to Joseph Priestley, LL.D. F.R.S. Occasioned by His Late Controversial Writings* (1787). As rector of St Philip's, Birmingham, from 1787 to 1809, Rev. Spencer Madan (1758–1836) played a prominent role in encouraging local hostility to Unitarianism and in opposing the Dissenters' campaign for the repeal of the Test and Corporation Acts. His sermon of 14 February 1790, published as *The Principal Claims of the Dissenters Considered*, gave rise to Joseph Priestley's *Familiar Letters Addressed to the Inhabitants of Birmingham, in Refutation of Several Charges, Advanced Against the Dissenters* (Birmingham, 1790), to which Madan responded in April 1790. In 1788, Madan was appointed chaplain in ordinary to the king, a position in which he served until 1832.

line. He has got one pupil at £100– ⅌ ann. a Russian. Mary still in Shropshire my wife owes Miss Nelly a l<sup>r</sup>.–

Adieu w<sup>th</sup>. our best wishes.<br>Yrs S. Kenrick.

## Letter 132: James Wodrow to Samuel Kenrick, 2 September 1787
Address: M<sup>r</sup>. Sam<sup>l</sup>. Kenrick
Notes: [JW's hand]: Sund<sup>y</sup>. night
        [SK's hand]: answ<sup>d</sup>. 28<sup>th</sup>. Sep<sup>t</sup>.

My Dear Friend

Miss Leslie Bailie[1] brought ^us^ a frank yesterday from Col. Fullarton[2] that must go tomorrow morn<sup>g</sup>. & having had Company at dinner & Tea I have just about half an hour to scrible a few lines in answer to your entertaining tho'

---

[1] Lesley Baillie (1768–1843) of Mayville House, Stevenston, approximately 300 metres east of JW's High Kirk. The subject of Robert Burns's 'Bonney Lesley' and 'Blythe hae I been on yon hill', he called her 'the most bewitching…a woman exquisitely charming, without the least seeming consciousness of it'. Robert Burns to Lesley Baillie of Mayville, May 1793, in Robert Chambers, ed., *The Life and Works of Robert Burns*, 4 vols (Edinburgh, 1896), III, p. 428. The daughter of Robert Baillie and May Reid, she married Robert Cumming at Stevenston on 22 June 1799. There is a monument to her in Glencairn street, Stevenston, that has the text of Burns's poem and her details as follows: 'Lesley Baillie wife of Robert Cumming Esq of Logie Morayshire. Born at Mayville Stevenston 6th March 1768, died in Edinburgh 12th July 1843 and her sister Grace Baillie died August 1841'. NRS, Old Parish Registers, Banns and Marriages 20/68; James Paterson, *History of the Counties of Ayr and Wigton* (Edinburgh, 1866), III, p. 566. JW travelled to Ireland with 'my neighbour Mr Baillie' in late 1793 (Letter 185); and in 1794 he declared that 'party spirit runs so high of late' that 'my good Neighbour M<sup>r</sup>. Baillie of Mayville' was the 'only friend just now within my reach to whom I would choose to communicate your Letters' (Letter 191). Robert Baillie declared that his sentiments 'were in perfect unison' with SK's (Letter 193).

[2] William Fullarton (1754–1808) inherited Fullarton near Irvine. A wealthy landowner, after education at Edinburgh University and a Grand Tour, he served as secretary in the British embassy at Paris 1775–78. Briefly an MP (1779–80) supporting Lord North's government, he was appointed lieutenant-colonel of the ninety-eighth regiment, which he raised on his estate. When this was criticized in Parliament, Fullarton challenged Lord Shelburne to a duel, and wounded him in the groin. His regiment sailed to India in 1781, where Fullarton rose to overall command of the British forces in the southern Carnatic, waging war against Haidar Ali of Mysore. He returned to Britain, published *A View of the English Interests in India* (1787), and was re-elected to Parliament for Haddington Burghs (1787–90). A strong critic of Warren Hastings, he joined the Portland Whigs in the 1790s, and incurred the wrath of Henry Dundas. In 1802 he became a commissioner in Trinidad, with antislavery ideas, but clashed there with the despotic Colonel Thomas Picton.

hurried letter of the 23ᵈ of August which reached us with in these three days & I am not a little tired with preaching all day[3] so that you can expect little worth reading from me. I thank you for your accᵗ. of Horne's book & woud wish to see it however little time I have at present for reading any thing. After all his discoveries of the origin & revolutions parts of Speech & his new & ingenious observations which in as far as I can judge from your Letter & from the Review are very just– Horne's rule will I apprehend be the prinˡ. one in that science verba valent usu.[4] Preistly controversy with Levi & Madan I am an entire stranger to.–

Macnight on the Thessⁿˢ. I got as soon as it was published but have read little ^more^ of it than what I saw in Manuscript. His abilities as a Critick on the Scripture I have a high oppinion of at the same time I cannot help thinking that he loses in many places the real simple ^plain^ sense of the sacred writers by his over ingenuity & refinement in searching after it.[5] I have been lately lecturing on the Thessⁿˢ. & as I write almost everything full in Short hand was enabled from this the better to judge of his explication of it. If he go on with the more difficult Epistles of the Romans Galⁿˢ. & Hebrews & the whole Epistolary writings as he proposes it will [be] a most voluminous work & I heartily wish him encouragement from the public to do so. For however different his sentiments are from mine which I can judge from several specimens he has read to me, I consider him as a most ingenious rational & judicious explainer of the scriptures in the main.

The Publication of Dʳ. Leechmans Sermons has been at a stand almost since my return from Edʳ. by reason of my parish bussiness particularly <–> the Sacᵗˢ. here & in the neighbourhood which are now over & I intend to begin & stick

---

[3] JW regularly preached three times each Sunday. Letter 119.
[4] 'Words get their meaning in their use'.
[5] Macknight's earlier *Harmony of the Gospels* had been similarly criticized by the eminent biblical scholar and Socinian, Nathaniel Lardner, in his pamphlet titled *Observations upon Dr Macknight's Harmony of the Four Gospels, so far as Relates to the History of Our Saviour's Resurrection* (1764). According to the Rational Dissenter, Andrew Kippis, in the conclusion of his tract Macknight 'bestowed extraordinary labour' upon a new interpretation of Christ's appearances following his resurrection. However, 'the efforts of his ingenuity and diligence had not the good fortune to satisfy Dr Lardner. It appeared to him, that certain suppositions...were all together without foundation....I have reason to believe, that there were other points in which Dr Lardner did not agree with Dr Macknight. In matters liable to difficulty, and involved in some degree of obscurity, a diversity of sentiments will take place between the most upright, able and serious enquirers after truth'. Kippis, *Works of Lardner*, I, pp. lxx–lxxi. See Letters 122 and 125 for references to Lardner's works.

to it as close as possible for some months to come.– Other matters have also unavoidably engrossed my attention such as M^r. Dow's illness & death one of the most pious benevolent & amiable of men with whom I have lived in a tender unbroken friendship for above 30 years.[6] The Presby appointed me against my will to preach his funeral Sermon which cost at least a forthnight. He has left his family in good circumstances for a mins^r. left them perhaps near £1200.

Do you know I myself & my small family have all sat for our pictures to a very young Painter but one who ^has^ taken off some likenesses surprisingly ^excellent^ & mine among others at least every body says so.[7] I wish his colours may stand.

I think of enlarging the Acc^t. of D^r. Le. Lectures a little as every literary person who has seen it seems to wish this. I think also the two vol^ms. shoud be printed at London for I see any books published in Scotland are never known in England let them have never so much merit ^or^ they are forgotten in a short time. This seems to be the case with my friend Magills publication. You have ^not^ given me your oppinion of it. I wish you woud fully & seriously consider that point of the comparative importance of printing at London & Ed^r. & write me your oppinion of it as you read so much & must be a perfectly well informed judge.

I must conclude. You will scarce be able to read this hurried scrawl. I left Helen in Carrick who is not yet returned & am uncertain if Peggy will have time to write in the Frank.

God bless you & yours prays

your affectionate Friend<br>J. Wodrow

---

[6] Robert Dow. See Letter 125.

[7] JW's own portrait is reproduced in *W-K*, I, p. 3, courtesy of Stevenston Church of Scotland, in whose building it hangs. It is in black and white, however, not in the colours to which JW refers here. The artist has not been identified.

## Letter 133: Samuel Kenrick to James Wodrow, 28 September 1787

Place: Bewdley
Addressed: Rev<sup>d</sup>. D<sup>r</sup>. Wodrow, / Irvine / Scotland
Postmarked: Bewdley September the Twenty eighth 1787
Franked: Free Westcote
Stamped: OC/3
Note: 6/3

My dear Friend,

I am much obliged to Miss Leslie Bailie[1] for her kind present of a frank to co^n^vey me your last favour of the 2nd. inst. for w<sup>ch</sup>. you will be so good as to make that Lady my kind acknowledgments.

In some respects, I am in the same predicament as you were when you wrote last. We have had a little bit of Borough skirmishing, w<sup>ch</sup>. has obliged Lord Westcote our member, & his friends who are Burgesses, to come together from all quarters to the election of a Bailiff in his interest ^& have gained a compleat victory^.[2] I could ^not^ help asking him for a frank as I usually do when I see him– & as I have got it I am under the necessity of scribbling something for it, whether to the purpose or not.

I still read & admire Macknight's writings having ^now^ got his harmony.[3] I think it a pity that [a] man of his abilities & extensive knowledge, particularly in the S.S.[4] was not professor of Divinity in some of your universities. He is certainly most eminently qualified for it. If you had time I should be happy to see your explication of some passages in these Epistles, w<sup>ch</sup>. you say is different from his.[5] I hope he will go on w<sup>th</sup>. his plan of explaining all the epistles. I am happy to find that my sentiments coincide so near with yours, who are a better judge.

---

[1] Leslie Baillie. See Letter 132.

[2] William Henry Lyttelton, created baron Westcote in 1776, was MP for Bewdley 1748–55 and 1774–90. The *History of Parliament* notes that Westcote maintained control of the borough of Bewdley, 'though not without some uneasiness. An opposition was threatened in 1780, and in 1787 there was a critical election for bailiff'. 'Bewdley: Single Member Borough', in HPO. See Letter 80.

[3] In 1756, James Macknight published *A Harmony of the Four Gospels: In which the Natural Order of Each is Preserved. With a Paraphrase and Notes*. This was followed in 1763 by a second single volume edition 'corrected and greatly enlarged'. See Letter 87.

[4] Presumably an abbreviation for 'Sacred Scripture(s)'.

[5] On 23 August 1787 (Letter 131) SK noted that he had got a copy of James Macknight's recent *Translation of the Epistles to the Thessalonians* (1787). See JW's comments in Letter 132.

I congratulate w^th. you on having finished this year's campaign & that you are now set down to revise D^r. Leechman's papers, w^ch. I hope you will be able to fit for the press before you are again interrupted. M^r. Wigan, who always remembers you with cordial affection, joins me in approving of the enlargements you mention to be made, in your account of his public lectures. This will be useful to gentlemen in his situation & pleasing to everybody else.

You have often mentioned to me the amiable virtues & christian graces of your late worthy friend M^r. Dow[6]– w^ch. Miss Wodrow confirmed by many pleasing little anecdotes of his harmless ingenuous nature & temper. It gives me pleasure to hear he has left such a comfortable provision for his surviving family.

It is kind of you to your friends, as well as to the ingenious artist, to have your pictures drawn. If it could be done in miniature so as to be conveyed in a letter, I should like to have it & place it in company with a cast I have of D^r. Priestley in my museum. There is a wonderfully ingenious man in Birm^m. who takes off the most striking likenesses in a small die– w^ch. forms a bas relief, rather stronger than this current coin or a common medal. And yet he is a poor drunken dog, as most of those ingenious artists are.

I approve much of your ^printing &^ publishing your intended work in London. Not that I know any thing of the relative excellence of this mode, as superiour to having done in Scotland. Your authors or Booksellers are the best judges of these matters. I infer it from the fact you mention, viz that all your late capital works have come forth in that manner. And if it should induce you to come into this country & take a peep at your old friends, it will still meet w^th. my stronger approbation.

I am much to blame for neglecting so long to thank you for the pleasure & comfort I & my family have received from D^r. M^cgill's Book.[7] I have the same to say of all my friends who have had copies: but particularly of an old Batchellor brother of mine,[8]– *abnormis sapiens crassaque Minerva*[9]– who says he likes it next to the Bible, it is so like to the Bible– & reads little else– none w^th. such relish. D^r. M. will probably think this a higher compliment than a more pompous one

---

[6] Rev. Robert Dow, minister of Ardrossan. Described in *W-K*, I, p. 161, as JW's 'orthodox friend and neighbour'.

[7] M'Gill, *Practical Essay on the Death of Jesus Christ*.

[8] William Kenrick (1729–93).

[9] Horace, *Satires*, II, ii, line 3. Translates literally as 'an unconventional philosopher (or scholar) with an uncultivated Minerva'. Horace is describing the philosopher/scholar's intelligence as that of a rustic autodidact, with all the strengths and weaknesses that tend to be associated with that type of person (Graeme Miles, University of Tasmania).

from some profound brother author. It is a good book. For it cannot be read, without our being made better thereby. We forget the author & style & think of nothing but the subject & our own feelings. I am sorry to think it should be so little attended to w<sup>th</sup>. you.

Our expectations here are much raised w<sup>th</sup>. the Acc<sup>t</sup>. in the Monthly Review of Professor Millar's historical deduction or View of the English constitution.[10] He seems to be an able & judicious writer– & more attached to liberty than our patriots generally think your neighbours are.[11]

By the bye I have just heard from L<sup>d</sup>. Valentia[12] of an old intimate friend of yours M<sup>r</sup>. Caldwell[13] of Dublin. He is a most respectable character & a man of business.

Mary is still in Shropshire let your amiable daughters know– or else she w<sup>d</sup>. have helped me in filling up this frank a little better than I do– from a multiplicity of avocations. We expect her home next tuesday & then you or ^at^ least they will soon hear from her.

Our dissenters are preparing again to petition parliament for abolishing the disgraceful test act– & will persist I hope till they find relief.[14] With my wife's & my own best respects to you & yours I ever am My dear Friend's

most affect<sup>te</sup>. S. Kenrick

---

[10] John Millar, *An Historical View of the English Government, from the Settlement of the Saxons in Britain to the Accession of the House of Stewart* (1787). See the *Monthly Review*, 77 (Aug. 1787), pp. 106–16.

[11] John Millar. See Letter 79.

[12] Arthur Annesley (1744–1816), eighth viscount Valentia since his father's death in 1761, and created first earl of Mountnorris in 1793. He married Lucy Fortescue Lyttelton (1742–83), daughter of George Lyttelton (1709–73), first baron Lyttelton, politician and man of letters. S. E. Brydges, *A Biographical Peerage of the Empire of Great Britain*, 4 vols (1808–17), IV, pp. 140–41. SK probably knew Lord Valentia through his connection to the Lyttletons of Hagley Hall, under whose cover he often posted letters. See Letters 53 and 54, *W-K*, I, pp. 327, 337.

[13] Andrew Caldwell (1733–1808), a former student at Glasgow University (1751–54), barrister and expert on architecture. He inherited a large Irish estate on the death of his father and was an MP in the Irish Parliament, 1776–90. He toured the Isle of Wight with SK in 1759. See *W-K*, I, pp. 264–65.

[14] See Letter 129. Having been defeated in the House of Commons on 28 March 1787 by 176 to 98 votes, the Dissenters did not succeed in having another motion put in the House of Commons until May 1789. Ditchfield, 'The Parliamentary Struggle over the Repeal of the Test and Corporation Acts, 1787–1790', p. 551. On the rise of Dissenting pressure for legislative change, see Andrew C. Thompson, 'Toleration, Dissent and the State in Britain', in Andrew C. Thompson, ed., *The Oxford History of Protestant Dissenting Traditions, Volume III: The Long Eighteenth Century, c. 1689–c. 1828* (Oxford, 2018), pp. 263–83, especially 277–82; James E. Bradley, *Religion, Revolution and English Radicalism* (Cambridge, 1990) Michael Watts, *The Dissenters: From the Reformation to the French Revolution* (Oxford, 1978), pp. 482–90.

## Letter 134: James Wodrow to Samuel Kenrick, 13 December 1787

Place: Stevenston
Addressed: M<sup>r</sup>. Kenrick Bewdley / Worcesters<sup>e</sup>.
Postmarked: Irvine Dec<sup>r</sup>. fourteenth 1787
Franked: E. Eglintoune
Stamped: DE/16
Note in SK's hand: answ<sup>d</sup>. 13 Feb. 88
Note: 88

My Dearest Friend

As I think of applying to my L<sup>d</sup>. Eglinton for a frank to London & another to Bewdley I take the Opportunity of acknowledging in a few lines your favour ^dated^ in End of Sept<sup>r</sup>.[1] leaving it to Nelly to fill up the prin<sup>l</sup>. part of it by her Answer to Miss Kenrick's long & entertaining Letter received since that time. Nelly ^& Peggy^ have also promised to copy & send to Miss Kenrick a mss<sup>p</sup>. poem of Burns which I had intended to do, as I think it superiour to many of his printed ones. It is an Elergy on Sir J. Hunter Blair of Dunskey.[2] M<sup>rs</sup>. Kenrick will know something of the family as it is a Carrick one.[3] He ^was^ marryed ^to^ the Heiress: & you will know something of his char<sup>r</sup>. even from the News Papers. He was at the head of the public spirited schemes for the Improvement of Ed<sup>r</sup>. & was suddenly cut off in the midst of them about two or three months ago <during> ^in^ his return from England.

Burns himself you know something of. An Airshire farmer, a self taught Poet with no other education, but what he acquired from reading a little in the evening after he returned from the Plow.[4] I was struck with the original painting of the

---

[1] Letter 133, SK to JW, 28 Sept. 1787.

[2] Robert Burns, 'On the Death of Sir J. Hunter Blair', in James Kinsley, ed., *The Poems and Songs of Robert Burns*, 3 vols (Oxford, 1968), I, pp. 340–42. It was first published, posthumously, in *The Works of Robert Burns*, ed. James Currie, 4 vols (1800), III, p. 381. Like Burns, Sir James Hunter Blair had been a freemason, and, as Lord Provost, he had welcomed the poet to Edinburgh in 1786. Burns left a note on one manuscript copy of the poem, stating of it that 'The Performance was mediocre, but my grief was sincere' and of Blair that he had been 'a worthy, public-spirited man'. *Poems and Songs of Robert Burns*, III, p. 1239. On Hunter Blair, see Letters 86 and 104. *Caledonian Mercury*, 1 Dec. 1781, carries a report of the St Andrews Day parade of the Edinburgh Grand Lodge, identifying Sir James Hunter Blair as the Grand Treasurer of Masons. We are grateful to Dr David Brown for this reference.

[3] Carrick, district of south Ayrshire of which Maybole is the principal town, where Elisabeth Kenrick's family lived.

[4] This caricature of Burns (1759–96) was a myth substantially established by Henry Mackenzie's review of Burns's *Poems, Chiefly in the Scottish Dialect* (Kilmarnock, 1786) in the *Lounger*, 9 (9 Dec.

scenes of nature & the scenes of low Life in the first Edition of his Poems printed at Kilmarnock[5] to gain him a few shill[s]. & said that if the book came to be read at Ed[r]. where the enthusiasm is strong for every thing Scottish it woud draw some attention. But I had no notion it woud have drawn so much. He was caressed last winter by the first people there in such a manner that it was a wonder it did not turn his head.[6] Another Edition of his Poems was printed there, corrected & much enlarged.[7] And I hear he has been now so wise as to betake himself to a farm with the little ^money^ he has made.[8] M[r]. Rose[9] writes me ~~Burns's~~ ^His^ poems have had a considerable run at London, merely because it was fashionable to read & admire them. & indeed I shoud imagine that few Englishmen coud understand the twentieth ^part^ of them & tho' they did, coud <-> relish the simple & beautiful pictures in them because they had never seen the original exhibited in real Life.[10] Cowper the English Poet[11] admires Burns, regrets that he must

---

1786), which described him as 'this Heaven-taught ploughman'. Indeed, Burns himself contributed to this impression by describing himself on the title-page of the Kilmarnock edition as a 'simple Bard, unbroke by rules of Art', and he had reason to flatter potential patrons by self-deprecation at the start of his career; but his father had been a subscriber to the Ayr Library, and had engaged a tutor for Burns and his siblings and the children of other local families, so he was far from 'self taught...with no other education'. See Donald Low, ed., *Robert Burns: The Critical Heritage* (1974), pp. 1–5; Robert Crawford, 'Robert Burns (1759–1796)', *ODNB*. Despite JW's reinforcement of this caricature, the Wodrow family were acquainted with Burns. See Letter 132 on Lesley Baillie; and JW's elder brother Patrick was the minister of Tarbolton, where Burns had lived from 1776 till 1781 and had founded the Tarbolton Bachelors' Club for debating. Patrick was the 'Auld Wodrow' mentioned in 'The Twa Herds' (*Poems and Songs of Robert Burns*, III, p. 1047).

[5] Robert Burns, *Poems, Chiefly in the Scottish Dialect* (Kilmarnock, 1786). This edition, of some 600 copies, was sold out in a month.

[6] Burns visited Edinburgh from Nov. 1786–May 1787. During this first visit he was celebrated and encouraged by luminaries such as Henry Mackenzie, Dugald Stewart, Hugh Blair, William Greenfield, the earl of Glencairn, Adam Ferguson, James Hutton, William Black, and John Home.

[7] This second edition, of 3,000 copies, was published by William Creech at Edinburgh in 1787.

[8] Burns had made something over £50 from his first edition, and Creech paid Burns £100 for the second. In fact, Burns devoted the rest of 1787 to tours of Scotland and the north of England, returning to Edinburgh in October, where he wintered again.

[9] Samuel Rose. See Letter 108.

[10] See also James Anderson's review of Burns's *Poems* (1786), *Monthly Review*, 85 (Dec. 1786), 439–48, which may have reinforced JW's view of the inaccessibility of Burns's poetry in Scots to readers outside Scotland. Neither were Anderson and JW unusual in this view: the prominent Scottish critics Henry Mackenzie and Hugh Blair focussed in print on the merits of Burns's English poetry at the expense of his work in Scots, at the time of the publication of his first collection, for fear that emphasizing the excellence of his vernacular poetry might diminish his readership. Donald A. Low, *Robert Burns: The Critical Heritage* (1974), p. 6; Emma Macleod, 'Burns and the Borders of Poetry in the Letters of James Wodrow and Samuel Kenrick', *Burns Chronicle*, special issue ed. Christopher A. Whatley, 133 (Sept. 2024), pp. 210–24.

[11] William Cowper (1731–1800), poet. Educated at Westminster school, in 1752 he took Chambers in the Middle Temple and was called to the bar in 1754. He suffered from serious

lose much deserved praise <-> because his Language is to many unintelligible, says "his candle is bright but shut up in a dark Lantern".[12] It is said of Ignorance that it begets contempt but I have often thought also that it begets ^or^ heightens Admiration. But I have run away with this subject perhaps uninteresting to you & forget to take up your Letter.

So you engage sometimes in the Politicks of your burrough I shoud think with no great relish for it, yet it is sometimes unavoidable.– I met D$^r$. Macnight not long ago accidentaly, but it was in the midst of a great Company so that I was obliged to take him to a window to obtain a few minutes conversation with him. I found he had printed only 500 copies of his late book[13] & disposed of a good many of them in Scotland– that he intends to print his whole commentaries if it gets a reasonable offer for them which he seems to expect.– As you were so nearly connected with the late M$^r$. Andrew Millar & sometimes ^lived^ with him,[14] I thought you woud have been innitiated into the whole mysteries of printing Bookselling & bargaining with Authours & possibly you may still give me some useful information if you woud recollect yourself.

I heartily wish success to the Dissenters second attempt.[15] Yet I am affraid your good friend Priestly has much hurt the cause he meaned to serve by irritating M$^r$. Pit who is sufficiently irritable.[16] If he sets his face against it it will be impossible to carry it. Few English Ministers have been so popular as he seems to be at present. For the same reason I am afraid we shall lose our cause of the Reformation of ^the^ constitution of Our borroughs tho' introduced & supported by the

---

depression, and in 1763 attempted suicide. He collaborated with the evangelical cleric, John Newton, to produce the *Olney Hymns* (1779). His major work was *The Task* (1785), a poem on rural themes.

[12] See McGinty, *Robert Burns and Religion*, pp. 87–111, at p. 88. Wodrow is quoting a letter of 27 Aug. 1787 from Cowper to Rose, who was a friend of Wodrow's, but who was particularly close to Cowper.

[13] James Macknight, *A New Literal Translation, from the Original, of the Apostle Paul's First and Second Epistles to the Thessalonians: With a Commentary and Notes* (1787). See Letter 87. His *New Literal Translation from the Original Greek of All the Apostolic Epistles* was published in four volumes in 1795.

[14] Andrew Millar (1705–68), bookseller in London, son of Rev. Robert Millar (1672–1752) of the Abbey Church, Paisley, who was married to Elizabeth, a cousin of SK's mother, Sarah Hamilton (1695–1775). SK stayed with Robert and Elizabeth Millar in university vacations, and also with another son of theirs, Henry ('Harry') Millar, minister of Neilston parish near Paisley. W-K, I, p. 227n; Sher, *Enlightenment and the Book*, pp. 275–79.

[15] To have the Test and Corporations Acts repealed by Parliament. See Letter 133.

[16] A judgement on William Pitt's temperament supported by his biographer. Erhman, *The Younger Pitt: The Years of Acclaim*, pp. 233–34.

Eloquence of a Sherridan.[17] Dundass is obstinate & has an Interest continuing matters on the old footing.[18] Pit will not take a side against him: nay seems to have imbibed prejudices against the ^proposed^ Reform ~~intended~~, as the scheme of a Mob; which is far from being the case, and will therefore act in this particular case against his own general & professed principles.[19]

I have now finished all that I intended respecting D^r. Leechmans Life & Lectures & also revised five Sermons 3 upon Religious Gratitude & two upon the Obligation & usefulness of attending Public Worship & put them into the hands of a Copier in Glasgow. These with the 4 sermons published by himself woud I apprehend make a large enough single Vol. but I must go on with the rest. We intend a family visit of three or four weeks this Winter to M^rs. Leechman in consequence of her ^earnest^ invitation. But she has ^been^ ill of late is beginning to recover & is still in a state of great weakness & perhaps not without danger. Poor Anderson has lost every one of the five or six processes which he commenced before the Lords of Session against the College for supposed injurious or unworthy treatment & this by an unanimous Sentence of the court on every point and is condemned in the whole Expenses. It is almost certain that D^r. Taylours process against him which draws <deep> will have a similar Issue; & thus his fortune as well as his character ^be^ compleatly ruined by his own folly & madness.[20]

The Plastering of the new Manse will be finished this week & the House shut up for some months except that it may be necessary to open the Windows in a good day & put on a fire in very severe frost. The last will scarce be necessary as the Plaister is only finished just now the most of it having been done two months ago

---

[17] A correct prediction. Scotland's municipal politics were not reformed till 1835. See Letter 121 for Richard Brinsley Sheridan's unsuccessful attempt to propose the motion for Scottish burgh reform to Parliament in 1787.

[18] Henry Dundas. See Letter 98. He was opposed to political reform; for instance, as Stephen Mullen argues, his opposition to the abolition of the slave trade helped to delay abolition by over a decade. Through the use of his powers of patronage he became Scotland's most powerful politician. In 1805 he was impeached for financial malpractices, and, although acquitted, it ended his career. *ODNB*; Stephen Mullen, 'Henry Dundas: A "Great Delayer" of the Abolition of the Transatlantic Slave Trade', *Scottish Historical Review*, 100 (2021), pp. 218–48.

[19] On Pitt's wavering support for reform, especially in relation to Dundas and the Scottish burghs by 1788, see Meikle, *Scotland and the French Revolution*, pp. 26–33, 41; R. C. Primrose, 'The Scottish Burgh Reform Movement, 1783–93', *Aberdeen University Review*, 37 (1957), pp. 27–41; Dalphy I. Fagerstrom, 'The American Revolutionary Movement in Scottish Opinion, 1763 to 1783' (PhD thesis, University of Edinburgh, 1951), pp. 103–44; David J. Brown, 'Henry Dundas and the Government of Scotland' (PhD thesis, University of Edinburgh, 1989), p. 85.

[20] Dr William Taylor was suing John Anderson for £2,000 for defamation of character. See Letters 98 and 117.

& pretty dry. I hope every thing will be ready & safe for us ag[t]. Whit[y].[21] if we live so long. We have been all very ill of the cold. I seldom have seen Louisa so ill of it accept our most aff[te]. Comp[s]. to you & yours.

J. Wodrow

## Letter 135: Samuel Kenrick to James Wodrow, 13 February 1788
Place: Bewdley
Addressed: The Rev[d]. D[r]. Wodrow / Irvine / North Britain
Postmarked: Birmingham February the Fourteenth 1788
Franked: Free Westcote

My worthy and dear Friend,

Your kind favour of the 13th. Dec[r]. came regularly to hand, w[th]. Burns' excellent elegy inclosed,[1] copied by the fair hand of one of your dear girls. Not long before my good friend Professor Richardson favoured me w[th]. a copy of his still more pathetic lines on the untimely death of an intimate friend of his and yours I believe, D[r]. Irvine.[2] When sentiments of this sort come from the heart, as I presume they do in both these instances, they cannot fail of their effect in any language; how much more powerful and pleasing must they be when set off with the imagery & harmony of poetry! The single circumstance of prematurity, fills the soul w[th]. a painful regret, w[ch]. disposes it to relish everything else that tends to heighten the loss.

I am much obliged to you for the farther particulars w[ch]. you have sent me of this self taught poet. He must be possessed of greatness of mind to receive even merited praises with moderation: & must have no small share of good sense and common prudence– not always the companions of genius– to betake himself to his original profession of a farmer. I look upon Cooper as an excellent poet[3]– altho'

---

[21] Whitsunday, or Pentecost Sunday, which would fall on 11 May 1788.

[1] Robert Burns (1759–96) published his first volume of poetry in the summer of 1786, his *Poems, Chiefly in the Scottish Dialect*. JW had sent SK an unpublished poem circulated locally, Burns's 'Elegy on Sir James Hunter Blair'. See Letter 134.
[2] William Irvine. See Letter 106. William Richardson's 'Elegaic Verses Occasioned by the death of Dr Irvine' are reproduced in Kent, *An Eighteenth-Century Lectureship in Chemistry*, pp. 149–50.
[3] William Cowper. See Letter 134. He had been converted to Evangelical Christianity in 1764 after a nervous breakdown and suicide attempt, and was supported by the Unwin family and

many of his moral and religious sentiments are much more congenial to his friend and admirer, honest Jesse's[4] ^than to mine: –^ & I am happy to find he has paid Burns so handsome a compliment. I grant you that ignorance may increase admiration. But for the honour of Burns' sanguine admirers who are supposed not to understand him– I should rather ascribe this excess of admiration to a more noble cause than ignorance. Every reader must understand something of him. What they do understand they admire, and *ex pede Herculem*,[5] conclude from thence that what they do not understand must be equally excellent.

I meddle very little in politics, I assure you, or w[th]. the world at all. But while one has friends or feelings it is as you observe, sometimes unavoidable. The less one does in this way, however, the better. For favours & services are much sooner forgot, than slights or offences. And I find too much peace & comfort at home and at my own fire side to have any inclination to stir abroad.

I am glad D[r]. M[c]Knight goes on w[th]. his work.[6] I hope he will meet w[th]. the encouragement he so justly deserves.– As to me you are quite mistaken, in supposing I had the least insight into the mystery of publication. Andrew Millar never gave me any. I remember in the true tradesman depreciating style he told me that he lost by twenty books, where he gained by one.[7]

I hear no more of the Dissenters petition– & therefore suppose it will be put off this session.[8] What you say of D[r]. Priestley & the minister is I am affraid too true:

---

John Newton in Olney, Buckinghamshire. This religious persuasion explains his appeal to Kenrick's friend William Jesse, but Cowper's poetry appealed to many who, like Kenrick, did not sympathize with his religious convictions. His poetry spanned narrative ballads (most famously, *The Task* and *John Gilpin*) and moral satires. The quality of his poetry was recognized by the Dissenting and reformist publisher Joseph Johnson, following Newton's introduction, and Cowper and Johnson enjoyed a lucrative and creatively rewarding partnership. Hay, *Dinner with Joseph Johnson*, pp. 117–30.

[4] William Jesse. See Letter 122.

[5] Literally, 'Hercules from his foot': inferring knowledge of the whole from one small part.

[6] See Letter 134.

[7] See Letter 134; also Letter 265, SK to JW, 16 Aug. 1808: SK had clearly been deeply impressed by this comment by Millar: 'My relation Andrew Millar is universally allowed to have been, however illiterate himself, the most generous Macenas, to living authors, during the last century. He told me himself that he had lost by many more publications then he had gained, & when his gains exceeded expectation, he was ready to allow the authors or their heirs to partake of them. & that for personal kindness & services to his young countrymen, I know of no man to whom they were under greater obligations.'

[8] SK's surmise was correct. The next motion for the repeal of the Test and Corporation Acts was on 8 May 1789, when it was defeated by a narrow margin of 122 to 102 votes. J. C. D. Clark, *English Society 1660–1832: Religion, Ideology, and Politics during the Ancien Regime* (Cambridge, 2000), p. 416.

& our antiministerial papers haveing been long charging Dundas,[9] with the very opposition you expect from him to the reform of your Boroughs, & his influence to bias the minister,[10] to act inconsistently w$^{th}$. his general principles– hitherto deemed in favour the liberty of the subject. You give us fresh hopes of soon seeing your first volume. When on your visit at Glasgow I hope you will get it into the press, when you will have time to correct the sheets as they are thrown off.

Poor Anderson, what will become of him! How does he find recollection and spirits to go thro' his College business? His must be a most uncomfortable situation to be at war with all the world– without one to befriend him. More wretched sure than Milton's Devil, who at the worst was surrounded with an *Innumerable host of spirits armed*.[11] I am most heartily sorry for him.– How comfortable you will soon be in your new manse! Long, long may you enjoy it!

Our sunday schools,[12] w$^{ch}$. continue to flourish equal to our most sanguine hopes, you will see are followed w$^{th}$. another most benevolent project, almost throughout the kingdom, namely to abolish slavery and the slave trade.[13] To this end, petitions are sending up to Parliament from all quarters, one of which from the University of Cambridge has been presented by Mr. Pitt, altho', we are told, he will not take an active part in the matter. The plan seems to have originated at Cambridge when a premium was given for the best Dissertation on the subject. This dissertation has been translated into English & circulated thro' the Kingdom.[14] This was followed by a very liberal subscription for the support of the plan by most of the Colleges– lead on I dare say by D$^r$. Watson the worthy

---

[9] See Letter 134.

[10] i.e. William Pitt, the prime minister.

[11] *Milton's Paradise Lost, A New Edition by Richard Bentley DD* (1732), book I, line 101: 'Innumerable force of Spirits arm'd'. Milton's Satan led a rebellion against God and the tyranny of heaven.

[12] See Letter 113.

[13] SK is technically incorrect here. Given the large scale of British investment in slavery, a tactical decision was made to focus on petitioning for abolition of the Atlantic slave trade. It was hoped that this might be politically achievable, and would encourage plantation owners to better care for their enslaved workforce. David Brion Davis, *Inhuman Bondage: The Rise and Fall of Slavery in the New World* (Oxford, 2006), p. 233.

[14] Thomas Clarkson, *An Essay on the Slavery and Commerce of the Human Species* (1786), was based on his prize-winning Latin essay at Cambridge in 1785 in response to the question, 'Is it lawful to make slaves of others against their will?', set by Vice-Chancellor Peter Peckard (1718–97), a heterodox latitudinarian. Along with some Quakers in London, Clarkson founded the Society for Effecting the Abolition of the Slave Trade in May 1787. John Oldfield, *Popular Politics and British Anti-Slavery: The Mobilisation of Public Opinion against the Slave Trade, 1787–1807* (1995). Prime Minister William Pitt consistently spoke in favour of abolition, but never made it a government measure owing to pro-slavery members of his cabinet and the royal family.

Bishop of Llandaff.[15]– By the papers, I see on the authority of Dolben, member for Oxford,[16] that the sister university is to cooperate– but I am afraid– in so reasonable a cause– but faintly. Indeed, I have too much reason to say so: for my friend M$^r$. Roberts was there last week to enter his son at Christ Church[17]– w$^{ch}$. is reckoned the first College: & at that time there was nothing done, or likely to be done, in the business. On the contrary, the gentlemen he conversed with represented it as a dangerous attempt, w$^{ch}$. threatened the ruin of our West India settlements.– I suppose you know that the Master or Head of a College has nothing to do w$^{th}$. the education of the students. D$^r$. Jackson the present Dean of Christ Church (as he is called) is reckoned eminent in his business, being a strict disciplinarian.[18] All he does, is to see that the students come to morning and evening prayers– at 7 in the morning in summer & 8 in the winter, & 9 at night– not in their gowns ownly, but in surplices above their gowns– & as to instruction, they must apply to what they call a tutor. This was the religious course of education, I dare say, at Glasgow two hundred years ago, as the custom of ringing the great bell at five in the morning and the little one at 6, morning and night still testify– the first to awaken & the other to summon the students to prayers.[19] All Colleges were

---

[15] Richard Watson (1737–1816), Bishop of Llandaff (1782–1816). Although not actively involved in the campaign for the abolition of the slave trade, he 'made it known that he thought its continuance as contrary to Christian doctrine'. In the debate on abolition in the House of Lords on 23 March 1807, he made a substantial speech in favour of abolition. Richard Watson, *Anecdotes of the Life of Richard Watson, Bishop of Llandaff; Written by Himself*, 2 vols (1818), II, pp. 288–99; Timothy John Brain, 'Some Aspects of the Life and Work of Richard Watson, Bishop of Llandaff, 1737–1816' (PhD thesis, University of Wales, 1982), p. 259.

[16] Sir William Dolben (1727–1814), MP for Oxford University (1780–1806).

[17] Wilson Aylesbury Roberts (1770–1853), eldest son of Wilson Aylesbury Roberts (1736–1819), SK's friend and banking partner. See W-K, I, 478n. He attended Christ Church, Oxford, in 1788 and Lincoln's Inn in 1790. He served as lieutenant in the Wolverly yeomanry in 1803 and was MP for Bewdley 1818–32. The family had property in Bewdley and an estate at Packwood, south-east of Birmingham. According to *HPO*, 'Roberts's father, a local attorney, became an increasingly "influential member" of the close corporation at Bewdley, which had his son returned without opposition in 1818. On his death the following year Roberts inherited canal shares and local property worth approximately £60,000, and assumed control of the family interest.' There is a portrait of *Wilson Aylesbury Roberts the Younger (1770–1853), of Bewdley, Worcs., as a boy* in the Packwood House, Warwickshire, collections that can be viewed at www.nationaltrustcollections.org.uk/object/557807.

[18] Cyril Jackson (1746–1819), dean of Christ Church, Oxford (1783–1809).

[19] In late seventeenth-century Glasgow, 'The College bell rang at five in the morning, and the roll being called, every student had to answer his name. The day was spent in private study and public exercises, and at nine in the evening the chambers were visited by the regents.' Coutts, *History of the University of Glasgow*, p. 156. The regenting system, by which one individual taught a cohort of students all the subjects in the curriculum, was replaced in Scotland by teaching by

I believe intended originally for nothing else but to keep up the ecclesiastical order– who engrossed all the great offices of State. As to instruction in the different branches of Science, being then unknown, ^they^ were of course entirely neglected. But is it not strange that at this time of day they should still continue to be so, & these old forms so strictly adhered to: while w^th. you, who pass for a religious people, the form should be dropped & the improvement of the human mind in every branch of Science should come in its room.

I mentioned to you formerly the respectable Book Society at Birm^m.[20]– where they constantly purchase Books & the stock acumulates.[21] They have one of the same sort at Manchester. That at Birm^m. consists of ab^t. 300 members. It was lately objected to take in controversial Books– particularly respecting the late great subject of contraversy, the Trinity– meaning D^r. Priestley's [w]ritings, who is a member. The D^r. w^th. great propriety [re]mained neuter, as the objection came from the clergy [of th]e establishment.[22] But this did not make the D^rs. friends [th]e less zealous. On the contrary, they insisted on the ques[t]ion being decided fairly & called together all the members, who could conveniently attend– when it appeared that there was a majority of 2 to one in favour of contraversy.[23]

---

subject specialists in the eighteenth century. D. A. Winstanley discusses the continued practice of Cambridge tutors being given responsibility for teaching across the curriculum in the late eighteenth century. D. A. Winstanley, *Unreformed Cambridge: A Study of Certain Aspects of the University in the Late Eighteenth Century* (Cambridge, 1935), pp. 274–76.

[20] Letter 92, SK to JW, 22 Feb. 1785. Joseph Priestley was not only a member but had also played an important part in founding the Birmingham Library in 1781. Its holdings grew from 277 volumes in 1781 to 4,696 in 1798, by which time it also had more than 450 members and a purposely erected building. Loveday Heritage and Sue Roe, 'Reading Sheffield: Sheffield Libraries and Book Clubs, 1771–1850', in Towsey and Roberts, eds, *Before the Public*, pp. 174–200, at p. 178; James Raven, 'Libraries for Sociability', in Mandelbrote and Manley, eds, *Cambridge History of Libraries in Britain and Ireland, Volume II, 1640–1850*, pp. 241–63, at p. 250; David Allan, *A Nation of Readers: The Lending Library in Georgian England* (2008), pp. 65–66.

[21] The book stock would grow incrementally as the rule was never to sell a book. In 1798, the Birmingham Library Society had advanced from the 277 volumes it had possessed in 1781 to 4,696 books. The pattern was first established in Liverpool and subsequently in Manchester, Leeds, and other towns. *Works of Joseph Priestley*, XIX, p. 583; Raven, 'Libraries for Sociability', in Mandelbrote and Manley, eds, *Cambridge History of Libraries in Britain and Ireland, Vol. II: 1640–1850*, p. 250.

[22] In fact, Priestley thought that books on controversy, including his own, should be excluded from the library until it was in a position to purchase works on all sides of the debate. Joseph Priestley, *Familiar Letters Addressed to the Inhabitants of Birmingham* (1790), in *Works of Joseph Priestley*, XIX, p. 277. Thanks to Josh Smith for this reference. See also Letter 89, in which SK refers to Priestley's enthusiasm for the publication of William M'Gill's *Death of Christ*, not only despite his disagreement with its position but because of it.

[23] The Birmingham subscription library was founded mainly by Dissenters, including Priestley. Books were purchased by a committee of persons chosen annually by a majority of

And what does still more honour, to the liberal spirit of this country & age, is what I was told of another book Society in the neighbourhood of Birm<sup>m</sup>. consisting of 31 members— when one member, a clergiman objected to D<sup>r</sup>. Priestley's obnoxious writings as they are called and was supported by another clergi ab<sup>t</sup>. four score years of age, but were opposed unanimously by the other 29, who were headed also by a clergiman, who did it he said for the Cause of Truth, w<sup>ch</sup>. could only be established by free enquiry. That for his part his sentiments were very different from D<sup>r</sup>. Priestley's on these subjects, & he was the more confirmed in them the more he read against them: & therefore should be the last man to oppose any thing that could be said.— My associates are far from being so liberal minded— particularly my friend M<sup>r</sup>. Jesse who shudders at the very name of Priestley. But he has now entered the lists w<sup>th</sup>. him.[24] He set out for London yesterday to correct the press on the spot. He has just published Lectures— in the name of the late Soame Jennings.[25]— Our B<sup>p</sup>. has just published Warburton's Works

---

subscribers. Every vote was by ballot. Although intended to be above civil or religious party, it ran into trouble in 1785 over the purchase of Priestley's *History of the Corruptions of Christianity*. The majority of the committee of subscribers voted for its purchase and for the principle of buying controversial works, but the local Anglican clergy, led by Spencer Madan, withdrew their subscriptions and by 1787 'the body of subscribers was irretrievably divided on party lines'. Jones, *Industrial Enlightenment*, p. 190; *Works of Joseph Priestley*, II, part II, p. 6, Priestley to Theophilus Lindsey, 1787; and XIX, pp. 462, 583–89.

[24] William Jesse, *A Defence of the Established Church or, Letters to the Gentlemen of Oxford and Cambridge who are in the Course of Education for the Christian Ministry in which Dr Priestley's Arguments against Subscription, and the Peculiar Doctrines of Christianity, are Examined and their Futility are Exposed. By William Jesse, Rector of Dowles, and Chaplain to the Right Honourable the Earl of Glasgow* (1788).

[25] William Jesse, *Lectures, Supposed to have been delivered, by the author of A View of the Internal Evidence of the Christian Religion to a Select Company of Friends: Dedicated to Edward Gibbon Esq* (1787). Jesse's amusing format for his defence of revealed religion is to imagine a dream of hearing a lecture by Soame Jenyns 'on the belief and profession of Christianity' (p. ii). His dream and the conversation which followed was interrupted by his favourite King Charles spaniel, and so he rushed to write down the lectures. They present the case for Evangelical Christianity as the only true Christianity. Jesse's targets were wide ranging, including 'philosophers, sceptics, Deists, and speculative professors of religion' (p. iii) and many who thought themselves Christian, including those who regarded themselves as rational, enlightened, or orthodox Christians. Soame Jenyns represented such trends, but not the Soame Jenyns of the dream lectures. There he argues that 'orthodoxy' should not be mistaken for faith and 'the moral part of Christianity...is in fact no characteristic part of it' (p. 13). Rational Christians were also 'essentially deficient' (p. 9). They confused the conclusions of reason with the faith of the gospel. It was in the gospel where true Christianity could be found, which 'proclaims Jesus Christ the only mediator between God and man' (p. 12). That was the persuasion 'by which men become real Christians' (p. 9), and was the essence of Jesse's evangelical faith which called for regeneration and being 'born again' (p. 31). This contrasted with Soame Jenyns's *A View of the Internal Evidence of Christianity* (1776), a natural target for Jesse as a popular work translated even into Polish, besides German and French.

7 Vol$^s$. 4$^{to}$.²⁶– which make as little noise here as they do w$^{th}$. you tho' he lives within 3 miles.²⁷ But I must leave you.– w$^{th}$. our united best wishes & respects. I ever am yours sincerely

S. Kenrick.

## Letter 136: James Wodrow to Samuel Kenrick, 28 May 1788
Place: Stevenston
Addressed: M$^r$. Samuel Kenrick / Bewdley / Worcestershire
Stamped: MY/30
Notes in SK's hand: May 28 1788 / answ$^d$. 9th. June 88¹

My very dear Friend

I have never yet I believe acknowledged the receiving your last dated so far back as the middle of Febr$^y$.² ~~or~~ ^nor^ thanked you for the various & entertaining com^m^unications it contained. I must not advert to them at the length they deserve in this Letter unfranked; which I give you the trouble of for reasons I shall soon Mention.– D$^r$. Irvine was indeed a beloved friend of mine. I was his Guest during the Prin$^{ls}$. illness & several visits I made to Glasgow ^soon^ after his Death and I enter with equal approbation & more sympathy than you can feel into Ritchardsons pathetick Lines on our common friend. His sudden Death was a great stroke to the University & city of Glasgow–³

Your Predictions as to ^the^ Dissenters Bill as to the probable fate of the Scotch reform bill & as to the coolness of the University of Oxford in their Application

---

²⁶ *The Works of the Right Reverend William Warburton, Lord Bishop of Gloucester*, 7 vols (1788). Richard Hurd, Bishop of Worcester, was responsible for the publication and contributed a biography of Warburton.
²⁷ Hurd lived at the bishop's residence, Hartlebury Castle, near Stourport, and 3 miles southeast of Bewdley, where he significantly expanded the library.

---

¹ Missing letter: SK to JW, 9 June 1788.
² Letter 135.
³ See Letters 106, 108, and 127. As well as having earned his MD at the age of twenty-three, and having served as president of the Faculty of Physicians in 1775–77 and 1783–85, William Irvine was a significant figure in academic chemistry, whose reputation might have taken him to Spain had he lived. From his role in Leechman's last days he was also clearly a significant figure within the Glasgow professoriate, as well as one for whom both Leechman and JW had substantial affection. He was only forty-four years old when he died.

of the abolition of Slavery have been all verifyed.[4] As to the last we were ^too^ long of being roused in Scotland to join in such a benevolent design which does honour to the age.[5] Even still, only a few of our towns have followed the Example of Ed$^r$.[6] but the Universities & the Clergy have taken up the cause from one End of the kingdom to the other which I suppose will be properly finished by a Petition from the Gen$^l$. Assembly now sitting.[7] The Synods were obliged to take it up not knowing whether ^the^ matter woud come on in Parl$^t$. before this time. The Synod of Glasgow and Air began. They also first started in an Application to the Asembly to appoint the 5th. of Nov$^r$. for a day of national Thanksgiving to impress the minds of our people with a sense of the blessings we have derived from the Revolution. Without doubt it will be appointed[8] and I hope the English nation will follow us.[9]

Our Quondam Friend Anderson made very light of the bad success of his Lawsuit talked of it like shuffling a bad Hand of Cards. The Court unanimously

---

[4] The campaign was to abolish the slave trade, not colonial slavery. Oxford University declined to petition in 1788 on the grounds that it would be inappropriate. Seymour Drescher, *Capitalism and Antislavery: British Mobilization in Comparative Perspective* (Oxford, 1987), pp. 76, 125.

[5] While the campaign inside and outside Parliament had begun in England in 1787, with the formation of the Society for the Abolition of the Slave Trade and the start of Thomas Clarkson's travels throughout England to rally support for the cause, petitions to Parliament in support of abolition did not emerge from Scotland until 1788. Sixteen of the petitions sent to Parliament that year came from Scotland, most from presbyteries and synods of the national church, though many did so in rather conservative terms, expressing their trust in Parliament to do what it thought best. William Dickson, who worked with Wilberforce and Clarkson from 1790, undertook a tour of Scotland, like Clarkson's in England, in Jan.–March 1792, resulting in 185 petitions to Parliament from Scotland in that year. Iain Whyte, *Scotland and the Abolition of Black Slavery, 1756–1838* (Edinburgh, 2006), pp. 70–85.

[6] The Edinburgh Chamber of Commerce, Glasgow and Aberdeen Universities, and the town councils of Dundee and Paisley were the only secular bodies to petition Parliament for the abolition of the slave trade in 1788. Whyte, *Scotland and the Abolition of Black Slavery*, p. 82.

[7] See Letter 137.

[8] The *Scots Magazine* reported in Nov. 1788 that 'The secular anniversary of the Revolution has been celebrated throughout Scotland with the greatest demonstration of joy and thanksgiving', and that 'a meeting of the Independent Friends at Edinburgh [was] held on Tuesday, Nov. 4' for the same purpose. On 5 Nov., the Revolution was commemorated by thanksgiving services in Scottish churches, and 'the clergy seemed to vie with each other, in doing justice to this important æra, and in making their hearers sensible of the blessings, ecclesiastical and civil, introduced by that event'. *Scots Magazine*, 50 (1788), pp. 567–68. See also Meikle, *Scotland and the French Revolution*, pp. 41–42, who also quotes Robert Wodrow's description of the 1688 Revolution as 'the glorious and never-to-be-forgotten' event.

[9] Rémy Duthille dates the earliest mention of the Revolution Society in London to the society's minute book, which began on 16 June 1788. Rémy Duthille, 'The London Revolution Society (act. 1788–1793)', ODNB.

condemned him in all the six or seven Processes & amerced[10] him in the Expenses of every one of them (except I suppose the one against M[r]. Ritchardson where they I immagine woud only give the cause against him).[11] To D[r]. Taylour they woud have given high damages which he with propriety & generosity declined judging his Char[r]. sufficiently vindicated by the unanimous Sentence of the Court ^& taking only his neat Expenses viz £260^. The College only exacted the half of their Expenses. With all these deductions It is thought he must be above £1500 out of Pocket.

To come to the Main purport of my writing. The Publication is not much advanced cheifly from my transcribing the Life which is long & now improved I hope by the corrections I have adopted & some additions I have made to it. There are however nine Sermons ready for the Press which with the four published by himself three of which will be divided, will make sixteen in all & I am going on with more as fast as I can. When I was in Glasgow at the Synod M[rs]. Leachman with much friendship assured me that she intended to leave me those of her husbands Mss[ps]. in my hands which are the best part of them & that she meaned I shoud have the profits of the present publication which it is likely may be the only one. She also seemed to wish that I would accept an invitation M[r]. Ritchardson gave me then, & which I have since upon the matter accepted even to accompany him to England in the month of Aug[st]. perhaps ^about^ the 18 or 19 & spend some time more or less at London. My Age & entire inexperience in the bussiness of publications makes me very diffident in undertaking such a Journey. Yet if I have G.W.[12] health & spirits to prosecute it it may [be] of some consequence to the success of the book. It is at least an ostensible Errand to my friends here. The sale I hope will be considerable in Scotland which however coud be easily managed by my numerous friends & acquaintances here. But I shoud hope also for some attention to the book among the English Dissenters & for this purpose ^wish^ to be introduced to D[rs]. Price[13] & Kippis[14] & other

---

[10] 'Amerce': to fine. *OED*; *DSL*.

[11] Because Anderson had sued Richardson, not the other way round as in the other lawsuits. See NRS, CS233/A/2/11, Professor John Anderson Ag[t]. Professor William Richardson.

[12] 'G.W.': God willing.

[13] Richard Price (1723–91), philosopher, demographer, and political radical. See Letters 84 and 117. Between 1758 and 1791 he pastored and preached for the Presbyterian chapels in London at Poor Jewry Lane, Newington Green, and the Gravel-Pit Meeting Place in Hackney. In 1787 he published his *Sermons on the Christian Doctrine: As Received by the Different Denominations of Christians*, and he was involved in founding the New College, Hackney.

[14] Andrew Kippis (1725–95), the Presbyterian minister at Princes Street, Westminster, writer, activist in the campaign for Dissenting rights, and biographer. See Letter 118.

principal people among them. These two I believe were both intimate friends of Dr. Leechman & <—> might by their advice or otherwise be of considerable use to Introduce this posthumous publication in case they approved of it. And any thing of this kind either with them or with Booksellers can be much better transacted on ^the^ place than by Letters. These are Mr Ritch^ns. Ideas as well as mine & I woud beg the favour you woud give me yours with the utmost frankness.

In case this scheme is prosecuted we woud take our directions from you as to the proper rout in going up for the Prof^r. has never been in the West of England we woud wish to see Liverpool, at least Manchester Birmingham spend eight or ten days with you & see the fine places in your neighbourhood. Yet the pleasure I can promise myself from these will be little compared to seeing yourself & my kind old friend M^rs. Kenrick & my amiable young friend once more before we leave this world & meet in a better. I promise myself some benefit from your corrections of the Scoticisms in my Mp. I think of bringing with me your & M^r. Warners translation of the Theorie &c,[15] & concerting some Measures with Prof. R. & you as to the revisal & publication of it by you. I think of fifty other thin[gs]– but there is one thing my kind & constant friend that I must mention beforehand & ask as one of the greatest favours you can do me– even that you would take such measures as to be able to accompany me to London (I say *Me* for I think it likely your friend Ritchardson will leave me with you) <-> to continue there with me a few days till I ^am^ able to look about me in that wilderness (a very improper image) & introduce me as your friend to Kippis & other Literary people there & give me what assistance you ^can^ as to the publication. I will absolutely depend on your friendship in this point.

I beg to hear from you as soon as convenient. I know that you & M^rs. & Miss Kenrick will approve of the Scheme & push it on but I need no spur. I woud rather you woud warn me of the Difficulties & embarassments so as that I may avoid them, suggest proper cautions to a young traveller tho an old man as to Expenses on the road & oeconomy ^&c^ & give what ^hints^ you can think of as to the princ^l. purpose of the journey. All my family join me in best wishes.

May God bless you & yours<br>J. Wodrow

We have not yet removed into the new Manse but are on the Eve of it.
Nelly wrote to Miss Kenrick some time ago.

---

[15] John Warner's translation of Louis-Jean Lévesque de Pouilly, *Théorie des Sentimens Agréables* (Geneva, 1747). See the notes on Thomas Christie's letter appended to Letters 143 and 144.

## Letter 137: James Wodrow to Samuel Kenrick, 3 July 1788

I return my best thanks to My Worthy friend for his last of the <->9th of June[1] & all the friendly information it contains relative to our Journey & to our Counsellours at London in the intended publication. I shall pay due regard to every thing he suggests in the proper time. In the mean time having occasionaly mentioned this English Excursion to my old Pupil & warm friend M$^r$. Arbuckle who within these two months has been made Collector at Do—dee[2] a place above £700 a year & is living there with his family. He presses me to come that way & take the opportunity of seeing himself his Aunt &c, whom I have not seen these thirty years. And as he himself is ordered to Harrowgate about the time we propose to set out, he woud transport us with him in his Revenue Barge to Whithaven. I have signified this Proposal to M$^r$. Rit.$^n$[3] & if he goes into it, it will save us the tedious part of Journey & some money also. If not I will follow his plan & meet him D.V.[4] at Glasgow.–

I intend to go there myself in a few days but do not expect to see R$^n$. as he lives in summer at his little Villa in Stirlingshire.[5] But I wish to see M$^{rs}$. Leechman now with her Neice M$^{rs}$. Ruet on Loch Lomond & settle every thing with her– to procure a Letter from D$^r$. Reid to his friend & Correspondent D$^r$. Price to get the translation from M$^r$. Arthur[6] in whose hands it is & settle some other affairs in Glasgow. I shall write to D$^r$. Magill this day for the first vol$^m$. of Lardeners works wishing indeed very much to see the Life you mention.[7] I have got a few more of the Sermons transcribed tho' I have been very busy of late other matters particularly giving the Sacrament here last Sabath & have been taken up this week with writing Letters cheifly in the view of this journey.

---

[1] Missing letter.
[2] Donaghadee. See W-K, I, pp. 264, 421 for JW's old pupil 'Mr Arbuckle', probably a member of a family of merchants and revenue collectors in Belfast.
[3] William Richardson.
[4] 'D.V.': '*Deo Volente*', God willing.
[5] William Richardson was born in Aberfoyle, 20 miles west of Stirling.
[6] Presumably a reference to John Warner's and SK's translation of Pouilly's *Théorie des Sentimens Agréables* (1747); see Letters 143 and 144. This was now in the hands of Archibald Arthur, professor of moral philosophy at Glasgow University. JW hoped that Arthur would edit a volume of Warner's sermons. See Letters 108, 114, and 146.
[7] See Letter 122, where SK had mentioned Andrew Kippis's then forthcoming *Works of Nathaniel Lardner*, 11 vols (1788). JW was keen to meet Kippis in London on his trip to arrange the publication of Leechman's sermons; see Letter 136.

I thank you for your kind promise of every assistance in your power & will fully depend upon it. I see from yours that you have been reading the last & lately published part of Gibbons History[8] which I shall not have time to do yet I have read lately the greatest part of D[r]. Reids last publication on the Active powers of the human mind.[9] Tho' the subject is dry & beatten yet the book is entertaining & in my judgement the best I ever read on the <u>Theory</u> of Ethicks there is perhaps too little <u>practical–</u> what of this there is, is excellent. Dr. R. is a most Acute Metaphysician & sound Moralist. His knowledge is so clear that you woud sometimes think it intuitive. He gives up the point at once when it exceeds his faculties: & states with great modesty & precision the bounds of human knowledge on these deep subjects. On the subject of Liberty & Necessity he takes the Opposite side to your friend Priestly treats him with sufficient decency tho' he takes all the advantage Dr. Pr. gives him in avowing the consequences of the Necessitarian Scheme which scarce anyone has done but He.[10] Yet I did not fully go through that part of the book.

Yes your friend Davidson was Moderator of the Assembly & I am told acquitted himself well after his bashfulness was a little rubbed off by being a day or two in the Chair.[11] They have appointed the 5th. of Nov[r]. for a day of National Thanksgiving here[12]– & expressed the grounds of their appointment in H. Erskine's[13] words, which must in due time be read in our Pulpits. They have also inserted into their records & published through the kingdom a very strong approbation of the Petitions in behalf of the Slaves but declined to petition themselves for what reason I do not know, if it was not a conception (foolish in my apprehension) that it was improper in an independant Court.[14] I am happy to see

---

[8] The final three volumes of Edward Gibbon's *Decline and Fall of the Roman Empire* were published in 1788.

[9] Thomas Reid, *Essays on the Active Powers of Man* (Edinburgh, 1788), a volume made up of material first delivered as lectures and papers he had presented at the Glasgow Literary Society. By the 1770s, Reid's principal intellectual focus from the 1770s was no longer the writings of David Hume, but now those of Joseph Priestley. Knud Haaksonssen and James Harris argue that the essays in this volume combined Reid's rejection of Hume's moral theory with his defence of human free will in response to Priestley's publications of the 1770s and 1780s on necessitarianism and materialism. Thomas Reid, *Essays on the Active Powers of Man*, eds Knud Haaksonssen and James Harris (Edinburgh, 2010), pp. xi–xii.

[10] See Letters 83 and 84.

[11] Archibald Davidson. See Letter 108.

[12] See Letter 136.

[13] Henry Erskine. See Letter 79. He regularly attended the General Assembly as a lay elder.

[14] The General Assembly did not petition Parliament in the abolitionist cause, despite overtures from the synods of Lothian and Tweeddale, Angus and Mearns, and Merse and Teviotdale,

this matter in such a train by Mr. Pit's late appearances.[15]– The Kings Letter to the Assembly had been drawn up by some young raw lad, the Secretary of State absent, & his principal Clerk sick, & contained some droll expressions about their <u>Social meetings</u> & exhibiting to others Temptations to Virtue &c, The Committee in drawing up their answer had very properly used more decent Language. H. Erskine in an admirable vein of Irony & Satire ridiculed the Letter & insisted that according to custom it should ^be^ re echoed verbatim to the throne in which he was supported by many Wags & a most entertaining Debate ensued. In the course of which the King's Commissioner allarmed lest any thing shoud have passed disrespectful to Majesty started forward several times on his throne in the attitude of adressing the Court; but happily Mr. Er$^{ne}$. & his friends preserved in their Irony such a decency of Language as left no room for his interference.[16] The only thing they erred in was, in carrying the matter a little too far by bringing it to a vote; in which Mr. Erskine received a proper check ^from the Court^ for ^how^ever well entertained they had been by his humour he was left in a Minority of five or six. I am obliged to conclude in a hurry by M$^r$. Boyle[17] & company coming to Dinner & the necessity of sending this to Irvine to night from the frank.

All happiness attend you & yours prays<br>
James Wodrow

---

because Alexander Carlyle persuaded its members that petitioning Parliament did not befit the Assembly's status. Instead, the Assembly declared its members' 'abhorrence of a traffic contrary to the rights of mankind and the feelings of humanity, and their desire that Parliament should swiftly relieve "that unhappy portion of their fellow creatures"'. Whyte, *Scotland and the Abolition of Black Slavery*, pp. 80–81, quoting the *Scots Magazine*, 50 (1788), p. 305.

[15] Pitt had appeared in the House of Commons first on 9 May 1788 to open a debate on a resolution to consider the slave trade early in the next session, and again on 3 July 1788 to support Sir William Dolben's bill to limit the number of enslaved people that a vessel of any given tonnage could transport. Ehrman, *Younger Pitt: The Years of Acclaim*, pp. 392, 394.

[16] The Scottish opposition Whigs sometimes exploited the General Assembly of the Church of Scotland as a political arena (in the absence of a Scottish parliament). Broadly speaking, the Popular party tended to support the Foxite Whigs, while the Moderates tended to align themselves with the Pitt administration, as here. See *Scots Magazine*, 50 (June 1788), p. 303; *Edinburgh Evening Courant*, 26 May 1788; Emma Macleod, 'The Scottish Opposition Whigs and the French Revolution', in Bob Harris, ed., *Scotland in the Age of the French Revolution* (Edinburgh, 2005), pp. 79–98.

[17] Patrick Boyle. See Letter 98.

## Letter 138: James Wodrow to Samuel Kenrick, 16 September 1788

Place: London Goldsmith street No. 11 / Cheapside
Addressed: M<sup>r</sup>. Samuel Kenrick / Bewdley / Worcestershire
Stamped: SE/88
Note in SK's hand: answ<sup>d</sup>. 18 Sept<sup>r</sup>. 88[1]

My Dear & kind Friend

I take the opportunity of a leizure hour to write a few lines to thank you & your family for all the kindness I experienced at Bewdley, too much, rather for my feelings & to let you know how matters stand here as to my main Errand. Neither D<sup>rs</sup>. Price nor Kippis were in town so that I coud profit nothing by their advice there is some chance they may be in town about the end of this week. I happened to have two Letters from my friends in Airshire to a M<sup>r</sup>. Christie[2] a young man in the Medical way here, but one who has a very Literary & even a theological turn; having begun his Studies in Scotland in that line & given them up from the liberal turn of his mind that was hurt by the shac^k^les of Subscription.[3] At my second meeting with Christie he represented Johnston[4] as almost the only bookseller here whose integrity I coud fully depend upon and who was a man of Principle &

---

[1] Missing letter: SK to JW, 18 Sept. 1788.
[2] Thomas Christie. See Letter 130.
[3] Having left Scotland for London in 1784 and trained for a year at the Westminster General Dispensary, Christie returned north to Edinburgh in 1785 to study medicine. He was back at the dispensary in Westminster in 1787. While subscription to the Westminster Confession of Faith was not required of most students at the Scottish universities (hence SK's enrolment at Glasgow), it was required of those studying for divinity degrees. Coutts, *History of the University of Glasgow*, pp. 376, 419. See also Letters 108 and 110 on subscription at Scottish universities.
[4] Joseph Johnson (1738–1809), publisher, born in Everton near Liverpool, son of a Baptist landowner and businessman, John Johnson. Joseph moved to London in 1752 and fulfilled a publisher's apprenticeship between 1754 and 1761, when he established his own business. From 1770 his premises were at 72 St Paul's Churchyard. He became a unitarian under Joseph Priestley, and he helped Theophilus Lindsey found the first unitarian chapel in London in 1774. He was particularly associated with publishing the works of radical Dissenting and political writers such as Anna Laetitia Aikin Barbauld, William Enfield, Richard Price, William Godwin, Thomas Paine, and Mary Wollstonecraft. As well as many important literary works and material on medicine and education, he published writing in support of the American colonists during the Revolution, including the first English edition of Benjamin Franklin's works in 1779, and in 1788 he established the radical *Analytical Review* with Thomas Christie, for which Wollstonecraft wrote many articles. See Bugg, *Joseph Johnson Letterbook*; Hay, *Dinner with Joseph Johnson*.

tast ^& zeal^ for such Compositions as D^r. Leechmans. In consequence of this I was introduced to him & have put the Mss^p's. into his hands & I wait an Offer from him as to the Copyright. M^r. Caddel[5] to ^whom<->^ I have a Letter as well as easy means of Introduction is on the continent, yet they seemed to expect him in about a week. Thus the matter rests till I shall hear from M^r. Johnston which he said woud not be long.

I called on your friend M^r. Taylour[6] whom I coud not have found without M^r. Hamiltons[7] assistance as he lodges with another person ^in^ the Square. He received me very kindly & I intend to call upon him again to day for since friday I have been in the Country with M^r. Hamilton. They have a Cottage as they call it about six miles from town on Blackheath a most delightful situation where I spent two or three days very agreably particularly on Saturday I dined in that neighbourhood with a Company of Scots people two or three ^of them^ my wife's relations.

Instead of being at a loss for acquaintances I am likely to get too many of them & all of them exceedingly obliging. My Nephew Capt Wodrow[8] is in town & seems acquainted with most places of it. And I am beginning to familiarize with this part of the city to form some notion of the principal streets so that I can venture by myself half a mile & sometimes a mile without any direction in these. The lanes and narrower streets I will not attempt for some time.

---

[5] Thomas Cadell the elder (1742–1806), bookseller, born in Bristol, trained by an apprenticeship with Andrew Millar in London in 1758–65, after which he became Millar's partner till Millar's death in 1768. He sometimes worked with William and Andrew Strahan. His business was located at 141 Strand and published many important works, including those of many Scots, such as Robert Burns, Henry Mackenzie, William Robertson, Hugh Blair, and Adam Smith. It is not surprising that JW had an introduction to him, from Leechman's successor as principal at Glasgow, Archibald Davidson. Sher, *Enlightenment and the Book*, p. 247.

[6] Probably Rev. Thomas Tayler (1735–1831), minister at Carter Lane 1766–1811. He was the grandson of Rev. Richard Serjeant, who had been ejected from Stone in 1662. He was born in Kidderminster, and educated at Northampton (1750–51) and Daventry (*c.* 1751–57) academies. Joseph Priestley was a fellow student at Daventry. Tayler was assistant tutor at the academy (1757–61), and domestic chaplain to Mrs Elizabeth Abney, at Stoke Newington (1766–78). Thereafter he was assistant minister Carter Lane (1766–78), minister (1778–1811), trustee of Coward's and Dr Williams's Trust, and manager of the Presbyterian Fund. He preached the funeral sermon for Thomas Urwick in 1807. *DAO*.

[7] John Hamilton, JW's brother-in-law. See Letter 84.

[8] Perhaps Andrew Wodrow (b. 1752), son of Robert Wodrow (1711–84) and his first wife Mary Craig (d. 1754), who had been an officer in America during the War of Independence. *W-K*, I, pp. 420, 429.

M^r. Ritchardson set out with his friend M^r. Allan[9] on friday for Essex where he continues till this day sennight. He approved of what I have done as to the Mss. & D^r. Geddes also.[10] The last I have not yet seen tho' we have called on one another. The distance of friends or acquaintances in this extensive city is the cheif thing I complain of <-> an inconvenience easily remedied by the Hackney Coaches yet being sometimes disappointed in the calls that I have made I am unwilling to throw away my money upon an uncertainty.[11]

I gave you the trouble of a line from Woodstock[12] about our great coats which we had thoughtlessly left behind us somewhere in Worcestershire. Whether it was owing to your Exertion or to the Honesty of Innkeepers to whom we wrote as soon as we missed them I cannot tell; but the great Coats followed their Masters faithfully to London & came up with us on Tuesday night.
1 after^n.

I have called on your friend[13] & missed him which I shall soon do again as he is not a great way from this. I have also seen M^r. Christie who seems to think that Johnston's offers will not be high– that is likely he may offer to take upon himself the risk of the loss & to divide with me the profits whatever they are of the book. This however M^r. Ch. only guessed at from some general conversation about it. He thought It might be unsafe to proceed in that way with any other Bookseller but that I might absolutely depend on Johnston's integrity as well as his exertion in such a case which woud be the same as if he had the whole profits of the sale.

---

[9] Unidentified. Possibly Rev. John Allan (1737–1812), minister of Row in Dunbartonshire, north-west of Glasgow. See Letter 125.

[10] Rev. Alexander Geddes (1737–1802), Roman Catholic priest and biblical scholar from Rathven, Aberdeenshire, but living in London from 1781, supported by Lord Petre. He was educated for the priesthood at the seminary of Scalan in the Braes of Glenlivet, and then in Paris (1758–64). A formidable scholar and radical thinker, his uncompleted translation of *The Holy Bible: Or the Books Accounted Sacred by Jews and Christians*, 2 vols (1792; 1797) was controversial and saw him suspended from holy orders. His biblical criticism was based on the view that 'divine authority as transmitted or embodied through human agency was perfect only in the case of Christ', according to Gerard Carruthers, 'Geddes, Alexander (1737–1802)', *ODNB*. The similarity to Joseph Priestley's rejection of the divine mission of Moses was noted at the time. *Works of Priestley*, II, part II, p. 120. See also Jonathan Sheehan, *The Enlightenment Bible: Translation, Scholarship, Culture* (Princeton, NJ, 2005), pp. 244–47.

[11] JW's experience of London as a first-time visitor was similar in many respects to John Galt's portrayal of an Ayrshire minister and his family visiting the British capital on legal business, in his first novel, *The Ayrshire Legatees: Or, The Pringle Family* (Edinburgh, 1821).

[12] Missing letter. Woodstock is a town 8 miles north-west of Oxford.

[13] Perhaps Thomas Tayler, as above.

Write your oppinion in case such an offer is made– I must conclude just now having received a Letter from Stevenston which gives me the comfort that my family & every thing there is well & which I intend to answer by this nights post. M^rs. Kenrick & your Daughter will accept of my best & kindest regards I ever am

My Dear Sir<br>
sincerely yours<br>
J. Wodrow

## Letter 139: James Wodrow to Samuel Kenrick, 27 September 1788

Place: London
Addressed: M^r. Kenrick Bewdley / Worcestershire
Stamped: SE/27/88
Note in SK's hand: Answ^d. 29th Sept. 88[1]
Note: 88

My Dear Friend

    I had the pleasure of your kind & agreable Letter of the 18th.[2] My time has been much engrossed ever since partly with the main bussiness for which I came here & also with other engagements unavoidable. Your good friend M^r. Tayl^r. sent me an invitation to Dine with him about the end of last week where I met M^r. Urwick[3] who came from Clapham on purpose & spent two or three very happy hours. Neither Urwick nor I shoud have known one another had we met in another place. He was so kind as to ride to town again on purpose in a very bad morn^g. Mond^y. to introduce me to D^r. Kippis who is both a pleasant & friendly man. He offered & did call on Johnston before he and ^I^ came to any Eclaircissement but cautioned me not to expect any <—> considerable offers from him or any Bookseller tho' he himself had no doubt but the Publication woud answer. I dined

---

   [1] Missing letter: SK to JW, 29 Sept. 1788.
   [2] Missing letter: SK to JW, 18 Sept. 1788.
   [3] Rev. Thomas Urwick (1727–1807), a leading Independent minister, educated at Northampton and Daventry academies (*c.* 1747–52) and Glasgow University (1752–54). Minister at Angel Street, Worcester (1754–75), Narborough (1775–79) and Grafton Square, Clapham (1779–1807). *ODNB*; *DAO*; *W-K*, I, p. 300. Like SK, Urwick had been a Dr Williams scholar at Glasgow University; JW had then been acquainted with him, but not closely.

with Johnston on Tues.^y with D.^r Geddes M.^r Christie & many others[4] & made an appointment with him on Wed.^y forenoon when we were a long time together. He made his calculations as to the bulk of ^the^ vol.^ms & will need four more Sermons. He offered me two Alternatives. Either to take the whole risk of the Impression of a 1000 copies on himself & divide the profits or 2^d to give me 200 Copies. The last is the best offer tho' I cannot specify the reasons.[5] I mentioned before we parted, my Letter to Caddel. He said very politely & frankly that my application to him or any ^other^ Bookseller so far from giving him any offense was what he rather wished. It was what I ought to do, & what my friends woud expect. If their offers were better than his, it was well. If not, he would abide by his. I like Johnston much on the slight acquaintance I have had with him. His Mind & manner seems superiour to the rest of the fraternity but his Opinion of the Sermons as a book for sale is not high whatever other regard he may have for them. I went on that day to Kensington where I was engaged to dine & called on D.^r Kippis in my way who agreed with me in thinking the last offer best. D.^r Thompson[6] who has a great School or Accademy there & is abundantly intelligent & acquainted with the booksellers has sent the Letter I brought from Prin.^l Davidson[7] supported by one of his own to Caddel who is at Isle Thanet in Kent[8] & will not return for some time. He (Thompson) is also to speak to Dilly[9] with

---

[4] Joseph Johnson commonly hosted literary people in this manner: Hay, *Dinner with Joseph Johnson*. The other guests mentioned were Thomas Christie and Alexander Geddes (1737–1802), Roman Catholic priest and biblical scholar (see Letter 138).

[5] On these negotiations, see Sher, *Enlightenment and the Book*, pp. 247–49. The second option offered to JW by Johnson left open the possibility of JW earning some profits from the sale of his copies without the risk of Johnson failing to make a profit, in the first scenario.

[6] Rev. Seth Thompson (c. 1731–1805) was born at Surfleet in Lincolnshire, became master of a school in Kensington, and was the afternoon preacher at Brompton Chapel, Kensington. He attended Clare College Cambridge in 1751, BA 1756, MA 1759; and held some minor preferments as rector of Foxley in Norfolk (1763–1805), and vicar of Thatcham (1773–93) in Berkshire. According to John Nichols, Thompson's 'character was ever mild, modest, and unassuming', and his 'eloquence as a plain, practical preacher, was very justly admired'. Nicholas Hans, *New Trends in Education in the Eighteenth Century* (1951), p. 240; *Clergy of the C of E*; *Alumni Cantabrigienses*; John Nichols, *Literary Anecdotes of the Eighteenth Century* (1815), p. 205.

[7] Archibald Davidson. See Letter 108.

[8] The Isle of Thanet, a peninsula at the north-eastern extremity of Kent.

[9] Charles Dilly (1739–1807), bookseller 'at the sign of Rose and Crown at 22 Poultry, London', originally in partnership with his brother Edward until Edward's death in 1779. James Boswell, Samuel Johnson, and Benjamin Rush were associated with their large and lively social circle. Charles Dilly was a Dissenter and a member of the Society for Constitutional Information, and was financially involved in the *London Magazine* and the *London Packet, or, New Lloyd's Evening Post*. See J. J. Caudle, 'Charles Dilly (1739–1807)', and 'Edward Dilly (1732–79)', *ODNB*; Leo Damrosch,

whom he is very intimate. I must now wait the result of this second transaction & also the return ~~of~~ ^to my^ letters ~~for~~ ^from^ friends in Scotland particularly M^rs^. Leechman relative to the first: I have sent for Prin^l^. Leechman's picture as M^r^. Johnston approved of having a good Print of him prefixed to the first vol^me^. & offered to include it in the Expense. I do not expect that Caddel's or Dillys offers will be any better than Johnstons with whom therefore I will probably close ^in the end^. But I beg you woud write me your oppinion & advice on the whole Matter together with M^r^. Wigans.

Offer ^him^ my kindest wishes & regards. It was your fault in part my good friend that I did not meet M^r^. Wigan in London for had you given me at Bewdley the same direction you sent in your Letter I should have found him immediately. But it is no matter, for I shall now have the consolation ^G. willing^ of spending a few perhaps but a very few days at Bewdley with him & You & my other dear friends there in my return to Scotland. Nothing is more agreable to my wishes & more soothing to my feelings than this prospect, after I get out of the present scene of business & Dissipation in which I am engaged which is not however without it's pleasures cheifly from <-> ^the^ Novelty of it & the conversation of some worthy people to whom I have been introduced. I shall indeed have a solitary journey home but enlivened with the hopes of meeting with my family in good health– perhaps you may give me a little convoy if it perfectly suits your convenience. Write me however exactly the Day & place of the Worcester dilligence for I shall not stay here a moment longer after every thing in my power as to the publication is finished. M^r^. Ritchardson sets out on Wed^y^. or Thurs^y^. next I have seen him little of late as he was near a forthnight in Essex. <-> I dined with him yesterday in a Coffeehouse with D^r^. Geddes, introduced <-> him to D^r^. Kippis agreable to an appointment at Tea, when we had two hours very agreable literary conversation & we supped together with M^rs^. & Miss Rose part of the family of your ^old^ friend of Chiswick.[10] I am obliged to dine abroad again to day as I have ^done^ every day this week & have taken a seat in the Clapham Stage coach on purpose to spend This night & to morrow with M^r^. Urwick & to preach for him if he will allow me.– And I have hurried this Letter that I might compose my own

---

*The Club: Johnson, Boswell, and the Friends who Shaped an Age* (New Haven, CT, 2019), pp. 287–90; Peter Moore, *Life, Liberty, and the Pursuit of Happiness: Britain and the American Dream* (New York, 2023), pp. 490–99.

[10] William Rose, Dissenting schoolmaster at Chiswick and frequent contributor to the *Monthly Review*. See Letter 116.

mind & look over something that will answer. Miss Stirling[11] is very well & remembers you all gratefuly as I also <shall> always do.

J. Wodrow

## Letter 140: James Wodrow to Samuel Kenrick, 15 October 1788
Place: London
Addressed: M^r. Kenrick Bewdley / Worcestershire
Stamped: OC/15/88
Note: 88

My Dear Friend

For several days past I have intended to write & give you the progress of this tedious but interesting bussiness of the publication. It has now ended (I think) much better than I once expected but at the same time left your friend busier than ever in preparing everything for the printing which is begun. After I had resolved to apply to M^r. Cadell I learned that he was 70 or 80 miles distant at Broadstairs Thanet.[1] D^r. Thom^n.[2] was so obliging as to send him the Prin^ls. Letter supported by one of his own. These brought me soon a very polite Letter from M^r. C. signifying that ^he^ woud consider it as an honour to be concerned in the Publication that he was obliged to continue there for his health till the end of Oct^r. hoped to find me in town then but if otherwise referred me to settle the business with M^r. Strahan.[3] I answered his ^Letter^ immediately & accepted the last offer but neither was M^r. Str. in town. It was ^not till^ the begin^g. of last week that I had any intercourse with him. His treatment of me was also polite & obliging. I asked at our first meeting 100£ & 100 Copies for the property of the two vol^s. & continued on this

---

[11] Unidentified. Possibly a descendant of John Stirling (1654–1727), principal of Glasgow University.

[1] Thomas Cadell (1742–1802), London bookseller. See Letter 138. Broadstairs Thanet is a coastal town with a beach in eastern Kent, near Margate, where Cadell, recently returned from the Continent, was taking the waters. Sher, *Enlightenment and the Book*, p. 248.

[2] Seth Thompson. See Letter 139.

[3] Andrew Strahan (1750–1831), printer and publisher. He inherited the printing, publishing, and stationer's businesses established by his father, William Strahan (1715–85). The Strahans were publishing partners with the Cadells. Fanny d'Arblay described Andrew Strahan as having 'all the appearance of a very worthy, sensible, unpretending man, well-bred and good natured'. *HPO*.

footing for two subsequent visits. He declined making the bargain on these terms as he was to see M^r. Cadell in a few days. ^But^ by his ^M^r. St^r.^ calculations (which were the same with M^r. John^n's.)^4 he brought me to abate a little in my offers & then woud have struck the barg^n. on these lower terms, which I on my part declined; telling him at the same time that I woud not flinch from my lowest offer but expected something better from his & M^r. C.'s honour & generosity when they shoud meet and consult about it. I parted with him on Sat^y. on this footing, ~~and in this view~~ & he left the town on Sund^y. In the mean time however he had without my knowledge com^m ^unicated my first offer to M^r. Cad^l. by Letters. In consequence of which I received a Letter from M^r. Cad^l. on Mond^y. offering me what I had first asked viz £100 & 100 copies which I immediately by another Letter accepted.[5]

Thus the Matter stands you will see there is a sort of confusion or ambiguity in it from the manner of the transaction but upon laying it open to Mr. Ham^n.[6] after his return to town He is of oppinion that the business is ^quite^ finished because M^r. C. was the Principal in it. In the meantime M^r. Preston[7] M^r. Strahans foreman (and a very sensible man) has got the Life which he intends to have printed before I leave the town And I have & will be exceeding^ly^ busy in preparing the rest of the work which was not so ready as I thought. Even the printed Sermons have cost me a good deal of trouble in correcting & comparing them with the last Edition in the Scotch Preacher.[8] I have only got through the two first which will be now five. They will need ^besides the 16^ three or four more new ^Ms^p^^ ones if they make the vol^mes. the same with Blairs 5/in sheets or boards:[9] M^r. Cad^ls. Letter

---

[4] See Letter 138.

[5] Sher, *Enlightenment and the Book*, pp. 248–49: 'Although the £100 and one hundred books that [JW] received as compensation may not seem impressive, it was a relatively large amount for a posthumous new book of sermons by an author who was only moderately well known outside Scotland.'

[6] John Hamilton. See Letter 84.

[7] William Preston (1740–1808).

[8] William Leechman, 'The nature, reasonableness, and advantages, of Prayer; with an attempt to answer the objections against it', Sermon V, in *The Scotch Preacher: Or, A Collection of Sermons. By Some of the Most Eminent Clergymen of the Church of Scotland*, 4 vols (Edinburgh, 1775–89), I, pp. 138–206; Leechman, 'The temper, character, and duty of a minister of the gospel', Sermons VIII and IX, ibid., vol. II (London and Edinburgh, 1776), pp. 136–87; Leechman, 'The Wisdom of God in the Gospel-Revelation', Sermons XII and XIII, ibid., pp. 215–80; Leechman, 'The Excellency of the Spirit of Christianity', Sermons XV and XVI, ibid., vol. III (London and Edinburgh, 1779), pp. 287–338. Thomas Cadell published vols I and II of *The Scotch Preacher* and, with Thomas Longman, vol. III.

[9] The first and second volumes of Hugh Blair's *Sermons*, 5 vols (Edinburgh, 1777–1801) had been published in 1777 and 1780; the third was not published till 1790. They were enormous

is on that plan. But if they shoud enlarge the vol^(me). to 6/it will take five or six more & I will not refuse. It will be friday sennight or most probably the Mond^(y). following before I can leave this busy town & the four days I hope to have the pleasure of spending with you will be partly occupied at the Mss. But this will not be disagreable to you.

I must leave many things in your last & former agreable Letters to be answered viva voce for I have met with so many persons & things in this new world if I may call it so as perfectly confuse my poor head when I sit down to give any account of them which I dare say you will fully see from my Letters tho' I did not tell it you. I have never seen good M^(r). Taylour[10] since I dined with him not that I thought myself the least neglected by him but from want of time. I knew his situation from Urwick. I dined by invitation with D^(r). Price (whom I love and revere) in a Company of his own friends D^(r). Rees[11] M^(r). Morgan[12] M^(rs). & Miss Morgan the D^(rs). Sister & Neice all Welsh people. To the conscientious the amiable & intelligent Lindsay[13] I was introduced soon after I came here by Christie.[14] I cultivated the Acquaintance or rather friendship, ^that immediately <comenced>^ as far as I coud in the hurry of other matters. Last sab^(th). forenoon I had the pleasure of joining in the reformed English Service in his Chapel & of hearing from him a most excellent Sermon.– of breakfasting with him on Mond^(y). He has loaded me

---

international bestsellers, hence JW's mentioning them as the model. The *Critical Review* described them as 'the most popular work in the English language other than the *Spectator*': 11 (1807), p. 87, quoted in Sher, *Enlightenment and the Book*, p. 33.

[10] Thomas Tayler. See Letter 138.

[11] Rev. Abraham Rees (1743–1825), Presbyterian minister and tutor, born in Wales like Price and Kenrick. He had taught mathematics at Coward's Academy, London (1762–85) and Hoxton Academy (1785–86), and had been tutor in Hebrew and mathematics at New College, Hackney since 1786. At the same time, he had been pastor to the Presbyterian congregation in St Thomas's, Southwark from 1768, followed by the Old Jewry congregation since 1783. He was a trustee of Dr Williams's foundation from 1774, secretary to the Presbyterian board from 1778, and was awarded a DD by the University of Edinburgh in 1775. He re-edited Ephraim Chambers's *Cyclopaedia*, and published his own *New Cyclopaedia; or, Universal Dictionary of the Arts and Sciences* (1802–20), which eventually ran to thirty-nine volumes.

[12] Either William Morgan (1750–1833), actuary to the Society for Equitable Assurances, or George Cadogan Morgan (1754–98), Dissenting minister and scientist, the two sons of Richard Price's sister Sarah (1726–1803). George Cadogan Morgan had been Richard Price's assistant at the Gravel Pit meeting-place at Hackney, Middlesex since 1787, and concurrently tutor at New College, Hackney. William Morgan also lived in London, in a large house at Stamford Hill, where he entertained his brother, uncle, and friends such as John Horne Tooke, Sir Francis Burdett, and Thomas Paine. Either brother, therefore, may have been at the gathering attended by JW.

[13] Theophilus Lindsey. See Letter 79.

[14] Thomas Christie. See Letter 130.

with presents of his Books & Pamphlets not as he says to disseminate his Heresy in the North but ^to^ gratify some friends he has there who may not have seen them. I ^have^ had the pleasure of joining in the Musick of the High mass in the Sardinian Chapel[15] & an opportunity of hearing in another Popish chapel a sermon delivered in the Scotch manner[16] but without Psalms or prayers equal in point of Elegance and Pathos to the most part of Blairs.[17] I was twice in the Jewish Portug^u^eese Synagogue[18] to hear their Prayers & then their singing or chanting during their great fast of the Annual Attonement[19] & carried Christie to one of their Houses where we were allowed to be present at the circumcision of an Infant, with several other sights & entertainments too tedious to mention to you who must have seen all these things and many more on a larger scale.

Our friend Urwick I have found to answer exactly your Description. He went on frid^y^. last with some Ladies to Bath & promised to call on me in his return. He is greatly interested in the Publication & has promised to revise the proof sheets. Some of my Quondam Scotch friends ^that were so^ thirty of forty years <acquaintance> ^ago^ have found me out & sent me invitations John Ingram M^rs^. Barbara Crawford, & her Brother Quintin now a Nabob. I cannot resist the impulse of renewing for a few hours these old connexions which are never likely to be repeated again in this world. It encroa[ches] a little upon my time, yet their

---

[15] Public access was available to the chapels of various London embassies of Catholic nations, and their baroque style of worship, in the seventeenth and eighteenth centuries. The Sardinian Chapel was a prominent Catholic church, which had been burned to the ground on the first day of the Gordon riots of 1780, but it was repaired with the help of British government compensation and reopened in 1781. Colin Haydon, *Anti-Catholicism in Eighteenth-Century England, c. 1714–1780* (Manchester, 1995), p. 213; Philip Olleson, 'The London Roman Catholic Embassy Chapels and Their Music in the Eighteenth and Early Nineteenth Centuries', in David Wyn Jones, ed., *Music in Eighteenth-Century Britain* (2000), pp. 101–18.

[16] See Ann Matheson, 'Theories of Rhetoric in the Eighteenth-Century Scottish Sermon' (PhD thesis, University of Edinburgh, 1979). The Moderates aimed to set high rhetorical standards for preaching; this had been the purpose of the publication of the volumes of *The Scotch Preacher*, in which some of Leechman's sermons had originally been published.

[17] Hugh Blair. See Letter 99.

[18] The synagogue of the Spanish and Portuguese Jews' congregation in Creechurch Lane in London was opened in 1657 after Oliver Cromwell ended the exclusion of Jews from England in 1656. It moved in 1701 to the larger Bevis Marks building it still occupies off Aldgate, on the limits of the City of London (in which Jews were barred from owning property). The arrival of Spanish and Portuguese refugees from the Inquisition was much diminishing by 1788 but had not yet ended. Sharman Kadish, *Bevis Marks Synagogue: A Short History of the Building and an Appreciation of Its Architecture* (2001), pp. 1–3; Richard D. Barnett and Abraham Levy, *The Bevis Marks Synagogue* (1998).

[19] i.e. Yom Kippur.

hours of dining are so late that it is not much. <-> Amidst all these things my Heart is at Bewdley & I long for the pleasure of ^passing^ a few days there with you & your family in ease & peace having now given up the thoughts of return^g to Scotland before our great Revolution Anniversary.[20]

God bless you & yours.<br>J. Wodrow

## Letter 141: James Wodrow to Samuel Kenrick, 25 October 1788
Place: London
Address: M^r. Kenrick Bewdley/Worcestershire
Stamp: OC/25/88

My Dear Friend

I have just ^now^ taken a Ticket in ^a^ Worcester Coach which goes from this neighbourhood on Mond^y. at 2 afternoon & arives at Wor^r. on Tues^y. morn^g. & I hope G.W. to be with you that night. In the meantime I wish you woud secure me a seat in the Bewdley Diligence[1] that I may not be dissapointed there. I have had my health here perfectly well till the beginning of the week when I took a cold in my Head which has fallen down on my breast so that I am not very fit for travelling today but hope to be better before Mond^y. & that the Journey will do me good.

I have been very busy hitherto in making further corrections on the Sermons the printed as well as the Mss. & have only finished today. The Life is printed all to the last sheet. I see from a Card of M^r. Strahan's[2] (who is just now with M^r. Cadell[3] in Thanet) that they wish to delay the engraving till a second Edition but I must insist on it to the first as the Picture is on the road & this, even tho' I shoud bear part of the Expense for it woud be pity to deprive D^r. Leech^ns. friends who will buy the first Ed^n. of the pleasure of looking at a good Print of him.[4] Besides I think a second Edition a little uncertain especially as they are printing 1250 copies of This.[5]

---

[20] i.e. 5 Nov. 1788, the centenary of the landing of William of Orange at Torbay on his way to seize the English and Scottish thrones from King James VII and II. See Letter 136.

[1] That is, the public stagecoach to Bewdley from Worcester.
[2] Andrew Strahan. See Letter 140.
[3] Thomas Cadell. See Letter 138.
[4] Sher, *Enlightenment and the Book*, p. 249.
[5] A shrewd assessment; no second edition was issued. Sher, *Enlightenment and the Book*, p. 249.

I spent two or three hours last night very agreably with D^r. Price at his nephew's at Black Friar's Bridge[6] & got a good deal of intelligence from him of different kinds. He has great hopes of the extension of Liberty from the present strugles in France.[7]

There have been some apprehensions of late about the King's state of health which I hope are without grounds.[8] Such as he is, may heaven spare him to us. We seldom know the value of our mercies till threatened with the loss of them.

In my hurry of writing or a multiplicity of things coming across my mind at once, one of which drives out another, I have always forgot to tell you any thing about the <u>Theorie</u>.[9] I cared not to say any thing about ^it^ to Johnston while matters were in dependance. I showed it to Mr. Strahan when I saw things woud come to an agreement. He considered it a little but gave an oppinion that it would scarce defray the Expense of printing for reasons that I shall give you at meeting. I have now put it & intend to leave it in Mr. Christie's hand to have his Judgment about it & also M^r. Johnston's to whom I have now mentioned it.

I bring with me the first vol^me. of Christie's Essays made up in a hurry for me.[10] The book will not be published till Jan^r.

I must break off as the last part of the life is now sent me & my spirits are not very good. I hope they will rise at Bewdley. In every situation I am

most sincerely yours<br>J. Wodrow

my kindest regards to M^rs. & Miss Kenrick

---

[6] William Morgan. See Letter 140. D. O. Thomas, 'William Morgan (1750–1833)', *ODNB*, says that he lived near Blackfriars Bridge (built in 1766) for seven years from 1775, when he started work with the Equitable Assurance Society. Evidently he still had accommodation there in 1788, whether or not still at the Society's offices, even if the house he built at Stamford Hill had been completed by then.

[7] An early comment on the pre-revolution tremors in France.

[8] King George III had suffered stomach pains in summer 1788, but he was very unwell by October and clearly mentally unstable.

[9] John Warner's translation of Louis-Jean Lévesque de Pouilly, *Théorie des Sentimens Agréables* (Geneva, 1747). For more on this, see the notes on Thomas Christie's letter appended to Letters 143 and 144.

[10] [Thomas Christie], *Miscellanies: Literary, Philosophical and Moral*, 4 vols (1788). See Letter 130.

## Letter 142: James Wodrow to Samuel Kenrick, 11 November 1788
Place: Kendal
Address: M[r]. Kenrick / Bewdley / Worce[ster]shire
Stamp: KENDAL
Notes: D[r]. Wodrow/88

My Dear Friend

I take the opportunity of a short stay at this place to return my best thanks to you for your friendly convoy & to M[rs]. & Miss Kenrick for their Sisterly kindness at Bewdley. I parted from you all with a heavy heart, I came here last night in perfect health & have been very fortunate in meeting with agreable fellow travellers & with much entertainment on the road.[1] After I parted with you ^& taking a good view of Shres[y].^ I had the coach to myself to Ellesmere.[2] There a young man like a Squire & a pretty Spaniel in his hand Breakfasted with me. He had come by his own account to purchase a house & bit of ground in that beautiful Country & had been looking at your friend Hatchets grounds[3] but I found he had not seen him & took my fellow traveller for an Irish adventurer we parted after four or five miles at that fine turn on the road that you mentioned before I entered Wales which is the most beautiful spot I have seen in England.[4] I missed your Nephew at Wrexham but chatted a few minutes with your neice & got on in Company with an old infirm lame Col[l]. to Chester about five. Drank Tea & sat till eight with M[r]. & M[rs]. Eddows[5] whom I like very much. I spent the whole Saturday at Chester

---

[1] JW must only have stayed with the Kenricks for a few days if he left London on Monday 27 October and arrived in Bewdley the next day, as he planned (Letter 141), since the journey from there to Kendal must have taken him more than a week.

[2] Ellesmere is a market town about 20 miles north of Shrewsbury.

[3] Hatchet appears to have been an old friend of SK. In 1767 Harry Millar expressed disappointment that 'we are not to see Buckley Hatchet & you this Season' at Neilston. Rev. Henry Millar to Samuel Kenrick, 4 Sept. 1767, Wynn Hall MSS, Bangor University, WYNN/1/1/14. He was probably the Buckley Hatchet who resided at Lee in Shropshire, halfway between Wrexham and Shrewsbury, and subscribed to Thomas Phillips, *The History and Antiquities of Shrewsbury* (Shrewsbury, 1779). Lee is around 10 km from Ruabon, where SK was raised.

[4] This will have pleased SK, who was born at Wynn Hall, Ruabon, 6 miles south-west of Wrexham.

[5] Ralph Eddowes (1751–1833) was the husband of SK's niece Sarah (m. 1777, d. 1815)—whom JW had missed at Wrexham (Letter 153). Educated at Warrington Academy as a pupil of Joseph Priestley, Eddowes became a unitarian and merchant in Chester. He waged a campaign in the 1780s to reform the town corporation, and was also active in the campaign to repeal the Test and Corporation Acts. In 1794 he emigrated to Philadelphia 'in disgust, being dissatisfied w[th]. the hostile measures, w[ch]. at that time threatened every friend to liberty & w[ch]. have not been much

breakfasted dined and drank Tea with M[r]. Moulson[6] & his family & M[r]. Chidlow who has stayed in his & his Father house for 34 years.[7] I had dressed myself & resolved to ^have^ preached tho' I had not promised to the old Gentleman in return for his obliging attention ^in showing me^ every thing in Chester worth seeing but ^a^company from shropshire ^ariving^ made it necessary for Paul to send his coach on Sund[y]. morn[g]. to Liverpool (which he had refused to me till the begin[g]. of the week & I coud not neglect such an opportunity & parted with Mr. Chidlow & Mr Moulson & his company after winning three Rubbers at Whist. They were the best whist players I have met with in England. Your Nephew found me in Chester & spent part of the day with me there. I was fortunate in getting good Companions tho' a crouded Coach & a fine fair wind to cross the water[8] on Sund[y]. Morn[g]. attended divine Service & heard a grand Anthem in the Octagon loft.[9] I saw a good deal of Liverpool left it yesterday morn[g]. at seven in the Kendal Coach & came here about 80 miles at 11[ck]. at night. I have ^come from Liv & am^ now in Company with a young Officer a Scots^man^ who has however spent near 18 years in England America &c, & we think of taking the Mail[10] onwards but have little chance of seats [so] that we may probably go on together in a post chaise to Penrith & take our chance of seats in it there. We have taken this resolution instantly so that I am obliged to break off abruptly begging to hear from you & particularly of the Health of your Nephew James[11] whom I am concerned

mitigated since– & carried w[th]. him very considerable property w[th]. a very large young family: & being an active intelligent tradesman, will, w[th]. the blessing of providence united w[th]. many more of the same sentiments, & inured in the similar habits, be the founders of a new colony of virtuous well informed citizens'. Letter 206, SK to JW, 17 March 1796; see also Letter 212, SK to JW, [20 Jan.] 1797; Letter 250, SK to JW, 22 March 1806. D. H. Weinglass, 'Eddowes, Ralph (1751–1833)', in Joseph O. Baylen and Norbert J. Gossman, eds, *Biographical Dictionary of Modern British Radicals*, 3 vols (Brighton, 1979–88), I, pp. 144–50; see also the Kenrick family tree in Norah Kenrick, *Chronicles of a Nonconformist Family: The Kenricks of Wynne Hall, Exeter and Birmingham. Edited by Mrs. W. Byng Kenrick* (Birmingham, 1932).

[6] Ralph Eddowes's former business partner, who had died by 1796. Letter 206, SK to JW, 17 March 1796.

[7] A clergyman: Letter 206, SK to JW, 17 March 1796.

[8] The River Mersey.

[9] The Octagon Chapel, a nonconformist congregation established in 1763, which used a liturgy with Arian tendencies, known as the 'Liverpool Liturgy': [Philip Holland, John Seddon, and Richard Godwin], *A Form of Prayer and a New Collection of Psalms, For the Use of a Congregation of Protestant Dissenters in Liverpool* (Liverpool, 1763); Smith, *Rational Dissenters*, pp. 89, 109; Anne Holt, *Walking Together: A Study in Liverpool Nonconformity, 1688–1938* (1938), pp. 133–36 on the liturgy and p. 49 on the Octagon, which leaves some ambiguity about its trajectory post-1776.

[10] i.e. the mail coach.

[11] James Kenrick (d. 1824), son of John (1725–1803) and Mary (d. 1801) Kenrick. See Letter 144.

about as he was in low spirits a little about his health– when I saw ^him^ it was nothing else in hast

> Yours ever aff<sup>y</sup>.
> James Wodrow

## Letter 143: James Wodrow to Samuel Kenrick, 25 December 1788

Place: Stevenston
Addressed: M<sup>r</sup>. Kenrick / Bewdly / Worcestershire
Postmarked: London Decr. Thirty First 1788
Franked: Free Ad: Fergusson
Stamped: EE
Note: answ<sup>d</sup>. 19th Jan<sup>y</sup>. 89

My kind & worthy friend's Letter of the 28 of Nov<sup>r</sup>.[1] reached me in course and he will certainly by this time be accusing me of negligence or Lukewarmness to my English connexions in consequence of my long silence. But I cannot accuse myself. Not to plead that all our M. of P. are at London & that I was forbidden at Bewdley to make use of L<sup>d</sup>. Westcote's direction. I have been busy four or five days every week in correcting & transcribing three excellent Sermons of D<sup>r</sup>. L. on Prov. XIX.27.[2] superiour I think to any in the Collection. I have had no assistance in the writing of them, our Schoolmasters being engaged with their night Schools. Pleasant as this Labour was, I am happy it is now over <blot> that I have it in my power to send the last Packet to morrow & hope to have little further trouble about the Publication. Our friend Urwick[3] has never acknowledged the Packet I sent him from Bewdley nor two others afterward sent him under the same direction containing a Tittle page some excellent verses on the Prin<sup>ls</sup>. Death Letters of bussiness to M<sup>r</sup>. Strahan &c. This gave me both much anxiety & some trouble in preparing new copies as I had little doubt that either He or his friend the Member were out of the kingdom. I changed my mode of conveyance &

---

[1] Missing letter: SK to JW, 28 Nov. 1788.
[2] Sermon XVIII, 'Youth guarded against licentious Pleasure', in *Sermons, by William Leechman*, II, pp. 129–50; Sermon XIX, 'Youth guarded against licentious Maxims', in ibid., pp. 151–68; Sermon XX, 'Youth guarded against hurtful Maxims and Books', in ibid., pp. 169–94. 'Cease, my son, to hear the instruction that causeth to err from the words of knowledge.' Proverbs 19:27.
[3] See Letter 139.

wrote under cover to Sir. A. Ferguson which produced me very lately a letter from Mʳ. Strahan's Clerk acknowledging the receipt of the packets ^signifying^ that the first volᵐᵉ was finished & the 2ᵈ begun. & going on & that Mʳ. Urwick ^was^ most attentive in correcting the press being there almost every day. Strange! that he should ride so often to London to oblige me & not send me a single line to remove my anxiety tho' I earnestly & repeatedly asked it & tryed to engage him in an interesting correspondence about his friend Farmer.[4] But why plague my Bewdley friend & take up so much room in this confined Letter with an Anxiety that is now almost over? Why not? say you. Well: I will just add That Messʳˢ Cadell & Strahan on their return to London declined any part of the Expense of the engraving which they said woud cost £30. I impute this to Mr. Strahan who knows that he coud have concluded the bargain ^on^ lower terms with me had it been left entirely to him, and has taken hold of this circumstance left a little loose in my Letters to bring down what he thought too high a price. Mʳ. Hamilton[5] to whom I left power to act for me has brought them to consent to be at the half of the Expense of the Engraving & I have agreed to bear the other half.[6]

My journey according to your hopes was prosperous to the end. Dod the agreable and obliging Officer <—> and I prosecuted our Scheme i.e. took Post Chaise from Kendal to Penrith; and travelling at rather a quicker rate than the Mail got full time to dine with ease at Penrith & to sit more than an hour after. When the Mail came up it was according to our fears quite full & according to our hopes dropt three of its Passengers at Penrith so that we stepped in immediately, and supped together at Carlisle where we parted not without half a promise on his part to beat up my Quarters here, & on mine to call on him at Edʳ. in case I shoud be there in half a year, to which his stay in Scotland is limited. I went on during the night with an honest good sort of Leather Merchᵗ. of Kendal who accompanied me the whole way to Glasgow a very different Companion from my former one but I had no objection to him as I got some hours confused sleep & tho' he had no talents for conversation he was in every other respect obliging & quite accustomed to the mail.[7] When the sun rose <—> I felt the inferiority of poor

---

[4] Presumably Hugh Farmer, Dissenting minister in Walthamstow, Essex, preacher at Salters' Hall, London, and theological writer, whose work JW admired. See Letter 87.

[5] John Hamilton. See Letter 140.

[6] Sher, *Enlightenment & the Book*, p. 249.

[7] That is, experienced in travelling on the mail coach, unlike JW, and so a helpful companion for JW.

Scotland, even some of the richest spots of it on Clyde <—> round Hamilton, to the fine cultivated Country I had just left. We got to Glasgow before two i.e. in 24 hours from Kendal notwithstanding some long stops. I found M^rs. Leechman in better health than I had seen her since her husbands Death. It happened to be Sacr^t. Week and I enjoyed the season of recollection & Devotion with some relish after the busy scenes I have been engaged with for three months before, especialy as I had no concern about preaching, the diets being ^all^ filled up. I was only called on to serve a single table.[8] I enjoyed my friends also, & did not move till Wed^y. morn^g. a week after my arival there, & soon met with a wellcome reception from my family & Parish. The last seemed to think that they had lost me entirely, being little accustomed to such long seperations.[9]

I now think with and speak with pleasure of my English Excursion especialy of the fortnight I spent at Bewdley by much the happiest part of part of it. Nelly had a thousand enquiries to make some of which I coud not answer. I shall always remember with pleasure & gratitude the reception I met with from your family and even from M^r. & M^rs. Roberts & Miss Caroline.[10] I hope she will always continue to think as little of her sweet sensible face, & her fine fortune as she seemed to do when I saw her. Had there been time to have spent <som> ^some^ days with your friends at Lee I am sure I shoud have enjoyed it much, from my knowledge of their char^rs. It seemed to be, too, a delightful part of the Country– You forgot to answer my too pressing enquiry about your nephew James's health yet from your Letter I can almost certainly conclude he is now very well. Remember me in the kindest manner to M^r. Wiggan. You will have already expressed my regret at not seeing ^him^ after his repeated calls the last night I was at Bewdley. It was

---

[8] For JW's description of a busy Scottish communion season in the Ayrshire town of Kirkoswald, see Letter 120. A Glasgow communion season would have been even larger. Hence the common practice of having several ministers present to serve the elements to different tables of congregants. See also W-K, I, p. 361.

[9] See John Galt's account of the triumphant return of Dr and Mrs Zachariah Pringle to their fictional parish of Garnock in North Ayrshire after a trip of several months to London to settle a legacy, in *The Ayrshire Legatees* (1821), chapter 10.

[10] SK's banking partner Wilson Aylesbury Roberts and his wife Betty Carolina Roberts. See Letter 103 in this volume, and W-K, I, p. 478n. Caroline Aylesbury Roberts (c. 1773–1830) was their only daughter and died unmarried. John and John Bernard Burke, *A Genealogical and Heraldic Dictionary of the Landed Gentry of Great Britain and Ireland*, 2 vols (1847), II, p. 1123; Warwickshire County Record Office; Warwickshire Anglican Registers; Roll: PG 3320; Document Reference: DRB 25. In addition, they had two sons: Wilson Aylesbury Roberts (1770–1853), who later became MP for Bewdley 1818–32 (see Letter 135); and Thomas Aylesbury Roberts (c. 1775–1804), who was briefly vicar of Hagley. *Alumni Oxonienses*, III, p. 1209; *Clergy of the Church of England Database*, id. 19598.

Mr. Roberts fault but it was perhaps as well to avoid a melancholy tho' a pleasant parting. Remember ^me^ to my young friend Mr. Rowan.[11] I had no opportunity of seeing any of his Relations at Glasgow. But last week Mr. White[12] (whose Sister is Mr. Rowan's Aunt) spent a day & night with me in his road to his s[page torn] Mr. Rowan's Relations with whom he was to spend several days. To Mr. Whyte I gave a particular acc$^t$. of the young Gent$^{ns}$. present situation & of his Tutor which woud be fully communicated to them.

The enclosed Letter from Mr. Christie I found lying for me at my Arival.[13] So occupied have I been that I had no time to Accknowledge the receipt of it till last week & this in a very few lines intimating that I considered the Ms$^p$. as yours rather than mine & that I shoud transmit his Letter or the Substance of it to <u>my</u> friend who was <u>his</u> also– you may consider the matter & return me the Letter with your thoughts about ^it^ before the end of Jan$^r$. about which time perhaps he may leave London.

I have left myself no time or room to say any thing about public affairs tho' very much interested in them & obliged to you for your present as I will be for your future communications about them. Only I am entirely on M$^r$. Pits side and in his views, thinking them the only ones supported by Revolution principles.[14] I am happy to see he has carried his point by such a majority in the H of C a greater might have been expected in any other Question <—> this one has been

---

[11] Unidentified member of SK's circle in Bewdley. A number of 'Rowans' and 'Rowands' appear in Addison, *Matriculation Albums*. See also Letter 236, SK to JW, 10 Nov. 1802.

[12] Unidentified.

[13] See the transcribed shorthand letter that follows this Letter 143. For Thomas Christie, see Letter 130.

[14] A reference to the Regency Crisis. King George III suffered a period of mental illness from late October 1788 until mid-February 1789. The length of this episode allowed the Foxite Whigs in opposition in Parliament to propose the necessity of a Regency, in which George, Prince of Wales would have assumed the duties of the monarch while his father remained incapacitated. Prime Minister William Pitt tried to delay the progress of the Regency Bill by debating the extent of executive power to be awarded to the Regent because, had the Prince of Wales become Prince Regent, he would undoubtedly have dismissed Pitt's administration and brought Charles James Fox and his followers into government. Fox, of course, argued that Parliament should not be allowed to limit the Regency powers of the prince. As John Cannon remarks, 'The piquancy of the reversal of roles, Pitt arguing for parliamentary sanctions, Fox for the prince's prerogative, was not lost on observers.' *ODNB*. Certainly Pitt seems to have convinced JW, though JW had previously been unimpressed by Fox's behaviour during his coalition government with Lord North in 1783, as had SK (Letters 79 and 80 above). See Ehrman, *Younger Pitt: The Years of Acclaim*, pp. 656–57.

decided in the face of the Rising Sun.[15] And tho' I have no Oppinion of City Wisdom & Politicks It gives me pleasure to see that the City of Lond^n. have supported him with their countenance likely to be followed by that of many other great bodies.[16] The struggle will be keener in the H. of L. but the point must be carried there also.[17] I am somewhat more doubtful of Mr. Pits 3^d. Proposi[ti]on not the limittations but the mode of passing a bill by commissioners. It is unprecedented. It looks like the two Houses assuming the whole Legislative Authority. They are in fact however in possession of the reality. The Sovereign's consent to their Bills is a mere form.[18]

My Wife & family join in Comp^s to M^rs. & Miss Kenrick & return their best thanks for the cask of Aples not yet come. M^rs. Wodrow intends next week to send M^rs. Kenricks Linnen Web[19] to Glasgow which was not ready for the Harvest conveyance. M^rs. Kenrick must not expect any Accounts to come allong with the Web. My wife will execute with the utmost pleasure any future Commission of the kind & transmit the accounts faithfuly. But you must forgive the ommision or neglect in the present instance, because you have given us several Precedents of late particularly a very strong one quite in point.

God bless you and yours prays
J. Wodrow

---

[15] The government had won the debate in the House of Commons on the Regency Bill on 16 Dec. 1788 by 268 votes to 204, a much better result for Pitt than the Foxites had expected. It was reinforced by a vote on 22 Dec. which the government won by 251 votes to 178. Ehrman, *Younger Pitt: The Years of Acclaim*, p. 656. The 'Rising Sun' may be a reference to the Prince of Wales with a play on the words 'sun' and 'son'. The king was sometimes depicted in graphic satires as the sun; e.g. see James Gillray, 'John Bull Ground Down', 1 June 1795.

[16] The City of London had raised a subscription of £100,000 from merchants and bankers in December 1788 to pay off Pitt's debts (which he refused to accept). In early January 1789 it also voted an address in his favour over the Regency question. Ehrman, *Younger Pitt: The Years of Acclaim*, p. 657.

[17] It was: on 26 and 29 December, by ninety-nine votes to sixty-six on the question of the right of Parliament to decide on the powers of the Regent. Ehrman, *Younger Pitt: The Years of Acclaim*, p. 656.

[18] Since George III was in no position to approve the Bills properly, and there was as yet no Regent.

[19] 'web' (or wab, or wob): 'a piece of woven cloth'. *DSL*.

## Enclosed copy, in SK's shorthand, of a letter by Thomas Christie to James Wodrow
No. 171 Fleet Street, Nov<sup>r</sup>. 3, 1788

Dear Sir,

My various occupations have rendered it impossible for me to read the M.S. in time, so as to write to you my opinion of it at Bewdley, but I have not delayed a moment after perusing it to enter upon the business.

I am much obliged to you for favouring me with the perusal of so truly ingenious a performance. I like it very much and am not a little surprised with such elegant well-digested ideas from a person in a remote corner of the world, and who lived a long time ago.[1] The merit of the work to sensible readers is unquestionable, and were all readers such, its publication must be attended with great success.

But I have some apprehensions that the amiable author has characterized his own work in one of the notes p. 27. "There is sometimes for instance a fine train of thinking to be found in certain literary compositions which altogether escapes the vulgar reader. It gives indeed a too high degree of pleasure to a person of the same attentive and delicate understanding, but as there are <u>few</u> readers of this sort, and as the vulgar sort of readers are apt to throw aside what ever costs them too much attention, or to despise what they cannot comprehend, it often happens that such performances lie neglected, &c."

M<sup>r</sup>. Wyatt[2] who has read the MS is pretty much of my opinion. He thinks that persons of taste who would relish it will know it in the original French, and that the notes appended to the <u>translation</u>, would be little attended to. We both regret that it should not be published and yet are both dubious of the success of the publication.

---

[1] Christie had read a manuscript work of translation and annotation composed by John Warner of Kilbarchan, in the late 1750s. In June 1759 SK wrote from London: 'When you see our common friend M<sup>r</sup>. Warner, please tell him that my reason of not writing to him all this time is– that I have not got a diterminate answer from M<sup>r</sup>. Hume yet...the papers are in his hands & he has promised to give me his sentiments impartially upon our friend's composition– I have reason to believe that there will be no publication from what I am given to understand'. Letter 32, SK to JW, 30 June 1759, *W-K*, I, p. 246. SK was working as a tutor in Warner's parish in the 1750s, and it appears that he helped with the translation. He considered Warner the 'best of men I ever knew' (Letter 144). The translated work was probably the *Théorie des Sentimens Agréables* (1747), by Louis-Jean Lévesque de Pouilly—see note 4 below.

[2] Unidentified.

Were it to be published, I think the style (though superior to what could possibly have been expected) would require a revisal and some alteration. There is a peculiarity in the orthography which should be changed, thus: <u>theorie</u>, <u>harmonicse</u>, <u>challanged</u>, <u>exicuted</u> repeatedly, <u>forreign</u>, <u>necessitys</u>, &c. And as really new books should come down to the present time, and contain the latest information that the public have had on its subject, some person should revise the present who is versant in the late writers of <u>happiness</u> and <u>pleasure</u> such as Paley, Sulzer, Kastner, &c.³ and add such particulars from them as are needful to confirm, explain or refute the opinions of M. Pouilly⁴ and Mʳ. Warner; for, without these I suspect that in some places snarling critics might alledge that the book contains imperfect views of what had been since perfectly elucidated. It is a pity so valuable a piece should have lain so long in obscurity. I see it is dated thirty years ago; it has in some degree passed the proper æra for its public.

Should you however wish to try it, I will do everything in my power for it here, and should you think it an object my name should be at your service as Editor. Spoke to Johnson⁵ who knows the work, but made him shy for the same reasons that struck myself and Wyatt. If you wish it returned, I shall deliver it to

---

³ The most influential works of these authors indicate that the subject of Warner's manuscript was of a philosophical nature. William Paley, *The Principles of Moral and Political Philosophy* (1785); Johann Georg Sulzer, *A General Theory of the Fine Arts* (Leipzig, 1771–74); Abraham Gotthelf Kästner's textbook on mathematics, *Mathematische Anfangsgründe*, was published in nine volumes between 1758 and 1791. Manfred Kuehn and Heiner F. Klemme, eds, *The Bloomsbury Dictionary of Eighteenth-Century German Philosophers* (2016), p. 408.

⁴ Louis-Jean Lévesque de Pouilly (1691–1751), French philosopher and author of *Théorie des Sentimens Agréables* (Geneva, 1747), published in English as *The Theory of Agreeable Sensations: In which the Laws Observed by Nature in the Distribution of Pleasure are Investigated; and the Principles of Natural Theology and Moral Philosophy are Established* (1749). It appears Warner's manuscript was a new translation with annotation and commentary, and that SK had transcribed a copy with an eye to having it published. There are several references to Warner's manuscript being a 'translation of Theorie &c' (Letters 88, 115, 121, 136, and 141), and JW describes one of Warner's sermons as reflecting a 'train of thought very similar to that of the Theorie &c' (Letter 146). Pouilly's only other major work was a critique of the sources for early Roman history. Pouilly was a 'disciple of Newton', and his *Théorie des Sentimens Agréables* can be considered 'important to dramatic criticism because it attempts to find a scientific basis for our aesthetic responses, and because it represents one important aspect of sentimentalism.... The parallel between Lévesque de Pouilly and Sulzer in Germany is close'. This comparison with Sulzer, combined with Christie's reference to Sulzer and multiple references in the correspondence to a 'translation of Theorie &c', suggests that it was the *Théorie des Sentimens Agréables* that Warner had translated and annotated. 'Louis Jean Levesque de Pouilly 1691–1750', in Henry Hitch Adams and Baxter Hathaway, eds, *Dramatic Essays of the Neoclassic Age* (New York, 1950), p. 297.

⁵ Joseph Johnson. See Letter 138.

M⁰. Hamilton[6] or anybody you desire. Or else if you leave it in my hands, I shall pledge myself to publish it at a future period in some form or other, as the subject has occupied my thoughts a good deal and I am collecting materials for a work on it, to be published when I have rendered more complete my acquaintance with speculative philosophy, and have added to it that interesting information relative to the human frame, which an attentive physician has such excellent opportunity of acquiring.[7]

Sermons by Mr. Warner would probably sell extremely well.

Your remarks on "Miscell, lit, philos. & moral" will be acceptable,[8] and the more faults you find it will be so much the better. This is no flourish. With best wishes for your health & happiness, & sincere assurances of the pleasure it will give me to be of any use to you here, I remain Dʳ Sir your fiend, Thoˢ Christie.

To Revᵈ. Dʳ. Wodrow

[The following shorthand note was added by Samuel Kenrick. For annotation, see Letter 144 where it is incorporated and elaborated]

In the year 1759, I showed this same manuscript to David Hume who was then in London, with my friend A. Millar's candidness if not by his directions and Anderson's too, who you may remember made that excursion along with us. Hume, who I dare say hardly read a page of it, having his mind a good deal ruffled at that moment with a pretty rough attack of Hurd, our present Bishop, upon his History of the Stuarts. Hume made then no useful objection as was made to Mʳ. C. that the readers of such ^a book would have it in the original^ as he has since shown in the memoirs of his own life.

---

[6] John Hamilton. See Letter 84.
[7] This work did not eventuate. Christie became involved in the debate over the French Revolution in the 1790s.
[8] [Thomas Christie], *Miscellanies: Literary, Philosophical and Moral*, 4 vols (1788).

## Letter 144: Samuel Kenrick to James Wodrow, 16 and 20 January 1789

Place: Bewdley
Addressed: The Rev<sup>d</sup>. D<sup>r</sup>. Wodrow, near Irvine, Scotland.
Postmarked: London January the Twentieth 1789
Franked: Free Westcote
Stamped: JA/20/89

My worthy & dear Friend

Though we were far from blaming you, knowing the multiplicity of different things you had to attend to, yet I own we were not a little uneasy at your long silence.[1] But your kind l<sup>r</sup>. of the 25th. ult<sup>o</sup>. has banished every gloomy fear & gratified every eager wish. I give you joy on having at length been able to say *exegi monumentum ære perennius*.[2] We all now long to see it & to enjoy the fruit of your labours. The trait you have given of my old friend Urwick[3] marks him the legitimate descendant of honest John Bull. To ride six miles every day in this cold season, w<sup>ch</sup>. I dare say he did w<sup>th</sup>. the same benevolent satisfaction as Fielding's Adams[4] would have done it, in the same circumstances, to serve his absent friend without ever thinking of his friend's anxiety or regarding his repeated requests, to know if the packets came safe– is to be sure extraordinary. But as long as he knew they were all safe & that the work ^was^ going on according to your warmest wishes– his own mind was satisfied & therefore he concluded yours must be so too– A pròpos I mentioned M<sup>r</sup>. Tayler[5] to you on a particular account[6]– who

---

[1] This may puzzle the reader, given that there is a run of eight JW letters since the last in this collection by SK nearly a year before (Letter 135, 13 Feb. 1788). There are at least three missing SK letters, however: 9 June, 18 Sept., and 28 Nov. 1788. It is not surprising that SK letters which were received by JW during the course of his travels were lost.

[2] Horace, *Odes*, III, xxx, line 1: 'I have finished a monument more lasting than bronze'. Loeb Classical Library.

[3] Thomas Urwick. See Letter 139. SK will have met him when he was a student at Glasgow and later when he was a minister at Worcester.

[4] Parson Adams is the travelling companion of Joseph Andrews in the picaresque novel by Henry Fielding, *The History of the Adventures of Joseph Andrews and of his Friend Mr Abraham Adams* (1742). He is erudite, absent-minded, and forever optimistic. His innocence makes him the prey of the less well intentioned, but his humour and belief in the goodness of human nature survive intact.

[5] Thomas Tayler. See Letter 138.

[6] i.e. for nomination for the award of a DD by the University of Glasgow.

by the bye is at last married & lives away, I am told, in a very high style. Upon second thoughts I think M$^r$. Urwick ^has a better claim^ to that honourable distinction, if you think it may be had. For he was educated at the university of Glasgow, studied divinity under D$^r$. Leechman, & has been so friendly to you in bringing forward to this publication– add to this his modesty, his simplicity of manners & truly christian spirit & character– w$^{ch}$. appear to me much higher titles to such distinctions, than the imposing parade of talent & learning. I shall not however do any thing in it without your approbation. All I w$^d$. pretend to, would be only to back you by writing to some of my remaining friends in the university– if you think proper to attempt it.

So M$^r$. Strahan has plaid you a bookseller's trick after all.[7] There is nothing acquired without experience: & you will now know better how to deal w$^{th}$. them the next time.

The happy closing of your long journey meeting w$^{th}$. so many affectionate friends at Glasgow & joining w$^{th}$. them in our most solemn act of devotion– & afterwards meeting your own family & parishioners, who never knew such an absence before, in comfort– are to us all matters of the highest joy & congratulation. Whatever attention was paid you by my family, w$^{ch}$. your goodness disposes you to think so favourably of, be assured it was far short of what I could have wished from many untoward circumstances. You now know that you have other friends here besides our family. And who knows what a kind Providence may yet have in reserve?– perhaps another opportunity of the same sort, where the rest of your family may partake of it w$^{th}$. you. This is not more improbable than your journey was twelve months ago. M$^r$. M$^{rs}$. & Miss Roberts[8] are most particular in their inquiries after you & your family. And we have had young M$^r$. Hatchett[9] here since repeating his own & family's regret in not having the pleasure of seeing you when you passed so near them.– It was in a great measure my fault or my fate– the shortness of the days &c &c w$^{ch}$. now cannot be helped. Let us rather look forward & expect better times.– M$^r$. Wigan says you have a good memory. He has feelings as well as you– tho' he puts on the face of a philosopher to us: I dare say he thinks as you do, that it was as well parting as you did. We agree w$^{th}$. you in

---

[7] i.e. he had managed to manoeuvre JW into bearing half of the expense of the engraving of Leechman's portrait for the frontispiece of the first volume of the sermons, despite his early suggestion that this cost would be borne by the publishers in the original agreement. See Letter 143.

[8] See Letter 143.

[9] See Letter 142.

politics & think that Pitt & his friends have clinched the nail w^ch. our ancestors had boldly driven in at the Revolution. Public liberty certainly now rests on a firmer basis than it ever did before in the annals of history & will entitle last year to be commemorated w^th. equal honour as its preceding centenary.– With regard to his majesty, it is the opinion of my friend D^r. Johnstone,[10] that there are little hopes of his recovery– that the apparent favourable symptoms were the effects of debility of body occasioned by the change of treatment, & it not to the removal of the cause or decrease of the disorder. It must have come to a crisis long ago. In short the disorder continues, the longer it is likely to continue.[11]

I am much obliged to you for M^r. Christie's letter w^ch. I return you inclosed.[12] It gives me the greatest pleasure to find that this fragment of our late worthy friend's should at last fall into the hands of a gentleman who seems to be blessed w^th. a congenial soul. His objections to publish it in its present form are unanswerable.[13] But had he read over the text as well as the notes– & compared it w^th. the original– I am afraid they would have been still stronger. And this I am most concerned for.[14] You must know that David Hume discouraged me from publishing it in 1759, on partly the same grounds. By my friend Andrew Millar's[15] request I took the M.S. w^th. me to London & w^th. his approbation & Anderson's[16] too (who you know was of our party) I shewed it to M^r. Hume & begged the favour of him to

---

[10] James Johnstone (1730–1802), physician in Kidderminster. See *W-K*, I, pp. 325–26n.

[11] See Letter 143. A retrospective diagnosis attributed the king's mental illness to porphyria, but it remains contentious. A more recent case has been made for bipolar disorder: e.g. Timothy Peters, 'King George III, Bipolar Disorder, Porphyria and Lessons for Historians', *Clinical Medicine*, 11 (2011), pp. 261–64.

[12] See the shorthand copy of Thomas Christie's letter to JW at the end of Letter 143.

[13] This was a manuscript translation of Louis-Jean Lévesque de Pouilly's *Théorie des Sentimens Agréables* (Geneva, 1747), with annotations by Rev. John Warner. See notes to Thomas Christie's letter appended to Letter 143.

[14] SK helped Warner with his translation of de Pouilly's *Théorie des Sentimens Agréables*. In the 1750s, SK worked as a tutor for the Milliken family in Warner's parish of Kilbarchan, and in Letter 136 JW refers to 'your & M^r. Warners translation of the Theorie &c'. It appears, however, that SK's main role was in transcribing a clean copy of the work with an eye to having it published. In December 1758 SK noted that he had been 'transcribing the first 16 pages (w^ch. reach to Æschila &c in the III. ch.) & intend to transmit them forthwith to M^r Millar' (Letter 26). Lévesque de Pouilly starts discussing Aeschylus on tragedy near the end of ch. 3. See the 1749 English edition of *The Theory of Agreeable Sensations*, p. 41. When JW found the manuscript among Warner's papers following his death in 1786, SK told him that 'if any of the Translation is mine I should doubt its fidelity to the original from my not understan^tg. French so well as I do now' (Letter 122).

[15] Andrew Millar. See Letter 134.

[16] Professor John Anderson who toured England with SK and James Milliken Jr in 1759. See *W-K*, I, Letters 31, 32, 34, 35, and 36.

peruse it. His objection was the same as M[r]. Wyatt's[17] that persons who had taste to relish such a work would certainly prefer the French original to a translation. And as to the notes I fancy he did not relish them himself– or at least take the trouble of dipping into them; otherwise he could not have returned them to me so coolly as he did. Indeed his mind was a little ruffled at the moment by a pretty rough attack of Hurd, our present Bishop, upon his history of the Stuarts.[18] That he was hurt, appears plain since from his own memoirs, where he mentions the Warburtonian ^school^ w[th]. no small degree of acrimony.[19] As to the orthography, there is only one peculiarity to be charged to my account– namely, the termination of plurals in -<u>ys</u> instead of <u>ies</u>. This you may have observed in many of my letters & w[ch]. I borrowed from our worthy Professor Hutcheson. But I think I have long since dropped it: as I would every other little peculiarity, w[ch]. in my younger years I was too fond of. As to the other words specified, the fault was either inattention or copying too scrupulously our friend's writing. These are trifles & easily amended. I am affraid of heavier charges, had the work appeared at that time, being brought against it by the snarly critics of that day, than what M[r]. C. mentions. I cannot help thinking how our ^late^ friend would have rejoiced to find this little work of his fallen into such hands. It may be the means of bringing forward & transmitting to posterity some of his other productions w[ch]. you may yet recover. It is certain that he was possessed of real original genius– & was indefatigable in polishing & finishing his labours. He used to say he never liked to see a M.S. that had not scratches & scores scattered through it: he was affraid it was not worth reading. And he was always quoting Horace's repeated injunctions to his young friends the Pisos.[20] But I do not think he had bestowed upon

---

[17] Christie's colleague. See appendix to Letter 143.

[18] Richard Hurd criticized David Hume's *The History of Great Britain, Volume I: Containing the Reigns of James I and Charles I* (Edinburgh, 1754) and his then recently published *The History of England, under the House of Tudor*, 2 vols (1759). Hume was called an 'apologist for the Stuarts' and accused of 'playing tricks with us' in a 'Post-Script' to Richard Hurd, *Moral and Political Dialogues: Being the Substance of Several Conversations between Divers Eminent Persons of the Present Age; Digested by the Parties Themselves, and now First Published from the Original MSS with Critical and Explanatory Notes* (1759), pp. 171, 245, 282–89. Hume published a second corrected edition of his *History of Great Britain, under the House of Stuart* in 1759.

[19] For Richard Hurd's criticism of Hume's histories of the Stuarts and Tudors, see SK's note at the end of Thomas Christie's letter attached to Letter 143. Hurd had also attacked Hume's religious views in *Remarks on Mr. David Hume's Essay on the Natural History of Religion: Addressed to the Rev. Dr. Warburton* (1757). Hume declared that the pamphlet was written with 'all the illiberal petulance, arrogance, and scurrility, which distinguish the Warburtonian school'. David Hume, *The Life of David Hume, Esq: Written by Himself* (1777), p. 9.

[20] Horace's *Ars Poetica* was addressed to Piso family.

the notes in question anything like the pains, w^ch. many of his sermons cost him. It was a new subject, w^ch. I accidentally threw in his way. His first view was merely to serve me by laying hold of a random promise of M^r. A.M.[21] at Paisley, to give us his assistance: w^ch., as I hinted above, I soon found to be an empty shadow. I should be glad to know if his Synod sermon is <u>to the fore</u>– Perfect love casteth out fear– as he took particular pains w^th. it & as it ^is^ the sum & substance of his just & elevated notions of divine Goodness– the sure foundation of all our hopes & comfort. Oh that I could find time, recollection & perseverance, to trace out & exhibit to the world that exce^l^lent character, in a manner worthy to be read.– it would be a pleasing task– & in some measure repay what I owe to the best of men I ever knew. But I am affraid I shall never be so happy.

20th Jan^y. 89

I am much obliged to you for your concern on my nephew James' acc^t.– & I am much to blame for my innattention in not notic^g. it before.[22] But it was as you judged owing to his feeling no bad effects from that allarming accident, that I thought no more of it. The numerous instances, however, of the contrary melancholy effects in that neighbourhood ha[ve] been the means of a most important discovery m[ade] by an apothecary at Oswestry of an easy & sure means of curing it– indeed the only means– except incision or rather excision, w^ch. is on the same principle but more difficult to perform. For the Ormskirk medicine, nor no other can be of any avail if ever the virus is communicated to the blood.[23] All that can be done is to prevent this. And this may be done merely by ablution [page torn] con[stant]ly washing the wound w^th. warm [page torn] 'till the whole saliva or poisonous matter [page torn] removed. It has succeeded in several instances– & never failed if persisted in.

What do you think of my friend Jesse, publishing by subscription a prose translation w^th. notes– of Juvenal's satyres?– not his own– but the work of that pious divine Martin Madan[24]—well known among the method[ists]. He puts his

---

[21] Andrew Millar. Despite SK's description of him here as 'at Paisley' in relation to events which took place in the 1750s, he had migrated to London in 1727, having completed his apprenticeship with James M'Euen in Edinburgh. Sher, *The Enlightenment and the Book*, p. 279.

[22] James Kenrick. See Letter 142.

[23] The Ormskirk Medicine originated in rural Lancashire and was claimed to cure madness caused by the bite of a rabid dog. Alan Mackintosh, *The Patent Medicines Industry in Georgian England Constructing the Market by the Potency of Print* (2017), p. 92.

[24] Rev. Martin Madan (1725–90), Church of England clergyman associated with Lady Huntingdon's circle and of the Calvinistic evangelical wing of Methodism. By the time he published his *A New and Literal Translation of Juvenal and Persius; with Copious Explanatory Notes, by which*

name boldly in the title page & Jesse says he loves & admires it almost as much as the bible. Madan makes his friend Jesse a present of it pr. 12/I have got him 6 subscriptions.–

But adieu remember us all most affet[ly]. to your fam[y]. & friends.<br>
Y[rs]. S.K.

## Letter 145: James Wodrow to Samuel Kenrick, 5 February 1789
Place: Stevenston
Addressed: M[r]. Kenrick / Bewdley / Worcester
Postmarked: Kilmarnock Eleventh February 1789
Franked: H. Montgomery
Stamped: KILMARNOCK
Note in SK's hand: answ[d]. this & that of 8 Mch then 20th to Glasgow

My Dear Friend

I have only time to acknowledge the receipt of your kind Letter of the 16th ult[mo]. as the Girls are sending a line to be franked by Col M[y]. which goes in a few minutes. The publication is in statu quo. The book is most certainly printed off before this time but I have not heard from London these three or four weeks tho' I have been expecting a Letter from M[r]. Strahan every post enclosing a ~~Con~~Assignment[1] to be signed by me previous to the publication. I care not to push Strahan by any more letters as he is best judge of the proper time possibly the engraving may not be ready. I wrote to our friend Urwick last week begging he woud inform me in a day or two after he received mine how matters stood. It is likely however I may have no answer from him.

Your Proposal about his degree I will consider & woud wish to obtain this honour for him as much as you can; yet it will be difficult to interest them in a man that none of them know any thing about.– Oh! That you coud find time to draw up some Memoirs of M[r]. Warners Life & Char[r]. the only way is to begin.

---

*these Difficult Satirists are Rendered Easy and Familiar to the Reader*, 2 vols (1789), he had retired from public life owing to the furore created by his advocacy of polygamy in a work titled *Thelyphthora; or, A Treatise on Female Ruin, in Its Causes, Effects, Consequences, Prevention, and Remedy; Considered On The Basis Of Divine Law* (1780). His *New and Literal Translation of Juvenal and Persius* (1789) was indeed stated on the title-page to have been 'printed for the Editor', as SK notes. LBS.

[1] Assignment: 'Legal transference of a right or property', *OED*, 2.

A thing fairly begun is half finished. Begin therefore I beseech you. Life is short. I complain greatly of want of time. My time is sadly encroached on by Company & myself hindered from finishing various pieces of business I have to do.

The apples we received above a month ago in fine Order & the best & Juiciest apples I have ever eaten at this Season.[2] We have not only been regaled with them ourselves but my Wife has given half dozens of them to our good neighbours– I will be glad to look at M$^r$. Jesse's or Madan's Juvenal yet I will not subscribe as I have been at a vast expense in purchasing books last year both at Lond$^n$. & at home. I am happy to be so fully assured of your Nephews wellfare & beg the favour you woud send me the receipt fully & disctinctly when you are at Leizure.

There is company in the house & I am confined to a few minutes so that I have rather sent you this confused scrawl as nothing. M$^r$. Pit has run a noble Carrier[3] now near a period.[4] I hope to live to see him start anew.

God bless you & yours prays<br>your friend James Wodrow

## Letter 146: James Wodrow to Samuel Kenrick, 8 March 1789
Place: Stevenston
Addressed: M$^r$. Kenrick / Bewdley / Worcestershire
Postmarked: Irvine Ninth March 1789
Franked: H. Montgomery
Stamped: MR/<->

I wrote a few hurried lines in answer to my Worthy Friends Letter of the twentieth of Jan$^r$., Sometime ago. I now sit down at more leisure but not in a fit state for writing, tired with preaching too long all day to a crowded audience. I seldom very seldom write on a Sunday but the frank sent me must be filled up by tomorrow morn$^g$. as I have engagements which will consume almost the whole day. Much obliged I am to M$^r$. & M$^{rs}$. Roberts & to other friends for their kind enquiries. I shall always remember them & my short stay at Bewdley with much

---

[2] The Kenricks sometimes sent apples to Wodrow.
[3] 'Carrier': 'a course; a career'. *DSL*.
[4] By 5 February it appeared that Pitt was likely to be unable to prevent the Regency Bill becoming law on 20 February. It was not until 13 or 14 February that signs of the king's recovery became clear. Ehrman, *Younger Pitt: The Years of Acclaim*, p. 662.

satisfaction.– That part of your Letter to M^r. Warner awakens also a very pleasing remembrance. Some of the best of his Sermons & the fittest as I thought for publication I put into M^r. Arthurs hands when I began to draw up D^r. Leechman's Life. Arthur is indolent to a high degree like you & me perhaps more so yet I do not despair of pushing him to do something to revive & preserve the Memory of a friend for whom he has the same enthusiastick veneration that you have & nearly on the same grounds. The last time we conversed about it he spoke of some peculiarities in M^r. W^rs. stile that he was doubtful about. No man that I know in Scotland is more fit to revise & correct a posthumous work than Arthur.– I must repeat my earnest request to you to begin & continue to make jottings of the Life & Char^r.–

You enquire about the Synod Sermon the very Man^p. that he ^preached or^ read before the Ass^ly. of his brethren is preserved in a very sullied state & besides it six or eight Scetches begun on the subject on a Larger scale & some of them acurately wrote as if for the Press but left totaly abrupt & unfinished after the first head, as if the attempt <—> of five or six discourses had been abandoned. These attempts are on a different plan or distribution of the Subject from the Synod Sermon & have a little in common with it or with one another. His Genius was various & fertile to an amusing degree & he found it difficult nay impossible to please himself. Hine illae Lachrimae![1] He always continued to polish but never finished anything. The Sermons in Arthur's hands on Prov. III.17[2] are the most regular & finished of any he has left about six in number. A Display of the immediate pleasure and the Utility of the three great branches of Religion, Piety Benevolence & Self denial, the Manner ingenious & almost peculiar to himself, yet the train of thought very similar to that of the Theorie &c.[3] I gave him ^Arth^r^ three or four Sermons more on free Enquiry into religion seemingly suggested by the abbot of Kilw^gs. Prosecution– these are incomparably less laboured than the former yet excellent in their way & woud please the ^liberal^ English Dissenters greatly.

You will be ready to think that ~~D^r. Ls.~~ the publication of D^r. L. Sermons has been strangled in its birth. I was almost of the same mind from & Interruption in my correspondence with London for about six weeks. I wrote Urwick our worthy friend a fourth Letter about a month ago requested a few lines in the most earnest

---

[1] 'Hence these tears', Terence, *Andria*, act I, line 99.
[2] 'Her [Wisdom's] ways are ways of pleasantness, and all her paths are peace.' Proverbs 3:17.
[3] Louis-Jean Lévesque de Pouilly, *Théorie des Sentimens Agréables* (Geneva, 1747). See notes to Thomas Christie's letter at the end of Letter 143.

man^r. yet he is still silent as the grave. I wrote to M^r. Hamilton & Strahan a second time. M^r. Hamilton had been very ^ill^ is now better. I had a letter from him ^only^ within these few days. I transcribe part of it. "I must confess that there may appear a dilatoriness in the Management of the Parties, which can only be accounted for from the various important bussiness in which they have been engaged. It is possible that M^r. Urwick may be averse to Letterwriting but he has paid the most unremitting attention as M^r. Preston[4] informs to the inspection of the book in its progress, and every thing goes on as it shoud do excepting that they are detained by the Print which is not yet finished (Feb^r. 27). M^r. Cadell assures me they have urged the Engraver as much as possible but he is not yet ready. The 2^d vol^me is half finished & will be, they expect, ready in a week or two, and before the Engraving is ready" &c. &c.

In my last letter to him I had ordered 11 copies for Bewdley. You already know my mind as to two of these. They will come to you <–> as soon as they are published in London. A copy of the first vol was sent ^for^ me some weeks ago. It is lying in Glasgow or on the road. I am vexed at the disappointment of D^r. L. friends in this Country by announcing it too early but there is no help for it now.

Mond^y. morn^g. 7 a clock

I expect allong with my first vol D^r. Kippis & some of the other Revolution Sermons[5] which I desired M^r. Preston to send me. We have had a few published in Scotland two of them in this neighbourhood by two particular friends of mine. One of them by M^r. Robertson Mins^r. at Kilmarnock[6] L^d. Glencairns[7] old Tutor whom you will remember. It was extorted from him by his hearers who printed it for themselves & presented copies to their friends but I hear a bookseller in Ed^r. has asked & got leave to throw off an Edition of it. The Composition is rather careless the sentences too long but sentiments woud delight you. He runs a parallel between the Jewish & the British nations & considers the last as set up by providence since the Reformation as an Example to other Nations to show them

---

[4] William Preston. See Letter 140.

[5] Andrew Kippis, *A Sermon Preached at the Old Jewry, on the Fourth of November, 1788, Before the Society for Commemorating the Glorious Revolution; Being the Completion of an Hundred Years Since that Great Event* (1788).

[6] John Robertson, *Britain the Chosen Nation: A Thanksgiving Sermon, Preached, November 5th, 1788* (Kilmarnock, 1788).

[7] Rev. John Robertson (1733–99), presented by William Cunningham (d. 1775), twelfth earl of Glencairn to the first charge of the parish of Kilmarnock on 8 October 1764 and ordained on 25 April 1765. *FES*, III, p. 106.

the value & to spread among them the grand blessings of religious light & knowledge and Civil Liberty.–

The Other Sermon is by our friend Magill a very short one giving a good view of the advantages of the Revolution.[8] He had no thought of publishing it but received an unexpected & unprovoked attack of the most cruel kind from one of his <—> Orthodox Neighbours M[r]. Peebles Mins[r]. of the Newtown of Air[9] who published his two Sermons of the 5th. of Nov[r]. & in six or eight pages and some Notes falls bloodily on the D[rs]. book whom he classes with Gibbon as an Adversary of X[ty]. and upon the great body of his own brethren even those called the Moderate Clergy of Scotland as a set of base Parricides & perjured Traitors for supporting Patronage & preaching & writing directly contrary to their Subscription.[10] It was wonderful how he coud think of patching in such things in a thanksgiving Sermon. This however has roused the D[rs]. Spirit who was unmoved by all the abuse that was cast upon him <—> in the pamplets of the Seceding & Relief Brethren & from the Pulpits of some of the established Clergy.[11] He has added an appendix much larger than his Sermon consisting of

---

[8] William M'Gill, *The Benefits of the Revolution: A Sermon, Preached at Ayr, on the 5th of November, 1788, by William M'Gill, D. D. To which are Added, Remarks on a Sermon, Preached on the Same Day, at Newton upon Ayr; Very necessary for all the Readers of said Sermon* (Kilmarnock, 1789).

[9] Rev. William Peebles (1753–1826), educated at Edinburgh University, became minister of Newton-upon-Ayr in 1778.

[10] 'It is a certain fact, that not a few in this country hold the Confession of Faith in the highest contempt...Alas! my brethren, they are not open separatists from this church—they dwell in her bosom; and without a blush at the dishonesty of their conduct.' William Peebles, *The Great Things Which the Lord Hath Done for This Nation, Illustrated and Improved; in Two Sermons Preached on the 5th of November, 1788* (Kilmarnock, 1788), pp. 34–36. Peebles justified the 'severity' of his paragraphs by noting that it was 'gentleness, in comparison with the keen invectives he has heard thrown out in conversation against the doctrines of our Confession' (p. 34 n). Their subscription to 'the Confession of Faith, only *so far as* it is agreeable to, or consistent with the word of God', was 'nothing', as anyone could equally subscribe to the Talmud, Koran, or 'the Creed of the Socinians' (p. 36 n). In addition, he pointed to M'Gill's *Death of Christ*, where 'that important and fundamental article of our Creed, the doctrine of Christ's *substitution*, has lately been ridiculed in a story concerning a British Governor and an Indian Chief'. In 1786 JW had noted that, before publication, 'all the obnoxious Strictures against the common Oppinions about the Satisfaction' had been 'struck out by my advice', but M'Gill had kept this 'one single note...as somewhat curious from the History of Carolina'. See Letter 125; and also Letter 84.

[11] John Jamieson, *Socinianism Unmasked* (1787). Rev. John Jamieson was an Evangelical who became an Anti-Burgher (see Letter 130); he addressed M'Gill directly: 'There is little reason to doubt your consciousness of the inconsistency of your doctrines with those of the Confession...Is perjury no crime except in civil concerns?...You may reply, indeed, that you believed the doctrines of the Confession, when you subscribed it. But does this really alter the case? Can your conscience be so seared, as to seek shelter in this refuge of lies?' (p. 128);

Observations on that passage of Peebles and a very masterly piece of controversy it is there is a mixture of mildness & keeness which cuts like a razor.[12] I had ^no conception^ that the D^r. had such Talents for Controversy. He did not write me of his intention till the Pamplet was in the press otherwise I woud have diswaded him from entering the lists with such a contemptible adversary tho' it woud have been to no purpose. I dissaprove of the <—> Spirit of Controversy yet if it be justifyable at all it is in Self defense. I am not without apprehension that it will provoke the whole party & draw on a prosecution of the book in the Ch courts. Yet this in your views & in the purposes of Providence will do good. As it has a Considerable resemblance to the picqueering[13] between Jesse & our Worthy friend tho' more important likely I wished to have sent you both Sermons & M^r. Wiggan D^r. Magills Sermon price only 6^d. & I wrote to Love[14] at Glasgow but he tells ^me^ there will be no opportunity of sending any small thing of that kind till the beginning of May when you may expect them if I do not get some franks sooner that will hold them.

Our honest & Worthy friend D^r. Campbell of Armagh has sent me both his Pamplets.[15] I have only had time yet to read the first it is ^sensible &^ & spirited. He

---

[Associate Synod of the Secession Church], *A Warning Against Socinianism: Drawn up and Published by a Committee of the Associate Synod. In which, Particular Notice is Taken of a Late Publication, Intituled, a Practical Essay upon the Death of Jesus Christ, by Dr. M'Gill* (Falkirk, 1788).

[12] The appendix is a robust defence of scriptural sufficiency, and obedience to conscience. McGill argued that subscription to articles of faith 'of human composition is altogether wrong'. In his view, abolishing subscription to the Westminster Confession would not lead it to 'fall into neglect and contempt'; rather, it would be understood 'in a reasonable and qualified sense; such as may not arrest the progress of religious knowledge' (pp. 23–52, cited at 42, 44–45).

[13] Cf. Letter 108. 'Pickeering': 'Wordy, playful, or amorous skirmishing; wrangling, bickering, petty quarrelling; an instance of this'. *OED*.

[14] Possibly 'John Love, merchant, Barr's land High-street opposite College', listed in *Jones's Directory; or, useful pocket companion, for the year 1789: containing an alphabetical list of the names and places of abode of the merchants, manufacturers, traders, and shopkeepers, in and about the City of Glasgow* (Glasgow, 1789), p. 36, though a 'Hugh Love and co., grocer, shop King's-street, No. 9' is also listed there.

[15] Rev. William Campbell (1727–1805), matriculated at Glasgow in 1744 and was licensed to minister at Armagh in 1750. Theologically he was an Arian. Ian McBride, *Scripture Politics: Ulster Presbyterians and Irish Radicalism in the Late Eighteenth Century* (Oxford, 1998), p. 59; *Dictionary of Irish Biography*, www.dib.ie/biography/campbell-william-a1435. The pamphlets were: *A Vindication of the Principles and Character of the Presbyterians of Ireland. Addressed to the Bishop of Cloyne, in Answer to his Book, Entitled, The Present State of the Church of Ireland* (Dublin, 1787); and *An Examination of the Bishop of Cloyne's Defence of his Principles; with Observations on Some His Lordship's Apologists, Particularly the Rev. Dr Stock: Containing an Inquiry into Establishment; and also, an Historical Review of the Political Principles and Conduct of Presbyterians and Episcopals in Great-Britain and Ireland. With A Defence of the Church of Scotland from the Charge of Persecution brought by His Lordship's Apologist. By William Campbell, D.D. Minister of Armagh* (Belfast, 1788).

beat ^the Bishop^ to Nothing. He wishes to have them introduced here but as that controversy is sopite[16] I am afraid it it is too late. I write in a hurry wishing to be in time to have this sent with our post to Irvine otherwise I must send my Ser[t]. & horse on purpose & unyoke the plow in this fine Weather.

The Girls desire me to make their excuse for not writing by this Opportunity which I have refused to do as I think they are inexcusable. Louisa has lost her eldest Sister about a month ago.[17] Her aged Mother[18] is ^still^ in good health & has bore this shock with her usual composure. My Wife thinks of going to [Edinburgh] next week & spending two months with her. M[rs]. & Miss K. will accept of my affectionate & best regards. I am ever

My Dear Friend<br>
most sincerely yours<br>
J. Wodrow

## Letter 147: Samuel Kenrick to James Wodrow, 20 March 1789

Place: Bewdley
Addressed: The Rev[d]. D[r]. Wodrow / Stevenston
Stamped: <GLASGOW>
Notes: 10z. 1/1789

My dear Friend

Both your kind favours of the 5th Feb[y]. & 8th Mch. came safe to hand. And however restricted you were in time & the pressure of indispensible engagements, as usual, they contained every mark of kindness & attention.

I am glad to find the publication is now so near ^a conclusion^. But Urwick's invincible silence astonishes me– nay it puts me out of all patience.[1] What can he mean– or what can he think? To <u>do</u> every thing that he possibly can, w[th]. the exactest punctuality to serve you– & to with-hold gratifying your request of

---

[16] 'Sopite': 'put to rest'. *OED*.
[17] This must be Anne Hamilton, dated in *ODNB* (1738–87), since Elizabeth (b. 1749) lived till *c*. 1842.
[18] Helen Hamilton (d. 1793), *née* Balfour, widow of the Edinburgh bookseller and paper-maker Gavin Hamilton (1704–67), and daughter of James Balfour (1681–1737), manufacturer and shipbuilder of South Leith, and Louisa Hamilton (1686–1750).

---

[1] Thomas Urwick. See Letter 139.

telling you of it— this is reversing the fable—for he generously gives you up the oyster & treasures up the shells himself.[2]

As to what I hinted— it rests entirely w^th. you. All I rest it upon is (1) That he is an alumnus a student of the university & ^was a^ pupil of D^r. Leechmans (2) that he has been useful in forwarding the publication. & (3) That he is one of those truly, gentle christian souls, who do more real honour to christianity than a thousand noisy disputants. This is all I have to say on the subject.

Thanks to my good friend for his warm wishes— they do not a little inspire me w^th. fresh courage to try something in honour of a character we both held in so high estimation— w^ch. has long employed my thoughts. Some facts will be necessary for you to ascertain— the year of his birth— where he went to school— & when he was settled at Kilbarchan &c—[3]

To tell you the truth I have a good deal of time in my hands w^ch. I employ ^mostly^ in cursor^il^y reading any thing that comes in my way, without any serious object in view. This is one valuable advantage I reap from my present situation in the Bank. For as my attendance is indispensable, it secures me from many idle visitors & still more from invitations to clubs & parties of pleasure & amusement, w^ch. consumed many precious hours in the former part of my life here. Being an entire stranger, I was in some measure under the necessity of making this sacrifice, for the sake of good neighbourhood. But it went always against the grain w^th. me— from long habits, you know, of a very different course of life. Now however, thanks to a kind providence, my character & situation are so well known, that I enjoy an undisturbed repose. But even this situation has it inconveniencies. For such slaves are we to habit & to our favourite pursuit, that it unfits us for everything else. I have been long conscious that I cannot write w^th. that ease w^th. w^ch. I could some years ago— owing I suppose to the routine letters on business I am every day obliged to write & to my employing so much attention in reading. This is I assure you, my good friend, a great obstacle in my way— founded I know in indolence & aversion to labour. For tho' there is nothing more pleasing to my heart & soul than to write to a friend— & to none more pleasing than to yourself— yet I could open any of the books w^ch. now lie within my reach, & doze over it w^th. more pleasure that I have in scrawling these words. This I know is

---

[2] One of the fables of Aesop (*c.* 620–564 BC), in which a traveller, asked to judge between two disputants which should retain the oyster they had found, awarded each a shell and took the oyster himself as payment.

[3] JW had urged SK to write a life of John Warner.

a fault– & it must be corrected. But whether I shall ever be able to correct it so far as to deserve your approbation– time only can tell. We are all happy to find the apples came safe– & escaped the effects of the severe frost– w^ch. was more than our own did.

I have looked into Madan's– now Jesse's Juvenal ^& Persius^.[4] It is very litteral indeed– as much so as poor Andrew's Virgil[5]– but not in verse– tho' every verse in the original is englished by a corresponding line– EG.

Ventilet ostevum digitis sudantibus aurum.

Can ventilate the summer gold on his sweating fingers.

Stirling, who is still more litteral & therefore generally flatter– is here more intelligible– must fan his summer gold ring on &c.[6]

Such versions may be of use to masters or schoolboys but must be disgusting to scholars & absolute nonsense to mere english readers. And to make it more useful to the first he has subjoined notes almost upon every word w^ch. makes it one must step more easy than Farnaby w^ch. is in every school boy's hands.–[7]

M^r. Pitt has run a noble carreer indeed! & has received every honour he was entitled to– And is now at liberty to start again. What an unexpected change have things taken? How little do our physicians know? And how lucky was it, that his Majesty was taken out of their hands & trusted to what they called a Quack![8] Never was ^there^ a more universal rejoicing. We too have thrown in our mite in the common mode of hilarity. But our neighbours at Kidderminster do not partake of the same good humour. Their most flourishing branch of manufacture is

---

[4] Martin Madan, *A New and Literal Translation of Juvenal and Persius; with Copious Explanatory Notes, by which these Difficult Satirists are Rendered Easy and Familiar to the Reader*, 2 vols (1789). See Letter 144.

[5] Robert Andrews. See Letter 81.

[6] *P. Virgilii Maronis Opera: Or the Works of Virgil...For the Use of Schools* by John Stirling, DD Late Vicar of Great Gaddesden in Hertfordshire, and Chaplain to His Grace the Duke of Gordon (1779).

[7] Thomas Farnaby (1574/5–1647) was a schoolmaster and grammarian. He annotated many of the classical authors for the use of schoolboys.

[8] Several doctors were called upon for their opinion particularly as to whether the king would recover. Pitt received conflicting opinions and decided to seek fresh advice from Dr Arthur Addington, his family doctor, who had at one time kept an asylum and proved to be optimistic that the king would recover. His opinion was reinforced when in December the queen called for an opinion from a clergyman and physician, Dr Francis Willis (1718–1807). As SK notes, many at the time thought that Willis's qualifications were suspect, so, for example, he was not a member of the Royal College of Physicians. He was not, however, a quack although he had original ideas on how to treat mental disorders based on his own experience in keeping a private asylum. Ehrman, *Younger Pitt: The Years of Acclaim*, pp. 650–53; for the king's treatment, see Jeremy Black, *George III: America's Last King* (New Haven, CT, 2008), pp. 275–80.

the fine called, Wilton Carpets.[9] The masters finding themselves undersold are under the necessity of lowering the wages– w^ch. the workmen do not choose to submit to: but to a man refuse.[10] So that that branch of business is at a stand & above a thousand people out of employ. This will soon be felt, not only in the town but through all the neighbourhoods where carding & spinning business is carried on.– I come now to your favour of the 8th. inst. I am glad you have some hopes of M^r. Arthur. To have our friend's remains revised by one who knew him so well must be of great advantage. Therefore you must persist in urging him to it. And if any loose hints will be worth his notice, I will try what I can do. What a pity that that great & good man was so hard to please! It was his favourite topic. Plato, he used to say, wrote an introduction to one of his dialogues six or seven times over– & Demosthenes[11] transcribed Thucydides[12] w^th. his own hand I do not know how many times to make himself perfectly master of the true attic style.[13] By this means composing became laborious & consequently tiresome. I should like much to see those discourses on free enquiry into religion, w^ch. you say are not so much laboured. I make no doubt of these becoming highly acceptable in this age & country where those subjects are now canvassed w^th. more spirit than ever.

Well! you must have had the patience of Job, to endure such usage. Strahan & Cadell are in such an immensity of business that I can easily excuse ^them^– but by no means, justify– them. But why Urwick should persist in such sullen silence is ^as^ I said before, quite inexplicable. I cannot imagine the shadow of an excuse for him. He must certainly have written & his letters must have been miscarried. M^r. Hamilton's good natured excuse– <u>his aversion to letter writing</u>– is not satisfactory. Let him be ever so averse he might write a few lines to make your mind easy.– I remember he wrote me a letter from Glasgow to Milliken– but it was in

---

[9] 'The looped-pile or Brussels carpet was first patented in England at Wilton in 1741 and the first loom for weaving it was built at Kidderminster in 1749. The construction was like that of terry-towelling but woven with multicoloured supplementary warps.' Gerald W. R. Ward, ed., *The Grove Encyclopedia of Materials and Techniques in Art* (Oxford, 2008), p. 86.

[10] This was an early example of collective strike action by workers. 'Carpets', in Arthur Marsh, Victoria Ryan, and John B. Smethurst, *Historical Directory of Trade Unions: Volume 4* (Aldershot, 1994).

[11] Demosthenes. See Letter 118.

[12] Thucydides (*c.* 460–*c.* 400 BC). Greek historian, author of the *History of the Peloponnesian War* between Athens and Sparta, in which he took part. His history, an eight-volume work, was not quite completed. Thucydides did not have time to revise his style which has been variously described as idiosyncratic, difficult, concise, energetic, and poetic.

[13] attic: the form of Greek used by the ancient Athenians.

short hand– & unsealed– & therefore put to defiance the impertinent curiosity of the Paisley postmaster– who could not help peeping into it. Who knows but he has forgot to write long-hand. But one would think he must have forgot to read it too– [page torn] he pays so little regard [page torn] your repeated requests. In short I should like to know what excuse he will offer. It is lucky, however, that he still minds the main business, in an unremitting attention to the press. This I give him credit for. And am glad to find upon the whole that every thing is in such forwardness. M^r. Wigan has just been w^th. ^me^ enquiring after ^you &^ it. I told him what you wrote me– we therefore expect it in a [page torn] or fortnight at farthest. He has ~~ordered~~ ^bespoke^ one copy [page torn] a friend.– I remember M^r. Robertson very well: & should like much to see his sermon– & shall be sure to order it when I see it advertized.[14] I like his method of treating the subject & hope it will induce him to prosecute his plan to a greater extent. Poor D^r. Magill! he has good sense to know that superiority & merit have always had, & will always have, enemies. Urit [en]im fulgore suo qui pregravat artes. Infra se positas–[15] But how a neighbour, a christian, a minister– & as you say, in a thanksgiving sermon should foist in such unneighbourly such unchristian such unbrotherly virulence, is to me passing strange.[16] I entirely agree w^th. you about controversy. It sours the temper & unhinges the mind when it becomes personal, & is the mark of a vain & little mind. And nothing is more mortifying to those little minds than to find themselves neglected & overlooked by their antagonist. This is the case of a neighbour of mine who addressed Gibbon w^th. all the tenderness of an affectionate brother & D^r. Priestley w^th. all the rancour & spleen of an inveterate enemy w^th. an attempt at ridicule.[17] The first I suppose despises & the latter pities him– but neither of them condescend to take notice of him, w^ch. shows his labour is lost & is indeed already forgotten. Yet I still say it is all right & will in the end produce the peaceable fruits of truth & righteousness to the honour of God.

---

[14] John Robertson. See Letter 146. SK would remember him from Glasgow University, where he obtained an MA in 1753. See Letter 146.

[15] 'Urit enim fulgore suo qui pregravat artes infra se positas'. Horace, *Epistles*, II, i, lines 13–14. 'For a man scorches with his brilliance who outweighs merits lowlier than his own'. Loeb Classical Library.

[16] See the previous Letter 146 for criticism of M'Gill in a sermon by William Peebles.

[17] A reference to William Jesse's publications titled *Lectures, Supposed to have been Delivered, by the Author of A View of the Internal Evidence of the Christian Religion, to a Select Company of Friends: Dedicated to Edward Gibbon, Esq.* (1787); and *A Defence of the Established Church or, Letters to the Gentlemen of Oxford and Cambridge who are in the Course of Education for the Christian Ministry in which Dr Priestley's Arguments against Subscription, and the Peculiar Doctrines of Christianity, are Examined and their Futility are Exposed* (1788). See the end of Letter 135.

I am glad you correspond w^th. our old friend D^r. Campbell[18]– Pray remember me to him–& assure him that his first pamphlet (for I have never seen nor heard before of the second) is much admired here.–

Your friends here are all much as you left them– constantly enquiring after you & yours.

Mary writes to her friend Nelly. We remain D^r. Sir w^th. our joint best wishes & respects

Yours most affect^ly.<br>
S. Kenrick.

## Letter 148: James Wodrow to Samuel Kenrick, 20 and 23 May 1789

Place: Stevenston
Addressed: M^r Kenrick / Bewdley / Worstershire
Postmarked: Maybole June Ninth 1789
Franked: Free Ad: Fergusson.
Stamped: MAYBOLE/JU/9/89
Notes in SK's hand: rec^d. the 16 June 89 at Bewdley/answ^d. the 10th. Aug^t. 89.

My kind Friends acceptable Letter with those from Miss Kenrick accompanying it came at last to my hand by post from Glasgow but not till a Month after date. I am happy to find you determined to write something like Memoirs of our most amiable & worthy friend[1] & shall as soon as the continued Labour of the publication in hand is over, second your views as far as possible. I have done nothing as yet with the College people for Urwick because it must be by personal application rather than Letter at least this will save much time & Labour & I have not been at Glasgow nor indeed any where since my return from England nor have I had half an hours assistance from a single friend. Urwick's Sermon in my view exhibits marks of true Genius as well as of a very liberal ^mind^, & most amiable heart.[2] I wish I had brought more copies of it from Shrewsbury. I dare say it will

---

[18] William Campbell. See Letter 146.

[1] John Warner.
[2] Probably Thomas Urwick's *A Sermon, Preached at Salters-Hall, May 3d, 1787. Before the Correspondent Board in London of the Society in Scotland (incorporated by Royal Charter) for Propagating Christian Knowledge in the Highlands and Islands* (1787).

please some of my friends among the Professors if the perfect Simplicity did not <—> throw a veil over it's Merit. At last & this only on Saturday ^the 16th.^ I had a long & kind Letter from him drawn forth it woud seem not by my requests but by a stop in the publication for want of sufficient Matter to complete the 2ᵈ. volᵐᵉ. & being at Dunstable on a journey he does not seem to have known that Mʳ. Hⁿ.[3] had written me at Strahan's desire a few days before requesting that I woud transmit with the utmost speed two and if possible three Sermons as the engraving was nearly finished & nothing now obstructed the publication but the want of these. Mʳ. Urwick asked only one. They are bad calculators as I was made to believe they had three too many. This call could not have come upon me at a more inconvenient & unlucky time the very day after I had advertised the Sacrᵗ. & engaged myself in diets of instruction of young Communicants &c besides assisting at ^a^ neighbouring Sacrᵗ. & all my ordinary work. Yet by an uncommon exertion & employing two Amanuenses in part, I made to shift to send to Mʳ. Urwick on Mondʸ. last two revised and corrected Sermons not inferiour to any of the rest & the third is in forwardness. Mʳ. Urwick says he has scarce had occasion to make any corrections on the Language Except in ^the^ <u>wills</u> & <u>shalls</u> & a few words become obsolete in S.B.[4] he writes in the strongest terms of the <inexpressible> pleasure he has had in perusing them ^Sermons^ even in the broken and interrupted way of sheet after sheet– presages a very extensive sale of them from the ^great^ body of good sense virtue & religion in the kingdom & paints from his own feelings in a very beatiful manner the impressions they are likely to make on the Pupils of this excellent master. You will easily conceive all this was very pleasing to me, though I am not without some doubts how far the prospect will be realized as he & you & I are partial & prejudiced Judges in this Matter. They have missed by their delays the opportunity of dispersing a considerable number of them at our Genˡ. Assˡʸ. which meets this week: but I coud easily see from my conversations with Mʳ. Strahan that they consider the Scots sale as nothing.

Dʳ. Magills Appendix has just as I forsaw irritated the party & raised a spirit of intollerance & persecution against him in this Country. Between 30 & 40 Country Elders were carried away from their ploughing & harrowing their grounds to the Synod at Glasgow in April & this with such secrecy that the Manoevre was not known till it was executed. An Overture was introduced & carried by 30 votes

---

[3] Hamilton.
[4] South Britain, i.e. England.

(not an Airshire mins^r. but Peebles[5] present) that ^in consequence of a Fama[6] that^ D^r. M. had in his Essay & appendix published some things Contrary to the Word of God the Con^n.[7] of Faith & his Ordination vows, therefore it was proper to make an Enquiry & his own Presby were enjoined to do it. Six or eight Mins^rs. in and about Glasgow entered a protest against this sentence craving Liberty to complain to the Gen^l. Ass^ly. & there the cause goes. I have not the least doubt that the Wisdom & Moderation of that court will give a proper check to ^the^ zeal of the Synod, as from the nonsensical fooling upon which it is taken up they have a full ground to do ^so^ without entering upon the points of Heresy Subscription &c, which our political Leaders at Ed^r. never chuse to bring above board. A fama clamosa upon Heresy is a perfectly ridiculous ground of process against an Author who has published his books & and then set his name to them. The Corpus delicti[8] is before the public and if any one thinks there is Criminality he must stand forth as the Accuser & take his hazard if he fails in the Accusation which by our Law is very considerable in the case of a Mins^r. that of being declared infamous by the court nam:[9] Defamer & Slanderer. I coud have done my friend no service by going to Ed^r. on the Contrary I ~~woud~~ ^must^ have been considered as a member of the Synod. And for private solicitation I hope there will be no need of it. I have corresponded with D^r. Blair who is entirely in these views. The court will be crouded exceedingly not from this cause which I wish may meet with sufficient attention but this Disposal of the prin^l. Clerkship just now vacant & a keen contest about this Lucrative Office.[10] The Magistrates & Council & the Parish or Kirk session of Air have published a noble attestation of their Mins^rs. Doctrine life & usefulness in all the Scots news papers & have denied that there is any fama to his disadvantage among them, in the face of the synod.[11]

---

[5] William Peebles. See Letter 146.
[6] 'Fama': 'a prevalent report of scandalous or immoral conduct by a church member'; a Scottish church legal expression, usually 'fama clamosa', as later in this paragraph. *DSL*.
[7] Confession, i.e. the Westminster Confession of Faith.
[8] Corpus delicti, i.e. evidence.
[9] i.e. namely.
[10] See Letter 149, JW to SK, 5 Aug. 1789 for JW's detailed account of the competition between Alexander Carlyle and Andrew Dalzel for the post of principal clerk to the General Assembly of the Church of Scotland in May.
[11] The *Caledonian Mercury*, 7 May 1789, carried both an extract from the minutes of the Ayr burgh council, signed by David Lamond, Town Clerk, and an extract from the minutes of 'a very full meeting of Elders' in the Kirk Session of Ayr, signed by the Moderator, M'Gill's colleague in ministry in Ayr, Rev. William Dalrymple. 'Had such a *fama* ever existed', noted the burgh council, 'it must have arisen among those who reside on the spot where that gentleman's doctrines

I have put up in a bundle a Copy of D^r. Magills Thankg. Sermon & Appendix & M^r. Robertson's, Peebles, I coud not find but you are at no great loss by the want of it.[12] I have also sent the three last Reports ~~from~~ ^about^ our Widdows Fund which last You will take the trouble to transmit some how to D^r. Price Hackney near London with some Card letting him know they have come from me & that I wished to have sent them sooner.–[13] This small bundle I intended to have sent to Glasgow but there is a family in this Neighbourhood M^rs. Blair of Blair a Dorsetshire Lady & her daughters going to England in a fortnight.– I think they will pass near your County which will ^be^ a quicker conveyance ^than the others^.

Remember me in the kindest manner to M^rs. & Miss Kenrick. I ever am most sincerely yours J^s. Wodrow

May 23 Stev^n.

I find the packet will not reach you by the Blair family till the end of July or ^beg^g. of^ Aug^t. I will therefore try it by Glasgow & put up another small thing ~~of~~ Extracts from D^r. Magills book made by his colleague & given gratis among the poor to co^u^nteract the prejudice raised ag^st. ^him^ by the Mad zeal of the Synod. In the first draught Of the Overture <u>the Word of God</u> was not inserted. A Member observed this. The framer of the Over^re. said he <u>woud</u> not object to this addition. The Other replyed you <u>dare</u> not Sir. It is pity it had been mended.

Since writing on Wed^y. I have had more packets & sheets from Lond^n. The 2^d. vol. is printed down to the new Sermons by this time in their hands & the plate finished so that I hope you will have little further delay.

---

are delivered, and his writings were published; but before reading the proceedings of the Synod [of Glasgow and Ayr], no such *fama* was ever heard among us.' Similarly, the Kirk Session denied 'in direct terms, that any such *fama clamosa* did ever exist, notwithstanding attempts of the most malignant nature were taken for that purpose, by the avowed enemies of our established Church, now supported from motives we have no right to judge upon, by some of her professed zealous friends'.

[12] See Letter 146.

[13] The General Assembly published annually a *Report of the Trustees for Managing the Fund Established for a Provision for the Widows and Children of the Ministers of the Church of Scotland, &c*, which JW helped to administer. See Letter 108; and for a thankful reply see Letter 281, Richard Price to James Wodrow, 20 Jan. 1790, printed here in Appendix B, and also in *Correspondence of Richard Price*, III, pp. 269–71. Price was a leading expert in actuarial statistics, having published *Observations on Reversionary Payments* (1771). See Aaron Allen, 'Corporate Charity for "the House": Craft Pensions and the Widows' Fund, 1670–1782', *Scottish Historical Review*, 101 (Aug. 2022), pp. 210–47 at pp. 237–38.

I have been reading D^r. Campbell's large book sent me from Lond^n. above 1500 pages 4^to. little do I read, now.[14] Yet have got through more than the half of the Dissertations. The spirit & plan of the book is excellent & the translation considerably improved yet I am dissapointed. Too too much verbal Criticism & <—> little on the Spirit & sentiments of the Sacred Writers compared to what I expected from such a great & Masterly Genius yet it will be a standing & valuable book.[15]

Yours ever JW

Nelly says the packet is too late for Glasgow so I must try the other way perhaps I may take D^r. Prices out & send them directly to London had you a place there to transmit Packets to you this woud be a better & speedier Method than by Glasgow's.

[The following is on the cover sheet, in SK's hand, with some in shorthand—translated by Tony Rail]

Warrington's H^y. of Wales[16]

I. The Strathclyde Britons over powered by the danes, Picts & Scots sought an asylum in Wales AD. 878 & were allotted the Vale of Clyid[17] Denbighshire which still retains their name out of which they drove the Saxons and the rest of the country between the Dee and by Conway.[18]

II. Fleance the son of Banquo escaping when his father was murdered fled into N. Wales where he was kindly received by the King Griffith ap Llewelyn. Here he intrigued with Nest the K's daughter and had by her a son named Walter. Griffith, incensed at these affronts, bad him to be put to death, and his daughter to be reduced to the lowest servile situation;

---

[14] George Campbell, *The Four Gospels, Translated from the Greek. With Preliminary Dissertations, and Notes Critical and Explanatory*, 2 vols (1789). In 1785 JW wrote that 'I long to see' this translation 'as I have heard a very favourable account of it from a good Judge' (Letter 87).

[15] In the following year, the *Monthly Review*'s assessment was the opposite of JW's. It praised Campbell's annotations, but claimed his translation only improved on the *King James* version in 'comparatively few' instances, while the text's 'simplicity and its energy have been frequently injured without any change, or at least any material change of sense'. Cited in Arthur E. Walzer, *George Campbell: Rhetoric in the Age of Enlightenment* (Albany, NY, 2001), p. 13.

[16] SK may have been using the 1788 edition of William Warrington, *The History of Wales, in Nine Books: With an Appendix*, 3rd edn, 2 vols (1788 [1st edn 1786]).

[17] Vale of Clwyd, Denbighshire.

[18] According to Warrington, 'the remains of the Strathclyde Britons... came into Wales: and having every motive of resentment and interest to urge them to valour, they easily disposed the Saxons of that country which is situated between the Dee and the Conway'. Warrington, *History of Wales*, I, p. 229.

but Walter the fruit of this illicit connection was spared and soon became distinguished at his grandfather's court. A dispute having arisen between him and one of his companions he was reproached with illegitimacy which so irritated him that he instantly killed his playfellow and fearing the anger of his grandfather he fled into Scotland where he joined the English adherents of Q. Marg$^t$ & Edgar the King. Here he soon became a favourite with the King of Scotland, then he was appointed Steward and thus became the ancestor of the Stuart tradition.[19]

## Letter 149: James Wodrow to Samuel Kenrick, 5 August 1789.
Place: Stevenston
Addressed: M$^r$. Kenrick / Bewdly / Worcestershire
Postmarked: Irvine August Fifth 1789
Franked: Cassillis
Note in JW's hand: afternoon
Notes in SK's hand: rec$^d$. 9th Aug$^t$., answ$^d$. 10th. Aug$^t$. 89.

My Dear Sir

There has been a great interruption in our correspondence as I have not heard from Bewdley for four or five months. The last packet I sent in the end of April or beginning of May, & it was unfortunate: first sent to Col Montgomery who returned it <-> he was uncertain whether his seat might be vacated. As it contained letters from Nelly & me troublesome to transcribe & send in another form, I inclosed it to Sir A. Fergusson then returned to Kilkerran. I have no doubt he would forward it if it reached him but your silence has rendered every thing about it doubtful. I have now got two franks one for you & another for London of this date. But I have very little time to fill them properly, being just allighted from a ride of ten miles & having been engaged for some days before at Largs Sacr$^t$. & yesterday at the marriage of my neice Mary Ann in the Island of little Cumbra to a very good sort of young man.[1]

---

[19] This paragraph is a paraphrase of Warrington's *History of Wales*, I, pp. 337–39.

[1] Mary Ann Wodrow (1762–1841) lived on the Isle of Little Cumbrae. See Letter 115. She married James Archbald, a farmer, who 'grew vegetables and hay; kept sheep, marketing lambs and wool; sold fur and meat from local rabbits; fished; and sold seaweed for fertilizer. In addition to

8. Margaret 'Peggy' Wodrow, watercolour by Mary Ann Wodrow, n.d., Mary Ann Wodrow Archbald Papers, Sophia Smith Collection, SSC-MS-00006, Smith College Special Collections, Northampton, Massachusetts.

9. Mary Ann Wodrow, watercolour self-portrait, n.d., Mary Ann Wodrow Archbald Papers, Sophia Smith Collection, SSC-MS-00006, Smith College Special Collections, Northampton, Massachusetts.

10. Professor William Leechman, by William Millar, oil painting, 1774/1775, © The Hunterian, University of Glasgow.

We have been all in our usual health since I wrote yet my Wife complains a little just now of her stomach. She was in Ed$^r$. above two Months, with her aged

her domestic chores, Mary Ann was an independent producer of textiles and knitted products and wove thread for professional weavers and tailors'. In 1807 they emigrated to New York state with their four surviving children (named James, Margaret Ann, Patrick Peter, and Helen Louisa—all longstanding Wodrow names). Smith College Libraries, Mary Ann Wodrow Archbald Papers, https://findingaids.smith.edu/repositories/2/resources/548, accessed 7 March 2023. Mary Ann confided her nervousness about the wedding in letters to her intimate friend,

Mother who lost the eldest of her two unmarried Daughters last spring.[2] Louisa returned in the beginning of June & brought with ^her^ Aunt M^rs. Leechman & her Sister in Law M^rs. Hamilton of London who were both our Guests about a Month & both seemed very happy tho' in a delicate ailing way. I know your veneration for the worthy Widow of the Principal, which woud not [have] been diminished had you spent that month with us. She carried Helen with her to Bell-ritiro to M^rs. Ruat's house where she still is & seems very happy from her Letters so that Miss Kenrick cannot hear from her by the present opportunity but Mar^t. has just now borrowed a pen from me to write to her amiable friend.– so much for family matters.

About the time that the last of the three additional Sermons reached London Mess^rs. Cadell & Strahan intimated to me by M^r. Hamilton that as many people who they expected would purchase the book had now left London that as the Impression was large & there was some risk part of it might ly on hand till next winter & be then considered as a stale publication, so, they thought of <—> keeping it by them till the Parl^t. sits down & then publishing. M^r. Hamilton remonstrated against this to no purpose. I approved of it in the present state of things as a wise measure; having always thought that it ought to have been published before the Month of April if it was to be done this season & that they had not

---

Margaret 'Peggy' Wodrow, and also described the wedding day in her journal, which provides insight into JW as both an uncle and minister. Unhappy about becoming a wife and no longer being 'Miss Wodrow', an 'anxious beating heart' led her to spend 'the forenoon in pulling pease'. After midday 'the boat arrived & my Dear Margaret came flying up to us...I saw her heart was sore but she had put on a face of gayety & contrived every method to amuse me'. Then JW 'my Uncle clasped me to his bosom & wished me happy', but 'I could not answer him'. Her fiancé's family came in and 'we drank only a glass of wine & then rose to prepare for the cerimony– I went into my Mothers room & leaned upon the bed– thought I should have fainted but scarce a tear would fall– Margaret said everything in her power to keep up my spirits [and] bad me look upon it all as a dream &c– the awful ceremony was performed [and] my Uncle went through with it in a very striking engaging manner– I made shift to support my self but towards the end of it felt my limbs begin to fail under me– it was endeed like a dream when I heard my self saluted round with wishes of long health & happiness &c– at tea my Uncle paid James much attention insisted upon seeing him soon, saying that he was now his nephew'. They then began a dance and 'Margaret & I took a reel & it was the chearful sounds to which my heart had often beat time– these sweet days of youth seemed now over forever & I thought it would have brock– Margaret was obliged to go with her Father– I bad her a sad adieu upon the Rocks– never till that moment did I feel her so very Dear'. Diaries of Mary Ann Wodrow Archbald, IV, Aug. 1789.

[2] Louisa Wodrow's mother, Helen Hamilton, née Balfour (d. 1793), had five children with Gavin Hamilton (1704–67): Louisa (1733–93), Anne (1738–87), John (1740–92, often mentioned in the Wodrow–Kenrick correspondence), Robert (1743–1829), and Elizabeth (1749–c. 1842). JW must refer here to Anne Hamilton, suggesting that she died in 1789 or 1788 rather than 1787, as ODNB.

<—> acted so handsomely to the Prin^ls. friends in this Country & to myself, in not having every thing ^ready^ against that time. Yet I willingly submit to the trifling loss for the sake of giving the book a better chance at Xmas. The Print was either the real or the Ostensible reason of the delay. I have within this week got a very few of the Prints.[3] After all the pains & expense that has been bestowed I am not quite pleased with the engraving. It is indeed a good engravin Print & a striking Likeness in one sense— but it wants the sweet & pleasant look that I think the picture had. The countenance is too grave or thoughtful. Yet our friend Gilbert Lang[4] to whom I carried one of them is highly pleased with it & he is a better Judge than I am. Had I got it a month ^or so^ sooner I woud have sent you one with a small packet containing D^r. Magill's & M^r. Robertsons Sermons which I gave about that time or earlier to the care of M^rs. Blair or her daughters & which, if it has not reached you already soon will, for after spending some time in Cumberland they were to pass through Worcester in their way to Glocestershire where they are likely to settle.

The poor D^r.[5] is now the Subject of persecution & the object of Popular Odium in the West of Scotland & his friends likely soon to be sharers in it. Lord Hales has proved a better prophet than D^r. Leechman <-> you'll recollect their Predictions in a Letter I sent you three or four years ago.[6] It was an unlucky Assembly for the D^r. The Contest for the Clerkship ran near & high & irritated the minds of the two parties. There were three or four Candidates. The friends of the losing Candidates united & threw themselves ^all^ into the scale against D^r. Carlyle[7] whose single

---

[3] That is, JW had been sent a few extra copies of the print of James Caldwall's engraving of William Millar's oil painting of Leechman (see Plate 10) which had been created to serve as the frontispiece to volume 1 of the edition of Leechman's *Sermons*. No doubt JW's opinion of the engraving was significantly coloured by his unexpected bill for half of its cost (see Letter 143 above), but it is possible to see a greater austerity in the expression engraved by Caldwall than in that painted by Millar. See Sher, *Enlightenment and the Book*, p. 190. They can be compared at ibid., pp. 192–93.

[4] See Letter 79.

[5] i.e. William M'Gill.

[6] See Letter 120, JW to SK, c. 9–15 Aug. 1786, and SK's reply, Letter 122, 28 Sept. 1786. Leechman had been optimistic that the age of heresy trials had ended, while Sir David Dalrymple, Lord Hailes, had believed that the rage for them had merely waned and was likely to blaze up again.

[7] Rev. Alexander 'Jupiter' Carlyle (1722–1805), minister of Inveresk parish (1748–1805), Midlothian, and a leading member of the Moderate party in the Church of Scotland. He preached political sermons against the American and French Revolutions, and he was centrally involved in various Moderate campaigns, such as those to support John Home's play *Douglas* (1756–57), a Scottish militia (1760 and later), and the presentation of the Rev. John Drysdale to Lady Yester's Kirk, Edinburgh (1762). He was a founding member of the Poker Club, an early member of the Select Society, and a literary Fellow of the Royal Society of Edinburgh.

party was however so strong as to carry it for him at the first meeting by 3 votes & he actualy sat a week as Clerk but by an artful scheme of Harry Erskine a Scrutiny was made & Dalziel <-> Professor Drysdale's son in Law[8] carried it by 5 votes. Among Dalziel's friends were perhaps 40 or fifty of what are <—> called the Moderate party of the Clergy. And when D^r. Magill's cause came on ^immediately after^ many of these seemed unwilling to desert the people they had voted with for a week before in the continued scrutiny about the Clerkship. There was however a long & voilent Debate which lasted two days. The Synod's sentence was reversed, but it was recommended to the Presby (of Air) to attend to the Matter & take if they shoud find it necessary measures for preserving the purity of Doctrine & the Authority of our standards.[9] This was also suggested by H. Erskine to get an unanimous sentence of the Assembly under the artful pretext that it was left in the power of the Presby to put an end to the matter if they pleased without doing any thing at all.

Had the Presby of Ayr been as friendly to the D^r. as our Presby was to the old Abbot in a similar Process, The tag to the Assemblys sentence woud have been considered as a mere formal Compliment to the established standards & there would have been an end of the matter. But unluckily a third or fourth part of the Mins^rs. are not friendly to Him, and they with the Country Elders the rotten part of our constitution are able to command a majority especially in such an allarming cause as Heresy. Accordingly their Presby met about three weeks ago.[10] The Ass^ly. sentence was read. A motion was made by Old M^r. Auld[11] of Mauchlin that

---

His *Autobiography* (1860) has been an important source for historians of eighteenth-century Edinburgh and Scottish culture. His involvement in various controversies, and particularly his role in the Moderate party, made him a divisive figure on more than one occasion. His attempt to secure the principal clerkship to the General Assembly in 1789 was one; his nomination to preach before that body thirty years earlier had been another. See Sher, *Church and University, passim*.

[8] Andrew Dalzel (1742–1806), professor of Greek at the University of Edinburgh, whose wife was Anne Drysdale (1751–1829), daughter of John Drysdale (1718–88), minister of the Tron Church, Edinburgh, and himself principal clerk to the General Assembly and twice its Moderator (1773, 1784). The death of Drysdale (see note above) in 1788 caused the vacancy discussed by JW here. Dalzel was supported by Principal William Robertson, but chose to have Henry Erskine nominate him in order to rally votes from Whigs and Evangelicals in the General Assembly. As well as *ODNB*, see the *Autobiography of the Rev. Dr Alexander Carlyle, Minister of Inveresk, Containing Memorials of the Men and Events of his Time*, ed. John Hill Burton, 3rd edn (Edinburgh, 1861), pp. 555–59.

[9] i.e. the Bible, and the Westminster Confession of Faith as the subordinate standard, in the Church of Scotland.

[10] NRS, CH2/532/8, Minutes of the Presbytery of Ayr, 1768–96, ff. 452–54, 15 July 1789.

[11] Rev. William Auld (1709–91), minister of Mauchline (1742–91), Ayrshire.

a Committee be appointed to draw up an Abstract of exceptionable Passages in D^r. M. publications if any such occurred & lay it before next meeting of Presby. Another Motion was made ^by M^r. Thomson of Daily^[12] that a Committee be named to meet this Afternoon & confer with D^r. M. concerning such passages in his publications as may have given offense, to receive what acknowledgements he might offer, and, thereupon finaly & amicably to terminate the matter & report to the Presby in the evening. This last motion was supported by the form of Process & acts of Ass^ly. requiring frequent & friendly conferences with Mins^rs. charged with Heresy before any thing at all ^be done^ in the Matter—by D^r. Magills singular work which entittled him to every attention and the peace of the Country which required that <——> the matter Should be speedily terminated. There was a long and interesting Debate. The D^r. himself spoke two hours affected every body even his zealous antagonists but coud not soften them. The second motion was lost by three votes ^though^ there was a majority of four Mins^rs. voted for it. A strong Dissent was entered by the D^r's. friends & thus the matter goes again to the Synod which meets at Glasgow in Oct^r.[13] I have a letter since this happened from my friend. He says he is entirely ignorant of what ^the Party against him^ intend to censure in his writings. They professed to be ig not to know it themselves but seemed disposed to go all the lengths against him that either right or wrong will carry them that if he had offended them by telling the truth or by just reasoning he coud not repent of it.

My mind woud be not to prosecute the dissent & appeal but protract the matter somehow till the Meeting of the Synod be over. Then his friends both in the Presby & out of it will have an opportunity of chusing new Elders which they cannot do till then. After which a strong push shoud be made to terminate the matter in his own Presby. If it is lost there, let it go to the Synod of April which meets in Air & where his friends are likely by a proper Effort to carry a sentence in his favour which will make some impression on the minds of the people ^joined with^ here. If his friends in his own Presby insist on being heard at Glasgow we must write to all the Mins^rs. in the Western Counties that have any regard to the sacred rights of Conscience & they are I hope not a few & endeavour to bring them up. This however will be difficult as the Synod is only an intermediate

---

[12] Rev. Thomas Thomson (1730–99), minister of Dailly parish (1756–99), Ayrshire.
[13] JW headed the list of dissenters from the presbytery's decision, followed by William Dalrymple, M'Gill's colleague at Ayr. NRS, CH2/532/8, Minutes of the Presbytery of Ayr, 1768–96, f. 454.

& insignificant court and at any rate it is doubtful if we shall be able to overpower the fanaticism in the City & neighbourhood of Glasgow supported by Country Elders. It is likely we must fall there but let it be decently; that is by a strong protest & Complaint against that Synods sentence which if signed by the most respectable Mins[rs]. in this part of the Country will show the Ass[ly]. our strength. Whatever happens I cannot think that Court will give any encouragement to a heresy Process but I have been tedious in this Matter. <—> The D[rs]. Eldest Daughter[14] has lately lost her Judgment and I dare say too much thought about this affair has hurt her though the disease ^is^ in the family, but little do these unfeeling Inquisitors think what effects their procedure may have on feeling hearts.

What think you of the state of France. I had flatered myself that a grand & glorious revolution in favour of Liberty woud have been effected without bloodshed & that it woud have made the Tyrants of Europe tremble on their Thrones; but now I see the purchase must be made by blood. The Tiers Etat[15] seem to have lost their influence & France from ~~the~~ one end of the kingdom to the Other to be under the power of an enrage Mob the most dreadful of tyrants. The cruelty & barbarity of their outrages put one in mind of the days of ^the^ League.[16] But I must stop as I have to write to London. Have you ever received the Linnen?

God bless you & yours.<br>J Wodrow

---

[14] Elizabeth M'Gill (1765–91) died two years later; another daughter named Douglas Heron M'Gill (1773–90) also died around this time; while another, Janet (1770–86), had died in the year M'Gill published his *Death of Christ*. *FES*, III, p. 12.

[15] *Tiers état:* third estate.

[16] A reference to the Thirty Years' War (1618–48). It began as a conflict between Catholics and Protestants, and led to atrocities, devastation, and depopulation of the German states. Among the multiple belligerents was a 'Catholic League' formed by states within the Holy Roman empire. This conflict was part of a broader crisis in the mid-seventeenth century, for which see Geoffrey Parker, *Global Crisis: War, Climate Change and Catastrophe in the Seventeenth Century* (New Haven, CT, 2013), ch. 8.

## Letter 150: Samuel Kenrick to James Wodrow, 10 August 1789
Place: Bewdley

My dear Friend

Your kind favours of the 20th & 23$^d$ May[1] (w$^{ch}$. I rec$^d$. under Sir A. F.'s frank the 16th of June)[2] have in vain stared me in the face: I was always expecting your parcel from London, & my impatience increased by repeated letters from friends & booksellers for your publication. Not satisfied w$^{th}$. writing to me & my answers, M$^r$. Fownes[3] ^of Shrewsbury^ called upon me some days ago, to know positively when he might expect it. I referred him to his townsman M$^r$. Urwick. This suspence, is all I have to offer in excuse for delaying so long to write to you. But your kind letter of the 5th. inst. has relieved my mind from an uneasy situation & determined me not to lose a moment longer to give you all the satisfaction I can– w$^{th}$. my sincere peccavi.[4]

I have also received ~~viewed~~ your parcel by M$^{rs}$. Blair ^last week^.[5] Of each in order.

I am happy to find you have such a favourable opinion of our friend Urwick– as worthy the notice of your learned <Courts> who like our Sovereign, have such power over mortals, to reward merit by flattering vanity. If I can meet w$^{th}$. an opportunity I will send you two or three copies of his sermon.[6] My imagination presages with his a welcome reception– as frivolous as this age is called: & who knows but this check of 4 months, may give a new spring to curiosity & produce a more extensive sale. Quoique il en soit,[7] the booksellers are certainly the best judges in these matters, & must know what they are about in their own business better than any body else.– (I am follow$^g$. your letter.)

D$^r$. McGill's appendix I have read w$^{th}$. equall pleasure & admiration.[8] Every impartial lover of Truth & of religious & civil Liberty as dictated by reason &

---

[1] Letter 148, written over 20 and 23 May 1789.

[2] Sir Adam Fergusson.

[3] Rev. Joseph Fownes (1715–89) minister at High Street, Shrewsbury (1748–89), co-pastor with Job Orton (1717–81) until 1765. SK's father had assisted in his ordination in 1743. Surman Index; id. 9436. See also W-K, I, p. 285n.

[4] peccavi: 'I have sinned'.

[5] 'M$^{rs}$. Blair of Blair a Dorsetshire Lady' (Letter 148).

[6] Probably Thomas Urwick's *A Sermon, Preached at Salters-Hall, May 3d, 1787. Before the Correspondent Board in London of the Society in Scotland (incorporated by Royal Charter) for Propagating Christian Knowledge in the Highlands and Islands* (1787). See Letter 148.

[7] quoi qu'il en soit: 'be that as it may'.

[8] William M'Gill, *The Benefits of the Revolution: A Sermon, Preached at Ayr, on the 5th of November, 1788, by William M'Gill, D. D. To which are Added, Remarks on a Sermon, Preached on the Same Day, at*

confirmed by our holy religion must value it– in proportion as bigots & hypocrites must shrink before it; & the greater strength of truth ~~that~~ it carries, ~~it~~ will be the more sure to rouse the carnal powers of virulence & animosity, w$^{ch}$. like fire on the rude elements of nature will separate the dross from the ore & bring it out pure gold. I sympathise w$^{th}$. him & w$^{th}$. his friends– to be interrupted in this manner in the conscientious discharge of their important duty:– I am sincerely sorry for his family– who cannot help their fears & anxieties: At the same time I congratulate w$^{th}$. him & w$^{th}$. every generous friend embarked in the same noble cause, whose minds & hearts must be warmed & elevated by the sublimest of motives, the consciousness of supporting & defending the best of causes, w$^{ch}$. will in the end triumph over all opposition.– But while his own parish of Air give such ample testimonies of their satisfaction w$^{th}$. their minister's doctrine life & usefulness, why should not this satisfy your ecclesiastical Courts; or at least have equal weight w$^{th}$. a similar declaration of the parish of Inch in favour of our old friend And$^w$. Ross? This is my wife's remark.[9] What a pity it was that the Conf. of Faith had not gone forth in the charge single? It must come to that tryal at last & will fall w$^{th}$. every other rotten appendage; however good & prudent as well as worldly & interested men, wish to ward it off as long as they can. I know <u>we</u> ^non cons^[10] are partial– perhaps prejudiced judges. Therefore I am not fond of saying much on the subject. But this I can see that our Leaders ^of the establishment^ like yours, & those of every cause w$^{ch}$. they are not able, or are ashamed to defend, are always for staving it off or pocketing small affronts.– This was particularly the case at Shrewsbury 7 or 8 years ago, when our B$^p$. Hurd was their Diocesan at Litchfield.[11] M$^r$. Tayleur, a gentleman of learning & fortune & of a most excellent character, joined the old dissenting Meeting House of w$^{ch}$. M$^r$. Fownes is one of the pastors on condition of them adopting M$^r$. Lindsey's Liturgy.[12] This gave a

---

*Newton upon Ayr; Very necessary for all the Readers of said Sermon* (Kilmarnock, 1789). See notes on this and William Peebles's Sermon in Letter 146.

[9] Rev. Andrew Ross (1726–87), minister of Inch in Stranraer, Galloway. He matriculated at the University of Glasgow in 1742 and presumably knew Kenrick and Wodrow there. In 1776 Ross asked to be relieved of the requirement of subscribing to the Confession of Faith. The presbytery rejected this request. After further discussion, however, Ross agreed to make a declaration of belief in fundamental Protestant principles, and to repudiate 'all doctrines and practices that are inconsistent with these principles'. Ditchfield, *Letters of Lindsey*, I, p. 217n; Addison, *Matriculation Albums*, p. 28.

[10] i.e. nonconformists.

[11] Richard Hurd (see Letter 79) was bishop of Coventry and Lichfield, 1775–81.

[12] William Tayleur (1712–96) was a landed gentleman of an old Shropshire family. Apparently he was intended for the Anglican church but developed doubts about the role of church

great alarm particularly among the hot headed clergy of the place who, like Peebles, wanted only the power, to devote these bold heretics to destruction.[13] M[r]. Tayleur's rank & character it was thôt w[d]. carry off many more. No time therefore was to be lost– & at the first visitation the Bishop was consulted, on this weighty matter. He gave them the strictest injunction to be quiet, & never to introduce the subject on any account into the pulpit. With the same spirit he has declined entering the lists w[th]. D[r]. Priestly, who has boldly thrown down the gauntlet to him more than once. This, D[r]. Horsley comends him for, as a mark of contempt for his antagonist: But a D[r]. Parr, no friend to D[r]. Priestley, judges otherwise; & tells him plainly that it is a proof of his pusilanimity.[14] He tells him many other severe truths respecting his adulation of Warburton, w[ch]. will not a little embitter the poor prelate's latter days. I do not see that the B[p]. or any of his friends have deigned to answer him. He blames the B[p]. for printing so few copies ^of Warburton's works^[15]– for not publishing his patron's life– for suppressing some of his juvenile works– w[ch]. Parr republishes– & poor performances they are indeed! but for that reason he thinks deserving of being preserved, to the curious– as it shews the progress of the human mind. For the same reason he w[d]. wish to recover from oblivion D[r]. S. Johnson's first production, w[ch]. was an english translation of a french translation of a portuguese or spanish account of a voyage.[16] He republishes 2 of Hurd's pieces, w[ch]. the author wishes were forgot– & for that reason: ^viz^ an attack of the learned Lealand[17] of Dublin & the most

---

authority and the Trinity. He was attracted to Theophilus Lindsey's Unitarianism and in 1775 began a correspondence with him which lasted a lifetime. Initially he organized private unitarian worship in his own house, then, with Lindsey's encouragement, persuaded Joseph Fownes, minister of the High Street Chapel, Shrewsbury, to adopt a unitarian liturgy based on Lindsey's own liturgy. Ditchfield, *Letters of Lindsey*, I, p. lxxxv.

[13] For William Peebles, see Letter 146.

[14] Rev. Samuel Parr (1747–1825), schoolmaster, Anglican clergyman, and writer. Parr had first met Joseph Priestley in the previous July at the induction of Parr's unitarian friend and future memorialist, William Field (1768–1857), at the High Street Chapel in Warwick. Warren Derry, *Dr Parr: A Portrait of the Whig Dr Johnson* (Oxford, 1966), p. 132.

[15] William Warburton. See Letter 109.

[16] In 1735 Samuel Johnson published his translation of *A Voyage to Abyssinia. By Father Jerome Lobo*, a Portuguese Jesuit.

[17] Richard Hurd, *A Letter to the Rev. Dr. Thomas Leland, Fellow of Trinity College, Dublin: in which His Late Dissertation on the Principles of Human Eloquence is Criticized; and The Bishop of Gloucester's Idea of the Nature and Character of an Inspired Language, as Delivered in his Lordship's Doctrine of Grace, is Vindicated From all the Objections of the Learned Author of the Dissertation* (1764). Thomas Leland (1722–85) was a historian and Church of Ireland clergyman. Following his appointment as professor of oratory at Trinity College Dublin in 1762, Leland published *A Dissertation on the Principles of Human Eloquence* (1764). A second edition soon followed in 1765 which included strictures on

excellent Jortin[18]– who had both disobliged Warburton. In short, he represents both Bishops as very moderate scholars. That Warb^n. had genius &^but^ all his ancient learning was derived from french & english translations– & Hurd is little better than an affected shallow scribbler.– What sh^d. provoke so much asperity I canot find– except envy, at seeing Hurd such a favourite. For all Parr's hopes of preferment are from the minority– w^ch. you know lately were very flattering– but are now at an end.[19]

I am sorry to find D^r. Campbell's voluminous work has disappointed you– tho' not surprized from the different Reviews I have seen of it.[20]– I am now come to your 2^d. kind letter of the 5th. inst. I rec^d. the 9th.– I am quite shocked again at my unaccountable delay & omission of acknowledging the recêt[21] of the cloth w^ch. M^rs. Wodrow was too good to send us. As I s^d. before I have rec^d. & just read D^r. McGills 2 pieces & M^r. Robertson's sermon: The sermon is a plain excellent discourse, containing proper information on that new subject & suitable

---

William Warburton's doctrine on grace. This led to a controversy about the style of the New Testament in which Bishop Hurd was Leland's chief opponent. SK was conversant with Leland's publications on ancient Greek history. W-K, I, p. 473.

[18] John Jortin. See Letter 122. Jortin upset Warburton by criticizing his interpretation of Virgil's *Aeneid* in his *Six Dissertations upon Different Subjects* (1755). Jortin had for a period (1747–50) acted as assistant to Warburton, hence the ironic title of Hurd's defence of Warburton, *On the Delicacy of Friendship* (1755).

[19] Known as 'the Whig Dr. Johnson', Samuel Parr's Whiggism survived the Fox–North coalition which he defended. His humanitarian views included criticism of child labour in a sermon for charity schools preached at Birmingham in October 1789 and later at Bewdley. Even more surprising was his praise for Priestley as 'one of the brightest ornaments of the age'. Despite holding some 'dangerous tenets', he was 'a profound philosopher, a Philanthropic citizen and a pious Christian'. At the time Parr and Priestley were only slightly acquainted but SK would soon learn that Parr was a true friend, as he later acknowledged in Letter 242, of 10 May 1804. In contrast to his praise for Priestley, Parr upset many of his Anglican contemporaries, although his spat with Hurd arose from an unflattering comment which Hurd had made of his preaching. Parr's response was to publish anonymously *Tracts by Warburton and a Warburtonian, not Admitted into the Collection of their Respective Works* (1789) which did not reflect well on their authors, Warburton and Hurd (who was the Warburtonian). They did not remain anonymous for long, as SK's comment indicates. Leonard W. Cowie, 'Parr, Samuel (1747–1825)', ODNB; Derry, *Dr Parr: A Portrait of the Whig Dr Johnson*, pp. 128–32.

[20] See JW's comment at the end of Letter 148. While praising George Campbell's *The Four Gospels*, the *Critical Review* concluded that he is 'perhaps, at times, a little too explicit, a little too copious in illustration: his remarks have occasionally too much minuteness, and a delicacy almost amounting in some instances to fastidiousness'. *Critical Review*, 67 (June 1789), pp. 401–09. The *Monthly Review*, most commonly cited by SK, did not review the book until June 1790.

[21] i.e. receipt.

application. The appendix, I repeat it, is a most spirited, accute & solid defence of the noblest of subjects, the rights of conscience & private judgment– w^ch. M^r. Fownes & many of my friends in that line will be happy to see. The parcel to D^r. Price I suppose you sent directly to London. And M^r. Robertson's sermon is a most excellent one, & shews the good sense & liberal turn of mind of his parishioners, in publishing it & making their fellow subjects partakers of the pleasure w^ch. is noble & enlarged view of Providence must give to every rational being & conscientious ^Christian^.[22] I remember him very well– I was at his first examination for orders in M^r. Warner's manse after a sacrament.– A propos, I lately wrote a random letter to Ben. Dawson[23]– giving him an acc^t. of your public^n. &c w^ch. he had never heard of. He remembers you well– & in his answer desires to be kindly rememb^d. to you.

[The remainder of this letter is missing. It may have contained SK's view of the French Revolution, a topic raised by JW at the end of Letter 149]

## Letter 151: James Wodrow to Samuel Kenrick, 9 November 1789

Place: Stevenston
Addressed: M^r. Samuel Kenrick / Bewdly / Worcester
Postmarked: Irvine Nov^r. Tenth 1789
Franked: Free Ad. Fergusson.
Stamped: NO/12
Note in SK's hand: answ^d. 16th Dec^r. 89

My Dear Friend

You will probably blame me for being so long acknowledging yours of the 10th of Aug^st. It is likely I would have done it sooner but a frank has been lying by me near a Month sent by D^r. Macnight the date of which he had foolishly put too far forward. Indeed I have been very busy for some [time] past, partly with secular business which I have been too much entangled with from the sudden death of a

---

[22] John Robertson, *Britain the Chosen Nation: A Thanksgiving Sermon, Preached, November 5th, 1788* (Kilmarnock, 1788). See Letter 146.
[23] Rev. Benjamin Dawson (1729–1814) was one of SK and JW's friends at Glasgow University, who subsequently conformed to the Church of England. He is frequently mentioned in the correspondence. See, for example, W-K, I, pp. 8, 28, 175, 248, 298, 443.

Factor to an estate entrusted to my care & partly from D^r. Magills cause of which by & by. In the meantime D^r. Macnight[1] paid me a visit six weeks ago preached for me half an hour & during the time he was with me & my parish Gentlemen with whom he is intimate we had much conversation about his great work which he is now determined to publish by subscription, in case he shall get as many subscriptions as will defray the Expense which he has not yet got. I understood from D^r. Kippis when I was in Lond^n. that the great Booksellers there woud make no offers at all or in his language woud not bite at the hook.[2] And I understand from D^r. M. that his returns to the Subscription Papers dispersed in Scotland were not numerous indeed the book is too dear for the fortunes of most Scotch Clergymen— that he had as yet had no regular returns to the Subscription papers sent to England & therefore coud not be certain whether there woud be a publication at all. And as I happened to mention you as wishing & approving the publication he asked the favour that I woud send two ^Papers^ to you one of which is enclosed & the other shall soon be sent you. At the same time Neither he nor I ask you to subscribe yourself but only make use ^of^ you as a friend to publish the proposals in your part of the Island that they who are more able & disposed to incourage such a work may have an opportunity of doing it; because I suspect that the Booksellers instead of promoting it will throw every obstruction in the way of it they can. I have not yet subscribed myself though I will probably do it to the £3"3 copy.[3] The D^r. wishes to publish it before he dyes though he shoud not gain a shill^g. & indeed every friend to Scriptural knowledge & inquiry must wish him success. He has taken infinite pains. It is the work of his Life. Yet with all his learn^g. & ingenuity he is too fanciful a Critick & Commentator to my tast.

When such great works as his & D^r. Campbells are issuing from Scotland it will appear surprising to a stranger that a furious persecution shoud be raised among us against such a man as D^r. Magill. Yet it is only by a desperate faction and I trust will in the end come to nought. The Committee appointed by their Presby after sitting week after week for two months at last laid their <u>report</u> before the Presby Sept^r. 30 consisting of above 50 folio pages chiefly extracts from the <u>Essay</u> & <u>Appendix</u> of such passages as they thought exceptionable i.e. contrary to the

---

[1] James Macknight (1721–1800), biblical scholar and minister of the Old Church, Edinburgh. His translation of the *Epistles to the Thessalonians* (1787) was followed by his *New Literal Translation from the Original Greek of All the Apostolic Epistles* in four volumes in 1795. See Letter 87.

[2] Andrew Kippis. See Letter 118.

[3] i.e. £3 and 3 shillings.

word of God & Confession of Faith with the respective passages of both cited, & scarcely any observations or reasoning mixed with them. This Paper without being either formaly received or rejected by the Presby was read in the Church of Ayr the Presby house being too small to contain the Crowd & suported by speeches of the Committee who were hissed by numbers of the D[rs]. congregation whom it was difficult to restrain within the bounds of decency. The D[rs]. friends who were a minority & not a large one first opposed the reading of the Paper & next insisted that it shoud ly on the Table to be seen & answered by the D[r]. Both of these requisitions were refused & the cause referred for advice to the Synod at Glasgow.[4]

There was little time to call friends & though there had been never so much It would have been difficult to cope with them in midst of the fanaticism of the town of Glasgow with all their Elders at their backs. I wrote only a single letter to M[r]. Bogue[5]. Without any Effort we had an equality if not a Majority of Ministers but all the Elders against us except three or four together with the Mob of Glasgow raised to a pitch of Enthusiam by some of their speeches & a Sermon at the opening of the synod.[6] The magistrates however checked both their ardour & that of their leaders by firmly refusing the request made to them by a deputation of the Synod for one of the Churches to meet in & confining us to their Court house our usual place of meeting which coud not admit above ^three or^ four or five hundred. The consequence of which was that we coud do no bussiness the first night the mob filling the house to the Exclusion of a part of the Synod. The next day a Guard of Soldiers placed at the door keept everything in order admitting no body till the Members were properly seated. Then we sat on the cause from 10 in the forenoon with very little respite till one next morn[g]. & after all they found it necessary for the sake of decency to grant the very thing that the D[rs]. friends in

---

[4] NRS, CH2/532/8, Minutes of the Presbytery of Ayr, 1768–96, 30 Sept. 1789, ff. 457–62; Fitzpatrick, 'Varieties of Candour', pp. 47–48.

[5] Presumably JW's friend Rev. Robert Boog (1746–1823), minister of the second and then first charges, Paisley (1745–82, 1782–1823), following SK's relative by marriage, Rev. James Hamilton (1721–82) in the first charge.

[6] On the Popular party's dominance in Glasgow Presbytery, see Ned C. Landsman, 'Presbyterians and Provincial Society: The Evangelical Enlightenment in the West of Scotland, 1740–1775', in John Dwyer and Richard B. Sher, eds, *Sociability and Society in Eighteenth-Century Scotland* (Edinburgh, 1993), pp. 194–209; Colin Kidd, 'Enlightenment and Anti-Enlightenment in Eighteenth-Century Scotland: An Ayrshire-Renfrewshire Microclimate', in Jean François Dunyachi and Ann Thomson, eds, *The Enlightenment in Scotland National and International Perspectives* (Oxford, 2015), pp. 59–84.

the Presby had insisted on and to remit it to the ^Presby^ with this single advice that the report shoud ly on their table for two or three Months for the D$^{rs}$. inspection.[7] He has begun to prepare his answers a good deal will depend on the Spirit of them. I have been exhorting him by Letters (for he was not present at Glasgow) to the meekness & Gentleness of Christ[8] not to return railing for railing but contrariwise blessing but you may judge from the Apendix that his Answers will be sufficiently spirited. We are likely to have another brush with them, at the Synod of April which meets at Air & a better chance to check their Madness. I have been doing what I coud to have proper Elders i.e. Gentlemen chosen from some parishes yet there is a lukewarmness & even a timidity to be expected in every establishment so that I am doubtful of an honourable Issue of the cause at the Synod & have some little apprehension though not much even of the Gen$^l$. Ass$^{ly}$.

Whatever may be the success in our Ch. courts these fools & bigots will be sufficiently lashed at the bar of the public. A specimen of which I send you of a Song printed at Glasgow.[9] It bears marks of the hand of Burns our ^Airshire^ Poet whom you may have heard of that is printed from a very imperfect and mutilated copy. Such as it is, it will amuse M$^{rs}$. & Miss Kenrick but will be scarcely intelligible without notes which I shall subjoin upon the Cover pointing out the names & Allusions to facts sufficiently known on the spot.[10]

At Glasgow I entered on a very serious conversation with M$^r$. Arthur about the Publication of a vol$^{me}$. of M$^r$. Warners Sermons & he has given me his promise that he will set about the revisal of them about the beginning of next summer when he ~~was~~ ^will be^ more disengaged than he has been for many years. Against that time I hope your Memoirs of his Life will be ready. I wish to have published

---

[7] NRS, CH2/464/4, Minutes of the Synod of Glasgow and Ayr, 1761–1803, 13 Oct. 1789, ff. 243, 247–9. JW's brother Patrick, minister of Tarbolton, was also in attendance, and took an active part in politicking on M'Gill's side.

[8] 'Now I Paul myself beseech you, by the meekness and gentleness of Christ…'. 2 Corinthians 10:1.

[9] This poem, sometimes as here titled 'The Tattered Garland', and sometimes as 'The Kirk's Alarm', was Robert Burns's satirical response to the lengthy heresy process carried out against his friend William M'Gill. It singled individual Ayrshire ministers out for praise or sharp mockery, and was not published till after the poet's death, but rather circulated in manuscript.

[10] See Letters 134 and 135 and Macleod, 'Burns and the Borders of Poetry'. JW's brother Patrick (see note 7 above) was 'Auld Wodrow' in Burns's poem 'The Twa Herds', though he was not a target of that ecclesiastical satire.

immediately ^some part of^ the Sermons I formerly mentioned on Rom. XIV.4[11]. as admirably adapted to the spirit of this Country at present, but as they consist of four long Sermons in a connected train They cannot be seperated & with the six Sermons on the Spirit of Religion & perhaps one or two more together with a preface, they will make a neat volume. I was ^therefore^ obliged to give up the thoughts of any separate Publication.

Nothing can excell some of the treatises of the Bangorian Controversy particularly those of Hoadly & Sykes[12] in points of <u>Argument</u> but in point of Unction as warm Scriptural adresses to the hearts of Mins$^{rs}$. & people I think M$^r$. Warners four Sermons superior to any thing I have read. They are however less Philosophical & less laboured in the Style & composition than most of his are yet they have been transcribed by himself. I brought them here with me.

I have looked over yours & have not time at present to advert to any thing in it thank you for your anecdotes. We have many Hurds in this Country & some of them not so conscientious & pious men as the Bishop. I hope to get something done about Urwick next time I go to Glasgow as I broke the Matter to Arthur but woud wish to have some copies of his Sermon.

God bless you & yours<br>J Wodrow

Notes on the Tattered Garland[13]

Stanza 3$^d$ alluding to what they published in favour of their Mins$^r$. in the N. Papers

    4. D$^r$. Dalrymple Mins$^r$. of Air[14]

---

[11] 'Who are thou that judgest another man's servant? to his own master he standeth or falleth. Yea, he shall be holden up: for God is able to make him stand.' Romans 14:4.

[12] The Whig latitudinarian Benjamin Hoadly, bishop of Bangor, criticized non-jurors and advocated erastianism in *A Preservative against the Principles and Practices of Non-Jurors* (1716). This provoked a storm of controversy, with Arthur Ashley Sykes (1684–1756) writing in support of Hoadly and the latitudinarian cause.

[13] 'garland': 'A collection of short literary pieces, usually poems and ballads; an anthology, a miscellany'. *OED*, 4.

[14] M'Gill's close colleague, Rev. William Dalrymple of the first charge in Ayr, to whom M'Gill's book had been dedicated. See Letter 125. Burns wrote: 'D'rymple mild! D'rymple mild, tho' your heart's like a child, / And your life like the new-driven snaw, / Yet that winna [will not] save you, auld Satan must have you, / For preaching that three's ane [one] an' twa [two], / D'rymple mild! For preaching that three's ane an' twa.'

6. The Rev^d. M^r. John Russel[15] Mins^r. of the Chapel of ease at Kilmarnock quite Characteristick. <u>Aidle</u> the refuse of the by[res]> in Scotland
7. M^r. James M^cKindlay[16] M^r. Robertsons[17] Collegue but a young man of a very different stamp. Killie dames. The Kilmarnock Dames[18]
8. The Rev^d. M^r. Alex^r. Moodie.[19] Sing't singed but the Scotch more contemptuous of this Gentleman my ~~collegue~~ ^friend^ D^r. Dow[20] upon hearing him harrangue at Synod at Irvine said "Poor thing! poor thing! The Head of him is as toom[21] as a ^halfpenny^ baubee-whistle
9. Father Auld Mins^r. of Machlin.[22] He prosecuted Clark Hamilton for Breach of the Sabath but the prosecution was found so unjust that the Presby ordered the Minutes of the Session relative to it to be erazed. He was prosecuted himself & fined by the Justices of Peace for non payment of duties in a Whyskie still he was concerned in.

---

[15] Rev. John Russel (1740–1817). He was minister of the chapel of ease at Kilmarnock from 1774 till 1800, when he was translated to the second charge at Stirling in 1800. He was described as 'an uncompromising disciplinarian, a strict Sabbatarian and a preacher of great power'. Donald Sage, *Memorabilia Domestica; or Parish Life in the North of Scotland* (Edinburgh, 1899), cited in *FES*, IV, p. 326. Responding to Russel's *The Reasons of our Lord's Agony in the Garden, and the Influence of Just Views of them on Universal Holiness, in a Sermon* (Kilmarnock, 1787), a severe critique of M'Gill's *Practical Essay*, Burns wrote: 'Rumble John! rumble John, mount the steps with a groan, / Cry the book is with heresy cramm'd; / Then out wi' your ladle, deal brimstone like aidle [liquid manure, *DSL*], / And roar ev'ry note of the damn'd. / Rumble John! And roar ev'ry note of the damn'd.'

[16] Rev. James MacKinlay (1756–1841), minister of the Laigh Kirk, Kilmarnock (second charge). See Letter 126. 'Simper James! simper James, leave your fair Killie dames, / There's a holier chase in your view: / I'll lay on your head, that the pack you'll soon lead, / For puppies like there's but few, / Simper James! For puppies like you there's but few.'

[17] Rev. John Robertson (1733–99), minister of the first charge of the parish of Kilmarnock. See Letter 146.

[18] i.e. the women of Kilmarnock.

[19] Rev. Alexander Moodie (1728–99), minister of Riccarton (1762–99). 'Singet Sawnie! singet Sawnie, are ye huirdin [hoarding] the penny, / Unconscious what evils await? / With a jump, yell, and howl, alarm ev'ry soul, / For the foul thief is just at your gate. / Singet Sawnie! For the foul thief is just at your gate.'

[20] Rev. Dr Robert Dow (1707–87), parish minister of Ardrossan, Ayrshire, and JW's Calvinist friend. See Letter 125.

[21] 'toom': 'empty'. *DSL*.

[22] Rev. William Auld of Mauchline, Ayrshire. See Letter 149. The kirk session of Mauchline Church had cited Burns to appear before it for his irregular marriage with Jean Armour, but had allowed him to give a donation to the poor fund in lieu of a fine. *FES*, III, p. 50. 'Daddy Auld! daddy Auld, there's a tod [fox] in the fauld [sheepfold], / A tod meikle waur [much worse] than

10. One Grant Mins^r. of Ochiltree[23] one of the most furious of ^the^ Committee he prosecuted or persecuted a ^reputed^ Witch in his parish. Was actualy Secretary to L^d. G. Gordon.[24]
11. <u>Jamie Goose</u>. James Young[25] Mod^r. of the Presby & Committee once a Coopar
12. M^r. Peebles[26] who has wrote many Poems & <—> printed an Ode to Liberty allong with his Sermon containing the Expression <u>Liberty's enduring chain</u>
13. M^r. Stephen Young[27] Mins^r. of the Parish of Barr

---

the clerk; / Tho' ye do little skaith [damage], ye'll be in at the death, / For gif ye canna bite, ye may bark, / Daddy Auld! Gif ye canna bite, ye may bark.'

[23] Rev. David Grant (1750–91), minister of Ochiltree (1786–91). Educated at the Universities of St Andrews and Edinburgh, he had previously ministered to the Groat Market Presbyterian Congregation in Newcastle-upon-Tyne (1781–86). *FES*, III, p. 62. 'Davie Bluster! Davie Bluster, for a saint ye do muster, / The corps is no nice o' recruits; / Yet to worth let's be just, royal blood ye might boast, / If the Ass were the king o' the brutes, / Davie Bluster! If the Ass were the king o' the brutes.'

[24] Lord George Gordon (1751–93), third son of the third duke of Gordon, president of the Protestant Association which marched on Parliament on 2 June 1780 to present a petition against the passing of Sir George Saville's Catholic Relief Bill, thus providing the catalyst for the Gordon Riots in which London was out of the control of the authorities for six days.

[25] Rev. James Young (1711–95), son of a cooper in Falkirk, minister of New Cumnock (1758–95). 'Jamie Goose! Jamie Goose, ye made but toom roose [empty praise, flattery. *DSL*] / In hunting the wicked Lieutenant; But the Doctor's your mark, for the Lord's holy ark, / He has cooper'd an' ca'd a wrang pin in't, / Jamie Goose! He has cooper'd an' ca'd a wrang pin in't.'

[26] William Peebles (1753–1826), minister of Newton-on-Ayr. See Letters 146 to 150, *passim*, on his sermons criticizing M'Gill. 'Poet Willie! poet Willie, gie [give] the Doctor a volley, / Wi' your 'Liberty's Chain' and your wit; / O'er Pegasus' side ye ne'er laid a stride, / Ye but smelt, man, the place where he sh–t. / Poet Willie! Ye but smelt, man, the place where he sh–t.'

[27] Rev. Stephen Young (1744–1818), minister of Barr. 'Steenie': a diminutive for 'Stephen'. *DSL*. 'Barr Steenie! Barr Steenie, what mean ye, what mean ye? / If ye meddle nae mair wi' the matter, / Ye may hae some pretence to havins [manners, *DSL*] and sense, / Wi' people that ken ye nae better, / Barr Steenie! Wi' people that ken ye nae better.'

## Letter 152: Samuel Kenrick to James Wodrow, 16 December 1789
Place: Bewdley
Postmarked: London December the Nineteenth 1789
Addressed: D[r]. Wodrow, / near / Irvine / Scotland
Franked: Free Westcote
Stamped: DC/89

My worthy Friend

As I see by the Newspaper that that to day is fixed upon at last by Mess[rs]. S. & C.[1] for publishing your long expected Work,[2] I am happy to congratulate you on the occasion & at the same time to thank you for your kind favour of the 9th. Ult[o]. I trust the copies will come directly to me by one of our Waggons, without any direction from hence.– When I receive them, you shall hear from me again.– & in case I should want more of them, you will be so kind as direct me where to apply.– Poor M[r]. Fownes, of Salop,[3] who repeatedly expressed his impatience to me, for a sight of this work, is gone to a better place without it. He died about a fortnight ago in the 75 year of his age.

I am truly sorry D[r]. Macknight should meet w[th]. so ungrateful a return from the christian world who are so well acquainted w[th]. his learned and useful labours. His former works are in high repute and he has therefore reason to expect great encouragement for the continuation of it. The specimen w[ch]. he has published on the Thessalonians seemed to give universal satisfaction & as I expected would have rouzed the curiosity of the learned to call with impatience for the whole.[4] After all I am affraid, w[th]. you, that the price is too high for many in the clerical line, here as well as w[th]. you. He may depend upon my doing every thing in my power to promote it, for his sake as well as for your's. I have sent the proposals by my nephew to Birmingham, to be shewn to D[r]. Priestley & the principal dissenters there; and when it comes back, will take care to have them exhibited at Worcester, Salop &c.

---

[1] The London publishers, Andrew Strahan and Thomas Cadell. See Letters 138 to 147, *passim*.

[2] The earliest surviving London advertisement for Wodrow's edition of Leechman's *Sermons* seems to have appeared in the *World*, on 16 Dec. 1789, at 'This Day is Published', priced 12s. in boards for the two octavo volumes. Other adverts in the London newspapers followed in early 1790. We are grateful to Richard B. Sher for this information.

[3] Joseph Fownes. See Letter 150. Salop was an old name for Shropshire.

[4] James Macknight, *A New Literal Translation, from the Original, of the Apostle Paul's First and Second Epistles to the Thessalonians: With a Commentary and Notes* (1787). See Letter 87 for his other works.

I am greatly obliged to you for the farther particulars you have sent me respecting D$^r$. Magill. It rejoices me to see matters are likely to come speedily to a crisis: that the charge now against him is open and he is called upon to defend the best cause in the world. This is better than your half smothered embers– ignes suppositos cineri doloso[5]– let them blaze out fairly– it will soon be over. You see the spirit of liberty and free enquiry is spread through the darkest retreats of superstition & despotism– why should it not reach fanaticism also, w$^{ch}$. thank heavens has not the powerful arm of flesh on its side. You see w$^{th}$. what undaunted spirit our little David[6] deals about his blows agt. against proud hierarchies, fashionable deists & a favourite prime minister. Instead of these haughty Philistines, your David[7] has only an untutored ill advised mob, headed by the lowest & most despicable of your establishment to encounter. This contest will I foresee soon bring down your ragged remnant of the old harlot's petticoat, of creeds & subscriptions, & establish Christianity upon its only true solid basis– *the Bible*– if you do not look sharp the French– and the Spaniards, for what I know, will have the start of you, in religious as well as civil liberty.[8] We poor dissenters are left far behind you all. You see what meetings we have in many counties; w$^{ch}$. will probably extend throughout the Kingdom– w$^{ch}$. looks well at the eve of an election. Many of them they have openly declared they will give their votes to none but the friends of civil and religious liberty. In return your spirited cousin D$^r$. Horsley[9] has sent a circular letter thro' his diocese (St Davids) to caution his clergy against voting for a member in that quarter, who voted in 1787 for the repeal of the test act.[10] And what is the mighty boon, do you think, we ask? Only to be put upon the same footing w$^{th}$. our protestant fellow subjects, in Scotland & Ireland,– & yet this is refused us, on no better ground than that it has been formerly refused– &

---

[5] Horace, *Odes*, II, i, lines 7–8. 'Incedis per ignes / Suppositos cineri doloso', translated as: 'walking, as it were, over fires hidden beneath treacherous ashes'. Loeb Classical Library. JW had quoted this line in Letter 120.

[6] Joseph Priestley.

[7] William M'Gill.

[8] The National Constituent Assembly in revolutionary France had issued a 'Declaration of the Rights of Man and Citizen' in August 1789, which included the principle of religious liberty. SK is alluding to the expected inclusion of this in the forthcoming French constitution. Lynn Hunt, *Inventing Human Rights: A History* (New York, 2007).

[9] Samuel Horsley. See Letter 80. He was a vigorous supporter of the establishment in church and state and critic of Dissent, particularly Rational Dissent.

[10] The MP referred to was John George Phillips (*c*. 1761–1816), member for Carmarthen, a Whig who voted for the repeal of the Test and Corporations Acts in March 1787 and in May 1789. The Dissenters' response was to appoint a delegation to meet Charles James Fox to draw his

because we have so long humbly submitted to a most oppressive imposition. If human nature in any shape should astonish us, I think it should be here. That the freest nation in the world, the pattern of every thing that is generous and good– in an enlightened age &c should withhold common justice from a peaceable industrious & respectable part of its community.– But it is my firm persuasion, as well as my heart's delight– that this like every other appointment of providence is to answer the wisest & best purposes: some of these we see, & the rest will appear in due time. This you, D$^r$. Magill & every good man knows and believes. He stands in need therefore of no motive that I can suggest to go on w$^{th}$. his defence & make the glorious cause better known among you.– On the 4th. of last Mo. D$^r$. Priestley preached a sermon at both the presbyterian meeting Houses in Birmingham, w$^{ch}$. is since published, exhorting the dissenters to persist in their application to parliament.[11] D$^r$. Price you see preached a revolution sermon on the same day[12]

---

attention to 'the unconstitutional and arbitrary interference of the Bishop of St David's for the purpose of obstructing the re-election of Mr Phillips'. They also asked Phillips as to whether he could provide them with a list of non-resident voters 'if he shall think it expedient, and if so, they would endeavour to engage their suffrages in [his] favour'. In the end it proved unnecessary to pursue remote voters. Horsley's action had proved counter-productive; Whig headquarters took measures to support Phillips and he was elected unopposed on 7 July 1790. Davies, *Committees for Repeal of the Test and Corporation Acts*, pp. 38–39; R. G. Thorne, 'Carmarthen, 1790– 1820', HPO; Donald E. Ginter, ed., *Whig Organization in the General Election of 1790: Selections from the Blair Adam Papers* (1967), pp. 80, 82, 97, 146, 148.

[11] Joseph Priestley, *The Conduct to be Observed by Dissenters, in Order to Procure the Repeal of the Corporation and Test Acts: Recommended in A Sermon, Preached before the Congregations of the Old and New Meetings, At Birmingham. November 5, 1789* (Birmingham, 1789). See also *Works of Joseph Priestley*, XV, pp. 389–404. SK thought that this had been preached on 4 November, an occasion when the birthday of King William III was celebrated. However, 5 November was also a celebratory occasion for the Revolution of 1688 as it was the date when William III and his invasion force landed at Torbay—though some Dissenters did not like to celebrate on that day as it coincided with the anniversary of the discovery of the Gunpowder Plot of 1605. For example, Joseph Towers, *An Oration Delivered at the London Tavern on the Fourth of November 1788* (1788).

[12] Richard Price, *A Discourse on the Love of our Country, Delivered on Nov 4, 1789, at the Meetinghouse in the Old Jewry, to the Society for Commemorating the Revolution in Great Britain* (1789). Minister at the Gravel Pit, Hackney (1770–91), Price was known for his support of the American cause, notably in *Observations on the Nature of Civil Liberty* (1776), and advocacy of parliamentary reform and religious liberty. He was a founder member of the Society for Constitutional Information (1780–94). The sermon that he preached on 4 Nov. 1789 before the London Revolution Society was in celebration of the centenary of the British 'Glorious Revolution', but it sparked off a major debate on the French Revolution after Edmund Burke attacked Price in his *Reflections on the Revolution in France* (1790). D. O. Thomas, 'Price, Richard (1723–1791)', ODNB. See also Martin Fitzpatrick, 'Richard Price and the London Revolution Society', *Enlightenment and Dissent*, 10 (1991), pp. 35–50; Martin Fitzpatrick and Anthony Page, 'Edmund Burke and Rational Dissent', in Martin Fitzpatrick and Peter Jones, eds, *The Reception of Edmund Burke in Europe* (2017), pp. 55–74; and *W-K*, I, p. 314. Discussion of the French Revolution will be a major theme in Volume 3 of *The Wodrow–Kenrick Correspondence*.

before L^ds. Stanhope[13] & Effingham[14] &c & after dinner offered the copy of an address to the National assemb[l]y at Paris, on their steadiness & success.[15]

I had much more to say– but must defer it at present. Many thanks for Burns– he has again made us laugh heartily– tho' I am no violent admirer of ridicule. Hypocricy & grimace[16] is certainly its fair game. But the satire is too local and personal to last long. Without your notes we sh^d. have been quite in the dark.

Mary rec^d. Miss Nelly's long entert^g. Epistle– w^ch. she means to answer soon. We all unite in every kind wish & affectionate for you & yours. I am as ever

Yours most aff^ly.
S.K.

## Letter 153: Samuel Kenrick to James Wodrow, 24 February 1790

Place: Bewdley
Addressed: D^r. Wodrow / near / Irvine / N. Britain
Postmarked: London February the Twenty sixth 1790
Franked: Free Westcote
Stamped: FE/26/
Note on printed sheet in SK's hand: NB The 2nd. Meet^g. The Resol^ns. were much fuller in the 1st.[1]

My dear Friend

The inclosed & annexed printed papers will shew that I have some excuse to plead in my favour for not acknowledging your kind l^r. of the 5th. Ult^o. sooner.[2]

---

[13] Charles Stanhope (1753–1816), third earl Stanhope, was a parliamentary reformer, an early member of the Society for Constitutional Information, a supporter of reform in church and state, favouring universal toleration, and chairman of the London Revolution Society.

[14] Thomas Howard (1747–91), third earl of Effingham, viewed by Dissenters as a friend. Davis, *Committees for Repeal of the Test and Corporation Acts*, p. 5, entry 16.

[15] For the London Revolution Society's 'Congratulatory Address to the National Assembly of France', unanimously resolved on 4 Nov. 1789, see *The Correspondence of the Revolution Society in London, with the National Assembly, and with Various Societies of the Friends of Liberty in France and England* (1792), p. 3.

[16] 'grimace': '1. a distortion of the countenance from habit, affectation, or insolence; 2. air of affectation'. Johnson's *Dictionary*.

---

[1] A single printed sheet is included with this letter titled *A Meeting of the Delegates from the Congregations of Protestant Dissenters in the County of Worcester*, 27 January 1790, signed S. Kenrick, Secretary (with a handwritten note added). See Plate 11.

[2] Missing letter by Wodrow, 5 Jan. 1790.

I duly rec^d. 11 Copies of your work, of w^ch. I accepted one as a token of your friendship in honour of the learned & worthy author our common Instructor– I gave one to M^rs. Roberts,[3] as it was your intention it sh^d. be so, & another to M^r. Wigan– w^th. the best inscriptions I could make in each. I also ordered one to Ben. Dawson[4] from London– as a mem^to. of your friendship & mine. From all whom I have received & now transmit to you the warmest & most affectionate acknowledgements. And inclosed I send you my Draft on Ja^s. Finlay of Glasgow[5] £5"8– for [ni]ne copies. So that matter is settled. How does the sale go on? Our neighbours here are very quiet about it: tho' they expressed great impatience before it came. The Life gives great satisfaction– particularly to your friends– who say they see you in every page of it. M^rs. Roberts will do herself the pleasure to write you her sentiments herself– she intended doing it to night: but some unexpected interruption put it out of her power. She & her charming daughter[6] beg to be remembered to you & yours in the most affectionate manner. So you may expect to hear from Bewdley very soon again. As to any trouble ab^t. D^r. M^cK.[7] proposals– I never thôt of it. I am only sorry my poor endeavours had so little effect– at least to my knowledge. They have been handed ab^t. at Worcester to the B^p. & his clergy by our fr^d. D^r. J.[8] who is happy to serve his friends & countrymen. My only wish & hope is that they have given their orders to the Booksellers– to me they have given none. They were warmly recommended to Birm^m. too– & now lie at Shrewsbury, w^th. my friends Mess^rs. Eddowes[9]– who advisd me that they had many orders for your work.

Your Critique on Campbell was highly pleasing to me & my friend W.[10]– whom you have almost tempted to get it & tred in your steps. But he says he has not eyes– & I know his hands are pretty full, having now 3 pupils. I wish w^th. you that ^the^ D^r. w^d. go on to the Acts.[11] To me it seems the easiest– & the most

---

[3] Betty Carolina Roberts. See Letter 103.
[4] Benjamin Dawson. See Letter 150.
[5] James Finlay of Finlay, Robert & Co., Merchants. See Letter 90.
[6] Caroline Aylesbury Roberts. See Letter 143.
[7] Dr James Macknight. See Letter 87.
[8] William Jesse.
[9] Presumably SK's nephew-in-law, Ralph Eddowes (see Letter 142); and Joshua Eddowes (1724–1811), a Dissenter and bookseller in Shrewsbury from 1749–1810, who printed and sold books in both English and Welsh. Isabel Rivers, *Vanity Fair and the Celestial City: Dissenting, Methodist, and Evangelical Literary Culture in England, 1720–1800* (Oxford, 2018), pp. 35–36.
[10] Thomas Wigan.
[11] JW provides a short critique of George Campbell, *The Four Gospels, Translated from the Greek* (1789), at the end of Letter 148. However, as he does not mention the book of Acts in that paragraph, JW probably said more in the missing letter of 5 Feb. 1790.

entertaining– pardon the familiarity of the expression– part of holy writ. Perhaps on that acc^t. it is supposed to stand in less need of elucidation. But its singularity– being an unique– & the variety of its subjects– are matters highly deserving notice in these enlightened times.

The independent unbiased sentiments of D^r. Campbell must make his work highly acceptable to every impartial mind– w^ch. his skill in languages & extensive knowledge must eminently qualify him for. As to his petulance to D^r. P.[12]– I am sorry for it on his own acc^t. & not on the D^rs. I believe them both to be honest & sincere searchers after truth– & equally deserving of honour & fame. Should not they have the same opinion of each other? If so why should one wish to hurt the other?

With regard to our present translation of the Bible it must carry a great bias w^th. it, from the preconceiv'd opinions w^ch. the translators then held of the controversial subjects of the times. They were it is presumed deeply tinged w^th. Calvinism. Most certainly they were Trinitarians. And consequently they would translate the Bible in conformity to their Trinitarian notions. A Socinian w^d. justly do the same. From this circumstance the english text must always have great weight on that sight the argument.[13] The plan therefore of D^r. C. must be of great advantage only in this point of view.

I long to see D^r. Magill's Answers & to hear farther particulars of that extraordinary transaction.[14] Yours was the advice of friendship, wisdom & christianity. If the good & honest could but keep up to, what a triumph would it be over their enemies!– only remember your friend D^r. Price– for you know him personally– I only from his writings– what bitter, what venimous, what hellish invectives are now poured out upon him– w^th. cutting sarcasms, whose the stings are perhaps the most irritating– He seems to smile w^th. sovereign contempt– or perhaps pity– for they certainly do not know what they ^do^:[15] Nay he continues on in his old

---

[12] Joseph Priestley.

[13] This is an accurate transcription of the Ms. However, SK surely meant to write 'on that side of the argument'.

[14] For a study of the controversy over M'Gill's *Practical Essay on the Death of Jesus Christ* (1786), see Fitzpatrick, 'Varieties of Candour'.

[15] 'Father, forgive them, for they know not what they do.' Luke 23:34. Two weeks before SK wrote this letter, in a parliamentary speech, Edmund Burke attacked the French Revolution and its British supporters. *Substance of the Speech of the Right Honourable Edmund Burke, in the Debate on the Army Estimates, in the House of Commons, on Tuesday, the 9th Day of February, 1790. Comprehending a Discussion of the Present Situation of Affairs in France* (1790). Price confided to a Dissenting MP that 'I think it very hard to be charged, as I now am, with being a Republican, after repeatedly in my

tract & rouses their envy, malice & animosity to a still higher pitch– in shewing every day new instances of respect & veneration from foreigners w<sup>ch</sup>. his own countrymen refuse him.– He has not only Horace's murus aeneus[16]– but the more impe^ne^trable christian panoply– to ward off all the darts of Satan.[17] I trust D<sup>r</sup>. Magill will put on the same & that I shall soon hear of his compleat victory. But how happy must he be to have so many able friends to assist him in the glorious cause! & that your established forms may be so easily reconciled to the sure & broad basis of Scripture. Your numerous opponents, w<sup>th</sup>. their intemperate zeal & self conceit– I know well are a most formidable host to contend w<sup>th</sup>.– and this brings me to our business, the Test Acts– w<sup>ch</sup>. you see in every newspapers– what a noise they make.[18]

This is but a trifling sample of what I intend to pester you w<sup>th</sup>. Our first & great tryal of skill comes on next tuesday the 2nd. Mch. M<sup>r</sup>. Fox has generously untertaken to introduce it into the House of Com. & we expect all his friends except Burke– who never liked us nor our cause[19]– upon our side but alas we have the K– god bless him & the minister[20]– tho' I cannot think so meanly of him that he is hearty– & the church– that is the high flyers– among whom your cousin Horsley makes a flaming figure. So that we do not expect to carry it even there. But we shall see who are our friends– for the call of the House it is expected will bring a greater number of members together than has been these 50 years at the fall of Walpole.[21]

---

publications declaring the contrary'. Richard Price to [William Smith], in *Correspondence of Richard Price*, III, p. 272. By November, Price was being criticized at length as a 'man much connected with literary caballers, and intriguing philosophers' in Burke's *Reflections on the Revolution in France: And on the Proceedings in Certain Societies in London Relative to that Event* (1790). Thomas, *Richard Price*, ch. 15, cited at p. 315.

[16] 'Walls of bronze'. Horace, *Odes*, III, iii, line 65.

[17] 'Put on the full armour of God...wherewith ye shall be able to quench all the fiery darts of the wicked.' Ephesians 6:11–16.

[18] Ditchfield, 'The Parliamentary Struggle over the Repeal of the Test and Corporation Acts, 1787–1790'.

[19] See Fitzpatrick and Page, 'Edmund Burke and Rational Dissent', especially pp. 71–74.

[20] George III and William Pitt, the prime minister.

[21] The call of the House ensured that the debate on 2 March was well attended. It was a device, occasionally used by back-benchers, to bring the government to heel. Instead, in this case, it was used by Pitt to bring them to voice their overwhelming prejudices against the Dissenters. The latter had been given what they thought was 'a flattering prospect of future success' following the narrow defeat of their repeal motion on 8 May 1789 by only twenty votes (102:122) in a poorly attended debate. When Fox gave notice on 15 February 1790 that he would move for the repeal of the Test and Corporation Acts, Pitt's immediate response was to move for a call of the House to take place before the repeal debate on 2 March, thus giving MPs notice to attend, ensuring that the Dissenters' hopes would be crushed by 105 to 294 votes. The

*1790, FEBRUARY 24*

*NB. The 2nd meet[in]g*
*The Resol[utions] were much fuller in the 1st*

At a MEETING of DELEGATES
From the several CONGREGATIONS of
## Proteſtant Diſſenters,
IN THE COUNTY OF WORCESTER,
Held at the ANGEL-INN, KIDDERMINSTER,
On WEDNESDAY the 27th of JANUARY, 1790.

NICHOLAS PEARSALL, Eſq. in the Chair,

IT WAS UNANIMOUSLY RESOLVED,

I. THAT we highly approve of the plan which has for its object the Union of all the Diſſenters into one compact and friendly body, that they may come forward by their Delegates, and with calmneſs and firmneſs claim our juſt rights, as men, as citizens, and as chriſtians.

II. THAT a County Meeting be held once a year, or oftener if neceſſary, to which each Congregation is expected to ſend Delegates, in order to maintain harmony and a friendly intercourſe among ourſelves.

III. THAT we eſteem ourſelves greatly obliged to the Birmingham Committee for their ſtrenuous exertions towards accompliſhing our common object, viz. the Repeal of the Teſt and Corporation Acts; but we think it more eligible to remain a diſtinct Diſtrict: at the ſame time we ſhall be always ready and happy to confer and unite with them upon any occaſion or emergency which may require our union or aſſiſtance.

IV. THAT Mr. WATSON of Kidderminſter, be appointed Delegate from the general Body of Proteſtant Diſſenters in this County, to attend the Committee in London; and in conjunction with the Secretary, to tranſact all matters relating to this buſineſs.

V. THAT a collection be made in each Congregation, in whatever mode they think proper, to defray the expences that may attend the proſecution of this buſineſs; and that the money collected be tranſmitted to the Treaſurer, as ſoon as may be convenient.

VI. THAT Mr. KENRICK of Bewdley, be appointed Treaſurer and Secretary for this Diſtrict; who, in conjuction with the Delegate, may ſummon an occaſional County Meeting whenever it ſhall appear to them neceſſary.

VII. THAT a reſpectful application be made by the Delegate and Secretary, in the name of this Diſtrict Meeting, to the Members for the County, for the City of Worceſter, and for the Boroughs of the County, requeſting their attendance and ſupport, when this Buſineſs ſhall be brought before the Houſe of Commons.

VIII. THAT our next County Meeting be held at the Star-and-Garter Inn, Worceſter, on Wedneſday the 4th of Auguſt, at ten in the morning, unleſs it ſhould be found neceſſary to call a meeting ſooner.

IX. THAT a number of theſe Reſolutions be immediately printed, and copies ſent to EDWARD JEFFERIES, Eſq. Chairman of the Committee in London; to SAMUEL SHORE, Eſq. Chairman of the Midland Diſtrict; to WILLIAM RUSSELL, Eſq. Chairman of the Birmingham Committee; and to the other Chairmen of the different Committees throughout the Kingdom who have honoured us with their correſpondence.

X. THAT the Thanks of this Meeting be given to the Rev. JOSEPH GUMMER, for his judicious management of the buſineſs ſince our laſt meeting; and likewiſe to the Chairman of this Meeting, for his acceptance of, and impartial conduct in the Chair.

S. KENRICK, Secretary.

11. Worcester Dissenters' Resolutions, 27 January 1790, printed enclosure, Letter 153.

But tho' we be baffled[22] it will not discomfit us. For we have already gained such an advantage as will in time gain us all we wish. We are united all as one man– tho' formally as discordant as different theological notions c$^d$. make us. We have all cordially adopted a plan, something similar to your ch. gov$^t$. w$^{ch}$. unites all prot. Dissenters throughout the whole Kingdom, by a chain of intercourse & communion advancing in order through successive gradations to a representation of the whole body in a general & national meeting in London[23]– But I must release you for the present w$^{th}$. our united best wishes & respects.

I am My d$^r$. Friends most affect$^e$.
S. Kenrick.

## Letter 154: James Wodrow to Samuel Kenrick, 2 June 1790
Place: Edinburgh
Addressed: Samuel Kenrick Esq. Bewdley / Worcestershire / June 2 1790
Postmarked: June 2 1790
Stamped: JU/<->
Notes: 90 / a single sheet
Notes in SK's hand: answ$^d$. 14th July 90 / 1st. Ann$^y$. of Fr. Rev$^n$.

My Dear friend

Your very agreeable letter of the 11th of May[1] was transmitted to me from Stev$^{tn}$. but I have been so wholly engrossed since I came here with the long sederunts of our Assembly & with the late dinners of friends that I have not found time to answer it & must now do it in a more hurried way than I woud wish as I am

---

Dissenters had to accept that they had met 'a very formidable opposition'. Davis, *Committees for Repeal of the Test and Corporation Acts*, pp. 34, 52, 56, 57. On 21 Jan. 1742, Walpole won a Commons vote which was 'essentially a motion of confidence' , in a very full House by only 253 to 250 votes. He resigned three weeks later. Stephen Taylor, 'Robert Walpole, first earl of Orford (1676–1745)', *ODNB*.

[22] 'to baffle': 'to elude, to confound, to crush; baffle, a defeat'. Johnson's *Dictionary*.

[23] The Dissenters' initial reaction to their defeat was to set up a united committee with delegates from England and Wales for the purpose of once more seeking repeal of the Test and Corporation Acts. With an atmosphere increasingly hostile to reform, it was unable to accomplish anything and disbanded in 1796. Davis, *Committees for Repeal of the Test and Corporation Acts*, pp. xii, 50–51.

---

[1] Missing letter: SK to JW, 11 May 1790.

obliged to leave this on friday. I <-> can therefore take but a very cursory view of the contents of yours. I am much obliged to M^r. & M^rs. Roberts for their continued regard & much grieved ~~for~~ ^at^ the accounts you have given me of the health of their amiable Daughter.[2] I hope for better accounts in your next. I thank you for the Extracts of Ben Dawsons & your Nephew's Letters.[3] Praise from such is soothing & too flattering. I am happy that the Sermons have been so well received both here & ^in^ England & that they are considered as little inferiour to those published by himself.[4]

The truce or Accomodation of D^r. Magills Prosecution though it did not please me yet gave much Satisfaction to the leaders of our Church & Indeed to all the sensible ^men^ in both parties at the same time great offense to the bigots & zealots.[5] Some Virulent things have been published Without effect, to rouse the zeal of the people not against the D^r. & his friends from whom no good ever was expected but against the Orthodox part of the Synod.[6] They have been accused as Traitors nothing better than Judas who betrayed his master with a kiss, as basely betraying the cause of truth & orthodoxy by accepting an ambiguous Decla^ra^tion (which they think means nothing) as satisfactory; though not one of the many damnable Errors ^in the book^ has been specifyed or retracted but left to infuse their poison into the minds of the people & not even any testimony given by the Church in support of the truth. I am the more reconciled to the quiet termination of that affair after having seen the Complexion of this Ass^ly. to which a great number had been chosen inimical to liberal sentiments who are much dissapointed at the loss of their great cause. Had it been canvassed here I am affraid it would not have been terminated without some censure on the D^r. or his

---

[2] Caroline Aylesbury Roberts. See Letter 143.

[3] Benjamin Dawson (see Letter 150); but as the SK letter is missing, the nephew is uncertain: possibly Ralph Eddowes, whom JW had met recently in Chester (Letter 142); or Timothy Kenrick, the unitarian minister in Exeter (Letter 112).

[4] i.e. those published by Leechman himself during his lifetime.

[5] For William M'Gill's 'declaration and apology', see *Proceedings of the Very Reverend the Synod of Glasgow and Ayr, held at Ayr on the 13th & 14th April 1790, Relating to some Late Publications of the Rev. Dr. William Mcgill, with the Final Decisions in that Cause* ([Glasgow], 1790).

[6] As well as James Russel, *The Reasons of our Lord's Agony in the Garden* (Kilmarnock, 1787) noted in Letter 152, see James Moir, *A Distinct and Impartial Account of the Process for Socinian Heresy against William M'Gill, D.D., One of the Ministers of Ayr: With Observations on his Explanations and Apology; And on the Proceedings and Final Decision of the Reverend Synod of Glasgow and Ayr, in that Dause. Dedicated to the Members, Commonly called the Orthodox Party without their Permission* (Edinburgh, 1790). James Moir was a minister of the Associate Synod (Burghers) at Tarbolton, Ayrshire from 1778 till 1800. John M'Kerrow, *History of the Secession Church* (Glasgow, 1841), p. 923; Strawhorn, *Ayrshire at the Time of Burns*, p. 127.

writings disgraceful to this poor Church. It was attempted to be revived by overtures from the Synod of Perth & Stirling to revive & inforce the old acts about purity of Doctrine. But these were strangled in their birth that is to say were <-> rejected by the Committee of Overtures & consequently never reached the Assembly but I must leave this for something more interesting to you.

Several different Overtures were transmitted by Synods and Presbys against the Test act all of which ^except one^ the Committee refused to transmit because they were conceived in high Language and by conjoining the cause of the Dissenters with ours must have involved us in an indecent & fruitless contest with the Parliament.[7] One of them only was brought into the Assembly from the Presby of Jedburgh the language of which was high enough as the test is ^here^ termed a profanation of that holy Ordinance ^sacred things^ but in this the Grievance is confined to Scotsmen members of this established Church ^& and the claim of freedom founded on the Articles of the Union^.[8] Thurs[y]. was appointed for the hearing of it. The debate lasted from 12 till after nine at night & it was incomparably the best & most interesting Debate I ever heard in our court.[9] Our leaders found themselves diserted by most of the conscientious men of their

---

[7] The Church of Scotland had refused to join in the wider campaigning in England and Wales for the repeal of the Test and Corporation Acts. This was a source of disappointment, but the Dissenters continued to hope for Scottish support. In March 1789 their repeal committee arranged for the distribution in Scotland of their *Case for Repeal*, and Samuel Heywood's influential *The Right of Protestant Dissenters to a Compleat Toleration Asserted* (1787, 2nd edn 1789), p. 71, which advocated the Scottish case, arguing, *inter alia*, 'If a Sacramental Test is really *necessary* for the security of an established religion, the kirk of Scotland is singularly unfortunate, since for holding the offices in Scotland none is required, and for holding those which it has in partnership in England, conformity to *another* church is necessary.' Only after the failure of the Dissenters' campaign on 2 March 1790 did the Scots attempt to secure repeal for themselves. Wodrow's letters are a valuable source for the campaign. Their case for repeal was put by Sir Gilbert Elliot on 10 May 1791, but the motion was defeated. See G. M. Ditchfield, 'The Scottish Campaign against the Test Act, 1790–1791', *Historical Journal*, 23 (1980), pp. 37–61; Davis, *Committees for Repeal of the Test and Corporation Acts*, minute 75, 6 March 1789.

[8] The Jedburgh overture read: 'The Test Act, or the obligation imposed upon Members of the Church of Scotland in Office to receive Sacrament according to the form of the Church of England, is not only a profanation of sacred things, but inconsistent with the doctrines & worship of the Presbytery established in Scotland at the revolution & confirmed by the Union'. Cited in Ditchfield, 'The Scottish Campaign against the Test Act', p. 39.

[9] For other accounts of this debate, see *Debates in the General Assembly of the Church of Scotland, on taking into Consideration an Overture from Jedburgh respecting the Test Act, May 27, 1790* (Edinburgh, 1790); George Cook, *The Life of the Late George Hill* (Edinburgh, 1820), pp. 274–78; *Scots Magazine*, 52 (July 1790), 351–52.

own party. The influence of the Commissioner[10] was tryed upon us in vain. His Minister[11] opened the Debate by a strong speech against the Overture which however hurt the cause as too much was said <-> or insinuated about the impropriety of the Application at the present time, the appearance of a factious spirit &c, &c. The Lord President[12] and the L$^d$. Advocate[13] spoke with decency & force on the same side. The last gave up the topick of Faction & inexpediency & said that in case we had any right from the Union ^Acts^ to be freed from the Grievance (which however he endeavoured to prove we had not) it was impossible our Application coud be considered as faction & pledged himself the Ministry woud not to consider it in that light. The ~~whole~~ cheif power however both of Argument & eloquence was on the opposite side. Harry Erskine[14] whom we consider as equal if not superiour to his Brother answered the President & Advocate with an energy Superiour to any thing I ever heard him to exert & this tho' he had been exhausted by some hours pleading in the court of the Session that same day. But without much preparation he was perfectly master of the cause & animated to a degree you cannot easily conceive. His speech had such an effect on a popular Assembly that though D$^r$. Hill[15] followed him by a very able speech on the

---

[10] David Leslie (1722–1802), sixth earl of Leven, and earl of Melville from 1797, was Lord High Commissioner of the General Assembly of the Church of Scotland from 1783 to 1801. *Acts of the General Assembly of the Church of Scotland, 1638–1842* (Edinburgh, 1843), pp. 815–82, *passim*.

[11] Rev. Samuel Martin (1740–1829), minister of Monimail, Fife, from 1776 until his death, and also chaplain to David Leslie, earl of Leven and lord high commissioner. FES, V, p. 166. Voted against the Jedburgh overture. *Scots Magazine*, 52 (July 1790), p. 352.

[12] Ilay Campbell (1734–1823), MP for Glasgow Burghs (1784–89), served as Lord President of the Court of Session from 1789 to 1808, for which he was created the first baronet Succoth in 1808. Though a quiet man and not a great orator, an impressive legal mind informed his written judgments. According to Henry Cockburn, Campbell 'was inferior to none of his brethren in depth or learning and was greatly superior to them all in a genuine and liberal taste for the law's improvement'. HPO, citing Henry Cockburn, *Memorials of His Time* (Edinburgh, 1856), p. 126. See Letter 80.

[13] Robert Dundas (1758–1819). Through the patronage of his uncle, Henry Dundas, he became solicitor general for Scotland in 1784, and then Lord Advocate in 1789. He also married Elizabeth (1766–1852), daughter of Henry Dundas, in 1787; and served as MP for Edinburghshire (1790–1801). See information in the entry on his father by J. A. Hamilton, revised by Michael Fry, 'Dundas, Robert, of Arniston (1713–1787)', ODNB; and in Michael Fry, *The Dundas Despotism* (Edinburgh, 1992), *passim*.

[14] Henry Erskine. See Letter 102. His younger brother was Thomas Erskine (1750–1823), Lord Chancellor in the Ministry of all the Talents (1806–07), but at this time he was a renowned barrister in the London criminal courts. He shared his brother's politics and was a highly successful defence counsel for the radical politicians tried for treason and sedition in London in the 1790s.

[15] Rev. Dr George Hill (1750–1819), minister of St Andrews and principal of St Andrews University. An impressive preacher, he helped found the Royal Society of Edinburgh in 1783,

opposite side yet he & his friends were obliged to give up the ground they had first taken,[16] ^viz the rejection of the Overture,^ & after a little softening of the first resolutions given in on our side– the Gen^l. Assem^ly. of the Ch. of Scotland *unanimously* adopted them ^in the^ following <—> terms

1. That by a fundamen^l. Art^le. in the treaty of Union the Prot^n. rel^n. & Presb^n. Ch. gov^t. are unalterably secured as the only estab^d. relig^n. & Ch. gov^t. within this part of the united King^m. & inseparable from the constitution of the British Empire.
2. That by the 4th. Art. of the Treaty of Un^n. it is provided that there shall be an equal communication of all rights priveledges & advant^gs. which belong to the subjects of either Eng^d. or Scotland except when it is otherwise explicitly agreed by the said Treaty.
3. That by an act of the Parl^t. of England passed in the 25 year of the reign of Char. II of a ^long^ recital[17] of the Test act,– and that in consequence of said act the Members of the Ch. of Sc. holding British Offices civil or military or receiving as British subjects any sallary fee &c, from his majesty &c, have been supposed liable to the penalty & forfeitures contained in said statute unless they receive the Sac^t. according to the usage of the Ch. of Eng^ld.
4. That as this construction of the Act constitutes a manifest inequality between the memb^rs. of the two establ^d. Churches of Gr. Br. injurious to the morals of the people of Scotland, & has a tendency to weaken & undermine the Ch. of Sc. it is the duty of the Gen^l. Ass^ly. as the Guardians of the religious establishment of Sc. to take every legal & constit^l. mode & to embrace the earliest proper oportunity to obtain effectual relief from the grievances arising from the said act of the Parl^t. of Eng: commonly called the Test act as affecting the Memb^rs. of this Ch[urch].

---

became professor of divinity and principal of St Mary's College, St Andrews, and served as moderator of the General Assembly of the Church of Scotland in 1789. FES, V, p. 236. Voted against the Jedburgh overture. *Scots Magazine*, 52 (July 1790), p. 352.

[16] In the original vote on the Jedburgh overture, other than those names noted above and below, the *Scots Magazine*, 52 (July 1790), p. 352 also reported the following as speaking for the overture: Mr Mitchell, Mr Fergusson of Craigdarroch, Professor Hamilton, and Mr Somerville (it had previously noted Dr [Thomas] Somerville; and against the overture, Dr Dalgleish.

[17] 'recital': 'restatement'. DSL.

5. The Appointment of a Committee of the Ass[ly]. instructed & impowered to carry the last resolution into effect viz the following Mins[rs]. & Elders The Moderator,[18] Prof[r]. Hill, D[r]. Carlysle[19] D[r]. Macnight Sir H. Moncrief[20] D[r]. Johnston[21] M[r]. Lapsley[22] M[r]. Dun[23] D[rs]. Charteris[24] & Somerville[25] M[r]. Walker[26] D[r]. Wodrow[27] & M[r]. Welsh[28] Mins[rs]. The L[d]. Prov[st]. of Ed[r].[29] The L[d]. President[30] L[d]. Advocate[31] The Earl of Lauderdale[32] ^The^ Solicitor

---

[18] Rev. Dr John Walker (1731–1803), minister of Colinton, south-west Edinburgh (1783–1803), having previously ministered at Glencorse (1758–62) and Moffat (1762–83); professor of natural history at the University of Edinburgh (1779–1803); moderator of the General Assembly of the Church of Scotland in 1790. In 1764 both the General Assembly and the Scottish Society for the Propagation of Christian Knowledge (SSPCK) had commissioned him to survey the Hebrides, and his report was published posthumously in two volumes in 1812. He was awarded an honorary MD by Glasgow in 1764 and a DD by Edinburgh in 1765. *FES*, I, p. 4.

[19] Rev. Dr Alexander Carlyle. See Letter 149.

[20] Rev. Sir Henry Moncrieff Wellwood (1750–1827), eighth baronet of Tullibole, minister of St Cuthbert's, Edinburgh (1775–1827); moderator of the General Assembly of the Church of Scotland in 1785; supporter of the SSPCK and of the Church of Scotland's Ministers' Widows' Fund, and he instigated the Society for Benefiting the Sons of the Clergy in 1790. Voted for the Jedburgh overture. *Scots Magazine*, 52 (July 1790), p. 352. *FES*, I, p. 98.

[21] Rev. Dr David Johnston (1734–1824), minister of North Leith (1765–1824). Voted for the Jedburgh overture. *Scots Magazine*, 52 (July 1790), p. 352. *FES*, I, p. 156.

[22] Rev. James Lapsley (1754–1824), minister of Campsie and Antermony (1783–1824), north of Glasgow. He was a principal actor in the effort to have Thomas Muir prosecuted for sedition in 1793, and had his manse set on fire in August 1797 because of his loyalty to the government. *FES*, III, p. 377. Voted for the Jedburgh overture. *Scots Magazine*, 52 (July 1790), p. 352.

[23] Rev. Alexander Dun (1718–90), minister of Cadder (1746–90), north of Glasgow. *FES*, III, p. 374. Voted for the Jedburgh overture. *Scots Magazine*, 52 (July 1790), p. 352.

[24] Rev. Dr Samuel Charters. See Letter 96. Voted for the Jedburgh overture. *Scots Magazine*, 52 (July 1790), p. 352.

[25] Rev. Dr Thomas Somerville (1741–1830), minister of Jedburgh (1772–1830) and author of *My Own Life and Times, 1741–1814* (1861). Voted for the Jedburgh overture. *FES*, II, pp. 127–28. *Scots Magazine*, 52 (July 1790), p. 352.

[26] Rev. Robert Walker (1755–1808), minister of the Canongate, Edinburgh (1784–1808), and the subject of Henry Raeburn's portrait known as 'The Skating Minister' (c. 1792–94), *FES*, I, pp. 25–26. Voted for the Jedburgh overture. *Scots Magazine*, 52 (July 1790), p. 352. *LBS*.

[27] JW.

[28] Rev. William Welsh (d. 1806), minister of Drumelzier in the Tweed Valley in the Scottish Borders (1787–1806). *FES*, I, p. 269. Voted against the Jedburgh overture. *Scots Magazine*, 52 (July 1790), p. 352.

[29] Thomas Elder of Forneth (1737–99), who had been lord provost of Edinburgh from 1788–90.

[30] Ilay Campbell (1734–1823), lord president of the Court of Session (1789–1808); see note above. Voted against the Jedburgh overture. *Scots Magazine*, 52 (July 1790), p. 352.

[31] Robert Dundas of Arniston, Lord Advocate (1789–1801); see note above. Voted against the Jedburgh overture. *Scots Magazine*, 52 (July 1790), p. 352.

[32] James Maitland (1759–1839), eighth earl of Lauderdale, Foxite Whig politician, first in the House of Commons as Viscount Maitland, and then as a Scottish Representative Peer from

Gen[l].[33] the Dean of Faculty (H. Erskine)[34] The Procurator for the Ch. (D[r]. Robison's Son)[35] Rob[t]. Macintosh Esq.[36] M[r]. Boyle of Shewalton[37] M[r]. Kennedy of Denure,[38] M[r]. Jo Clark Advocate[39] & Prof[t]. Dalziel[40] ruling Elders.

June 3[d] I must finish this long affair briefly as I go tomorrow & have too much to do. Sir H. Moncrief our Convener thought prop[r]. to call a meeting of the Comm[tee]. before we seperated viz on Tues[y]. The Officers of the Crown did not honour us with their presence nor L[d]. Lauderdale who is however a strong friend of the Measure– most of the Other Members were present. The Ass[ly]. debate was revived but soon repressed & confined to this point what are we to do. Two plans were proposed. First to apply in the name of the G. Assembly to the next Parliament. Second before that or any other step was taken to lay the Matter before the Gov[t]. i.e. the ^Kings^ Ministers. The last was opposed by many of us not that we were unwilling to honour or court them by every honest means but that in case they put their negative upon it we woud then go with a bad grace to Parl[t]. & with little hope of success. The Motions were voted only D[rs]. Hill & Carlysle (Chaplains) voted for the 2[d]. & then entered a protest that they shoud be free from blame if any bad consequence followed a measure which they considered as improvident. They then left us. And we went on to appoint a strong Memorial stating the grounds of our right to be freed from the grievance to be ~~laid~~ drawn up & laid before the next meeting. This will probably be sent immediately to the Ministry, and to all the Members of Parl[t]. I am somewhat affraid that we may be hurt by ^our conexion with^ M[r]. Ereskine L[d]. Laud[le]. & others who are strong fr[ds]. of the Minority.

---

1790. He was generally reformist, except on slave trade abolitionism; he only stopped defending slavery in 1806.

[33] Robert Blair of Avontoun (1741–1811), solicitor general for Scotland (1789–1806), who succeeded Ilay Campbell as lord president of the Court of Session.

[34] Henry Erskine, the Dean of the Faculty of Advocates. See Letter 79. Voted for the Jedburgh overture. *Scots Magazine*, 52 (July 1790), p. 352.

[35] William Robertson, son of Professor William Robertson, Procurator for the Church of Scotland. See Letter 99. Voted for the Jedburgh overture. *Scots Magazine*, 52 (July 1790), p. 352.

[36] Robert McIntosh or Macintosh. Unidentified. Voted for the Jedburgh overture. *Scots Magazine*, 52 (July 1790), p. 352.

[37] Patrick Boyle of Shewalton. See Letter 114.

[38] Thomas Kennedy of Dunure and Dalquharran. See Letter 84.

[39] John Clerk of Eldin (1757–1832), advocate and Foxite Whig politician in Edinburgh. He was solicitor general in the Ministry of All the Talents in 1806–07, and became a judge in the Court of Session in 1823.

[40] Andrew Dalzel. See Letter 149.

Yet it seemed wrong not to avail ourselves of their Abilities & mean to petition Minis^ry^ for what we consider our just & full right. For my own share independant of the Union treaty which was so much canvassed pro & con in the debate I cannot bring myself to think that the Wisdom & Equity of the Parliament will hesitate a moment in pronouncing that an Act of the Kingdom of England made more than twenty years before Scotland ~~were~~ ^was^ connected with ~~them~~ ^it^ can by any <—> construction bind Scotsmen. We surely can be bound only by British acts we need therefore no <u>repeal</u> but only a Declaratory statute. D^r^. Macnight[41] stood single & wished the point of law to be ascertained by Scots Officers refusing & standing trial before an English Jury. But this was thought to[o] little to satisfy the scruples of a whole Kingdom. The <u>Unanimity</u> of our ^As^^ly^^ Resolutions is a grand point towards their success. I know not if M^rs^. Wodrow has thanked M^rs^. K. <— —> when I left home.

God bless you all<br>J Wodrow

## Letter 155: Samuel Kenrick to James Wodrow, 25 September 1790

Place: Bewdley
Addressed: The Rev^d^. D^r^. Wodrow / Irvine / N. Britain
Postmarked: Bewdley Sep^r^. the twenty fifth 1790
Franked: Free G F Lyttelton[1]
Stamped: AIR

My dear Friend

Many thanks for your kind letter of the 23^d^ July (as dated on the frank):[2] ~~particularly~~ ^especially^ for the farther particulars respecting your Memorial,[3]

---

[41] Rev. Dr James Macknight. See Letter 87. Voted against the Jedburgh overture. *Scots Magazine*, 52 (July 1790), p. 352.

---

[1] i.e. George Fulke Lyttelton (1763–1828), MP for Bewdley (1790–96). See note 14 below.

[2] Missing letter: JW to SK, 23 July 1790. Missing except for the cover sheet: Addressed: Samuel Kenrick Esq^re^./Bewdley/Worcestershire. Postmarked: Irvine July twenty third 1790. Franked: W. Macdowall. Stamped: IRVINE/FREE/C/JU/27/90.

[3] The *Memorial of the Committee of the General Assembly of the Church of Scotland, Concerning the Test Act*, for presentation to Parliament, as noted by JW in Letter 154. In the event it was prepared

w[ch]. we are impatient to see presented & to know the effect.– Even to know the mode, you propose to adopt, would be kindly received.

As I am happy to send you every thing however trifling that passes here ^on that to me interesting subject^, you have the annexed Resolutions w[ch]. were agreed to at our last meeting at Worcester.[4] We had a most suitable sermon on the occasion preached by M[r]. Gentleman[5]– w[ch]. was the more striking as it was (by accident) the memorable St Bartholomew ^on^ whose day in 1662, above 2000 conscientious ministers were turned out of their churches by the infamous act of uniformity:[6] in w[ch]. he introduced many pertinent observations & anecdotes, that could not fail making lasting & useful impressions, particularly on the younger part of his audience.– As to the address mentioned on the other side, it went off well enough, by its novelty, among so many partial friends– but w[d]. make a very poor figure, among so many able & masterly productions, before an impartial– much more– censorious Public.

Your account of the proceedings of the general assembly on this subject met w[th]. the same applause it did at the [other associations]. Some indeed objected to the narrowness of its extent– w[ch]. was fully answered by your own argument– that in no other shape could it have promised the least shadow of success:

---

in Nov. 1790 and presented to Parliament on 18 April 1791. Ditchfield, 'The Scottish Campaign Against the Test Act', p. 42. See Letters 161, JW to SK, 29 Apr. 1791, and 164, JW to SK, 16 June 1791.

[4] See Plate 12.

[5] Rev. Robert Gentleman (1743–95), born in Shrewsbury, the son of Robert Gentleman (1701/2–57), a Scot. He grew up under Job Orton's wing (see Letter 119). Later in life he facilitated the publication of Orton's most important work, *A Short and Plain Exposition of the Old Testament*, 6 vols (1788–91). From Orton's care he proceeded to Daventry Academy (1764–67). In 1767 he was appointed minister of the congregation at Shrewsbury which had seceded following Job Orton's retirement in 1765. Orton had helped them build a new place of worship at Swan Hill, Shrewsbury. Gentleman supplemented his income with tutoring and running a boarding school. In 1779, he became minister of Llamas Street, Carmarthen and divinity tutor at Carmarthen Academy (1779–84). Returning to Worcestershire in 1784, he was appointed minister of the New Meeting, Kidderminster. He was a popular preacher of the Arian tendency. E. D. Priestley Evans, *History of the New Meeting House, Kidderminster* (1900), pp. 43–48; DAO; W-K, I, p. 285n.

[6] The Act of Uniformity of 1662 required all clergy to consent to the Book of Common Prayer, to renounce the Solemn League and Covenant (1643), and to subscribe to the Thirty-Nine Articles. It was a matter of coincidence that the deadline for its acceptance was on 24 August, the anniversary of the notorious St Bartholomew's Day Massacre of Protestants in Paris in 1572. It has been estimated that in the period 1660–62 just over 2,000 ministers and teachers in holy orders refused to submit to Anglican authority and lost their livelihoods. David J. Appleby, 'From Ejectment to Toleration in England, 1662–89', in Alan P. F. Sell, ed., *The Great Ejectment of 1662: Its Antecedents, Aftermath, and Ecumenical Significance* (Eugene, OR, 2012), pp. 67–124.

whereas if it do succeed to this extent, there will be the highest probability it will pave the way to the completion of all we ask. On the other hand what think you of our liberal friend Ben. Dawson, who in the same breath speaks in raptures of the French Revolution, commending the <u>spirit</u> & <u>prudence</u> of the Church ^of Scotland^, for confining their claim to the members ~~of the members of~~ of their communion residing in Scotland, holding offices of trust & power, & having nothing to do w[th]. those (miscreants) of another country, who dissent from both of the established churches?– was there ever greater John Bullism, in one who resided so long in Scotland?[7] Quantum mutatus![8]– I have tried to set him right– & impatiently wait his answer. I can only account for it by poor Ben's smarting, I am affraid under some strictures of our Bigotto Mastix[9] neighbour D[r]. P. who does not spare him:[10] & coming from nearly the same spot (near Leeds),[11] is perhaps more sensibly felt. But after all he supposes me to cry out– *"Lord, what stuff! What high church rant?"*– w[ch]. to be sure I did. This made me think it was all a hum– did he not subjoin that all we can advance appears to him only <u>specious</u>– but so it is– *and he cannot help his poor judgment*. When D[r]. Dawson can speak thus what can we to expect from those who have sucked in their prejudices w[th]. their mothers' milk, & have had them fostered, by education, example, interest, & every dazzling worldly advantage? What opposition must we still expect? To our comfort,

---

[7] This appears to refer to private correspondence from Dawson, as he did not publish anything on the French Revolution and the Church of Scotland at this time. Some insight into his general attitude toward government can be gained, however, from Benjamin Dawson, *The Benefits of Civil Government, a Ground of Praise to God. A Sermon, Preached on Occasion of the Late General Thanksgiving, for the Restoration of His Majesty's Health, April 23, 1789* (1789).

[8] Virgil, *Aeneid*, II, line 274: 'Quantum mutatus ab illo', translated as 'how changed he was'. Loeb Classical Library.

[9] Opponent of bigots.

[10] Kenrick was going over old ground here. There was no love lost between Priestley and Dawson. The latter responded to Priestley's charge that many of the clergy subscribed to the Thirty-Nine Articles insincerely in his edition of John Jones's *Free Thoughts on the Subject of a Farther Reformation of the Church of England; in Six Numbers: To Which are Added, the Remarks of the Editor* (1771) in which he accused Priestley of being 'more than uncandid and indecent'. Priestley responded with his *A Letter of Advice to those Dissenters who Conduct the Application to Parliament for Relief from Certain Penal Laws* (1773), which included section III: 'Of the Offence which the Author of this Pamphlet has given to those Dissenters who have Conformed to the Church of England, Particularly Dr Benjamin Dawson'. He argued that despite his conformity, Dawson's theology was Socinian. *ODNB*; *Works of Joseph Priestley*, XXII, pp. 464–72; Ditchfield, *Letters of Lindsey*, I, p. 149n. There is no later mention of Dawson in Priestley's publications, except in a letter that Priestley left Thomas Belsham to publish at his discretion after he had emigrated to the United States.

[11] Priestley was born in Fieldhead, some 6 miles south-west of Leeds, and Ben Dawson in nearby Halifax.

however, all the clergy do not seem~~ed~~ to ^have their minds^ ~~be~~ soured & perverted w^th. such monstrous prejudices. Two of my neighbours M^r. Wigan & M^r. Butt vicar of Kidderm^r. & King's chaplain[12]– both high bred Oxonians, entertain very different sentiments. They have the candour to acknowledge our merits– our undeserved hardships– & the equity, good policy, ^magnanimity^ & christian charity of granting us all we ask.

But there is no end to me, when I get upon this subject– I will return to your letter– Meanwhile remaining w^th. our united most affect^te. Regards
Yours S.K.

How different my good friend are your generous feelings of our ill usage– You have set me again on the subject. But ^I^ cannot be so ungrateful as to pass by such marked kindness & esteem, w^ch. every word of yours conveys, in our favour.– even if we sh^d. lose our point– you sh^d. deem it honourable to <u>fall</u> with <u>us</u>. How grateful is such a declaration to the heart of every– I was going to say, honest dissenter– but that does not do it justice– but to every enlightened mind & generous heart– to every sincere disciple of our gracious Lord & master, who declared his Kingdom was not of this world.

It is a pleasure to think we have such sensible men as Sir Ad. Fergusson[13]– he honoured me w^th. a letter, ^in answer to one^ w^ch. I wrote ^him^ in my official character, expressing the same sentiments in the most explicit terms. And last night I had a long conversation on the subject w^th. our member, who is a young man & near relation of M^r. Pitt's.[14] He joined me w^th. the greatest cordiality in every thing I asserted– & assured me that we must succeed, when our government has the wisdom & sound policy, to do what is right & just.

---

[12] Rev. George Butt (1741–95), vicar of Kidderminster 1787–1794. A pluralist for most of his life, he maintained a good relationship with the Dissenters in the town. Born at Lichfield, the son of a surgeon and apothecary, Butt had matriculated at Oxford University in 1761 as a member of Christ Church (BA 1765, MA 1768, and BD and DD 1793). After being ordained deacon in 1765, he was successively private tutor to Edward Winnington, rector of Stanford, and vicar of Clifton upon Teme. In 1783 he was appointed chaplain-in-ordinary to George III; he was also chaplain to James Ogilvy, seventh earl of Findlater and fourth earl of Seafield.

[13] Sir Adam Fergusson of Kilkerran, MP for the county of Ayrshire. See Letter 79.

[14] George Fulke Lyttelton (1763–1828) of Hagley succeeded his father (then Lord Westcote) as MP for Bewdley (1790–96). A supporter of William Pitt's administration, he did not fulfil his youthful promise and made no mark in the Commons. In 1791 he was reckoned hostile to the repeal of the Test Act in Scotland. He made way for a friend of the family in 1796, and his life thereafter was marred by bouts of mental illness. *HPO*.

I sh^d. like to know if you met w^th. D^r. Barnes[15]– or how he was received at Glasgow. It was a pity he sh^d. be there when so many of the Litterati were abroad.

Your warm panegyric on the French Revolution charmed me & many hearty friends to whom I communicated it. Our hearts & souls beat in unison w^th. you in every word.

I took the first opportunity of communicating your grateful regards & Miss Wodrow's, to our incomparable friend M^rs. R.[16] who rec^d. it w^th. all the kindness you c^d. wish– & begged always to be numbered among your affectionate friends.

We are much obliged w^th. your kind enquiry. Thanks to a kind & good providence, we have long enjoyed & do still, a great share of health with numberless other comforts.– My complaint was not dangerous– being a violent eruption on my skin–whc. is now got into my legs– but is almost gone.

In the last M. Rev^w. you will see a high encomium on a Sermon preached by M^r. Belsham[17] before the patrons of the New College at Hackney on the <u>importance of truth &c.</u>[18] It shews an enlarged & enlightened mind– & cannot fail to give eclat to our cause in general as well as to that Institution. But at the end there is a note w^ch. will interest you & some of your neighbours. "That reformation is still a distance." Note. "The Synod of Ayr have given recent proof, that the worst part of the spirit of popery, *persecution*, is not limited to the members of the Romish ~~Church~~ communion. But let not too severe a censure fall upon the unhappy sufferer, who, sinking under the pressure of infirmities & domestic woes, fainted

---

[15] Rev. Thomas Barnes (1747–1810), Presbyterian minister and reformer. He completed his education at the Warrington Academy (1764–68). His first charge was Cockey Moor (Ainsworth, near Bolton), following which he became co-minister·in 1780, with the Rev. Ralph Harrison, at Cross Street Chapel, Manchester, an influential congregation in the region. Through his influence Arianism remained the dominant form of heterodoxy among Dissenters in the north-west of England during his lifetime. He was awarded an honorary DD by Edinburgh University in 1784. Having helped to establish the Manchester Academy in 1786, he served as its first principal and ensured its survival during the difficult foundational years of the 1790s when Dissent was under threat. Although Joseph Priestley thought him hostile to Unitarianism, in 1792 Barnes signed the petition to Parliament for the repeal of the penal laws against unitarians and was said to be 'very hearty for the thing'. *ODNB*; Theophilus Lindsey to John Rowe, 6 March, 1792, in Ditchfield, *Letters of Lindsey*, II, p. 171.

[16] Betty Carolina Roberts. See Letter 103.

[17] Thomas Belsham, now at Hackney Academy since 1786. See Letter 112.

[18] *'The Importance of Truth, and the Duty of making an Open Profession of It: Represented in a Discourse delivered on Wednesday the 28^th of April, 1790, at the Meeting-house in the Old Jewry, London, to the Supporters of the New College, Hackney. By Thomas Belsham'*, *Monthly Review*, n.s., 2 (Aug. 1790), pp. 476–79. See also Fitzpatrick, 'Varieties of Candour', p. 49.

in the day of trial, & intimidated by threats of deprivation, renounced those principles, w^ch. in better days, as the result of calm enquiry, he had honestly avowed. The most ignorant & unrelenting of his inquisitors, cannot wish him severer torture than his own sad feelings & reflexions upon the present unfortunate occasion will necessarily create in a thoughtful & ingenuous mind. Need I mention the name of D^r. McGill the author of an excellent Treatise on the death of Christ– Quis talia fando–

Temperet a lachrymis![19] Adieu adieu.

---

[19] 'Who, in speaking such things, can refrain from tears?' A phrase derived from Virgil, *Aeneid*, II, lines 6–8: 'quis talia fando Myrmidonum Dolopumve aut duri miles Ulixi temperet a lacrimis?'; translated as 'what Myrmidon or Dolopian, or soldier of the stern Ulysses, could refrain from tears in telling such a tale?'. Loeb Classical Library.

At a numerous and respectable MEETING of the WORCESTERSHIRE DISTRICT

OF

## PROTESTANT DISSENTERS,

Held at the STAR-AND-GARTER, in WORCESTER,

The 24th of AUGUST, 1790,

JOSEPH HANCOX, Esq. in the Chair,

IT WAS AGREED UNANIMOUSLY,

THAT our warmest thanks be given to the Committee in *London*, for their unremitting zeal and perseverance in trying every legal and constitutional means for procuring the repeal of those unjust and impolitic acts, under which we have so long and so unmeritedly laboured.

To assure that respectable Committee of our hearty concurrence in the new mode they have adopted, of admitting an Agent from the different County Districts, as specified in the proceedings of the Meeting of Deputies and Delegates on the 4th and 5th of March last, and confirmed at their adjourned general meeting of the 13th of May.

That THOMAS RICKARDS, Esq. of *Hackney*, be appointed resident Agent for the County of *Worcester*, and our representative in the absence of our Delegate, in the standing Committee of Protestant Dissenters in *London*.

That thanks be returned to Mr. WATSON, of *Kidderminster*, our Delegate, for his faithful and cheerful discharge of the trust reposed in him, in assisting at the different meetings and conferences held in *London*, in March last; and that he be requested to continue our Delegate.

That our thanks, with every token of friendship and respect, be given to the Committees of the different Districts, who have favoured us from time to time with their friendly communications, which they may be assured will always be gratefully received and punctually acknowledged, with whatever may occur to us worthy of being transmitted to them in return.

In short, we wish to offer our warmest acknowledgements to all the friends of civil and religious liberty, whether in or out of Parliament, for every exertion they have made on this occasion, remembering " THAT NO EFFORT CAN BE LOST:" but especially to the authors of several excellent publications, whom we could with pleasure name, as an honour to our cause, but it is unnecessary; for the manly, liberal, and christian sentiments, which this contest has induced them to bring to light, will hand down the memory of their virtues and talents to future ages.

That the Secretary be requested to publish in the *Worcester* paper, the Address to the People of *England* from the Committee of Protestant Dissenters in *London*, appointed to conduct the application to Parliament for the Repeal of the Test Laws.

That the propriety of an address to the King, as proposed by the Midland District, be referred to the general Meeting of Delegates of the Protestant Dissenters in *London*.

That the thanks of this meeting be given to the Secretary, for his assiduity in transacting the business of the Dissenters in this County: that he be requested to continue in his office; and to publish the Address which he delivered this day to the County Meeting.

That the thanks of this Meeting be given to the Rev. ROBERT GENTLEMAN, for his excellent sermon, delivered this day, in favour of religious liberty.

That the next County Meeting be at *Bromsgrove*, at the *Golden-Cross*, on the Wednesday after the second Sunday in May next.—Service to begin at eleven of the clock.

That the Rev. JOHN BARRETT be appointed to preach at the next Meeting; and that the Rev. Mr. BUTTERWORTH, of *Evesham*, be his substitute, in case Mr. BARRETT should be prevented by any unforeseen accident.

That the nomination of the preacher be left to the select Committee.

That the Chairman of the day nominate that Committee.

That a number of these resolutions be printed, for the use of our District and other friends.

That the thanks of this Meeting be given to the Chairman, for his attention to the business of the day.

JOSEPH HANCOX, Chairman.

N.B. *It is desired that all correspondence relating to this business, be directed to our Secretary,* Mr. KENRICK, *of* Bewdley.

12. Worcester Dissenters' Resolutions, 24 August 1790, printed enclosure, Letter 155.

# APPENDIX A
## EXTRACT FROM NRS, CH2/197/6/519, MINUTES OF THE PRESBYTERY OF IRVINE, 13 FEBRUARY 1787

## Stevenston Manse

The old manse of this Parish of Stevenston being in a fragile condition having been reported by workmen to be unfit for any repairs we the Subscribing Heritors have resolved that it shall be pulled down and that it shall be rebuilt in a very convenient and sufficient manner by days wages together with an office house adjoining to it we adJudge that the sum of Two hundred and sixty pounds Sterling will be an adequate sum which we are to put into the hands of our Minister for that purpose together with the Sum of twelve pounds ten Shillings as a rent for one year and a half of a house in which he and his family are Lodged at present and ten Shillings more to James Auld Wright in Saltcoats whom we appoint Collector of the above and we hereby promise to pay our proportions according to our respective valuations of the above sums amounting in all to two hundred and seventy three pounds Ster the one half payable the first of April and the other half at Martinmas next.

You will please acquaint the Rev#. Presb#. with this and request them in our name to pass their decreet in the usual way for the above Sum that it may be raised in the Parish for the foresaid purposes. We are Revd Sir your obedient Servts. Signed Robert Cunningham Pat. Warner Robert Baillie Eliza. Cunningham Alexander Hamilton—Directed to the Mod#. of the Presb#. of Irvine.

D#. Wodrow also produced to the Presb#. and read a Letter from M#. Fairlie Esq#. of Fairlie Manager for the Right Hon#. the Earl of Eglintoun Signifying that in his Lordships name he concurred with the rest of the Heritors of the Parish of Stevenston in what relates to the above—All this being duely Considered by the Presb#. the Presb#. did and hereby do unanimously approve of and heartily concur with this generous free and voluntary agreement of the Heritors of the Parish of Stevenston among themselves—and they appoint that D#. Wodrow bring into next Presb#. a Signed Cess Roll[1] of the Parish of Stevenston with the Proprotions of the Several Heritors annexed thereto in the aforesaid sum of 273 pounds Ster in order that the Presb#. may then pass their Decreet upon the Same in Common form.

[1] 'Cess': 'an assessment tax or levy'. *DSL*.

APPENDIX B

## Letter 281: Richard Price to James Wodrow, 20 January 1790[1]

Place: Hackney
Addressed: D[r]. Wodrow / Stevenston / near Irvine / N.B.
Postmarked: London Twenty first January 1790
Franked: free Cha. Gould[2]
Note: from D[r]. Price

Dear Sir,

I return you my best thanks for the kind and agreeable letter with which I was favoured by you some time ago, and for sending me the Reports of the Trustees of the Widows Fund.[3] Having bestowed much attention on this Fund and held for many years a correspondence with the late D[r]. Webster[4] on the Subject of it, it cannot but be agreeable to me to be informed of its state and progress.

——I have received also the two volumes of D[r]. Leechman's Sermons.[5] I can scarcely tell you how kindly I take this present, and how much I have been affected and edify'd, particularly by your introduction containing the Analysis of his Lectures and the account of his life and death. May Heaven help me to imitate him in what may remain of a life now in its last stage and grant me such an end.

---

[1] This letter is also printed in in *Correspondence of Richard Price*, III, pp. 269–71.

[2] Charles Gould (1726–1806), also known as Charles Morgan, of Ealing, Middlesex. Lawyer and MP for Brecon (1778–87) and Breconshire (1787–1806). He seldom spoke in Parliament and supported the governments of Lord North and William Pitt. From 1773 until his death he served as president of the Equitable Life Assurance Society. *HPO*.

[3] *Report of the Trustees for Managing the Fund Established for a Provision for the Widows and Children of the Ministers of the Church of Scotland, &c. to the General Assembly of the said Church, held at Edinburgh*, published after its annual meeting in May.

[4] Dr Alexander Webster (1707–84), minister of the Tollbooth Kirk, Edinburgh. A leading member of the Popular party, he helped found a fund for the Widows and Children of the Ministers of the Church of Scotland. See *The Correspondence of Richard Price*, eds D. O. Thomas and W. Bernard Peach, 3 vols (Durham, NC, and Cardiff, 1983–94), I, pp. 104–13, 118–20.

[5] Leechman, William, *Sermons, by William Leechman, D.D., Late Principal of the College of Glasgow, to which is prefixed Some Account of the Author's Life, and of his Lectures, by James Wodrow, D.D., Minister at Stevenston*, 2 vols (1789).

APPENDIX B

I must farther thank you for D[r]. M'Gill's thanksgiving Sermon,[6] which I read with pleasure. I respect his character and abilities as well as his principles, and am sorry he should be made uneasy by the opposition of ignorance and bigotry. But such opposition must be expected, and it generally defeats its own end by promoting discussion and spreading liberal and just principles.

You will, I hope, Soon receive a Discourse which I delivered on the 4th of Nov:[r] last to the Revolution Society in London, and which it has not been possible for me to avoid publishing.[7] I have left it at M[r]. Hamilton's[8] with another for D[r]. Reid.[9] M[r]. Hamilton tells me he has now an opportunity of conveying them by a Gentleman who is returning to Scotland. You will learn from this Sermon and the Appendix to it, how much I agree with you in rejoicing in the events that have lately happen'd on the Continent. Never perhaps did an event happen more favourable to civil and religious liberty than the late Revolution in France. A glorious prospect seems, as you say in your letter, to be opening. A spirit is gone forth which is likely to shake to the foundations the long establish'd fabricks of superstition and tyranny.

I have sent you the Second Edition; but there is a third Edition just publish'd, which differing in nothing very material from the former Editions, I have sent you only the additions to it which have been printed separately in order to accommodate the purchasers of former editions.

I am, Dear S[r], with very great esteem and affection, your obliged and very humble Serv[t].

Rich[d]. Price

[6] William M'Gill, *The Benefits of the Revolution: A Sermon, Preached at Ayr, on the 5th of November, 1788, by William M'Gill, D. D. To which are Added, Remarks on a Sermon, Preached on the Same Day, at Newton upon Ayr; Very necessary for all the Readers of said Sermon* (Kilmarnock, 1789). See Letter 146.
[7] Richard Price, *A Discourse on the Love of our Country, Delivered on Nov 4, 1789, at the Meeting-house in the Old Jewry, to the Society for Commemorating the Revolution in Great Britain* (1789).
[8] Presumably John Hamilton (1740–92), a London merchant and Louisa Wodrow's brother.
[9] Thomas Reid (1710–96), professor of moral philosophy at University of Glasgow (1764–96).

# VOLUME 2
# PRIMARY SOURCES CITED

A Letter by Students of Divinity, Law, Medicine, and Philosophy, in Glasgow College, to the Reverend William Taylor, D.D. Minister of the Inner High Church in Glasgow; Who, by Holding that Office, is appointed by the Foundation Charter of Glasgow College to be one of its Ordinary Visitors (Glasgow, 1785).

A Letter from a Blacksmith to the Ministers and Elders of the Church of Scotland: In which the Manner of Public Worship in that Church is Considered (1759).

A Meeting of the Delegates from the Congregations of Protestant Dissenters in the County of Worcester ([Kidderminster?], 1790).

A Short Catechisme, or Playne Instruction, Conteynynge the Sume of Christian Learninge, Sett Fourth by the Kings Maiesties Authoritie, for all Scholemaisters to Teache... Published by the Kinges Maiesties Authoritie (1553).

A Speech, Addressed to the Provincial Synod of Glasgow and Ayr, Met at Ayr, 14th April 1784, by one of the Members of that Court, upon Patronage (Edinburgh, 1784).

Acts of the General Assembly of the Church of Scotland, 1638–1842 (Edinburgh, 1843).

Ainsworth, Robert, Thesaurus Linguae Latinae Compendiarius: Or, A Compendious Dictionary of the Latin Tongue: Designed for the Use of the British Nations, 2 vols (1736).

An Universal Etymological English Dictionary: Comprehending the Derivations of the Generality of Words in the English Tongue, Either Ancient or Modern (1721).

Anstey, Christopher, The New Bath Guide (1766).

Arnot, Hugh, The History of Edinburgh (Edinburgh, 1779).

Arthur, Archibald, Discourses on Theological and Literary Subjects. By the Late Rev. Archibald Arthur, M.A. ...with an Account of Some Particulars in His Life and Character by William Richardson (Glasgow, 1803).

[Associate Synod of the Secession Church], A Warning Against Socinianism: Drawn up and Published by a Committee of the Associate Synod. In which, Particular Notice is Taken of a Late Publication, Intituled, a Practical Essay upon the Death of Jesus Christ, by Dr. M'Gill (Falkirk, 1788).

Bagot, Lewis, A Sermon Preached at the Cathedral Church in Norwich, on Thursday August 21, 1783. On Occasion of the Anniversary meeting of the Governors of the Norfolk and Norwich Hospital. By Lewis Lord Bishop of Norwich (Norwich, 1783).

*Bailey's Northern Directory; or, Merchant's and Tradesman's Useful Companion for the Year 1781...in every principal town from the River Trent to Berwick upon Tweed; with the Cities of London and Westminster, Edinburgh and Glasgow* (Warrington, 1781).
*Bailey's Western and Midland Directory...for the Year, 1783* (Birmingham, 1783).
Baron, Richard, *The Pillars of Priestcraft and Orthodoxy Shaken* (1752; 2nd edn 1768).
Bayle, Pierre *Dictionnaire Historique et Critique* (Rotterdam, 1697).
Beattie, James, *Evidences of the Christian Religion* (Edinburgh, 1786).
Bellamy, George Anne, *An Apology for the Life of George Anne Bellamy* (1785).
Belsham, Thomas, *The Importance of Truth, and the Duty of making an Open Profession of It: Represented in a Discourse delivered on Wednesday the 28th of April, 1790, at the Meeting-house in the Old Jewry, London, to the Supporters of the New College, Hackney* (1790).
Belsham, William, *Memoirs of the Reign of George III. To the Session of Parliament Ending A.D. 1793*, 4 vols (1795).
Belsham, Thomas, *Freedom of Enquiry, and Zeal in the Diffusion of Christian Truth, Asserted and Recommended in a Discourse Delivered at Bristol, July 9, 1800, Before the Society of Unitarian Christians, Established in the West of England, for Promoting Christian Knowledge and the Practice of Virtue, by the Distribution of Books* (1800).
Belsham, Thomas, *Memoirs of the Late Theophilus Lindsey* (1812).
Blackburne, Francis, *Memoirs of Thomas Hollis*, 2 vols (1780).
Blair, Hugh, *Lectures on Rhetoric and Belles Lettres* (1783; 2nd edn 1785).
Blair, Hugh, *Sermons*, 5 vols (Edinburgh, 1777–1801).
Boswell, James, *An Account of Corsica: The Journal of a Tour to that Island; and Memoirs of Pascal Paoli* (1768).
Boswell, James, *Letter to the People of Scotland: On the Present State of the Nation* (Edinburgh, 1783).
Boswell, James, *Journey of a Tour to the Hebrides* (1785).
Boswell, James, *Letter to the People of Scotland on the Alarming Attempt to Infringe the Articles of Union and Introduce a Most Pernicious Innovation by Diminishing the Number of Lords of Session* (Edinburgh, 1785).
Boswell, James, *The Life of Samuel Johnson*, 2 vols (1791).
Boswell, James, *Boswell on the Grand Tour: Germany and Switzerland 1764*, ed. Frederick A. Pottle (1953).
Boswell, James, *Boswell: The Applause of the Jury, 1782–1785*, eds I. S. Lustig and F. A. Pottle (1981).
Bourne, Samuel, *Twenty Sermons on the Most Serious and Practical Subjects of the Christian Religion, Fitted for the Use of Private Families Preached by the Late Revd Samuel Bourn, to which is Added Some Memoirs of the Life of the Author* (1755).
Brown, Stephen W. and Warren McDougall, eds, *The Edinburgh History of the Book in Scotland: Vol. 2, Enlightenment and Expansion, 1707–1800* (Edinburgh, 2012).
Brutus, *Vindiciae, Contra Tyrannos: Or, Concerning the Legitimate Power of a Prince over the People, and of the People over a Prince*, trans. and ed. George Garnett (Cambridge, 2003).
Brydges, S. E., *A Biographical Peerage of the Empire of Great Britain*, 4 vols (1808–17).

Brydone, Patrick, *A Tour through Sicily and Malta: In a Series of Letters to William Beckford, esq. of Somerly in Suffolk*, 2 vols (1773).
Bull, George, *The Primitive and Apostolical Tradition of the Doctrine Received in the Catholic Church, Concerning the Divinity of our Saviour Jesus Christ* (1703).
Burke, Edmund, *Reflections on the Revolution in France: And on the Proceedings in Certain Societies in London Relative to that Event* (1790).
Burke, Edmund, *Substance of the Speech of the Right Honourable Edmund Burke, in the Debate on the Army Estimates, in the House of Commons, on Tuesday, the 9th Day of February, 1790. Comprehending a Discussion of the Present Situation of Affairs in France* (1790).
Burney, Charles, *An Account of the Musical Performances in Westminster Abbey and the Pantheon, May 26th, 27th, 29th; And June the 3d and 5th, 1784* (1785).
Burns, Robert, *Poems, Chiefly in the Scottish Dialect* (Kilmarnock, 1786).
Burns, Robert, *The Works of Robert Burns*, ed. James Currie, 4 vols (1800).
Burns, Robert, *The Poems and Songs of Robert Burns*, ed. James Kinsley, 3 vols (Oxford, 1968).
Campbell, Alexander, *A Journey from Edinburgh through Parts of North Britain*, 2 vols (1802).
Campbell, George, *Dissertation on Miracles: Containing an Examination of the Principles Advanced by David Hume, Esq; in an Essay on Miracles* (Edinburgh, 1762).
Campbell, George, *The Four Gospels, Translated from the Greek, with Preliminary Dissertations, and Notes Critical and Explanatory*, 2 vols (1789).
Campbell, Thomas, *The Life and Letters of Thomas Campbell*, ed. William Beattie, 2 vols (1850).
Campbell, William, *A Vindication of the Principles and Character of the Presbyterians of Ireland. Addressed to the Bishop of Cloyne, in Answer to his Book, Entitled, The Present State of the Church of Ireland* (Dublin, 1787).
Campbell, William, *An Examination of the Bishop of Cloyne's Defence of his Principles; with Observations on Some His Lordship's Apologists, Particularly the Rev. Dr Stock: Containing an Inquiry into Establishment; and also, an Historical Review of the Political Principles and Conduct of Presbyterians and Episcopals in Great-Britain and Ireland. With A Defence of the Church of Scotland from the Charge of Persecution brought by His Lordship's Apologist. By William Campbell, D.D. Minister of Armagh* (Belfast, 1788).
Cappe, Newcome, *Remarks in Vindication of Dr Priestley, on that Article of the Monthly Review for June, 1783, Which Relates to the First Part of Dr Priestley's History of the Corruptions of Christianity* (1783).
Carlyle, Alexander, *Autobiography of the Rev. Dr Alexander Carlyle, Minister of Inveresk, Containing Memorials of the Men and Events of his Time*, ed. John Hill Burton, 3rd edn (Edinburgh, 1861).
Chambers, Ephraim, *Cyclopaedia; or, An Universal Dictionary of Arts and Sciences... Compiled from the Best Authors*, 2 vols (1728).
Chambers, William and Robert, *Chambers's Information for the People: A Popular Encyclopedia* (Edinburgh, 1849).
Chapman, George, ed., *Original Essays and Translations* (Edinburgh, 1780).

Charters, Samuel, *A Sermon Preached at the Anniversary Meeting of the Society in Scotland for Propagating Christian Knowledge, on Thursday, June 3. 1779* (Edinburgh, 1779).
Charters, Samuel, *A Sermon on Intercession* (Hawick, 1785).
Charters, Samuel, *Sermons* (Edinburgh, 1786).
Christie, Alexander, *The Holy Scriptures the Only Rule of Faith, and Religious Liberty* (Montrose, 1790).
[Christie, Thomas], *Miscellanies: Literary, Philosophical and Moral*, 4 vols (1788).
Cicero, Marcus Tullius, *Cato; An Essay on Old-Age. By Marcus Tullius Cicero: With Remarks*, ed. William Melmoth (1773).
Clarkson, Thomas, *An Essay on the Slavery and Commerce of the Human Species* (1786).
Coleridge, H. N., *Specimens of the Table Talk of the Late Samuel Taylor Coleridge*, 2 vols (1835).
Collins, Anthony, *A Discourse of Free-Thinking* (1713).
Cowper, William, *The Task: A Poem* (1785).
Coxe, William, *Travels into Poland, Russia, Sweden and Denmark*, 3 vols (1784).
Crawfurd, George, *A General Description of the Shire of Renfrew* (Paisley, 1818).
Dalrymple, David, Lord Hailes, *Annals of Scotland, From the Accession of Malcolm III, surnamed Canmore, to the Accession of Robert I* (Edinburgh, 1776).
Dalrymple, David, Lord Hailes, *Annals of Scotland: From the Accession of Robert I, surnamed Bruce, to the Accession of the House of Stewart* (Edinburgh, 1779).
Dalrymple, David, Lord Hailes, *An Inquiry into the Secondary Causes which Mr. Gibbon has Assigned for the Rapid Growth of Christianity* (Edinburgh, 1786).
Dalrymple, William, *A History of Christ, for the Use of the Unlearned: With Short Explanatory Notes and Practical Reflections. Humbly Recommended to Parents, and Teachers of Youth in Schools* (Edinburgh, 1787).
Dalrymple, William, *A Sequel to the Life of Christ, Lately Published, For the Use of the Unlearned; Containing Practical Reflexions, Suited to Each Section* (Ayr, 1791).
Dashkova, Ekaterina Romanovna, *The Memoirs of Princess Dashkova*, trans. and ed. Kyril Fitzlyon (Durham, NC, 1995).
Dawson, Benjamin, *The Benefits of Civil Government, a Ground of Praise to God. A Sermon, Preached on Occasion of the Late General Thanksgiving, for the Restoration of His Majesty's Health, April 23, 1789* (1789).
*Debates in the General Assembly of the Church of Scotland, on taking into Consideration an Overture from Jedburgh respecting the Test Act, May 27, 1790* (Edinburgh, 1790).
*Dictionarium Britannicum* (1730; 2nd edn 1736).
Emlyn, Thomas, *An Humble Inquiry into the Scripture Account of Jesus Christ* (1702).
Equiano, Olaudah, *The Interesting Narrative and Other Writings*, ed. Vincent Carretta (New York, 2003).
Evanson, Edward, *A Letter to the Right Reverend the Lord Bishop of Litchfield and Coventry [Richard Hurd]; wherein the Importance of the Prophecies of the New Testament, and the Nature of the Grand Apostacy Predicted in Them, are Particularly and Impartially Considered* (1777).
Fagaras, Josephus Pap de, *Dissertation sur la Force Primitive, qui a Remporté le Prix Proposé par L'Académie Royale des Sciences et Belles-Lettres pour l'année MDCCLXXIX* (Berlin, 1780).

Farmer, Hugh, *Inquiry into the Nature and Design of Christ's Temptation in the Wilderness* (1761).
Farmer, Hugh, *A Dissertation on Miracles* (1771).
Farmer, Hugh, *An Essay on Demoniacs* (1775).
Ferguson, Adam, *An Essay on the History of Civil Society* (Edinburgh, 1767).
Ferguson, Adam, *The History of the Progress and Termination of the Roman Republic*, 3 vols (Edinburgh, 1783).
Fielding, Henry, *Joseph Andrews* (1742).
Fielding, Henry, *The History of the Adventures of Joseph Andrews and of his Friend Mr Abraham Adams* (1742).
Fordyce, James, *Addresses to the Deity* (1785).
Fullarton, William, *A View of the English Interests in India* (1787).
Fullerton, Alexander, *The Measures of Toleration: A Sermon, Preached before the Synod of Aberdeen, at Aberdeen, October 8th, 1782* (Aberdeen, 1783).
Galt, John, *The Ayrshire Legatees: Or, The Pringle Family* (Edinburgh, 1821).
Geddes, Alexander, *The Holy Bible: Or the Books Accounted Sacred by Jews and Christians*, 2 vols (1792; 1797).
Geddes, James, *An Essay on the Composition and Manner of Writing of the Antients, Particularly Plato* (Glasgow, 1748).
Gentleman, Robert, *A Short and Plain Exposition of the Old Testament*, 6 vols (1788–91).
Gerard, Alexander, *The Influence of the Pastoral Office on the Character Examined* (Aberdeen, 1760).
Gerard, Alexander, *The Corruptions of Christianity Considered as Affecting its Truth: A Sermon, Preached before the Society in Scotland for Propagating Christian Knowledge* (Edinburgh, 1792).
Gibbon, Edward, *History of the Decline and Fall of the Roman Empire*, 6 vols (1776–88).
Gibbon, Edward, *Memoirs of My Life*, ed. Betty Radice (1984).
Goldie, John, *Essays on Various Important Subjects, Moral and Divine. Being an Attempt to Distinguish True from False Religion*, 3 vols (Glasgow, 1779).
Goldie, John, *The Gospel Recovered from Its Captive State*, 5 vols (1785).
Hakewill, George, *An Apologie of the Power and Providence of God in the Government of the World* (1627).
Hamilton, Robert, *An Introduction to Merchandise* (Edinburgh, 1777).
Harris, James, *Hermes: Or, A Philosophical Inquiry Concerning Language and Universal Grammar* (1751).
Hayley, William, *Triumphs of Temper: A Poem* (1781).
Hayley, William, *An Essay on Epic Poetry; in Five Epistles to the Revd Mr Mason* (1782).
Hayley, William, *Plays of Three Acts; Written for a Private Theatre* (1784).
Hewat, Alexander, *An Historical Account of the Rise and Progress of the Colonies of South Carolina and Georgia*, 2 vols (1779).
Heywood, Samuel, *The Right of Protestant Dissenters to a Compleat Toleration Asserted* (1787).
*Historical Account of Newcastle-upon-Tyne, Including the Borough of Gateshead* (Newcastle-upon-Tyne, 1827).

Hoadley, Benjamin, *A Preservative against the Principles and Practices of Non-Jurors* (1716).

[Holland, Philip, John Seddon, and Richard Godwin], *A Form of Prayer and a New Collection of Psalms, For the Use of a Congregation of Protestant Dissenters in Liverpool* (Liverpool, 1763).

Home, Henry, Lord Kames, *Loose Hints upon Education, Chiefly Concerning the Culture of the Heart* (Edinburgh, 1781).

Horace, *Satires. Epistles. The Art of Poetry*, trans. H. Rushton Fairclough (Cambridge, MA, 1926).

Horne, George, *A Letter to the Reverend Doctor Priestley, by an Undergraduate* (Oxford, 1787).

Horne Tooke, John, *Epea Pteroenta. Or, The Diversions of Purley*, 2 vols (1786).

Horsley, Samuel, *A Charge, Delivered to the Clergy of the Archdeaconry of St Albans, at a Visitation Holden May 22d 1783* (1783).

Horsley, Samuel, *Letter from the Archdeacon of Saint Albans, in reply to Dr Priestley, with an Appendix, Containing Short Strictures on Dr Priestley's Letters by an Unknown Hand* (1784).

Horsley, Samuel, *On the Incarnation: A Sermon, Preached in the Parish Church of St Mary Newington, in Surrey, Dec. 25, 1785* (1786).

Horsley, Samuel, *Remarks upon Dr Priestley's Second Letters to the Archdeacon of St Albans with Proofs of Certain Facts Asserted by the Archdeacon* (1786).

Horsley, Samuel, *An Apology for the Liturgy and Clergy of the Church of England* (1790).

Howes, Thomas, *A Discourse on the Abuse of the Talent of Disputation in Religion, Particularly as Practiced by Dr Priestley, Mr Gibbon, and Others of the Modern Sect of Philosophic Christians. Preached in the Cathedral Church, Norwich... on June 23, 1784* (Norwich, 1784).

Hume, David, *The History of Great Britain, Volume I: Containing the Reigns of James I and Charles I* (Edinburgh, 1754).

Hume, David, *The History of England, under the House of Tudor*, 2 vols (1759).

Hume, David, *The Life of David Hume, Esq: Written by Himself* (1777).

Hurd, Richard, *On the Delicacy of Friendship* (1755).

Hurd, Richard, *Remarks on Mr. David Hume's Essay on the Natural History of Religion: Addressed to the Rev. Dr. Warburton* (1757).

Hurd, Richard, *Moral and Political Dialogues: Being the Substance of Several Conversations between Divers Eminent Persons of the Present Age; Digested by the Parties Themselves, and now First Published from the Original MSS with Critical and Explanatory Notes* (1759).

Hurd, Richard, *A Letter to the Rev. Dr. Thomas Leland, Fellow of Trinity College, Dublin: in which His Late Dissertation on the Principles of Human Eloquence is Criticized; and The Bishop of Gloucester's Idea of the Nature and Character of an Inspired Language, as Delivered in his Lordship's Doctrine of Grace, is Vindicated From all the Objections of the Learned Author of the Dissertation* (1764).

Hurd, Richard, *A Charge Delivered to the Clergy of the Diocese of Lichfield and Coventry, at the Bishop's Primary Visitation in 1775 and 1776* (1776).

Hutcheson, Francis, *An Essay on the Nature and Conduct of the Passions and Affections* (1728).

Hutchinson, John, *Moses's Principia. Of the Invisible Parts of Matter; Of Motion: Of Visible Forms; And of their Dissolution, and Reformation. With Notes* (1724).

[Jamieson, John], *Socinianism Unmasked: In Four Letters to the Lay-Members of the Church of Scotland, and Especially to those of the Collegiate Church of Ayr: Occasioned by Dr M'Gill's Practical Essay on the Death of Jesus Christ. Proving that he Denies the Great Doctrines of the Atonement, and of the Deity of our Lord. To which are added, a Letter to the Doctor, and an Humble Address to the Members of the General Assembly of the Church of Scotland. By a Friend to Truth* (Edinburgh, 1787).

Jenyns, Soame, *A View of the Internal Evidence of the Christian Religion* (1776).

Jenyns, Soame, *The Works of Soame Jenyns, Esq.*, ed. Charles Nason Cole, 4 vols (1790).

Jervis, Thomas, *A Sermon Preached by the Rev. Thomas Jervis; and a Charge Delivered by the Rev. Thomas Belsham; at the Ordination of the Rev. Timothy Kenrick; in the New Meeting, Exeter, on Thursday the 28th of July, 1785* (1785).

Jesse, William, *Parochialia; Or Observations on the Discharge of Parochial Duties, in which Defects and Errors are Pointed out and Improvements Suggested and Recommended to The Parochial Clergy: in Seventeen Letters to Clericus with Remarks on a Letter Containing Strictures on a Discourse Lately Preached in Bewdley Chapel* (Kidderminster, 1785).

Jesse, William, *The Importance of Education: A Discourse, Preached in Bewdley Chapel, on Sunday the 27th day of March, 1785. By William Jesse, Rector of Dowles, and Chaplain to the Right Honourable the Earl of Glasgow* (Kidderminster, 1785).

Jesse, William, *Lectures, Supposed to have been Delivered, by the Author of A View of the Internal Evidence of the Christian Religion to a Select Company of Friends: Dedicated to Edward Gibbon Esq* (1787).

Jesse, William, *A Defence of the Established Church or, Letters to the Gentlemen of Oxford and Cambridge who are in the Course of Education for the Christian Ministry in which Dr Priestley's Arguments against Subscription, and the Peculiar Doctrines of Christianity, are Examined and their Futility are Exposed. By William Jesse, Rector of Dowles, and Chaplain to the Right Honourable the Earl of Glasgow* (1788).

Johnson, Samuel, *Taxation no Tyranny* (1775).

Jones, John, *Free Thoughts on the Subject of a Farther Reformation of the Church of England; in Six Numbers: To Which are Added, the Remarks of the Editor* (1771).

*Jones's Directory; or, Useful Pocket Companion for the year 1787* (Glasgow, 1787).

*Jones's Directory; or Useful Pocket Companion for the Year 1789: containing an Alphabetical List of the Names and Places of Abode of the Merchants, Manufacturers, Traders and Shopkeepers in and about the City of Glasgow* (Glasgow, 1789).

Jortin, John, *Remarks on Ecclesiastical History*, 5 vols (1751).

Jortin, John, *Six Dissertations upon Different Subjects* (1755).

Kästner, Abraham Gotthelf, *Mathematische Anfangsgründe*, 9 vols (Göttingen, 1758–91).

Kay, John, *A Series of Original Portraits and Caricature Etchings by the Late John Kay, with Biographical Sketches and Illustrative Anecdotes* [by Hugh Paton], 2 vols (Edinburgh, 1877).

Kaye, Richard, *A Sermon Preached at the Anniversary Meeting of the Sons of the Clergy, in the Cathedral Church of St Paul, on Thursday, May 22, 1783* (1784).

Kippis, Andrew, ed., *Biographica Britannica: Or, The Lives of the Most Eminent Persons Who have Flourished in Great-Britain and Ireland, From the Earliest Ages, to the Present Times*, 5 vols, 2nd edn (1778–93).

Kippis, Andrew, *A Sermon Preached at the Old Jewry, on the Fourth of November, 1788, Before the Society for Commemorating the Glorious Revolution; Being the Completion of an Hundred Years Since that Great Event* (1788).
Kippis, Andrew, ed., *The Works of Nathaniel Lardner*, 11 vols (1788).
Knox, Vicesimus, *Liberal Education: Or a Practical Treatise on the Methods of Acquiring Useful Knowledge and Polite Learning* (1781).
Knox, Vicesimus, *Essays, Moral and Literary*, 2 vols (1782).
Lardner, Nathaniel, *Observations upon Dr Macknight's Harmony of the Four Gospels, so far as Relates to the History of Our Saviour's Resurrection* (1764).
Leechman, William, *The Excellency of the Spirit of Christianity: A Sermon, Preached before the Society in Scotland for Propagating Christian Knowledge, at their Anniversary Meeting, in the High Church of Edinburgh, on Friday, June 5. 1767* (Edinburgh, 1768).
Leechman, William, 'The Nature, Reasonableness, and Advantages, of Prayer; With an Attempt to Answer the Objections Against It', Sermon V, in *The Scotch Preacher: Or, A Collection of Sermons. By Some of the Most Eminent Clergymen of the Church of Scotland*, vol. I (Edinburgh and London, 1775), pp. 138–206.
Leechman, William, 'The Temper, Character, and Duty of a Minister of the Gospel', Sermons VIII and IX, in *The Scotch Preacher: Or, A Collection of Sermons. By Some of the Most Eminent Clergymen of the Church of Scotland*, vol. II (London and Edinburgh, 1776), pp. 136–87.
Leechman, William, 'The Wisdom of God in the Gospel-Revelation', Sermons XII and XIII, *The Scotch Preacher: Or, A Collection of Sermons. By Some of the Most Eminent Clergymen of the Church of Scotland*, vol. II (London and Edinburgh, 1779), pp. 215–80.
Leechman, William, 'The Excellency of the Spirit of Christianity', Sermons XV and XVI, in *The Scotch Preacher: Or, A Collection of Sermons. By Some of the Most Eminent Clergymen of the Church of Scotland*, vol. III (London and Edinburgh, 1779), pp. 287–338.
Leechman, William, *Sermons, by William Leechman, D.D., Late Principal of the College of Glasgow, to which is prefixed Some Account of the Author's Life, and of his Lectures, by James Wodrow, D.D., Minister at Stevenston*, 2 vols (1789).
Leland, Thomas, *A Dissertation on the Principles of Human Eloquence* (1764).
Levi, David, *A Succinct Account of the Rites and Ceremonies of the Jews* (1782).
Levi, David, *Letters to Dr Priestley, in Answer to those he Addressed to the Jews; Inviting them to an Amicable Discussion of the Evidences of Christianity* (1787).
Levi, David, *Dissertation on the Prophecies of the Old Testament*, 2 vols (1793–1800).
Lindsey, Theophilus, *The Letters of Theophilus Lindsey (1723–1808)*, ed. G. M. Ditchfield, 2 vols (Woodbridge, 2007–12).
Lobo, Jerome, *A Voyage to Abyssinia. By Father Jerome Lobo*, trans. Samuel Johnson (1735).
Locke, John, *An Essay Concerning Human Understanding* (1690).
Lowth, Robert, *A Short Introduction to English Grammar: With Critical Notes* (1762).
Lucretius, *De Rerum Natura, with an English Translation by W. H. D. Rouse*, revised by Martin Ferguson Smith (1975).

Lunardi, Vincenzo, *An Account of Five Aerial Voyages in Scotland in a Series of Letters to his Guardian, Chevalier Gerardo Compagni* (1786).
M'Gill, William, *The Prayer of Our Saviour for the Union of His Followers Considered: A Sermon by William M'Gill, A.M. one of the Ministers of Ayr* (Glasgow, 1768).
M'Gill, William, 'A Humble Remonstrance Against Some Prevailing Vices of the Present Age: A Fast Sermon', in William Dalrymple and William M'Gill, *The Judgements of God Against Impiety, &c.: Illustrated and Improved, in Two Sermons, Preached at Ayr, December 24, 1772. On Occasion of a Fast Appointed by the Presbytery of Ayr* (Edinburgh, 1773).
M'Gill, William, *The Friends: A Sermon; Preached December 27, 1778 at the Annual Meeting of the Society of Free Masons at Ayr* (Edinburgh, 1779).
M'Gill, William, *A Practical Essay on the Death of Jesus Christ* (Edinburgh, 1786).
M'Gill, William, *The Benefits of the Revolution: A Sermon, Preached at Ayr, on the 5th of November, 1788, by William M'Gill, D. D. To which are Added, Remarks on a Sermon, Preached on the Same Day, at Newton upon Ayr; Very necessary for all the Readers of said Sermon* (Kilmarnock, 1789).
[Mackenzie, John], *The Religious Establishment in Scotland Examined Upon Protestant Principles: A Tract, Occasioned by the Late Prosecution Against the Late Reverend Mr. Alexander Fergusson, Minister in Kilwinning* (1771). Note: This publication has often been incorrectly attributed to John Graham.
Macknight, James, *A Harmony of the Four Gospels: In which the Natural Order of Each is Preserved. With a Paraphrase and Notes*, 2 vols (1756).
Macknight, James, *A New Literal Translation from the Original, of the Apostle Paul's First and Second Epistles to the Thessalonians: With a Commentary and Notes* (1787).
Macknight, James, *A New Literal Translation from the Original Greek of All the Apostolic Epistles*, 4 vols (Edinburgh, 1795).
Maclaine, Archibald, *A Series of Letters Addressed to Soame Jenyns, Esq., on Occasion of His View of the Internal Evidence of Christianity* (1777).
Madan, Martin, *Thelyphthora; or, A Treatise on Female Ruin, in Its Causes, Effects, Consequences, Prevention, and Remedy; Considered On The Basis Of Divine Law* (1780).
Madan, Martin, *A New and Literal Translation of Juvenal and Persius; with Copious Explanatory Notes, by which these Difficult Satirists are Rendered Easy and Familiar to the Reader*, 2 vols (1789).
Madan, Spencer, *Letters to Joseph Priestley, LL.D. F.R.S. Occasioned by His Late Controversial Writings* (1787).
Madan, Spencer, *The Principal Claims of the Dissenters Considered* (1790).
Mason, William, *The English Garden: A Poem in Four Books* (1772–81).
Mason, William, *An Heroic Epistle to Sir William Chambers* (1773).
Melmoth, William, ed., *Cato and Laelius: Or, Essays on Old-Age and Friendship. By Marcus Tullius Cicero: With remarks by William Melmoth* (1785).
*Memorial of the Committee of the General Assembly of the Church of Scotland, Concerning the Test Act* (Edinburgh, 1790).

Millar, John, *An Historical View of the English Government, from the Settlement of the Saxons in Britain to the Accession of the House of Stewart* (1787).
Milton, John, *Milton's Paradise Lost, A New Edition by Richard Bentley DD* (1732).
Mitford, William, *The History of Greece*, 5 vols (1784–1818).
Moir, James, *A Distinct and Impartial Account of the Process for Socinian Heresy against William M'Gill, D.D., One of the Ministers of Ayr: With Observations on his Explanations and Apology; And on the Proceedings and Final Decision of the Reverend Synod of Glasgow and Ayr, in that Cause. Dedicated to the Members, Commonly called the Orthodox Party without their Permission* (Edinburgh, 1790).
Montesquieu, Charles-Louis de Secondat, *De l'Esprit des Lois* (Geneva, 1748).
Montesquieu, Charles-Louis de Secondat, *The Spirit of Laws by Baron De Montesquieu*, trans. Thomas Nugent, 2nd edn, 2 vols (1752).
Moor, James, *Essays; Read to a Literary Society; at their Weekly Meetings within the College, at Glasgow* (Glasgow, 1759).
Mure, William, ed., *Selections from the Family Papers Preserved at Caldwell*, 2 vols (Glasgow, 1854).
*New Cyclopaedia; or, Universal Dictionary of the Arts and Sciences*, ed. Abraham Rees, 39 vols (1802–20).
Newton, Issac, *Philosophiae Naturalis Principia Mathematica* (1687).
Newton, Issac, *Opticks: Or, A Treatise of the Reflexions, Refractions, Inflexions and Colours of Light* (1704).
Paley, William, *The Principles of Moral and Political Philosophy* (1785).
Palmer, Samuel, *The Protestant Dissenter's Catechism…Designed to Instruct and Establish Young Persons among the Dissenters, in the Principles of Nonconformity* (1772).
[Parr, Samuel, ed.], *Tracts by Warburton and a Warburtonian, not Admitted into the Collection of their Respective Works* (1789).
Peebles, William, *The Great Things Which the Lord Hath Done for This Nation, Illustrated and Improved; in Two Sermons Preached on the 5th of November, 1788* (Kilmarnock, 1788).
Pennant, Thomas, *A Tour in Scotland. MDCCLXIX [1769]* (Chester, 1771).
Pennant, Thomas, *A Tour in Scotland and Voyage to the Hebrides. MDCCLXXII [1772]* (Chester, 1774).
Pennant, Thomas, *A Tour of Wales*, 2 vols (1784).
Phillips, Thomas, *The History and Antiquities of Shrewsbury* (Shrewsbury, 1779).
Philostratus, Flavius, *Vita Apollonii Tyanei*, ed. Gerard Boter (Berlin, 2022).
Philostratus, Flavius and Eunapius, *Philostratus, Lives of the Sophists; Eunapius, Lives of Philosophers and Sophists*, ed. and trans. Graeme Miles and Han Baltussen (Cambridge, MA, 2023).
Piozzi, Hester Lynch, *Anecdotes of the Late Samuel Johnson, LL.D. During the Last Years of his Life* (1786).
Pouilly, Louis-Jean Lévesque de, *Théorie des Sentimens Agréables* (Geneva, 1747).
Pouilly, Louis-Jean Lévesque de, *The Theory of Agreeable Sensations: In which the Laws Observed by Nature in the Distribution of Pleasure are Investigated; and the Principles of Natural Theology and Moral Philosophy are Established* (1749).

Price, Richard, *Observations on Reversionary Payments* (1771).
Price, Richard, *Sermons on the Christian Doctrine: As Received by the Different Denominations of Christians* (1787).
Price, Richard, *A Discourse on the Love of our Country, Delivered on Nov 4, 1789, at the Meeting-house in the Old Jewry, to the Society for Commemorating the Revolution in Great Britain* (1789).
Price, Richard, *The Correspondence of Richard Price*, eds Bernard Peach and D. O. Thomas, 3 vols (Durham, NC, and Cardiff, 1983–94).
Priestley, Joseph, ed., *Theological Repository: Consisting of Original Essays, Hints, Queries, &c. Calculated to Promote Religious Knowledge* (1769–71 and 1784–88).
Priestley, Joseph, *An Appeal to the Serious and Candid Professors of Christianity* (1771).
Priestley, Joseph, *The Triumph of Truth; Being an Account of the Trial of Mr E. Elwall, for Heresy and Blasphemy, at Stafford Assizes, before Judge Denton. To Which are Added, Extracts from Some Other Pieces of Mr Elwall's, Concerning the Unity of God* (Leeds, 1771).
Priestley, Joseph, *A Familiar Illustration of Certain Passages of Scripture Relating to the Power of Man to do the Will of God, Original Sin, Election and Reprobation, the Divinity of Christ and Atonement for Sin by the Death of Christ* (1772).
Priestley, Joseph, *Institutes of Natural and Revealed Religion*, 3 vols (1772–74).
Priestley, Joseph, *A Letter of Advice to those Dissenters who Conduct the Application to Parliament for Relief from Certain Penal Laws* (1773).
Priestley, Joseph, *An Examination of Dr. Reid's Inquiry into the Human Mind, Dr. Beattie's Essay on the Nature and Immutability of Truth, and Dr. Oswald's Appeal to Common Sense in Behalf of Religion* (1775).
Priestley, Joseph, *Hartley's Theory of the Human Mind, on the Principle of the Association of Ideas; With Essays Relating to the Subject of It* (1775).
Priestley, Joseph, *Disquisitions Relating to Matter and Spirit. To Which is added, the History of the Philosophical Doctrine Concerning the Origin of the Soul, and the Nature of Matter; with its Influence on Christianity, Especially with Respect to the Doctrine of the Pre-Existence of Christ* (1777).
Priestley, Joseph, *The Doctrine of Philosophical Necessity Illustrated: Being an Appendix to the Disquisitions Relating to Matter and Spirit. To Which is Added, an Answer to the Letters on Materialism, and on Hartley's Theory of the Mind* (1777).
Priestley, Joseph, *An History of the Corruptions of Christianity*, 2 vols (Birmingham, 1782).
Priestley, Joseph, *A General View of the Arguments for the Unity of God; and Against the Divinity and Pre-existence of Christ, from Reason, from the Scriptures, and from History* (Birmingham, 1783).
Priestley, Joseph, *Letters to Dr Horsley, in Answer to His Animadversions on the History of the Corruptions of Christianity: With Additional Evidence, that the Primitive Christian Church was Unitarian* (Birmingham, 1783).
Priestley, Joseph, *Reply to the Animadversions on the History of the Corruptions of Christianity in the Monthly Review* (Birmingham, 1783).
Priestley, Joseph, *Letters to Dr Horsley, Part II: Containing Farther Evidence that the Primitive Christian Church was Unitarian* (Birmingham, 1784).

Priestley, Joseph, *The Importance and Extent of Free Inquiry in Matters of Religion: A Sermon, Preached Before the Congregations of the Old and New Meeting of Protestant Dissenters at Birmingham, November 5, 1785. To which are added, Reflections on the Present State of Free Enquiry in this Country...* (Birmingham, 1785).

Priestley, Joseph, *An History of Early Opinions Concerning Jesus Christ* (Birmingham, 1786).

Priestley, Joseph, *Letters to Dr Horsley, Part III: Containing an Answer to His Remarks on Letters, Part II* (Birmingham, 1786).

Priestley, Joseph, *Letters to the Jews* (Birmingham, 1786).

Priestley, Joseph, *A Letter to the Right Honourable William Pitt,... on the Subjects of Toleration and Church Establishments; Occasioned by His Speech Against the Repeal of the Test and Corporation Acts, on Wednesday the 28th of March, 1787* (1787).

Priestley, Joseph, *Letters to a Philosophic Unbeliever. Part II. Containing a State of the Evidence of Revealed Religion, with Animadversions on the Two Last Chapters of the First Volume of Mr Gibbon's History of the Decline and Fall of the Roman Empire* (Birmingham, 1787).

Priestley, Joseph, *Letters to Dr Horne, Dean of Canterbury; To the Young Men who are in the Course of Education for the Christian Ministry at the Universities of Oxford and Cambridge; to Dr Price; and to Mr Parkhurst, on the Subject of the Person of Christ* (Birmingham, 1787).

Priestley, Joseph, *Letters to the Jews, Part II: Occasioned by Mr David Levi's Reply to the Former Letters* (Birmingham, 1787).

Priestley, Joseph, *Lectures on History, and General Policy* (Birmingham, 1788).

Priestley, Joseph, *The Conduct to be Observed by Dissenters, in Order to Procure the Repeal of the Corporation and Test Acts: Recommended in A Sermon, Preached before the Congregations of the Old and New Meetings, At Birmingham. November 5, 1789* (Birmingham, 1789).

Priestley, Joseph, *Familiar Letters Addressed to the Inhabitants of Birmingham, in Refutation of Several Charges, Advanced Against the Dissenters* (Birmingham, 1790).

Priestley, Joseph, *Discourses on the Evidence of Revealed Religion* (1794).

Priestley, Joseph, *A General History of the Christian Church*, 2 vols (Northumberland, PA, 1802).

Priestley, Joseph and Richard Price, *A Free Discussion of the Doctrines of Materialism, and Philosophical Necessity, in a Correspondence Between Dr. Price, and Dr. Priestley* (1778).

*Proceedings of the Very Reverend the Synod of Glasgow and Ayr, held at Ayr on the 13th & 14th April 1790, Relating to some Late Publications of the Rev. Dr. William Mcgill, with the Final Decisions in that Cause* ([Glasgow], 1790).

Ratramnus, *The Book of Bertram, or, Rathram, Priest and Monk of Corbey, Concerning the Body and Blood of Jesus in the Sacrament* (Dublin, 1753).

Reid, Thomas, *Essays on the Active Powers of Man*, eds Knud Haaksonssen and James Harris (Edinburgh, 2010 [1788]).

Richardson, William, *A Philosophical Analysis and Illustration of Some of Shakespeare's Remarkable Characters* (1774).

Richardson, William, *Anecdotes of the Russian Empire; In a Series of Letters, Written, a Few Years Ago, from St. Petersburg* (1784).

Richardson, William, *Essays on Shakespeare's Dramatic Characters of Richard the Third, King Lear, and Timon of Athens* (1784).

Robe, James, *The Remarks of the Committee of the Presbytery of Glasgow, upon Mr Leechman's Sermon on Prayer, with His Replies Thereunto* (Edinburgh, 1744).
Robertson, John, *Britain the Chosen Nation: A Thanksgiving Sermon, Preached, November 5th, 1788* (Kilmarnock, 1788).
Robertson, William, *The History of Scotland during the Reigns of Queen Mary and James VI* (1759).
Robertson, William, *The History of the Reign of Charles V* (1769).
Robertson, William, *The History of America* (1777).
Robertson, William, *An Historical Disquisition Concerning the Knowledge which the Ancients had of India* (1791).
Rose, William, *The History of Catiline's Conspiracy, and the Jugurthine War. By C. C. Sallust. With a New Translation of Cicero's Four Orations against Catiline. To which is Prefixed, the Life of Sallust* (1751).
Rufinus, Tyrannius, *The Sacred Writings of Rufinus*, ed. Johann Peter Kirsch (Altenmunster, 2012).
Russel, John, *The Reasons of our Lord's Agony in the Garden, and the Influence of Just Views of them on Universal Holiness, in a Sermon* (Kilmarnock, 1787).
Shaw, Duncan, *The History and Philosophy of Judaism: Or, A Critical and Philosophical Analysis of the Jewish Religion. From which is Offered a Vindication of its Genius, Origin, and Authority, and of its Connection with the Christian, against the Objections and Misrepresentations of Modern Infidels* (Edinburgh, 1787).
Smith, Adam, *The Theory of Moral Sentiment* (1759).
Smith, Adam, *An Inquiry into the Nature and Causes of the Wealth of Nations* (1776).
Smith, Adam, *Lectures on Rhetoric and Belles Lettres*, ed. J. C. Bryce (Indianapolis, IN, 1985).
Sterne, Laurence, *The Life and Opinions of Tristram Shandy (1759–67)*, ed. Graham Petrie, intro. Christopher Ricks (1985).
Sulzer, Johann Georg, *A General Theory of the Fine Arts* (Leipzig, 1771–74).
Sykes, Arthur Ashley, *Principles and Connexion of Natural and Revealed Religion* (1740).
Tait, John, *Directory for the City of Glasgow, Villages of Anderston, Calton, and Gorbals; Also for the Towns of Paisley, Greenock, Port-Glasgow, and Kilmarnock, from the 15th May 1783, to the 15th May 1784* (Glasgow, 1783).
Taylor, John, *The Scripture Doctrine of Original Sin* (1740).
*The Correspondence of George, Prince of Wales, 1770–1812: Volume I, 1770–1789*, ed. A. Aspinall (1965).
*The Correspondence of the Revolution Society in London, with the National Assembly, and with Various Societies of the Friends of Liberty in France and England* (1792).
*The Means of Effectually Preventing Theft and Robbery; Together with Our Present Cruel Punishments of those and Other Crimes: The Means of Immediately Suppressing Vagrant Beggary: of Speedily Abolishing Our Poor's Rates: and of Relieving the Present Oppression of our Labouring Commonalty* (1783).
*The Parliamentary History of England, From the Earliest Period to the Year 1803*, ed. William Cobbett, 36 vols (1812–20).

*The Scotch Preacher: Or, A Collection of Sermons. By Some of the Most Eminent Clergymen of the Church of Scotland*, 4 vols (Edinburgh, 1775–89).
*The Works of Virgil, Englished by Robert Andrews* (Birmingham, 1766).
Thucydides, *History of the Peloponnesian War* (c. 400 BC).
Toulmin, Joshua, *Memoirs of the Life, Character, Sentiments and Writings of Faustus Socinus* (1777).
Towers, Joseph, *An Oration Delivered at the London Tavern on the Fourth of November 1788* (1788).
Tullideph, Thomas, *Enquiry Concerning the Intention of the Evangelists and the Writer of the Book of Acts of the Apostles in Quoting Passages from the Old Testament* (c. 1734).
Urwick, Thomas, *A Sermon, Preached at Salters-Hall, May 3d, 1787. Before the Correspondent Board in London of the Society in Scotland (incorporated by Royal Charter) for Propagating Christian Knowledge in the Highlands and Islands* (1787).
Virgil, P., *Virgilii Maronis Opera: Or the Works of Virgil... For the Use of Schools by John Stirling, DD Late Vicar of Great Gaddesden in Hertfordshire, and Chaplain to His Grace the Duke of Gordon* (1779).
[Walcot, John], *Bozzy and Piozzi: Or the British Biographers, a Town Eclogue by Peter Pindar Esq.* (1786).
Warburton, William, *The Works of the Right Reverend William Warburton, Lord Bishop of Gloucester*, ed. Richard Hurd, 7 vols (1788).
Warrington, William, *The History of Wales, in Nine Books: With an Appendix*, 3rd edn, 2 vols (1788 [1st edn 1786]).
Warton, Thomas, *The History of English Poetry from the Close of the Eleventh to the Commencement of the Eighteenth Century*, 3 vols (1774, 1778, 1781).
Watson, Richard, *Anecdotes of the Life of Richard Watson, Bishop of Llandaff; Written by Himself*, 2 vols (1818).
[Wigan, Thomas] Clericus, *A Defence of the Clergy of the Church of England; in a Letter to the Rev. William Jesse, Rector of Dowles, Occasioned by his Parochialia* (Gloucester, 1786).
Williamson, Peter, *Williamson's Directory for the City of Edinburgh, Canongate, Leith, and Suburbs, From June, 1784, to June, 1785* (Edinburgh, 1784).
Williamson, Peter, *Williamson's Directory for the City of Edinburgh, Canongate, Leith, and Suburbs, From June, 1788, to June, 1789* (Edinburgh, 1788).
Witherspoon, John, *Ecclesiastical Characteristics; Or, The Arcana of Church Policy: Being an Humble Attempt to Open Up the Mystery of Moderation; Wherein is Shewn a Plain and Easy Way of Attaining to the Character of a Moderate Man, as at Present in Repute in the Church of Scotland* (Glasgow, 1753).
Witherspoon, John, *The Works of John Witherspoon*, 4 vols (Philadelphia, PA, 1802).
Wodrow, James, 'The Parish of Stevenston', in *The Statistical Account of Scotland, Drawn Up from the Communications of the Ministers of the Different Parishes*, ed. Sir John Sinclair, 13 vols (Edinburgh, 1791–99), VII (1793), pp. 1–41.
Wodrow, Robert, *The Life of James Wodrow, A.M., Professor of Divinity in the University of Glasgow from MDCXCII to MDCCVII. Written by his Son Robert Wodrow, A.M., Minister of the Gospel at Eastwood* (Edinburgh, 1828).

Wright, James, *A Recommendation of Brotherly Love, Upon the Principles of Christianity. To which is Subjoined, an Inquiry into the True Design of the Institution of Masonry... By James Wright, A.M., Minister of the Gospel at Maybole* (Edinburgh, 1786).
Young, Edward, *The Complaints: Or, Night Thoughts on Life, Death and Immortality* (1742–46).
Young, Edward, *Conjectures on Original Composition* (1759).
Zwicker, Daniel, *Irenicum Irenicoram* (Amsterdam, 1658).

# VOLUME 2
## SECONDARY SOURCES CITED

*A History of the Society of Writers to Her Majesty's Signet, With a List of the Members of the Society from 1594 to 1890 and an Abstract of the Minutes* (Edinburgh, 1890).

Adams, Henry Hitch and Baxter Hathaway, eds, *Dramatic Essays of the Neoclassic Age* (New York, 1950).

Ahnert, Thomas, *The Moral Culture of the Scottish Enlightenment, 1690–1805* (New Haven, CT, 2014).

Alexander, Derek and Gordon McCrae, *Renfrewshire: A Scottish County's Hidden Past* (Edinburgh, 2012).

Alford, B. W. E., *W.D. & H.O. Wills and the Development of the UK Tobacco Industry, 1786–1965* (1973).

Allan, David, *A Nation of Readers: The Lending Library in Georgian England* (2008).

Allan, David, *Scotland in the Eighteenth Century: Union and Enlightenment* (2016).

Allen, Aaron, 'Corporate Charity for "the House": Craft Pensions and the Widows' Fund, 1670–1782', *Scottish Historical Review*, 101 (2022), pp. 210–47.

Allen, Richard C., *David Hartley on Human Nature* (New York, 1999).

Andrews, Corey E., *Inventing Scotland's Bard: The British Reception of Robert Burns, 1786–1836* (Columbia, SC, 2022).

Andrews, Stuart, *Unitarian Radicalism: Political Rhetoric, 1770–1814* (Basingstoke, 2003).

Annan, Thomas, John Guthrie Smith, and John Oswald Mitchell, *The Old Country Houses of the Old Glasgow Gentry*, 2nd edn (Glasgow, 1878).

Appleby, David J., 'From Ejectment to Toleration in England, 1662–89', in Alan P. F. Sell, ed., *The Great Ejectment of 1662: Its Antecedents, Aftermath, and Ecumenical Significance* (Eugene, OR, 2012), pp. 67–124.

Appleby, John H., 'St Petersburg to Edinburgh: Matthew Guthrie's Introduction of Medicinal Plants in the Context of Scottish-Russian Natural History Exchange', *Archives of Natural History*, 14 (1987), pp. 45–58.

Balfour-Melville, Barbara, *The Balfours of Pilrig: A History for the Family* (Edinburgh, 1907).

Barlow, Richard B., *Citizenship and Conscience* (Philadelphia, PA, 1962).

Bartlett, Thomas, 'Ireland: From Legislative Independence to Legislative Union, 1782–1800', in H. T. Dickinson and Michael Lynch, eds, *The Challenge to Westminster: Sovereignty, Devolution and Independence* (East Linton, 2000), pp. 61–70.

Basker, James G., 'Scotticisms and the Problem of Cultural Identity in Eighteenth-Century Britain', in John Dwyer and Richard B. Sher, eds, *Sociability and Society in Eighteenth-Century Scotland* (Edinburgh, 1993), pp. 81–95.

Batchelor, Jennie, *The Lady's Magazine (1770–1832) and the Making of Literary History* (Edinburgh, 2022).

Batchelor, Jennie and Manushag, N. Powell, *Women's Periodicals and Print Culture in Britain, 1690–1820s: The Long Eighteenth Century* (Edinburgh, 2018).

Baylen, Joseph O. and Norbert J. Gossman, eds, *Biographical Dictionary of Modern British Radicals*, 3 vols (Brighton, 1979–88).

Beales, Derek, *Joseph II*, 2 vols (Cambridge, 1987 and 2009).

Beavan, Iain and Warren McDougall, 'The Scottish Book Trade', in Michael F. Suarez and Michael L. Turner, eds, *The Cambridge History of the Book in Britain. Vol. 5, 1695–1830* (Cambridge, 2009), pp. 352–65.

Bee, Michele, 'The Nurse of Fanaticism: Adam Smith on the Origin of Anti-Establishment Movements', *History of Political Thought*, 44 (2023), pp. 92–115.

Beedell, A. V. and A. D. Harvey, *The Prison Diary (16 May–22 November 1794) of John Horne Tooke* (Leeds, 1995).

Benchimol, Alex, 'The "Spirit of Liberal Reform": Representation, Slavery and Constitutional Liberty in the *Glasgow Advertiser*, 1789–94', *Scottish Historical Review*, 99 (2020), pp. 51–84.

Berg, Maxine and Pat Hudson, *Slavery, Capitalism and the Industrial Revolution* (Cambridge, 2023).

Berry, Christopher J., *The Social Theory of the Scottish Enlightenment* (Edinburgh, 1997).

Bieler, Ludwig, *Theios Anēr: Das Bild des 'göttlichen Menschen' Spätantike und Frühchristentum* (Vienna, 1935).

Birch, Jonathan C. P., *Jesus in an Age of Enlightenment* (New York, 2019).

Black, Jeremy, *British Foreign Policy in an Age of Revolutions, 1783–1793* (Cambridge, 1994).

Black, Jeremy, *George III: America's Last King* (New Haven, CT, 2008).

Blanning, T. C. W., *Joseph II* (1994).

Boeker, Ruth, 'Francis Hutcheson on Liberty', *Royal Institute of Philosophy Supplement*, 88 (2020), pp. 121–42.

Bold, Alan, *A Burns Companion* (Basingstoke, 1991).

Bond, W. H., *Thomas Hollis of Lincoln's Inn: A Whig and His Books* (Cambridge, 1990).

Bossenga, Gail, 'Financial Origins of the French Revolution', in Thomas E. Kaiser and Dale K. Van Kley, eds, *From Deficit to Deluge: The Origins of the French Revolution* (Stanford, CA, 2011), pp. 37–66.

Boudri, J. C., *What Was Mechanical about Mechanics? The Concept of Force Between Metaphysics and Mechanics from Newton to Lagrange* (Dordrecht, 2002).

Bradley, James E., *Popular Politics and the American Revolution in England: Petitions, the Crown, and Public Opinion* (Macon, GA, 1986).

Bradley, James E., *Religion, Revolution and English Radicalism: Nonconformity in Eighteenth Century Politics and Society* (Cambridge, 1990).

Brady, Frank, *Boswell's Political Career* (New Haven, CT, 1965).

Brady, Frank, *James Boswell: The Later Years, 1769–1795* (New York, 1984).
Brekke, Luke, 'Heretics in the Pulpit, Inquisitors in the Pews: The Long Reformation and The Scottish Enlightenment', *Eighteenth-Century Studies*, 44 (2010), pp. 79–98.
Brockett, Allan, *Nonconformity in Exeter* (Manchester, 1962).
Brown, C. G., *Religion and Society in Scotland since 1707* (Edinburgh, 1997).
Brown, Carys, *Friends, Neighbours, Sinners: Religious Difference and English Society, 1689–1750* (Cambridge, 2022).
Brown, Christopher L., *Moral Capital: Foundations of British Abolitionism* (Chapel Hill, NC, 2006).
Brown, David J., 'Henry Dundas and the Government of Scotland' (PhD thesis, University of Edinburgh, 1989).
Buchan, James, *Capital of the Mind: How Edinburgh Changed the World* (2003).
Bugg, John W., *The Joseph Johnson Letter Book* (Oxford, 2016).
Burke, John, *A Genealogical and Heraldic Dictionary of the Peerage and Baronetage of the British Empire* (1869).
Burton, Anthony, *The Canal Builders: The Men Who Constructed Britain's Canals* (Barnsley, 1972).
Burton, J. R., *A History of Bewdley: With Concise Accounts of Some Neighbouring Parishes* (1883).
Butt, John, *John Anderson's Legacy: The University of Strathclyde and Its Antecedents, 1796–1996* (East Linton, 1996).
Cairns, John W., 'Knight v Wedderburn', in David Dabydeen, John Gilmore, and Cecily Jones, eds, *The Oxford Companion to Black British History* (Oxford, 2007), pp. 244–46.
Cairns, John W., 'After *Somerset*: The Scottish Experience', *Journal of Legal History*, 33 (2012), pp. 291–312.
Campbell, R. H., *The Rise and Fall of Scottish Industry, 1707–1930* (Edinburgh, 1980).
Campbell, R. H., 'The Making of the Industrial City', in Devine and Jackson, eds, *Glasgow, Volume 1*, pp. 184–213.
Cannon, John, *The Fox-North Coalition: Crisis of the Constitution, 1782–4* (Cambridge, 1969).
Cannon, John, *Parliamentary Reform 1640–1832* (Cambridge, 1973).
Carey, Brycchan and Geoffrey G. Plank, eds, *Quakers and Abolition* (Urbana, IL, 2014).
Carnie, Robert Hay, 'Scottish Printers and Booksellers 1668–1775: A Second Supplement (II)', *Studies in Bibliography*, 15 (1962), pp. 105–20.
Carretta, Vincent, *Equiano, the African: Biography of a Self-Made Man* (Athens, GA, 2005).
Carruthers, Gerard and Satinder Kaur, 'Thomas Muir and Staff and Student Politics at the University of Glasgow', in Gerard Carruthers and Don Martin, eds, *Thomas Muir of Huntershill: Essays for the Twenty-First Century* (Edinburgh, 2016), pp. 112–40.
Chalus, Elaine, *Elite Women in English Political Life c. 1754–1790* (Oxford, 2005).
Chambers, Robert, ed., *The Life and Works of Robert Burns*, 4 vols (Edinburgh, 1896).
Chernock, Arianne, *Men and the Making of Modern British Feminism* (Stanford, CA, 2010).
Chifflet, Pierre-François, ed., *Victoris Vitensis, et Vigilii Tapsensis, Provinciae Bizacenae Episcoporum Opera* (Dijon, 1664).
Claeys, Gregory, *Thomas Paine: Social and Political Thought* (1989).

Claeys, Gregory, ed., *Utopias of the British Enlightenment* (Cambridge, 1994).
Clark, Ian D. L., 'Moderatism and the Moderate Party in the Church of Scotland, 1752–1805' (PhD thesis, University of Cambridge, 1963).
Clark, Ian D. L., 'From Protest to Reaction: The Moderate Regime in the Church of Scotland, 1752–1805', in Nicholas T. Phillipson and Rosalind Mitchison, eds, *Scotland in the Age of Improvement* (Edinburgh, 1970), pp. 200–24.
Clark, J. C. D., *English Society, 1660–1832: Religion, Ideology, and Politics during the Ancien Regime* (Cambridge, 2000).
Clark, Peter, *British Clubs and Societies, 1580–1800; The Origins of an Associational World* (Oxford, 2000).
Clayden, P. W., *The Early Life of Samuel Rogers* (1887).
Coffey, John, '"Tremble, Britannia!": Fear, Providence and the Abolition of the Slave Trade, 1758–1807', *English Historical Review*, 127 (2012), pp. 844–81.
Colley, Linda, 'The Apotheosis of George III: Loyalty, Royalty and the British Nation 1760–1820', *Past and Present*, 102 (1984), pp. 94–129.
Constantine, Mary-Ann, Nigel Leask, Lisa Cardy et al., 'Curious Travellers: Thomas Pennant and the Welsh and Scottish Tour (1760–1820)', https://curioustravellers.ac.uk/en.
Cooke, Anthony, *A History of Drinking: The Scottish Pub since 1700* (Edinburgh, 2015).
Coutts, James, *History of the University of Glasgow: From Its Foundation in 1451 to 1909* (Glasgow, 1909).
Crawford, Ronald Lyndsay, *The Lost World of John Witherspoon: Unravelling the Snodgrass Affair, 1762 to 1776* (Aberdeen, 2014).
Crawford, Ronald Lyndsay, *The Chair of Verity: Political Preaching and Pulpit Censure in Eighteenth-Century Scotland* (Edinburgh, 2017).
Crawford, Ronald Lyndsay, *Scotland and America in the Age of Paine: Ideas of Liberty and the Making of Four Americans* (Aberdeen, 2022).
Cunningham, Hugh, *The Reputation of Philanthropy since 1750: Britain and Beyond* (Manchester, 2020).
Damrosch, Leo, *The Club: Johnson, Boswell, and the Friends Who Shaped an Age* (New Haven, CT, 2019).
Daniel, Dafydd Mills, 'Modern Infidels, Conscientious Fools, and the *Douglas* Affair: The Orthodox Rhetoric of Conscience in the Scottish Enlightenment', *Journal of Religion*, 100 (2020), pp. 327–60.
Davidoff, Leonore and Catherine Hall, *Family Fortunes: Men and Women of the English Middle Class, 1780–1850*, 2nd edn (2002).
Davis, David Brion, *Inhuman Bondage: The Rise and Fall of Slavery in the New World* (Oxford, 2008).
Davis, Thomas W., ed., *Committees for Repeal of the Test and Corporation Acts: Minutes 1786–90 and 1827–8* (1978).
Derry, John W., *Politics in the Age of Fox, Pitt, and Liverpool: Continuity and Transformation* (New York, 1990).
Derry, Warren, *Dr Parr: A Portrait of the Whig Dr Johnson* (Oxford, 1966).

Devine, T. M., *The Tobacco Lords: A Study of the Tobacco Merchants of Glasgow and Their Trading Activities, c. 1740–90* (Edinburgh, 1975).
Devine, T. M., 'A Glasgow Tobacco Merchant: Alexander Speirs of Elderslie, 1775 to 1781', *William and Mary Quarterly*, 33 (1976), pp. 501–13.
Devine, T. M., 'The Golden Age of Tobacco', in T. M. Devine and Gordon Jackson, eds, *Glasgow, Volume 1* (Manchester, 1995), pp. 166–76.
Devine, T. M., ed., *Recovering Scotland's Slavery Past: The Caribbean Connection* (Edinburgh, 2015).
Devine, T. M. and Gordon Jackson, eds, *Glasgow, Volume 1: Beginnings to 1830* (Manchester, 1995).
Dickinson, H. T., *The Politics of the People in Eighteenth-Century Britain* (New York, 1994).
Dictionary of Irish Biography, www.dib.ie.
Ditchfield, G. M., 'The Parliamentary Struggle over the Repeal of the Test and Corporation Acts, 1787–1790', *English Historical Review*, 89 (1974), pp. 551–77.
Ditchfield, G. M., 'The Scottish Campaign against the Test Act, 1790–1791', *Historical Journal*, 23 (1980), pp. 37–61.
Ditchfield, G. M., 'The Subscription Issue in British Parliamentary Politics, 1772–79', *Parliamentary History*, 7 (1988), pp. 35–80.
Ditchfield, G. M., 'Anti-Trinitarianism and Toleration in Late Eighteenth Century British Politics: The Unitarian Petition of 1792', *Journal of Ecclesiastical History*, 42 (1991), pp. 39–67.
Ditchfield, G. M., 'The Changing Nature of English Anticlericalism, c. 1750–c. 1800', in Nigel Aston and Matthew Cragoe, eds, *Anticlericalism in Britain c. 1500–1914* (Stroud, 2000), pp. 93–114.
Ditchfield, G. M., *George III: An Essay in Monarchy* (Basingstoke, 2002).
Doyle, William, *The French Revolution: A Very Short Introduction* (Oxford, 2001).
Drescher, Seymour, *Capitalism and Antislavery: British Mobilization in Comparative Perspective* (Oxford, 1987).
Drescher, Seymour, *Abolition: A History of Slavery and Antislavery* (Cambridge, 2009).
Drescher, Seymour, *Econocide: British Slavery in the Era of Abolition*, 2nd edn (Chapel Hill, NC, 2010).
Dumas, Paula E., *Proslavery Britain: Fighting for Slavery in an Era of Abolition* (Basingstoke, 2016).
Dunlop, Jean, *The British Fisheries Society 1786–1803* (Edinburgh, 1978).
Dwyer, John and Alexander Murdoch, 'Paradigms and Politics: Manners, Morals and the Rise of Henry Dundas, 1770–1784', in John Dwyer, R. A. Mason, and Alexander Murdoch, eds, *New Perspectives on the Politics and Culture of Early Modern Scotland* (Edinburgh, 1983), pp. 210–48.
Dybikowski, James, 'Joseph Priestley, Metaphysician and Philosopher of Religion', in Rivers and Wykes, eds, *Joseph Priestley: Scientist, Philosopher, and Theologian*, pp. 91–104.
Ehrman, John, *The Younger Pitt*, 3 vols (1969–96).
Eltis, David and David Richardson, *Atlas of the Transatlantic Slave Trade* (New Haven, CT, 2015).

Emerson, Roger, *Academic Patronage in the Scottish Enlightenment: Glasgow, Edinburgh and St Andrews Universities* (Edinburgh, 2008).

Emerson, Roger L., *An Enlightened Duke: The Life of Archibald Campbell (1682–1761), Earl of Ilay, 3rd Duke of Argyll* (Edinburgh, 2013).

Emerson, Roger and Paul Wood, 'Science and Enlightenment in Glasgow, 1690–1802', in Charles W. J. Withers and Paul Wood, eds, *Science and Medicine in the Scottish Enlightenment* (East Linton, 2002), pp. 79–142.

Endelman, Todd M., *The Jews of Georgian England, 1714–1830: Tradition and Change in a Liberal Society* (Ann Arbor, MI, 1999).

Endelman, Todd M., 'The Jews of Great Britain (1650–1815)', in Jonathan Karp and Adam Sutcliffe, eds, *The Cambridge History of Judaism: Volume 7, The Early Modern World, 1500–1815* (Cambridge, 2017), pp. 949–71.

Evans, E. D. Priestley, *A History of the New Meeting House Kidderminster* (Kidderminster, 1990).

Fagerstrom, Dalphy I., 'The American Revolutionary Movement in Scottish Opinion, 1763 to 1783' (PhD thesis, University of Edinburgh, 1951).

Ferguson, William, 'Electoral Law and Procedure in Eighteenth and Early Nineteenth Century Scotland', 2 vols (PhD thesis, University of Glasgow, 1957).

Ferguson, William, *Scotland: 1689 to the Present* (Edinburgh, 1968).

Fisher, Linford D., 'Evangelicals and Unevangelicals: The Contested History of a Word, 1500–1950', *Religion and American Culture*, 26 (2016), pp. 184–226.

Fitzpatrick, Martin, 'Varieties of Candour: English and Scottish Style', *Enlightenment and Dissent*, 7 (1988), pp. 35–56.

Fitzpatrick, Martin, 'Richard Price and the London Revolution Society', *Enlightenment and Dissent*, 10 (1991), pp. 35–50.

Fitzpatrick, Martin, 'Dissenting Academies', in Anthony Grayling, Andrew Pyle, and Naomi Goulder, eds, *The Continuum Encyclopedia of British Philosophy* (2006), II, pp. 862–64.

Fitzpatrick, Martin, 'The Enlightenment, Politics and Providence: Some Scottish and English Comparisons', in Haakonssen, *Enlightenment and Religion*, pp. 64–98.

Fitzpatrick, Martin and Anthony Page, 'Edmund Burke and Rational Dissent', in Martin Fitzpatrick and Peter Jones, eds, *The Reception of Edmund Burke in Europe* (2017), pp. 55–74.

Fitzpatrick, Martin, Peter Jones, Christa Knellwolf, and Ian McCalman, eds, *The Enlightenment World* (2004).

Fleet, Christopher and Daniel MacCannell, *Edinburgh: Mapping the City* (Edinburgh, 2023).

Fruchtman, Jack, 'Joseph Priestley and Early English Zionism', *Enlightenment and Dissent*, 2 (1983), pp. 39–46.

Fry, Michael, *The Dundas Despotism* (Edinburgh, 1992).

Fyfe, Aileen and Colin C. Kidd, eds, *Beyond the Enlightenment: Scottish Intellectual Life, 1790–1914* (Edinburgh, 2023).

Gardham, Julie and Lesley Richmond, Research Resources in the University of Glasgow for Adam Smith and the Scottish Enlightenment, University of Glasgow Library, 2009, rev. 2013, www.gla.ac.uk/media/Media_138989_smxx.pdf.

Garrett, C. W. F., 'Bewdley and the Stinking Ditch: An Exposition', in Snell, ed., *Essays towards a History of Bewdley*, pp. 1–14.

Gerber, David A., 'Mary Ann Wodrow Archbald: Longing for Her "Little Isle" from a Farm in Central New York', in *Authors of Their Own Lives: Personal Correspondence in the Lives of Nineteenth Century British Immigrants to the United States* (New York, 2006).

Gibbs, F. W., *Joseph Priestley: Adventurer in Science and Champion of Truth* (1965).

Ginter, Donald E., ed., *Whig Organization in the General Election of 1790: Selections from the Blair Adam Papers* (Berkeley, CA, 1967).

Glover, Julian, *Man of Iron: Thomas Telford and the Building of Britain* (2017).

Glover, Katharine, *Elite Women and Polite Society in Eighteenth-Century Scotland* (Woodbridge, 2011).

Gonzalez, Justo L., *A History of Christian Thought, Volume 2: From Augustine to the Eve of the Reformation* (Nashville, TN, 2010).

Grafton, Anthony, *The Footnote: A Curious History* (Cambridge, MA, 1999).

Graham, Eric, *Burns and the Sugar Plantocracy of Ayrshire* (Edinburgh, 2014).

Graham, Eric J., *Robert Reid Cunninghame of Seabank House, Entrepreneur and Life Time Manager of the Stevenson Coal Company 1770–1814*, Ayrshire Monographs, 19 (Ayrshire Archaeological and Natural History Society, 1997).

Graham, Eric J., 'The Scots Penetration of the Jamaican Plantation Business', in Devine, ed, *Recovering Scotland's Slavery Past*, pp. 82–98.

Haakonssen, Knud, ed., *Enlightenment and Religion: Rational Dissent in Eighteenth-Century Britain* (Cambridge, 1996).

Halsey, Katie, 'Types of Libraries, Books and Borrowing 1750–1830: An Analysis of Scottish Borrowers' Registers', 9 Nov. 2020, https://borrowing.stir.ac.uk/types-of-libraries.

Hancock, David, *Citizens of the World: London Merchants and the Integration of the British Atlantic Community, 1735–1785* (Cambridge, 1995).

Hanley, Ryan, *Beyond Slavery and Abolition: Black British Writing, c. 1770–1830* (Cambridge, 2018).

Hanley, Ryan Patrick, 'Adam Smith on the "Natural Principles of Religion"', *Journal of Scottish Philosophy*, 13 (2015), pp. 37–53.

Harrison, J. F. C., *The Second Coming: Popular Millenarianism 1780–1850* (1979).

Hay, Daisy, *Dinner with Joseph Johnson: Books and Friendship in a Revolutionary Age* (2022).

Haydon, Colin, *Anti-Catholicism in Eighteenth-Century England, c. 1714–1780* (Manchester, 1995).

Heath, Eugene, 'Alexander Gillies and Adam Smith: Freemasonry and the Resonance of Self-Love', *Scottish Historical Review*, 103 (2024), pp. 289–304.

Hesse, Carla, 'Print Culture in the Enlightenment', in Fitzpatrick, Jones, Knellwolf, and McCalman, eds, *The Enlightenment World*, pp. 366–81.

Himmelfarb, Gertrude, *The People of the Book: Philosemitism in England, from Cromwell to Churchill* (New York, 2011).

Hitchin, Neil W., 'The Politics of English Bible Translation in Georgian Britain: The Alexander Prize', *Transactions of the Royal Historical Society*, 9 (1999), pp. 67–92.

Hobson, Joan, 'A Short History of the "Free Grammar School of King James in Bewdley"', in Snell, ed., *Essays towards a History of Bewdley*, pp. 105–14.

Hobson, Kenneth, 'Every Other House ... Bewdley Inns', in Snell, ed., *Essays towards the History of Bewdley*, pp. 115–22.

Holcomb, Kathleen, 'Thomas Reid in the Glasgow Literary Society', in Hook and Sher, eds, *The Glasgow Enlightenment*, pp. 95–110.

Holt, Anne, *Walking Together: A Study in Liverpool Nonconformity, 1688–1938* (1938).

Honeyman, Valerie, '"That Ye May Judge for Yourselves": The Contribution of Scottish Presbyterianism towards the Emergence of Political Awareness amongst Ordinary People in Scotland between 1746 and 1792' (PhD thesis, University of Stirling, 2012).

Hook, Andrew, *Scotland and America: A Study of Cultural Relations, 1750–1835* (Glasgow, 1975).

Hook, Andrew and Richard B. Sher, eds, *The Glasgow Enlightenment* (East Linton, 1995).

Hunt, Lynn, *Inventing Human Rights: A History* (New York, 2007).

Hutchison, I. G. C., *Industry, Reform and Empire: Scotland, 1790–1880* (Edinburgh, 2020).

Ingram, Robert G., 'William Warburton, Divine Action, and Enlightened Christianity', in William Gibson and Robert G. Ingram, eds, *Religious Identities in Britain, 1660–1832* (Aldershot, 2005), pp. 97–118.

Ingram, Robert G., *Reformation without End: Religion, Politics and the Past in Post-Revolutionary England* (Manchester, 2018).

Israel, Jonathan, *Radical Enlightenment: Philosophy and the Making of Modernity, 1660–1750* (Oxford, 2002).

Israel, Jonathan, *Enlightenment Contested: Philosophy, Modernity, and the Emancipation of Man, 1670–1752* (Oxford, 2008).

Israel, Jonathan, *Democratic Enlightenment: Philosophy, Revolution, and Human Rights, 1750–1790* (Oxford, 2011).

Israel, Jonathan, *The Enlightenment That Failed: Ideas, Revolution, and Democratic Defeat, 1748–1830* (Oxford, 2019).

Jackson, Clare, 'Progress and Optimism', in Fitzpatrick, Jones, Knellwolf, and McCalman, eds, *The Enlightenment World*, pp. 177–93.

Jackson, Gordon, 'New Horizons in Trade', in Devine and Jackson, eds, *Glasgow, Volume 1*, pp. 214–38.

Jacob, Margaret C., 'Polite Worlds of Enlightenment', in Fitzpatrick, Jones, Knellwolf, and McCalman, eds, *The Enlightenment World*, pp. 272–87.

Jennings, Judi, *The Business of Abolishing the British Slave Trade, 1783–1807* (1997).

Jones, Brad, 'The American Revolution, Glasgow, and the Making of the Second City of the Empire', in Simon Newman, ed., *Europe's American Revolution* (Basingstoke, 2006), pp. 1–25.

Jones, Peter M., *Industrial Enlightenment: Science, Technology, and Culture in Birmingham and the West Midlands, 1760–1820* (Manchester, 2008).

Kadish, Sharman, *Bevis Marks Synagogue: A Short History of the Building and an Appreciation of Its Architecture* (2001).
Katz, David S., 'Hutchinsonians and Hebraic Fundamentalism in Eighteenth-Century England', in D. S. Katz and J. I. Israel, eds, *Sceptics, Millenarians and Jews* (Leiden, 1990), pp. 237–55.
Keen, Paul, 'The "Balloonomania": Science and Spectacle in 1780s England', *Eighteenth-Century Studies*, 39 (2006), pp. 507–35.
Kelly, Paul, 'Radicalism and Public Opinion in the General Election of 1784', *Historical Research*, 45 (1972), pp. 73–88.
Kelly, Paul, 'British Parliamentary Politics, 1784–1786', *Historical Journal*, 17 (1974), pp. 733–53.
Kennedy, Alison, 'Historical Perspectives in the Mind of Joseph Priestley', in Rivers and Wykes, eds, *Joseph Priestley: Scientist, Philosopher, and Theologian*, pp. 190–93.
Kennedy, Thomas D., 'William Leechman, Pulpit Eloquence and the Glasgow Enlightenment', in Hook and Sher, eds, *The Glasgow Enlightenment*, pp. 56–72.
Kenrick, Norah, *Chronicles of a Nonconformist Family: The Kenricks of Wynne Hall, Exeter and Birmingham*. Edited by Mrs. W. Byng Kenrick (Birmingham, 1932).
Kent, Andrew, ed., *An Eighteenth-Century Lectureship in Chemistry* (Glasgow, 1950).
Kidd, Colin, 'North Britishness and the Nature of Eighteenth-Century British Patriotisms', *Historical Journal*, 39 (1996), pp. 361–82.
Kidd, Colin, 'Subscription, the Scottish Enlightenment and the Moderate Interpretation of History', *Journal of Ecclesiastical History*, 55 (2004), pp. 502–19.
Kidd, Colin, 'Enlightenment and Anti-Enlightenment in Eighteenth-Century Scotland: An Ayrshire-Renfrewshire Microclimate', in Jean-François Dunyach and Ann Thomson, eds, *The Enlightenment in Scotland: National and International Perspectives* (Oxford, 2015), pp. 59–84.
Kidd, Colin, 'The Fergusson Affair: Calvinism and Dissimulation in the Scottish Enlightenment', *Intellectual History Review*, 26 (2016), pp. 339–54.
Kidd, Colin, 'Satire, Hypocrisy and the Ayrshire-Renfrewshire Enlightenment', in Gerard Carruthers and Colin Kidd, eds, *International Companion to John Galt* (Glasgow, 2017), pp. 15–33.
Knott, Sarah and Barbara Taylor, eds, *Women, Gender and Enlightenment* (Basingstoke, 2005).
Kot, Stanislas, *Socinianism in Poland: The Social and Political Ideas of the Polish Antitrinitarians in the Sixteenth and Seventeenth Centuries*, trans. Earl Morse Wilbur (Boston, MA, 1957).
Kuehn, Manfred and Heiner F. Klemme, eds, *The Bloomsbury Dictionary of Eighteenth-Century German Philosophers* (2016).
Lana, Renata, 'Women and the Foxite Strategy in the Westminster Election of 1784', *Eighteenth-Century Life*, 26 (2002), pp. 46–69.
Landsman, Ned C., 'Presbyterians and Provincial Society: The Evangelical Enlightenment in the West of Scotland, 1740–1775', in John Dwyer and Richard B. Sher, eds, *Sociability and Society in Eighteenth-Century Scotland* (Edinburgh, 1993), pp. 194–209.
Leneman, Leah, *Alienated Affections: Divorce and Separation in Scotland 1684–1830* (Edinburgh, 2019).

Leonard, Dick and Mark Garnett, *Titans: Fox vs. Pitt* (2019).
Lewis, A. R., 'The Builders of Edinburgh's New Town, 1767–1795' (PhD thesis, University of Edinburgh, 2006).
Livingstone, Elizabeth A. and Frank Leslie Cross, eds, *Oxford Dictionary of the Christian Church*, 4th edn (Oxford, 2005).
Llarman, Michael J., *The Framers Coup: The Making of the United States Constitution* (Oxford, 2016).
Lock, F. P., *Edmund Burke, Volume I: 1730–1784* (Oxford, 1998).
Lock, F. P., *Edmund Burke, Volume II: 1784–1797* (Oxford, 2006).
Low, Donald A., *Robert Burns: The Critical Heritage* (1974).
M'Kerrow, John, *History of the Secession Church* (Glasgow, 1841).
MacCulloch, Diarmaid, *The Boy King Edward VI and the Protestant Reformation* (Chapel Hill, NC, 2002).
Mackenzie, Robert Dunbar, *Kilbarchan: A Parish History* (Paisley, 1902).
Mackie, J. D., *The University of Glasgow 1451–1951: A Short History* (Glasgow, 1954).
Mackintosh, Alan, *The Patent Medicines Industry in Georgian England Constructing the Market by the Potency of Print* (Basingstoke, 2017).
Macleod, Emma, 'The Scottish Opposition Whigs and the French Revolution', in Bob Harris, ed., *Scotland in the Age of the French Revolution* (Edinburgh, 2005), pp. 79–98.
Macleod, Emma, 'British Attitudes to the French Revolution', *Historical Journal*, 50 (2007), pp. 689–709.
Macleod, Emma, *British Visions of America, 1775–1820: Republican Realities* (2013).
Macleod, Emma, 'Revolution', in Aaron Garrett and James Harris, eds, *Scottish Philosophy in the Eighteenth Century, Volume I: Morals, Politics, Art, Religion* (Oxford, 2015), pp. 363–69.
Macleod, Emma, 'A Proper Manner of Carrying on Controversies: Richard Price and the American Revolution', *Huntington Library Quarterly*, 82 (2019), pp. 277–302.
Macleod, Emma, 'Burns and the Borders of Poetry in the Letters of James Wodrow and Samuel Kenrick', *Burns Chronicle*, special issue ed. Christopher A. Whatley, 133 (2024), pp. 210–24.
MacRobert, A. E., *The 1745 Rebellion and the Southern Scottish Lowlands* (Ely, 2006).
MacRobert, A. E., 'The Myths about the 1745 Jacobite Rebellion', *Historian*, 99 (2008), pp. 16–23.
Mailer, Gideon, *John Witherspoon's American Revolution* (Chapel Hill, NC, 2017).
Mandelbrote, Scott, 'The English Bible and Its Readers in the Eighteenth Century', in Isabel Rivers, ed., *Books and Their Readers in 18th Century England, Volume 2: New Essays* (2003), pp. 35–78.
Manley, Keith, *Books, Borrowers, and Shareholders: Scottish Circulating and Subscription Libraries before 1825: A Survey and Listing* (Edinburgh, 2012).
Marshall, P. J., *Remaking the British Atlantic: The United States and the British Empire after American Independence* (Oxford, 2012).

Mather, F. C., *High Church Prophet: Bishop Samuel Horsley (1733–1806) and the Caroline Tradition in the Later Georgian Church* (Oxford, 1992).

Maver, Irene, *Glasgow* (Edinburgh, 2000).

McBride, Ian, *Scripture Politics: Ulster Presbyterians and Irish Radicalism in the Late Eighteenth Century* (Oxford, 1998).

McElroy, D. D., 'Literary Clubs and Societies of Eighteenth-Century Scotland, and Their Influence on the Literary Productions of the Period from 1700 to 1800' (PhD thesis, University of Edinburgh, 1951).

McElroy, Davis D., *Scotland's Age of Improvement: A Survey of Eighteenth-Century Literary Clubs and Societies* ([Pullman], WA, [1969]).

McGinty, J. Walter, *Robert Burns and Religion* (Aldershot, 2003).

McIntosh, John R., *Church and Theology in Enlightenment Scotland: The Popular Party, 1740–1800* (East Linton, 1998).

McLean, Ralph, 'Professors, Merchants, and Ministers in the Clubs of Eighteenth-Century Glasgow', in Mark C. Wallace and Jane Rendall, eds, *Association and Enlightenment: Scottish Clubs and Societies, 1700–1830* (Lewisburg, PA, 2020), pp. 85–102.

Mee, Jon, 'Transpennine Enlightenment: The Literary and Philosophical Societies and Knowledge Networks of the North, 1781–1830', *Journal for Eighteenth-Century Studies*, 38 (2015), pp. 599–612.

Mee, Jon, *Networks of Improvement: Literature, Bodies and Machines in the Industrial Revolution* (Chicago, IL, 2023).

Meikle, Henry W., *Scotland and the French Revolution* (Glasgow, 1912).

Midgley, Graham, *University Life in Eighteenth-Century Oxford* (New York, 1996).

Miller, Henry, *A Nation of Petitioners: Petitions and Petitioning in the United Kingdom, 1780–1918* (Cambridge, 2023).

Moore, Peter, *Life, Liberty, and the Pursuit of Happiness: Britain and the American Dream* (New York, 2023).

Mortimer, Sarah, 'Exile, Apostasy and Anglicanism in the English Revolution', in Philip Major, ed., *Literatures of Exile in the English Revolution and Its Aftermath, 1640–1690* (Farnham and Burlington, VT, 2010), pp. 91–104.

Mullen, Stephen, 'Henry Dundas: A "Great Delayer" of the Abolition of the Transatlantic Slave Trade', *Scottish Historical Review*, 100 (2021), pp. 218–48.

Mullen, Stephen, *Glasgow's Sugar Aristocracy in the British Atlantic World, 1776–1838* (2022).

Munck, Thomas, *The Enlightenment: A Comparative Social History, 1721–1794* (2000).

Munck, Thomas, *Conflict and Enlightenment: Print and Political Culture in Europe, 1635–1795* (Cambridge, 2019).

Murdoch, Alexander, 'Patronage and Party in the Church of Scotland, 1750–1800', in Norman Macdougall, ed., *Church, Politics and Society: Scotland, 1408–1929* (Edinburgh, 1983), pp. 197–220.

Mutch, Alistair, *Religion and National Identity: Governing Scottish Presbyterianism in the Eighteenth Century* (Edinburgh, 2015).

Nangle, Benjamin Christie, *The Monthly Review, First Series, 1749–1789* (Oxford, 1934).
Nisbet, Stuart, 'Renfrewshire's Slave Legacy 3: The Cunninghams of Craigends', Renfrewshire Local History Forum, 2019, https://rlhf.info/renfrewshires-slave-legacy-3-the-cunninghams-of-craigends.
Nisbet, Stuart, 'Early Scottish Sugar Planters in the Leeward Islands, c. 1660–1740', in Devine, *Recovering Scotland's Slavery Past*, pp. 62–81.
Nockles, Peter B., *The Oxford Movement in Context: Anglican High Churchmanship, 1760–1857* (Cambridge, 1994).
Nockles, Peter B., 'Church Parties in the Pre-Tractarian Church of England, 1750–1833: The "Orthodox"—Some Problems of Definition and Identity', in Walsh, Haydon, and Taylor, *Church of England c. 1689–c. 1833*, pp. 334–59.
Noll, Mark, *Princeton and the Republic, 1768–1822: The Search for a Christian Enlightenment in the Era of Samuel Stanhope Smith* (Princeton, NJ, 1989).
Norris, Clive Murray, *The Financing of John Wesley's Methodism c.1740–1800* (Oxford, 2017).
O'Gorman, Frank, *Voters, Patrons, and Parties: The Unreformed Electoral System of Hanoverian England 1734–1832* (Oxford, 1989).
O'Gorman, Frank, 'Ordering the Political World: The Pattern of Politics in Eighteenth-Century Britain (1660–1832)', in Diana Donald and Frank O'Gorman, eds, *Ordering the World in the Eighteenth Century* (Basingstoke, 2006), pp. 83–111.
Oldfield, J. R., *Popular Politics and British Anti-Slavery: The Mobilisation of Public Opinion against the Slave Trade, 1787–1807* (1998).
Olleson, Philip, 'The London Roman Catholic Embassy Chapels and Their Music in the Eighteenth and Early Nineteenth Centuries', in David Wyn Jones, ed., *Music in Eighteenth-Century Britain* (Aldershot, 2000), pp. 101–18.
Oslington, Paul, ed., *Adam Smith as Theologian* (2011).
Pagan, James, *Sketch of the History of Glasgow* (Glasgow, 1847).
Page, Anthony, 'The Enlightenment and a "Second Reformation": The Religion and Philosophy of John Jebb (1736–86)', *Enlightenment and Dissent*, 17 (1998), pp. 48–82.
Page, Anthony, *John Jebb and the Enlightenment Origins of British Radicalism* (Westport, CT, 2003).
Page, Anthony, 'Rational Dissent, Enlightenment and Abolition of the British Slave Trade', *Historical Journal*, 54 (2011), pp. 741–72.
Page, Anthony, *Britain and the Seventy Years War, 1744–1815* (Basingstoke, 2015).
Page, Anthony, 'Rational Dissent and Blackstone's Commentaries', in Anthony Page and Wilfrid R. Prest, eds, *Blackstone and His Critics* (Oxford, 2018), pp. 78–81.
Parker, Geoffrey, *Global Crisis: War, Climate Change and Catastrophe in the Seventeenth Century* (New Haven, CT, 2013).
Paterson, James, *History of the Counties of Ayr and Wigton* (Edinburgh, 1866).
Peters, Carolyn Marie, 'Glasgow's Tobacco Lords: An Examination of Wealth Creators in the Eighteenth Century' (PhD thesis, University of Glasgow, 1990).

Peters, Timothy, 'King George III, Bipolar Disorder, Porphyria and Lessons for Historians', *Clinical Medicine*, 11 (2011), pp. 261–64.
Phillipson, N. T. and Rosalind Mitchison, eds, *Scotland in the Age of Improvement: Essays in Scottish History in the Eighteenth Century* (Edinburgh, 1996).
Phillipson, Nicholas, *Adam Smith: An Enlightened Life* (2010).
Phillipson, Nicholas T., *The Scottish Whigs and the Reform of the Court of Session 1785–1830* (Edinburgh, 1990).
Pietenholz, Peter G., 'Daniel Zwicker's Views on Religious Peace and Unity', in C. Berkens-Stevenlinck, J. Israel, and G. H. Posthumus Meyjes, eds, *The Emergence of Tolerance in the Dutch Republic* (Leiden, 1997), pp. 117–30.
Pietenholz, Peter G., *Daniel Zwicker 1612–1678: Peace, Tolerance and God, the One and Only* (Florence, 1998).
Pittock, Murray, *Enlightenment in a Smart City: Edinburgh, 1680–1750* (Edinburgh, 2018).
Pocock, J. G. A., 'Conservative Enlightenment and Democratic Revolutions: The American and French Cases in British Perspective', *Government and Opposition*, 24 (1989), pp. 81–105.
Pocock, J. G. A., *Barbarism and Religion*, 6 vols (Cambridge, 1999–2018).
Ponting, Betty, 'Mathematics at Aberdeen: Developments, Characters, Traits, 1717–1860', *Aberdeen University Review*, 48 (1979–80), pp. 162–76.
Popkin, Jeremy D., *A Short History of the French Revolution*, 6th edn (Upper Saddle River, NJ, 2015).
Popkin, Richard H., 'David Levi, Anglo-Jewish Theologian', *The Jewish Quarterly Review*, 87 (1996), pp. 79–101.
Porter, Roy, *Enlightenment: Britain and the Creation of the Modern World* (2000).
Primrose, R. C., 'The Scottish Burgh Reform Movement, 1783–93', *Aberdeen University Review*, 37 (1957), pp. 27–41.
Rauser, Amelia F., 'The Butcher-Kissing Duchess of Devonshire: Between Caricature and Allegory in 1784', *Eighteenth-Century Studies*, 36 (2002), pp. 23–46.
Raven, James, 'Libraries for Sociability: The Advance of the Subscription Library', in Giles Mandelbrote and Keith A. Manley, eds, *The Cambridge History of Libraries in Britain and Ireland, Volume II: 1640–1850* (Cambridge, 2006), pp. 241–63.
Rediker, Marcus, *The Fearless Benjamin Lay: The Quaker Dwarf Who Became the First Revolutionary Abolitionist* (Boston, MA, 2017).
Redwood, John, *Reason, Ridicule and Religion: The Age of Enlightenment in England 1660–1750* (1976).
Reid, David A., 'Rational Dissent and the Rhetoric of Educational Philanthropy in the Dissenting Academies of Lancashire, Hackney and Exeter', *Northern History*, 47 (2010), pp. 97–116.
Rendall, Jane, '"Women That Would Plague Me with Rational Conversation": Aspiring Women and Scottish Whigs, c. 1790–1830', in Knott and Taylor, eds, *Women, Gender and Enlightenment*, pp. 326–47.
Renton, Alex, *Blood Legacy: Reckoning with a Family's Story of Slavery* (Edinburgh, 2021).

Renwick, Robert, John Lindsay, and George Eyre-Todd, *History of Glasgow*, 3 vols (Glasgow, 1921–34).

Richard, Robert, 'An Examination of the Life and Career of Rev William McGill (1732–1807): Controversial Ayr Theologian' (PhD thesis, University of Glasgow, 2010).

Riordan, Michael D., 'Mysticism and Prophecy in Scotland in the Long Eighteenth Century' (PhD thesis, University of Cambridge, 2015).

Rivers, Isabel, *Vanity Fair and the Celestial City: Dissenting, Methodist, and Evangelical Literary Culture in England, 1720–1800* (Oxford, 2018).

Rivers, Isabel and David L. Wykes, eds, *Joseph Priestley: Scientist, Philosopher, and Theologian* (Oxford, 2008).

Robbins, Caroline, *The Eighteenth-Century Commonwealthman* (Cambridge, MA, 1959).

Roberts, Andrew, *George III: The Life and Reign of Britain's Most Misunderstood Monarch* (2021).

Robertson, John, *The Scottish Enlightenment and the Militia Issue* (Edinburgh, 1985).

Rolli, Chiara, *The Trial of Warren Hastings Classical Oratory and Reception in Eighteenth-Century England* (2019).

Roper, Derek, *Reviewing before the Edinburgh, 1788–1802* (1978).

Ross, Ian Simpson, 'Adam Smith's "Happiest" Years as a Glasgow Professor', in Hook and Sher, eds, *Glasgow Enlightenment*, pp. 73–94.

Ruddock, E. C., 'The Building of the North Bridge, Edinburgh: 1763–1775', *Transactions of the Newcomen Society*, 47 (1974), pp. 9–33.

Ruderman, David B., *Jewish Enlightenment in an English Key: Anglo-Jewry's Construction of Modern Jewish Thought* (Princeton, NJ, 2018).

Rule, John, *The Vital Century: England's Developing Economy, 1714–1815* (1992).

Ryan, Yann Ciarán and Mikko Tolonen, 'The Evolution of Scottish Enlightenment Publishing', *Historical Journal*, published online 2024, pp. 1–33, doi: 10.1017/S0018246X23000614.

Sage, Donald, *Memorabilia Domestica; or Parish Life in the North of Scotland* (Edinburgh, 1899).

Saville, Richard, *Bank of Scotland: A History, 1695–1995* (Edinburgh, 1996).

Schofield, Robert E., *The Enlightenment of Joseph Priestley: A Study of His Life and Work from 1733 to 1773* (University Park, PA, 1997).

Schofield, Robert E., *The Enlightened Joseph Priestley: A Study of His Life and Work from 1773 to 1804* (University Park, PA, 2004).

Scott, William Robert, *Francis Hutcheson: His Life, Teaching and Position in the History of Philosophy* (Cambridge, 1900).

Seed, John, 'The Spectre of Puritanism: Forgetting the Seventeenth Century in David Hume's "History of England"', *Social History*, 30 (2005), pp. 444–62.

Seed, John, *Dissenting Histories: Religious Division and the Politics of Memory in Eighteenth-Century England* (Edinburgh, 2008).

Seed, John, '"A Set of Men Powerful Enough in Many Things": Rational Dissent and Political Opposition in England 1770–1790', in Haakonssen, ed., *Enlightenment and Religion*, pp. 140–68.

Sell, Allan P. F., 'Priestley's Polemic against Reid', *The Price-Priestley Newsletter*, 3 (1979), pp. 41–52.
Sell, Alan P. F., *Christ and Controversy: The Person of Christ in Nonconformist Thought and Ecclesial Experience, 1600–2000* (Eugene, OR, 2011).
Sheehan, Jonathan, *The Enlightenment Bible: Translation, Scholarship, Culture* (Princeton, NJ, 2005).
Sher, Richard B., 'Scotland Transformed: The Eighteenth Century', in Jenny Wormald, ed., *Scotland: A History* (Oxford, 2005).
Sher, Richard B., *Church and University in the Scottish Enlightenment: The Moderate Literati of Edinburgh* (Edinburgh, 2015).
Sher, Richard B., 'Commerce, Religion and the Enlightenment', in Devine and Jackson, eds, *Glasgow, Volume 1*, pp. 312–59.
Sher, Richard B. and Alexander Murdoch, 'Patronage and Party in the Church of Scotland, 1750–1800', in Norman Macdougall, ed., *Church, Politics and Society: Scotland, 1408–1929* (Edinburgh, 1983), pp. 197–220.
Sher, Richard B. and Jeffrey R. Smitten, eds, *Scotland and America in the Age of the Enlightenment* (Edinburgh, 1990).
Sher, Rick B., 'The Book in the Scottish Enlightenment', in *The Culture of the Book in the Scottish Enlightenment: An Exhibition, with Essays by Roger Emerson, Richard Sher, Stephen Brown, and Paul Wood*, Thomas Fisher Rare Book Library (Toronto, 2000), pp. 40–60.
Sher, Rick B., *The Enlightenment and the Book: Scottish Authors and Their Publishers in Britain, Ireland, and America* (Chicago, IL, 2006).
Short, L. Baker, *Pioneers of Scottish Unitarianism* (Narbeth, 1963).
Simonton, Deborah, 'Negotiating the Economy of the Eighteenth-Century Scottish Town: Female Entrepreneurs Claim Their Place', in Katie Barclay and Deborah Simonton, eds, *Women in Eighteenth-Century Scotland: Intimate, Intellectual and Public Lives* (Farnham, 2013), pp. 211–32.
Skjönsberg, Max, *The Persistence of Party: Ideas of Harmonious Discord in Eighteenth-Century Britain* (Cambridge, 2021).
Smethurst, John B., *Historical Directory of Trade Unions: Volume 4* (Aldershot, 1994).
Smith, Valerie, *Rational Dissenters in Late Eighteenth-Century England: 'An Ardent Desire of Truth'* (Woodbridge, 2021).
Smitten, Jeffrey R., *The Life of William Robertson: Minister, Historian, and Principal* (Edinburgh, 2017).
Smout, T. C., 'The Landowner and the Planned Village in Scotland, 1730–1830', in Phillipson and Mitchison, eds, *Scotland in the Age of Improvement*, pp. 73–106.
Snell, Lawrence S., ed., *Essays towards a History of Bewdley* (Bewdley, 1972).
St Clair, William, *The Reading Nation in the Romantic Period* (Cambridge, 2004).
Strawhorn, John, ed., *Ayrshire at the Time of Burns* (Kilmarnock, 1959).
Strong, Joy and Rowan Strong, 'Elspeth Buchan and the Buchanite Movement', in James Crossley and Alastair Lockhart, eds, *Critical Dictionary of Apocalyptic and Millenarian Movements*, 27 April 2021, www.cdamm.org/articles/buchanites.

Struthers, Gavin, *The History of the Rise, Progress and Principles of the Relief Church* (Glasgow, 1843).
Suderman, Jeffrey M., *Orthodoxy and Enlightenment: George Campbell in the Eighteenth Century* (Montreal and Ithaca, NY, 2001).
Suderman, Jeffrey M., 'Religion and Philosophy', in Aaron Garrett and James A. Harris, eds, *Scottish Philosophy in the Eighteenth Century*, I, *Morals, Politics, Art, Religion* (Oxford, 2015), pp. 196–238.
Swaminathan, Srividhy, *Debating the Slave Trade: Rhetoric of British National Identity, 1759–1815* (Farnham, 2009).
Swiderska, H., 'Socinian Books with the Raków Imprint in the British Library', *The British Library Journal*, 8 (1982), pp. 206–17.
Sykes, Norman, *Church and State in England in the XVIIIth Century* (Cambridge, 1934).
Symington, Graeme, 'William Symington 1764–1831: Engineer, Inventor and Steamboat Pioneer', revised 3 Nov. 2022, https://sites.google.com/view/william-symington/introduction-and-contents.
Tapper, Alan, 'The Beginnings of Priestley's Materialism', *Enlightenment and Dissent*, 1 (1982), pp. 73–82.
Taylor, Barbara, 'Mary Wollstonecraft and the Wild Wish of Early Feminism', *History Workshop Journal*, 33 (1992), pp. 197–219.
Thomas, D. O., *The Honest Mind: The Thought and Work of Richard Price* (Oxford, 1977), pp. 260–83.
Thompson, Andrew C., 'Toleration, Dissent and the State in Britain', in Andrew C. Thompson, ed., *The Oxford History of Protestant Dissenting Traditions, Volume III: The Long Eighteenth Century, c. 1689–c. 1828* (Oxford, 2018), pp. 263–83.
Towsey, Mark, *Reading the Scottish Enlightenment: Books and Their Readers in Provincial Scotland, 1750–1820* (Leiden, 2010).
Towsey, Mark and Kyle B. Roberts, eds, *Before the Public Library: Reading, Community, and Identity in the Atlantic World, 1650–1850* (Leiden, 2018).
Turnbull, Paul, 'Gibbon's Exchange with Joseph Priestley', *British Journal for Eighteenth-Century Studies*, 14 (1991), pp. 139–58.
Vickery, Amanda, *The Gentleman's Daughter: Women's Lives in Georgian England* (1998).
Voges, Friedhelm, 'Moderate and Evangelical Thinking in the Later Eighteenth Century: Differences and Shared Attitudes', *Records of the Scottish Church History Society*, 22 (1985), pp. 141–57.
Walker, David M, 'The Background of the Institutions', in David M. Walker, ed., *Stair Tercentenary Studies* (Edinburgh, 1981), pp. 69–78.
Walsh, John, Colin Haydon, and Stephen Taylor, eds, *The Church of England, c. 1689–c. 1833: From Toleration to Tractarianism* (Cambridge, 1993).
Walvin, James, *The Zong: A Massacre, the Law and the End of Slavery* (New Haven, CT, 2011).
Walvin, James, 'Why Did the British Abolish the Slave Trade? Econocide Revisited', *Slavery & Abolition*, 32 (2011), pp. 583–88.
Walvin, James, 'The Slave Trade, Quakers, and the Early Days of British Abolition', in Carey and Plank, eds, *Quakers and Abolition*, pp. 165–79.

Walzer, Arthur E., *George Campbell: Rhetoric in the Age of Enlightenment* (Albany, NY, 2001).
Ward, Gerald W. R., ed., *The Grove Encyclopedia of Materials and Techniques in Art* (Oxford, 2008).
Watts, Michael, *The Dissenters: From the Reformation to the French Revolution* (Oxford, 1978).
Webb, R. K., 'Price among the Unitarians', *Enlightenment and Dissent*, 19 (2000), pp. 147–70.
Webb, R. K., 'The Emergence of Rational Dissent', in Haakonssen, ed., *Enlightenment and Religion*, pp. 12–41.
Whatley, Christopher A., *Scottish Society, 1707–1830: Beyond Jacobitism, Towards Industrialisation* (Manchester, 2000).
Whatley, Christopher A., 'The Experience of Work', in T. M. Devine and Rosalind Mitchison, eds, *People and Society in Scotland, Vol. 1: 1760–1830* (Edinburgh, 1988), pp. 234–39.
Whatley, Christopher A., 'Reformed Religion, Regime Change, Scottish Whigs and the Struggle for the "Soul" of Scotland, c.1688–c.1788', *Scottish Historical Review*, 92 (2013), pp. 66–99.
Whatmore, Richard, *The End of Enlightenment: Empire, Commerce, Crisis* (2023).
Whyman, Susan E., *The Pen and the People: English Letter Writers 1660–1800* (Oxford, 2009).
Whyte, Iain, *Scotland and the Abolition of Black Slavery, 1756–1838* (Edinburgh, 2006).
Wiles, Maurice, *Archetypal Heresy: Arianism through the Centuries* (Oxford, 2004).
Winstanley, D. A., *Unreformed Cambridge: A Study of Certain Aspects of the University in the Late Eighteenth Century* (Cambridge, 1935).
Wood, Paul, '"Jolly Jack Phosphorous" in the Venice of the North; or, Who Was John Anderson?', in Hook and Sher, eds, *Glasgow Enlightenment*, pp. 111–32.
Yeager, Jonathan, *Enlightened Evangelicalism: The Life and Thought of John Erskine* (New York, 2011).
Young, B. W., *Religion and Enlightenment in Eighteenth-Century England: Theological Debate from Locke to Burke* (Oxford, 1998).
Young, Ronnie, 'Thomas Muir at Glasgow: John Millar and the University', in Gerard Carruthers and Don Martin, eds, *Thomas Muir of Huntershill: Essays for the Twenty-First Century* (Edinburgh, 2016), pp. 112–40.
Youngson, A. J., *The Making of Classical Edinburgh* (Edinburgh, 1966).

# INDEX

Aberdeen, 47, 119, 137 n., 162, 193, 289, 347
   see Universities, Aberdeen, King's College
   see Universities, Aberdeen, Marischal College
Aberfoyle, 376 n.
Abney, Elizabeth, 380 n.
Abolitionism (slave trade), 53, 61–6, 157 n., 368, 373, 456 n.
Abraham, 250
Achinairn, near Glasgow, 235, 258, 277
Act of Uniformity (1662), 458
Act of Union (1707), 61, 215, 452, 453, 454, 457
Adam, James, 129 n.
Adam, John, 287
Adam, Robert, 95 n.
Adam's Court, Glasgow, 114–15
Addington, Arthur, 414 n.
Addison, Joseph, 126
Adrian, Emperor, 288
Advocates' Library, Edinburgh, 102 n.
Aesop, 413
Africa / Africans, 62, 63, 64, 65
Agriculture, 12 n., 83, 111, 156, 273, 412
Aikin, John, 348 n.
Ailesbury, Lord, 78 n.
Ainsworth, Robert, 220
Alcohol, 82–4, 213, 301, 360
Ali, Haidar, of Mysore, 356 n.
Allan, John, 166 n., 325, 381 n.
Alva, see Maxwell
Amalfi, 293
America, 1, 56
   American Revolution, 63, 199 n., 444 n.
   College of New Jersey, see Universities, College of New Jersey
   Congress, 263
   Constitution, 56
   Declaration of Independence, 98 n., 132 n.
   Emigration to, 391–2 n.
   New York, 289 n.
   Peace of Paris (1783), 129, 130
   Philadelphia, 391 n.
   Religion, 39, 202 n.
   Seven Years' War, 134 n.
   South Carolina, 82 n., 103 n., 157 n., 325, 410 n.
   United States of, 53, 88, 263
   Trade with, 56, 178 n., 180 n., 300
   Virginia, 130, 179, 289 n.
   War of Independence, 53, 54, 56, 62, 64, 78 n., 79 n, 130, 174, 199 n., 246 n., 251, 306 n.
Amsterdam, 86 n.
Anacreon, 292
Anastasius, Pope, 204 n.
Anatomy, 189 n., 190
Anderson, James, 363 n.
Anderson, John, 178, 184
   Campaign against the College (University) of Glasgow and Principal William Leechman (1785), 28–30, 151–2, 154, 160–1, 164, 165–70, 176, 181–91, 193, 207, 216–17, 224, 237, 278, 334
   Career at Glasgow University, 28, 158 n., 177, 188, 232 n.
   Hostility to Adam Smith in the 1750s, 29, 154
   Lawsuit at the Court of Session against the College (University) of Glasgow, 216, 237, 278, 365, 373–4
   Lawsuit at the Court of Session against William Richardson, 29, 188, 189, 278, 365, 373–4
   Lawsuit against, at the Court of Session, by William Taylor, 29, 189, 278, 365, 373–4
   Tour of England (1759) with SK and James Milliken, 28, 151 n., 154, 399, 402
   Wodrow, Gavin, and, 28
Andrews, Robert, 92–3, 414
Anglicanism, see Church of England
Ankerville, see Ross
Anne, Queen, 170
Annesley, Arthur, eighth viscount Valentia, 361
Anstey, Christopher, 113
Apollonius of Tyana, 281
Apostles, 74 n., 75, 151, 160, 271, 318, 319
Arabic, 259 n.
Arbuckle, Mr, 376
Archbald, James, 422, 426 n.
Archbald, Mary Ann, née Wodrow, 12, 36, 267, 270, 422–6 n.

503

# INDEX

Ardrossan, Ayrshire, 79 n., 440 n.
Argyll, *see* Campbell
Aristotle, 352
Arkwright, Robert, 300 n.
Armagh, Ireland, 411
Arminians / Arminianism, *see* Theology, Arminians / Arminianism
Armour, Jean, 440 n.
Arnot, Hugo, 17, 138, 148–9
Arran, island of, 105 n.
Arthur, Archibald, 230–2, 233, 240–1, 248, 266, 269, 275, 277, 294, 295, 307, 323, 376, 408, 415, 438, 439
Ashgrove, Ayrshire, 184 n.
Ashworth, Caleb, 258
Association movement, 77
Aston, 81 n.
Astronomy, 193, 300
Athanasius of Alexandria, 80
Athanasians / Athanasianism, *see* Theology, Athanasians / Athanasianism
Atheist / atheism, *see* Theology, Atheist / atheism
Athens, 415 n.
Attercliffe Dissenting Academy, 249 n.
Atonement, *see* Atonement, Day of; Theology, Atonement
Auchenharvie House, 105 n.
Auchincruive or Auchincrue, 129
Auld, James, 465
Auld, William, 428–9, 440
Automatons, 31, 221, 239
Ayr, 109 n., 150
  Ayr Bank, 20, 35, 99, 104, 123
  Ayr, first charge, 327 n.
  Ayr, second charge, 48, 327 n.
  Circulating library, 15 n.
  Kirk Session, 419, 420
  Library Society, 15, 363 n.
  Magistrates and Town Council, 419–20
  Presbytery of Ayr, 50–2, 70, 72 n., 440, 441
  Synod of Glasgow and Ayr, 22, 32, 50–2, 72 n., 101, 102 n., 165, 166 n., 167, 189, 283 n., 308, 373, 440
Ayrshire, 95 n., 106 n., 108, 129, 130 n., 134 n., 298, 362
  Address in favour of William Pitt (1784), 77
  Ardrossan, 79 n., 440 n.
  Ashgrove, 184 n.
  Ayr, *see* separate entry
  Ayrshire Local Militia, 340 n.
  Ayrshire-Renfrewshire theological 'microclimate' (Kidd), 35, 72 n., 103 n.
  Barr, 441
  Beith, 15 n., 98 n., 132, 240
  Craigie House, 109 n.
  Cumnock, New, 441 n.
  Cumnock, Old, 106, 120
  Dailly, 429
  Dalry, 340 n.
  Dunlop, 109, 118 n.
  Election (1784), 77–9, 90
  Fenwick, 140 n.
  Freeholders' meeting (1785), 214–16
  Galston, 224
  Kerelaw *or* Kerrylaw Castle, 340 n.
  Kilbirnie, 132
  Kilmarnock, 15 n., 106, 329 n., 340 n., 363, 409, 440
  Kilwinning, 94, 98 n., 198 n., 291
  Loudoun, 167 n.
  Mauchline, 121, 428, 440
  MPs, 78–9, 95 n., 215
  Ochiltree, 441
  Riccarton, 440 n.
  Saltcoats, *see* separate entry
  Stevenston, *see* separate entry
  Stewarton, 131 n.
  Tarbolton, 128, 277, 296, 297, 298, 363 n., 451 n.
  'Sugar plantocracy' (Graham), 65
  'Yorkshire of Scotland', the (Boswell), 215 n.

Badcock, Samuel, dissenting minister, 73–5, 85–6, 203 n.
Bagot, Lewis, 142
Bailey, Nathan, 179
Bailey, William, 179, 184
Baillie, Grace, 356 n.
Baillie, Lesley, 356, 359, 363 n.
Baillie, May, *née* Reid, 356 n.
Baillie, Robert, 356 n., 465
Baines, James, 287
Balfour, George, 341 n.
Balfour, James, 341 n., 412 n.
Balfour, John, 119, 303
Balfour, Major and Mrs, 46, 231
Balloons, hot-air, 31, 226, 248, 299
Bampton Lectures, 259, 274
Bangorian controversy, 439
Banking
  Ayr Bank, 20, 35, 99, 104, 123
  Christie, Thomas, 348 n.
  Coutts, Thomas, & Co., Edinburgh, 131 n.
  Sir W. Forbes, J. Hunter, & Co., 131 n.
  Glasgow Arms Bank, 184 n.
  Kenrick, James, 392
  Roberts, Skey, S. Skey and Kenrick, 96
  Rogers, Thomas, 285
  Speirs, Alexander, 178 n.
Banks, Sir Joseph, 311 n.
Barbauld, Anna Laetitia, 379 n.
Barnes, Thomas, 461
Baron, Richard, 85
Barr, Ayrshire, 441

504

# INDEX

Barrowby, Lincolnshire, 142 n.
Bastille, Paris, 67
Bath, 43, 388
Baxter, Andrew, 133
Bayle, Pierre, 294
Beattie, James, 98, 102 n., 195, 279, 293, 347
Beaufoy, Henry, 59
Bedford, 157 n.
Beith, Ayrshire, 15 n., 98 n., 132, 240
Belfast, 376 n.
Bellamy, George Anne, 178
Belles lettres, 193
'Belretiro', Dunbartonshire, 298, 303, 345, 426
Belsham, Thomas, 52, 258, 270 n., 290, 461–2
Bennett, Richard, 217
Benson, George, 133 n.
Bentinck, William Henry Cavendish Cavendish-, third duke of Portland, 356 n.
Bertram (Ratramnus), 92
Bethune, John, 141 n.
Bewdley, 1, 33, 41, 141 n., 178, 207
   Bailiffs, 359
   Bank, 96
   Book societies, 16, 155, 159
   Burgesses, 359
   Canal, Severn to Mersey, 30, 31, 264, 292
   Charity school, 41
   Franchise, 359
   Grammar School, 203 n.
   Hagley Hall, 27, 82 n., 96, 361 n.
   Library, 15
   Lyttelton interest, 82 n.
   Merchants, 217, 227, 264
   Methodists, 260–1
   MPs, 359, 364, 395 n., 460 n.
   Religious debate, 41
   Trade, 264
   Unitarians, 217 n.
   Wesley's visit, 40, 260, 274
   See also Wodrow, Helen, Visit to the Kenricks
   See also Wodrow, James, Bewdley, Visits to (1789)
Biblical scholarship, see Theology, Biblical scholarship
Biggar, Margaret, née Wodrow, 117, 301, 312
Biggar, Matthew, 117 n., 131, 181, 301, 312
Biographies, 240, 249
Birmingham, 33, 83, 99 n., 205, 206, 375, 446
   Automaton, 221
   Book societies, 155, 370–1
   Commercial traffic, 7, 206
   Industrial growth, 30, 83, 206, 292
   New Meeting, 39, 42, 315 n.
   Old Meeting, 290
   Poor rate, 83
   Post office, 210
   Priestley, Joseph, 42, 99, 370–1, 442
   St Philip's Church, 355 n.
   Trade, 263
   Wedgwood, Josiah, 64
Birse, Aberdeenshire, 273 n.
Bishops, see Church of England
Black, Joseph, 232 n.
Black, William, 363 n.
Blackburne, Francis, 39, 14 n., 118 n.
Blackstone, Sir William, 34
Blair, Hugh, 175, 196, 197–8, 363 n., 380 n., 388, 419
   Lectures on Rhetoric and Belles Lettres (1783), 17, 126, 138, 148
   Sermons, 5 vols (1777–1801), 386–7
Blair, James Hunter, see Hunter Blair
Blair, Jane, 131 n.
Blair, Mrs, 'a Dorsetshire lady', 420, 427, 431
Blair, Robert, of Avontoun, 456
Bogue, see Boog
Bohemia, 147
Bolton, Lancashire, 316 n.
Boog, Rev. Robert, 166 n., 437
Book clubs and societies, 15, 16, 155, 159, 370–1
Bookselling and publishing, 15, 19–26, 46, 119 n., 123, 136, 261, 297 n., 312 n., 347, 360, 364, 367, 379–90, 398–400, 402–3, 418, 426–7, 431
   Authors, and, 19–20, 102–3, 146, 147, 159, 329, 346, 358, 374–5, 381, 383, 385–7, 388, 389, 394, 402, 409, 418, 436
   Cadell, Thomas, see separate entry
   Copyright, 20, 385–6
   Johnson, Joseph, see separate entry
   Millar, Andrew, see separate entry
   Printing, 358, 360, 364, 386
   Subscription, publication by, 20, 21, 46, 101 n., 102–4, 123, 146, 239, 275, 302, 326, 329, 346, 436
   Strahan, Andrew, see separate entry
Borrowstouness, now Bo'ness, Lothian, 167 n.
Boswell, Alexander, 77 n.
Boswell, James, 77–8, 87–8, 102 n., 154 n., 209, 215, 327 n.
   Tour to the Hebrides (1785), 212, 275, 279, 292, 320
Botany, 231 n., 270 n.
Bourn, Samuel (1689–1754), 76
Bourn, Samuel (1714–96), 77 n.
Bowman, John, 184
Boyd, William, 140
Boyle, Elizabeth, née Ross, Lady Glasgow, 114, 127, 129, 304
Boyle, Mr, of Irvine, 142
Boyle, Patrick, Lord Shewalton, 186, 267, 270, 321, 340 n., 378, 456
Bradfute, John (1725–93), 297
Bradfute, John (1763–1820), 297 n., 338

505

INDEX

Brecon, Wales, 178 n.
Bridgewater, *see* Egerton
Bridgnorth, 92, 97
Brightling, Sussex, 95 n.
Brindley, James, 264 n.
Brisbane, Mary, 114–15, 126
Brisbane, Robert, 93, 98, 109, 114–15, 124–5, 154, 258
Bristol, 142 n., 217, 280, 292, 380 n.
British Fisheries Society, 300 n.
British Museum, 311 n.
Broadstairs Thanet, Kent, 385
Brompton Chapel, Kensington, 383 n.
Brown, Malcolm, 132
Brunswick, 157 n.
'Brutus, Stephen Junius', 294
Brydone, Patrick, 197
Buccleuch, duke of, 78 n.
Buchan, Elspath or Elspeth, *née* Simpson, 40, 106–8, 120–1
Buchan, Robert, 106 n.
Buchanites, 40, 105–9, 120–1, 124, 142–3
Bull, George, 86 n., 87
Bull, John, 82, 97, 401, 459
Burdett, Sir Francis, 387 n.
Burgh reform campaign, 53, 60, 306, 339, 343, 364–5, 368
Burke, Edmund, 53, 168 n., 312 n.
    Dissent, and, 59, 68, 448
    Hastings, Warren, trial of, 55
    Rector of Glasgow University, 169, 183, 217, 267
    *Reflections on the Revolution in France* (1790), 53, 68, 444 n.
    *Speech…in the Debate on the Army Estimates* (1790), 447
    Regency crisis 1788–89, 57
Burnett, James, Lord Monboddo, 320, 354
Burney, Charles (1757–1817), 273 n., 304
Burns, Robert, 9, 18–19, 134 n., 327 n., 329 n., 356 n., 366, 380 n.
    M'Gill, William, and, 49, 51, 438
    'On the Death of Sir J. Hunter Blair', 362
    *Poems, Chiefly in the Scottish Dialect* (1786, 1787), 363
    Scots and English language, use of, 363–4
    'The Tatter'd Garland' or 'The Kirk's Alarm', 51, 327 n., 438, 439–40, 445
Burt, Robert, 263 n.
Butt, George, 460

Cadder, Lanarkshire, 455 n.
Cadell, Thomas, 273 n., 380, 383, 384, 385–6, 389, 394, 409, 415, 426, 442
Caithness, 129 n.
Caldwall, James, 427 n.
Caldwell, Andrew, 361

Caldwell, Renfrewshire, 338
Calvin, Jean, 271
Calvinists / Calvinism, *see* Theology, Calvinists / Calvism
Cambridge, University of, *see* Universities, Cambridge
Cambuslang, 202 n.
Campbell, Archibald, fifth duke of Argyll, 78 n., 186
Campbell, George, 47, 137, 194, 195, 196, 200, 436, 446–7
    *The Four Gospels, Translated from the Greek* (1789), 47, 347, 421, 434, 446
Campbell, Ilay, 78, 90, 168 n., 183, 186 n., 214 n., 215, 453, 455
Campbell, Ann, 171 n.
Campbell, John, fourth earl of Breadalbane, 142 n.
Campbell, Dr John, 312, 354
Campbell, Robert, of Downie, 171 n.
Campbell, Thomas, 171 n.
Campbell, William, 411–12, 417
Campbell, Willielma, Viscountess Glenorchy, 142
Campsie and Antermony, Stirlingshire, 455 n.
Canals, 30, 292, 299, 305–6
Canterbury, 58, 80 n., 343 n.
Cappe, Newcome, 74–5, 85, 93, 122
Caribbean, *see* West Indies
Carlisle, 6, 90 n., 269, 394
Carluke, 114 n.
Carlyle, Alexander, 50 n., 419 n., 427–8, 455, 456
Carmarthen, 443 n., 458 n.
Carrick, 262, 300, 358, 362
Carstares, William, 216 n.
Cassillis, *see* Kennedy
Cathcart, Renfrewshire, 232
Cathcart, Archibald Hamilton, 225, 328, 332, 334
Cathcart, Charles Schaw, ninth Lord Cathcart, 225, 332, 334
Cato, Marcus Porcius the elder, 227
Cawood, John, 203 n.
Chambers, Ephraim, 220
Charles I, 354 n.
Charlotte, Queen, 228, 261 n.
Charters, Samuel, 175, 180, 191–2, 275, 293, 455
Chaucer, Geoffrey, 353
Chemistry, 193, 270 n., 372 n.
Cheshire, 158
Chester, 262, 270, 289, 311, 317, 391, 392
Chidlow, Mr, of Chester, 392
Chiswick, 237 n., 273 n., 384
Christology, *see* Theology, Christology
Christie, Alexander, 348 n.
Christie, Thomas, 18, 25–6, 140 n., 348–9, 375 n., 379, 381, 383, 387, 388, 390, 396, 398–400, 403–4

506

# INDEX

Christie, William, 348 n.
Church of England
  Archbishop of Canterbury, 46, 58, 80 n.
  Bishops, 37, 42, 58, 84, 116, 142, 270, 292, 354 n., 369 n., 400, 404, 432–3, 439, 443
  Diocese of Norwich, 142
  Diocese of St David's, 443
  Establishment status, 14, 454
  Evangelicals, 280, 285–6
  *see* William Jesse, separate entry
  Heterodoxy, 46, 162, 326
  Parish clergy, 84, 310
  Sacrament, 218
  Test and Corporation Acts, 58, 339, 342–3, 361, 364, 367, 448
  Thirty-Nine Articles, 39, 58, 118 n., 342, 458 n.
  Tithes, 84
  *see also* Latitudinarians; Feathers Tavern Petition
Church of Scotland
  Abolition of the slave trade, and, 66, 191 n., 373, 377–8
  Act of Union (1707), 61, 71 n.
  Anderson, John, cause against William Leechman and others (1785), 165–70, 181–2
  Ayrshire-Renfrewshire theological 'microclimate' (Kidd), 35, 72, 103 n.
  Calvinists / Calvinism, *see* Theology, Calvinists / Calvinism
  Chapels of ease, 440
  Clergy, public opinion of, 70–1, 84
  Communion seasons, 209, 214, 232, 299, 301, 395, 418, 422
  Deposition of minister for fornication, 351
  Disputed settlements, 350–1
  Disruption (1843), 71 n.
  Elders, 50, 170, 213, 295, 350, 428
  Establishment status, 452, 454
  Evangelicals, *see below*, Popular party
  Fast days, 192
  General Assembly of, 22, 32, 50–2, 61, 66, 71, 102 n., 165–71, 175, 176, 186 n., 197, 283 n., 350–1, 373, 377, 378, 419, 427–9, 451, 454, 455 n.
    Clerkship dispute (1789), 50, 427–9
    Committee of Overtures, 452
    Kilbarchan settlement (1787), 350–1
    Patronage debate (1785), 169–70
    Test and Corporation Acts repeal debate (1790), 452–7
  Heresy charges, *see* Heresy
  Heritors, 170, 330, 350
  Kirk Sessions, 70 n., 145, 295
  Lord High Commissioner, 378, 453
  Ministers' and Scottish University Professors' Widows' Fund, 167 n., 235, 420, 455 n., 466
  Moderate party, 33, 34–5, 126 n., 166, 191 n., 410, 427
    Divided (1789, 1790), 428, 452–3
    Heterodoxy, and, 35, 49–53, 162
    Latitudinarianism, 137 n.
    Leechman, William, influence of, 21, 84, 166 n.
    Patronage, and, 71 n., 410
    Robertson, William, leadership of, 175 n.
    Subscription to the Westminster Confession of Faith, and, 35, 119 n., 237, 410–11, 429 n.
    Test and Corporation Acts, repeal of, 60–1, 191 n.
  Moderators, 22, 197, 347, 377, 429 n., 454 n., 455
  Parish business, 34, 70, 295, 296
  Patronage, 34, 35, 49, 71, 84, 101–2
    Act (1712), 71, 34–5
    dispute, 34, 71 n., 101–2, 199 n., 287 n.
    debated in the General Assembly (1785), 169–70, 350–1
  Party politics, and, 378 n.
  Patrons, 170, 350–1
  Poor relief, 2, 69–70, 82, 97, 139, 145, 287 n.
  Popular Party, 34, 35, 48–53, 61, 71 n., 98 n., 166 n., 170, 175 n., 199–200, 287 n., 298, 329–30
  Preaching, 295, 296, 301, 357
  Presbyterian / presbyterianism, 71 n., 219 n.
  Presbytery of Ayr, 50–2, 70, 72 n., 440, 441
  Presbytery of Glasgow, 21, 116, 166, 167, 177, 282–3 n.
  Presbytery of Irvine, 50, 118, 198 n., 340 n., 465
  Presbytery of Jedburgh, 452, 453 n., 455 n.
  Presbytery of Paisley, 266, 350
  Presbytery of Stranraer, 119 n.
  Procurator, 456
  Revolution of 1688–89, centenary, 49, 373, 377, 389
  Roman Catholic relief, and, 199 n.
  Secessions, 70–1
  Society for Benefiting the Sons of the Clergy, 455 n.
  Synod of Aberdeen, 119
  Synod of Glasgow and Ayr, 22, 32, 50–2, 72 n., 101, 102 n., 165, 166 n., 167, 189, 283 n., 308, 373, 440
  Synod of Perth and Stirling, 452
  Test and Corporation Acts, campaign for repeal, 40, 60–1, 191 n., 452–7, 460 n.
  *Memorial of the Committee…Concerning the Test Act* (1790), 456, 457–8
  'Village Calvinists', 36, 71–2, 84
  Westminster Confession of Faith, 34, 35, 51, 119 n., 237 n., 249 n., 379 n., 411 n., 419, 428 n., 452

Cicero, Marcus Tullius, 227
Clarke, Samuel, Anglican theologian and philosopher, 132, 133
Clarke, Samuel, dissenting minister at St Albans, 288
Clarke, Samuel, dissenting schoolmaster and minister at Birmingham, 290
Clarke, Sarah, 289
Clarkson, Thomas, 63, 64, 66, 368, 373
Clement I, Pope, 318
Clerk, John, of Eldin, 456
Clifton upon Teme, Worcestershire, 460
Closeburn, Dumfries, 108, 142
Clow, James, 158 n., 186
Clwyd, Denbighshire, 421
Clyde, river, 26, 47 n., 178 n., 395
Clydesdale, William, 166 n.
Coal, 2, 32, 35 n., 264
Cockburn, Henry, 138 n., 453 n.
Coldstream, Berwickshire, 197 n.
Coleridge, Samuel Taylor, 38, 316 n.
Collins, Anthony, 91
Colquhoun, Elizabeth, 325 n.
Colquhoun, Humphrey, 325 n.
Colquhoun, Patrick, 305–6
Common sense school of philosophy, 44, 195
Communion seasons, *see* Church of Scotland
Constantinople, 305
Controversy, 34, 370–1
Copland, Patrick, 195
Cornwall, 262
Cornwallis, Charles, first marquess, 130
Corruption, 305–6
Corsica, 212
Cotton, 141, 299–300
Couper, James, 166 n.
Court of Session, Edinburgh, 29, 78 n., 131 n., 188, 209 n., 214–16, 339, 453, 455 n., 456 n.
Covenanters / Covenanting, 2 n., 149
Cowper, William, 237 n., 348 n., 363–4, 366–7
Coxe, William, 17, 157
Craig, Mary, 12 n.
Craig, William, 240, 245, 282, 326 n.
Craig, William jr, 340
Craigends, Renfrewshire, 266
Craigie, Thomas, 245 n.
Craigie House, Ayrshire, 109 n.
Craufurd, John, 78, 90
Crawford, Barbara, 388
Creech, William, 363 n.
Creich, Sutherland, 141 n.
Crellius, Johannes, 174
Crime, 262
Cromwell, Oliver, 388 n.
Culcreuch estate, Renfrewshire, 178 n.

Cullen, William, 9, 270
Culzean castle, 95 n., 117 n.
Cumberland, 427
Cumbrae, two islands of, 267 n., 422
Cumming, Robert, 356 n.
Cumnock, New, Ayrshire, 441 n.
Cumnock, Old, Ayrshire, 106, 120
Cunningham, Alexander, 266
Cunningham, Elizabeth, 465
Cunningham, George, of Monkredding, 339 n.
Cunningham, James, thirteenth earl of Glencairn, 329 n., 363 n., 409
Cunningham, William, twelfth earl of Glencairn, 409 n.
Cunninghame, Robert Reid, of Seabank, 35, 105, 465
Currie, James, 348 n.

Dailly, Ayrshire, 429
Dale, David, 131, 300 n.
Dalquharran Castle, 117, 118 n.
Dalry, Ayrshire, 340 n.
Dalrymple, Sir David, third baronet, Lord Hailes, 17, 102–3, 123, 138, 149, 298–9, 310, 349, 427
Dalrymple, Sir James, second baronet, 102 n.
Dalrymple, William, 72 n., 327, 347–8, 419 n., 429 n., 439
Dalzel, Andrew, 50 n., 419 n., 428, 456
Dalzel, Anne, *née* Drysdale, 429 n.
Danzig (Gdansk), 86 n.
D'Arblay, Fanny, *née* Burney, 385 n.
Daventry Academy, 249 n., 258, 458 n.
Davidson, Archibald, 236, 248, 294, 377, 380 n., 383
Davidson, John, 237 n.
Dawson, Benjamin, 435, 446, 451, 459
Dean of the Faculty of Advocates (Scotland), 456
Deaths, 7, 94, 105, 118, 123–4, 150, 171, 222–6, 229–41, 241, 300, 366, 372, 412, 426
*see also* Wills and executry
Deism / Deists, 37, 42, 77 n., 133 n., 284, 316, 324, 371 n.
Demosthenes, 286, 415
Dempster, George, 31, 79, 306, 340 n.
Denham, Sir James Steuart, 78 n.
Devotions, popular, 219
Dickson, William, 373 n.
Dictionaries, 179
Directories, 179
Dilly, Charles, 383, 384
Dilly, Edward, 383 n.
Dinwiddie, of Redvale, 192, 205, 214
Dissent / Dissenters, 275, 293, 374
  Baptists, 379 n.

# INDEX

Burke, Edmund, and, 59, 68, 448
Blasphemy Act (1698), 34
Establishment, criticisms of, 432
Evangelical Dissenters, 34
Feathers Tavern petitions (1772, 1774), 39, 80 n., 118 n.
Fox, Charles James, and, 54, 59
Heterodoxy, 37–8, 162
Leechman's sermons, and, 374–5, 382, 383
Libraries, subscription, 370–1
Nonconformist Relief Act (1779), 39
'Old Dissenters', 284
Orthodoxy, 284, 292
Quakers, 368 n.
Petitions, 58
Political reform, 53, 274 n., 391 n.
Political rights, 58
Presbyterian Fund, 380 n.
Public houses, and, 82–4
Rational Dissent, 20, 33–53, *passim.*, 142 n., 284, 326
Religious liberty, 40, 58, 86 n., 282 n., 443
Scotland, 84
   Anti-Burghers, 410 n.
   Burghers (Associate Synod), 451 n.
   Fife, 70–1
   Methodists, 142
   Old Scots Independents, 131 n.
   Old Seceders, 71
   Relief Church, 71 n., 120, 214, 287 n., 410
   Roman Catholics, 238
   Secession Churches, 70–1 n., 410
   Western Scotland, 70–1
Subscription, relief from, 36, 249, 342, 379; *see also* Theology, Subscription
Test and Corporation Acts, campaigns for repeal, 39–40, 53, 58–9, 157 n., 259 n., 274, n., 339, 342–3, 361, 364, 367, 372–3, 391 n., 443–4, 448–50, 452 n.
Thirty-Nine Articles, and, 34, 39, 58, 342
Toleration Act (1689), 34, 39
Universities, and, 34
Worcester Protestant Dissenters, 445 n., 449, 458, 463
Dissenting Academies, 28, 260
   Attercliffe, 249 n.
   Carmarthen Academy, 458 n.
   Coward's, London, 387 n.
   Derby, 28, 260
   Exeter, 28, 258 n., 260, 285
   Hackney (New College), 28, 31, 283 n., 300, 304–5, 311 n., 323, 374 n., 387 n., 461
   Kendal, 28, 260
   London, 28, 260
   Manchester (New College), 28, 284
   Northampton / Daventry, 249 n., 258, 260, 270 n., 273 n., 289, 290, 380 n., 382 n., 458 n.
   Taunton, 28, 260
   Warrington, 28, 260, 284, 391 n.
Doddridge, Philip, 249 n., 258 n., 259
Dodsley, James and Robert, 312 n.
Dolben, Sir William, 259 n., 369, 378 n.
Dolphington, Lanarkshire, 240
Donaghadee, County Down, 376
Doric language, 353 n.
Dornoch, Sutherland, 141, 300 n.
Dorsetshire, 420
Douglas case, 1761–7, 79 n.
Douglas, Dunbar Hamilton, fourth earl of Selkirk, 85
Douglas, Gavin, 353
Douglas-Hamilton, Archibald, ninth duke of Hamilton, 78
Doune Castle, 98 n.
Dow, Robert, 13 n., 41, 322, 358, 360
Dowles, Worcestershire, 41, 203 n.
Dr Williams's Library / Trust, 28, 180, 284, 310 n., 380 n., 382 n., 387 n.
Dron, Fife, 137 n.
Drumelzier, Scottish Borders, 455 n.
Drysdale, John, 427 n., 428
Dublin, 361
Dudgeon, William, 133 n.
Dumbarton, 339 n.
Dumfries, 108
Dun, Alexander, 455
Dundas, Henry, 60, 61, 78 n., 79 n., 168 n., 183, 187, 209 n., 214 n., 307 n., 356 n., 365, 368, 453 n.
Dundas, Robert, of Arniston, 61, 453, 455
Dundee, 348, 373 n.
Dunkeld, Perthshire, 353 n.
Dunlop, Ayrshire, 109, 118 n.
Dunlop, Alexander, 216, 332–3
Dunlop, Elizabeth, *see* M'Gill
Dunlop, John, of Dunlop, 109 n.
Dunlop, Sarah, 216, 227, 332–3
Dunlop, William, 216 n.
Dunlop-Wallace, Thomas, 109 n.
Dunskey, Wigton, 362
Dunstable, 418
Dunsyre, South Lanarkshire, 297
Dunure, 117

East India Company, 54, 55
Eddowes, Ralph, 391–2, 446
Eddowes, Joshua, 446 n.
Eddowes, Sarah, 391 n.
Edgar Ætheling, 422

# INDEX

Edinburgh, 48, 77 n., 78 n., 79 n., 94, 95, 114 n., 131 n., 161, 183 n., 306, 340, 344, 394
  Advocates' Library, 102 n.
  Assembly Rooms, 172 n.
  Bankers, 306 n.
  Booksellers, 409
  Canongate, 455 n.
  Castle, 172
  Chamber of Commerce, 373 n.
  Charlotte Square, 172 n.
  Colinton, 455
  Corruption, 305–6
  Court of Session, 29, 78 n., 131 n., 188, 209 n., 214–16, 277, 339, 453, 455 n., 456 n.
  Cowgate, 131 n., 173
  Expansion, 171–2, 177
  General Assembly at, 32, 33, 191, 277, 340
  Grand Lodge, Freemasons', 301
  High Street, 172, 173
  History of, 138, 148–9
  Lady Yester's Kirk, 287 n., 427 n.
  Literati, 91, 191, 196–200, 206, 228 n., 277, 304, 352, 363
  Lord Provost, 455
  Meadows, the, 138 n.
  Merchants, 179 n., 222 n., 306 n.
  Mound, The, 33, 172
  New Town, 32, 172, 300
  North Bridge, 33, 172
  Old Greyfriars parish church, 175 n.
  Old Town, or Southside, 172, 173
  Petition for abolition of the slave trade, 1788, 66
  Popular party or 'the orthodox', 298
  Poker Club, 427 n.
  Post, 97
  Printing and publishing in, 358, 360, 363, 364
  Relief Church, 287 n.
  Revolution Society, 102 n.
  St Andrews Square, 32, 172 n.
  St Cuthbert's church, 455 n.
  Select Society, 102 n., 427 n.
  South Bridge, 131 n., 173
  Speculative Society, 137 n.
  Tron Church, 172, 173, 429 n.
  *See* Universities, Edinburgh
  Urban development, 32–3, 171–2, 177, 362
Education, 23, 27–8, 173–4, 236, 242–4, 262
  *see also* Universities
Edwards, Jonathan, 200 n.
Edward VI, King, 271
Effingham, *see* Howard
Egerton, Francis, third duke of Bridgewater, 30
Eglinton, *see* Montgomerie
Elderslie, Renfrewshire, 178 n.
Election, doctrine of, 38, 107
Elections, general, 54, 55
  1784, 54–5, 77–9, 89–90
  1790, 57, 444 n.
Ellesmere, Shropshire, 391
Elliot, Sir Gilbert, 61, 452 n.
Emlyn, Thomas, 151
Empedocles, 281 n.
Empire, British, 264
Enfield, William, 379 n.
English, Thomas, 312 n.
English accents, 84 n., 125, 177–8
English language, 103, 109, 140, 177–8, 209, 221, 266, 280, 352, 433
*English Review, see* Periodicals, *English Review*
Engraving, 346
Enlightenment/s, 13–32
  *see* Dissent, rational
  Glasgow Literary Society, 232, 236, 266 n., 309, 377 n.
  *see* Liberty
  progress, 26–7, 255
  *see* Reason
  'Reformation, second', 37
  *see* science
  Stadial theory, 26–7, 255–6, 257, 273–4
  'Transpennine', 14, 33, 204
  'useful knowledge', 14, 30, 33
Epiphanius, 288
Epicurus, 113
Equiano, Olaudah, 64
Equitable Assurance Society, 390 n.
Erskine, near Glasgow, 179 n.
Erskine, David Steuart, eleventh earl of Buchan, 77 n., 283 n.
Erskine, Henry, 77, 170, 209, 212, 377, 378, 428, 453–4, 456
Erskine, John, 132 n., 175 n., 196, 199–200
Erskine, John, of Carnock, 200 n.
Erskine, Thomas, 77 n., 453 n.
Esk, river, 348 n.
Est, Willem Hessels van, 138
Estates-General of France, 67, 430
Ethics, 232 n.
Eton College, 91 n., 102 n., 157 n., 353 n.
Euclid, 252
Euler, Leonard, 256
Eunapius, 280–1
Europe, 88, 246, 262
Eusebius, 75 n., 204 n.
Evangelicals / Evangelicalism, *see* Theology, Evangelicals / Evangelicalism
Evanson, Edward, 11, 80, 91
Everton, 379 n.
Evidence for Christianity, works on, 23, 42, 47, 48, 73, 80, 85, 86, 112, 195, 248, 267, 269, 279, 313, 324, 338, 343, 355, 371, 419
Ewing, David, 214 n.

510

# INDEX

Executry, *see* Wills and executry
Exeter, 28, 258
Ezekiel, 87 n.

Faculty of Physicians, 372 n.
Fagaras, Josephus Pap de, 112
Failsworth, Lancashire, 316 n.
Fairlie of Fairlie, 465
Fairlie, Renfrewshire, 117
Falkirk, 98 n., 441 n.
Farmer, Hugh, 137, 196, 394
Farnaby, Thomas, 414
Feathers Tavern Petition (1772, 1774), 80 n.
Fenwick, Ayrshire, 140 n.
Ferguson, Adam, 26, 227, 363 n.
Fergusson, Sir Adam, 15, 31, 56, 65, 77 n., 78–9, 90, 102, 105, 115, 129, 130, 139, 143–4, 215, 239, 306 n., 350, 394, 422, 431, 460
Fergusson, Rev. Alexander
  'Abbot of Kilwinning', 48 n., 98 n., 119, 408
  Heresy process, 35, 118–19, 132, 197, 428
  Mentor in ministry to JW and others, 29 n., 72 n., 119 n., 198 n.
Fergusson, George, Lord Hermand, 79 n.
Fergusson, Sir James, Lord Kilkerran, 79 n.
Fergusson, William, 160
Ferry Bridge, 95, 217
Festus, Porcius, 342–3
Field, William, 433 n.
Fielding, Henry, 99, 401
Findlay, Robert, 224, 334
Finlay, James, 148, 326, 446
Fishing villages, 31, 32, 300, 306
Fitzherbert, Maria, *née* Smythe, 262–3
Fitzherbert, Thomas, 263
Fitzroy, Augustus Henry, third duke of Grafton, 38
Fleet prison, 263
Fleming, John, 76, 88
Fleming, Peter, 32 n.
Flintshire, 158 n.
Footnotes, 17–18, 163
Fordyce, David, 220–1
Fordyce, James, 219–21, 239, 250
Forfar, Angus, 79 n.
Fort William, 306
Forth, river, 30
Forth and Clyde canal, 30, 305–6
Foulis, Andrew, 117, 232 n., 251
Foulis, Robert, 24 n., 117, 232 n., 236 n., 251
Fownes, Joseph, 431, 432–3, 435, 442
Fox, Charles James
  Dissenting campaign for repeal of the Test and Corporation Acts, 58–9, 339, 340 n., 342, 443 n., 448
  East India Bill (1783), 54, 77 n.
  Election (1784), 77–8, 90

Fox-North Coalition (1783), 53–5, 77 n., 78, 89, 90 n., 396 n., 434 n.
Foxite Whigs, 16, 54–5, 57, 58–9, 77 n., 396 n., 397 n., 434 n., 455 n., 456
  Regency Crisis (1788–89), 57, 396 n.
  Tain burghs, 55, 90
  Westminster, 55
Foxley, Norfolk, 383 n.
France, 92 n., 192
  Declaration of the Rights of Man and the Citizen, 443 n.
  Mob, in, 430
  National Assembly, 445
  National Constituent Assembly, 443 n.
  Revolution in, 53, 59, 67, 348 n., 390, 400 n., 430, 443, 450, 459
  Violence, 430
Franchise, 54
Franciscans, 258
Franklin, Benjamin, 132 n., 379 n.
Franks, *see* Post, franks
Fratres Poloni, 138, 147, 174
Freeholders' meetings (Scotland), 214–16
Freemasonry, 115, 301–2, 362 n.
Freethinking, 13, 45, 77 n.
French language, 221, 268, 371 n., 433, 434
Fullarton estate, Renfrewshire, 356 n.
Fullarton, John, 340 n.
Fullarton, Col. William, 356
Fullerton, Alexander, 119
Fulton, William, 111
Futtie, Aberdeen, 119 n.

Gaelic language, 227 n.
Galloway, 108 n., 117, 119 n., 129, 432 n.
Galston, Ayrshire, 224 n.
Galt, John, 11, 381 n., 395 n.
Gdansk (Danzig), 86 n.
Geddes, Alexander, 46, 238 n., 348 n., 381, 383, 384
Geddes, James, 251
General Assembly, *see* Church of Scotland
General Associate Synod, 451 n.
Geneva, 228, 271
Gentleman, Robert, 458
Geology, 194 n.
George III, king
  Fox-North coalition, 53–5
  Petitions to, 152, 182–4
  Popularity, 57, 228
  Regency crisis, 1788–89, 53, 56–7, 390, 396–7, 402, 414
  Test and Corporation Acts, 58, 448
George, Prince of Wales, future George IV
  Clandestine marriage, 262–3, 275
  Foxite Whigs, 55, 396 n.
  Regency crisis, 1788–89, 57, 396 n., 397 n.

# INDEX

Gerard, Alexander, 195
German language, 200, 371 n.
Germany / Germans, 109, 271
Gibbon, Edward, 17, 42, 123, 163, 195–6, 228 n., 257, 313, 326–7, 348, 410, 416
   *History of the Decline and Fall of the Roman Empire* (1776–89), 274 n., 377
Gibson, Mrs, 161, 222
Gibson, [Peter], 222
Gladsmuir, East Lothian, 198 n.
Glasgow, 8, 23, 49, 93, 94, 100, 106, 109, 111, 113, 119, 127, 132, 156, 202 n., 214, 218, 222, 226, 227, 235, 267, 273, 291, 297, 299, 311, 317, 333, 335, 340, 345, 372, 376, 395, 402, 415, 417, 420, 461
  American trade, 56, 179–80
  Banking, 178 n., 306 n.
  Burgh Council, 184 n.
  Burghs, 78, 90, 453
  Burgh reform, 339, 343 n.
  Chamber of Commerce, 161, 305 n.
  Craft incorporations, 190 n.
  Dean of Guild, 184 n.
  Directory, 179
  Elders, 437
  Electorate, 60
  Evangelicalism, 298
  *Glasgow Journal, see* Newspapers, *Glasgow Journal*
  Grammar school, 98
  Irish in, 152, 169, 177, 178, 184, 190, 238 n., 278
  Jacobites, 1745–6, 28–29, 59, 98
  Literary Society, 21, 23 n., 24 n., 184 n., 232, 236, 312, 377 n.
  Literati, 352, 461
  Lord Provost, 184 n., 305–6
  Magistrates, 437
  Merchants, 7, 123, 177, 306 n., 317, 326, 411 n.
    Colquhoun, Patrick, 305 n.
    Dale, David, 131 n.
    Finlay, James, 148, 326, 446
    Oswald, Richard, 56, 129, 130
    Ritchie, James, 179 n.
    Speirs, Alexander, 178–80, 184–5
  Mob, 189, 437
  North or High Church, 189 n., 278 n.
  Popular party or 'the orthodox', 298, 330, 430, 437
  Post, 97, 420, 421
  Poverty, 83
  Presbytery, *see* Church of Scotland, Presbytery of Glasgow
  Prosperity, 56, 174
  Slave wealth, 65
  St Andrew's Church, 226, 240
  St David's Church, 224
  Statue for John Howard considered, 305
  Stockwell, 148
  Sugar, 178 n., 180 n.
  Synod of Glasgow and Ayr, *see* Church of Scotland, Synod of Glasgow and Ayr
  Tobacco, 65, 178 n., 180 n.
  Tontine tavern and coffee-room, 152, 189
  Town council, 190 n.
  Trades, 160, 168, 183, 190–1
  University of, *see* Universities, Glasgow
Glencairn, *see* Cunningham
Glencorse, 455 n.
'Glorious' Revolution, *see* Revolution of 1688–89
Gloucester, 90 n., 244 n., 259 n., 261, 274, 291, 305, 312, 313, 427
Gloucestershire, 125, 292
Gnostics, 74 n.
Godwin, William, 379 n.
Goldie, John, 80 n., 104 n.
Gordon, Cosmo George, third duke of Gordon, 441 n.
Gordon, Lord George, 441
Gordon riots (1780), 388 n.
Gordon, Jane, *née* Maxwell, duchess of Gordon, 195
Gould (or Morgan), Charles, 466
Grafton, *see* Fitzroy
Graham, James, marquess of Graham, 78, 90, 168, 182, 183, 190–1, 217
Graham, John, 118 n.
Grand Tour, *see* Travel, Grand Tour
Grange House, 340 n.
Grangemouth, 306 n.
Grant, David, 441
Great Bedwyn, Wiltshire, 78 n.
Greece, ancient, 22 n., 162–3
Greek language, 189 n., 216 n., 232 n., 242 n., 268, 286, 309 n., 352, 415, 429 n.
Green, Ashbel, 132 n.
Greenfield, William, 363 n.
Greenock, 117, 131, 287 n.
Gregory I, Pope, 254 n.
Gregory of Tours, 204, 218
Grey, Charles, 157 n.
Griffith ap Llewellyn, King of Wales, 421
Griffiths, Elizabeth, *née* Clark, 290–1
Griffiths, Isabella, 290 n.
Griffiths, Ralph, 18, 273 n., 290–1
Guthrie, William, 149 n.

Hackney, 28, 31, 276 n., 283 n., 284 n., 285 n., 293, 300 n., 310 n., 311 n., 374 n., 387 n., 420, 444 n., 461
Haddington, 356 n.
Haddow (or Hadow), Mr, 94, 105, 118, 123–4, 171
Hagley Hall, 96, 361 n., 460
Hague, The, 112 n., 157 n.
Hakewill, George, 26, 257

# INDEX

Halkhead estate, 115, 129 n.
Hamilton, Lanarkshire, 394
Hamilton, *see* Douglas-Hamilton
Hamilton, Alexander, of Grange, 340, 465
Hamilton, Anne, 412, 426 n.
Hamilton, Lord Archibald, ninth duke of Hamilton and sixth duke of Brandon, 177
Hamilton, Douglas, 327 n.
Hamilton, Elizabeth, 426 n.
Hamilton, Elizabeth, *née* Millar, 101
Hamilton, Frederick, 177
Hamilton, Gavin, 109 n., 119 n., 193, 412 n., 426 n.
Hamilton, Helen, *née* Balfour, 109 n., 117 n., 412, 426 n.
Hamilton, James, 94, 101, 437 n.
Hamilton, Jane, *née* Morrison, 193
Hamilton, John, 110–11, 116, 142, 159, 161, 175, 180, 192, 200–1, 208, 210–11, 214, 222, 380, 386, 394, 400, 409, 415, 418, 426, 467
Hamilton, John, *see* McCormick
Hamilton, Louisa (1686–1750), 412 n.
Hamilton, Robert (1743–1829), 137, 193–5, 200, 426 n.
Hamilton, Robert (d. 1809), 177 n.
Hamilton, Thomas, 189
Hamilton, William (1669–1732), 22, 46 n.
Hamilton, Sir William (1731–1803), 225 n.
Hamilton, William Douglas (1634–94), 177 n.
Hargreaves, James, 141 n.
Harris, Howel, 202
Harris, James, 354
Harrogate, 376
Hartley, David, 26, 44, 252, 257, 346
Hastings, Selina, Countess of Huntingdon, 142 n., 202 n., 286, 405 n.
Hastings, Warren, 55, 356 n.
Hatchet, Buckley, 391, 402
Hawick, Roxburghshire, 226
Hawkes, William (1732–96), 315
Hawkes, William (1759–1820), 315–16 n.
Hayley, John, 95 n.
Hayley, William, 17, 81, 90, 113, 126
Hayley, William Burrell, 95 n.
Hays, Mary, 348 n.
Heaven, *see* Theology, Heaven
Hebrew language, 177, 286
Hebrides, 455 n.
Herbert, George, eleventh earl of Pembroke, 157 n.
Herefordshire, 90
Heresy
  Fergusson, Alexander, 118–19, 197, 428
  Leechman, William, 21–2, 282–3, 298, 308, 329
  McGill, William, 298–9, 427–9
  Simson, John, 188

Herschel, William, 299, 300
Hervey, James, 250
Heywood, Samuel, 343 n., 452 n.
Highlands / Highlanders, 227 n., 306
Hill, George, 453–4, 455, 456
Hill, Jane, 142 n.
Hill, John, 220 n.
Hill, Rowland, 142 n.
History
  Ancient and modern, 195
  Ecclesiastical, 157 n., 189 n., 195, 216 n., 231 n., 347, 348
  Gibbon, Edward, *see* separate entry
  Greek, 162–3, 236 n., 255
  Hume, David, *see* separate entry
  Jewish, 22 n., 47
  Leechman, William, *see* separate entry
  Levi, David, *see* separate entry
  Priestley, Joseph, *see* separate entry
  Roman, 22 n., 123 n., 163, 227 n., 236 n., 245, 255, 353
  Robertson, William, *see* separate entry
  Saxon, 354
  Shaw, Duncan, *see* separate entry
  Welsh, 421–2
Hoadly, Benjamin, 439
Holland, 83, 109
Hollis, Thomas, 84, 294
Home, Henry, Lord Kames, 13, 26, 191
Home, John, 363 n., 427 n.
Homer, 17, 163
Hope, Lord Charles, 157
Hops, 83, 213, 217, 330
Horace, Quintus Horatius Flaccus, 199, 286, 294, 299, 312, 316, 360, 401, 404, 416, 443, 448
Horne, George, 343
Horne Tooke, John, 352–5, 357, 387 n.
Horsley, Anne, *née* Hamilton, 46 n.
Horsley, Samuel, 37, 85–7, 116, 127, 142, 171, 248, 270–1, 287, 315, 316, 317, 320, 324, 433, 443, 444 n., 448
House of Commons, 54, 58–9, 64, 66, 77 n., 259 n., 264, 292, 305–6, 339 n., 342, 361 n., 372–3, 378 n., 397 n., 448–50
House of Lords, 54, 58, 64, 148, 292, 305–6, 342, 369 n., 397
Howard, Charles, earl of Surrey, then eleventh duke of Norfolk, 90
Howard, John, 261, 291, 305
Howard, Thomas, third earl of Effingham, 445
Howes, Thomas, 288
Huet or Huetius, Pierre-Daniel, 87
Hull, 264
Humber estuary, 264, 292
Hume, David, 13, 22 n., 23, 24 n., 102 n., 232 n., 236 n., 245, 253, 297 n., 377 n., 398 n., 399, 403–4

513

Humphreys, Alexander, 166 n., 190, 278
Hunter, Andrew, 172 n.
Hunter, Peter, 108, 121, 143
Hunter, William, 15, 130–1
Hunter Blair, James, first baronet, 131, 215–16, 362
Huntingdon, *see* Hastings
Hurd, Richard, 42, 80, 270, 280, 285, 314, 322, 371–2, 400, 404, 432–3, 434, 439
Hutcheson, Francis, 21, 22, 77 n., 84, 85, 111, 112, 216 n., 227, 240, 308, 404
Hutchinson, Alexander, 166 n.
Hutchinson, John, 286 n.
Hutton, James, 363 n.

Illness and medicine, 345, 392–3
　Amputation, 267
　Asthma, 114
　Bipolar disorder, 402 n.
　Blisters, bleeding, 298, 303
　Blood, loss of; or blood-letting, 297–8, 303, 405
　Colds, 242, 366, 389
　Dog bites, 405
　Erysipelas (rose), 216, 223, 229, 332, 333
　Fever, 267
　Flux (discharge), 223, 333–4
　Frailty, general, 426
　Gravel (kidney stones), 11, 44, 114, 265
　Medical practice, 99 n.
　Mental illness, 344, 348 n., 390 n., 396 n., 402, 414 n., 460 n.
　'Ormskirk medicine', the, 405
　Porphyria, 402 n.
　Skin complaints, 461
　Stomach pains, 390 n., 425
　Stroke, 11, 100–1, 223, 265
　*See also* Physicians
Improvement, *see* Agriculture
Inch, Galloway, 48 n.
Inchinnan, Renfrewshire, 236
Independent country gentlemen, 215 n.
India, 356 n.
Industry, 30
　Canals, 30, 32, 275, 292, 299, 305–6
　Coal, 2, 32, 35 n., 264
　Fishing, 31
　Harbours, 32
　Inventions, 299–300
　Investment, 32
　Lead, 30
　Rope, 32
　Shipbuilding, 32
　Steam engines, 30–1
Infidelity, *see* Theology, Atheism
Ingram, John, 388
Innes, Dorothea, 105 n.
Inventions, 299–300
Inveresk, Lothian, 427

Investment, 31–2
　*See also* Subscriptions (financial)
Ireland, 251, 258, 290, 356 n.
　Church of, 433 n.
　Commercial regulations, 56, 246
　Constitution, 56
　Estates, 361 n.
　Parliament, 361 n.
Irish, *see* Glasgow, Irish in
Iron manufacture, 83, 292
Irvine, 29, 98 n., 106, 120, 121, 143, 198 n., 226, 335, 356 n., 378
　*see* Buchanites
　Circulating library, 15 n.
　Postal centre, 144, 412
　Presbytery of, *see* Church of Scotland, Presbytery of Irvine
　Relief Church, 107, 120
Irvine, William, 223, 226, 229, 231, 238, 333, 335, 366, 372
Isle of Thanet, Kent, 383, 389
Isocrates, 316
Italian language, 221, 268
Italy, 157 n.

Jackson, Cyril, 369
Jacobites / Jacobitism, 97–8, 149
Jamaica, 82 n., 157 n., 162, 225, 266 n.
Jamieson, John, 49 n., 349, 410–11 n.
Jardine, George, 167, 226, 235, 323, 345
Jay, John, 132 n.
Jebb, John, 56, 118 n.
Jedburgh, 61, 452, 455 n.
Jefferson, Thomas, 67
Jeffray, James, 115 n.
Jenyns, Soame, 112 n., 293, 371
Jerome, 204 n., 288
Jervis, Thomas, 258 n.
Jesse, William, 13 n., 41, 42, 202–3, 261, 321, 322, 367, 405–6, 407, 414, 416, 446
　Criticism of Joseph Priestley, 42, 203, 371, 416
　Pamphlet debate with Thomas Wigan, 41–2, 202–3, 238–9, 251, 270, 279–80, 285, 303, 311, 313–14, 321–2
Jews / Jewish, 22 n., 47–8, 75, 79, 244, 251, 336, 347, 388
　Atonement, Day of, 388
　Circumcision, 388
　JW's visit to the Bevis Marks synagogue in London, 388
Job, Old Testament patriarch, 415
John, apostle, 44, 73, 319 n.
John O'Groats, 90
John the Baptist, 318
Johnson, Joseph, 348 n., 379–80, 381, 382, 383, 384, 386, 390, 399

# INDEX

Johnson, Samuel, 63, 77 n., 99 n., 179 n., 212, 219, 220, 273 n., 279 n., 293 n., 320, 352, 354, 433
Johnston, David, 455
Johnstone, Edward, 99
Johnstone, James, 402
Jones, John, 459 n.
Jortin, John, 310, 434
Joseph II, 263
Judaism, 47–8, 79
  see Levi, David
Judges, 277 n.
Judges Bill (1785), 214–16
Julianus, Flavius Claudius, 22 n., 24 n., 236 n., 245, 257–8, 280
Juries, 215–16
Justin Martyr, 74
Juvenal, 354, 405, 414

Kames, see Home
Kästner, Abraham Gotthelf, 399
Kaye, Sir Richard, 262
Kelburn Castle, 114, 117
Kelvin, river, 306 n.
Kemble, Roger, 178 n.
Kendal, 392, 394
Kennedy, David, tenth earl of Cassillis, 95, 118 n., 128 n., 129, 139, 181, 215, 241, 250, 296, 301
Kennedy, Thomas, ninth earl of Cassilis, 95 n., 302
Kennedy, Thomas, of Dunure and Dalquharran, 117, 456
Kenrick, Elisabeth, née Smith, 8, 91, 98 n., 128, 192, 201, 217 n., 301, 397, 432, 457
  Apples sent to Stevenston, 397, 407, 417
  Jamaica, and, 65, 162
  Linen received from Stevenston, 208, 218, 330, 397, 430, 434
  Scottish identity, 8, 47, 98 n., 117, 362
Kenrick, James, 392, 395, 405, 407
Kenrick, Mary, 7–8, 97, 160, 171, 192, 201, 361, 397
  Ayrshire friends, 268, 339
  Bewdley friends, 95
  Friendship with Nell and Peggy Wodrow, 180, 205–6, 210, 227, 239, 341, 361, 417, 445
  Participation in the family business, 7–8, 9, 213, 217
  Visit to the Wodrows (1784), 1, 7–8, 11, 21, 22–23, 24, 25, 28, 81, 92, 93–4, 97, 99, 100, 101, 109–11, 114–15, 116–17, 118, 119, 120, 122, 128, 139, 201, 205–6
Kenrick, John, 249 n., 392 n.
Kenrick, Mary (d. 1801), 392 n.
Kenrick, Samuel
  Anderson, John, 154, 160, 164, 176–8, 218, 248–9, 295, 368
  Banking, 16, 96, 126, 145, 163, 413
  Bewdley, 34, 413
  British liberty, 444
  Burns, Robert, 19, 366–7, 445
  Book-buying, 416
  Career, 1, 16, 27, 65, 163–4
  Devotional practice, 219
  Dissent, 34
  Dr Williams's Library scholarship, 28, 284, 382
  Education, 163
  Family, 7–9, 97, 249 n., 264
  Free will, 125–6
  French Revolution, support for its early stages, 68, 450, 461
  Glasgow, 29, 154
  Hops, 213, 217, 330
  Jacobites, volunteer against, 98
  Jesse, William, 41, 202–3, 261, 285–6, 314, 355, 371, 405–6
  Language and dialect, 19, 124–5, 352–5, 366, 367
  Leechman, William, 3, 114, 118, 123, 127, 153, 159, 163, 164, 176, 218, 227, 247, 248, 249, 256–7, 259, 290, 294, 310, 341, 426, 446
  Macknight, James, 46, 98, 147, 180, 355, 359, 367, 442, 446
  M'Gill, William, 3, 9, 20–1, 52, 101–2, 104, 115, 122–3, 135–6, 145–7, 148, 150, 153, 159, 162, 250, 275, 293, 310, 326, 329, 336, 344, 358, 360–1, 370 n., 416, 431–2, 434–5, 443, 444, 447, 448, 462
  Millikens of Kilbarchan, 31 n., 65, 100 n., 122, 402 n.
  *Monthly Review*, 290–1
  'Museum', 43, 360
  Optimism, 18
  Orthography, 404
  Politics
    Burke, Edmund, 89
    Charlotte, Queen, 55, 89
    Fox, Charles James, 55, 89, 90, 342
    George III, King, 55, 57, 89, 402
    George, Prince of Wales, 89
    Interest, loss of, 56, 251, 367
    North, Lord Frederick, 55, 89, 342
    Pitt, William, 57, 89, 342, 402, 414, 443
    Prince of Wales, 55
    Regency crisis, 1788–89, 55, 57, 402, 414
    Revolution of 1688–89, 57, 389, 402
  Price, Richard, 68
  Priestley, Joseph, 16, 26, 38, 42–3, 58, 85–8, 92–3, 98–9, 123, 145–7, 153, 203, 204, 252, 257, 312, 314–16, 326, 336, 342–3, 360, 443, 444
  Progress, 257, 290, 310
  Providence, 163

515

Kenrick, Samuel (*Continued*)
  Reading, 15–19, 157, 163, 218, 227, 314–15, 317–20, 377, 413
  Recommendations for Glasgow University to confer DD degrees, 259, 401–2, 406, 413, 417, 431, 439
  Religious liberty, support for, 432, 443, 444
  Scotland, 12–13, 28–29, 32, 218, 443
  Short-sightedness, 248
  Slave trade / slavery, abolition of, 65–6, 368
  Stevenston, urged to visit, 117
  Test and Corporation Acts, campaign for repeal of, 58–9, 63, 342–3, 361, 367, 372–3, 443–4, 448–50, 457–63
  Theology
    Atonement, 72 n., 153, 154
    Biblical scholarship, 446–7
    Miraculous conception, 43, 312
    Providence, 27, 402
    Subscription, 42, 52, 119 n., 249, 314, 432, 443
    Unitarianism, 34, 38, 271, 447
  Tobacco, 65, 217 n., 264 n.
  Tour of England (1759), 28, 151 n., 154, 399 n., 400
  Tours of Europe (1760–3, 1765), 11, 47, 289, 293
  Travel for business, 156, 158, 272
  Wales, 391
  Warner, John, 11, 12, 25, 153, 159, 163, 269, 290, 293, 294, 307, 336, 399, 403, 408, 415
    Biography and gravestone inscription, SK urged to write, 26, 266, 269, 275, 406–7, 408, 413, 417, 438
    Translation of Pouilly's *Theorie des Sentimens Agréables* (1747), 25–6, 140, 313, 390, 396, 398–400, 403–5
  Wigan, Thomas, 41–2, 202–3, 261, 290, 293, 308, 312, 314, 335, 359, 446, 460
  Wodrow, Helen (Nell), 7, 8, 20, 24, 28, 124, 125, 128, 156, 164, 180, 201–2, 204, 205–6, 210–12, 218, 227, 247, 272, 360, 445, 461
  Wodrow, James
    Affection for, 28, 114, 115, 210–11, 269, 291, 295, 336, 360, 402
    Edition of Leechman's sermons, 21, 23, 88, 247, 248, 249, 250–1, 290, 294–5, 297, 308–10, 312, 328, 336, 341, 352, 359, 368, 382, 401, 408–9, 412–13, 420, 431, 435, 442, 446, 451
    Family, affection for, 150, 153, 265, 407
    Theological influence of, 290, 359
    Urged by SK to publish his scholarship, 146–7
    Urged by SK to visit Bewdley, 202, 211, 360, 402
    Urges SK to visit Stevenston, 47, 205
    *see also* Wodrow-Kenrick correspondence

  Worcester Protestant Dissenters, secretary to, 40, 59, 445 n., 449, 458, 463
Kenrick, Timothy, 258, 270 n., 273, 285, 299
Kenrick, William, 360
Kerelaw *or* Kerrylaw Castle, Ayrshire, 340 n.
Kidderminster, 83, 96, 99, 292, 380 n., 414, 458 n., 460
Kilbarchan, 25, 95, 100, 105, 118, 122, 265, 266, 267, 272, 344 n.
  *see* Warner, John
  Disputed settlement at (1787), 350–1
Kilbirnie, Ayrshire, 132
Kilmarnock, Ayrshire, 15 n., 106, 329 n., 340 n., 363, 409, 440
Kilnwick, Berwick Chapel, 203 n.
Kilsyth, 283 n.
Kilwinning, Ayrshire, 94, 98 n., 198 n., 291
  *see* Fergusson, Rev. Alexander
King's College, Aberdeen, *see* Universities, King's College, Aberdeen
Kippax, Yorkshire, 225 n.
Kippis, Andrew, 46, 58, 240 n., 249 n., 258 n., 282, 283 n., 309, 311 n., 357 n., 374, 375, 376 n., 379, 382, 383, 384, 409, 436
Kirkcudbright, 277 n.
Kirkoswald, 117, 128, 299, 301, 312, 395 n.
Knight, Joseph, 62, 65
Knox, John, 255, 271
Knox, Vicesimus, 28, 251, 279, 283

Lamond, David, 419 n.
Lanarkshire, 30, 78
Lancashire, 33, 141 n.
Land speculation, 129 n.
Landowning, 30, 130
Lang, Gilbert, 76, 88, 427
Languages, 266 n., 311 n.
  Arabic, 259 n.
  Doric, 353 n.
  English, 103, 109, 140, 177–8, 209, 221, 266, 352, 433
    Accents, 84 n., 125, 177–8
    For public preaching, 280
  French, 221, 268, 371 n., 433, 434
  Gaelic, 227 n.
  German, 200, 371 n.
  Greek, 189 n., 216 n., 232 n., 242 n., 268, 286, 309 n., 352, 415, 429 n.
  Hebrew, 177, 286
  Italian, 221, 268
  Latin, 10, 177, 209, 227 n., 231 n., 232 n., 242 n., 266, 271, 308, 352, 354 n., 368
  Oriental, 28 n., 157 n., 186 n.
  Polish, 371 n.
  Portuguese, 221, 433
  Scots, 19, 109, 209, 352, 439–41
  Spanish, 221, 433

# INDEX

Lapsley, James, 455
Lardner, Nathaniel, 309–10, 325, 357 n., 376
Largs, 117, 422
Latimer, Hugh, 271
Latin, 10, 177, 209, 227 n., 231 n., 232 n., 242 n., 266, 271, 308, 352, 354 n., 368
Latitudinarians / Latitudinarianism, *see* Theology, Latitudinarians / Latitudinarianism
Lauchlan(e), Mr, 144
Lauderdale, *see* Maitland
Laurie or Lawrie, George, 166 n., 167
Lausanne, 228 n.
Lavater, Johann Caspar, 200
Lawyers, 159, 162, 187
Lead mining, 30
Leadhills, 30–1, 299, 311
Lee, Shropshire, 391 n., 395
Lee, George Henry, third earl of Litchfield, 255
Leechman, Bridget, *née* Balfour, 10, 21, 29, 114, 160, 216, 222–6, 229, 231, 232, 235, 236, 237, 242, 247, 267, 273, 276, 277, 295, 297–8, 303, 310, 312, 323, 333–6, 340, 345, 352, 365, 374, 376, 384, 395, 426
Leechman, William
    Accusations of heterodoxy, 21–2, 282–3, 308, 329
    Anderson, John, campaign against Leechman (1785), 28–30, 151–2, 154, 160–1, 164, 165–70, 176, 181–91, 207, 216–17, 237, 345
    JW's actions in the church courts in support of Leechman in the Anderson 'stramash' (1785), 166–70, 176, 184, 189, 197
    Leechman's deathbed forgiveness of Anderson, 224, 234, 235, 247, 334
    Arminian theology, 36
    Biblical scholarship, 23, 159
    Correspondents, 77, 276
    Death, 7, 10, 222–6, 229–41, 241, 247, 328, 331–2, 333–5, 338, 372, 393, 395
    Devotional practice, 23, 219, 249 n., 259, 309, 332, 333
    Divinity professor at Glasgow, 10, 21–2, 282, 283, 308, 322, 329, 402, 413
    Early life, 322, 329, 338
    Education, on, 23, 24 n., 26, 236, 242–4, 250–1
    Essays, secular, 21–4, 47, 269, 302–3
    Evidences of Christianity, lectures on, 23, 248, 269, 322, 329, 338
    Executors, 226, 235
    Extempore prayer, 23, 240, 249
    Family, 235
    Funeral, 231–5
    Glasgow Literary Society, 21, 23 n., 24 n., 232, 236, 242, 244 n., 245, 309
    Health and ill-health, 3, 10, 11, 44, 80, 114, 140, 165, 216, 222, 332, 372
    Heresy, on, 53, 116, 298–9, 427
    History, 22, 47, 244, 245, 253–5, 274, 290
    Horsley, Samuel, 45
    Hume, David, 22 n., 23, 24 n., 253–5, 256–7
    Hutcheson, Francis, 21, 22, 85, 308 n.
    Influence on Moderate theology in Scotland, 21, 84
    Influence on Gavin Wodrow, 10, 47
    Influence on JW and SK, 3, 114, 118, 123, 127, 159
    Jews, on, 47, 244, 251
    JW's edition of Leechman's sermons with his memoir (1789), 19, 21–5, 66, 236, 294–5, 296–7, 302–3, 365, 379–90, 393, 406, 408–9, 412–13, 418, 426–7, 442, 446, 451
    M'Gill, William, *Practical Essay*, 115–16, 326 n.
    Latitudinarianism, 122, 123
    Liberty, on, 255, 258
    Lowth, Robert, 116
    Moderator of the General Assembly, 22
    Moral philosophy, 245
    Mure, William, of Caldwell, tutor to, 78 n., 297 n.
    'New light', 18
    Obituary, 230, 231–2, 240–1, 248
    Paganism, on, 22 n., 244–5, 251
    Papers given to JW after his death, 18, 21–5, 88, 236, 242–5, 267, 276, 295, 303, 338
    Parish ministry at Beith, 294–5, 310
    Posthumous reputation, 21–5
    Portrait by William Miller, 24, 346, 384, 389, 402 n., 409, 427
    Prayer, on, 283 n.
    Principal of Glasgow University, 3, 21, 22, 25, 27, 28–30, 233, 242, 283, 309, 323, 334, 345
    Progress, on, 255–6, 257, 290
    Providence, 27, 274
    Revealed religion, 332
    Roman Catholicism, 253–5
    Rouet / Ruat, William, 158 n.
    Sermons, 21, 119–20, 276, 338, 365, 374, 386–7, 393, 418, 451
    Stadial theory, on, 255–6, 257, 273–4, 290
    Theological lectures, 245, 248, 269, 322, 329, 338
    Will, 10, 235
Leeds, 258 n., 269, 459
Leibnitz, 112 n.
Leith, 412 n., 455 n.
Leland, Thomas, 433
Leslie, David, sixth earl of Leven, 453
Leveson-Gower, George Granville, viscount Trentham, 114 n.
Levi, David, 47–8, 79 n., 355, 357
Liberty, 40, 97–8, 212, 215, 218, 236 n., 255, 258
Libraries, 15, 16 n., 30, 231 n., 370–1
Lichfield, 432
Lincoln / Lincolnshire, 142 n., 262

Lindsay, Hercules, 158 n.
Lindsey, Theophilus, 38, 45, 76, 90 n., 279 n., 287 n., 311, 315, 379 n., 387–8, 432–3
Linen trade, *see* Trade
Literary criticism, 103
Literary Society, *see* Glasgow, Literary Society
Literati, *see under* Edinburgh & Glasgow
Little Cumbrae, 36
Liverpool, 33, 217, 264, 292, 370 n., 375, 379 n., 392
  'Liverpool Liturgy', 392 n.
  Octagon Chapel, 392
Loch, James, 141 n.
Loch Lomond, 376
Locke, John, 26, 27, 354
Logic, 186 n., 231 n., 232 n.
Logierait, Perthshire, 227 n.
London, 110, 114 n., 131, 137 n., 176, 193, 204, 205, 211, 239, 289, 339, 450
  Banking, 285
  Billingsgate, 278
  Blackfriars Bridge, 390
  Blackheath, 380
  Bookshops, 80
  Carter Lane, 380 n.
  Chiswick, 237 n., 273 n., 384
  City, 397
  Clapham, 382
  Commercial traffic, 7
  Covent Garden, 178 n.
  Cripplegate, 284 n.
  Critics, 363
  Drury Lane, 178 n.
  Equitable Assurance Society, 390 n.
  Gordon riots (1780), 441 n.
  Gravel Pit, Hackney, 276, 374 n., 387 n.
  Greenwich, 304 n.
  Hackney, 284 n., 420
  Kensington, 383
  Lindsey's chapel, Essex Street, 45, 90, 287 n., 379 n., 387
  Merchants, 397
  Monkwell Street Presbyterian chapel, 219 n., 250
  Newington Green, 276, 374 n.
  Old Jewry, 276, 387 n.
  Poor Jewry Lane, 276, 374 n.
  Portuguese (Bevis Marks) synagogue, 388
  postal networks, 264, 268, 269, 272, 421
  printing and publishing in, 358, 360, 374
  Revolution Society, 444 n., 445 n.
  Salters' Hall, 137 n., 394 n.
  St Paul's Churchyard, 379 n.
  St Thomas's, Southwark, 387 n.
  Sardinian chapel (Roman Catholic), 388
  Stamford Hill, 387 n., 390 n.
  Stoke Newington, 380 n.
  Strand, 380 n.
  Westminster General Dispensary, 348 n., 379 n.
  *See also* Wodrow, James, London
Longdon, Worcestershire, 80 n.
Lord Advocate (Scotland), 183 n., 453 n.
Loudoun, Ayrshire, 167 n.
Loudoun, John, 308
Louis XVI, king of France, 67
Lowth, Robert, 116, 354
Lucretius, 113 n.
Lunardi, Vincenzo, 226, 248
Luther, Martin, 255, 271
Lyttelton, George, first baron Lyttelton, 361 n.
Lyttelton, George Fulke, 457, 460
Lyttelton, Lucy Fortescue, 361 n.
Lyttelton, Thomas, 82 n.
Lyttelton, William Henry, Lord Westcote, 82 n., 92 n., 96, 210, 218, 282, 289, 355, 359

Macintosh / Mackintosh, James, 351
Macintosh / McIntosh, Robert, 456
Mackenzie, Henry, 237 n., 362 n., 363 n., 380 n.
Mackenzie, John, 40, 118–19
MacKinlay, James, 329–30, 340 n., 440
Macknight, Elizabeth, 268
Macknight, James, 46–7, 98, 137, 147, 175, 197–8, 326 n., 435, 455, 457
  *New Literal Translation of the Epistles to the Thessalonians* (1787), 46, 137–8, 175, 180, 199, 347, 348, 355, 357, 364, 442
  *New Literal Translation from the Greek of All the Apostolic Epistles* (1795), 46–7, 357, 364, 436
Macknight, William, 198 n.
Maclaine or Maclean, Archibald, 112
Macleod, Hugh, 167, 189
Macreddie, Mrs, 105, 124
Madan, Martin, 74 n., 405–6, 407, 414
Madan, Spencer, 355–6, 357, 371 n.
Maitland, James, viscount Melville, eighth earl of Lauderdale (1790–1839), 455, 456
Manchester, 30, 33, 64, 155, 192, 204, 205, 206, 207, 208, 210, 214, 263, 316 n., 348 n., 370, 375
Mansfield, *see* Murray
Manufacturing, manufactures
  Ale / small beer, 83–4, 213
  Carpets, 415
  Cotton, 131 n., 141, 299–300
  Flax, 141 n., 300
  Iron, 83, 292
  Paper, 193
  Porter, 157 n., 213
  Salt, 143–4
  Wages, 83
  Whisky, 141 n., 440

## INDEX

Margaret, Queen of Scotland, 422
Marischal College, *see* Universities, Marischal College, Aberdeen
Markinch, Fife, 137 n.
Martin, Samuel, 453
Mason, William, 17, 81, 91
Mathematics, 193–4
Matthew, gospel of, 79, 80, 91
Maty, Paul Henry, 311
Mauchline, Ayrshire, 121, 428, 440
Maurice, emperor, 254 n.
Maxwell, Elizabeth Hairstanes, Lady Alva, 141
Maxwell, Patrick, 350–1
Maybole, 95 n., 98 n., 117, 198 n., 301, 362 n.
Mayville House, 356 n.
M'Aulay, Alexander, 166 n.
M'Aulay, John, 166 n.
McCormick, Edward, 268
McCormick, Mrs John ('Jack'), 268
McDowell, Elizabeth, 200
McDowall estate, 65, 315 n. 13
McDowall, Col. William (1678–1748), 65, 101 n., 266 n.
McDowall, Col. William (1719–84), 266
McEuen, James, 405 n.
M'Gill, Douglas Heron, 430 n.
M'Gill, Elizabeth, *née* Dunlop, 72 n., 99 n., 104, 330
M'Gill, Elizabeth (d. 1791), 430
M'Gill, Janet, 430 n.
M'Gill, William
  Ayr, second charge, 48, 50, 348, 432, 437
  Ayr Bank crash (1772), 20, 104, 326 n.
  *Benefits of the Revolution, The* (1789), 49, 410–11, 418–19, 420, 427–30
  Booksellers, and, 102–3, 146, 147
  Burns, Robert, friendship with, 49, 51, 72 n., 438
  DD (University of Glasgow, 1785), 150
  Dalrymple, William, 327, 419 n.
  Deism, on, 327
  Fergusson, Sir Adam, 102
  Financial difficulties, 35
  General Assembly, 50, 330, 350, 419, 427, 438, 451–2
  Heresy process, 9, 35, 48–53, 72 n., 411, 419, 427–30, 436–8, 451–2
  Kenrick, Samuel, 135–6, 145–7, 148, 150, 153, 159, 162
  Kirk Session, 419, 420, 432
  *Practical Essay on the Death of Jesus Christ* (1786), 3, 19–21, 48–53, 101–4, 118, 128, 145, 150, 162, 239, 275, 298–9, 302, 325, 329, 337, 340, 370 n.
    Initial reactions, 329–30
    Mounting hostility, 349–50, 410–11, 427–30, 436–8, 462

Peebles, William, 49–50, 102 n., 410–11, 416, 419, 433, 441
Presbytery of Ayr, 50–2, 301 n., 428–9, 436–8, 462
Priestley, Joseph, 3, 21, 48, 76 n., 135–6, 145–7, 150–1
  Responses to critics, 3, 21, 49, 410–11, 427–30, 438
Scots language, use of, 19, 326
Sermons, printed, 33, 45, 102, 115, 118, 145, 410–11
Socinian theology, 20, 48, 50–1, 72, 103–4, 146, 150–1, 325, 348, 410, 436–7
*Speech on Patronage* (1784), 101
Subscription to the Westminster Confession of Faith, 50–1, 410–11
Synod of Glasgow and Ayr, 50–52, 101, 418, 420, 428, 429, 437–8, 451
McGrugar, Thomas, 306–7 n.
M'Indoe, David, 166 n., 167, 169, 181–2, 189
McKenzie, John, 105 n.
M'Turk, William, 189 n.
Meason, George, 299 n.
Mechanics, 193
Medicine, *see* Illness and medicine
Medicine, academic discipline, 270 n.
Meek, James, 160 n., 166 n., 278 n.
Melanchthon, Philip, 271
Melmoth, William, the younger, 227
Melton, Suffolk, 259 n.
Mennons, John, 189 n.
Mersey, river, 292, 392
Methodists / Methodism, 40, 41, 142, 202, 260–1, 274
Methley, Yorkshire, 225 n.
Midlands, 30, 64, 292
Middle Temple, 102 n.
Millar, Andrew, 94 n., 364, 367, 380 n., 399, 403, 405
Millar, Elizabeth, *née* Hamilton, 94 n., 364 n.
Millar, Henry, 94, 125, 364 n., 391 n.
Millar, John, 77, 256, 257, 273, 361
Millar, Miss, 367
Millar, Robert, 94 n., 101 n., 364 n.
Millar, William, 24, 427 n.
Millennialism / millennium, 48, 286 n., 355 n.
Miller, Thomas, 106
Milliken estate, 95, 100, 101, 118, 122, 266, 402 n., 415
Milliken, Alexander, 171 n.
Milliken, Major James (1669–1741), 65
Milliken, James (1710–76), 64, 101 n., 351 n.
Milliken, James (1741–63), 28, 157, 171 n.
Milliken, Jane or Jean, *née* Macdowall, 65, 101, 122, 171 n., 350
Miln, James, 166 n.
Milton, Lanarkshire, 114 n.

519

## INDEX

Milton, John, 354, 368
Ministry of All the Talents (1806–7), 64, 456 n.
Mitcham, Surrey, 80 n.
Mitford, William, 17, 162–3
Moderates / Moderatism, *see* Church of Scotland, Moderate party
Moffat, 455 n.
Moir, James, 52 n., 451 n.
Monboddo, *see* Burnett
Moncrieff Wellwood, Sir Henry, 455, 456
Monimail, Fife, 453 n.
Monteath, Ann, *née* Cunningham, 339
Monteath, James, 339 n.
Monteath, James Stewart, 142
Montesquieu, Charles-Louis Secondat, Baron de la Brède, 255, 257, 273
Montgomerie, Alexander, eleventh earl of Eglinton, 77 n., 134, 144, 162, 214, 215, 226, 241, 300, 327–8, 331, 341, 362, 465
Montgomerie, Frances, *née* Twysden, 327 n.
Montgomerie, Hugh, of Coilsfield and Skelmorlie, twelfth earl of Eglinton, 78 n., 79, 90, 215, 296, 300, 302, 327, 328, 331, 406, 422
Montgomerie, Mary, 327 n.
Montgomeryshire, 156
*Monthly Review*, *see* Periodicals
Montrose, 106, 348 n.
Moodie, Alexander, 440
Moor, James, 158 n., 309
Moral philosophy, 22 n., 221 n., 227 n., 231 n., 266
Moravia / Moravians, 147, 318
Moray Firth, 141 n.
More, Hannah, 27
Morgan, Miss, 387
Morgan, Sarah, 387
Morgan, William or George, 387, 390
Morthland, Matthew, 165 n., 187
Moulson, Mr, 392
Mount Etna, 118
Moy and Dalarossie, Inverness-shire, 351 n.
Muir, George, 266
Muir, John, 194
Muir, Thomas, 168 n., 455 n.
Mure, Elizabeth, of Caldwell, 297, 338
Mure, William, of Caldwell, 78, 297 n.
Murray, John, 18
Murray, John, fourth earl of Dunmore, 289
Murray, William, first earl of Mansfield, 62, 353
Music, 33, 204, 205

Nairn, 339 n.
Napier, Robert, 351 n.
Napier, Col. William, of Culcreuch, 178 n.
Narborough, Leicestershire, 382 n.
National Assembly, France, 67–8, 445

National Constituent Assembly, France, 443 n.
Natural history, 193, 455 n.
Natural philosophy, 28, 186 n., 194, 228 n., 232 n.
Neilston, Renfrewshire, 364 n., 391 n.
New Jersey, College of, *see* Universities, New Jersey, College of
New Lanark, 300
New Light churches, 47
Newark castle, 95 n.
Newcastle-upon-Tyne, 167, 441
Newspapers, 66, 78, 160, 161, 204, 216, 261
   *Caledonian Mercury*, 32 n., 152, 160 n., 230, 240–1, 306 n., 419 n.
   *Edinburgh Advertiser*, 60
   *Edinburgh Evening Courant*, 175 n.
   *Edinburgh Weekly Magazine*, 5 n.
   *Glasgow Journal*, 36 n., 45, 85, 105–6, 115, 119–21, 152, 160 n., 165 n.
   *Gloucester Journal*, 261, 312 n.
   *World*, 442 n.
New Testament, 44, 73, 79, 80, 91, 120, 123, 151, 198, 296, 318, 319, 333, 347, 357, 446–7
Newton, John, 364 n.
Newton, Isaac, 132 n., 252, 399 n.
Newton-upon-Ayr, 49, 410
Nicaea, Council of, 80 n.
Nicoll, Mr, 162
Nithsdale, 129
Nonconformist Relief Act (1779), 39
Nonconformists, *see* Dissent
North, Frederick, Lord, second earl of Guilford, 3, 53–5, 63, 77 n., 89, 90 n., 95 n., 342, 356 n., 396 n., 434 n., 466 n.
Northampton Academy, 249 n., 380 n., 382 n.
Norwich, 142, 276
Novels, 148

Oban, Argyll, 300 n.
Ochiltree, Ayrshire, 441
Old Sarum, 78 n.
Old Scots churches, 131 n.
Old Testament, 79, 121, 198, 296, 319
Oldswinford, Worcestershire, 41, 141 n.
Origen, 204 n., 288, 318
Ormskirk, Lancashire, 405
Orton, Job, 293, 458 n.
Osborne family, Dumfriesshire, 142 n.
Oswald, George, 129
Oswald, James, 129 n.
Oswald, Richard, 56, 129, 130
Oswestry, Shropshire, 405
Oughterson, Arthur, 340 n.
Owen, Robert, 131 n.
Oxford, 125, 264
Oxford University, *see* Universities, Oxford
Oxfordshire, 292

Packwood, Warwickshire, 208 n.
Paganism, 22 n., 75, 244–5
Paine, Thomas, 26, 379 n., 387 n.
Pairman, William, 24 n., 117, 224, 225, 235–6, 276, 277, 295, 334
Paisley, 56, 100, 110, 118, 122, 132, 294, 364 n., 373 n., 405, 416
   Abbey Kirk (first and second charges), 101 n., 437 n.
   Directory, 179
   High Kirk, 266 n., 287 n.
   Laigh / St George's parish, 98 n., 132 n., 224
   Poverty, 83
   Presbytery of Paisley, *see* Church of Scotland, Presbytery of Paisley
   Prosperity, 174
   Trade, 56
Paley, William, 399
Palmer, John, 6, 268–9
Palmer, Samuel, 293, 294
Paris, 67, 317, 356 n., 445
Parliament, 8 n., 30, 61, 64, 96, 143, 264, 339
   Acts of, 144, 454
   Sessions, 144 n., 148, 241, 426
   *see* House of Commons
   *see* House of Lords
Parliamentary reform, 55, 56, 10, 157 n., 445 n
Parr, Samuel, 304 n., 433, 434
Paterson, John, of Craigton, 179
Patronage Act (1712), *see* Church of Scotland
Paul, apostle, 135–6, 151, 153, 177, 318, 342
Peckard, Peter, 368 n.
Peebles, William, 49–50, 102 n., 410, 416, 420, 433
Pembroke, *see* Herbert
Pennant, Thomas, 17, 158
Penrith, 6, 392, 394
Percival, Thomas, 348 n.
Periodicals, 9, 16
   *Analytical Review*, 18, 348 n., 379 n.
   *Annual Register*, 312
   *Critical Review*, 18, 78 n., 305, 387 n., 434 n.
   *Edinburgh Weekly Magazine*, 73 n.
   *English Review*, 18, 305, 311
   *London Magazine*, 383 n.
   *London Packet, or, New Lloyd's Evening Post*, 383 n.
   *Lounger*, 362 n.
   *Monthly Review*, 18, 69, 73–5, 77, 78 n., 85–8, 91, 112, 142, 256, 259, 273 n., 274, 289, 290–1, 305, 311, 317, 323, 342, 352, 357, 361, 363 n., 384 n., 421 n., 434 n., 461
   *New Annual Register*, 18, 311
   *Rambler*, 220
   *Scots Magazine*, 36 n., 105 n., 118 n.
   *Spectator*, 387 n.
   *Theological Repository*, 48 n., 72 n., 101 n., 116, 204, 218, 316
Persius, or Aulus Persius Flaccus, 414

Perth, 137 n., 194
Perthshire, 142 n.
Pétau, Denis, *or* Petavius, 87
Peter, apostle, 153, 254, 318
Petitions to the King, 152, 160, 166 n., 168–9, 176, 182–4, 189
Petitions to Parliament, 39 n., 54, 58, 60, 61, 63, 64, 66, 77 n., 144–5, 339 n., 368–9, 373 n., 377–8
Petty, William, second earl of Shelburne, 129 n., 258 n., 356 n.
Philanthropy, 261
Philostratus, 281
Phillips, John George, 443–4 n.
Phocas, emperor, 254
Physicians, 223, 298, 348 n., 414
Picton, Thomas, 356 n.
Pindar, *see* Walcot
Piozzi, Hester Lynch, previously Thrale, 279, 292
Piozzi, Gabriel Mario, 279 n., 293 n.
Piso family, 404
Pitt, William, the Younger, 53
   Abolition campaign, 66, 368, 378
   Appointment as prime minister, 1783, 53, 54
   Debts, 397 n.
   Election of 1784, 54, 77, 89–90
   Ireland, 56
   Pittites, 16, 79 n.
   Popularity, 364
   Postal reforms, 6, 96
   Reform, 55, 364–5, 368
   Regency crisis, 1788–89, 57, 396–7, 402, 407, 414
   Smuggling, and, 144
   Tax, 96, 246
   Test and Corporation Acts, campaign for repeal, 59, 340 n., 342, 364, 367, 443, 448
Planned villages, 31, 32
Plantations (coffee, sugar, tobacco), 62, 64, 178 n., 180 n.
Plato, 251 n., 316, 415
Playfair, John, 194
Plutarch, 280–1, 320
Poets / poetry, 81, 193
Poland, 147, 157
Portsmouth, 157 n.
Polycarp, 318–19
Poor / poverty
   Charity, 141 n., 214
   English poor rates system, 69, 82
   Liberty, and, 28
   Medical assistance, 99 n.
   Public houses, and, 82–4, 97
   Scottish parish poor relief scheme, 69–70, 82, 97, 139, 145, 287 n.
Pope, the, 254, 263

Popular Party, *see* Church of Scotland, Popular Party
Population, 32, 33, 70
Portland, *see* Bentinck
Portpatrick, Galloway, 118 n., 131 n.
Portugal, 62, 82 n.
Portuzon, Hugh, 105 n.
Post, the
  Address panels, 4–6, 150, 337 n.
  Anderson, John, and, 278
  By private hand, 69, 100, 150, 207, 222, 420, 431
  Cost, 3, 6, 10, 12, 27–28, 79, 82, 222
  Delays, 6, 69, 207, 253, 417
  Franks, 3, 4, 12, 25, 27, 28, 94, 96, 97, 121, 128, 134, 144, 145, 148, 181, 190, 207, 208, 226, 239, 241, 250, 256, 296, 300–1, 337 n., 339, 341, 344, 356, 359, 361, 362, 372, 378, 393, 407, 411, 421, 431, 435
  Horses, 246 n.
  Improvements, 6, 268–9
  Lost letters, 139, 207, 210, 328
  Mail coach, 6, 268 n., 392, 394
  Packaging and seals, 149–50, 210
  Postmarks, 5–6, 337 n.
  Post chaise, 392, 394
  Post masters and post mistresses, 6, 10, 12, 79, 82, 148, 149–50 , 152–3, 253, 256, 416
  Post office, 3, 96, 210
  Post roads, 268 n.
  Postal system, 5–6, 96, 265
Potter, Margaret, 287 n.
Potter, Michael, 282 n., 308 n.
Pouilly, Louis-Jean Lévesque de, 25–6, 140, 268, 307, 313, 375, 376, 390, 398–400, 402–3, 408
Prattinton, William, of Bewdley, 217 n.
Preaching, 197, 239, 357, 388
Predestination, *see* Theology, Predestination
Presbyterians / Presbyterianism, 33, 219 n.
Preston, William, 386, 409
Price, Richard, 82 n., 379 n.
  Actuarial statistics, 420
  America, United States of, 56, 444 n.
  Arianism, 39
  Civility in the face of criticism and invective, 447–8, 467
  Correspondence with JW, 420, 421, 435, 447, 466–7
  Correspondence with William Leechman, 276, 374
  Dinners with JW in London, 1788, 67, 374, 376, 379, 387, 390
  *Discourse on the Love of Our Country* (1789), 68, 444–5, 467
  Free will, 76 n., 111 n.
  French Revolution, 67, 467
  M'Gill, William, 467
  Ministry, 285
  Parliamentary reform, 444 n.
  Priestley, Joseph, 76 n., 111 n., 343
  Religious liberty, 444 n.
  'Republicanism', 447–8 n.
  Unitarianism, 39
  JW's edition of Leechman's sermons, 466
Priestley, Joseph, 3, 5 n., 9, 17, 88, 249 n., 380 n., 447
  Accent, Yorkshire, 125
  Amanuensis, 17
  *Appeal to the Serious and Candid Professors of Christianity, An* (1771), 136 n., 147
  Appearance, 92–3
  Arianism, 38, 288 n., 319–20, 342
  Arminianism, 76
  Atonement, 174
  Attacked by William Jesse, 42, 416
  Attacks on Hume and Oswald, Reid, and Beattie, 98
  Badcock, Samuel, 73–5, 85–6, 203 n.
  Birmingham (New Meeting), 42, 315 n.
  Birmingham Library Society, 370–1
  Calvinism, 38, 76
  Cappe, Newcome, 74–5, 85
  Christology, 39, 45 n., 76, 150–1, 317–20
  *Conduct to be Observed by Dissenters* (1789), 444
  Criticized by JW, 43–5, 59, 73–6, 88, 111–13, 127, 135, 146–7, 151, 174, 324–5, 346
  Dawson, Benjamin, 459
  Debating style, 74, 86–7, 127, 270, 342, 433, 459
  Deism, 317, 324
  *Discourses on the Evidence of Revealed Religion*, 313 n.
  *Disquisitions Relating to Matter and Spirit* (1777), 320 n.
  *Doctrine of Philosophical Necessity Illustrated* (1777), 43–4, 111
  Education, on, 27, 112
  *Examination of Dr Reid's Inquiry, Dr Beattie's Essay, and Dr Oswald's Appeal* (1775), 44 n., 98, 129 n., 252
  *Familiar Illustration of Certain Passages of Scripture* (1772), 136 n., 147
  *Familiar Letters Addressed to the Inhabitants of Birmingham* (1790), 355 n.
  *Free Discussion of the Doctrines of Materialism, and Philosophical Necessity, in a Correspondence between Dr Price, and Dr Priestley, A* (1778), 76 n.
  *General History of the Christian Church, A* (1802), 86 n.
  *General View of the Arguments for the Unity of God, A* (1783), 72 n.
  Gibbon, Edward, correspondence with, 313

## INDEX

Hartley, David, influence of, 44, 252, 346
Heterodoxy, 317
*History of Early Opinions Concerning Jesus Christ, An* (1786), 39, 43 n., 86 n., 271 n., 287 n., 303, 312, 314–15, 317–20
*History of the Corruptions of Christianity* (1782), 43, 45 n., 72 n., 76, 86 n., 135–6 n., 171, 174, 204 n., 271, 313 n., 371 n.
Horsley, Samuel, 316
*Importance and Extent in Free Inquiry in Matters of Religion* (1785), 259
*Institutes of Natural and Revealed Religion* (1772–74), 87 n.
Jews, conversion to Unitarianism of, 47–8
SK's admiration, 16, 26, 38, 42–3, 58, 85–8, 92–3, 98–9, 123, 315–16, 442
*Letter of Advice to those Dissenters... Relief from Penal Laws* (1773), 459 n.
*Lectures on History, and General Policy* (1788), 99 n.
*Letters to a Philosophical Unbeliever* (1780), 43 n., 343, 346
*Letters to Dr Horne, to Dr Price, and to Mr Parkhurst* (1787), 343
*Letters to Dr Horsley, in Answer to His Animadversions* (1783), 85 n., 86 n., 87 n., 142
*Letters to Dr Horsley, Part II: Containing Further Evidence* (1784), 127, 136 n., 142
*Letters to Dr Horsley, Part III* (1786), 259, 270 n., 287–8
*Letter to the Jews* (1786), 355
*Letter to the Jews, Part II* (1787), 355
*Letter to the Right Honourable William Pitt* (1787), 43, 58–9, 342
Levi, David, debate with, 47, 355
Library, 316
'man with the bee in his bonnet', 43, 75, 78, 87–8, 92, 98, 113, 209, 324
M'Gill, William, and, 21, 48, 72, 123, 135–6, 145–6, 148, 150–1, 326
Millenarianism, 47–8
Miraculous conception, 43, 80, 288, 324
*Monthly Review*, and, 73–6, 85–6, 136 n., 142, 324
Moses, 381 n.
Necessarianism, 43–4, 76, 111, 112, 252, 377
New Meeting, Birmingham, 39, 42, 315 n.
Parr, Samuel, support from, 434 n.
Piety, 112
Polygamy, 74
Predestination, 113
Price, Richard, 76 n., 343
Progress, and, 26, 43, 257
Providence, 112–13
Reading, 16–17, 204, 218, 238, 316
*Remarks on the Monthly Review of the Letters to Dr. Horsley* (1784), 85 n.

*Reply to the Animadversions... in the Monthly Review* (1783), 74 n. 76 n., 85
Scotland, familiarity with, 99
Smith, Adam, admiration for, 99
Socinianism, 38, 39, 72 n., 76, 146, 150–1, 309 n., 459
Subscription, 249 n.
*Theological Repository*, see Periodicals
Unitarianism, 34, 38, 39, 43, 146, 150–1, 259 n., 342
Test and Corporation Acts, campaign to repeal, 58–9, 342–3, 364, 367, 444, 459
Trinitarianism, 318, 342
*Triumph of Truth, The* (1771), 137 n.
Warrington Academy, 391 n.
Writing, 316
Priestley, Mary, née Wilkinson, 125
Prior, Matthew, 113
Prison reform, 261
Pro-slavery attitudes, 369
'Profligacy of the age', 275
Progress, 22 n., 26–7, 255, 258
Prophets / prophecy, 319
Protestant Association, 441 n.
Proverbs, Old Testament book of, 272, 275
Providence, see Theology, Providence
Public houses, 82–4
Publishing, see Bookselling and publishing
Puritans, 354 n.

Quakers, 63, 368 n.

Raeburn, Henry, 455 n.
Raikes, Robert, 261, 274, 281–2, 291, 305, 312–13, 316
Ramsay, Allan, the younger, 85 n.
Ramsay, James, 63
Raphael, 117
Rathven, Aberdeenshire, 381 n.
Rational Dissent, see Dissent
Rayner, Elizabeth, 287, 315
Rayner, John, 287 n.
Reading, 3, 15–19, 155
Rees, Abraham, 387
Reformation / Reformers, 39, 254, 409
Regency crisis (1788–9), 56–7, 396–7, 414
Reid, Thomas, 44, 98, 151, 165 n., 187–8, 194 n., 231 n., 232 n., 238 n., 276 n., 300, 303, 346, 376, 377, 467
Relief Church, 71, 107, 120, 214, 287 n.
Renfrewshire, 78 n., 100 n., 117, 178 n., 231 n.
Theological 'microclimate' (Kidd), 35, 72, 103 n.
Representation, 215
Reprobation, doctrine of, 38, 107
Revelation, book of, 80, 232–5

523

# INDEX

Revolution of 1688–89, 402
   Centenary of, 49, 373, 389, 402
   Sermons on, 409–11, 444–5
   Revolution Society, Edinburgh, 102 n., 373
   Revolution Society, London, 444 n., 445 n.
Ribbesford, Worcestershire, 203 n.
Riccarton, Ayrshire, 440 n.
Richard III, 160
Richardson, William, 10, 90, 188, 189, 225, 237, 238, 240, 249, 272, 282, 283 n., 289, 297, 303, 307, 308, 309, 313, 323, 328, 331, 334, 337, 366, 372, 374, 375, 376, 381, 384
Ridley, Nicholas, 271
Risk, John, 166 n.
Ritchie, James, 179 n.
Robe, James, 283 n.
Roberts, Betty Carolina, 208, 212, 395, 402, 407, 446, 451, 461
Roberts, Caroline Aylesbury, 395, 402, 446, 451
Roberts, Thomas Aylesbury, 395 n.
Roberts, Wilson Aylesbury (1736–1819), 208 n., 369, 395, 402, 407, 451
Roberts, Wilson Aylesbury (1770–1853), 369, 395 n.
Robertson, David, 196 n.
Robertson, Eleanor, 197 n.
Robertson, Janet, 197 n.
Robertson, John, 409–10, 416, 420, 427, 434, 435, 440
Robertson, James, 196 n.
Robertson, Mary, née Nisbet, 197
Robertson, Mary, 197 n.
Robertson, William (1721–93), 35, 102 n., 175, 196–7, 200, 380 n., 429 n.
Robertson, William (1753–1835), 33 n., 196 n., 197, 456
Rochester, 86 n.
Rockingham, see Wentworth
Rogers, Mary, née Radford, 285
Rogers, Thomas, 284, 311
Romans, epistle to the, 272, 275
Rome, 22 n., 123 n., 157 n.
Rose, Samuel, 18, 237, 272, 276, 277, 289, 304, 312, 323, 363
Rose, William, 18, 273, 274, 277, 289, 291, 303, 304, 384
Ross, Andrew, 119 n., 432
Ross, David, Lord Ankerville of Tarlogie, 277
Ross, George, thirteenth Lord Ross, 115 n.
Rothsay, 262
Rouet / Ruat, William, 157, 158 n., 175, 180
Rouet / Ruat, Mrs, 175 n., 180, 231, 277, 298, 345, 376, 426
Rousseau, Jean-Jacques, 13, 27, 77 n.
Rowan, Mr, 396
Royal College of Physicians, 414 n.
Royal Marriages Act (1772), 263

Royal Society, 86 n., 176, 282 n., 311
Royal Society of Edinburgh, 197 n., 231 n., 309, 427 n., 453 n.
Royal visitations, 152, 161, 165 n., 166 n., 176, 191 n., 216 n.
Ruabon, Wales, 391 n.
Ruat, see Rouet
Ruet, see Rouet
Rufinus, Tyrannius, 204, 218
Russel, John, 440, 451 n.
Russia, 157, 178
Ruthven, Anne, 12 n.

Sacrament, see Church of Scotland, Communion season
Salop, see Shropshire
Sallust, otherwise Gaius Sallustius Crispus, 289
Saltcoats, Ayrshire, 32, 101, 143–4
   Brewery, 213–14
   Canal, 32
   Harbour, 32, 143–4
   Investment, 32, 143
   Ropeworks, 32
   Salt works, 32, 101, 143–4
   Shipbuilding, 32
   Shipwrecks, 144 n.
   Subscription library, 15
   Tourism, 144 n.
   JW, and, 323
Salter's Hall, London, 137 n.
Satire, 81 n., 438–41, 445
Satisfaction, see Atonement
Sceptics / scepticism, 91 n.
Science, 193
Scot, James, 166 n.
Scotland, 8, 355
   Abolition of the slave trade, 66, 373, 456 n.
   Alcohol, and, 82–3
   American Revolution, 59
   Banking, 131 n.
   Burgh reform campaign, 53, 60, 306–7, 339, 343, 364–5, 368, 372–3
   Calvinism, 35
   Canals, 30, 305–6
   Church of Scotland, see separate entry
   Clearances, 114 n., 141 n.
   Convention of royal burghs, 307 n.
   Corruption, 305–6
   County reform campaign, 53, 60, 215
   Denominations other than the Church of Scotland, 70–1, 84, 410
      Anti-Burghers, 410 n.
      Burghers (Associate Synod), 451 n.
      Fife, 70–1
      Methodists, 142
      Old Scots Independents, 131 n.
      Old Seceders, 71

## INDEX

Relief Church, 71 n., 120, 214, 287 n., 410
Roman Catholics, 238
Secession Churches, 70–1 n., 410
Western Scotland, 70
Dundas, Henry, *see* separate entry
Economic development, 30
Electorate, 60
Emigration, 132 n., 133
Enlightenment, 14
Faculty of Physicians, 372 n.
Fictitious votes, 60
Fishing villages, 31, 32
Franchise, 306 n.
Freeholders' meetings, 214–16
Heterodoxy in, 162
Highlands, 114 n., 227 n.
Jacobites / Jacobitism, *see* separate entry
Juries, 215–16
Landscapes, 8
Language, 19, 40, 109, 326, 345, 363–4, 439–41
Law, 183
Liberty, 40, 218
Lowlands, 227 n.
Magistrates, 339
Medicine, 270 n.
Militia, 59, 78, 427 n.
Political reform, 53
Poor relief / poverty, 12–13, 97, 139, 141 n., 145, 287 n.
Representation, 215
Slave wealth, 62, 129 n., 266
Theological controversy, 34
Tours of, 158 n.
Universities, *see* separate entry
*Scots Magazine*, *see* Periodicals, *Scots Magazine*
Scottish representative peers, 95 n., 134 n., 289 n., 455 n.
Scottish University Professors' Widows' Fund, 167 n., 235, 420 n., 455 n., 466
Seabank House, 105 n.
Secession Churches, 70–1
Secker, Thomas, 46
Seddon, John, 284
Sedition, 455 n.
Select Society, Edinburgh, 102 n., 427 n.
Selkirk, *see* Douglas
Serjeant, Richard, 380 n.
Severn, river and canals, 30, 31, 158, 264, 275, 292, 305–6
Shaw, Duncan, 47, 347
Sheffield, 249 n.
Shelburne, *see* Petty
Sheridan, Richard Brinsley, 60, 307 n., 339 n., 365
Sheriffs, 340
Shipbuilding, 32
Shipwrecks, 144 n., 258
Shorthand, 23, 184, 272 n., 416

Shrewsbury, 176, 293, 391, 417, 446, 458
High Street Chapel, 431, 432
Shropshire (or Salop), 13, 14, 90, 156, 158, 292, 293, 361, 392, 432 n., 442
Siddons, Sarah, *née* Kemble, 99 n., 178
Simson, John, 77 n., 188 n.
Simson, Robert, 158 n., 232 n.
Sinclair, Sir John, *Statistical Accounts of Scotland* (1791–99), 327 n.
Slavery (chattel), 61–6, 79 n., 129 n., 130 n., 185 n., 266 n., 456
Abolitionist campaign, 53, 61–6, 157 n., 191 n., 356 n., 365 n., 368–9, 373, 377–8, 456 n.
Smith, Adam, 13, 26, 154 n., 158 n., 186, 232 n., 237 n., 245 n., 304, 380 n.
Anderson, John, and, 29, 154
Glasgow Literary Society, 232 n.
Johnson, Samuel, on, 220
Religion, on, 342
Stadial theory, 26, 256, 257, 273
*Theory of Moral Sentiments* (1759), 99 n.
Universities in Scotland, on, 29–30
*Wealth of Nations* (1776), 99
Smith, Elisabeth, *see* Kenrick, Elisabeth, *née* Smith
Society for Effecting the Abolition of the Slave Trade, 63, 368 n., 373 n.
Society for Constitutional Information, 383 n., 444 n., 445 n.
Society for Promoting Knowledge of the Scriptures, 116, 127
Society for Propagating Christian Knowledge, 191 n.
Society in Scotland for the Propagation of Christian Knowledge, 455 n.
Society of Antiquaries, 282 n.
Socinus, Faustus, 76, 138 n.
Socrates, 88
Solicitor General (Scotland), 455–6
Somerset, 125, 263, 354
Somerset, James, 62
Somerton, 263
Somerville, Thomas, 61, 326 n., 455
South Carolina, *see* America
South Mimms, Hertfordshire 80 n.
Southwark, 258 n.
Sparta, 415 n.
Speirs, Alexander, of Elderslie, 178–80
Spens, Graham, 171
Spens, Nathaniel, 171, 173, 201, 344
Spinning jenny, 141, 300 n.
Stadial theory, 26–7, 255–6, 257, 273–4
Staffordshire, 90, 263 n., 292 n.
Stanhope, Charles, third earl Stanhope, 445
*Statistical Accounts of Scotland*, *see* Sinclair, Sir John
Steam power, 30–1, 299, 300 n.
Sterne, Laurence, 164, 191

# INDEX

Steuart, James, 30 n.
Stevenson, Alexander, 223, 333
Stevenston, Ayrshire, 117, 165, 224, 277, 298, 300, 450
   Baptisms, 70
   Burghers and Antiburghers, 71 n.
   Charity, 70, 214
   Church building, 1
   Coal Company, 105 n.
   Coalfield, 32, 70
   Elders, 213
   Glencairn Street, 356 n.
   Heritors, 330–1, 340, 465
   High Kirk, 356 n.
   Kirk session, 145
   Manse, 1, 323, 330–1, 340, 346, 351, 365–6, 368, 375, 465
   Marriages, 70
   Mayville House, 356 n.
   Parish, 11
   Poor relief, 70, 83, 97, 139, 145
   Population, 32, 70
   Relief Church, 71, 214
   Schoolmasters, 393
   Weaving, 70
Stewart, Dugald, 106 n., 363 n.
Stewart, Janet, 106 n.
Stewart, John, 193 n.
Stewart, Keith, 328
Stewarton, Ayrshire, 131 n.
Stirling, Stirlingshire, 440 n.
Stirling, James, 455
Stirling, John (1654–1727), 188, 385 n.
Stirling, John (fl. 1779), 414
Stirlingshire, 376
Stockingfield, 306 n.
Stockwell, Glasgow, 148
Stourport, 164 n.
Strahan, Andrew, 25, 273 n., 380 n., 385–6, 389, 390, 393, 394, 402, 406, 409, 415, 418, 426, 442
Strahan, William, 380 n., 385 n.
Stranraer, Galloway, 117 n., 118 n., 119 n., 432 n.
Strathclyde, 421
Stuart, Andrew, 78
Stuart dynasty,
   see also Jacobites / Jacobitism
Stuart, Gilbert, 18
Stuart, Robert, 105 n.
Students, see Universities, Students
Subscription (to a confession of faith), see Church of Scotland, Moderate party; Dissent
Subscription, publication by, see Bookselling and publishing
Subscriptions (financial), 21, 31–2, 46, 102, 103, 104, 146, 147, 261, 264, 284, 292, 300, 305, 311
Surfleet, Lincolnshire, 383 n.

Surrey, see Howard
Sutherland, county of, 114 n.
Sutherland, Elizabeth, countess of Sutherland, 79 n., 114, 127, 141–2
Sutherland, William, eighteenth earl of Sutherland, 114 n., 141 n.
Stanford, Norfolk, 460
Stillingfleet, Edward or James, 280
Sulzer, Johann Georg, 399
Sunbury on Thames, Middlesex, 287 n.
Sunday Schools, 261–2, 291, 368
Swynnerton, 263 n.
St Andrews, 453 n.
St Asaph, 86 n., 142 n.
St Bartholomew's Day, 458
St Davids, 86 n., 443
St Kitts and Nevis, 65, 101 n.
St Petersburg, 157
Switzerland, 83
Sydney, see Townshend
Sykes, Arthur Ashley, 91, 439
Symington, William, 31, 299 n.
Synods, see Church of Scotland

Tain burghs, 55, 90 n.
Tait, Peter, 115
Tarbolton, Ayrshire, 128, 277, 296, 297, 298, 363 n., 451 n.
Taxation, 56, 69, 96, 246, 252, 376
Tayler, Thomas, 380, 381, 382, 387, 401–2
Tayleur, William, 432–3
Taylor, John, 77, 133 n., 137, 138, 276
Taylor, William, 29, 160 n., 189–90, 237, 248, 278, 365, 374
Telescope, 300
Test Act (1673), 40, 60–1, 454
Tewkesbury, 80 n.
Textiles, see entries under Manufacturing; and Trade
Thames, river, 264
Thatcham, Berkshire, 383 n.
*Theological Repository*, see Periodicals
Theology
   Antinominanism, 322
   Arians / Arianism, 38, 44, 73 n., 75, 80 n., 86, 87, 132 n., 133 n., 137 n., 138 n., 204 n., 288, 349, 392 n., 411 n., 458 n.
   Arminianism, 36, 40, 76, 260, 349
   Athanasianism, 37 n., 80, 86, 116, 138 n., 310 n.
   Atheist / Atheism / Infidelity, 149
   Atonement, 38, 41, 48, 151, 154, 349
   Biblical scholarship, 37, 39, 44, 45–7, 48, 199, 347–9, 381 n., 436
   Buchanites, 40–1, 105–9, 120–1, 124, 142–3
   Calvinists / Calvinism, 35, 36, 38, 41, 72, 76, 113, 119 n., 132, 151, 199 n., 202, 260, 321, 322, 349, 405 n.

Christology, 37–8, 48, 51, 72, 103, 120–1, 132–3, 151, 174, 314 n., 347, 349
Conversion, 106, 107
Crucifixion, 102–3, 123, 151, 154
Election, doctrine of, 107
'Enthusiasm', 106, 107, 109, 121, 214
Eternal punishment, 38, 252
Evangelicals / Evangelicalism, 153, 405 n.
Evidences for Christianity, 195, 324
Heaven, 12–13, 233, 234, 269
Holy Spirit, 120, 121
Hutchinsonians, 286
Intercession, 192
Judgement, 199, 233, 234
Latitudinarians / Latitudinarianism, 37, 41, 91 n., 137 n., 368 n.
Methodism, 202, 260–1, 321, 322, 405 n.
Millenarianism, 120, 355 n.
Miracles, 80, 195 n.
Miraculous conception, 80, 324
Original sin, 38, 76 n., 80 n., 113, 120
Piety, 106
Predestination, 36, 112 n., 113
Providence, 27, 43, 44, 84, 97, 109, 112, 122, 151, 233, 234, 256, 257, 274, 290, 392n., 402, 409–10, 411, 413, 435, 444, 461
Reprobation, 38, 107
Revealed religion, 191 n., 195, 332
Roman Catholics / Roman Catholicism, 16, 22 n., 52, 87, 138, 262–3, 381n.
  Anti-Catholicism, 84 n., 441 n.
  Catholic Relief Bill (1780), 441 n.
  JW's visit to the Sardinian chapel, London, 388
Sabbatarianism, 440, 440 n.
Second coming of Christ, 233
Socinians / Socinianism, 20, 38, 44–5, 46, 48, 50–1, 72–4, 86, 103–4, 132, 133 n., 151, 174, 271, 310, 349, 411 n.
Subscription to a confession of faith, 35, 36, 40, 118–19, 237–8, 249, 342, 379, 410–11, 429 n.
Transubstantiation, 92, 254
Trinitarianism, 132–3, 279 n., 311 n., 343 n., 355 n.
Unitarians / Unitarianism, 38, 138 n., 271
  Belsham, Thomas, see separate entry
  Cappe, Newcome, see separate entry
  Christie, Alexander, William and Thomas, see separate entry
  Eddowes, Ralph, see separate entry.
  Essex Street chapel, London, see separate entry
  Evanson, Edward, see separate entry
  Grafton, Duke of, see separate entry
  Jebb, John, see separate entry
  Johnson, Joseph, see separate entry

Kenrick, Samuel, see separate entry
Kenrick, Timothy, see separate entry
Kidderminster, see separate entry
Lindsey, Theophilus, see separate entry
Prattinton, William, see separate entry
Priestley, Joseph, see separate entry
Tayleur, William, see separate entry
Toulmin, Joshua, see separate entry
Theocritus, 353
Thirty-Nine Articles, see Church of England; Dissent
Thirty Years' War, 430 n.
Thom, William, 166 n.
Thompson, Seth, 383, 385
Thomson, Thomas, 429
Thrale, Henry, 293
Thucydides, 415
Thurlow, Edward, 353
Tobacco, 178 n., 180 n., 217 n.
Toland, John, 86
Toleration, 445 n.
Toleration Act (1689), 34, 39
Tonbridge, Kent, 251 n.
Torbay, Devon, 444 n.
Toulmin, Joshua, 45, 76 n., 138 n., 348 n.
Towers, Joseph, 444 n.
Townshend, Thomas, first viscount Sydney, 168–9, 182–4, 191 n., 217, 218
Trade / tradesmen, 263–4
  Benefits of, 82
  British, 306
  Coal, 105 n., 264
  Coffee, 62
  Cotton, 131 n.
  Directories, 179
  Fishing, 31
  Hops, 213, 217, 330
  Horses, 129 n.
  Industrial action, 415
  Iron, 30, 292
  Irish, 306
  Leather, 394
  Slaves, 62, 129 n., 266 n.
  Sugar, 61, 129 n., 178 n., 180 n.
  Tobacco, 62, 129 n., 178 n., 180 n., 217 n.
  Weaving, 117 n., 415 n.
Trail, Robert, 245
Trail, William, 194
Travel and infrastructure, 11, 290
  Balloons, 31, 226, 248, 299
  Boswell's *Tour to the Hebrides* (1785), 212, 275, 279, 292, 320
  Canals, 30, 31, 151, 264, 275, 292, 299, 305–6
  Correspondence during, 11
  Cost, 40, 381
  Grand Tour, 157 n., 221 n., 356 n.
  Hackney coach, 381

# INDEX

Travel and infrastructure (*Continued*)
  Horseback, 99, 299
  Improvements in, 9
  Innkeepers, 381
  Mail coach, 6, 268 n., 392, 394
  Post chaise, 236 n., 392, 394
  Roads, 94, 272
  SK's tour to England (1759), 28, 151 n., 154, 399 n., 400
  SK's tours to Europe with James and Alexander Milliken (1760–63, 1765), 11, 47, 289, 293
  Shipwreck, 220–1
  Stage coaches, 6, 205, 246 n., 384, 389, 391–6
  Steam, 299
  JW's journey home from London via Bewdley (1788), 389–96
  *See also*
    Kenrick, Mary, Visit to the Wodrows
    Wodrow, Helen, Visit to the Kenricks
    Wodrow, James, Bewdley
    Wodrow, James, London
Trent, river, 292
Trials for sedition and treason, 453 n.
Trimmer, Sarah, 27
Trinidad, 356 n.
Tullibole, Perthshire, 455 n.
Tullideph, Thomas, 137
'Two Acts', 1795, 77 n.
Tyrawley, Lord, 178 n.
Tytler, James, 226 n.

Unitarians / Unitarianism, *see* Theology, Unitarians / Unitarianism
Universities, 27–9, 154, 166 n., 195, 283, 359
  Aberdeen, King's College, 98 n., 194 n., 195 n., 304 n.
  Aberdeen, Marischal College, 47, 137 n., 193–5, 219 n., 221 n., 273 n., 373 n.
  Cambridge, 28, 61, 66, 81 n., 157 n., 283, 320, 368, 370 n.
    Clare College, 383 n.
    Corpus Christi College, 91 n.
    Gonville and Caius College, 304 n.
    King's College, 91 n., 157 n.
    St John's College, 353 n.
    Trinity College, 311 n.
  Dublin, Trinity College, 433 n.
  Edinburgh, 31, 86 n., 95 n., 98 n., 99 n., 106 n., 126 n., 129 n., 175 n., 216 n., 227 n., 228 n., 251 n., 270 n., 282 n., 286 n., 287 n., 348 n., 356 n., 387 n., 428 n., 441 n., 455 n.
  Glasgow, 1, 3, 10, 14, 22, 27–8, 28–9, 47, 77 n., 78 n., 80 n., 85, 86 n., 91 n., 98 n., 99 n., 112 n., 137 n., 140, 151–2, 154–5, 157 n., 168, 176, 183 n., 188 n., 190, 194 n., 195, 198 n., 216 n., 219 n., 224 n., 225 n., 231 n., 233, 236, 237–8, 251 n., 270 n., 283, 287 n., 320, 369–70, 372, 373 n., 382 n., 401 n., 402, 411 n., 416 n., 435 n., 455 n.
  *see* Anderson, John
    Blackstone examination, 232
    Chapel, 232, 307
    Library, 231 n., 236, 346
    Professors, 238, 278
    Scottish, 369–70
    Students, 166–9, 181–4, 188–9, 190, 238, 249
  Königsberg, 86 n.
  Leiden, 86 n.
  New Jersey, College of, 98 n., 132 n., 133–4
  Oxford, 27, 30, 61, 154–5, 157 n., 225 n., 283, 320, 334, 354 n., 369, 372–3, 395 n.
    Bampton Lectures, 259
    Christ Church College, 66, 142 n., 369, 460
    Hutchinsonians, 286 n.
    Oriel College, 158 n.
    Queen's College, 158 n.
    St John's College, 251 n.
    Trinity College, 203 n.
    Wadham College, 259 n.
  Religion, and, 370
  Scottish, 27, 29–30
  St Andrews, 194 n., 227 n., 441 n., 453–4 n.
  Slave trade, abolitionism and anti-abolitionism at, 66, 368–9, 372–3
  Strathclyde, 151 n.
  Students, 166–9, 181–4, 188–9, 190, 238, 249, 369–70, 379
  Subscription, and, 237–8, 249, 379
  Utrecht, 86 n., 102 n.
Uranus, 299 n.
Urwick, Thomas, 380 n., 382, 384, 387, 388, 393, 401, 402, 406, 408, 409, 412–13, 415–16, 417–18, 431, 439
Utrecht, 33 n., 102 n., 157 n.

Vagrancy, 70
Valentia, *see* Annesley
Vatican, 117
Vesuvius, 118
Vigilius Tapsensis, 204, 218
Viret, Pierre, 271
Virginia, *see* America
Virgil, or Publius Vergilius Maro, 304, 353, 414, 434 n., 459, 462
Volcano, 145 n., 156 n.
Voltaire, François-Marie Arouet, 348

Wages, 83
Walcot, John (*pseud*. Peter Pindar), 293
Wales, 90, 158, 178 n., 262, 387, 391, 421–2
Wallace, Frances Anna, 109 n.
Wallace, Robert, 455
Walpole, Sir Robert, 157 n., 448, 450 n.
Walthamstow, Essex, 137 n., 394 n.

# INDEX

Wanlockhead, South Lanarkshire, 299 n.
Warburton, William, bishop of Gloucester, 244, 251, 314 n., 371–2, 404, 433, 434
Warburton, William, of Worcester, 294
Warley Hall, Worcestershire, 217 n.
Warner, John, of Kilbarchan, 132, 325, 340 n.
  Death, 7, 11, 12, 25–6, 265, 272, 344 n.
  Defence of those accused of heresy, 266
  Friendship with JW and SK, 11, 13 n., 100–1, 122, 159, 192, 265, 268, 269, 402, 406, 413, 435
  Incapacity after stroke, 11, 100–1, 122, 139–40
  Papers and sermons, 11–12, 25–6, 140, 265, 267, 269, 277, 307, 400, 404, 405, 408, 438–9
  Scholarship, 159, 265, 404, 405, 408, 415
  Translation of Pouilly's *Theorie des Sentimens*, 25–6, 140, 268, 307, 313, 375, 376, 390, 398–400, 403–5, 408
  Visited by Mary Kenrick, 11, 25, 100
Warner, Patrick, 150 n., 265, 340, 465
Warrington, William, 421–2
Warton, Thomas, 354
Warwick, High Street Chapel, 433 n.
Watson, Richard, 369–70
Wat(t), Hugh, 213, 227, 330, 337, 344
Watts, Isaac, 286
Weather, 80, 90–1, 94, 97, 100, 109, 111, 114, 134, 145, 156, 214, 250, 272, 299, 301, 365, 392, 412, 414
Webster, Alexander, 266
Wedderburn, Sir John, 62, 65
Wedgwood, Josiah, 64
Welsh, William, 455
Wentworth-Watson, Charles, second marquess of Rockingham, 130 n.
Wesley, John, 40, 260, 274, 286
West Bromwich, 203 n.
West Indies, 65, 129 n., 178 n., 266 n., 289 n., 369
West Kilbride, 129 n., 340 n.
West Midlands, 264
Westcote, *see* Lyttelton
Westminster, 55, 86 n., 90 n., 204, 205, 258 n., 374 n.
Westminster Confession of Faith, 119 n., 237, 249, 429 n.
Westminster School, 353 n., 363 n.
Westmoreland, 125
Whigs
  Foxite Whigs, 16, 54–5, 57, 77 n., 155, 157 n., 274 n., 396 n., 434 n., 455 n., 456
  Pittites, 16, 55, 155
Whist, 392
Whitbread, Samuel, 157
Whitchurch, Shropshire, 95, 168 n., 270 n.
White, Hugh, 107, 120, 121
White, Joseph, 259, 274, 290
Whitefield, George, 202, 260
Whitehall, 259

Whitehaven, 376
Wigan, Thomas, 13 n., 23 n., 26 , 41, 229, 232, 274, 290, 301, 308, 312, 322, 359, 395, 402, 416, 446, 460
  Called a Methodist, 261
  Critical of Priestley, 342
  Enjoyment of William M'Gill's publications, 21, 141, 411
  Friendship with SK, 41, 122 n., 141, 293, 335, 359, 460
  Pamphlet debate with William Jesse, 41–2, 202–3, 238–9, 251, 270, 279, 280, 285, 311, 313–14, 321
  Politics, 314
  Tutoring, 355–6
Witchcraft, 441
Wilberforce, William, 64, 66, 340 n., 373 n.
Wilkes, John, 353 n.
William III and II, 170, 444 n.
Willis, Francis, 414 n.
Wills and executry, 159, 162, 226, 277
Wilton, near Hawick, 175 n.
Wilton Carpets, 415
Wiltshire, 78 n.
Windsor, 228
Wine, 154, 231, 426 n.
Wishart, George, 172 n.
Witherspoon [or 'Wotherspoon'], John, 42, 56, 98, 131–4, 202
  *Ecclesiastical Characteristics* (1753), 42, 202, 203
  Heresy processes, 266
  Priestley, Joseph, 133
  Scotland, visit to (1784), 131–3
Wodrow, Andrew, 12, 267 n., 380
Wodrow, Anne, *née* Ruthven, 267 n.
Wodrow, Elizabeth, *née* Balfour, 225 n., 277 n., 298
Wodrow, Gavin, 10, 28, 47, 118
Wodrow, Helen ('Nell'), 93, 117, 165, 214, 222, 328, 330, 333, 358
  Bewdley friends, 206, 208, 226, 395
  Character / temperament, 109, 156
  Dyslexia, 9, 109
  Family, wider, 426
  Friends, 128, 135, 148, 339
  Friendship with Mary Kenrick, 161, 205–6, 210, 218, 222, 239, 247, 253, 268, 277, 302, 328, 338, 362, 375, 412, 422, 426
  Money, 110, 125, 152, 155, 161, 164, 192, 200
  Manchester, visit to, 29, 205, 206, 207, 208, 210
  Music, 110, 204, 205
  Scots dialect, 19, 109, 124, 125, 140
  Social skills, 8, 124
  Visit to the Kenricks (1784–5), 1, 2, 6, 7, 8, 9, 20, 33, 93–4, 97, 100, 101, 109–11, 114, 118, 122, 124, 125, 128–9, 134, 135, 139, 140, 141, 145, 148, 156, 161, 164, 176, 178, 180, 192, 201, 204, 205–6, 210, 218, 222, 247

529

# INDEX

Wodrow, James (1730–1810)
Anderson, John
campaign against William Leechman, 28–30, 151, 160–1, 165–70, 181–4, 187–91, 193
character, 185–7
court cases, and, 365
Anxiety to receive letters from SK and Nell Wodrow, 139, 144, 148, 149, 207–8, 210
Bereavements, 10, 12, 118, 150, 153, 159, 229–41, 358
Bewdley, visits to (1789), 1, 2, 6, 7, 10–11, 375, 379, 384, 387, 389, 390, 391, 393, 394–5, 398, 402, 407, 446
Book buying, 10, 171, 192, 407, 409, 417
Buchanites, 40–1
Burns, Robert, 363
Communion seasons, 209, 214, 218, 299, 301, 302, 357, 376, 395, 402, 418, 422
DD (University of Glasgow, 1786), 1, 278, 295
Devotional literature / practice, 239, 395
Dow, Robert, 13 n., 41, 322, 358, 440
Early life, 10
Edinburgh, visits to, 16, 32
Eglinton, earl of, JW's patron, 134, 331, 341, 362
Elders, 437, 438
Evangelicals / Popular party, and, 40, 41, 48–53
Family, 8–9, 23, 118, 159, 201, 207, 382, 384, 426
Farming, 111, 117, 412
Fergusson, Alexander, JW's support for, 35, 118–19, 197
Free will, 44
Freebairn, Robert, 236 n.
French Revolution, early support for, 67–8, 390, 430, 461, 467
General Assembly of the Church of Scotland, 50–2, 61, 165–6, 340, 344, 430, 450–7
Member of the committee on the repeal of the Test and Corporation Acts (1790), 455
Opportunity to socialise, 170–1, 175, 191, 196–200, 344–5, 450
Glasgow, 31, 374
Health and illness, 273, 275, 389, 391
Hospitality, 31, 117, 253, 346, 407, 426
Irenicism, 45, 51, 103, 153, 324
Jesse, William, 41, 238–9, 303, 321–2, 325, 328, 411
Judaism, interest in, 47
Kenrick, Elisabeth, 375, 438
Kenrick, Mary, 7, 31, 100, 110, 114, 117, 118, 128, 134, 138, 207, 222, 268, 375, 391, 417, 426, 438
Kenrick, Samuel
Admiration for his teaching gifts, 159
Affection for, 134, 222, 265, 296, 302, 375, 417

Friendship for, 1, 10, 53, 162, 291, 382, 384
Urged to visit Stevenston, 9–10, 31, 47, 205
Urges JW to visit Bewdley, 9–10, 100, 202, 206, 360
Kirk session (Stevenston), 295
Language, Scots and English, 109, 326, 345, 363–4, 375, 439–41
Leechman, William and Bridget
Admiration for Leechman's extempore prayer and devotion, 23, 240
Edition of Leechman's sermons with JW's memoir (1789), 1, 19, 21–5, 66, 240, 253, 277, 282, 294–5, 296–7, 302–3, 322, 323, 328–9, 337–8, 345–6, 357–8, 365, 374, 375, 376, 379–90, 393–4, 406, 408–9, 417, 418, 420, 426–7, 442, 446, 451, 466
JW's actions in the church courts in support of Leechman in the Anderson 'stramash' (1785), 166–70, 176, 184, 189, 197, 278
Papers of Leechman given to JW after his death (1786), 10, 21–5, 88, 236, 242–5, 275, 282, 295, 338, 374
Relationship with, 3, 10, 118, 165, 185, 277, 296, 297–8, 303, 334, 338, 340, 345, 365, 374
Sermon following Leechman's death, 232–5
London, trip to have Leechman's sermons and life printed (1789), 1, 2, 7, 10–11, 25, 33, 45, 46, 67, 374–5, 376, 379–90
Manse, 1, 323, 330–1, 340, 346, 351, 365–6, 368, 375
M'Gill, William, 139, 328, 340
Admiration for, 325
Advice to, 48–53, 102–4, 325, 329, 346, 410 n., 411, 438, 448
Friendship, 102, 150, 302, 376
Help to publish his *Practical Essay* (1786), 19–21, 48–9, 102–4, 135–6, 148, 150, 159, 275, 302, 325, 326
Support during his heresy process, 1789, 35, 48–53, 66, 68, 429–30, 436, 448
Moderates / Moderatism, 34, 48–53
Parish business, 16, 97, 100, 117, 139, 143–4, 145, 160, 213, 269, 282, 294–5, 296, 357, 395, 418
Parish visitations, 46, 296, 322–3
Parliamentary reform, 79
Patronage Act (1712), 170
Piety, 106, 395
Philosophy, 44
Politics, 55, 131, 396–7, 407
Portrait, 358, 360
Preaching / lecturing, 31, 100, 159–60, 199, 232, 295, 296, 357, 407
Presbytery of Ayr, 50–2, 428, 429

530

# INDEX

Priestley, Joseph, 43–5, 59, 73–6, 88, 111–13, 146–7, 151, 171, 191, 324–5, 325, 328, 346, 357
Reading, 15–19, 138–9, 148–9, 159–160, 238, 275, 357, 377, 407, 421
Reid, Thomas, 44, 346, 377
Saltcoats, 323
Scholarship, 146–7
Slavery and abolition, 65–6, 185 n., 456 n.
*Statistical Accounts of Scotland* (1793), 70 n., 101 n., 144 n.
Stevenston, 1, 11, 395
Synod of Glasgow and Ayr, 50–2, 165–6, 374, 429–30
Test and Corporation Acts, campaigns to repeal, 40, 58–9, 60, 339, 364, 450–7, 460
Theology
    Arians / Arianism, 73 n., 75, 324
    Arminianism, 36
    Atonement, 151, 296, 325, 326 n.
    Bible / biblical scholarship, 45–7, 48, 73, 137–8, 143, 197, 199, 357, 421, 434, 436
    Caution / dislike of disputes, 36, 43, 45, 103–4, 127, 411, 416
    Christology, 44–5, 72–4, 150–1, 296, 326 n.
    Deism, 327
    'Enthusiasm', 'enthusiasts' / fanaticism, 22, 105, 143, 214, 325, 438
    Heaven, 233–5, 340, 375
    Hebrews, book of, 136
    Methodism, 325
    Miracles, 80
    Miraculous conception, 80, 324
    Morality, 325
    Paul, apostle, 136
    Providence, 27, 43, 44, 411
    Rational belief, 72, 325
    Socinians / Socinianism, 72–3, 86 n., 138 n., 150–1, 324
    Subscription, 40, 118–19, 237–8, 410–11, 429
    Unitarianism, 150–1
Visiting (non-parish), 128, 129, 387, 390
Warner, John
    Friendship with, 11, 31, 272, 403, 408
    papers of, 11–12, 25–6, 265, 267, 275, 277, 282, 294–5, 307, 408, 438–9
Wigan, Thomas, 238–9, 282, 302, 321, 324, 384, 411
Wills and executry, 159, 226
Witherspoon, John, 132
Wodrow, Louisa, 297
Wodrow, James (1637–1707), 149 n.
Wodrow-Kenrick correspondence
    Books acquired for each other, 226, 238, 251, 259, 264, 268, 270, 273, 290, 311, 317, 323, 329, 340, 409, 411, 420

Candour and disagreement, 3, 35, 135
Conversation, as, 14–15
Copying, 97
Delays in writing, 3, 69, 81, 90, 145, 158, 247, 256, 265, 269, 321, 328, 331, 337, 413, 422, 431, 434, 435
Enlightenment, 2, 8, 13–32
Family, 2–3, 7–13
Friendship in, 1, 2, 3, 10, 12–13, 28
Humour, 336
Missing letters, 2, 11, 55, 66, 67, 68, 72 n., 79 n., 81 n., 165 n., 201 n., 210, 295 n., 339 n., 372 n., 376 n., 381, 382, 393, 401 n., 445 n., 450 n., 457 n.
Pleasure in, 1, 2, 3, 12, 20, 25, 82, 94, 296
Wodrow, Louisa, *née* Hamilton, 8, 127, 134, 135, 160, 192, 217, 222, 247, 297, 457
    Apples received from Bewdley, 397, 407, 417
    Family, 8, 10, 86 n., 160, 161, 170, 193, 207, 216, 222, 298, 303, 332, 337, 345, 412, 426
    Health, 170
    Linen sent to the Kenricks at Bewdley, 208, 218, 330, 397, 430, 434
    Temperament, 109
Wodrow, Margaret, *see* Biggar, Margaret
Wodrow, Margaret ('Peggy'), daughter of JW, 35, 105, 110, 127, 134, 135, 180, 217, 239, 247, 299, 302, 358, 362, 412, 424, 426
    Friendship with Mary Ann Wodrow, 36, 424
Wodrow, Marion ('Mainy'), sister of JW, 128, 150, 153, 159
Wodrow, Mary, *née* Craig, 380 n.
Wodrow, Mary Ann, *see* Archbald, Mary Ann
Wodrow, Patrick, son of JW, 10
Wodrow, Patrick, brother of JW, 225, 277 n., 298 n., 334, 363 n., 438 n.
Wodrow, Robert, brother of JW, 12, 267 n., 380 n.
Wodrow, Robert, father of JW, 23, 149 n., 204, 218
Wollstonecraft, Mary, 26, 27, 348 n., 379 n.
Wolverhampton, 292
Women, 7–9, 81 n., 82, 107–8, 124
    *see also* individually named women
Woodstock, 381
Worcester, 80 n., 97, 260, 384, 389, 427, 442, 446
    Angel Street chapel, 382 n.
    Banking, 27
    Canals, 264, 275, 292, 305–6
    Cathedral / diocese, 270, 322, 446
    Protestant Dissenters, 40, 59, 293, 401 n., 445 n., 449
    Rivers Severn and Teme, 292
    Travel from London, 384, 389
Worcestershire, 8, 82, 99, 141 n., 381
    Accent, 125
    Bewdley, *see* separate entry
    Birmingham, *see* separate entry

Worcestershire (*Continued*)
   Bridgenorth, *see* separate entry
   Canals, 30, 264, 275, 292, 305–6
   Clifton upon Teme, 460
   Dowles, 41, 203 n.
   Hagley, 82 n., 96, 361 n., 395 n.
   Industry, 30
   Iron, 30, 292
   Kenrick family move to, 32
   Kidderminster, *see* separate entry
   Longdon, 80 n.
   Oldswinford, 41, 141 n.
   Ribbesford, Worcestershire, 203 n.
   Severn, *see* separate entry
   Stourbridge, 141 n., 210
   Stourport, *see* separate entry
   Warley Hall, 217 n.
   Worcester, *see* separate entry
   Wribbenhall, 141 n.
Worsley, Lancashire, 30
Wrexham, 123, 156, 264, 270, 391
Wribbenhall, Worcestershire, 141 n.
Wright, James, 301–2, 312

Writers to the Signet (WS), 108, 341
Wyatt, Mr, 398, 399, 404
Wynn Hall, Ruabon, 391 n.
Wyvill, Christopher, 77 n.

Xenophon, 320

Yate, Benjamin, 269–70
York, 77, 122, 225 n., 304
York, Frederick, Duke of, 56
Yorke, Sir Joseph, 157
Yorkshire, 125, 269
Yorkshire Association, 77
Yorktown, 78 n.
Young, Edward, 90
Young, James, 441
Young, John, 189, 237
Young, Mrs John, 237
Young, Stephen, 441

Zeno, 112 n.
*Zong* massacre, 1781, 63
Zwicker, Daniel, 86, 87 n., 204, 218